WORD
BIBLICAL
COMMENTARY

General Editors
David A. Hubbard
Glenn W. Barker

Old Testament Editor
John D. W. Watts

New Testament Editor
Ralph P. Martin

WORD
BIBLICAL
COMMENTARY

VOLUME 32

Micah-Malachi

RALPH L. SMITH

WORD BOOKS, PUBLISHER • WACO, TEXAS

Word Biblical Commentary:
Micah–Malachi
Copyright © 1984 by Word, Incorporated

Library of Congress Cataloging in Publication Data
Main entry under title:

Word biblical commentary.
  Includes bibliographies.
  I. Bible—Commentaries—Collected works.
BS491.2.W67   220.7'7   81–71768
ISBN 0–8499–0231–2 (v. 32) AACR2

Printed in the United States of America

Unless otherwise indicated, Scripture quotations in the body of the commentary are from the Revised Standard Version of the Bible, copyright 1946 (renewed 1973), 1956, and © 1971 by the Division of Christian Education of the National Council of the Churches of Christ in the USA, and are used by permission. Those marked NIV are from the New International Version of the Bible, copyright © 1973 by New York Bible Society International. The author's own translation of the text appears in italic type under the heading "Translation."

239 AGF 987654

To my wife
DOROTHY

Proverbs 31:29

Contents

Author's Preface

Thanks are due the editors of this Old Testament series, Dr. J. D. W. Watts and Dr. David A. Hubbard, and Floyd Thatcher, the editor-in-chief of Word Books, for the opportunity to contribute to this series. I would also like to thank Cathe Caves, a student at Southwestern Seminary, for typing and checking the original manuscript. She has rendered invaluable service to this project. I hope that this work will make this portion of God's written word more understandable to those who read these pages and that the readers catch the love and respect for the Word of God that the writer has discovered.

RALPH L. SMITH

Southwestern Baptist Seminary
Forth Worth, Texas

Editorial Preface

The launching of the *Word Biblical Commentary* brings to fulfillment an enterprise of several years' planning. The publishers and the members of the editorial board met in 1977 to explore the possibility of a new commentary on the books of the Bible that would incorporate several distinctive features. Prospective readers of these volumes are entitled to know what such features were intended to be; whether the aims of the commentary have been fully achieved time alone will tell.

First, we have tried to cast a wide net to include as contributors a number of scholars from around the world who not only share our aims, but are in the main engaged in the ministry of teaching in university, college and seminary. They represent a rich diversity of denominational allegiance. The broad stance of our contributors can rightly be called evangelical, and this term is to be understood in its positive, historic sense of a commitment to scripture as divine revelation, and to the truth and power of the Christian gospel.

Then, the commentaries in our series are all commissioned and written for the purpose of inclusion in the *Word Biblical Commentary*. Unlike several of our distinguished counterparts in the field of commentary writing, there are no translated works, originally written in a non-English language. Also, our commentators were asked to prepare their own rendering of the original biblical text and to use those languages as the basis of their own comments and exegesis. What may be claimed as distinctive with this series is that it is based on the biblical languages, yet it seeks to make the technical and scholarly approach to a theological understanding of scripture understandable by—and useful to—the fledgling student, the working minister as well as to colleagues in the guild of professional scholars and teachers.

Finally, a word must be said about the format of the series. The layout in clearly defined sections has been consciously devised to assist readers at different levels. Those wishing to learn about the textual witnesses on which the translation is offered are invited to consult the section headed "Notes." If the readers' concern is with the state of modern scholarship on any given portion of scripture, then they should turn to the sections on "Bibliography" and "Form/Structure/Setting." For a clear exposition of the passage's meaning and its relevance to the ongoing biblical revelation, the "Comment" and concluding "Explanation" are designed expressly to meet that need. There is therefore something for everyone who may pick up and use these volumes.

If these aims come anywhere near realization, the intention of the editors will have been met, and the labor of our team of contributors rewarded.

General Editors: *David A. Hubbard*
Glenn W. Barker
Old Testament: *John D. W. Watts*
New Testament: *Ralph P. Martin*

Abbreviations

AB	Anchor Bible
AJSL	*American Journal of Semitic Languages*
ANET	*Ancient Near Eastern Texts,* J. B. Pretchard, ed.
ASV	American Standard Version
ATD	Das Alte Testament Deutsch
Atlas	*The Macmillan Bible Atlas,* ed. Y. Aharoni and M. Avi-Yonah.
ATR	*Anglican Theological Review*
BBC	*Broadman Bible Commentary*
BDB	Brown, Driver, and Briggs, *Hebrew and English Lexicon of the Old Testament*
BHK	*Biblia Hebraica,* ed. R. Kittel
BHS	*Biblia Hebraica Stuttgartensia*
Bib	*Biblica*
Bright	J. Bright, *A History of Israel.* 3rd ed.
BS	*Bibliotheca Sacra*
BZAT	Beiträge zur alttestamentliche Theologie
BZAW	Beihefte zur *ZAW*
CamB	Cambridge Bible (Old Series)
CB	Century Bible (New Series)
CBC	Cambridge Bible Commentary
CBQ	*Catholic Biblical Quarterly*
CCHS	*Catholic Commentary on the Holy Scriptures*
CeB	Century Bible (Old Series)
CHAL	*Concise Hebrew-Aramaic Lexicon,* ed. Holladay
Childs	B. Childs, *Introduction to the Old Testament as Scripture*
CNEB	Cambridge New English Bible Commentary
DSH	Dead Sea Scroll: Habbakkuk Commentary
EBib	Etudes bibliques
Eissfeldt	O. Eissfeldt, *The Old Testament: An Introduction*
EPC	Epworth Preacher's Commentary
EvQ	*Evangelical Quarterly*
ExB	Expositor's Bible
ExpT	*Expository Times*
FRLANT	Forschungen zur Religion und Literatur des Alten und Neuen Testaments (Göttingen)
FS	Festschnift

GKC	*Gesenius' Hebrew Grammar*, ed. E. Kautsch, trans. A. E. Cowley
HAT	Handkommentar zum Alten Testament
HTR	*Harvard Theological Review*
HUCA	*Hebrew Union College Annual*
IB	*Interpreter's Bible*
ICC	International Critical Commentary
IDB	*Interpreter's Dictionary of the Bible*
IDBSup	*Interpreter's Dictionary of the Bible, Supplementary Volume*
IER	*Irish Ecclesiastical Review*
Int	*Interpretation*
JAOS	*Journal of the American Oriental Society*
JB	*Jerusalem Bible*
JBL	*Journal of Biblical Literature*
JJS	*Journal of Jewish Studies*
JNES	*Journal of Near Eastern Studies*
JQR	*Jewish Quarterly Review*
JSOT	*Journal for the Study of the Old Testament*
JSS	*Journal of Semitic Studies*
JTS	*Journal of Theological Studies*
Jud	*Judaica*
KAT	*Kommentar zum Alten Testament*, ed. E. Sellin
KB	Köhler, L. and Baumgartner, W. *Lexicon in Veteris Testamenti Libros*
KD	Keil and Delitzsch, *Biblical Commentary on the Old Testament*
KJV	King James Version
LXX	*Septuaginta*, ed. A. Rahlfs
MS(S)	Manuscript(s)
MT	Masoretic Text
NAS	*New American Standard Version*
NCB	New Century Bible
NEB	*New English Bible*
NICOT	New International Commentary on the Old Testament
NIV	*New International Version*
OT	Old Testament
OTL	Old Testament Library
OTS	*Oudtestamentische Studien*
OTT	G. von Rad, *Old Testament Theology*
OTWSA	*Die Ou Testamentiese Werkgemeenskap in Suid-Afrika*
PCB	*Peake's Commentary on the Bible*, rev. ed. Black and Rowley
PEQ	*Palestine Exploration Quarterly*
POUT	*De Prediking van het Oude Testament*
RB	*Revue Biblique*

RevExp	*Review and Expositor*
RevQ	*Revue de Qumran*
RSV	*Revised Standard Version*
RTR	*Reformed Theological Review*
RV	*Revised Version*
SB	**Sources Biblique**
SBL	**Society of Biblical Literature**
SBT	*Studies in Biblical Theology*
SEÅ	*Svensk Exegetisk Årsbok*
SJT	*Scottish Journal of Theology*
StTh	*Studia Theologica*
Syr	**Syriac Version: Peshitta**
TB	*Tyndale Bulletin*
TBC	**Torch Bible Commentary**
TDOT	*Theological Dictionary of the Old Testament*
TEV	*Today's English Version*
TOTC	**Tyndale Old Testament Commentary**
TR	*Theologische Rundschau*
TTZ	*Trierer theologische Zeitschrift*
Vg	**Vulgate**
VT	*Vetus Testamentum*
VTSup	**Vetus Testamentum Supplements**
WC	**Westminster Commentary**
Wester-mann, BFPS	Westermann, C. *Basic Forms of Prophetic Speech*
WMANT	**Wissenschaftliche Monographien zum Alten und Neuen Testament**
ZAW	*Zeitschrift für die alttestamentliche Wissenschaft*
ZDMG	*Zietschrift der deutschen morgenlandischen Gesellschaft*
ZTK	*Zeitschript für Theologie und Kirche*

Introduction

This volume is a study of the last seven "minor prophets" according to the Hebrew canon. They are: Micah, Nahum, Habakkuk, Zephaniah, Haggai, Zechariah, and Malachi. Their dates range from the eighth century (Micah) to the end of the sixth or the beginning of the fifth century B.C. The Book of the Twelve minor prophets is a collection of miscellaneous prophetic materials from the eighth century possibly to the fourth century B.C. It is counted as one book in the Hebrew canon. The purpose of placing all of this material in one scroll seems to have been to make a balance in the Hebrew prophetic canon between the four books of the former prophets (Joshua, Judges, Samuel, and Kings), and the four books of the latter prophets (Isaiah, Jeremiah, Ezekiel, and the Twelve).

As early as 180 B.C., Ben Sira refers to this fourth section of the latter prophets as "the twelve prophets" (Ecclus. 49:10). Augustine was probably the first to call them "the minor prophets," because of the size of the individual books in comparison with the books of Isaiah, Jeremiah and Ezekiel.

It is difficult to discover the principle or principles by which these "twelve prophets" are arranged. There may be a chronological principle at work here. Hosea and Amos were among the earliest of the twelve, but it is generally agreed today that Amos preceded Hosea and that Joel might have been the last of the minor prophets. Size or length could have been a factor in the arrangement. Hosea with fourteen chapters and Amos with nine are among the longest. But again Joel, one of the shorter ones, is placed between Hosea and Amos, and Zechariah with fourteen chapters is near the end. Certain phrases such as, "the day of Yahweh" and "the Lord roars from Zion" may explain the arrangement of Joel, Amos, and Obadiah.

The fact that the LXX has a different arrangement for the first six of the minor prophets suggests that these six at one time formed an independent collection (Curt Kuhl, *The Old Testament: Its Origins and Composition,* trans, C. T. M. Herriott [Richmond: John Knox Press: 1961], 202). For a thorough discussion of the arrangement of the Minor Prophets see Budde, "Eine folgenschwere Redaction des Zwölfprophetenbuchs," *ZAW* 39 (1922) 218–29; Wolfe, "The Editing of the Book of the Twelve," *ZAW* 53 (1935) 90–127. The LXX apparently classified them according to length: Hosea, Amos, Micah, Joel, Obadiah, and Jonah. Jonah was placed at the end of this first group even though it is longer than Obadiah, because it is mainly a story about a prophet rather than a collection of prophetic oracles.

The seven books treated in this volume cover the whole period of classical prophets in the OT. Micah is the only one to speak of the Assyrian crisis before the fall of Samaria in 722 B.C. Nahum, Habakkuk, and Zephaniah spoke during the Babylonian crisis prior to the fall of Jerusalem in 586 B.C. Haggai and Zechariah spoke of the post-exilic community in Jerusalem about 520–516 B.C. Malachi probably addressed the discouraged and disillusioned Jews in Jerusalem about 450 B.C. And the writer or writers of Zech

9–14 probably worked in Jerusalem immediately before and after 500 B.C.

The times and circumstances of these seven prophets varied greatly. Their messages were always addressed to the needs of their people in the various times. Each prophet had words of warning and judgment, and also a message of future hope. Their messages of judgment and hope were grounded in their understanding of the nature of Yahweh. Yahweh was a holy, righteous, just, and loving God who was sovereign over history and the world. The day of Yahweh meant judgment for the wicked, but a day of hope for the fearers of Yahweh's name and for those who were faithful to their covenant with him (Mal 3:16–18). The last chapters of Zech (9–14) lapse over into apocalyptic material. In contrast to the regular prophets, the apocalyptists despaired of seeing the kingdom of God come in this present evil age. They began to project a cosmic battle between the forces of evil and Yahweh around Jerusalem. After a time of great sorrow and suffering Yahweh would be victorious. Evil would be eradicated from the earth and all the survivors of all the nations would "go up year by year to worship the King, the Lord of hosts, and to keep the feasts of booths" (Zech 14:16).

But this prophetic canon as it now stands does not end with a message of hope but with a warning. The last word in the book of Malachi is "ban" or "curse." There is a stern warning to the people of the OT era to "repent" and return to God or he will come and smite the land with a ban (Mal 3:24, 4:6 Eng.).

These seven books still speak the words of God. We, like Israel, need the warnings and should "repent" as needed. But we also need the messages of hope for a new day when the kingdom will come in its fullness.

Bibliography

Commentaries on Two or More Books

Allen, L. C. *The Books of Joel, Obadiah, Jonah, and Micah.* NICOT. Grand Rapids: Eerdmans, 1976. **Baldwin, J.** *Haggai, Zechariah, Malachi.* TOTC. Downer's Grove, IL: Inter-Varsity Press, 1972. **Beuken, W. A. M.** *Haggai-Sacharja 1–8. Studien zur Uberliefe-rungsgeschichte der fruhnachexilischen Prophetie.* Studia Semitica Neerlandica 10. Assen: Van Gorcum, 1967. **Buchholtz, K. D.** *Haggai, Sacharja, Maleachi.* Stuttgart: Quell, 1960. **Cornill, C. H.** *The Prophets of Israel.* Trans. S. F. Corkran. Chicago: Open Court, 1895. **Chary, T.** *Agee-Zacharie, Malachi.* Sources Bibliques. Paris: J. Gabalda et Cie, 1969. **Davidson, A. B.** *The Books of Nahum, Habakkuk, and Zephaniah.* Cambridge: Cambridge University Press, 1896. **Driver, S. R.** *The Minor Prophets.* CB. Edinburgh: T. C. and E. J. Jack, 1906. **Elliger, K.** *Das Buch der Zwölf Propheten II.* ATD 25. Gottingen: Vandenhoeck and Ruprecht, 1956. **Eiselen, F. C.** *The Minor Prophets,* in Whedon's Commentary. New York: Eaton and Mains, 1907. **Ewald, H.** *Commentary on the Prophets of the Old Testament.* Vol. 2. Edinburgh: Williams and Norgate, 1875. **Horst**—See **Robinson and Horst. Jones, D. R.** *Haggai, Zechariah, Malachi.* TBC. London: SCM, 1962. **Keil, C. F.** and **Delitzsch, F.** *The Twelve Minor Prophets.* 2 vols. Biblical Commentary on the Old Testament, vol. 24. 1868; rpt. Grand Rapids: Eerdmans, 1949. **Marti, K.** *Das Dodekapropheton.* Tübingen: J. C. B. Mohr, 1904. **Mason, R.** *The Books of Haggai, Zechariah, and Malachi.* CNEB. Cambridge: Cambridge University Press, 1977. **Mitchell, H. G.** *Haggai, Zechariah, Malachi.* ICC. Edinburgh: T. and T. Clark, 1912. **Nowack, W.** *Die Kleinen Propheten.* HKAT. Göttingen: Vandenhoeck and Ruprecht, 1897. **Robinson, T. H.** and **Horst, F.** *Die Zwölf Kleinen Propheten.* HAT. Tübingen: J. C. B. Mohr, 1938. **Rudolph, W.** *Haggai-Zacharja 1–8-Sacharja 9–14-Malachi.* KAT. Neukirchen: Neukirchener Verlag, 1976. ———. *Micah-Nahum-Habakkuk-Zephaniah.* KAT. Gutersloh: Gerd Mohn, 1975. **Sellin, E.** *Das Zwölfprophetenbuch.* KAT. Leipzig: A. Diechert, 1929–30. **Smith, G. A.** *The Books of the Twelve Prophets.* ExB 14. Garden City, NY: Doubleday, Doran, and Co., 1929. **Smith, J. M. P., Ward, W. H.,** and **Bewer, J. A.** *Micah, Zephaniah, Nahum, Obadiah, and Joel.* ICC. Edinburgh: T. and T. Clark, 1911. **Stonehouse, G. G.** *The Books of the Prophets Zephaniah and Nahum.* London: Methuen and Co., Ltd., 1929. **Torrey, C. C.** *The Lives of the Prophets.* JBL Monograph 1. Philadelphia: SBL, 1946. **Wade, G. W.** *Micah, Obadiah, Joel, and Jonah.* WC. London: Methuen and Co., 1925. **Watts, J. D. W.** *The Books of Joel, Obadiah, Jonah, Nahum, Habakkuk, and Zephaniah.* CNEB. London: Cambridge University Press, 1975. **Wellhausen, J.** *Die Kleinen Propheten.* Berlin: W. DeGruyter and Co., 1963.

Source Books

Ackroyd, P. *Exile and Restoration.* Philadelphia: Westminster Press, 1968. **Bentzen, A.** *Introduction to the Old Testament,* 2 vols. Copenhagen: G. E. C. Gad, 1948–49. **Childs, B.** *Introduction to the Old Testament as Scripture.* Philadelphia: Fortress Press, 1979. **Eissfeldt, O.** *The Old Testament: An Introduction.* Trans. P. R. Ackroyd. New York: Harper and Row, 1965. **Finegan J.** *Handbook of Biblical Chronology.* Princeton: Princeton University Press, 1964. **Hanson, P.** *The Dawn of Apocalyptic.* Philadelphia: Fortress Press, 1975. **Nielsen, E.** *Oral Tradition: A Modern Problem in Old Testament Introduction.* Chicago: A. R. Allenson, 1954. **Soggin, J. A.** *Introduction to the Old Testament.* Trans. J. Bowden. OTL. Philadelphia: Westminster Press, 1976. **Welch, A. C.** *Post Exilic Judaism.* Edinburgh: Blackwood and Sons, Ltd., 1935. **Westermann, C.** *Basic Forms of Prophetic Speech.* Trans. H. C. White. Philadelphia: Westminster Press, 1967.

Micah

Micah

Bibliography

Books

Copass, B. A. and **Carlson, E. L.** *A Study of the Prophet Micah.* Grand Rapids: Baker Book House, 1950. **Lescow, T.** *Micha 6:6–8. Studien zu Sprache, Form und Auslegung.* Stuttgart: Calwer Verlag, 1966. **Marsh, J.** *Amos and Micah.* TBC. London: SCM, 1959. **Mays, J. L.** *Micah.* OTL. Philadelphia: Westminster, 1976. **McKeating, H.** *Amos, Hosea, Micah.* CNEB. Cambridge: University Press, 1971. **Nielsen, E.** *Oral Tradition.* SBT 11. London: SCM, 1954. **Renaud, B.** *Structure et attaches litteraraires de Michee* iv–v. Paris: Gabalda, 1964. ———. *La Formation du Livre de Michee. Tradition et Actualisation.* Paris: Gabalda, 1977. **Scoggin, B.** "Micah." *BBC* 7. Nashville: Broadman Press, 1972. **Snaith, N.** *Amos, Hosea, Micah.* EPC. London: Epworth Press, 1956. **Willis, J. T.** *The Structure, Setting and Interrelationships of the Pericopes in the Book of Micah.* Dissertation: Vanderbilt Divinity School, 1966. **Wolfe, R. E.** "The Book of Micah: Exegesis." *IB* 6. Nashville: Abingdon, 1956. **Wolff, H. W.** *Dodekapropheton 4: Micha.* BK xiv/4. Neukirchen: Verlag der Erziehungsverein, 1982. ———. *Micah's Cultural and Intellectual Background.* Trans. R. D. Gehrke. Philadelphia: Fortress Press, 1981. **van der Woude, A. S.** *Micha.* POuT. Nijkerk: Callenbach, 1976.

Articles

Cannawurf, E. "The Authenticity of Micah iv 1–4." *VT* 13 (1963) 26–33. **Carreira, J. N.** "Micha—ein Ältester von Mereshet?" *TTZ* 90 (1981) 19–28. **Fensham, F. C.** "Righteousness in the Book of Micah and Parallels from the Ancient Near East." (Afrikaans) *TGW* 7 (1967) 416–25. ———. "The Divine Subject of the Verb in the Book of Micah." *OTWSA* (1973) 62–72. **Fohrer, G.** "Neue Literatur zur alttestamentlichen Prophetie. 6. Micha." *TR* 45 (1980) 212–16. **Gunkel, H.** "The Close of Micah: A Prophetical Liturgy." *What Remains of the OT and Other Essays.* Eng. tr. New York: Macmillan (1928) 115–49. **Hyatt, J. P.** "On the Meaning and Origin of Micah 6:8." *ATR* 34 (1952) 232–39. **Jepperson, K.** "New Aspects of Micah Research." *JSOT* 8 (1978) 3–32. **Jeremias, J.** "Die Deutung der Gerichtsworte Michas in der Exilzeit." *ZAW* 83 (1971) 330–54. **Kapelrud, A. S.** "Eschatology in the Book of Micah." *VT* 11 (1961) 392–405. **Lescow, T.** "Das Geburtsmotiv in den messianischen Weissagungen bei Jesaja und Micha." *ZAW* 79 (1967) 172–207. **Mays, L.** "The Theological Purpose of the Book of Micah." BZAT. FS W. Zimmerli (Göttingen: Vandenhoeck und Ruprecht 1977) 276–87. **von Rad, G.** "The City on the Hill." *The Problem of the Hexateuch and Other Essays.* Eng. tr. (New York: McGraw-Hill, 1966) 232–42. **Reicke, B.** "Liturgical Traditions in Micah 7." *HTR* 60 (1967) 349–67. **Schwantes, S. J.** *A Critical Study of the Text of Micah.* Dissertation: Johns Hopkins University, 1962. **Tucker, G. M.** "Prophetic Superscriptions and the Growth of a Canon." *Canon and Authority,* eds. Coats and Long. Philadelphia: Fortress (1977) 56–70. **Waard, J.** "Vers une identification des partifipants dans le livre de Michee." FS E. Jacob. *RHPR* 59 (1979) 509–516. **van der Woude, A. S.** "Micha 2.7a und der Bund Jahwes mit Israel." *VT* 18 (1968) 372–79. **Willis, J. T.** "On the Text of Micah 2:1aαβ." *Bib* 48 (1967) 534–41. ———. "Some Suggestions on the Interpretation of Micah 1:2." *VT* 18 (1968) 372–79.

————. "Micah 4:14–5:5—A Unit." *VT* 18 (1968) 529–47. ————. "A Note on וַאמר in Micah 3:1." *ZAW* 80 (1968) 50–54. ————. "The Structure of Micah 3–5 and the Function of Micah 5:9–14 in the Book." *ZAW* 81 (1969) 191–214. ————. "The Authenticity and Meaning of Micah 5:9–14." *ZAW* 81 (1969) 353–68. ————. "The Structure of the Book of Micah." SEÅ 34 (1969) 5–42. ————. "Fundamental Issues of Contemporary Micah Studies." *Restoration Quarterly* 13 (1970) 77–90. ————. "Thoughts on a Redactional Analysis of the Book of Micah." *Seminar Papers of SBL* (1978) 97. **Wolff, H. W.** "Wie verstand Micha von Moreshet sein prophetisches Amt?" VTSup 29 (1978) 403–17. ————. "Mica the Moreshite—The Prophet and His Background." *Israelite Wisdom*. Theological and Literary Essays in Honor of S. Terrien. New York: Union Theological Seminary (1978) 77–84. **van Zyl, A. H.** "Messianic Scope in the Book of Micah." *OTWSA* (1973) 62–72.

Introduction

The Place in the Canon

The book of Micah is sixth in order in the Book of the Twelve in the Hebrew canon but third in the list of the Minor Prophets in the LXX, which places Micah immediately after Hosea and Amos, two of his older contemporaries.

The Prophet

Micah's name was a rather common one in ancient Israel. At least nine different individuals are called Micah or Micaiah in the OT: an Ephraimite in the time of the Judges (Judg 17–18); a descendant of Reuben (1 Chr 5:5); a grandson of Saul (1 Chr 8:34; 2 Sam 9:12); a Levite of the family of Aseph (1 Chr 9:15); a Kohathite (1 Chr 23:20); a messenger of Josiah (2 Chr 34:20); a prophet in the time of Ahab (1 Kgs 22:8); a Levite who sealed the covenant with Nehemiah (Neh 10:11); and our prophet, who is mentioned by name in only two places in the Scriptures (Mic 1:1; Jer 26:18). Micah means "Who is like Yahweh." For Micah God was incomparable. In 7:18 there is probably a play on his name "who is a God like thee?"

The name is appropriate for a book like this because Yahweh is exalted in it. From the opening lines which announce Yahweh's coming, to the closing assertions about God's faithfulness to his covenant promise Yahweh is recognized as sovereign. He is no local or national deity here, but God of the whole world and all nations. He is a God of justice, judgment, and grace.

Some OT prophets are identified by their occupation or by their father's name. Neither Micah's occupation nor his father's name is given. He is not even called a prophet in his book. We know the name of the father of Isaiah, Jeremiah, Ezekiel, Hosea, Joel, Jonah, Zephaniah, and Zechariah, but Micah's father's name is not mentioned, perhaps because his family was not prominent. Micah, like Nahum the Elkoshite and Amos from Tekoa, was known from his hometown. When a person becomes known by his place of origin two factors are usually involved: (1) the person no longer lives in his place of origin. If he did there would be nothing to distinguish him from his fellows. Micah's small town origin probably stood out because he lived and worked in Jerusalem; and (2) although Micah lived and worked in Jerusalem he was actually a citizen of the small town, Moresheth, and still identified with the people there.

The Time of Micah

The superscription suggests the time of the ministry of Micah as being during the reigns of Jotham (742–735 B.C.), Ahaz (735–715 B.C.) and Hezekiah (715–687 B.C.). These figures allow a maximum period of fifty-five years for

Micah's ministry, but it is not likely that he was active as a prophet during all of that time. The references to Samaria (1:1, 6), to idols (1:7; 5:12–13, Eng. 5:13–14) and to Omri and Ahab (6:16) have led some to argue that Micah's ministry began during the fall of Samaria in 722 B.C. Other scholars have denied these references to Micah, arguing that they are the work of a later redactor. Lescow even assigns the references to Samaria to the conflict which brought about the Samaritan schism in the fourth century B.C. The evidence, however, is not strong enough to deny that Micah preached before the fall of Samaria.

There is a strong similarity between Mic 6:10–11 and Amos 8:5–6. Each accuses their wealthy listeners of cheating the poor by using false weights, small measures, and rigged scales. Such similarity would support a pre-722 B.C. date for part of Micah's ministry.

Perhaps the earliest identifiable historical reference in the book of Micah is in 1:10–16. This pericope probably describes the march of Sennacherib from Lachish to Jerusalem in 701 B.C. If this section is the work of Micah we have evidence that he prophesied at least to the end of the eighth century B.C. Jer 26:18 tells us that Micah predicted the fall of Jerusalem (3:12) during the reign of Hezekiah (715–687 B.C.)

Historical Setting

Cultural Background. Micah rails against his listeners for their apostate life style. The transgressions of the people involved two primary aspects: perversion of the worship practices (1:7; 3:5–7, 11; 5:11–13, Eng. 5:12–14) and injustice toward others (2:1–2, 8–9; 3:2–3, 9–11; 7:2–6). The former iniquity is a common complaint of the prophets, who rebuked religious leaders for earning their wealth at the expense of pure religious practice. Professional prophets and priests of local shrines behaved more like merchants than servants of God. Furthermore, the widespread practice of worshiping domestic idols revealed blatant spiritual decay. Nude goddesses with ornate hair designs have been found in Palestine archeological sites dating from 2000 to 700 B.C. This lends credence to Micah's complaint about the proliferation of Canaanite worship practices (G. Cornfeld, *Archaeology of the Bible: Book by Book* [New York: Harper and Row, 1976] 185).

The sin of abusing one's fellow man was a target of Micah's rebuke as well. As Israel's society shifted to a merchant economy and the use of money replaced barter as the basis for transactions, the separation between rich and poor broadened. Unethical merchants were able to increase their profits by using a light weight to balance the amount of a product they sold and a heavy weight to balance the gold they charged for the product. The laws of the jubilee year and the provisions for the helpless—the poor, the widow, the orphan, the sojourner—were all but forgotten. Because no effective system of justice was enforced, the strong were able to oppress the weak.

International Situation. The list of cities in 1:10–16 indicates the march of Sennacherib. As king of Assyria (705–681 B.C.) Sennacherib was challenged in 703 B.C. by a coalition of tribes led by Merodach-baladan. When this rival took Babylon, he sought support by sending messengers to other countries—

among them Israel. While Sennacherib focused his efforts on regaining Babylon, Hezekiah seized the Assyrian envoy and joined Tyre and Sidon in withholding tribute. After a successful campaign in the East, Sennacherib turned
to the other end of his empire and defeated the armies of Egypt and the
Philistines. Finally from the defeated city of Lachish he demanded surrender
and tribute from Hezekiah. According to Sennacherib's records he defeated
forty-six Israelite cities and laid siege to Jerusalem. This siege is recorded
in 2 Kgs 18. The march from Lachish to Jerusalem is depicted in Mic 1
(C. F. Pfeiffer, *The Biblical World* [Grand Rapids: Baker Book House, 1966]
516–17).

The Book—Authorship

Until the middle of the nineteenth century very little critical work was
done on the book of Micah. Ewald was the first to raise serious questions
about the authorship of Micah. He first argued that chaps. 4–5 were written
by another prophet contemporary with Micah because of a difference in style.
Later he defended Micah's authorship of chaps. 4–5 urging similarities of
form, thought and diction. But in 1867 Ewald argued that chaps. 6–7 were
not the work of Micah but rather the work of another prophet living during
the dark days of the reign of Manasseh. Ewald said that chaps. 1–5 are complete
in themselves and need nothing added to them, but there is a complete change
in style and historical background in chaps. 6–7. Writing in 1878, Wellhausen
agreed with Ewald that 6:1–7:6 comes from the time of Manasseh but concluded that 7:7–20 was added during the exile (cf. J. M. P. Smith 13). In
1881, B. Stade wrote an article in *ZAW* in which he denied chaps. 4–5 to
Micah *in toto* largely on the grounds that Micah would not have blunted his
prophecies of doom in chaps. 1–3 with such promises of hope in 4–5. Following
Stade's work there was a veritable flood of materials produced by OT literary
critics who denied almost all of the book after chap. 3 to Micah.

Are there sections in the book that are earlier or later than Micah? Few
OT scholars today would defend the Mican authorship of the entire book.
However, some scholars attribute much more of the materials to Micah than
others. L. C. Allen assumes that Micah could have written all of the book
with the exception of three passages. He believes that 4:1–4 is earlier than
Micah and 4:6–8 and 7:8–20 are exilic or early post-exilic. Allen posits an
editor who collected, arranged and added to the oracles of Micah in the
early post-exilic period (Allen 251–52).

Structure

In the twentieth century the work of the literary critic has been augmented
by that of the form critic and that of the history of tradition scholar. The
form critic has been concerned with isolating the pericopes, identifying the
Sitz im Leben, and with tracing the oral transmission of the text. Hermann
Gunkel, the father of form criticism, did a study on the close of Micah (7:7–
20) and demonstrated how four different pericopes of varying literary types
were connected to form a prophetic liturgy which was sung by different singers

in Jerusalem on one of the days of grief about the time of Trito-Isaiah (Hermann Gunkel, "The Close of Micah," in *What Remains of the OT,* trans. A. K. Dallas [New York: Macmillan, 1928] 146–47).

Eduard Nielsen was one of the first scholars to do a history of tradition study on any portion of Micah. In his *Oral Tradition* (1954) he made a thorough study of Mic 4–5. Nielsen reviews the radical views of Marti (1904) and Hylmo (1919) in which Marti denied to Micah anything in the book after chap. 3. Nielsen demonstrates the traditio-historical approach to Mic 4–5. He believes that an inner core of material can be found in 4:9–5:6 made up of four pericopes which contrast the present distress with the promises of future deliverance. On either side of this center are pericopes (4:1–5; 5:10–14) which state that all nations will be brought into the kingdom of God. Then Nielsen suggests that 4:1–5 may have been written by the same hand that wrote chap. 3 because of the deliberate contrast between the passages.

Ten years after Nielsen's work, B. Renaud published a study on the structure of Mic 4–5. Renaud arranged the materials in these chapters in a chiastic order rather than as layers around a central core. According to Renaud sections A and A' go together, A = 4:1–4; A' = 5:9–13 (Eng. 5:10–14). Sections B and B' are alike, B = 4:6–7 (2:12–13) and B' = 5:6–7 (Eng. 5:7–8). Section C = 4:8–14 (Eng. 4:8–5:1) is closely related to C' = 5:1–5 (Eng. 5:2–6). Renaud viewed these chapters as a coherent theological unit written by a Jerusalem priest-scribe of the fifth century. They are a midrash which combines many earlier sources into an eschatological synthesis.

In 1969 John T. Willis published a critique of Renaud's views along with his own theories about the structure of Micah 4–5 (*ZAW* 81 [1969] 191–214). Willis argues that chaps. 4–5 are a unit made up of seven parallel pericopes (4:1–5; 6–8; 9–10; 11–13; 4:14–5:5, Eng. 5:1–5:6; 5:6–8, Eng. 5:7–9; 5:9–14, Eng. 5:10–15) each of which starts with the present hopeless situation of Israel and concludes with a promise of future victory and hope. Willis argues that the hope elements are "not attempts by a later generation to offset the severity of the doom oracles of the pre-exilic period" (p. 203).

Leslie Allen (257–61) draws on the work of Nielsen and Willis and arranges the materials in chaps. 3–5 in concentric circles around a center section made up of three pericopes: 4:9–10; 4:11–13; 4:14–5:5 (Eng. 5:1–6.) The two passages on either side of this center material (4:6–8; 5:6–8, Eng. 5:7–9) deal with the remnant. The two outside sections 3:1–4:5 and 5:9–14 (Eng. 5:10–15) contain long sections on judgment (3:1–12; 5:9–13, Eng. 5:10–14) followed by short sections of hope (4:1–5; 5:14, Eng. 5:15).

What can we say about the structure of the book of Micah? Have the materials in this book been arranged in a logical, or chronological, or a theological pattern? Von Rad says, ". . . the prophetic corpus lies before us in what are . . . very shapeless collections of traditional material, arranged with almost no regard for content or chronological order, and apparently quite unaware of the laws with which we are familiar in the development of European literature" (G. von Rad, *Old Testament Theology,* vol. 2 [Edinburgh: Oliver and Boyd, 1965] 33, n.1). Von Rad quotes Martin Luther as saying the prophets "have a queer way of talking, like people who instead of proceeding in an orderly manner, ramble off from one thing to the next so that you cannot make head or tail of them or see what they are getting at" (Ibid.). G. W. Wade says that the book as a whole lacks any systematic structures: ". . . its contents comprise a number of sections of which many stand in no logical or orderly relation to one another" (Wade, xx).

But some scholars try to organize the seemingly unorganizable. Almost every scholar who has written on Micah has offered some outline or scheme by which the materials are to be arranged. Ewald, Mays and Lescow divide the materials into two sections (chaps. 1–5 and 6–7), although Mays in his commentary simply discusses the materials in the book in thirty-one separate sections.

Many writers on Micah divide the book into three major sections: 1–3 (judgment); 4–5 (hope); 6–7 (judgment and hope). J. M. P. Smith and George Adam Smith used this system of arrangement. John T. Willis and L. C. Allen have made a strong case for arranging the material into three major divisions (1–2; 3–5; 6–7). F. C. Eiselen in his old but valuable commentary on the Minor Prophets used this outline for the book. In support of this outline we note that chaps. 1, 3, and 6 all begin with the words "Hear ye." Each of these sections begins with a message of judgment and ends with a note of hope.

The careful reader of the Hebrew text will notice obvious "catch-words" and other devices that are used to join pericope to pericope. But there is no definitive way to outline the book. This should be obvious when one considers how many different ways it has been outlined. Even the number and limits of pericopes in the book is not precise. Willis says that the modern critic should not expect to find a structure in biblical literature similar to modern literary canons. But ". . . it seems only fair to give ancient literary works the benefit of the doubt and allow them the possibility of containing coherent principles of organization" (J. T. Willis, *Seminar Papers SBL* [1978] 92). Scholars still disagree on the outline, date, and authorship of the book. Hans Walter Wolff, writing in 1978, said, "the extent of the secondary material in the Book of Micah is as controversial as ever" (H. W. Wolff, "Micah the Moreshite," *Israelite Wisdom* 77).

It is always difficult to discern major divisions in the materials of the OT prophets. In the commentary below the material is arranged in twenty pericopes. If larger units are present, then the grouping of chaps. 1–2; 3–5; and 6–7 together as three judgment/hope oracles seems to have the most support from the text.

Date

Extreme dates are assigned to various sections of the book. For example: J. Dus assigns the origin of 7:7–20 to the period just after the battle of Ebenezer in which the Philistines captured the ark about 1100 B.C. (J. Dus, "Weites zum nordisraelitischen Psalm Micah 7:7–20," *ZDMG* 115 [1965] 14–22. cf. Willis, *Restoration Quarterly* 13 [1977] 89). Stade, Marti, Haupt, Nowack and T. H. Robinson assigned the same passage to the Maccabean period in the second century.

I believe that the prophet Micah furnished the inspiration for the entire project. The materials may have been edited and supplemented in the time of Jeremiah and again in the exilic or early post-exilic period by the prophetic disciples of Isaiah and Micah. But the basis for the entire book is found in the life and teachings of the prophet Micah and so dates back to his lifetime— about 700 B.C.

The Text

The MT of Micah shows signs of corruption in a few places. Following the translation of each pericope is a list of notes on the text. In some cases the person, gender, and/or number of certain words must be changed to fit the context (i.e. 1:2, 9, 10; 3:10; 6:4; 7:12, 14, 15, 19). Some necessary words are missing from the text (i.e. 1:7; 2:6; 6:10). מִי "who?" is used for מַה "what?" in 1:5. Wrong voweling in particular words is used in 1:8; 2:12; 3:10. Words are divided improperly in 2:12; 6:9. The consonants ר and ד are confused in 6:9; 7:12. One word must be omitted (6:11). The text must be emended in 1:5, 12; 4:10; 5:5 (Eng. 5:6); 6:2, 9, 14. The most difficult verse in the book is 6:14. A glance at different translations of this verse will demonstrate the variety of conjectures that are based on this text.

There is a rich variety in the witness of the various versions to the text. Brief portions of a commentary on Micah have been found in caves one and four at Qumran, and a portion of the scroll of the Minor Prophets found at Wadi Muraba'at (Mur 88) contains a section from Micah. For a recent, brief study of the text of Micah see Matthew Collin, "Recherches sur L'histoire textuelle Du Prophete Michee," *VT* 21 (1971) 281–97. For an older but thorough study of the text of Micah see John Taylor, *The Masoretic Text and the Ancient Versions of the Book of Micah* (Edinburgh: William and Norgate, 1891).

The Message of Micah

For many years the bulk of OT scholarship was primarily interested in dissecting and analyzing the biblical materials according to their literary sources. But recently scholars have moved behind the literary sources to the origin of the biblical traditions in the worship, judicial, and political centers of Israel. They have attempted to trace the history of these traditions from their origins to the time of the final editorial work of each part of the OT. Along with all these processes they look for the theological thrust. This attempt to discover the theological thrust of a passage is actually a rediscovery of a vital aspect of biblical exegesis which was lost during the sway of the positivistic History of Religion School.

Before one does a theological study of the book of Micah, one should make a thorough study of the text, establishing the original reading wherever possible. One should mark off each pericope and isolate the literary sources. One should identify the literary genre, propose a *Sitz im Leben*, and attempt a reconstruction of the history of tradition for each pericope. In the commentary below I have studied the text, marked off the pericopes and identified the literary genre for each section. It is not always possible to determine the *Sitz im Leben* or reconstruct the history of each pericope. But it is possible to look for the theological thrust of each section and to arrange such findings in an orderly fashion. Even though the book may contain materials earlier than and later than Micah, the theology is essentially the same. If Micah used earlier materials he shaped them according to his theology. If a later disciple of Micah put this material together he did it in the spirit of the theology of his predecessor. However, the purpose and use of the materials in Micah might change from generation to generation. For example, Micah's message of judgment was probably intended to bring his generation to repentance so that the judgment might be avoided. But for the people of the exile who had already experienced judgment the purpose was to assure them that God had not abandoned them. James Ward says that "the oracles of doom functioned in the exile to justify the destruction of Jerusalem and to elicit a spirit of contrition among survivors" (*IDBSup* 592–93).

What is the message of Micah? The most prominent theme in Micah is judgment. Judgment is coming (1:2–4) and has come (7:7–20). The judgment motif is so strong in this book that several scholars have claimed that Micah only preached judgment. Judgment in Micah is seen in the destruction of Samaria (1:6–7), in the coming of an invader against Jerusalem (1:15), in the greedy land-grabbers' loss of their land (2:3–5) and in their being abandoned by Yahweh (3:4), in shame for the false prophets (3:6–7), in the siege of Jerusalem and the humiliation of their king (3:9–12; 5:1), in the cleansing of the land from idolatry and militarism (5:9–13, Eng. 5:10–14), in the removal of the wicked, the violent, the liars and cheats (6:9–16), and in the judgment on the nations (1:2; 4:13; 5:4–5, Eng. 5:5–6, 8–9, 15).

What causes God's judgment? The book of Micah answers quickly, "Sin brings judgment" (1:5). "Sin" חטא and "rebellion" פשע are used as word pairs in 1:5, 13; 3:8; 6:7. "Iniquity" עון occurs in 7:18–19. Sin here takes many forms ranging from idolatry (1:7; 5:12, Eng. 5:13) to murder (7:2). Abuse of judicial and political power leads to the oppression of the poor (2:1–2). Lying (6:12), stealing (6:11), and turning to the occult (5:11, Eng. 5:12) are condemned. How does God's judgment work? The basic principle by which judgment is meted out in the book of Micah is the law of retaliation. Judgment is related to the crime. Those who plan evil will find Yahweh planning evil against them (2:1–3). Those who snatch lands away from others will have their own lands and posterity taken away (2:4–5). Those who turn a deaf ear to the cry of their helpless victims will find that God will not hear them when they cry (3:1–4).

The reason for judgment is found in the nature of God. He is a God of anger and wrath against iniquity (5:14, Eng. 5:15). God cannot forget wickedness (6:10) nor acquit the guilty (6:11). He is a God who hides his face from disobedient people (3:4) and comes to judge them (1:2).

Yahweh is the covenant God of Israel. This can be seen in the covenant lawsuit language in chap. 6. Mic 7:20 is full of covenant language. But Yahweh is more than the God of Israel. He is sovereign over the whole world (1:2–4; 5:14, Eng. 5:15; 7:17). Because he is sovereign he can exercise his grace and forgiveness. God is a savior (2:12–13; 7:15), a redeemer (4:10), and a shepherd (7:14). God does not keep his anger forever, but is compassionate and forgiving (7:18–19). God is faithful to his promises (7:20).

What does God seek from man? Does God want lavish sacrifices or groveling servitude from man? That question is asked in 6:6–7. In one of the great summaries of prophetic religion Micah reminds his people that God has declared what is good and what he seeks from man. Nothing is said about sacrifices. God is concerned that man's acts (what he does עשׂה) be just (משׁפט); that his loves, desires, and motives (אהב) be true and faithful (אמת); and that his relationship to God be one of humility and cautious fellowship (צנע). Micah's attitude toward sacrifice was essentially the same as that of Isaiah (1:11–13) and Amos (5:21–22). Sacrifices in themselves were of no value. Their value depended upon the attitudes and actions of the worshiper.

Is there any hope in the book of Micah? There certainly is. If the book is arranged in three large sections—1–2; 3–5; 6–7—each section ends with a message of hope. Most of the hope-oriented material is in chaps. 4–5 and 7:7–20. Are these hope messages from Micah or from a later redactor? The time is past when all of the hope passages in pre-exilic prophets can automatically be assigned to a post-exilic editor. Earlier scholars thought that Micah could not have preached any messages of hope because the people of Jeremiah's day remembered him only as a prophet of doom (Jer 26:18–19). But such reasoning gives too much weight to an argument from silence.

A study of the cultic materials from pre-exilic Israel and the Ancient Near East has shown a very strong doom-hope motif. In every lament in the Psalms there is a note of hope. Undoubtedly many of them are pre-exilic. The basic pattern of Israel's holy history, the exodus-conquest motif, is that of suffering-salvation. Therefore, we should not expect a radical difference between pre-exilic, exilic, and post-exilic materials as far as hope is concerned, since they are all grounded in the same covenant theology, transmitted largely through the cult.

Hope, to be hope, must be oriented toward the future. Micah speaks often of the present evil situation. The greed and fraud of merchants (6:10–11), the crimes of land grabbers (2:1–2; 3:2–3), the corruption of spiritual leaders (2:11; 3:11), in addition to the ominous approach of an enemy nation, all present a dark picture. But the prophet said that those conditions would not prevail forever. Judgment would come but a saved, chastened, and faithful remnant would survive (2:12; 4:7; 5:6, 7, Eng. 7, 8; 7:19). A new king from the line of David would be born in Bethlehem and replace the present weak king on the throne. He would reign in the majesty of the name of Yahweh. His people would dwell securely and he would be great to the ends of the earth (5:1–3, Eng. 5:2–4).

OUTLINE

Superscription 1:1
1. Yahweh is coming   1:2–7
2. The prophet's lament   1:8–16
3. Woe to the wealthy wicked   2:1–5
4. Micah and the land-grabbers   2:6–11
5. A remnant to be restored   2:12–13
6. Guilty rulers   3:1–4

Superscription (1:1)

Bibliography

Tucker, G. M. "Prophetic Superscriptions and the Growth of the Canon." *Canon and Authority* ed. Coats and Long. Philadelphia: Fortress (1966) 56–70. **Willis, J. T.** in *Seminar Papers of SBL* (1978) 97. **Wolff, H. W.** in *Israelite Wisdom* 77–84.

Translation

[1] *The word of Yahweh which came to Micah* [a] *the Moreshite* [b] *in the days of Jotham, Ahaz, Hezekiah, kings of Judah, which* [c] *he saw* [d] *concerning Samaria and Jerusalem.*

Notes

a. LXX "and the Lord's word came to Micah" makes this heading like that in Jonah.

b. Lxx[B] τὸν τοῦ Μωρασθι "who was of Morash." This seems to make מרשתי the name of his father (cf. Wolff, 1). Tg דממרשא and Syr refer to a place, Moresha (cf. 1:15).

c. LXX ὑπὲρ ὧν makes the relative pronoun refer to the kings of Judah. Vg *quod* correctly relates to דבר יהוה *verbum Domini* "the word of Yahweh." אשר "which" is properly accusative. Wolff (1) notes that חזה "saw" always has an object in comparable settings.

d. Tg דאתנבי "he prophesied." But LXX εἶδεν "he saw."

Explanation

All OT prophetic books with the exception of Haggai and Zechariah begin with a superscription. A superscription is a statement prefixed to a written work which usually gives the historical setting of the book. A superscription differs from a title and an introduction. A title is simply a name and stands outside the work itself. An introduction usually describes the purpose, extent, and method of the work of which it is an integral part. A superscription is more than a title and less than an introduction. In the OT Prophets the superscription was usually affixed to the beginning of the completed work by the editor or collector of the materials in the book. In the case of Micah, the superscription was probably attached at the time the Book of the Twelve was put together.

The superscription of Micah is a phrase followed by two relative clauses. There are four elements in this superscription. First is the title, "The word of Yahweh which came to Micah." This title asserts that what follows is authoritative because it is the word of Yahweh, Israel's covenant God. The superscriptions of Hosea, Zephaniah, and Joel begin with these same words. The word of Yahweh is described as one which "came." "Came" like "happened" points to the fact that it had its origin outside the prophet.

This word of God came to a particular man מיכה המרשתי "Micah the Moreshite," at a specific time, "in the days of Jotham, Ahaz, and Hezekiah," and for a specific purpose, "concerning Samaria and Jerusalem." The name

Micah is an abbreviated form of מיכיה *Micayah* (Jer 26:18) and means "who is like Yahweh?" There is probably a play on his name in 7:18. Micah was a common name in Israel. It was an expression of praise and wonder at the incomparable God of Israel.

Of all the Micahs in the OT (Judg 17–18; 2 Sam 9:12; 1 Kgs 22:8; 1 Chr 5:5; 9:15; 23:20; 2 Chr 34:20; Neh 10:11; Mic 1:1) there was only one who lived in Moresheth and he was a prophet. Moresheth probably is to be identified with the modern village of Tell el Judeideh about twenty-five miles southwest of Jerusalem on the road from Azekah to Lachish. Although Micah grew up in a small village and lived there long enough to be identified with it, he probably spent much of his life in Jerusalem. Like Nahum the Elkoshite and Amos from Tekoa, Micah was known by his place of origin. Such an identification was given to a man away from home by his associates who knew of his origin.

The time of Micah's ministry is indicated by the names of the three kings (Jotham, Ahaz, Hezekiah) who occupied the throne in Jerusalem. A maximum period of fifty-five years (742–687 B.C.) is covered by the kings' reigns. It is unlikely that Micah was active as a prophet during all of those years. However his message to Samaria (1:2–7) must be dated prior to 722 B.C. According to Jer 26:18–19 Micah preached the oracle concerning the destruction of Zion during the reign of Hezekiah probably about 701 B.C.

Two words are used in the superscription to describe how Micah received his message. It is said that the word of Yahweh "came" (היה) unto Micah. The word "came" is the same as the verb "to be." It can also mean "to become" or "to happen." The Hebrew language is action-oriented. Therefore the force here is that the word "happened," "came in power" to Micah (cf. 3:8). The other word in this verse which describes the manner in which Micah received his message is חזה "he saw." There are two Hebrew words which mean "he saw" (ראה and חזה). These two terms are synonyms and represent only dialectical differences. חזה is probably of Aramaic origin and ראה is of Arabic origin (H. H. Rowley, *The Servant of the Lord.* London: Lutterworth Press [1952] 100; J. Lindblom, *Prophecy in Ancient Israel.* Philadelphia: Muhlenberg Press [1962] 109). Micah does not use ראה but uses חזה three times (1:1; 3:7; 4:11). The use of the term "see" indicates that Micah was a man who had the gift of seeing and revealing hidden things which the common man could not see (Lindblom 88, 94).

According to the superscription, the immediate addresses of the word of Yahweh according to Micah were the cities of Samaria and Jerusalem. At least two OT scholars doubt that Micah himself addressed Samaria. According to James Mays and T. Lescow all references to Samaria in this book come from a later redactor. But there is not sufficient evidence to prove that Micah did not preach to or about Samaria. These two capital cities represented their nations (1:5, 6). Therefore any word directed to these cities was also addressed to the nations of Israel and Judah. But the word of Yahweh in Micah is directed to all ages in the sense that the conditions that called for an announcement of judgment then must all the more call for judgment today. And the basis of hope which Micah and his editors saw must serve as the basis of hope for us.

Yahweh Is Coming (1:2–7)

Bibliography

Crenshaw, J. L. "Wedorek 'al-Bamote 'ares." *CBQ* 34 (1972) 39–53. **Willis, J. T.** "Some Suggestions on the Interpretation of Micah 1:2." *VT* 18 (1969) 372–79.

Translation

2 *Hear ye peoples, all of you (them);* [a]
  Listen, O earth and all her fullness;   3+3
  And let the Lord [b] *Yahweh be a witness against you,*
  The Lord from his holy temple.   4+3
3 *For behold, Yahweh is going forth from his place,*
  and he will come down and walk [a] *upon the high places of the earth.*   4+4
4 *And the mountains will melt under him,*
  and the valley shall be split   3+2
like wax before the fire,
  like water poured down a slope.   3+3
5 *All this is for the transgression of Jacob,*
  and the sins of the house of Israel.   3+3
What [a] *is the transgression of Jacob?*
  Is it not Samaria?   3+2
And what is the sin [b] *of Judah?*
  Is it not Jerusalem?   3+2
6 *And I will make Samaria*
  a heap for the field,
  planting places for a vineyard.   2+2+2
And I will pour out her stones into the valley
  and her foundations I will uncover.   3+2
7 *And all her images shall be smashed,*
  and all of her harlot's fees [a] *shall be burned with fire,*
  and all of her idols I will make desolate,   3+3+3
because from the hire of a harlot she gathered (them), [b]
  and to the hire of a harlot they will return.   3+3

Notes

2.a. כלם "all of them" should be כלכם "all of you." These words are a quote from 1 Kgs 22:28 connecting Micah with Micaiah.

2.b. LXX deletes אדני "Lord." It does lengthen the line.

3.a. LXX and Vg delete ודרך "and walk." Crenshaw defends MT on the basis of its similarity to other similar passages (Amos 4:13; Job 9:8; Hab 3:15, 19; Deut 32:13; 33:29; Isa 58:14).

5.a. מי may be used in the neuter sense of "what" when a person is implied (GKC 137a). Here it is the author of sins (KD, 427).

5.b. Read חטאת בית "sins of the house" with LXX. Jerusalem was not known for its high places.

7.a. Mays, following Wellhausen, reads אשריה for אתנניה but this would require a fem. verb (ICC, 35).

7.b. Tg, Syr and Vg read קבצו, "they were gathered." MT has קבצה "she gathered." "Them" is omitted in MT.

Form/Structure/Setting

The first pericope (1:2–7) begins with Yahweh's call to the nations to listen to his witness against them (v 2) and concludes with the announcement of judgment on Samaria (v 7). Micah's lament (v 8) introduces the next pericope which ends in a call for mourning (v 16). The genre of the first pericope is in the form of a lawsuit. Yahweh as judge calls the whole world to attention. He testifies against them in a general way (v 2) then brings specific charges against Samaria and Jerusalem (v 5). Finally he announces judgment on Samaria (vv 6–7). There has been much debate about the unity and authorship of this pericope. The problem is that vv 2–4 seem to be an oracle against all nations while vv 6–7 clearly contain an oracle against Israel and Judah. This has led several scholars (B. Stade, Marti, Cheyne, Hölscher, Pfeiffer, Marsh, Mays, and Wolff) to conclude that the original beginning of the book was v 5b, and that vv 2–4 were added later by a post-exilic redactor who connected them to vv 5b–7 by inserting v 5a. John T. Willis defends the unity and Micah's authorship of this pericope by arguing that the covenant lawsuit form was a common form used by pre-exilic prophets (Isa 1:2–9; Hos 4:1–3; Jer 2:4–13; Mic 6:1–8); that neither v 5a nor 5b is a good beginning for a pericope; and that vv 2–4 do not form a complete pericope since they announce an impending judgment which is not described.

Willis points out that Yahweh is a witness against the nations in v 2, which makes the nations the defendants. In other covenant lawsuit passages the mountains or heavens (Mic 6:1–2; Isa 1:2) are witnesses not as accusers but as verifiers of the truth. The peoples are addressed in the second person in v 2 while Israel is referred to in the third person in v 5. Willis concludes that such a summons to the nations is appropriate in an oracle which announces judgment on Israel because the prophets considered Yahweh's punishment of Israel as a model of Yahweh's future punishment of the nations. The nations are to see Yahweh's witness against them (vv 2–4) in his punishment of his own people (vv 5–7). "If Yahweh does not spare His own people, the nations need not expect that He will spare them" (Willis, *VT* 18 [1968] 378). G. Hylmo said, "By his judgment of sinful Israel, Yahweh will even yet awaken the sleeping conscience of the sinful nations of the world" (p. 18, quoted by Willis, *VT* 18 [1968] 378).

Explanation

Micah uses the imperative of the verb "hear" (שמע) to call the nations to listen to his witness against them. The call was a summons to court. "Hear" was a favorite term of the eighth century prophets (cf. Amos 3:1, 13; 4:1; 5:1; 7:16; 8:4; Hos 4:1; 5:1; Isa 6:9; 7:13; 28:14; 33:13; 36:13; Mic 1:2; 3:1, 9; 6:1, 2, 9). Why does the Lord call all nations to listen without bringing specific charges against them at this time? Charges are brought against Samaria and Jerusalem (1:5). Some have suggested that עמים here means "tribes" rather than "peoples" as it does in Gen 49:10; Deut 32:8; 33:3; Hos 10:14; Zech 11:10. The parallel "the earth and her fullness" supports the universal interpretation of "peoples." However those who see "peoples" referring to the tribes of Israel point out that the term translated "earth" (1:2) can also mean "land" (of Palestine). The exact same words, "Hear ye peoples all of you," are used by Micaiah probably speaking of the tribes or the people of Israel in 1 Kgs 22:28. However since this expression is not in the LXX version of 1 Kgs 22:28 no weight should be put upon it in interpreting this passage in Micah.

James L. Mays believes that the phrase refers to "all the nations of the earth" but that it is the work of a later redactor who gave Micah's message a universal setting. The book of Micah is interested in the motif, "Yahweh, Israel and the nations," according to Mays (40–41). It is true that after the nations are introduced in 1:2 they are not mentioned again until 4:1 where they are to come to the temple in the new Jerusalem to learn the law of Yahweh. In 5:6, 7 (Eng. 5:7, 8) Israel is to become a remnant in the midst of many nations. But in 5:14 (Eng. 5:15) and 7:16, 17 the nations are to experience the judgment of God. At this point it is impossible to tell how much of this book is the work of Micah and how much is the work of redactors. However, there is no compelling reason to deny that the opening call of Yahweh to the nations in 1:2 is the work of Micah.

"His holy temple" refers to God's dwelling place in heaven as v 3 implies. Although Israel believed that God visited his people on earth and his name dwelt in the temple in Jerusalem, his true dwelling place was in heaven (Ps 11:4; Isa 63:15; 64:1; Hab 2:20; Zech 2:13).

The announcement of Yahweh's coming to earth is made in v 3. The theophany is clothed in strong anthropological language. Yahweh, like a giant, will come down and tread on the high places of the earth (Amos 4:13). The high places were not just mountain tops, but were also places of pagan or syncretistic worship which were to be destroyed at his coming. Crenshaw sees an influence of Ugaritic myths on this language (p. 44).

The effects of Yahweh's coming are described in v 4. Like wax melts before a fire, the valleys will be cleft by rushing torrents of water. Many have understood this language as that of the thunderstorm that often accompanied a theophany (Exod 19:16). The lightning is the fire and the waters poured down a slope are the torrents of rain. In the land south of Jerusalem rain was a rare event. When it did rain however the claylike soil would refuse to absorb the moisture, forming an almost waterproof covering over the ground. Because of this even a rain of less than half an inch created large, gushing streams and waterfalls powerful enough to move boulders and dig channels in the earth. In any case the similes are designed to teach that when Yahweh appears in judgment on the earth ruin and destruction result. Nothing can abide his immediate presence (Pss 18:7–15; 68:2; 97:3; Nah 1:5; Mal 3:2).

The reason for "all this" (the coming of Yahweh), is the transgression of Jacob and the sins of Israel. The precise meaning of the names Jacob and Israel is not clear. Normally they are synonyms either for the patriarch, the nation, or for the Northern Kingdom. However, the issue is confused here by the second half of the verse where Jacob stands for the Northern Kingdom designated as Samaria, and Israel is parallel with Judah.

The capital cities, Samaria and Jerusalem, are identified as the offenders which call forth God's judgment. Two rhetorical questions in 1:5b ask literally "who is the transgression of Jacob" and "who is the high place (sin) of Judah?" "Who" is used rather than "what" because the capital cities are personified as the guilty ones. "High places" in the MT is changed to "sin of" by the LXX, Syr, Tg and many modern versions because the high places as centers of pagan worship were constant occasions of sin (2 Chr 28:25).

The immediate result of God's coming will be judgment on Samaria. She will be made a "heap" (ruin) in an open field. A heap of stones or "ruin" usually marked the site of an intentional destruction (cf. Josh 8:28). The place where the city of Samaria stood was to be cleared of houses, rubble, and stones so that vineyards might be planted there. Her building stones were to be poured down the mountain (cf. v 4) and her foundations were to be laid bare.

V 7 emphasizes the fact that it is Samaria's idolatry that causes her destruction. Her graven images will be smashed, her profits from sacred prostitution burned, and her idols devastated. Some scholars see a problem with the first use of the word אתנן in this verse. In the last part of the verse אתנן refers to the "hire" of a harlot. But "hire" of a harlot does not seem to fit the context in the first part of the verse. The context calls for three different words for image or idol. The terms for image and idol are there; therefore אשריה "Asherah" could be read for אתנן "harlot's fees" in 1:7a (cf. Mays 46n).

Again an explanation for the judgment is given. The images had been gathered with the hire of a harlot. The hire of a harlot probably should not be interpreted literally, but as a reference to the false idea of the people that their prosperity was the gift of Baal. However, idol worship probably was practiced in Israel and Judah at this time. Micah says that the smashed, burned, and devastated images will become the property of the pagan invaders who smashed and burned them.

In 722/21 B.C. Samaria was captured by the Assyrians. At that time the city experienced little physical damage. It certainly was not destroyed. Sargon II, King of Assyria, claims to have restored the city and made it more habitable than before. The restored city served as the capital of the province of Samaria until its capture by Alexander the Great. Then it became a Greek city with pagan shrines. It was destroyed by John Hyrcanus ca 107 B.C. but was soon rebuilt. It has been occupied constantly since that date (D. Winton Thomas, *Archaeology and Old Testament Study* [Oxford: Clarendon Press, 1967] 348).

The first pericope in Micah is one of judgment. Judgment at first has a universal dimension; then both Samaria and Jerusalem are involved; finally the judgment on Samaria is detailed. Micah may be following the lead of Amos in the form of his message. Just as Amos began preaching against Israel's enemies, then after getting his hearer's attention announced judgment on her; so Micah began preaching about the nations and Judah, before announcing the coming judgment on Samaria.

The Prophet's Lament   (1:8–16)

Bibliography

Schwantes, S. J. "Critical Notes on Micah 1:10–16." *VT* 14 (1964) 454–561. **Stine-spring, W. F.** "No Daughter of Zion." *Encounter* 26 (1965) 133–41. **Thomas, D. W.** "A Pun on the Name of Ashdod in Zephaniah 2:4." *ET* 74 (1962) 63.

Translation

8 *For this I will beat my breast and howl*	
I will go barefoot [a] *and naked.*	3+3
I will lament like jackals.	
And mourn like the daughter of an ostrich.	3+3
9 *Because incurable is her wound,* [a]	
because it has come to Judah;	3+2
it has touched the very gate of my people,	
even Jerusalem.	3+2
10 *In Gath do not tell it,*	
weep not at all;	2+2
in Beth-le-Aphrah	
roll yourselves [a] *in the dust.*	2+2
11 *Cross over,* [a]	
inhabitant of Shapir,	
in nakedness and shame.	2+2+2
The inhabitants of Zaanan	
did not come out.	
Lamentation will be in Beth-ezel,	2+2
when he takes away his support from you.	3+3
12 *The inhabitant of Maroth*	
waited [a] *for good,*	2+2
but evil came down from Yahweh	
to the gate of Jerusalem.	2+2+2
13 *Harness the chariot to the steeds,*	
O inhabitant of Lachish,	3+2
who are the beginning of sin	
for the daughter of Zion	2+2
For in you were found	
the transgressions of Israel.	2+2
14 *Therefore you shall give parting gifts*	
to Moresheth-gath,	3+3
houses of Achzib intended to be deceitful	
to the kings of Israel.	3+2
15 *I will again bring a possessor in* [a] *to you,*	
inhabitant of Moreshah.	3+2

> To Adullam will come
>> the glory of Israel.   2+2
> ¹⁶ Make bald and cut your hair
>> for the sons of your pamperings;   2+2
> make broad your baldness like an eagle
>> because they go from you as captives.   ʼ   3+2

Notes

8.a. Read the *Qere* שׁוֹלָל "barefoot" (cf. *CHAL* 364; Mays 48; Job 12:19).

9.a. מכותיה "her wounds" should be read as sing.

10.a. Read 2 mas. pl. impv. התפלשׁוּ "roll yourselves" with LXX, Syr and Vg instead of התפלשׁתי "I have rolled."

11.a. No emendation is necessary. לכם "for yourselves" completes imperv.

12.a. Read יחל "to hope" for חלה "to be sick."

15.a. אבי lcs qal impf. from בוא (cf. 1 Kgs 21:29) "I will bring in."

Form/Structure/Setting

The second pericope in the book of Micah is a lament over the fate of Judah (1:8–16). V 8 may be a transition verse connecting the following lament with the judgment on Samaria in 1:6–7. "Upon this" or "For this" at the opening of v 8 probably refers to the approaching judgment on Judah.

The lament is largely a series of puns on the names of twelve cities. The names of twelve cities in the Shephelah are given meaning symbolic of the judgment which God was bringing on them in the form of an invader, probably the king of Assyria. Many of the textual problems in the pericope may be due partially to faulty transmission of the text. Elliger, followed by Schwantes, argued that the original manuscript at this point was damaged on the right side of the column. Hence lacunae and other corruption resulted. Specific problems with the text will be noted in the comments below.

The prophet's personal reaction described in v 8 is one of outward demonstration of his sorrow. He says, "I will beat my breast and howl." For many of us mourning is a private affair. We wear black, seclude ourselves, and suffer in silence. The mourner in the OT gave full expression to his grief. "Barefoot and naked" describes the appearance of a mourner and/or a prisoner. Slaves and captives usually wore only loin cloths and no shoes. This act by the prophet not only symbolized his mourning but also indicated the fate of many of his fellow countrymen. Jackal and ostrich are frequently mentioned together (Isa 34:13; 43:20; Jer 50:39; Job 30:29). They were famous for their howls and mourning sounds.

V 8 makes clear the reason for the prophet's mourning—the imminent judgment on Judah. Her wound will be fatal. It has touched the heart of the nation—the gate of Jerusalem.

The historical situation to which this language refers is probably Sennacherib's invasion of Judah in 701 B.C. According to 2 Kgs 18:13–16 and Sennacherib's own accounts, the Assyrian king came into Palestine attacking Tyre which was one of the leaders of the rebellion against the empire. Sennacherib then marched against Ashkelon and Ekron putting down their resistance. He met and defeated an Egyptian army at Eltekeh, near Ekron, then turned on Judah. He reports that he reduced forty-six cities of Judah and deported their population. He shut up Hezekiah, king of Judah and the remnant of his troops in Jerusalem "like a bird in a cage" (Bright 269). The twelve cities mentioned in Micah 1:10–15 were in the path of Sennacherib's march to Jerusalem.

Vv 10–15 are a lament over the fate of twelve cities ranging from Gath to Jerusalem. There is a word-play on the names of the cities. The word-plays are not to be taken lightly. The prophet was very serious in describing the misfortune that was coming on his home territory. It is difficult to discover the pun intended with every city. In fact there was probably no word-play intended on the name of the first city, Gath. Instead the prophet began his lament with a quotation from David's lament over Saul and Jonathan, "Tell it not in Gath" (2 Sam 1:20). He probably used this line because this lament over Judah was to be like the mourning for a loved one, and because the Assyrian invasion was to begin at Gath. Although there is no textual problem with this line some scholars would emend the text to read, "In the gardens of Giloh," to secure the word-play and make the passage refer to a known city in SW Judah (Josh 15:51; 2 Sam 15:12). The second line in v 10, "Weep not at all," is also correct although George Adam Smith reads with the LXX "Weep not in Acco." But Acco is too far north to be included in this list. JB leaves out the supposed city, "in . . . shed no tears." Mays and others believe that the negative should be dropped because the prophet was probably calling for more weeping not less. But that interpretation misses the point. The point is that there was to be no weeping in Judah because the Assyrian invasion would leave the people in a state of shock.

There is an obvious word-play on the name Beth-le-Aprah "House of dust." According to the marginal reading and the LXX the inhabitants of Beth-le-Aphrah were to roll themselves (MT "I will roll myself"). To roll in the dust was an expression of sorrow and mourning (cf. Jer 6:26; Ezek 27:30).

The name of the third city, Shaphir, means "beautiful." Her inhabitants are to be reduced to nakedness and shame by the invaders and they will pass over to exile. The fourth city, Zaanan (found only in this text), means "one who goes out" (to battle). This brave city will not go out to fight when the enemy approaches. Beth-ezel, the fifth city (found only in this text), means "house by the side of another" suggesting a helper or place of refuge. But also the king of Assyria will take away any help or refuge the city might be able to give to the victims of the attack. Maroth, the sixth city (known only from this text), means "bitterness." She looks for good but only evil comes down from Yahweh to the gate of Jerusalem. In the last line of v 12 two earlier themes are repeated: evil comes down from the Lord, a reminder of the earlier theophany (v 3), and "the gate of Jerusalem" recalls the line in v 9 at the opening of the lament. Jerusalem is the seventh city in the list.

Lachish was the chief city in southwest Judah. It was a fortified chariot city. The word-play on its name is seen in the Hebrew word (לרכש) for a team of horses (1:13). The prophet says that the horses in Lachish were to be harnessed to the chariots because the day of battle has come. In the last part of v 13 the prophet accuses Lachish as being the starting place for the sin of Jerusalem. The nature of the sin is not identified. Most commentaries identify the sin as that of introducing the trust in horses and chariots into the nation. But the text does not actually say that. "The beginning of the sin of the daughter of Zion" could refer to some Egyptian heresy imported into Jerusalem through Lachish. Elmo Scoggin believes that the sin was some form of idolatry practiced in the temple at Lachish. The ruins of a temple were discovered at the ancient site of Lachich in 1968 (cf. Scoggin, 195–96).

The ninth city, Moresheth-gath, is best known as the home of the prophet Micah. It is included in this list of towns, however, because it was in the path of the Assyrian invader and because its name, Moresheth, sounds very much like the Hebrew word מאׂרשׂת "dowry," "possession," or "gift." The word probably suggested to the hearers the idea of a parting gift to a bride leaving her father's house for that of her husband (1 Kgs 9:16; Deut 22:23). Micah says that the inhabitants of his home town will be departing for captivity.

The name Achzib (the tenth city) is very similar to the Hebrew word for "lie." Jeremiah uses this word "lie" to refer to a deceitful brook that becomes dry, disappointing, and unreliable (Jer 15:18). Now the city of Achzib has failed the kings of Israel. They expected help in resisting the Assyrians but found none in Achzib.

The last word-play is on the name of the eleventh city, Moreshah (not to be confused with Moresheth). Moreshah is similar to the word מֹורשׁ "possessor," "heir," or "conqueror." The idea is that the possessor will be possessed. And the glory of Israel, that is, her wealth and nobles, will flee for refuge in the cave of Adullum (twelfth city) where David escaped from Saul (1 Sam 22:1; 2 Sam 23:13). The lament began with the words, "Tell it not in Gath" which probably recalled the words, "The glory has departed." Now at the end of the lament the glory of Israel departs to the cave at Adullam.

So far archeologists have been unable to locate all these cities. A Bible map will give some help in visualizing the location of cities (see *Atlas* #154; Wolfe 896; McKeating 158).

The lament ends with a call for the mourners to cut their hair and make themselves bald as an expression of their grief. Although such action was forbidden in the law (Lev 21:5; Deut 14:1), the practice was common among Israel's neighbors and in Israel (Isa 3:24; 15:2; Jer 7:29; 16:6; Amos 8:10). At this time, hair was believed to have special powers and to contain the essence of life. Possibly because of its preservation after death, hair was a symbol of one's self. Holy men and women often allowed their hair to grow without cutting (Num 6:1–21) and kings displayed their power by long hair and a beard. The shaving of one's head went beyond mourning, for mourning only required disheveled hair. Micah's call to baldness may have been a symbol of Israel's helplessness and shame before the approaching armies and before the wrath of God (*IDBSup* 386; J. Lindblom, *Prophecy in Ancient Israel* [Philadelphia: Muhlenberg Press, 1962] 68–69). The one addressed in this call to mourning in v 16 is not identified. However, since the imperatives are in the feminine singular, we may assume that it is "the daughter of Zion" (v 13). The expression "daughter of Zion" here as in 4:8, 10, 13 should be taken as an apposition and read "daughter Zion" (cf. Stinespring, *Encounter* 26 [1965] 133–42).

Perhaps there is a bit of irony in the expression, "children of your delight." Literally it is, "sons of your pamperings." Now these pampered children are going into exile. The last verb גלה is a perfect form of the verb which suggested completed action. The question is: Is the action thought of as complete in the present, "They have gone captive" (NEB, JB, ASV), or in the future, "They will go into captivity" (KJV, RSV)? Those who read it as complete in the past regard this verse as a post-exilic addition to the work of Micah.

Woe to the Wealthy Wicked   *(2:1–5)*

Bibliography

Clifford, R. J. "The Use of Hoy in the Prophets." *CBQ* 28 (1966) 458–64. **Gerstenberger, E.** "The Woe-Oracles of the Prophets." *JBL* 81 (1962) 249–63. **Willis, J. T.** "On the Text of Micah 2:1a-b." *Biblica* 48 (1967) 534–41.

Translation

¹ *Woe to the devisers of wickedness*
 and plotters ^a *of evil on their beds.*   3+3
In the light of the morning they do it
 because there is power in their hands.   3+3
² *And they covet fields and seize them,*
 and houses and take them away.   3+2
And they do violence to a man and his house,
 a man and his inheritance.   3+2
³ *Therefore thus says Yahweh,*
 "Behold I am devising evil against this family,
 from which you will not withdraw your necks.   4+5+4
Do not walk haughtily
 for it is an evil time."   3+4
⁴ *In that day one will take up against you a taunt song,*
 and he will sing a lament (It has happened), ^a   4+4
and will say, ^b *"We are utterly devastated!*
 He changes the portion of my people."   3+3
How does he remove it from me?
 To the rebel ^c *he assigns* ^d *our fields.*   3+3
⁵ *Therefore there will be none of you* ^a
 casting a line by lot
 in the congregation of Yahweh.   3+3+2

Notes

1.a. פעלי "doers" in the sense of "planners."
4.a. *K-D* consider נהיה niph. part. "It has happened." L. C. Allen makes it a noun, "moaning." Mays thinks it is a dittography.

4.b. BHS adds waw consecutive. L. C. Allen omits as a scribal note.
4.c. Probably mas. noun (cf. *CHAL*, 364).
4.d. Mays reads piel as a hophal "are divided."
5.a. L. C. Allen reads לכם "for you" (pl.) instead of לך "for you" (sing.).

Form/Structure/Setting

The third pericope in the book of Micah (2:1–5) is a woe oracle, combined
with an announcement of judgment which will consist in a reversal of fortunes
for the evil-doers. The woe oracle is a common oral and literary form in
the prophets (Isa 5:8, 11, 18, 20; 10:1; 29:15; 31:1; 33:1; 45:9, 10; Jer 22:13;
Ezek 13:18; Amos 5:18; Hab 2:6, 9, 12, 15, 19; Zeph 3:1). It only occurs
once in Micah. The woe oracle is introduced by the interjection, הוֹי "alas,"
which sets the tone for the bad news that follows. The interjection is almost
always followed by an indefinite participle as in this case. The participle identifies the person or persons guilty of covenant-breaking who are in imminent
danger of experiencing judgment from God. It is not always easy to determine
the end of the woe oracle. It seems clear that this pericope ends with the
threat in v 5. The correspondence of the crimes (vv 1–2) to the punishments
(vv 3–4) indicates that the whole passage is intended to be a kerygmatic
unit (Gerstenberger 253).

Comment

In this pericope the prophet makes specific the charge against his people.
The chief offenders were a relatively small group of greedy, powerful business
men who spent their nights devising schemes to get possession of the land
of the small farmers. The next day they carried out their schemes because
they had sufficient economic, political and judicial power to accomplish their
goals even when their goals deprived a man and his household of their inheritance which was a part of covenant right. According to the covenant every
man in Israel was equal before God and the law, and the land of each tribe
and family was not to be transferred to another.

The sin here is the covetousness which produced the violent disregard
for justice. By adding field to field (Isa 5:8) these land monopolizers controlled
all the instruments of production in that agricultural society. Today there
is still the threat that all the farming land might be controlled by a few land
holders giving them abnormal power in the market. Although we are no
less dependent on agriculture for our food than were our ancestors, ours is
an industrial society. The instruments of production are not just land but
factories, raw materials, and capital. The concentration of these instruments
of production, distribution, and communication in the hands of a few may
threaten our society.

From the charges of greed and the violent seizure of other's property,
Micah turns to announce the outcome of such conduct. God himself is devising
a plan that will thwart the plan of the evil-doers. Micah speaks with divine
authority, "Therefore thus says Yahweh." Micah was convinced that the
wrongs in this world would eventually be made right because he believed
that his God was just and sovereign. There is some ambiguity in the meaning
of "this family" (v 3). Family in this context usually indicates the whole nation

(Amos 3:1). Is Micah saying that because of the sins of a few the whole family of Israel will be subjected to the conqueror's yoke? Or does he refer only to the guilty ones as "this family"?

It is not at all clear who the speaker is in v 4. Is it one of the guilty land-grabbers or is it one of their captors taunting them? The MT calls for a singular subject for the verbs, although RSV, NEB, and JB all use the plural "they" as the subject. It is best to understand the verse as the voice of one speaking for the rich land holders on whom the judgment of God has come. Micah quotes them as saying, "We are utterly devastated, he (God) changes the portion of my (the rich man's) people, how he (God) removes it (property) from me (the rich). To the rebel he (God) divides our fields."

The prophet speaks for God in v 5. The lot of the guilty will be completely cut off. They will no longer have any descendants to claim their heritage in the assembly of the Lord. When the Hebrew tribes came into Canaan with Joshua, he divided the land into various sections and cast lots to determine each tribe's territory (Josh 18:8–10). Here Micah seems to be looking forward to a new day when the land of Canaan will be redistributed among the families of his people. In that time Micah says that the guilty land-grabbers will have no one to claim their lot, either because their family will be completely decimated or because they will all be in exile.

Micah and the Land-Grabbers   (2:6–11)

Bibliography

Van der Woude, A. S. "Micah in Dispute with the Pseudo-prophets." *VT* 19 (1969) 244–60.

Translation

6 "Stop preaching," they preach.
"One (they) ᵃ must not preach these things.
Calamity will not overtake ᵇ us." ᶜ   2+2+2
7 Should it be said,ᵃ "O house of Jacob?
Has the Spirit of Yahweh become annoyed?
Are these his deeds?"   3+3+3
Do not my words cause good to happen
to him who walks uprightly?   3+3
8 But yesterday ᵃ my people rose up as an enemy.
"You strip off the mantle with (from) the robe   4+4
from the ones passing by (travelers) in trust,
from those averse ᵇ to war.   2+2
9 You have driven out the women of my people
from their pleasant houses.   3+2
You have taken away from their children
my glory forever.   3+2

¹⁰ *Arise, go,*
  for this is no resting place,   2+2
because of uncleanness you will be destroyed
  with a painful destruction.   3+2
¹¹ *If a man, walking*
  (in) spirit and deceit, lies saying,   2+3
"I will preach to you
  of wine and strong drink,"   2+2
then he would be the preacher
  for this people."   2+2

Notes

6.a. יַטִּפוּ "preach" is pl. but indefinite.
6.b. Read יִסַּג "overtake" as hiph. from נסג.
6.c. "Us" is not in MT.
7.a. Many scholars emend הֶאָמוּר "should it be said?" to הֲאָרֻר "Is it cursed?" But the MT is clear.
8.a. וְאֶתְמוּל "yesterday" is often divided וְאַתֶּם "you" and לְ attached to the following עַמִּי to form וּלְעַמִּי "and to or against my people." Such is possible but not imperative. The "my people" could refer to the wealthy wicked.
8.b שׁוּבֵי is a qal pass. part. "ones being returned from war/or averse to war." The latter fits the context better.

Form/Structure/Setting

This pericope 2:6–11 is subject to various interpretations. The MT is very difficult, so many emendations have been suggested. Another difficulty in this passage is that the speaker is not clear. Is this passage a dialogue or a dispute between Micah and the wealthy land-grabbers he addresses in 2:1–5, or are the opponents of Micah here a group of false prophets? Some scholars (Allen, Van der Woude) believe that false prophets are speaking in behalf of the greedy land-grabbers.

This is a disputation passage but it is not necessary to assume that false prophets were Micah's opponents here. It would be a perfectly natural reaction for the wealthy land-holders to try to silence Micah. Attempts to silence prophets are recorded in Amos 2:12, 7:12–13; Hos 9:8; Isa 30:10; Jer 11:21; 20:7–10.

Comment

Micah's wealthy hearers could not accept his message. They found it so offensive that they commanded him to stop saying such things as he had said in 2:1–5. These greedy laymen were commanding the prophet not to preach, yet they preached to him the worst kind of message. They were saying, "Calamity will not overtake us." The greedy oppressors were confident that no evil would come upon them. They believed that Micah was wrong when he said that God was devising evil against them and that the day would come when these swindlers would have no representative in the congregation of the Lord.

The reason for their confidence that no evil would befall them was to be found in their theology. They did not feel that such a subject should even be mentioned: "Should it be said, O house of Jacob?" Many scholars prefer to emend the MT from חאמר "should it be said" to הארר "is the house of Jacob accursed?" Van der Woude prefers to read the form האמין "He affirmed the house of Jacob" as in Deut 26:17–18. This would be a reference to the covenant between Israel and Yahweh. All such emendations are unnecessary. Micah's opponents using rhetorical questions were saying, "Do not even mention judgment. God is not annoyed. His spirit or power is not short. Are these things that you say will happen the deeds of God?"

The last line in v 7 is often emended to read "his words" for "my words." The meaning is the same regardless of who the speaker is. If the people speak, the reading should be "his, i.e. God's words." If Micah is speaking for God the reading should be "my words." The point in any case is that God's words or promises cause good to happen to the one who walks uprightly. "Walk" here refers to the manner of one's life and according to Micah his opponents had not been walking uprightly.

In v 8 Micah continues to describe the offenses of his hearers. He said, "Only recently (yesterday) you have illegally stripped the clothes from innocent and peaceful travellers. Women and children were victims of these greedy land-grabbers."

They had driven widows away from their pleasant homes and from their children they took away God's glory forever. God's glory in this context probably refers to a godly heritage which all children in Israel should enjoy.

Now the prophet's opponents are told to arise and depart for they who had evicted others from their land were about to be evicted themselves (v 10). "Rest" is a significant term in the OT and the NT. Israel's settlement in Canaan after wandering in the wilderness is described in terms of "rest" (Deut 12:10; Ps 95:11). But it meant more than physical rest. It referred to the accomplishment of the purpose of God (Heb 3:11, 18; 4:1, 3, 5, 10, 11).

The end of the pericope in v 11 returns to the beginning (v 6) and picks up the word "preach." Micah says that his hearers are so confused and out of touch with Yahweh that if a peripatetic, charismatic (man of the spirit) preacher were to come along preaching the gospel of wine and strong drink, they would hire him immediately.

A Remnant to Be Restored   (2:12–13)

Bibliography

Smith, L. P. "The Book of Micah." *Int* 6 (1952) 210–27.

Translation

[12] "*I will certainly gather all of you, Jacob;*
      I will surely assemble the remnant of Israel.   4+4
 I will place them together
      like sheep in a fold. [a]   2+2
 Like a flock in the middle of its pasture [b]
      they will bleat for fear of man."   3+2
[13] *The one who breaks out has gone up before them.*
      They have broken out and they passed over.
      There was a gate and they went out by it.   3+2+3
 And their king passed before them,
      Yahweh at their head.   3+2

Notes

12.a. MT has "Bozrah" בָּצְרָה. The same consonants with different vowels בַּצְרָה mean "sheepfold" (*CHAL* 310).

12.b. Read הַדֹּבֶר "the pasture" place the final ו on the next verb (cf. *CHAL* 68).

Form/Structure/Setting

This pericope has been the subject of much debate. Some interpreters such as John Calvin and T. H. Robinson have understood it as a continuation of the previous oracles of judgment. According to this view God is gathering the remnant for further judgment (for a history of the interpretation of this passage see J. M. P. Smith 66; L. P. Smith, *Int* 6 [1952] 219). Other scholars, beginning with Ewald and most recently Van der Woude (*VT* 19 [1969] 257) have taken these verses to be the words of false prophets (v 11) who preach a pleasant message of hope and salvation. It is best to take these words as a message of salvation by a true prophet—Micah or one of his disciples.

Because this oracle is a message of hope some scholars automatically deny it to Micah, saying that Micah was a prophet of doom and judgment. The language could easily be understood in terms of gathering the people of God who were scattered by the deportations of 597 and 586 B.C. Perhaps the majority of OT scholars hold this view. Some (Renaud, Moffatt, Condamin) believe that 2:12–13 is exilic or post-exilic, but they also believe that it is misplaced and should follow another message of hope in 4:7. But this pericope can also be understood as a reference to the gathering of the refugees of the villages and countryside of Judah who fled from the advance of Sennacherib toward Jerusalem in 701 B.C.

OT scholars no longer insist that a true prophet had to be a prophet of woe only. Scholars are beginning to understand that the basic pattern of the faith of the OT is one of a cry for help based on a hope that God would deliver the individual or the nation from trouble. The exodus experience was basis enough for such faith. The book of Judges presents a scenario of sin, judgment, cry, and deliverance. All of the laments in the Psalms are a cry for help plus an assurance of being heard. Is it surprising that the true prophets of the OT would follow their messages of judgment with a note of hope?

There is a sudden shift in emphasis between 2:11 and 2:12. Is it possible and probable that 2:12–13 was not delivered at the same time or to the same audience as 2:6–11? Von Rad suggested that messages of hope might have been given by the prophet only to his disciples, not to the people who had rejected earlier messages of judgment (von Rad, *OTT* II, 171).

There is even a shift in style between vv 12 and 13. The Lord speaks in v 12 while the prophet speaks about God in v 13. James Mays traces the supposed history of this pericope. Mays believes that the original saying is in 12ab. 12c is a comment on the original promise and v 13 is an expansion of v 12 (Mays 74).

All attempts to move 2:12–13 or to explain the history of the tradition of the passage are problematical. Let us acknowledge that the passage is subject to various interpretations but try to understand that it is a message of hope from Micah to the refugees who fled to Jerusalem because of Sennacherib's invasion of Judah in 701 B.C.

Comment

The promise to gather the remnant Israel into a safe place is expressed by the use of the infinitive absolute before the cognate verb in the first two lines of v 12. This is a strong way of expressing certainty. The place where the remnant is to be gathered for safety is not named. Many interpreters believe that the place is Babylon during the exile. However, Babylon was never understood as place of refuge or as a fold or pasture for the sheep who bleat or make a loud noise out of fear of the man, Sennacherib.

In v 13 the Sennacherib threat is over. The time has come for the refugees to return to their villages. Yahweh will break through the gate of the city of Jerusalem that had protected them but now confines them. The way to freedom is open and the remnant of Israel will go through the gate with Yahweh their king at their head.

Here is the first reference to a remnant שְׁאֵרִית in Micah. The term occurs five times in Micah (2:12; 4:7; 5:6, 7 [Eng. 5:7, 8]; 7:18). The idea of a remnant grew out of the idea of war and judgment. Amos spoke of an invader coming against Israel. The effect on Israel would be like those on sheep after a lion attacked the flock. Only a fragment of the original would be left (Amos 3:12), perhaps ten percent (Amos 5:3; 6:9). It was Isaiah who popularized the idea of only a remnant of Israel surviving the holocaust of judgment by naming his son *Shear-jashub,* "a remnant shall return." In Mic 4:6–7 the remnant is identified with the afflicted, poor and the lame (cf. Zeph 2:3). However Micah stresses the power of the remnant in 5:6–7 (Eng. 5:7–8) by comparing them to a lion which tramples and tears its enemies. In Mic 7:18 the remnant is a forgiven and cleansed group (cf. Zeph 3:12; Mays 101).

It is always difficult to discern major divisions in the materials in the books of the OT prophets. If the book of Micah is not a continuous series of pericopes without a major division, this oracle of hope (2:12–13) ends the first division. The pattern of judgment and hope marks the three main divisions in the book (chaps. 1–2, 3–5, 6–7).

Guilty Rulers   (3:1–4)

Bibliography

Bartlett, J. R. "The Use of the Word ראש as a Title in the OT." *VT* 19 (1969) 1–10. Willis, J. T. "A Note on ואמר in Micah 3:1." *ZAW* 80 (1968) 50–54.

Translation

> ¹ *And I said,*[a]
> *"Hear, heads of Jacob*
>   *and leaders of the house of Israel.*   3+3
> *Is it not for you*
>   *to know justice?*   2+2
> ² *Haters of good,*
>   *and lovers of evil,*   2+2
> *tearers of skin,*
>   *and strippers of flesh from the bone."*   3+3
> ³ *"They eat the flesh of my people*
> *and strip off their skin from them,*
>   *and they break in little pieces.*   4+3+2
> *They chop them up like flesh in the pot,*
>   *like meat in the midst of the cauldron.*   3+3
> ⁴ *Then they will cry out to Yahweh,*
>   *but he will not answer them.*   3+3
> *But he will hide his face from them*
>   *at that time,*
>   *according to the wickedness of their deeds."*   3+2+3

Notes

1.a. Many take ואמר "and I said" as a remnant of a narrative omitted from an original version (*ZAW* 80 [1968] 50–54.). Van der Woude sees it as proof of his disputation theory that Micah is now replying to the false prophets. Mays sees it as a simple report form in the first person in which Micah states the kind of response he makes to the opposition.

Form/Structure/Setting

This pericope is a judgment oracle. It establishes the guilt of the heads and leaders of Israel. They are guilty because they have disregarded their responsibility to administer justice (v 1) and instead have consumed the ones they were responsible to protect (v 2). They were acting like cannibals left in charge of missionaries or lions assigned to care for lambs (v 3). Because of their guilt these leaders will be abandoned by Yahweh in their hour of need (v 4).

Comment

The expression "And I said" at the beginning of v 1 poses a problem. If chapter 3 is the beginning of a second major section of this book, such an expression can be explained as a carryover from an earlier form of the oracle. The prophet is speaking for Yahweh. There is a call for a hearing. The imperative "hear ye" stands at the beginning of the three major divisions of the book (1:2; 3:1; 6:1).

The addressees of this oracle are the "heads" and "leaders" of Israel. These "heads" and "leaders" were not kings or priests but officials who functioned as judges in the city gates. They were most likely professional judges or rulers who served to decide legal matters on a local level. In the early stages of Israel's history the judges were merely heads of extended families who met to resolve disputes between people not of the same clan. With the rise of the monarchy this responsibility was passed on to the king. Unfortunately the king often did not or could not devote enough time to judicial matters. Finally in the ninth century B.C. Jehoshaphat instituted judicial reform that gave rise to paid regional judges (2 Chr 19:4–7). (K. W. Whitelam, *The Just King*, JSOT Supplement Series, No. 19 [Sheffield: JSOT Press, 1979] 189.)

It was their responsibility to know justice. "Know" includes the administration of justice as well as an intellectual understanding that justice is good. But these judges were always hating (participle=continuous action) the good and continuously loving evil. The word pair good/evil was important to the eighth-century prophets. Amos said:

Seek good, and not evil,
     that you may live.
Hate evil, and love good,
     and establish justice in the gate (Amos 5:14–15).

Isaiah said:

Cease to do evil,
     learn to do good;
seek justice,
     correct oppression (Isa 1:16c–17b).

It is very difficult for those in power politically to resist using that power for their own personal advantage and abusing the rights and persons of others. Those who held the reins of political and judicial power in Micah's day had cast aside all pretense for justice and were openly using their power to consume the poor and powerless.

But Micah knew of a greater power than that of the heads and leaders of Israel. God was sovereign over all earthly powers. Ironically Micah saw a time in the not too distant future when these very powerful men would cry out to God for help, but God would not answer them. Yahweh would hide his face from them in their time of crisis just as they had not turned a friendly face toward their victims. God's negative actions are explained on the basis that Israel's leaders have made their deeds evil.

Peace Prophets and Micah   (3:5-8)

Bibliography

Sanders, J. A. "Hermeneutics in True and False Prophecy," in *Canon and Authority*, eds. Coats and Long, 21–41. **Van der Woude, A. S.** "Micah in Dispute with the Pseudoprophets." *VT* 19 (1969) 244–60.

Translation

> 5 *Thus says Yahweh concerning the prophets,*
>   *the ones leading my people astray,*
> *the ones who bite with their teeth* [a]
>   *and proclaim peace.*   3+2
> *But they commit themselves to war against*
>   *the one who puts nothing in their mouths.*   3+3
> 6 *Therefore it shall be night to you without vision*
>   *and darkness* [a] *for you without divination.*   4+3
> *And the sun will go down upon the prophets,*
>   *and the day will become black for them.*   3+3
> 7 *And the seers shall be ashamed,*
>   *and the diviners will be confused,*   3+3
> *and all of them will cover their lip*
>   *because there is no answer from God.*   3+3
> 8 *On the other hand I am full of power,*
>   *the spirit of God,*
>   *and justice and might,*   4+2+2
>   *to tell to Jacob his transgression*
>   *and to Israel her sin.*   3+2

Notes

5.a. "To bite with the teeth" here refers to eating the things their clients give them.
6.a. MT has a verb "to be dark."

Form/Structure/Setting

This pericope is a disputation as well as a judgment oracle. It begins with one of only two messenger formulas in Micah (cf. 2:3). A charge or an indictment is brought against the "peace" prophets that their message was based on economic expediency (v 5). Therefore, Micah says, God will no longer speak to or through them (vv 6–7). In contrast to the "peace" prophets Micah witnesses to his own sense of calling and equipment for his God-given mission of declaring to Israel her sin and transgression.

This pericope witnesses the first open clash between Micah and other prophets who did not agree with him. Such a conflict was hinted at in 2:11 when Micah said, "If a man, walking in spirit and deceit, lies saying, 'I will preach to you of wine and strong drink,' then he would be the preacher for this people." It seems that every true prophet had his counterpart in a false prophet. Elijah had his prophets of Baal (1 Kgs 18:20–41). Micaiah had his "peace" prophets (1 Kgs 22:6–13). The classical controversy between a true prophet and a "peace" prophet was between Jeremiah and Hananiah (Jer 28:1–17). Ezekiel experienced similar difficulties (Ezek 13:1–23). These "peace" prophets were overly optimistic. They believed that their God, Yahweh, was sovereign over the whole world. They also believed that Yahweh had made an everlasting covenant with David and had promised that Jerusalem would always be the city of God. Their problem was that they did not understand the conditions of the covenant. Micah knew that sins violated the covenant and could not go unpunished (v 8). Thus conflict between Micah and the "peace" prophets was inevitable.

Comment

In v 5 Micah accuses his "prophetic" counterparts of leading "my people" astray. The people were Micah's people. Nine times Micah calls the people "my people" (1:9; 2:4, 8, 9; 3:3, 5; 6:3, 5, 16; cf. Mays 55). He identified with them. Their cause was his cause. The "peace" prophets only thought of their stomachs. As long as their hearers would give them something to eat they would preach what the people wanted to hear. But they would declare war on anyone who did not contribute to their cause.

In vv 6 and 7 Micah says that the "peace" prophets and diviners will be humiliated and embarrassed when the judgment of God falls on the city. Then their peace prophecies will be shown to be empty deceptions.

Interestingly enough, Micah does not call these men "false prophets" and he speaks as though they truly had received a vision. Rather, he threatens the prophets with a darkness when "there is no answer from God." Prophets often delivered contradictory messages. This may have been due to political pressure (2 Kgs 22:13), personal immorality (Isa 28:7), greed (Ezek 13:19), or confusion (Jer 14:14). Indeed God himself may deceive the wicked prophet (Ezek 14:9). The people had to choose who the true prophet was, based on the fulfillment of the prophecy (Deut 18:22), a sign from God (1 Kgs 18:23–24), and ultimately if the prophecy led the people closer to God (Deut 13:1–3). Micah claims that these men will not meet the requirements of a true prophet (*IDBSup* 701–2).

With a strong adversative ואולם "on the other hand," and an emphatic use of the pronoun "I," Micah contrasts his ministry with that of his opponents (v 8). Whereas the "peace" prophets were preaching for personal gain and proclaiming a message of peace "when there was no peace" (Jer 6:14), Micah was preaching because he was sent by the spirit and power of God. V 8 is a kind of call narrative for Micah. In it he shares his understanding of his calling, his divine gifts, and the kind of ministry he was to have. His ministry was concerned with justice and a courageous declaration of Israel's sins. Micah knew that only as Israel was righteous would she be strong (6:8). Righteousness makes a nation great, not its gross national product. It is only as the guilty see themselves under the judgment of God that they can understand what is happening to themselves and their society and, it is to be hoped, want to change their ways. A true prophet preaches judgment then hope. A false prophet preaches only false hope.

Corrupted Leaders and Zion's Fall
(3:9–12)

Translation

> ⁹ *Hear this, heads of the house of Jacob*
>   *and leaders of the house of Israel,*   2+2+2
> *the ones hating justice*
>   *and distort all that is upright;*   2+2
> ¹⁰ *the ones* ᵃ *building Zion with blood*
>   *and Jerusalem with perversity.*   3+2
> ¹¹ *Her heads judge for a bribe,*
>   *and her priests teach for a price.*   3+3
> *Her prophets divine for silver,*
>   *and upon Yahweh they lean,*   3+2
> *saying, "Is Yahweh not in our midst?*
> *Evil shall not come upon us."*   3+3
> ¹² *Therefore, on your account Zion*
>   *shall become a ploughed field*   2+3
> *and Jerusalem shall become a ruin,*
> *and the mount of the house*
>   *a forest high place.* ᵃ   3+2+2

Notes

10.a. MT בְּנֶה is sing. LXX, Syr, Tg have pl., suggesting Heb. בֹּנִי. See BHK.
12.a. במות "high places" probably should be singular במת "high place." Cf. LXX and BHK. The parallel word "ruin" suggests that the word is used in a physical rather than a cultic sense.

Form/Structure/Setting

This pericope is an oracle of judgment very similar to 3:1–4. The same groups are addressed—the land-grabbers (heads and leaders of the people) and the "peace" prophets (11b) with the priests being included in this oracle (11a). There is a call to hear (9a) followed by the charge of wrongdoing on the part of the leaders, priests, and prophets (9–11b). Then the evil-doers state their defense (11c). Finally, there is the pronouncement of judgment—Jerusalem and the temple will be destroyed (12).

Comment

What a bombshell this oracle must have been in Jerusalem. The city of Jerusalem and the temple were sacred. How could any disaster fall on the city? It was unbelievable. The prophets, priests, judges, and government leaders "leaned on" Yahweh. They believed in the Davidic covenant. They "trusted" Yahweh. They did not consider it relevant to the covenant that they constantly hated justice and always perverted the way of righteousness. They saw no inconsistency between their taking bribes and "payola," and mouthing religious shibboleths.

These leaders sought to increase the power of Jerusalem, but only so their power could grow with it. Because of their personal motives, the rulers killed and cheated anyone who stood between them and greater authority. Nevertheless they could justify their greed by claiming that Yahweh supported them in their efforts.

But Micah, who understood his mission as a prophet to be one who declared to Israel her sins, said, "Because of you (your doings) Jerusalem and the temple will be destroyed." Micah's description of Jerusalem's fate is a vivid picture of a defeated city. The inhabitants were killed or enslaved and the city was destroyed to prevent future uprisings. The city wall was broken down into rubble, along with the palace and temple, and the entire city was burned. Anything left of value was taken as spoil (2 Kgs 25:9–11; 2 Chr 36:17–21).

Jerusalem was not destroyed immediately. Micah spoke these words probably around 711 B.C. or 701 B.C. at the latest. Jerusalem continued as it was for another hundred years. Then in 609 B.C. Jeremiah preached in the gate of the temple that the time of the destruction of the temple had come. Jeremiah was arrested but some elders who remembered what Micah had said a century earlier, quoted his words about the destruction of Jerusalem (Jer 26:1–19). Perhaps there is a lesson here not only for Micah's and Jeremiah's days but for our own as well. Any attempt to use the service of God for one's own glory and profit carries great risks. We cannot accept God's love and reject his lordship. We should be careful to see that our creed and conduct are consistent.

Zion's Future Exaltation (4:1–5)

Bibliography

Cannawurf, E. "The Authenticity of Micah IV 1–4." *VT* 13 (1963) 26–33. **Clements, R. E.** *God and Temple.* Oxford: Basil Blackwell, 1965. 81–106. **Porteous, N. W.** "The Prophets and the Problem of Continuity." *Israel's Prophetic Heritage,* eds. Anderson and Harrelson. New York: Harper and Brothers, 1962. 11–25. **von Rad, G.** "The City on the Hill." *The Problem of the Hexateuch and Other Essays.* 232–42. **Willis, J. T.** "The Structure of Micah 3–5." *ZAW* 81 (1969) 191–214.

Translation

¹ *And it shall be in the latter days,*

  the mountain of the house ^a *of Yahweh*   3+3

shall be established at the top of the mountains,

  and shall be lifted up above the hills.   3+3

² *And many nations will come,*

  and they will say,

"Come, let us go up ^a *to the mountain of Yahweh* ^a

  to the house of the God of Jacob.   3+3

Let him teach us his ways ^b

  and we shall walk in his paths."   2+2

Because from Zion the law will go out

  and the word of Yahweh from Jerusalem.   3+3

³ *He will judge between many peoples*

  and settle disputes for strong nations far away.   4+4

They shall beat their swords into plowshares, ^a

  and their spears into pruning hooks.   3+3

Nation shall not lift up sword against nation,

  and they shall not train again for war.   4+4

⁴ *They will sit—each under his vine*

  and under his fig tree with nothing to fear;   4+4+4

because the mouth of Yahweh has spoken.

⁵ *Because all people walk,*

  each in the name of his god,   3+3

then we will walk

  in the name of Yahweh our God

  forever and ever.   2+2+2

Notes

1.a. בית "house" not in LXX.

2.a.-a. אל הר יהוה "unto the mountain of Yahweh" not in DSIa.

2.b. MT "from his ways."

3.a. Or "hoe."

Form/Structure/Setting

This is a salvation oracle. It is freighted with eschatological overtones. It seems that it was deliberately placed after the oracle of judgment on Jerusalem (3:9–12) to say that Jerusalem and the temple may be destroyed but they will be restored in a grander style than before. Rather than being the worship center for the tribes of Israel the renewed Jerusalem will be the worship center for all people.

The oracle begins with an announcement that in the future, Jerusalem and the temple will be exalted (v 1). All nations will make pilgrimages to

Zion to learn the law of Yahweh and to walk in his ways (v 2). Universal
peace among nations will result. Instruments of war will be turned into imple-
ments of peace and an ideal age will be ushered in (v 4). V 5 seems to be
a liturgical response of commitment from the congregation to Yahweh.

Before we can interpret this pericope we should ask: What is the relation
of this pericope to 3:9–12? And what is its relation to Isa 2:2–4? Edward
Nielsen said, ". . . it is no accident that Micah 1–3 is followed by Micah 4–
5" (*Oral Tradition* 93). Willis says that "the contrasts between 3:9–12 and
4:1–5 are so striking that one is almost compelled to conclude that the final
redactor intended for chaps. 3 and 4 to be taken together" (*ZAW* 81 [1969]
196). 3:9–12 concerns the imminent future while 4:1–5 concerns the remote
future; in the former, Zion is to become a ploughed field, in the latter Zion
will be exalted; the former describes Jerusalem as a city built with blood—
the latter presents Jerusalem as a city of peace. There is a very close relationship between 4:1–5 and 3:9–12.

But who is responsible for this close relationship? Was it Micah or a later
redactor? This question is involved with another question, namely, who was
the original author of 4:1–5? Some scholars have argued that Micah was
the original author because the text seems to be in better condition than
that of the parallel passage in Isa 2:2–4 (cf. Cannawurf, *VT* 13 [1963] 30).
Some have argued that Isaiah was the author of the oracle 2:2–4 and Micah
borrowed it and inserted it in 4:1–5. Vriezen ("Prophecy and Eschatology"
VTSup 1 [1953] 213) defended this view as did Wildberger ("Die Völkerwall-
fahrt zum Zion" *VT* 7 [1957] 66). Von Rad, L. C. Allen, and J. T. Willis
argue that Isaiah and Micah might have used an earlier oracle. Weiser, Eissfeldt
(*The Old Testament* [New York: Harper, 1965] 410), Mays, and Cannawurf
all argue for a post-exilic date for 4:1–5. We will assume that 4:1–5 is the
work of Micah or a contemporary until it can be proved otherwise. However,
the arrangement of the various pericopes in the book could be from a hand
other than Micah's.

Comment

4:1–5 is one of the best known pericopes in the OT. It looks forward to
the day when the enmity that separated the nations at Babel (Gen 11) will
be put aside and all peoples of the world will worship the one true God.
They will be taught Yahweh's law and not the ways of war. A universal reign
of peace will prevail and each individual will participate in it (v 4).

In ancient times mountains were associated with the mysterious. Because
they were not suitable for agriculture, the rugged hills were often left to
bands of thieves and to foraging animals. Perhaps this contributed to the
mystique of mountains that led to their being worshiped. The kings of Israel
were rated on their devotion to Yahweh by their attitude toward the "high
places" which had become centers of idolatry (1 Kgs 22:43; 2 Kgs 12:3; 18:4).
Abraham offered Isaac on a mountain (Gen 22:2), Moses received the Ten
Commandments on a mountain (Exod 19:16), and the city of Jerusalem was
on top of a large hill. Yahweh's power is often expressed in terms of his
authority over mountains (Ps 90:2; Isa 40:12; Nah 1:5) and particularly in
Micah the figure of Mount Zion is a portrayal of Yahweh's presence. That

Yahweh's mountain will be an attraction for all nations is a message of hope strongly amplified by the threat in 3:12 that the mountain would become a forest.

However, v 5 is a stark reminder that such an idyllic hope is not yet a present reality. In Micah's day the nations did not come to Jerusalem to worship Yahweh. In fact Sargon and Sennacherib, kings of Assyria, had come to Jerusalem to raid, pillage, and destroy. So, the congregation in Judah said, "Even though other nations still walk after their gods, we will not. We (emphatic) will walk continually (imperfect action) in the name of Yahweh our God forever and ever."

Note that the nations are mentioned in these verses for the first time since 1:2. They will be mentioned many times in chaps. 4–5. Israel did not live in a vacuum. What Israel did affected other nations and what they did affected her.

Restoration of a Remnant and the Reign of Yahweh (4:6–8)

Bibliography

Stinespring, W. F. "No Daughter of Zion." *Encounter* 26 (1965) 133–41.

Translation

> 6 *In that day, Oracle of Yahweh,*
> *I will gather the lame ones,*   2+2
> *and the scattered ones I will collect*
> *and those whom I have injured.*   2+2
> 7 *And I will make the lame ones a remnant*
> *and the ones who have strayed afar* [a] *a strong nation.*   3+2
> *And Yahweh shall reign over them*
> *in Mount Zion*
> *from now until eternity.* [b]   2+2+2
> 8 *But you, tower of the flock,*
> *hill of Maiden Zion,* [a]   2+2
> *unto you it will come,*
> *the former rule will come*
> *the kingdom to Maiden Jerusalem.* [a]   2+3+2

Notes

7.a. הנהלאה niph. fem. part. of הלא a hapax. Some read הנחלא niph. part. of חלה "wounded," or "sick."

7.b. עולם means "hidden ages."

8.a. בת ציון "daughter or maiden Zion." בת is used in apposition to Zion and Jerusalem (cf. Stinespring, *Encounter* 26 [1965] 136–38).

Form/Structure/Setting

This pericope is an oracle of salvation. The limits are marked by the opening phrase, "In that day" and the closing words, ". . . will come the kingdom of the maiden Jerusalem" (v 8). Some would end the pericope with the words in v 7 "from now to eternity." After the introductory phrase marks the pericope as eschatological, the first of two uses of יהוה נאם "Oracle of Yahweh" in the book (cf. 5:9), validates the authority of the oracle. The oracle itself speaks of gathering the lame and the scattered (sheep) of Zion whom Yahweh himself has injured (v 6). Then God promises to make the remnant of lame ones into a mighty nation over which he will rule in Zion (v 7).

What is the setting of this pericope? Who are the lame, scattered, and injured of Zion? Is the reference to the damage done to Judah during Sennacherib's invasion of Judah in 701 b.c. (cf. Isa 1:5–8)? Or, is the reference to the Babylonian captivity? Certainly the language about God gathering the lame and scattered sheep is very similar to that of Isa 40:1–11. The "reign of Yahweh" (v 7) echoes the language of the "enthronement Psalms" (93, 95, 97, 99), but scholars are divided on whether or not these psalms are pre-exilic or post-exilic. L. C. Allen concludes largely on the basis of the positive use of the "remnant" in v 7 that this pericope originated in the time of exile (Allen 245). The preponderance of the evidence supports his conclusion.

Explanation

This is the second hope oracle in chap. 4. It too is for the latter days in contrast to the evil present. The message of hope is for evil times. God has brought Zion to her state of brokenness and disunity and he will restore her former dominion and rule in the future (v 8). Jesus may have been influenced by these words when he saw the crowds and was moved with compassion "because they were harassed and helpless, like sheep without a shepherd" (Matt 9:36). Certainly the promise to the lame and the outcasts represented a remarkable change in Israel's thinking, for these people were specifically prohibited from serving as priests (Lev 21:16–23). Now they are being singled out as recipients of God's blessing.

From Distress to Deliverance—(4:9–10)

Translation

⁹ *Now why do you cry loudly?*
Is there no king in you?   3+2
Or has your counselor perished,
that writhing grips you
like a woman giving birth?   2+3

> [10] *Writhe and bawl,*[a] *Maiden Zion,*
>   *like a woman giving birth.*   2+2
> *Because now you shall go out from the city*
>   *and live in a tent in the field,*
>   *and you shall go to Babylon;*   2+2+2
> *there Yahweh will redeem you*
>   *from the hand of your enemies.*   3+2

Notes

10.a. גחי is uncertain. *CHAL* takes it from גיח or גוח "bawl" (*CHAL* 59; *BDB* 161). LXX ὤδινε καὶ ἀνδρίζου καὶ ἔγγιζε "be in travail and be brave and draw near."

Form/Structure/Setting

This pericope is a salvation oracle with a heavy emphasis on the present predicament of Jerusalem. The people are crying loudly and writhing in pain like a woman in childbirth. The cause of the terror is not indicated, but it was probably due to an enemy invader. The time of the oracle is pre-exilic because of the reference to the king and counselor, who seems to be helpless at this point (v 9).

V 9 comments on the wails of distress heard in the city. The prophet asks satirically why the people did not get help from their king or counselor. The truth is their human leaders had failed. They were powerless to help. The pain of the present situation is compared to the pains of a woman in childbirth (vv 9–10). The pains in childbirth can be excruciating but they normally conclude with a new life. There may be a suggestion here between the present suffering and future deliverance (cf. Mays 106).

Is there any connection between Zion's childbirth pains here and those of the expectant mother in 5:3? Lescow (199–205) and Mays (116–17) say yes. The one about to give birth in 5:3 is still Zion. The pains are brought on by the attack of enemies; "the image is concerned only with the writhing of labour not an expected birth" (Mays 116). But it is better to follow the traditional view that the words in 5:3 are a prophecy of the birth of the coming Davidic king (cf. Isa 7:14; 9:6).

In the second line of v 10 there is an ironic use of exodus language. Instead of going out of Egypt and tenting in the wilderness, on their way to Canaan, this generation will go out of Zion and tent in a field on their way to Babylon. Van der Woude (*VT* 18 [1968] 388–91) and L. C. Allen (334) believe that this is Micah's satirical reply to the peace prophets who preached that the covenant meant that no harm could come to Israel. It is only after judgment in Babylon that Yahweh will deliver Israel.

Comment

Mays sees this pericope as having a history beginning with the taunting questions about the king in the pre-exilic period. He thinks that these oracles of salvation then were assembled and used by the small group who continued to worship at the ruined temple in Jerusalem during the exilic period (Mays 26). Though such a theory is entirely possible, we do not have enough information to make a definitive judgment on the matter. The emphasis in this pericope is not on exile but on redemption. The only occurrence of גאל "kinsman redeemer" in Micah is here. God will redeem his people.

From Siege to Victory (4:11–13)

Translation

11 *And now many nations*
are assembled against you, — 3+2
the ones saying, "Let her be desecrated
and let our eyes gaze ª *on Zion."* — 2+3
12 *But they do not know Yahweh's thoughts,*
nor do they understand his plan — 3+2
to gather them like sheaves of the threshing floor. — 3+3
13 *Arise and thresh, Maiden Zion,*
because I will make your horn iron — 3+3
and your hooves I will make bronze.
And you shall crush many peoples, — 3+3
and you will put under the ban ª *their profit,* ᵇ
and their substance shall be for the Lord of all the earth. — 3+3

Notes

11.a. חזה here means "to gaze on" in the sense of "to gloat over."
13.a. חרם "to put under the ban" was a term used in holy war. The spoil of battle was to be entirely dedicated to Yahweh.
13.b. בצע "profit" is a technical weaver's term meaning to cut off the threads of the woof, "to make one's cut," "to make a profit" (*CHAL* 45).

Form/Structure/Setting

Like the previous pericope this is a salvation oracle. It begins with the present calamity ("now") brought on by the attack on Jerusalem by many nations (v 11). However, the nations do not know that they are simply doing the will of Yahweh (v 12). This is his plan to destroy them. They will come against Jerusalem only to be threshed like sheaves on a threshing floor (v 13). Many passages in the prophets and Psalms tell of an attack on Jerusalem by the nations (cf. Isa 17:12–14; 29:5–8; Ezek 38–39; Zech 14:1–3, 12–15; Joel 3:1–3, 9–12; Pss 46:6; 48:4–5; 76:3–6). In most of these God himself intervenes in the battle and defeats the enemy.

Explanation

This is the second of three pericopes which begin with "now." The purpose of the prophet is to encourage the people in a difficult and trying time. The oracle probably comes from the time of Sennacherib's invasion of Judah in 701 B.C. The land had been stripped bare. Many people were in Jerusalem as refugees from their homes in the villages of Judah. Micah, like Isaiah, knew that Sennacherib's success was only temporary, and that Israel would be victorious over her enemies. The time of the victory was left indefinite.

From Helpless Judge to Ideal King
(4:14–5:3 [5:1–4])

Bibliography

Harrelson, W. "Nonroyal Motifs in the Royal Eschatology." *Israel's Prophetic Heritage.* FSJ. Muilenberg. New York: Harper Brothers (1962) 155–59. **de Vaux, R.** "The Remnant of Israel According to the Prophets." *The Bible and the Ancient Near East.* Trans. D. McHugh. Garden City, N.Y.: Doubleday and Co., Inc., 1971. 16–30. **Willis, J. T.** "Micah IV 14–V 5 a Unit." *VT* 18 (1968) 529–47.

Translation

14(1) a *Now you are slashing yourself,*[b] *O daughter under attack.*[c]
   Siege is set against us.   3+3
With the rod they smite the cheek
   of the Judge of Israel.   3+3
1(2) *But you, Bethlehem Ephrathah,*
   small among the clans of Judah,   3+3
from you shall come forth for me
   one to be a ruler in Israel,   3+3
whose origin is from of old
   from ancient days.   3+2
2(3) *Therefore he will give them up until the time*
   one who is about to give birth bears a child.   3+2
Then the rest [a] *of his brothers shall return*
   to the children of Israel.   3+2
3(4) *And he shall stand and shepherd in the power of Yahweh,*
   in the majesty of the name of Yahweh his god.   4+4
They shall dwell (safely) because now [a] *he will be great*
   to the ends of the earth.   3+2

Notes

14.a. The verses are numbered differently in chap. 5 in Hebrew and English versions. Cf. p. 193.
   14.b. RSV, JB, NEB follow LXX and read גָּדֵר "wall" for גָּדַד "to slash."
   14.c. גְּדוּד refers to a band of marauders (cf. 1 Sam 30:8, 15, 23).

2.a. The word יֶתֶר is not the usual word for remnant. De Vaux notes that שְׁאָר or שְׁאֵרִית denotes a remnant which escapes death when a company or group of men is scattered or massacred. יתר means "that which is over and above." It draws attention not to the remnant which survives but the remnant that was joined.

3.a. "Now" refers to the future reign of the new king.

Form/Structure/Setting

This is a salvation oracle. There has been much debate about the starting and concluding points of this pericope as well as about the unity of the passage. 4:14 (5:1) should be considered as the origin of the pericope. It describes the present predicament of the people of Jerusalem. They are slashing themselves in lamenting their plight. גדד could mean "gather in troops" in the qal (Ps 94:21). Jerusalem is being invaded and the present ruler is being insulted by a slap on the face. But a new ruler will be born in Bethlehem whose heritage goes back a long time—to the beginning of David's line (v 1). The present evil situation will continue until the one about to give birth (the mother of the new king of Jerusalem, cf. 4:9), brings forth her child (v 2). Then the rest of his brothers will return from exile. Mays believes that v 3 interrupts the thought moving from v 2 to v 4. This new king will be crowned and rule in the glory and name of Yahweh. The people will dwell secure and the new king will be great to the ends of the earth (v 3). Does the pericope end with v 3? Probably so. The words "the ends of the earth" furnish a natural conclusion. The next verse begins with another reference to peace when Assyria is conquered. There is no reference to the new David in the next pericope.

Comment

The language of 4:14 (5:1) is difficult. The RSV, JB and NEB follow the LXX and read "you are walled about with a wall." The KJV and TEV read "gather your forces" (cf. Ps 94:21). Harrelson (155) suggests, "Now you are in mourning, besieged one." But the first meaning of the Hebrew root גדד is "to slash." The hithpolel form used here and in 1 Kgs 18:28 means "to slash oneself with knives" either as a part of pagan worship or as mourning for the dead (Deut 14:1; Jer 16:6). The thought here seems to be that the people of Jerusalem had been slashing themselves like Baal worshipers, thinking that would help save them. Zion is now suffering attack. Her ruler (Judge) is being treated shamefully by his enemies. The word "Judge" probably was used to call attention to the impotency of the present ruler. The earlier judges were charismatic deliverers or saviors. The present king could not even save himself.

But there is hope. Deliverance will come from the least expected place. Bethlehem Ephrathah was the smallest, most insignificant clan in Judah. The word צָעִיר is not the regular word (מְעַט) for "little or small" but a word rarely used to call attention to the trifling or insignificant (Ps 68:27). Out of Bethlehem would come a new ruler (מוֹשֵׁל), one who would rule in strength, whose origins were from "old times" (קֶדֶם) and from ancient (עוֹלָם) days. The ancient days could be referring to the origin of the new ruler in terms of the first Adam in the garden of Eden. Edmond Jacob says that the messianic hope has "deep roots which go further back than the institution of kingship, though the latter gave it its dominant orientation. Since the return of the golden age formed part of the most ancient patrimony of Israel it is quite natural to suppose that it also included the hope of the return of man as he existed at the beginning" (*Theology of the Old Testament* [New York: Harper, 1958] 327, 335). Whether or not the image of primitive man was in Micah's mind, the idea of a new David certainly was. The days of David are spoken of as בימי עולם "the ancient days" in Amos 9:11, so such language would not be out of place in Micah.

The deliverer had not yet come. Until he did Yahweh would give the people of Judah into the hands of their enemy until one about to give birth (the qal active participle suggests that in the mind of the prophet the event was imminent) brought forth (same word is in Isa 7:14) a child "for me" לי. The child was to be Yahweh's ruler (5:1 [5:2]). Then the rest (יתר "remnant") of his brothers (in exile) will return to the children of Israel.

Explanation

This is one of the most familiar pericopes in Micah for Christians. Matthew quoted 5:1 in reference to Jesus' birth in Bethlehem (Matt 2:6). However, the OT text is slightly altered in Matthew's account. Instead of saying, *"little to be among the clans of Judah,"* Matthew says, *"by no means least among the rulers of Judah."* Also Matthew omits "Ephrathah," and adds, "my people" Judah.

This passage has been widely referred to as "messianic" and as similar to Isaiah's promise of the birth of a new king in 7:14. Although some scholars have questioned assigning this pericope to Micah there is no compelling reason for not doing so. Granting that all of these pericopes might have undergone some editing, it is possible to understand Micah saying essentially the same thing as Isaiah said, namely, that the present king is weak and embarrassing. The only solution to the problem is for a new king to be born not in Jerusalem (it was too corrupt for Micah) but in Bethlehem where the line of David began. Micah sees a new beginning for the kingdom of God which would extend through the earth. This last thought was probably influenced by some of the royal psalms (Pss 2, 17, 72).

Peace by the Overthrow of Assyria
(5:4–5 [5:5–6])

Bibliography

Porteous, N. *Living the Mystery.* Oxford: B. Blackwell, 1967. 102, 121. **Thomas, D. W.** "Micah." *Peakes' Commentary.* New York: Thomas Nelson, 1962. 630.

Translation

4(5) *And this* ᵃ *shall be peace.*
When Assyria comes into our land
   and when he treads upon our palaces, ᵇ   3+3+3
we shall set up over him seven shepherds
   and eight leaders of men.   4+3
5(6) *They will shepherd the land of Assyria with the sword,*
   the land of Nimrod with her bare blades. ᵃ   4+3
He will deliver from Assyria,
   when he comes into our land,
   when he treads on our borders.   2+2+3

Notes

4.a. זֶה "this" is indefinite. Sometimes read, "this one."
4.b. LXX, Peshitta suggest אַדְמָתֵנוּ "our soil or ground," instead of ארמנתינו "our palaces."
5.a. Read בפתיחה "her swords" for בפתחיה "her entrances" (Ps 55:21).

Form/Structure/Setting

This is a salvation oracle. Some scholars include these verses with the previous pericope (Willis, Allen, Wolfe). Some include 4a in the previous pericope (NEB, TEV, JB, Bewer). But 5:4–5 (Eng. 5:5–6) should be considered a separate oracle (Thomas, Mays). "This" in 4a probably does not refer to the new king but to a coming period of peace after Assyria is conquered. There is too much difference between this pericope and the previous one for them to be a unit. 4:14–5:3 (Eng. 5:1–4) is addressed to Bethlehem and speaks of a new king to be born there. In 5:4–5 (Eng. 5:5–6) Israel is the speaker and the subject is the conquest of Assyria.

Explanation

This passage is difficult to interpret. If 4:14–5:3 (5:1) refers to the messianic age, does 5:4–5 (5:5–6) follow chronologically the coming of the Messiah according to the prophet's understanding? If so, Micah expected the Messiah to come at the end of the Assyrian crisis. It appears that Isaiah at one time expected the new king of the line of David to appear when the Assyrians were cut down (cf. Isa 10:34–11:1).

The seven shepherds and eight leaders are not to be taken literally. This is a Hebrew literary device to indicate that an indefinite yet adequate number of leaders will arise to overthrow the Assyrians (Prov 30:15, 18, 21, 29; Eccl 11:2). They will even possess the land of Assyria. Land of Nimrod probably refers to Assyria although it could refer to Babylon also (Gen 10:8–9). "He" in 5b "he will deliver" probably refers to God rather than the new king.

The Remnant Among the Peoples
(5:6–8 [5:7–9])

Translation

6(7) *And the remnant of Jacob shall be*
    in the midst of many peoples   3+3
like dew from Yahweh,
    like showers upon the plants   3+3
which does not wait for man
and does not tarry for the sons of men.   3+4
7(8) *And the remnant of Jacob shall be among the nations,*
    in the midst of many peoples   4+3
like a lion among the beasts of the forest,
    like a young lion among flocks of sheep   3+3
who if he passes through,
    tramples and tears with none to deliver.   3+3
8(9) *May your hand be raised* a *against your foes*
    and all your enemies be cut off.   3+3

Notes

8.a. Mays and JB take תָּרֹם as a jussive to express a prayer. RSV, NEB, TEV, KJV read it as a regular impf. "your hand shall be raised."

Form/Structure/Setting

Here are two salvation oracles and a prayer or a promise (v 8). The two oracles have the same form. The first line states the theme, "The remnant among the nations." The second part is a simile describing the remnant, "as dew" or "as a lion." The third part (v 8) either prays for Israel's victory over her enemies or gives assurance of such a victory. Scholars are divided as to the date of this passage. Some (Mays, D. W. Thomas, H. W. Robinson) assign it to a post-exilic period largely on the basis of the remnant idea. Others (Eiselen, L. C. Allen, Willis) defend Mican authorship.

Explanation

The remnant's relation to the nations is first compared to dew on grass or shrubs, and then to a lion among sheep. Are these two metaphors, dew and lion, symbols of judgment, or does dew symbolize blessing and the lion judgment? Some interpreters say this figure of speech refers to the numberless drops of dew which are a blessing. So the verse would emphasize the great growth of Israel. But this interpretation is not likely. It does not fit the context even though the Abrahamic promise included numberless heirs. Dew here is a beneficent gift to the nations "like showers upon the plants." This gift is wholly the work of God, "which does not wait for man." It is not the work of Israel or of the nations. Just as the formation of dew is an act which man cannot perform, so the salvation of the Gentiles is the work of God (cf. Gal 1:11–12). God's intention is to bless and save the world through the remnant represented as dew. But it is possible that dew could signify judgment on the nations. In 2 Sam 17:12 Hushai says that Absalom's army might overwhelm David and his party like dew falling on the ground and not a man of his family or followers will be left alive. McKeating (180) says that the point of the simile is that dew is silent, irresistible, and thorough. So both metaphors, dew and lion, might be symbols of judgment. Therefore, the nations that do not hear and obey the word of God will experience the wrath of God (5:14 [Eng. 5:15]). The wrath or judgment of God is depicted in terms of the remnant as a lion tearing and destroying the sheep in vv 7–8. V 8 may be a prayer for victory over all of the enemies of Israel, or it may be a word of promise.

Purge of the Military and False Religions *(5:9–14 [Eng. 5:10–15])*

Bibliography

Dahood, J. *Psalms I.* AB. Garden City: Doubleday, 1966. 55–56. **Mendenhall, G.** "The Vengeance of Yahweh," *The Tenth Generation.* Baltimore: Johns Hopkins University Press, 1973. 69–104.

Translation

9(10) *And it shall be in that day,*	
oracle of Yahweh,	3+2
that I will cut off your horses from your midst	
and cause your chariots to perish.	3+2
10(11) *And I will cut off the cities of your land*	
and throw down all your fortresses.	3+2
11(12) *And I will cut off the sorceries from your hand*	
and soothsayers shall not be for you.	3+2
12(13) *And I will cut off your graven images*	
and your pillars from your midst.	2+2
And you shall not bow down again	
to the work of your hands.	2+2
13(14) *And I will root out your Asherim*	
from your midst	
and I will destroy your cities. [a]	3+2

14(15) *And I will take vengeance in anger and wrath*
upon the nations which have not hearkened. ª   3+3

Notes

13.a. Some emend עָרֶיךָ "your cities" to בְּעָלֶיךָ "your Baals," for parallelism. Dahood posits an Aramaic word אָרִים meaning "gods" and points to puns in Jer 2:28 and 19:15 to support his theory (Dahood, *Psalms I*, 55–56).

14.a. שָׁמְעוּ means "to hear and obey."

Form/Structure/Setting

The pericope begins with נְאֻם יהוה. It is an oracle of judgment on those things that might take the place of Yahweh in people's minds. It is easy for people to rely on the military rather than God. Chariots, horses, fortresses then were comparable to hydrogen bombs, guided missiles and bomb shelters today. Militarism was not the only threat to this people's trust in God. Pagan symbols and practices were prevalent in Micah's time also (cf. Isa 2:6, 8, 15, 18). The dominant meter is 3+2 which is typical of the lament. God seems to be lamenting the necessity for judgment on his people. In v 15 the oracle of judgment is broadened to include the nations who would not acknowledge the sovereignty of Yahweh.

Comment

This is the concluding pericope in chap. 5 and is the end of section two of Micah. Some scholars (Lescow, Mays) argue that all of chaps. 1–5 compose section one. 1:2 begins with an opening summons to all the peoples of the earth to hearken to Yahweh's witness. Now 5:14 (Eng. 5:15) says that those nations which do not hearken will experience the judgment of Yahweh's anger and wrath.

Israel herself will be purged of militarism and idolatry in the latter days. The nations which hearken to God and come to the temple to learn to walk in his ways (4:2) will avoid God's judgment.

All of the prophets condemned trusting in horses and chariots for the security of the nation (Isa 2:7; 30:15–17; Hos 10:13; Ps 20:7). Uzziah, one of the great kings in Judah, was famous for his military establishment, but it became an occasion for sin for him (2 Chr 26:15–16).

Idolatry was common in Israel and Judah until the time of the exile. "Sorceries" כְּשָׁפִים (v 11) is a term for some form of the occult or magical arts (cf. 2 Kgs 9:22; Isa 47:9, 12–13; Nah 3:4). The word for "soothsayers" מְעוֹנְנִים is a polel participle from a word meaning "to cause to appear." The root is used in the sense of augury in Lev 19:26; Deut 18:10, 14; 2 Kgs 21:6; Isa 2:6; 57:3; Jer 27:9. Another meaning of the root is "clouds." There may be a connection between the shape of the clouds and ancient use of magic.

There are three terms in vv 13–14 which refer to an idol or some representation of deity. The "Asherim" usually were evergreen trees planted near the altar to represent the female deities. Such practices were common in Canaanite worship but forbidden to Israel.

The word נקם "vengeance" (v 14) needs some explanation. We often associate the idea of revenge, retaliation, vindictiveness, excessive punishment with the word "vengeance." Those concepts do not apply when this word is used of God in the OT. It is used of a judge or suzerain whose responsibility it was to determine the innocence or guilt of an accused, then to administer grace or punishment as the case demanded. Here Micah says that Yahweh acting as the Judge of the world will punish those nations who rebel against him (cf. Mendenhall, *The Tenth Generation*, chap. 3; G. E. Wright, "The Nations in Hebrew Prophecy," *Encounter* 26 [1965] 235).

God's Lawsuit (6:1-8)

Bibliography

Anderson, G. W. "A Study of Micah 6:1–8." *SJT* 4 (1951) 191–97. **Brownlee, W. H.** "Anthropology and Soteriology in the Dead Sea Scrolls." *The Use of the OT in the NT*, ed. James M. Efird. Durham, N.C.: Duke University Press, 1972. 219–21. **Hyatt, J. P.** "On the Meaning and Origin of Micah 6:8." *ATR* 34 (1952) 232–39. **Lescow, T.** *Micah 6:6–8*. Stuttgart: Calver Verlag, 1966. 1–72. **Thomas, D. W.** "The Root צנע in Hebrew." *JJS* 1 (1949) 182–88.

Translation

1 *Hear ye what Yahweh is saying,*	3
Arise, plead your case before the mountains	
and let the hills hear your voice.	3+3
2 *Hear, ye mountains, the Lord's case,*	3+3
and give ear,[a] *foundations of the earth.*	3+3
For Yahweh has an indictment against his people	
and with Israel he argues.	3+3
3 *My people, what have I done to you,*	
and how have I wearied you? Answer me.	3+3
4 *For I brought you up from the land of Egypt*	
and from the house of slaves I ransomed you.	3+3
And I sent Moses before you,	
Aaron and Miriam with him.[a]	3+3
5 *Remember, my people, what Balak the king of Moab advised,*	3+3
And what Balaam, son of Beor,	
answered him,	2+2
from Shittim to Gilgal—	
in order to know	
the righteous[a] *acts of Yahweh.*	2+2+2
6 *With what shall I come before Yahweh*	
and bow myself before God most high?	3+3
Shall I come before him with burnt offerings,	
with year-old calves?	3+3

7 *Will Yahweh be pleased with thousands of rams*
    with ten thousand rivers of oil?   3+3
Shall I give my first-born for my rebellion,
    the fruit of my belly for the sin of my life?   3+2
8 *He has declared to you, O man, what is good.*
    And what is Yahweh seeking from you?   3+3
Nothing but ª *to do justice, to love devotion,* ᵇ
    and to walk humbly ᶜ *with your God.*   3+2+3

Notes

2.a. Emend האתנים which means "unfailing streams" to האזינו "cause to give ear."

4.a. Read עמי which is now at the beginning of v 5 here at the end of v 4, as עמו "with him" to balance the meter.

5.a צדקות often translated, "saving deeds" (cf. 1 Sam 12:7; Ps 103:6).

8.a. כיאם "except," "nothing but" (*CHAL* 156).

8.b. חסד "covenant love."

8.c. הצנע usually taken as hiph. inf. abs. used adverbally. A hapax. In DSS it carries the connotation of "being wise" (cf. NEB; Brownlee 219–21).

Form/Structure/Setting

6:1–5 is a covenant lawsuit and 6:6–8 is a Torah liturgy. The unity of 6:1–8 is subject to question. It is generally agreed that it contains two kinds of literary material—a lawsuit form and a question-answer form. The question-answer pattern could have its *Sitz im Leben* in a cultic entrance liturgy, a prophetic sermon, or in a wisdom teaching situation. In this context they should be considered together. The question-answer section is the people's response to the suit brought against them. V 8 is the prophet's response to the people's questions. Lescow, followed by Mays, separates the pericopes. L. C. Allen following Willis holds to the unity of the passage. It is possible that all of chap. 6 is a lawsuit genre (cf. Willis 278; McKeating 186).

Scholars are not agreed on the date of the material in chap. 6. Mays and others would assign it to the exilic period, Eissfeldt and many others attribute it to Micah. There is no substantial reason for denying it to Micah.

Explanation

This is one of the great passages of the OT. It, like Amos 5:24 and Hos 6:6, epitomizes the message of the eighth-century prophets. The passage opens with a beautiful example of a covenant lawsuit in which the prophet summons the people to hear the charge Yahweh has against them. The mountains and hills are the jury because they have been around a long time and have witnessed God's dealing with Israel. Rather than directly charging Israel with breaking the covenant, God asks Israel if they have any charges against him. "What have I done? How have I wearied you?" In the face of injustice some of the poor people may have become "weary in well doing." In the face of opportunities to get rich quick some of the land-owners might have grown weary of keeping the covenant laws. In reality it was God who had a right to be weary. Isaiah asked unbelieving Ahaz, "Is it too little for you to weary men, that you weary my God also?" The prophet of the exile accused Israel of wearying God with their iniquities (Isa 43:24). Malachi said, "You have wearied the Lord with your words" (Mal 2:17).

Instead of wearying Israel, Yahweh redeemed her. There is a play on words here, "I have not (הלאתיך) wearied you, I have (העלתיך) brought you up from Egyptian bondage." The prophets were always reciting the great redemptive acts of God to their people. They constantly reminded them of what God had done for them. God ransomed them; he sent spiritual leaders, "Moses, Aaron and Miriam" (v 4). Balaam attempted to curse their ancestors as they marched through the wilderness, but God thwarted all of Balaam's efforts and safely led them from Shittim on the east of the Jordan to Gilgal on the west (v 5).

If vv 6–8 are related to vv 1–5, they supply Israel's response to the implied charge against her. She had displeased Yahweh but she claims ignorance. She asks God what he wants. What must she bring with her when she comes into his presence that will make her acceptable? This question represents one of the two basic ideas about religion. How can a man approach God? One answer is: with sacrifice, things, good works. The other answer is reflected in v 8. God requires not some external gifts from his worshiper, but a humble communicant who loves to serve God and practice justice toward his fellowman.

The questions about sacrifice are comprehensive. Burnt offerings represented total dedication. Calves a year old represented the most desirable kind of sacrificial animal. Thousands of rams and ten thousand rivers of oil represented lavish sacrifice. One's first-born represents one's most valuable possession.

The implied answer to all of these questions is that none of these things is required. Then what about the whole sacrificial system and cultic worship? Sacrifices were required in the Mosaic law (Lev 1–6). Is there no need for sacrifice? Yes, there is. What Micah was speaking about, and Isaiah (1:11–17), and Amos (5:21–24), and the Psalmist (40:6–8; 50:7–11; 51:16–17), was not that sacrifice was wrong, but in and of itself without a proper relationship to God and neighbor, sacrifice is useless.

God has told man what he seeks from him. He has told him what is good: "To practice justice"; "to love devotion"; and "to walk humbly (wisely) with one's God." So when we come before God we must remember that it is not so much what is in our hands but what is in our hearts that finds expression in our conduct that is important. Norman Snaith said (104), "To say that God requires ultimately nothing that men can bring does not mean that men ought not to worship Him. Worship is necessary for man, because it is the outward expression of true humility before God, of that humble trust which is essential. It is when worship ceases to be this that it is a hindrance and not a help; so long as it is the outcome of true and humble conscious devotion to God, it can and does strengthen those bonds which bind God and man together through Christ. Worship is also necessary because a man should be full of praise and thankfulness to God; but as soon as the aim of hymns and songs and music generally becomes aesthetic, it is the time to beware."

More Charges and the Sentence (6:9–16)

Bibliography

Pope, M. "The Word שחת in Job 9:31." *JBL* 83 (1964) 270.

Translation

⁹ *The voice of Yahweh calls to the city;*
 and the wise man ^a *fears* ^b *thy name.*   4+3
Hear, O tribe ^c
 and assembly of the city, ^d   2+2
¹⁰ *Are there* ^a *in* ^b *the house of wickedness*
 storehouses of wickedness
 and the scant ephah which has been cursed? 4+2+3
¹¹ *Shall I count pure the one with* ^a *wicked scales*
 or with a bag of deceitful weights?   3+3
¹² *Her* ^a *rich men are full of violence,*
 her inhabitants speak lies,
 and their tongues in their mouths are deceitful. 3+3+3
¹³ *And also I will smite* ^a *you with illness,*
 making you desolate because of your sins.   3+3
¹⁴ *You will eat but not be full,*
 but garbage ^a *will be in your inward part.*   3+2
You shall carry off but not save,
 and that which you save I will put to the sword. 3+4
¹⁵ *You shall sow and not reap.*   2+2
You shall tread olives
 and not anoint yourself with oil,   2+2
You will possess grapes,
 and not drink wine.   2+2
¹⁶ *For the statutes of Omri are kept*
 and all the works of the house of Ahab
 and you walked in their counsels,   3+3+3
in order that I might make you a desolation,
 and your inhabitants an object of whistling,
 and you shall bear the people's scorn.   3+2+3

Notes

9.a. תושיה is a questionable form. BDB (444) take it from ישח (meaning unknown). The derived form תושׁיה is considered a technical term of Wisdom Literature meaning "sound wisdom." KB (1024–25) take it from ישׁי meaning "to work effectively," "to succeed." Scoggin (223) leaves the text as it is and reads,
 "The voice of Yahweh declares to the city—
 O, thy name always provides understanding
 Listen, O Tribe! now who assembled it (the city?)"

9.b. יראה "he will see" should be read with LXX, Syr, and Vg יִרָא "he fears."

9.c. מטה can be "tribe" or "rod." Read "tribe" here as a vocative, with the LXX.

9.d. וּמִי יְעָדָהּ עוֹד "And who appointed it still?" should be redivided וּמוֹעֵד עִיר "and assembly of the city" (cf. Mays 143; Allen, 375).

10.a. הָאֶשׁ should be הַאֶשׁ "is there?" (*CHAL* 29).

10.b. בֵּית as an adverbial accusative.

11.a. ב on בְמֹאזְנֵי is translated "with."

12.a. There is no antecedent for אֲשֶׁר at the beginning of the verse. It is probably a dittograph for the next word עָשִׁיר "rich."

13.a. Many read with the LXX and Syr הַחִלּוֹתִי "I have begun" for הֶחֱלֵיתִי "I have made you sick."

14.a. יֶשְׁחֲךָ is a hapax legomenon and is obscure. The LXX took the root as חָשַׁךְ "dark"; the Vg as שָׁחַח "humiliation." The meaning "filth" or "garbage" is based on Scott's study of שׁחת. Some understand the reference to be semen and translate פלט "to give birth" rather than "to save" (cf. NEB; Mays, 143).

Form/Structure/Setting

The form is that of a judgment oracle. 6:9–12 may be a continuation of the lawsuit form which began in 6:1. Vv 9–12 give the reasons for the lawsuit and vv 13–15 furnish the threat or the sentence.

Explanation

In v 9 we learn that the city of Jerusalem is the accused in the lawsuit. Then the tribe (of Judah) and the ruling council of the people are addressed. They are told that it is wise to fear (worship) Yahweh as 6:8 had said.

But instead of justice, loyalty, and humble fellowship with God the city was a storehouse of wickedness. Micah accuses the people in Jerusalem of committing the same sins that Amos pointed to in Samaria. They were using wicked scales, giving small measures, and charging exorbitant prices. Her rich men were full of violence (cf. 2:1–2; 3:2–3). The sentence phase of the trial begins with v 13. Illness and desolation will be the lot of the inhabitants of Jerusalem. They will eat, but not be nourished. They will fill their stomachs with filth or garbage (14a). They will try to carry off their children and/or their prized possessions to save them from the enemy but God will put what they save to the sword. They will sow and not reap; tread olives and not use the oil; tread grapes and not drink wine. All of their work will come to naught. For the statutes of Omri are observed. Omri assassinated Zimri and seized the throne of Israel, only to lead her into worse evil. When he died his son Ahab assumed control and went to the further extremes of child sacrifice (1 Kgs 16:34) and widespread Baalism (1 Kgs 18). After his death in battle the entire house of Ahab—including seventy sons—were violently slain by Jehu. Furthermore, all who followed them into Baalism were killed at a pagan festival. Micah is now accusing Israel of being like Ahab and is warning them of a similar punishment. The same sins which led to the demise of the northern kingdom will bring an end to Judah. The people of Jerusalem will become the objects of scorn and derision among the peoples of the world (v 16).

Lament over a Decadent Society   (7:1-6)

Bibliography

Kapelrud, A. S. "Eschatology in the Book of Micah." *VT* 11 (1961) 392–405. **Reicke, B.** "Liturgical Traditions in Micah 7." *HTR* 60 (1967) 349–67.

Translation

¹ Woe to me because I am like the gatherings
     of the summer fruit,
          like the gleanings of the vintage.   2+2+2
     There are no clusters of grapes to eat,
          no first-ripe fig that I ^a crave.   3+3
² The godly man has perished from the earth
          and there are no upright men.   3+3
     All of them lie in ambush for blood,
          each hunts his brother with a dragnet.   3+4
³ They do evil with both hands. ^a
          The prince and the judge ask for a reward.   3+4
     And the great one speaks the desire of his soul,
          and they twist (tie) it up. ^b   4+2
⁴ The best of them is like a briar,
          the upright worse than a thorn hedge.   2+2
     The day of thy watchmen and thy visitation has come;
          their confusion is now.   3+3
⁵ Do not believe in a neighbor.
          Do not trust in a companion.   2+2
     Keep the doors of your mouth
          from the one lying in your bosom.   2+2
⁶ For a son considers his father a fool, ^a
          a daughter rises against her mother,   3+3
     a daughter-in-law against her mother-in-law.
          A man's enemies are the men of his house.   2+3

Notes

1.a. Lit. "my soul" (נפשׁי).
3.a. Lit. "upon the evil, both their hands to do."
3.b. Text is very difficult. "To twist" or "to tie" means to finish the evil deeds.
6.a. Lit. "for a son considers foolish a father."

Form/Structure/Setting

There can be little doubt that the form of this pericope is that of a lament. The opening interjection אללי "woe" is not the expression most prophets use. אללי is only used here and in Job 10:15 but the meaning is clear. The writer is bemoaning the fact that no righteous people can be found. The beginning of the pericope is obvious, the end is not. Some scholars think the unit stops with v 6. Others include v 7, while others (Reicke) include all of chap. 7. V 7 is a transition verse. One problem in interpreting this pericope is knowing who the speaker is. Is he an individual or is he the king, priest, or prophet speaking for the nation? V 1 is an expression of lament. Vv 2–6 recount the reasons for the lament. No righteous people are left. Everyone is trying to capture or kill everyone else. Every member of society—prince, judge and great one—is greedy and corrupt. The best are useless (v 4a). The announcement is made that the day of judgment has come (4b). Then follows a warning not to trust anyone (v 5), with the observation that family relationships had disintegrated (v 6).

Explanation

Here, like Abraham before him (Gen 18:23–33) and Jeremiah and Ezekiel after him (Jer 5:1–5; Ezek 22:30), Micah tries to find a righteous man. His search is like that of a man who goes into an orchard after the summer fruit has been picked or into a vineyard after the grapes have been gathered hoping to find some fruit, but he finds none. No righteous, faithful, loyal man could be found. Instead everyone hunted his neighbor for his blood. Again like Jeremiah, Micah might have expected such wicked conduct from the poor. Jeremiah said that they did not have any sense because they had not been taught the way of the Lord (Jer 5:4). But the great ones, the prince and judge, should know better, but they did not do any better. They asked for and received bribes and "pay-offs." Anyone who expected justice from them would become entangled in a hedge of intrigue and avarice (briars and thorns). But it was not only the public sector of society that was corrupt. Normal family relationships had disintegrated. Sons considered their fathers fools. Daughters and daughters-in-law rebelled against their mothers. A man could not trust his closest friend—even his wife. And a man's worst enemies were those in his own house. Such a society cannot stand.

Jesus used the message of v 6 in Matt 10:21, 35–36 to say that these terrible social conditions characterized the end of the OT and the beginning of the gospel age. He was claiming to be the inaugurator of the messianic age and was preparing his followers for persecution from their own families.

A Prophetic Liturgy (7:7–20)

Bibliography

Barre, M. L. "A Cuneiform Parallel to Ps 86:16–17 and Mic 7:16–17." *JBL* 101 (1982) 271–75. **Eissfeldt, O.** "Ein Psalm aus Nord-Israel. Mica 7, 7–20." *ZDMG* 112 (1962) 259–68. **Gordon, R. P.** "Micah VII 19 and Akkadian Kabasu." *VT* 28 (1978) 355. **Gunkel, H.** "The Close of Micah." *What Remains of the OT.* New York: Macmillan

(1928) 115–49. **Willis, J. T.** "A Reapplied Prophetic Hope Oracle." *Studies on Prophecy.* VTSup (1974) 64–76.

Translation

⁷ *But I will watch for Yahweh,*
I will wait for the God of my salvation,
my God will hear me.   3+3+2
⁸ *Do not rejoice over me, my enemy!* ᵃ
Although I have fallen I will arise.   3+2
Although I sit in darkness
Yahweh will be light to me.   2+2
⁹ ᵃ *The rage of Yahweh I will bear*
because I sinned against him.   3+2
Until he pleads my case
and brings about my justice.   3+2
He will bring me out to the light,
and I will see his righteousness (salvation).   2+2
¹⁰ *Then my enemy* ᵃ *shall see*
and shame shall cover her.   2+2
The one saying to me,
"Where ᵇ *is Yahweh your God?"*
My eyes will gloat over her.   2+3+2
Now she shall be trampled
like clay of the street.   3+2
¹¹ *A day* ᵃ *for the building of your walls!*
That day ᵇ *to extend your border!*   3+3
¹² *In that day* ᵃ *they* ᵇ *will come to you* ᶜ
from ᵈ *Assyria to* ᵉ *the cities of Egypt,*   4+4
and from Egypt to the river
and from sea to sea and mountain to mountain. ᶠ   3+4
¹³ *And the earth shall become a desolation*
over her inhabitants
as the fruits of her deeds.   3+3+2
¹⁴ *Shepherd your people with your staff,*
the sheep of thy inheritance   3+2
who dwell ᵃ *alone in a forest,*
surrounded by ᵇ *a garden land.*   3+2
Let them feed in Bashan and Gilead
as in ancient days.   3+2
¹⁵ *Like the days when you went out*
from the land of Egypt,
let us see ᵃ *wonders.*   2+2+2
¹⁶ *May the nations see and be ashamed*
of all their strength.   3+2
Let them lay a hand on their mouth;
may their ears be deaf.   3+2

¹⁷ *Let them lick dust as the serpent,*
  like the crawling things of the earth.   3+2
Let them come trembling from their dungeons.
  Let them turn in dread toward Yahweh our God.
And let them fear you.   2+3+2
¹⁸ *Who is a God like thee,*   2+2
  the one taking away guilt
and passing over the rebellion   2+2
  of the remnant of his heritage?
He does not keep his anger strong forever,   3+3
  for he delights in steadfast love.
¹⁹ *He will turn and show us compassion.*   2+2
  He will tread down ^a *our iniquities,*
and he will cast all our ^b *sins*   3+2
  into the depths of the sea.
²⁰ *You will give truth to Jacob,*   3+2
  steadfast love to Abraham
which you swore to our fathers   3+2
  from days of old.

Notes

8.a. איבתי "my enemy" is fem., suggesting a nation is intended. Tg adds רומי "Rome" pointing to the major enemy of that time.

9.a. Tg adds at the beginning of the verse אמרת ירושלם "Jerusalem says" thus identifying the speaker of the verse (cf. Wolff 188).

10.a. See 8.a.

10.b. MT אֵיוֹ makes no sense. It should probably be read as אַיֵּה "where." This may have occurred because יהוה "Yahweh" follows, leading some scribe to think this is a repetition of the abbreviation יה (see Wolff 188).

11.a. Three brief statements begin with יום "a day." None of them fit the rules of grammar.

11.b. יום ההוא cannot be translated "in that day" since neither the article nor the prep. is present. הוא may be understood as a rel. particle.

12.a. See 11.b. Here the pronoun occurs without an article. Cf. G. W. Nebe, "הואהא in IQS 8, 13–14." *ZNW* 63 (1972) 288.

12.b. MT יבוא "he will come." LXX ἥξουσιν "they will come." I. Willi-Plein ("Vorformen der Schriftexegese." BZAW 123 [1971] 106–109) explains the corruption as "metathesis of ו in א." Read plural with LXX.

12.c. MT ועדיך uses a mas. pronoun "to you." V 11 leads one to expect a fem. for the city. A mas. refers to the inhabitants (cf. Wolff 188).

12.d. למני is an extended form of מן (*CHAL* 200).

12.e. Read עד "to" for ערי "cities." The ד has been confused with ר.

12.f. MT ההר "the mountain." Eissfeldt (*ZDMG* 112 [1962] 266–68) translates "Sea for sea, mountain for mountain." Some LXX MSS. correct this καὶ ἀπὸ θαλάσσης ἕως θαλάσσης καὶ ἀπὸ ὄρους ἕως (τοῦ) ὄρους "and from sea to sea and from mountain to (the) mountain." Renaud (361) finds in וים and והר an unusual accusative of "motion toward." Vg translates *et ad mare de mare et ad montem de monte*. Perhaps the easiest way is to emend ההר to מֵהָר "from a mountain" to parallel the first pair as Wellhausen suggested long ago.

14.a. MT שֹׁכְנִי "one who dwells" is a ptc. with yodh-compaginis, *GKC* 90n. The form appears in Deut 33:16 of God's dwelling. LXX κατασκηνοῦντας, Vg *habitantes*, Syr and Tg have plural forms referring to God's people. Wolff (188) does not find enough reason to support a plural reading שֹׁכְנִי with BHS. The antecedents "people" and "flock" are both collective nouns which may well explain this sing.

14.b. Lit. "in the midst of."

15.a. MT אֶרְאֶנּוּ "I will see him" changes the person from second "you" to third "him." Wellhausen suggested emending to הראנו "let us see." This suggests that "your" in the first line refers to Yahweh.

19.a. The Akkadian equivalent of MT יכבש is "kabasu" which can mean "forgive" (cf. *Chicago Assyrian Dictionary;* R. P. Gordon, *VT* 28 [1978] 335).

19.b. MT חטאותם ="Their sins." LXX, Syr, Tg read "our sins" in conformity with 1 per. pl. pronominal suffixes in lines one and two of the verse.

Form/Structure/Setting

A prophetic liturgy, 7:7–20 is a unit. There is some question about the beginning of the pericope. Does it begin with v 7 or v 8? V 7 is definitely transitional. The word "watching" in v 7 points back to the word "watchmen" in 7:4. But the content of v 7 contrasts too much with that of vv 1–6 to be an integral part of it. 7:7–20 is made up of four distinct parts which should be considered together. First is a psalm of trust (vv 7–10) in which the nation speaks of her trust in Yahweh. She understands that she is suffering for her sins (v 9), but her enemies should not gloat over her plight because God will give her victory and they will become like mire in the streets (v 10). Second is an oracle (vv 11–13) in which a prophet announces that the city walls will be enlarged, exiles will return from north to south and from east to west, but the lands of her enemies will be desolate. Third is a prayer for God to bless Israel and punish her enemies (vv 14–17). Fourth is a hymn praising Yahweh for his forgiveness and devotion to his covenant which he promised his people as far back as the days of Abraham.

This pericope was probably put together by Micah's disciples shortly after the fall of Jerusalem. It may have been used in cultic celebrations during the exile to voice the hope and assurance that God would restore the fortunes of Jerusalem. For a reconstruction of the history of this pericope see Willis, *Studies on Prophecy.*

Explanation

The speaker in vv 7–10 says that although society may be corrupt (vv 1–6), it will not always be that way. Calamity has come. Jerusalem has fallen (8b). Her people sit in the darkness of prison, poverty, or exile. But Yahweh will be a light to her (cf. Ps 27:1). Now for the first time in Micah we read of the people's confession of sin (7a), and a willingness to suffer because of it. But there is assurance that God will defend her and give her victory over her enemies. Those who now are taunting Israel by asking, "Where is your God?" (cf. Ps 42:3, 10) will one day become the mire of the streets (v 10).

In many cultic rituals in Israel there was a moment when a priest or prophet stepped forward and gave the congregation an assurance from God that he had heard their petitions. Vv 11–13 seem to be such a prophetic utterance. The walls will be rebuilt; the borders enlarged; the exiles will return and the enemies' land will be desolate. Some scholars have questioned whether or not the city referred to here is Jerusalem. Eissfeldt, Reicke, and others have argued that the city was Samaria because Jerusalem is not mentioned and there are many North Israelite names, i.e. Carmel, Bashan, and Gilead (v 14), in the passage. The word for wall גדר generally refers to a stone fence (Num 22:24; Ps 62:4). קיר is more commonly used for city wall. However these arguments do not militate against taking this pericope to be about Jerusalem.

Vv 14–17 are a prayer for God to care for his people like a shepherd and for the subjection of the nations to Yahweh. Israel is God's inheritance as a result of the covenant (v 14). Now Israel dwells alone in a forest, abandoned on a lonely mountain top as Micah had predicted (3:12). The prayer is for Israel's fortunes to be changed. Still using the analogy of sheep, the people pray that they will be restored to the best grazing lands of Bashan and Gilead (v 14c). Then recalling how God led them out of Egypt the people pray to see the wonders again (v 15). What Israel sees as God's mighty acts of salvation for her will become acts of terror and fear for the nations (v 16, cf. Exod 15:14–16). They will become speechless and deaf (cf. Isa 33:3).

V 17 prays that "the nations" be like snakes, licking dust, and living in underground holes in view of Yahweh's awesome display of power. Then it prays that, thus humiliated, they will emerge into God's presence with fitting dread. "Let them fear you" is a prayer for their humble worship of Yahweh. Their total capitulation before Yahweh has made possible their worship of him (cf. for Jonah 1:16 in relation to the sailors; cf. Wolff 204). Paul speaks of a time when "every knee shall bow and every tongue confess . . ." (Phil 2:10).

The last section of this liturgy is a hymn or a doxology (vv 18–20). The first line states that God is incomparable and unique. There is a play on Micah's name in this statement, for his name means "who is like Yahweh?" The congregation believes that its prayers will be answered because it believes that God forgives sins. His anger does not last forever (v 18, cf. Ps 30:5). He will get victory over our sins and bury them in the depths of the sea because he will always be true to his covenant promise which he made with Abraham. The two words חסד and אמת in v 20 are often translated "grace and truth" in the OT to refer to God's faithfulness to his covenant. The prologue to John's Gospel claims that "the law came through Moses, but *grace* (חסד) and *truth* (אמת) came through Jesus Christ" (Jn 1:17). Thus Jesus is the fulfillment of God's covenant promise to Abraham and Jacob.

SUMMARY OF THE MESSAGE OF MICAH

As we have seen, Micah is composed of twenty pericopes loosely connected into three cycles of judgment and hope. The material stems from the prophet Micah, or at least from those who were closely associated with him. The book contains a sharp polemic against corruption on all levels; judges, prophets, merchants, and priests fall under Micah's condemnation. Vivid imagery and the skillful use of metaphors give his utterances the flavor of emotional outbursts, yet the hatred with which Micah addresses the wicked is matched by the joy he communicates in his promise of redemption.

The first cycle of judgment/hope is contained in chaps. 1–2. The message is open to all who will hear and the invective is addressed to the entire nation. After an introductory passage that levels a condemnation at all of Judah, Micah describes the punishment of Yahweh by listing the cities attacked by Sennacharib's army. He then focuses on the immoral businessmen who cheat, steal, and kill to gain profit and power, regardless of who is impoverished or displaced as a result. Ironically it is these very refugees who are chosen as the true Judah, the remnant which Yahweh will lead.

The second main division focuses on the leaders of the nation—judges (3:1), prophets (3:5), rulers (3:9), and priests (3:11). These people who should be establishing justice and righteousness are the very ones who will cause the nation's demise (3:12). Again, the message of hope is a contrast to the objects of judgment. The Lord will establish Jerusalem as a place for learning his ways. He will judge fairly, teach the people to "walk in the name of the Lord" (4:5), and will establish peace. The authorities who oppressed the weak will be replaced by a Davidic king who will serve as a shepherd for the remnant. All of the old accouterments of government—strong armies, sorceries, and idolatry—are to be destroyed and supplanted with a reign of peace and holiness.

The final division of Micah is devoted to the people of the Lord. Yahweh passionately asks why they have neglected centuries of his care and have taken up wicked ways. Their offerings and sacrifices cannot overcome the lack of compassion displayed in their daily affairs. So the Lord must turn their wealth into a desolation. In this section lies the ultimate contrast between judgment and hope. Those who live in violation of God's laws are condemned and those who love Yahweh are vindicated. The whole nation will be judged, even Micah himself; however, the remnant which repents will be delivered and granted honor.

Micah is a complex work containing a large number of textual and conceptual problems. Nevertheless, a greater insight into the book is achieved by seeing it as a study in contrasts. The unethical merchants are condemned while those they abused are redeemed; the corrupt political and religious leaders are replaced with a Davidic king led by Yahweh; every individual who rejects the Lord is destroyed but those who trust in him are refined and stand in his favor.

The community of Judaism that used the book as it was becoming canonical scripture were made by it to see themselves "standing between judgment and salvation" in a stance not unlike that of the prophet. It "is still very compatible for its ongoing liturgical use" (Childs *IOTS* 439; cf. Wolff 210).

Nahum

Nahum

Bibliography

Books

(For a complete bibliography see Schulz, *Das Buch Nahum* 156–63.) **Bickell, G.** *Beiträge zur semitischen Metrik, I Das alphabetische Lied in Nahum 1:2–2:3.* SAW Phil-hist. Kl. 131, 5 (1894) 1–12. **Cathcart, K. J.** *Nahum in the Light of Northwest Semitic.* Rome: Biblical Institute Press, 1973. **Dalglish, E. R.** "Nahum," in *The Broadman Bible Commentary*, vol. 6. 1972. **Haldar, A.** *Studies in the Book of Nahum.* Uppsala: A. B. Lundequistska Bokhandeln, 1946. **Hyatt, J. P.** "Nahum" in *Peake's Commentary on the Bible*, eds. Black and Rowley, 1962. **Maier, W. A.** *The Book of Nahum.* St. Louis: Concordia Publishing House, 1959. **Parrot, A.** *Nineveh and the Old Testament.* London: SCM Press, 1955. **Schulz, H.** *Das Buch Nahum.* BZAW 129. Berlin: deGruyter, 1973. **Taylor, C. L.** "Nahum," in *The Interpreter's Bible*, vol. 6 (1956).

Articles

Allegro, J. M. "Further Light on the History of the Qumran Sect." *JBL* 75 (1956) 89–95. ———. "More Unpublished Pieces of a Qumran Commentary on Nahum 4Qp Nah." *JSS* 7 (1962) 304–08. **Allis, A. T.** "Nahum, Nineveh, Elkosh." *EvQ* 27 (1955) 67–80. **Arnold, W. R.** "The Composition of Nahum 1–2:3." *ZAW* 21 (1901) 225–65. **Christensen, D. L.** "The Acrostic of Nahum Reconsidered." *ZAW* 87 (1975) 17–30. **Gaster, T. H.** "Two Notes of Nahum." *JBL* 63 (1944) 51–52. **Gunkel, H.** "Nahum 1." *ZAW* 13 (1863) 223–44. **Humbert, P.** "Essai d'analyse de Nahum 1:2–2:3." *ZAW* 44 (1926) 266–78. **Mihelic, J. L.** "The Concept of God in the Book of Nahum." *Int* 2 (1948) 199–208. **Rowley, H. H.** "Nahum and the Teacher of Righteousness." *JBL* 75 (1956) 188–93. **Saggs, H. W. F.** "Nahum and the Fall of Nineveh." *JTS* 20 (1969) 220–25. **van Doorslaer, J.** "No Amon." *CBQ* 11 (1949) 280–295. **de Vries, S. J.** "The Acrostic of Nahum in the Jerusalem Liturgy." *VT* 16 (1966) 476–81. **Weiss, R.** "A Comparison Between the Massoretic and the Qumran Texts of Nahum III, 1–11." *RQ* 4 (1963–64) 433–39.

Introduction

Place in the Canon

In all forms of the Bible Nahum stands seventh in the list of "The Twelve." It follows Micah in the Hebrew Bible, the Peshitta, the Vulgate and modern versions, but follows Jonah in the LXX. It invariably precedes Habakkuk. The order of "The Twelve" appears generally to be determined by the historical period with which their prophecies have to do.

The Prophet

Very little is known about the life of Nahum. His name occurs only once in the OT (in the superscription to his book), and once in the NT (Luke 3:25). It occurs frequently in Northwest Semitic inscriptions, once in the Arad ostraca (seventh century B.C.) and once in the Lachish letters (seventh century B.C.). It occurs often in the Mishnah. There is no reason to doubt the authenticity of the name. The name probably means "consolation," or "comforter." Nahum is not called a prophet but the book is classified as an "oracle" משא and as a חזון "vision," classifications associated also with Habakkuk, Obadiah, Malachi, and throughout Isaiah.

Nahum is called an Elkoshite, which means that his home was Elkosh. The location of Elkosh is not known. Various traditions have arisen, however, as to its location. In the preface to his commentary on Nahum, Jerome said that he visited a village in Galilee by the name of "Elkesi" which a guide identified as the home of Nahum. In the *Lives of the Prophets* Elkosh is identified with Beth-gabre in the tribe of Simeon and is believed to be the same as the modern Beit-Jebrin, the ancient Eleutheropolis, which is about twenty miles southwest of Jerusalem. Another tradition identified Nahum's home with a village about twenty-five miles north of the ancient city of Nineveh. This tradition cannot be traced back beyond the sixteenth century. Hitzig and Knobel claimed that Elkosh was the original site of Capernaum, the "village of Nahum," on the north shore of the Sea of Galilee. None of these locations can be verified as the home of Nahum. The most logical one is Beit-Jebrin in Judah. If Elkosh is Beit-Jebrin, Nahum lived in the same vicinity as Micah of Moresheth.

The Time of Nahum

Nahum lived during the supremacy of the Assyrian Empire. Nineveh was the capital at the time (see *IDB* k–q 551–3). Although no specific dates are given in the book (no king's names are mentioned), two events give us a clue as to when Nahum delivered his message. One was the sack of No-Amon (Thebes), the capital of Egypt by Ashurbanipal, king of Assyria in 663 B.C. The other event was the fall of Nineveh in 612 B.C.

In one of Ashurbanipal's inscriptions found in the ruins of Kuyunjik in 1878, the king tells how he captured Thebes. Urdamane was the son of the sister of Pharaoh Tirhakah who died in 664 B.C. Ashurbanipal said,

> In my second campaign I marched directly against Egypt (Musur) and Nubia. Urdamane heard of the approach of my expedition (only when) I had (already) set foot on Egyptian territory. He left Memphis and fled into Thebes to save his life. The kings, governors, and regents whom I had installed in Egypt came to meet me and kissed my feet. I followed Urdamane (and) went as far as Thebes, his fortress. He saw my mighty battle array approaching, left Thebes and fled to Kipkipi. Upon a trust (inspiring) oracle of Ashur and Ishtar I, myself, conquered this town completely. From Thebes I carried away booty, heavy and beyond counting: silver, gold, precious stones, his entire personal possessions, linen garments with multicolored trimmings, fine horses, (certain) inhabitants, male and female. I pulled two high obelisks, cast of shining zahalu-bronze, the weight of which was 2,500 talents, standing at the door of the temple, out of their bases and took (them) to Assyria. (Thus) I carried off from Thebes heavy booty, beyond counting. I made Egypt (Musur) and Nubia feel my weapons bitterly and celebrated my triumph. With full hands and safely, I returned to Nineveh, the city (where I exercise) my rule. (*ANET* 295)

Nahum was well aware of the fall of Thebes. In 3:8 he reminds Nineveh that what she did to Thebes, others will do to her. Evidently the fall of Nineveh was imminent in Nahum's day. Nineveh fell to a combined attack by the Medes, Babylonians, and Scythians in 612 B.C. A record of that event has been preserved in one of the Babylonian Chronicles (British Museum, no. 21901):

> (In the fourteenth year, 613/12 B.C.) the king of Babylonia called out his army and marched to . . ., the king of the Umman-manda and the king of Babylonia met each other in . . . Kyaxares made . . . the king of Babylonia to cross and they marched along the Tigris river bank and pitched camp by Nineveh. From the month of Sivan to the month of Ab they (advanced?) only three. . . . They made a strong attack on the citadel and in the month of Ab, (on the . . . the day the city was taken and) a great defeat inflicted on the people and (their) chiefs. On that same day Sin-shar-ishkun, the Assyrian king, (perished in the flames). They carried off much spoil from the city and temple-area and turned the city into a ruin-mound and heap of debris . . . of Assyria moved off before (the final attack?) and the forces of the Babylonian king (followed them). On the twentieth of Elul Kyaxares and his army returned to his land; the Babylonian king and his army marched as far as Nisibin. Booty and prisoners . . . and of the land of Rusapu were brought before the Babylonian king at Nineveh. In the month of (. . . Ashur-uballit) sat on the throne in Harran as king of Assyria. (*DOTT* 75–76)

Evidently Nahum witnessed the height and the eclipse of Assyria's power. By sheer military strength, Assyria, the lion of the Ancient Near East, with its capital in Nineveh, was able to conquer and rule most of the known world. Tiglath-Pileser III had overrun Israel, which he called "Omriland." A few years later Sargon II and Sennacherib were to make Judah a vassal state. Ashurbanipal devastated Thebes in Egypt and burned Babylon. Ishtar, goddess of war and ancient queen of the universe, who was originally revered in Nineveh, came to be exalted from Mesopotamia, throughout Babylonia and the kingdoms of Palestine, even in Egypt. The lion had roared from its den and the seventh-century world trembled at the sound.

But with the death of Ashurbanipal in 627 B.C., coalitions of Medes, Babylonians, and Sythians sought revenge for the ravages of Assyria. By 612 B.C., these armies could lay siege to Nineveh and destroy her. The rise and fall of the Assyrian Empire took less than a century-and-a-half. Unbelievably, the great city of Nineveh lay in fiery ruins, hardly to rise again. In these years Nahum, the prophet, spoke for God.

The Book

The book of Nahum is divided into three chapters and forty-seven verses. The Hebrew and English numbering of chapters and verses do not always coincide. 2:1–14 in Hebrew is equivalent to 1:15–2:13 in English. The first chapter describes the nature and purposes of God toward those who oppose and those who trust him. It begins with a hymn about the nature of God. Chaps. 2 and 3 are songs or oracles about the siege and fall of Nineveh.

The attention of most of the critical study of the book of Nahum has concentrated on the nature of chap. 1. In the 1867 edition of his *Commentary on Psalms* (Edinburgh: T. & T. Clark), Franz Delitzsch said that Pastor G. Frohnmeyer of Württemberg had noted at least a partial acrostic in Nahum 1:3–7. In 1880, shortly after Frohnmeyer's death, G. Bickell, *Beiträge* 1–12, reconstructed Nahum 1:2–10 into a sixteen-bicola acrostic containing the entire Hebrew alphabet; cf. Christensen, *ZAW* 87 (1975) 17. Soon after Bickell's initial work Gunkel, *ZAW* 13 (1893) 223–44, argued that chap. 1 was a broken acrostic and was added by a post-exilic editor of Nahum's oracles. Gunkel "restored" what he thought was the original alphabetical text of chap. 1 and extended the poem to v 3 of chap. 2. Gunkel's work began a scholarly debate about the form and date of chap. 1 of Nahum. In the third edition of *Die Kleinen Propheten* (Berlin: De Gruyter, 1898) J. Wellhausen asserted that the acrostic could not be maintained beyond 1:2–8 and branded the reconstructions of Bickell and Gunkel as total failures. In 1901 W. R. Arnold, *ZAW* 21 (1901) 225–265, accused Bickell and Gunkel of "decapitating a masterpiece of Hebrew literature." However, Arnold proceeded to emend the text of 1:1–2:3, dividing it into eight parts, four of which he assigned to a late fourth-century redactor, who remembered vaguely an alphabetical poem which he thought would make an appropriate introduction to Nahum.

In 1907 Paul Haupt argued that the book of Nahum was not prophecy at all but was festival liturgy composed for the celebration of the Day of Nikanor on the thirteenth of Adar, 161 B.C. Haupt believed that the acrostic continued through the letter ס in 1:10 and explained the omission of the last seven lines (ע through ת) as "not quoted by the compiler . . . because they did not suit his purpose" (P. Haupt, "The Book of Nahum," *JBL* 26 [1907] 1–53).

Although Haupt's Maccabean date was rejected, his idea that the book was a festival liturgy influenced later research. In 1926 P. Humbert (*ZAW*

44 [1926] 266–78) argued that the book was a prophetic liturgy used at the New Year festival in Jerusalem in 612 B.C. to celebrate the fall of Nineveh earlier that year. Humbert believed that the acrostic is limited to 1:2–8 and contains precisely the first half of the Hebrew alphabet through the letter כ, and that it consists of thirteen stiches with one uniform (3+3) rhythm. Humbert also cited Pss 9 and 10 as an important parallel to the acrostic in Nahum. George Fohrer in his *Introduction to the Old Testament* (trans. D. E. Green [Nashville: Abingdon] 1968) purports to find two prophetic liturgies in the book. The cultic interpretation has been sharply rejected by many scholars including Elliger, Rudolph, and Jörg Jeremias (*Theophanie*. Neukirchen-Vluyn: Neukirchener Verlag, 1965).

In 1946 A. Haldar published his unique view that the book of Nahum was the work of cultic prophets who used the language of ritual combat in the New Year festival as a curse on their political enemies, the Assyrians. Haldar suggested that the book was written ca 614 B.C., shortly before the fall of Nineveh. Haldar's views have found few supporters although many admire his confidence in the MT, his rejection of the presence of an acrostic in chap. 1, and his support of the unity of the book.

In 1959 Walter A. Maier's comprehensive (386 pages) commentary on Nahum was published posthumously. Maier took a very conservative approach to the materials in the book of Nahum, but he discussed extensively all of the scholarly theories and debates about the book and gave a thorough exegesis of the Hebrew text. He thought the book of Nahum was written about 654 B.C., when Ashurbanipal was king. The burden upon Nineveh should not be seen as a product of Manasseh's cult. It was a true vision of the prophet's poetic imagination predicting the justice of God on the cruelest of cities.

Recently S. J. de Vries (*VT* 16 [1966] 476–81) and Duane L. Christensen (*ZAW* 27 [1975] 17–30) have made thorough studies of the acrostic in Nahum 1:2–8. Each agrees that the acrostic goes through the letter כ. De Vries (479) is freer in emending the text than Christensen and thinks it is probable that the acrostic was written by Nahum since there are linguistic affinities between it and the oracles against Nineveh. Christensen reconstructs the acrostic using Frank Cross' "new syllabic theory" for scanning Hebrew poetry. By dropping some articles and pronominal suffixes, restoring and relocating a word or two, Christensen brings order to the poem. He sees it as a hymn "which portrays a theophany of the Divine Warrior who has come in the storm-wind to vindicate his name, together with mythical allusions to cosmic entities which collapse and languish in his presence" (23). As to the date, Christensen believes that any date after Ashurbanipal's last western campaign ca 639–637 B.C. could fit the occasion. But an earlier date is possible. Christensen says that the Chronicler's account of Manasseh's revolt against Assyria (2 Chr 33:14–16) is not a figment of his imagination (29). If such a revolt occurred, it probably happened between 652–648 B.C. Christensen believes that the book of Nahum presents the very message that might have persuaded the Judean king to take part in such a revolt—the assurance that Assyria's fall was certain, "in fact that it was ordained of Yahweh the Divine Warrior" (29).

In 1973 Kevin J. Cathcart published his dissertation at the Pontifical Biblical Institute, *Nahum in the Light of Northwest Semitic.* This work is a word-by-word study and translation of the book of Nahum in the light of the materials now available as a result of "epigraphical discoveries and subsequent advances in the study of comparative Semitic philology and comparative ancient Near Eastern literatures." Cathcart brings together an amazing amount of valuable information about the text of Nahum, and reviews the current literature in the field. His study indicates that many difficulties which cause scholars to emend the text can be explained in the light of modern discoveries in Northwest Semitic languages. Like Haldar, he would caution against changing a text that has been handed down so faithfully. In 1975 John D. W. Watts wrote *Cambridge Bible Commentary* on Joel, Obadiah, Jonah, Nahum, Habakkuk, and Zephaniah. Watts believes that Obadiah, Nahum, and Habakkuk were liturgical expansions of foreign prophecies and were part of the "day of the Lord" section of the annual Royal Zion Festival in Jerusalem. Such a hypothesis certainly would provide an excellent *Sitz im Leben* for chap. 1.

One may divide the book into three almost equal parts. Chap. 1 is about the nature of God. Because Yahweh is a jealous God he will judge the enemies of his people and he will give refuge to those who trust in him because he is good (v 7). Chap. 2 is a vivid description of the battle for Nineveh along with a taunt song against Nineveh. Chap. 3 is an oracle on the fate of Nineveh. A more detailed outline of the book will show that 1:9–2:2 contains alternating judgment oracles against Assyria and salvation oracles for Judah based on the contrast in the psalm between the enemy and those who seek Yahweh's protection. The psalm is not a typical hymn of praise because it lacks the imperatives which are usual in the call to thanksgiving in Israel. The thematic relation of the judgment oracle against Assyria to the psalm is marked in 1:8–9 by the idea of "making an end" כלה. The salvation oracle promises deliverance for Judah in that day. Then the King of Assyria is told of his ultimate annihilation. The oracles of judgment and salvation are expansions of the themes introduced in the hymn fragment. In vivid contrapuntal manner the oracles introduce the reader, filled with the knowledge of a zealous God, to the descriptive passages about Nineveh and Thebes, the final destruction of the Assyrian king, and the joy of those who must no longer endure his tyranny. As Childs says, "The implications of the divine claim voiced in the Psalm are spelled out in the second half of the chapter in the direct addressing of the two historical entities, Assyria and Judah" (*Introduction* 443).

The Text

The Hebrew text of Nahum is fairly clear. Several passages are subject to different readings. Some scholars in the past have emended the text freely to produce an assumed original acrostic in chap. 1, but the Dead Sea Scrolls and the materials from Wadi Murabba'at and the fragments of Greek text of the Minor Prophets from Nahal Hever indicate that the consonantal text of the Hebrew Bible has been handed down with amazing accuracy for almost 2000 years.

There are some very difficult passages in the book. 1:10 is extremely hard to understand. Words may not be divided properly in 1:12 (see notes). An enclitic is found in 1:14. Several hapax legomena are used causing some uncertainty in meaning. The antecedent of "he" is unclear in 2:6. חַצָּב is a major problem in 2:8. 2fs forms must be changed to 3fs forms in 2:14; 3:7. In this commentary the Masoretic reading has been retained wherever possible. The chapter and verse numbers differ in the Hebrew and English Bibles: (1:15–2:13 in English is 2:1–14 in Hebrew. Cf. *Note* 1.a.p. 193).

The Message of Nahum

Nahum has been criticized because he has no word of condemnation of Israel's sins and no call for her to repent. He appears to be an avowed nationalist, and has been accused of being a "false prophet" like those who opposed Micah and Jeremiah (see Maier 74; J. M. P. Smith 281).

Such criticism of Nahum is much too harsh and reflects a failure to understand or appreciate Nahum's real message, which is to stress the sovereignty of God over history and the world. God is good and just. Therefore he is the champion of the outraged and helpless and "will by no means justify the guilty" (1:3). In the final analysis, the threat against Nineveh does not stem from personal hatred of the human author or some historical event in the seventh century B.C. but from the nature of God who is jealous for the right, wrathful toward his enemies, and claims dominion over the world. The vision of Nahum renders intelligible this imminent sovereignty of Israel's God over the history of nations. "What nation can withstand the God who overcame the primordial chaos?" (Childs, *Introduction* 444).

The glee of Nineveh's victims over her fall is easily understood when one remembers the scourge of such rulers as Adolph Hitler and Idi Amin. Assyrian kings boasted on tablets that have survived the years of the way they were able to drag women and children away from their dead husbands and fathers as the spoils of conquest to the great fortress at Nineveh. Their annals reflect their pride in the complete devastation of their enemies. There may be another message beyond the literal meaning of the text. Watts (120) says, "Nineveh is no ordinary city for the prophet, nor is Assyria just another degenerating civilization. They stand for the ultimate supernatural evil that frustrates and suppresses the purposes and people of God. Their defeat is a sign of the victory of God and the basis for hope that his power and justice will ultimately conquer all evil" (cf. Childs, *Introduction* 444–45).

Outline

Superscription 1:1
1. A psalm in praise of Yahweh 1:2–8
   a. Yahweh—a jealous God 1:2–3a
   b. Yahweh—God of creation 1:3b–5
   c. Yahweh—God of love and judgment 1:6–8
2. Prophetic responses 1:9–2:3 (Eng 1:9–2:2)
   a. Disputation speech and judgment oracle against Assyria 1:9–11
   b. Salvation oracle for Judah 1:12–13

   c. Judgment oracle against the king of Assyria   1:14
   d. Salvation oracle for Judah   2:1,3 (Eng 1:15, 2:2)
3. Mocking judgment in the battle for Nineveh   2:2, 4–11 (Eng 2:1, 3–10)
4. Taunt song against Nineveh   2:12–14 (Eng. 11–13)
5. Judgment oracle against Nineveh   3:1–7
6. The analogy of Thebes   3:8–13
7. Satirical warnings for Nineveh   3:14–17
8. Rejoicing over ultimate defeat   3:18–19

Superscription (1:1)

Bibliography

Gehman, H. S. "The Burden of the Prophet." *JQR* 31 (1940) 107. **Johnson, A. R.**
The Cultic Prophet in Ancient Israel. Cardiff: University of Wales Press, 1944. 40–41
n4.

Translation

Oracle of Nineveh; book of the vision of Nahum, the Elkoshite.

Comment

The superscription of Nahum has two parts. The first part identifies the
form (oracle or burden) and the object of the oracle (Nineveh). The second
part identifies the burden-bearer or oracle-giver as Nahum from Elkosh. The
oracle did not originate with Nahum. It came to him in a vision. The message
was from Yahweh. The word מַשָּׂא can mean either "burden" (Jer 23:33),
or "oracle," or "utterance" in the sense of "lifting up the voice" (Isa 3:7;
42:11). The term is often used in the OT in a technical sense to introduce
an oracle of a prophet (Isa 13:1; 14:28; 15:1; 17:1; 19:1; Ezek 12:10; Hab
1:1; Zech 9:1; 12:1; Mal 1:1).

Nineveh was a large and ancient city in Nahum's day (*IDB* k–q 551–3).
It was probably founded about 5000 B.C. on the east side of the Tigris river
just opposite the modern city of Mosul. It had a checkered history until Sennacherib made it his capital city at the end of the eighth century. Sennacherib
spent twenty-five years restoring, enlarging and beautifying the old city. He
built temples, ramparts, palaces, aqueducts, and gardens. He was followed
on the throne by two other strong kings and builders, Esarhaddon (680–
669 B.C.) and Ashurbanipal (669–626 B.C.). This was Assyria's golden age.
The empire covered the entire fertile crescent from Egypt to the Persian
Gulf. Its palaces were filled with the wealth of the subject nations. Behind
its double line of ramparts Nineveh seemed invulnerable. She was the undis-
puted master of the world.

The theme of the book of Nahum is the fall of Nineveh, an event which
occurred in 612 B.C. How was it that this greatest nation on earth fell from
its zenith to its total destruction in a quarter of a century? Dalglish suggests
that the sudden decline and fall of Nineveh can be attributed to Ashurbanipal's
illness during the last part of his reign; to his preoccupation with Babylonian
lore and letters; and to the growing civil wars within the empire (*BBC* vol.
7, 232).

The appearance of the name Nineveh in the title is important, otherwise
the reader would not know that the fall of Nineveh is the subject of the

book. The name Nineveh does not occur in the book until 2:9 (Eng. 2:8). The only other place the name appears is 3:7.

The second part of the superscription contains two more descriptions of the work. ספר "book" appears only here in a prophetic title. Nahum is self-consciously a piece of literature. חזון "vision" also appears in the title of Isaiah and Obadiah (cf. p. 63). The verb "to see a vision" is used more widely to describe the unique prophetic function of revealing what is otherwise unseen, unknown, or unrecognized of God's will for his people. It points to God as the source of the message to come. It contains the visual aspects of prophecy with the auditory aspects emphasized by the title דבר "word."

The name Nahum occurs only here in the OT but it is frequently attested in Northwest Semitic inscriptions (cf. p. 63). The name is intensive in form like *rahum* "full of compassion," *hannun* "full of grace." So *nahum* should mean "full of comfort." It could be a short form of Nahum-Yah, i.e. Yahweh is "full of comfort," like Nehemiah. Other names from the same root in the OT are Nahum (1 Chr 4:19), Nahamani (Neh 7:7) and Menahem (2 Kgs 15:14).

"The Elkoshite" identifies Nahum's hometown (Elkosh). Three other OT prophets are identified by their hometown: Amos—Tekoa; Micah—Moresheth; Jeremiah—Anathoth. The location of Elkosh is unknown.

A Psalm in Praise for Yahweh (1:2-8)

Bibliography

Childs, B. S. *Introduction to the Old Testament As Scripture* 441–46. **Christensen, D. L.** "The Acrostic of Nahum Reconsidered." *ZAW* 87 (1975) 17–29. **De Vries, S. J.** "The Acrostic of Nahum in the Jerusalem Liturgy." *VT* 16 (1966) 476–81.

Comment

The nature and date of the first chapter of Nahum has been debated since Gunkel published his first article on "Nahum 1" (*ZAW* 13 [1893] 223–44). Gunkel "reconstructed" 1:2–2:3 to make an acrostic using the entire Hebrew alphabet. Bickell and Arnold followed Gunkel in the "reconstructing process." Gunkel also was the first to assign the first chapter to a post-exilic date. He was followed in his dating by Bickell and Arnold also. Haupt took the date down to the Maccabean period before scholars started moving the date back (see Introduction for details). Today many scholars hold to a unity for the book pointing out that the oracles against Assyria and for Judah are keyed linguistically and theologically to the psalm in praise of Yahweh (1:2–8).

Chap. 1 as it stands is not alphabetically arranged. However, there seems to be a broken acrostic in 1:2–8. Yet the letters ד and ז are missing and מ comes before ל. Many scholars (including the translators of NEB) still try to rearrange the text to produce an acrostic for the first half of the Hebrew alphabet but such a procedure has been highly subjective until now. Christensen claims to have put his work on the basis of metrics which "avoids much of the arbitrariness of earlier studies" (*ZAW* 87 [1975] 20).

Whether Nahum or a later redactor is responsible for the psalm in 1:2–8, it serves as an introduction to the following oracles concerning the destruction of Nineveh. Actually there is nothing specific in chap. 1 about the destruction of Nineveh. Outside the superscription, Nineveh is not mentioned until 2:9 (Eng. 2:8). However, much is said about God's wrath and vengeance on his enemies and his protection for his friends. Chap. 1 is a theological introduction extolling Yahweh's power over nature and nations. Such an introduction makes the book adaptable for use in a cultic celebration of the fall of Nineveh. It is Yahweh who is responsible for her fall.

Yahweh a Jealous God (1:2–3a)

Bibliography

Mendenhall, G. "The Vengeance of Yahweh," in *The Tenth Generation*. Baltimore: Johns Hopkins U. P., 1973. 69–104. Westermann, C. *The Praise of God in the Psalms*. Richmond: John Knox Press, 1965.

Translation

> ² *Yahweh is a jealous and avenging God*
> ᵃ *Yahweh is avenging,ᵃ and is a lord ᵇ of wrath.* 4+4
> *Avenging ᶜ is Yahweh against his enemies,*
> *and he rages ᵈ against his foes.* 3+3
> ³ᵃ *Yahweh is slow to anger*
> *and great ᵃ in power.*
> *Yahweh will certainly not clear the guilty.* 3+2+4

Notes

2.a–a. Omitted in LXX.

2.b. בעל חמה "lord of wrath" is parallel to אֵל קַנּוֹא. RSV has "wrathful." NEB has "quick to anger." Could *El qano'* perhaps be a play on האלקשי "the Elkoshite" in 1:1?

2.c. Some translators omit second נקם יהוה on basis of some G MSS. Others (NEB) transpose this line to v 9 or 11 for the ו strophe.

2.d. נטר has a second meaning "rage" as in Akkadian *ndr-smr* (cf. Amos 1:11; Jer 3:5). See Cathcart 43.

3.a. K וגדול an adj. which should follow the noun. Q וּגְדָל is probably considered an inf. const. The meaning is hardly altered.

Form/Structure/Setting

The form of 1:2–8 is a hymn. Although it does not have an imperative call to worship, the hymn may be compared to Ps 113 (cf. Westermann,

Praise of God 122). It is a descriptive psalm, not concerned with the attributes of Yahweh, but with his actions. The praise they illicit from his worshipers is response to his intervention in their history. The participles נֹקֵם "avenging" (v 2), נוֹטֵר "raging" (v 2), גֹּעֵר "rebuking" (v 4) and יֹדֵעַ "knowing" (v 7), are typical of this kind of hymn and make God's historical presence very vivid.

There is a broken acrostic here. 1:2–3a celebrates God's zeal for action against his enemies, while 1:3b–8 celebrates his judgment on them in the world. The setting of this hymn was probably as a part of a New Year festival liturgy. Haldar and Mowinckel reconstruct this liturgy along the lines of the Babylonian New Year festival in which God does battle with cosmic forces. The liturgy here stresses the fact that God's enemies are the enemies of his people and his purpose. His power is supreme over the whole world.

Explanation

Yahweh is proclaimed to be a jealous God. The form קַנּוֹא occurs one other place in the OT (Josh 24:19) and may have been an old Canaanite form. The more common word קַנָּא is used in Exod 20:5; 34:14; Deut 4:24; 5:9; 6:15. אֵל is used only here in Nahum and may indicate that the hymn is from an independent source. God is often presented as a jealous God in the OT (Num 25:11; Deut 6:15; Isa 59:17; Ezek 5:13; 38:18–19). Jealousy in essence is an intolerance of rivals. It can be a virtue or a sin depending on the legitimacy of the rival. God would allow no rivals in the covenant between him and Israel. He bound Israel exclusively to his service and he swore to protect her against all enemies.

Jealousy, wrath and vengeance of Yahweh go together in the OT. Vengeance is a word that troubles many people. To the modern reader, it suggests private retaliation. Mendenhall made a thorough study of the root נקם in the OT and in other Ancient Near Eastern texts and concluded that in only a very few instances is the term used of blood vengeance on the part of an individual. Most of the time it refers to judgment of a group or God to defend one of its/his own. Mendenhall emphasizes the importance of the covenant background to a proper understanding of the use of this term in the OT. Since Israel was Yahweh's covenant people, he was acting in her behalf in destroying Nineveh (1:13; 2:1). Yahweh is a jealous God who pours out his wrath and brings vengeance (judgment) against his enemies.

1:3 must be a part of a cultic confession. Parts of it are found in Exod 34:6; Num 14:18; Neh 9:17; Pss 86:15; 103:8; 145:8; 147:5; Joel 2:13; Jonah 4:2. In some places the patience of God is paired with his kindness חסד. Here and in Ps 147:5 power is paired with patience. This passage calls for a demonstration of God's power כֹּחַ.

The expression, "Yahweh will certainly not clear the guilty," is omitted by NEB. Haldar took the negative לֹא to be an emphatic lamed and reads "and, indeed, complete annihilation Yahweh will make" (18), a reading that is not much different from the negative reading. The meaning is clear, "Yahweh will not clear the guilty."

Yahweh—the God of Creation   (1:3b-5)

Translation

3b *His way is in the whirlwind and in the storm*
   and the clouds are the dust of his feet.   3+3
4 *The one rebuking the sea and drying it up;*
   and he causes all the rivers to go dry.   3+3
   Bashan and Carmel wither a
   and the flower of Lebanon withers.   3+3
5 *The mountains quake before him,*
   and the hills melt.   3+2
   The earth is laid waste a *before him*
   the world and all the inhabitants in her.   3+3

Notes

4.a. The first אֻמְלַל "wither," (GKC 55 d 2) is often altered to the verb דאר "to languish" to fit the acrostic but there is no MSS evidence for such. 4QpNah has אמלל twice like MT.

5.a. MT וַתִּשָּׂא] must be identified as a qal impf. from נשׂא meaning "then (the earth) raised" or "lifted up." No object is given, although the sense requires one. *BHS* and many scholars emend ט to שׁ meaning "(the earth) is laid waste" (nif. or passive from שׁאה: BDB I 980).

Form/Structure/Setting

The language in this part of the psalm reflects the ancient struggle between the Creator God and the powers of chaos represented by the sea and rivers. Whether there was a New Year cultic drama in Israel or not, the language from such a drama became a part of Israel's theological language. The prophet in this section is asserting that Yahweh is sovereign over all creation and capable of exercising his authority in it.

Explanation

The coming or an appearance (theophany) of Yahweh is often accompanied by a storm or whirlwind in the OT (Exod 19:16; Isa 28:2; 29:6; 66:15; Jer 23:19; Zech 7:14; 9:14; Ps 18:10–15; Job 38:1). Yahweh is called the rider of the clouds (Ps 68:4; cf. Isa 14:14). In the Canaanite myths of Baal found at Ugarit, Baal is captured by Prince Yamm (sea), alias Judge River, but Baal (a rider of the clouds) subdues his captors and becomes king of the gods. Ahab had once built a temple for Baal in Samaria (1 Kgs 16:31–33). Elijah stood up in the name of Yahweh to oppose him. The description of Yahweh here, like the fire Elijah witnessed on Carmel, shows Yahweh doing what Baal cannot do. No one can capture him. No one can stop him.

This part of the psalm says that not only are the sea (chaos) and the river under Yahweh's control, but the hills, mountains, the earth and her inhabitants are also subject to the power of God.

Yahweh—God of Love and Judgment
(1:6–8)

Bibliography

Ackroyd, P. R. and **Lindars, B.** *Words and Meanings.* Festschrift for D. W. Thomas. (London: Cambridge University Press, 1968) 11.

Translation

> 6 *Who can stand before his fury?*
>   *And who can rise up against the heat of his anger?*   4+4
> *His wrath is poured out like fire,*
>   *And the rocks are broken by him.*   3+3
> 7 *The Lord is good,* [a]
>   *a fortress in the day of trouble.*   2+2+2
>   *He knows* [b] *(cares for) those who seek refuge in him.*
> 8 *But* [a] *with an overflowing flood*   4+4
>   *he will make an end of her place,* [b]
>   *and pursue his enemies into* [c] *darkness.*   2+3+3

Notes

7.a. Cathcart translates ל . . . טוֹב "better than a fortress . . ."

7.b. ידע can mean "to know," "to care," or "to be made submissive"; (cf. Ackroyd and Lindars, *Words and Meanings* 11).

8.a. Christensen takes the waw as emphatic, repoints the other words in 8a and takes it as a continuation of the thought in v 7, "Yea, those who pass through the flood" (*ZAW* 87 [1975] 22).

8.b. מְקוֹמָהּ "her place" presents a problem. There is nothing in the immediate context to which "her" can refer. "Her place" might refer to Assyria's temple or to "the world" as in v 5. The LXX has "those who rise against him" τοὺς ἐπεγειρομένους = מְקָמָיו. James Barr (*Comparative Philology* 334 word 279) and Driver ("Vocabulary of the OT VIII," *JTS* 36 [1935] 300) take מקום to mean "opposition." J. D. W. Watts suggests that if "her place" is allowed to stand it must refer to Nineveh or to her patron goddess, Ishtar (105).

8.c. The prep. "into" is not in the MT or LXX.

Form/Structure/Setting

These verses are still part of the psalm. But the style changes with the two questions in v 6. By asking these questions the prophet is teaching that no one can withstand the fury of God's wrath.

Comment

V 7 has been variously translated. טוֹב יהוה is usually read "Good is Yahweh" (JB), "The Lord is good" (RSV). Cathcart takes טוֹב as an adverb and reads "Yahweh is better than a fortress." The NEB reads, "The Lord is a sure refuge." Then the NEB inserts a phrase from the LXX "for those who look to him." NEB also reconstructs the text in v 8.

Explanation

1:6–8 tells us that God is a God of wrath and judgment, but he is also a good God. Although none can stand against him, he protects and cares for those who seek him for refuge. The last word in the psalm is a word of judgment on his enemies. He will pursue them into darkness.

Prophetic Responses
Disputation Speech and Judgment Oracle against Assyria (1:9–11)

Translation

⁹ *Whatever* ᵃ *you plot against*
Yahweh,
he will put an end to anyone doing it.
His foe ᵇ *will not arise a second time.*   3+3+3
¹⁰ *For like entangled thorns*
and like sodden drunkards, ᵃ
     they are consumed as stubble fully dry.   3+3+3
¹¹ *From you has come out*
one plotting evil against Yahweh;
one counselling wickedness. ᵃ   2+4+2

Notes

9.a. מַה may be an indefinite pronoun instead of an interrogative. Cf. GKC, 137c.

9.b. צָרָה "oppression" is the subject of the sentence. *BHK*³ emends to צָרָיו "his oppressors." LXX ἐπὶ τὸ αὐτὸ ἐν θλίψει "on him who is affliction" makes it the object of the verb.

10.a. V 10 is very difficult. עַד which usually means "until," or "as far as," must be translated here by the rare meaning, "like." BDB (724) lists only two other references with this meaning (1 Chr 4:27; 2 Sam 23:19) and says the text is dubious. סִירִים means "thorns," but the fem. pl. סִירוֹת means "pots." סְבֻבִים is a qal pass. part. mas. pl. "entangled." So it is better to read these two words "entangled thorns." וּבְסָבְאָם סְבוּאִים the first word could be a qal. inf. cst with a mas. pl. suffix "their drink." BDB (685) takes it as a corrupt pass. part. dittograph of the next word (qal pass. part.) and suggests that both words be omitted from the translation. James Barr notes that the final ם on the first word could be an enclitic so the text could read, "and as the drunken are getting drunk" (*Comparative Philology* 33). JB, RSV and NEB do not translate the phrase. KJV has an adequate translation.

10.a. Recently בְלִיַּעַל has been taken as a proper name "Belial" for a demon comparable to Satan in Christian teaching (cf. Watts 106; Cathcart 63).

Form/Structure/Setting

The form is that of a judgment oracle on the leaders of Nineveh. These leaders are mas. in vv 9a, 11 but fem. in 9b. The fem. must refer to Nineveh and to her patron goddess. The passage is linked to the preceding poem by the repetition of the phrase "he will make an end" (cf. v 8). It differs from the previous poem by using direct address.

Comment

The emphasis in this pericope is upon the certainty and the finality of Yahweh's judgment on Nineveh and her patron deity. Nineveh can "devise," "plot," or "plan" any evil imaginable, but Yahweh will make a full end. Dalglish says that "the vocabulary of the poetical literature of Assyria is replete with such expressions as 'conceiving of a wicked plan,' 'plotting openly,' 'a planner of evil,' 'a plotter of iniquity'" (*BBC*, 7, 239). Dalglish also notes that v 9c is very similar to an Assyrian proverb, "The word of the deity is not spoken the second time" (ibid). V 10 seems to contain three similes of approaching disaster; like entangled thorns in a brush pile, like drinking drunkards, and like dry stubble they will all be fully consumed (intensive form of the verb). The word "fully" is at the end perhaps as the last word. The same likening of Yahweh's foes to thorns and stubble appears in Isa 33:11, 12. The thrust of the passage is that Yahweh is sovereign. All of his enemies, including the cosmic powers of evil, will be put down firmly and finally. V 11 may refer to Sennacherib as the one who came out of Nineveh plotting evil against Yahweh and counseling wickedness (cf. 2 Kgs 18–19). However, the term Belial suggests that the human enemy, whoever he was, represented the Assyrian goddess.

Salvation Oracle for Judah (1:12–13)

Translation

12 *Thus says Yahweh,*
  Though they are [a] *strong* [b] *and many,*
    they shall be cut down and he will pass over.   4+3
  Though I have oppressed you, [c]
    I will not oppress you [c] *again.*   1+3
13 *Now I will break his yoke from upon you,* [c]
    and your bonds I will tear off.   4+2

Notes

12.a. "They are" must be supplied from the verb in line 2.
12.b. שלמים can mean "strong." Some divide the word and read following LXX κατάρχων

ὑδάτων πολλῶν, מ֫שֵׁל מַיִם רַבִּים "ruler of many waters." Others (Haldar 34, n. 5) אמשל מים "I shall be like water."

12–13.c. All four pronouns are fem. sing. and probably refer to Judah.

Form/Structure/Setting

The oracle is introduced by the messenger formula, "Thus says Yahweh." It is an oracle of salvation with the pattern: a) Yahweh's intervention, b) the consequences, and c) the purpose. It assures Judah that though her oppressor is strong and numerous and Judah has been oppressed, Yahweh is now ready to break the Assyrian yoke that has bound her for so long.

Explanation

Assyria's oppression of Judah had been great. Although Judah had been allowed to keep her own king and temple, she did not enjoy political or religious freedom. For more than a hundred years Judah had been forced to pay tribute to Assyria and bow to her gods. When she asserted her independence she was beaten into submission. In 3:8 Nahum calls Nineveh "the bloody city." In 2:12 he describes Nineveh's treatment of her captives as a lion strangling its prey and tearing its flesh. Now God will put an end to all of that.

Judgment Oracle Against the King of Assyria (1:14)

Bibliography

Hummel, H. D. "Enclitic *Mem* in Early Northwest Semitic." *JBL* 76 (1975) 85–107.

Translation

> [14] Yahweh has commanded concerning you,
>> Your name [a] shall not be sown again;   3+3
> From the house of your god
>> I will cut off the graven and molten images.
> I will appoint [b] your grave
>> because you are small. [c]   2+2

Notes

14.a. The first ם on משמך is probably enclitic (cf. Cathcart 65).

14.b. Many scholars read אשׁים hiph. pf. of שמם "to make desolate" instead of אשׂים "I will set or appoint."

14.c. קָלוֹתָ is 2nd mas. sing. qal pf קלל "to be light or small." Some scholars read as a noun "shame," or "fall." RSV "vile," NEB "fickle."

Form/Structure/Setting

This is a very short judgment oracle addressed to the king of Nineveh. It is a part of a series of brief oracles of judgment and salvation addressed to Nineveh and Judah which form the prophetic responses to the partial hymn. First Assyria (2nd fem. pl. in vv 9–11) was addressed, then Judah (2nd fem. sing. in vv 12–13), and here the King of Assyria in a series that continues into the next chapter where Yahweh's purposes are revealed. In this verse the consequences of God's intervention are announced.

Explanation

This is one of the few references to the commands of God in the prophets (cf. Isa 23:11; 34:16; Jer 47:7; Ezek 37:10). God's command carries authority and certainty. The mas. sing. pronoun (you, your) refers to the king of Nineveh. The king's name will not be sown again, that is, his descendants will be no more. The power of Assyria's gods will be cut off. The carved and molten image in the temple will be destroyed. Assur, Nabu, Marduk, Bel, Ishtar, and a host of other divinities in the Assyrian Empire, from Hammurabi to Sin-shar-ishkun, its last emperor in 612 B.C., demanded the spoils of war for their benefit. Ishtar, goddess of all the world, was also the goddess of war. Descriptions of her dealings with the nations are unprintable. The kings of the empire were dedicated to pleasing the gods and making their temples and images famous. Thus their gods must fall with them, and Yahweh will select a grave site for the king of Nineveh. Because he, in contrast to his self-estimate, is actually of little consequence, God will provide a grave suitable for his true importance.

Salvation Oracle for Judah (2:1, 3 [Eng. 1:15; 2:2])

Translation

1(1:15) *Behold, upon the mountains the feet*
of one bringing good news,   2+2+2
the one proclaiming peace.
Keep your feasts, Judah.
Pay your vows,   3+2
because never again ᵃ *will Belial*
cross over ᵇ *against you.*
He is completely ᶜ *cut off.*   4+3+2

³⁽²:²⁾ *Because Yahweh is about* ᵃ *to restore the glory* ᵇ *of Jacob*
   as the pride of Israel;   5+2
because plunderers ᶜ *plundered them*
   and destroyed their branches.   3+2

Notes

1.a. LXX has a plural verb.
1.b. K לַעֲבִיר Q לַעֲבָר. BDB 717 recognizes both as inf. const. "to cross over."
1.c. כָּלֹה pu. inf. abs. LXX συντετέλεσται "be finished, completed."
3.a. שָׁב can be a qal part. "restoring."
3.b. גָּאוֹן "glory" is often changed to גֶּפֶן "branch" (cf. *BHK*³ and JB) as the antecedent of "branches" in the second line. But this is neither necessary nor justified.
3.c. בָּקַק can mean "profuse," "abundant," "empty" (BDB I 132). Here it means "lay waste" (BDB II 132).

Form/Structure/Setting

Once again the prophet changes the literary form of his message. The new motif is that of a messenger bearing good news that the enemy has fallen. The term "behold" introduces an announcement that the battle has been won reminiscent of the one in Isa 40:9. Judah is free to celebrate her feasts and to pay vows she made during her suffering. The consequences of Yahweh's intervention are realized with the admonition to renew her worship in the temple. "Behold" is a typical beginning for a salvation speech. The imperative actions of "keeping festival" and "paying vows," missing in the call of the earlier hymn, are now possible in Judah. She is free at last! An appendix in 2:2 should be considered a part of this oracle. Nahum has hopes that the northern tribes, taken captive in the fall of Samaria in 722 B.C., will also be set free. Prophetic faith never gave up hope of the restoration of all the tribes (cf. Rev 7:4–8). Both Israel and Judah had been stripped and pillaged as a vine without regard for the branches (2:2).

Comment

2:1 in Hebrew is 1:15 in the English versions. This verse marks a new oracle. These two verses 2:1, 3 should be taken together. 2:2 marks the beginning of the account of the battle for Nineveh. The term מְבַשֵּׂר usually means "one bringing good news" (2 Sam 18:31; 1 Kgs 1:42; Isa 40:9). But it can refer to the bearer of bad tidings (1 Sam 4:17). Here the message is good news for Judah. The plunderers have been destroyed. Yahweh "is about to return." שָׁב probably should be taken as a qal part. of שׁוּב (to express imminent action) "Yahweh is about to restore the glory of Jacob." God is going to return Judah to her previous greatness. The first גָּאוֹן "pride" possibly should be גֶּפֶן "vine" as an antecedent to branches in the last line. Israel is compared to a vine in Isa 5:1–7; Jer 5:10; Ps 80:8.

Mocking Judgment in the Battle for
Nineveh   (2:2, 4–11 [Eng 2:1, 3–10])

Bibliography

Driver, G. R. "Farewell to Queen Huzzab!" *JTS* 15 (1964) 296–98. **Pritchard, J. B.**
ANET 303–306. **Saggs, H. W. F.** "Nahum and the Fall of Nineveh." *JTS* 20 (1969)
220–24.

Translation

2(1) *The scatterer* [a] *has come up against you.*	
Guard the fortress;	
watch the road.	3+2+2
Strengthen your loins;	
gather much power.	2+3
4(3) *The shield of his mighty ones is red.* [a]	
The strong men are dressed in scarlet. [b]	3+3
Like fire the chariot flashes [c]	
in the day of its array,	
and the spears [d] *are shaken.*	3+2+2
5(4) *The chariots race wildly through the streets.*	
They rush to and fro in the squares.	3+2
Their appearance is like torches;	
they run like lightning.	2+2
6(5) *He (the king) remembers* [a] *his officers.*	
They stumble as they go.	2+2
They hasten toward the wall	
and the mantlet is set up. [b]	2+2
7(6) *The river gates are opened,*	
and the palace reels.	3+2
8(7) *The mistress* [a] *is stripped, carried away.*	
Her maidens are sobbing like the sound of doves,	
beating [b] *upon their breast.* [c]	3+4+2
9(8) *Now (because) of her water.* [a]	3+2
They [b] *are fleeing!*	
Stop! Stop!	
But none turns back.	2+2+2
10(9) *Plunder silver, plunder gold.*	2+2
No end to the treasure;	
heaps of every precious thing.	3+4
11(10) *Desolation, devastation and destruction,*	
melting hearts and shaking knees.	3+4
Trembling in all loins	
and all faces grow pale!	3+3

Notes

2.a. Some read מֵפֵץ "war-club" (Jer 51:20) for מֵפִיץ "scatterer."

4.a. מְאָדָּם is a pu. part. "is red." LXX misunderstood the term and read מֵאָדָם "from man."

4.b. מתלעים is a hapax, a pu. part. of תלע (BDB 1069).

4.c. פלדות is a hapax. It could mean "steel" (BDB 811). *BHK³* suggests כְאֵשׁ לַפִּד֫ת "like fire of torches" (BDB 542).

4.d. RSV and others read with the LXX and Syr פרש "horses" instead of MT ברש "spears."

6.a. No subject is expressed for יִזְכֹּר "he remembers" (BDB 811). Is the reference to the invader or the king of Nineveh? LXX μνησθήσονται, Syr nê'ḥ'dûn "they will be reminded" pl. pass. = יִזָּכְרוּ. Eng transl have tended to read יַזְכִּיר "cause to remember, remind, call out." *BHK³* records two suggested emendations: יֶדְהֲרוּ "they dash" (BDB 187) cf. Nah 3:2 and יְכַרְכְּרוּ "they dance or whirl" (BDB 503) cf. 2 Sam 6:14, 16. Read MT.

6.b. הכן is a hoph. perf. of כון "is set" (BDB 466).

8.a. הֻצַּב is a major problem. The AV and many older scholars read it as a hoph. perf. of נצב "to stand," "be established, decreed" (BDB 662). Ewald and Wellhausen took it as an epithet of or reference to the queen. It could be a reference to a statue of the goddess of Assyria like נְצִיב. G. R. Driver read it as a noun from an Arabic root צוב "train" (cf. NEB). The Greek text of the Minor Prophets from Naḥal Ḥever took הצב to mean "wagon," "chariot" (Cathcart 97).

8.b. LXX φθεγγόμεναι "making a sound."

8.c. Lit. "their hearts" (cf. BDB 523).

9.a. MT מֵימֵי הִיא "waters of her" is awkward Heb. LXX τὰ ὕδατα αὐτῆς = מֵימֶיהָ = "her waters."

9.b. *BHK³* suggests the הֵמָּה "they" be deleted. But the reference is to the soldiers and must be kept.

Form/Structure/Setting

Here is a battle account in poetry. Nahum may have witnessed such a battle. This version was designed to be sung. The number of accents in the poetic lines seem to imitate the fierce action of battle. The poet, with the imperatives in vv 9b–10a, takes his readers into the tumultuous sights and sounds of floods and chariots. One can hear commanders of Assyrian forces shouting their orders: "Stop them! Stop them!" and then see the people of Nineveh fleeing their once-great city as her temples crumble before the combined assault of floods and armies. V 2 (Eng. 1) calls for the Assyrians to prepare for invasion. Vv 4–5 describe the appearance of the invading soldiers with their scarlet uniforms, gleaming spears, and chariots. It seems they are already in the streets and squares of the city. However, vv 6–7 put the invader outside the walls while the king of Nineveh frantically tries to shore up his defenses (v 6), but the river gates are opened and the palace melts. The mistress of Nineveh (the queen or goddess) is carried away (v 8). Nineveh is plundered and ruined (vv 9–11).

Comment

This is a very graphic account of the battle of Nineveh. The invader approaches. The leaders of Nineveh are warned. The appearance and actions of the enemy troops are described. The frantic, futile attempts at defense are recounted (v 6). The flooding of the city and the capture of the queen are described. Nineveh is helpless in spite of her great treasure. All of her people are terrified.

A Babylonian account of the fall of Nineveh was published first by G. J. Gadd. The tablet was number 21,901 in the British Museum. The tablet chronicles the events in the tenth to the seventeenth year of Nabopolassar, king of Babylon (616–609 B.C.; cf. ANET 303–306). Most of the events in the tablet revolve around the battle for Nineveh. Nineveh fell to a coalition of the Babylonians, Medes, and "Scythians" (cf. Bright 315 n. 16). The tablet is not as graphic in its details of the actual battle as is Nahum's account.

Explanation

The battle account opens with an announcement to Nineveh that an attack is pending. The king is commanded to prepare his defenses: guard the fort, watch the road, strengthen the loins exceedingly (2:2). The approach of Nineveh's enemy as a well-dressed and well-equipped army is described in vv 4–5. V 6 is difficult. It seems to say that the king of Nineveh hastily summons his nobles (war council) and they stumble (perhaps due to drunkenness) toward the city wall to man their stations (mantlets). Stonehouse and Wade, NEB, Taylor, and Dalglish take this verse to refer to the invaders. S. R. Driver and A. B. Davidson take it as reference to the defenders.

The city of Nineveh was built on the east bank of the Tigris river, and the river Husur ran through the city. According to a Greek story it was the sudden rise of this river, causing a stretch of the wall to collapse, that brought disaster to the city (cf. E. G. Kraeling, *Rand-McNally Bible Atlas* [Chicago: Rand-McNally, 1956] 310). Nahum says that the gates of the rivers are opened and the palace melts (2:7). The queen or goddess (הָאָב) is stripped and carried away (2:8). Nineveh, like a pool whose waters have fled, will find her people fleeing the city. Nothing can stop them. This is the first use of the word "Nineveh" since the superscription. V 10 is a graphic description of the wealth—gold and silver—treasures of Nineveh. V 11 is a classic example of paronomasia in Nahum: בוקה ומבוקה ומבלקה "desolation, devastation, and destruction." Fear grips all that are left in Nineveh.

A Taunt-Song Against Nineveh   (2:12–14 [Eng. 2:11–13])

Translation

12(11) *Where is the lair of lions*
 and the feeding place ª *for young lions,*
to which the lion and the lioness went?
There were the lion's cubs with no disturbance.

3+3
5+4

¹³⁽¹²⁾ *The lion tears for the needs of his cubs,*
      and strangles for his lioness.   4+2
  He fills his holes with prey
      and his caves with torn flesh.   3+2
¹⁴⁽¹³⁾ *Behold I am against you,*
      oracle of Yahweh of hosts,   2+3
  and I will burn your ^a *chariots in smoke,*
  and your young lions the sword will devour.   3+3
  I will cut off your prey from the land,
  and the voice of your messengers ^b *will be heard no more.*   3+4

Notes

12.a. Many change מִרְעֶה "pasture" to מְעָרָה "cave," (*BHK*³) but without MS evidence. "Pasture" may refer to the feeding grounds of lions. Of course, "cave" fits a lion's den better.

14.a. 3rd fem. suf. should be 2nd fem. referring to Nineveh as are the others in the verse. LXX πλῆϑός σοῦ "your multitude" apparently read רֻבֵּךְ.

14.b. LXX, Syr τὰ ἔργα σοῦ "your deeds" uses the second meaning of the Heb. and reading מְלַאכֹתֵךְ. As in the previous verse the 3rd fem. sing. suf. should be read as 2nd fem. sing., as LXX has done.

Form/Structure/Setting

This section is a taunt song addressed to Nineveh. It could have been used in a cultic celebration. The language shifts from that of a battle account to a metaphor of a lion's den. The passage opens with two rhetorical questions asking where the lions' dens are, now that Nineveh has been destroyed. It recalls how Assyria as a lion had plundered other peoples, strangling, tearing flesh, and carrying off prey to her cubs in their safe places in Nineveh. But now the tables have been turned. Behold, Yahweh is against Nineveh. That sealed her fate (cf. 3:5). Her military power will certainly be broken. Her soldiers will die by the sword, and her messengers (tax collectors) will no longer threaten other people.

A Judgment Oracle Against Nineveh
(3:1–7)

Bibliography

Dalglish, E. R. "Nahum." *BBC* 7 242. **Gerstenberger, E.** "The Woe-Oracles of the Prophets." *JBL* 81 (1962) 249–63. **Westermann, C.** *Basic Forms of Prophetic Speech.* Philadelphia: Westminster Press (1967) 189–94.

Translation

¹ *Woe to the city of bloodshed—*
    full of lies,   3+2
    full of plunder!
    The prey never ceases.   2+3
² *Sound of the whip*
    and sound of the clatter of the wheel.   2+3
    The horse galloping
    and chariot bounding.   2+2
³ *Horse prancing*
    and sword flashing,
        and spear gleaming.   2+2+2
    Hosts of slain;
    and heaps of corpses.   2+2
    No end to the bodies—
    They stumble on their bodies.   3+2
⁴ *Because* ᵃ *of the multitude of the harlotries of the harlot,*
    fair and gracious,
    a mistress of sorceries—   3+2+2
    the one trading ᵇ *her harlotries to the nations,*
    and her sorceries to the clans.   3+2
⁵ *Behold I am against you,*
    oracle of Yahweh of hosts.   2+3
    I will lift your skirts over your face,
    and cause nations to see your nakedness
    and kingdoms your shame.   3+3+2
⁶ *And I will throw filth upon you.*
    I will treat you with contempt, and make you a gazingstock.   3+3
⁷ *And it shall be that everyone who looks at you will flee from you*
    and will say, "Devastated is Nineveh!"   4+3
    Who will express sympathy ᵃ *for her?*
    Whence shall I seek comforters for you? ᵇ   3+4

Notes

4.a. מִן has a causal force "because" (*CHAL* 200).
4.b. מכרת is a fem. sing. qal act. part. of מכר "selling." Cathcart, following Dahood, takes it as a pu. part. from נכר "to know" and reads "the one who is known by."
7.a. ינוד "to express sympathy" literally means "to sway," "to shake the head."
7.b. לך should be לָהּ "for her" (cf. LXX).

Form/Structure/Setting

This is the only oracle in Nahum to begin with "woe." This account of the fall of Nineveh is similar to the account in 2:2, 4–11 except that this one is much more gruesome. Blood, lies, plunder, harlotries, corpses, filth, and sorceries characterize this section. This passage ends with two rhetorical questions: who will express sympathy for Nineveh, and where does one get comforters for such an evil nation?

Comment

Von Rad and Dalglish see this woe oracle of Nahum as a kind of curse on Nineveh. It was a malediction spoken in the name of deity impregnated with power to secure its fulfillment. Both von Rad and Dalglish assign 36 of the 51 uses of הוֹי "woe" in the prophets to that of the curse. But Gerstenberger argues effectively that none of the uses of הוֹי in the prophets can be connected with the idea of a curse. Gerstenberger says that the woe oracle in the prophet is a part of a kerygmatic unit (*JBL* 81 [1962] 253) perhaps derived from wisdom circles.

Explanation

The announcement of the woe on Nineveh as the city of blood (i.e. "bloodshed," acts of bloody violence) is given in v 1. The reason for the woe or judgment is her deceit and cruelty as seen in her military prowess (vv 2–3). The deceit is described as the wiles of a harlot in v 4. The threat begins in v 5. She will be treated as a harlot. Her shame will be exposed to the nations (v 5). She will be defiled with abominable filth (v 5). People will flee from her in horror and disgust. No one will be found to comfort her.

The Analogy of Thebes   (3:8–13)

Bibliography

Bullough, S. "Nahum." *A Catholic Commentary.* eds. D. B. Orchard and E. F. Sutcliffe. New York: Thomas Nelson (1953) 716. **van Doorslaer, J.** "No Amon." *CBQ* 11 (1949) 280–95.

Translation

[8] *Are you better than Thebes,*[a]	
the one sitting by the Nile,	
surrounded by water;	
whose strength was the sea,	3+2+3
and water a wall?	3+2
[9] *Cush was her*[a] *strength,*	
Egypt too, and that without end.	
Put and Libyans	2+3
were her[b] *helpers.*	2+2

TIAN THEOLOGICAL SEMINARY BOOKSTORE

00 WEST 42ND STREET • INDIANAPOLIS, INDIANA 46208 • (317) 924-1331

32-64-5252   DATE 11-23-92

COUNT   ☐ CREDIT ACCOUNT   ☐ CASH RECEIPT

m Crenshaw

PHONE

SUBTOTAL	22 99
TAX	1 15
SHIPPING	
TOTAL	24 14

RECEIVED BY

PLEASE PUT THE INVOICE NUMBER ON YOUR CHECK.   #   32814

¹⁰ *She too became an exile.*
   She went into captivity.   3+2
   Also her infants were dashed in pieces
      at the head of every street.   3+2
   And lots were cast over her honored men,
   and all her great ones were bound in chains.   4+3
¹¹ *You* ᵃ *also will be drunk.* ᵇ
   You will be hidden. ᶜ   2+2
   Even you will seek
      a refuge from the enemy.   2+2
¹² *All of your fortifications*
   are fig trees with first-ripe fruit.   2+2
   If shaken they fall
      into the mouth of the eater.   2+2
¹³ *Behold your troops* ᵃ *are women in your midst.*
   To your enemies
      the gates of your country are open.   4+1+4
   Fire will devour your bars.   3

Notes

8.a. נֹא אמוֹן "city of Amon" (see *Comment*).

9.a. עצמה should be עצמה "her strength" with LXX, Syr, Tg.

9.b. "Your helpers" should be "her helpers" with LXX and Syr. בעזרתך could mean "in your army" (cf. Cathcart 135).

11.a. את is fem. "you" referring to Nineveh.

11.b. Driver, Gaster, Dahood, and Cathcart all read תשכרי "you will hire yourself out," instead of תשכרי.

11.c. Dahood and Cathcart take the construction to be from עלמה "to be ripe," "mature," "young" rather than עָלָם "hidden." NEB has "flaunting your sex" without explanation.

13.a. Cathcart reads עם as "troops" rather than "people."

Form/Structure/Setting

This pericope begins with an interrogation, "Are you better than?" There could be some Wisdom influence on this form. However, interrogation is a common device of the prophets of this general period (Habakkuk, Haggai, Zechariah). Vv 8–9 describe Thebes' strength which is all the more reason to be surprised by Thebes' fall. V 10 recounts Thebes' fate. Her children were killed and her men were taken as captives. Vv 11–13 describe Nineveh's weakness and ultimate destruction.

Comment

Thebes, the capital of Egypt, is often called נֹא for the Egyptian word *n.t*, "city" (Jer 46:25; Ezek 30:14–16). In Nahum 3:8 it is called נֹא אמוֹן "city of Amon." However in translating Nahum for the Vulgate, Jerome adopted an old Rabbinic interpretation based on a pun on the god's name

נֹא הֲמוֹן "the multitude of No" in Ezek 30:15. Jerome translated נֹא אָמוֹן in Nahum 3:8 *populorum No,* which became "populous No" in the KJV. In fact, Jerome identified "No-Amon" with the later Alexandria. Bullough says that Jerome was conscious of the anachronism and explained that he was merely giving the modern name "—though the identification happens to be wrong" (*New Catholic Commentary,* 716). Van Doorslaer (*CBQ* 11 [1949] 280–95) reviewed much of the evidence for Jerome's view and concluded that his interpretation deserves renewed consideration (295). However, no one seems to have been persuaded by van Doorslaer's materials. (See Introduction for Ashurbanipal's account of his capture of Thebes.)

Explanation

Thebes or No-Amon, "city of Amon," was the capital of Egypt during much of her history. It was in upper Egypt, approximately 440 miles south of Memphis and 150 miles north of Aswan and the first cataract. The city is situated on a large bend in the Nile at the point where the river is closest to the Red Sea. Here the river opens into a broad and fruitful valley. Thebes has been called the world's first great monumental city. Even today the visitor is overwhelmed by the vastness and the magnitude of the ruins of ancient temples and palaces. Larger Thebes is made up of Luxor and Karnak on the east side of the river and Thebes proper with the ruins of Hatshepsut's temple and the tombs of the kings on the west. The city is mentioned five times in the OT (Jer 46:25; Ezek 30:14, 15, 16; Nah 3:8). It was captured and partially destroyed by Ashurbanipal in 663 B.C. (See Introduction for Ashurbanipal's account of his capture of Thebes.)

The greatness of Thebes was legendary in Nahum's time. So was her fall. Nahum reminded Nineveh and in turn his own people that even the greatest kingdoms can fall. He was firmly convinced that Nineveh's demise was inevitable. All of the references to the sea and waters in v 8 seem to go beyond a factual description of the city's position. (Watts explains this language as due to the Egyptian belief that Thebes as a sacred city was built on the first dry land to emerge from primeval waters. "They considered the river Nile to be the supreme manifestation of creation's blessings, and based their faith and security on its powers. Nahum sees it, rather, as a symbol of their arrogant and heathen attitude against the Lord" [Watts 119]). But No-Amon had some powerful allies and helpers according to v 9. Cush (Ethiopia), Egypt, Put, and the Libyans added their strength to No-Amon. The twenty-fifth Egyptian dynasty (716–663 B.C.) was composed of Ethiopian kings (Bright 289).

In spite of Thebes' greatness and that of her allies, she became an exile. Her infants were dashed in pieces. Her honored and great men were put in chains. Now, Nineveh too will be treated shamefully. Her fortification will be like first ripe figs—they will fall into the mouth of the eater. Her soldiers are weak and unprepared for battle. The gates of the city will be opened to the invader and the bars on the city gates will be burned with fire.

Satirical Warnings for Nineveh (*3:14–17*)

Translation

14 Draw for yourselves water for the siege.	2+2
Strengthen your forts.	3+2
Go into the mud	
and trample on the clay.	
Seize the brick mold.	2+2+2
15 There a the fire will devour you.	
The sword will cut you off.	
It will devour you like the locust.	3+2+2
Multiply yourselves like the locust.	
Multiply yourselves like the grasshopper.	2+2
16 You multiplied your merchants	
more than the stars of the heavens.	
The locust sheds its skin and flies away.	2+2+3
17 Your pair of guards a are like grasshoppers,	
and your officers b are like a swarm c of locusts	2+2
clinging to the walls	
on a cold day.	2+2
The sun rises and they d flee.	
No one knows where they e are.	3+3

Notes

15.a. Dahood and Cathcart (143) read שָׁם as "Behold."

17.a. מנזר is a hapax. Its meaning is uncertain, but it does have a dual form. NEB "your secret agents."

17.b. טפסר "scribes" (BDB 381) were military recruiting officers (Jer 51:27).

17.c. *CHAL* (54, 57) reads כגוב as a dittograph of the next word גֹּבָ֫י "a plague of locusts." Used only here and in Amos 7:1.

17.d. נודד should be נוֹדְדוּ "they flee" (hoph. perf. of נדד). See *BHK³*.

17.e. Lit. "not is known his place. Where (are) they?" LXX οὐαὶ αὐτοῖς "Woe to them!" read אוֹי לָהֶם. Some commentators read אים as אוֹי "woe," put it at the beginning of v 18, and join ם with the following word (see *BHK³*).

Form/Structure/Setting

A satirical warning calls on Nineveh to prepare for the siege, then tells her that her efforts will be futile. V 14 is the call to prepare and vv 15–17 tell of her coming defeat.

Explanation

Preparations for the siege included drawing water, strengthening the fortress, and making new mud bricks to repair buildings and walls. But such

efforts were to prove useless. Sword and fire would devour the people like
locusts devour vegetation. In 3:15b the prophet compares Nineveh to locusts.
They multiply greatly but then shed their skin and fly away (v 16). Nineveh's
military officers are like locusts sitting on a fence on a cold day. They are
numbed by the cold. Then the sun rises and warms them. They flee and
the city is left unguarded and helpless.

Rejoicing over Ultimate Defeat   (*3:18-19*)

Translation

¹⁸ *Your shepherds are asleep,*
    O king of Asshur.
    Your mighty ones are at rest;
your people are scattered ^a *upon the mountains*   2+2+2
    and no one gathers them.
¹⁹ *No healing* ^a *for your hurt;*   3+2
    your wound is incurable.
All who hear the report about you   3+2
    clap their hands over you,
for upon whom has not come   3+3
    your unceasing evil.

                                                     2+2

Notes

18.a. Read נָפֹצוּ for נָפֹשׁוּ. See *BHK*³.
19.a. כֵּהָה is a hapax (BDB 462).

Explanation

The king of Assyria is addressed. His officers are asleep. This may mean
that they are dead. At least they are deactivated. The people (or troops)
are scattered as sheep on the mountains, and since the officers are the shepherds, they are unable to gather the people or troops together. In v 19,
Nineveh is compared to an incurably sick person. Then the prophet observes
that instead of sympathy or mourning for Nineveh, there will be universal
joy, for the whole world had borne the brunt of Nineveh's cruel treatment.

Habakkuk

Habakkuk

Bibliography

Books and Commentaries

Brownlee, W. H. *The Text of Habakkuk in the Ancient Commentary from Qumran.* Philadelphia: JBL Monograph Series, 1959. ————. *The Midrash Pesher of Habakkuk.* Missoula, MT: Scholars Press, 1979. **Duhm, B.** *Das Buch Habakkuk.* Tübingen: J. C. B. Mohr, 1906. **Garland, D.** "Habakkuk," in *BBC* 7. Nashville: Broadman Press, 1972. **Gowan, D.** *The Triumph of Faith in Habakkuk.* Atlanta: John Knox Press, 1976. **Humbert, P.** *Problèmes du Livre D'Habacuc.* Neuchatel: Secretariat de L'Universite, 1944. **Hyatt, J. P.** "Habakkuk," in *Peake's Commentary on the Bible,* eds. H. H. Rowley and M. Black. London: Thomas Nelson and Sons, 1962. **Stonehouse, G. G. V.** *The Book of Habakkuk.* London: Rivingtons, 1911.

Articles

Brownlee, W. H. "The Composition of Habakkuk." *Hommages a Andre Dupont-Sommer.* Paris: Librairie D'Amerique et D'Orrent Adrien-Maisonneuve (1971) 255–275. **Cannon, W. W.** "The Integrity of Habakkuk 1–2." *ZAW* 43 (1925) 62–90. **Good, E. M.** "The Barberini Greek Version of Habakkuk III." *VT* 9 (1959) 11–30. **Gowan, D. E.** "Habakkuk and Wisdom." *Perspective* 9 (1968) 157–66. **Keller, C. A.** "Die Eigenart des Propheten Habakuks." *ZAW* 85 (1973) 156–67. **Nielsen, E.** "The Righteous and the Wicked in Habaqquq." *ST* 6 (1953) 54–78. **Peake, A. S.** "Recent Criticism of Habakkuk." *The Problem of Suffering in the OT.* London: Primitive Methodist Publishing House, 1904. **Torrey, C. C.** "The Prophecy of Habakkuk." *Jewish Studies in Memory of G. A. Kohut.* Philadelphia: Jewish Publication Society, 1935. **Vischer, W.** *Der Prophet Habakuk.* BST 19 (1958). **Walker, H. H.** and **Lund, N. W.** "The Literary Structure of the Book of Habakkuk." *JBL* 53 (1934) 355–70. **van der Woude, A. S.** "Der Gerechte wird durch seine Treue leben." *Studia Biblica et Semitica T. C. Vriezen dedicata.* Wageningen: H. Veenman, 1966.

Introduction

Bibliography

Eissfeldt, O. *The Old Testament: An Introduction.* New York: Harper and Row (1965) 416–422. **Peake, A. S.** *The Problem of Suffering in the OT.* London: Kelly, 1904. 150–71.

The Place in the Canon

The book of Habakkuk stands in the eighth position among "The Twelve" in the Masoretic and Greek texts. It follows Nahum and precedes Zephaniah. It is generally acknowledged that these three prophets were contemporaries and shared a common conviction that Yahweh was sovereign in the affairs of men and would judge the wicked and deliver the righteous.

The Prophet

Little is known about the prophet Habakkuk. His name occurs only in the titles to chaps. 1 and 3 of his own book (1:1; 3:1). The name Habakkuk is not a typical Hebrew word. Some ancient rabbis connected his name to the word חֲבָקֶת "embrace" in 2 Kgs 4:16. Most modern scholars consider the name to be an Accadian word for a garden plant. If Habakkuk's name is a foreign word, that might indicate a high degree of foreign influence on Israel at that time.

Numerous legends have grown up around Habakkuk's identity. Some rabbis identified him with the son of the Shunammite woman because of the Hebrew word "embrace" in 2 Kgs 4:16. Another rabbi argued that Habakkuk was the watchman referred to by Isaiah (21:6) because Habakkuk stood on his tower (2:1). According to C. C. Torrey (*Lives of the Prophets* [Philadelphia: SBL, 1946]) Habakkuk was of the tribe of Simeon and lived in Beth-Zachariah (1 Macc 6:32) which was about ten miles southwest of Jerusalem.

In *Bel and the Dragon* (one of three additions to the book of Daniel) Habakkuk is described as being on his way to the field to take some pottage to the reapers. An angel met him and commanded him to take the pottage to Daniel in the lion's den in Babylon. Habakkuk told the angel that he had never been to Babylon and did not know the location of the lion's den. Whereupon the angel lifted Habakkuk by his hair and set him down over the den. After Daniel ate, the angel returned Habakkuk to his place.

One manuscript of *Bel and the Dragon* says that Habakkuk was the son of Jesus of the tribe of Levi. This later tradition that Habakkuk was of the tribe of Levi, along with the fact that he is one of only three men in the OT to be called a prophet in the superscription of his book, and the fact that he is presented as a prophet in the musical chapter (3:1) of his book, suggests that he may have been a Levite and a professional or temple prophet. Prophets and seers were musicians near the end of the OT period (1 Chr 25:1–8)

Date and Unity

We do not know when Habakkuk lived and preached. No date is given in the superscription to the book. One solid clue to the date of the prophet seems to be the reference to the "rise of the Chaldeans" (1:6). If the "Chaldeans" were the Neo-Babylonians the date would probably be between the fall of Nineveh (612 B.C.) and the battle of Carchemish (605 B.C.). However, the book speaks not only of the rise of the Babylonians but also reflects a time after the Babylonians had ruthlessly and violently overrun many small nations (2:5–17).

Bernard Duhm considered the term "Chaldeans" a reference to "the Kittim" (Greeks). He dated the book about 332 B.C. Happel went even further than Duhm and assigned the book to the Seleucid period (*Das Buch Des Propheten Habakuk,* 1900).

The questions of the date and unity of the book are related to the question of the identity of the wicked (רָשָׁע) in 1:4 and 1:13b. Traditionally the wicked in 1:4 have been identified as the wicked within Judah (those oppressing their neighbors). However, the wicked who are "swallowing up the righteous" in 1:13b were Chaldeans. Should the wicked be the same in both places? Is the wicked in 1:2–4 some foreign oppressor as Budde, Giesebrecht, Wellhausen, George Adam Smith and others have supposed? If the wicked refers to a foreign oppressor, was it Babylon, Assyria, or Greece? The foreign oppressor could not be the Babylonians in 1:2–4 if the Babylonians are the punisher of the oppressor in 1:5–11. Giesebrecht was the first to point out this problem in 1891. His solution was to remove 1:5–11 from 1:2–2:8, assign 1:2–2:8 to the exile and 1:5–11 to an earlier period. In 1893 Budde published a new theory that the oppressor of Judah in 1:2–4 and 1:12–2:4 was Assyria. Babylon was to punish Assyria, as 1:5–11 indicates, but that passage (1:5–11) should follow 2:4. Budde's views were adopted by Cornill (1896) and by G. A. Smith (1898). However, after considering Giesebrecht's and Budde's theories A. B. Davidson and S. R. Driver returned to the traditional view that the wicked are rebellious Israelites and Babylon is their punisher in 1:5–11.

More recently the unity and traditional order of the book has been defended largely on the basis of its cultic function. Sellin, Humbert, Mowinckel, Bentzen, and Nielsen have all defended the cultic function. Lindblom agrees with this view. He says, "The book of Habakkuk is not the work of a secondary collector of prophetic revelations, but a composition by the prophet himself, who was certainly a cultic prophet at the temple in Jerusalem" (*Prophecy in Ancient Israel.* [Philadelphia: Muhlenberg, 1962] 254). The majority of OT scholars would probably date a large portion of the book of Habakkuk in the period between 612 and 587 B.C., although some editing was probably done later.

Structure and Setting

The major units of the book are obvious. After the superscription (1:1) there is the prophet's first lament complaining about the oppression of the righteous by the wicked (1:2–4). The prophet asks why Yahweh allows sin to go unpunished. The evil here seems to be within the community of Israel.

The problem is a lack of social justice. Such a situation could have existed almost any time in the history of Israel. The next division (1:5–11) seems to be a direct answer from Yahweh to the prophet's complaint in the form of an oracle (1:2–4). Yahweh says that the wicked will be punished by a new nation then on the rise. That new nation will be the Chaldean, or Neo-Babylonian nation.

A new cycle in the dialogue between the prophet and Yahweh begins with the prophet's second lament (1:12–17). This cycle may have come later than the first. Babylon in this passage is a ruthless world conqueror, not a new nation on the rise. A probable date for the origin of this section is 597 B.C. Yahweh's answer to Habakkuk's second lament is in 2:1–5. The prophet says that he will wait for God's answer (2:1). Yahweh speaks in 2:2–5. He first tells Habakkuk that the vision is to be publicly recorded on tablets in plain, easy-to-read language (2:2). Then he tells Habakkuk that the ultimate solution to the problems of evil and theodicy will be worked out in history. That will take a long time. Evil will be overthrown. The righteous will survive and thrive, but that will not always seem to be the case. In the meantime the righteous is to continue in his faithfulness to God.

A major division comes after 2:5. Brownlee and Humbert make the division in the middle of v 5. 2:6–20 contains a series of five woes addressed to the oppressor. Each woe indicates that the oppressor or the evil one is doomed. (See the commentary at this point for a detailed explanation of each woe.) Some questions of unity, date, and identity of the oppressor are raised by this passage. These questions are discussed in the commentary section.

The last chapter of Habakkuk is a prayer in the form of a psalm. The reference to Habakkuk as a prophet in the superscription, along with the reference to the *Shigionoth,* may indicate that Habakkuk was a cultic or a temple prophet. The musical title and subscription of chap. 3 suggest that the chapter may have been used separately, apart from chaps. 1–2. Among the Dead Sea Scrolls that were found in Cave I in 1948 was a commentary on the first two chapters of Habakkuk. There is no evidence that the people of Qumran ever wrote a commentary on chap. 3 of Habakkuk. Chap. 2 ends inside the scroll without a trace of chap. 3. However, this evidence does not militate against the view that chap. 3 was an original part of Habakkuk. It is likely that the covenanters at Qumran could use the material in chaps. 1–2 for their purposes better than they could use chap. 3. Brownlee cites many scholarly opinions for and against the view that chap. 3 was an original part of the book of Habakkuk. He notes that chap. 3 is in all the complete manuscripts of the LXX and says that some copies of the Book of the Twelve already contained chap. 3 of Habakkuk by 200 B.C. (*The Text of Habakkuk,* 92). Now we know that the third chapter was in the Murabba-'at scroll about the beginning of the second century A.D. (J. T. Milik, *Ten Years of Discovery in the Wilderness of Judea,* trans. J. Strugnell [Naperville. Ill.: A. R. Allenson, 1957] 14, 18). Brownlee also notes that what took place at Jamnia was at most "only standardization" of what was already present in the scrolls (op. cit.).

Chap. 3 is made up of four parts after the superscription (3:1). First, the prayer for God to renew his work of salvation-history (3:2). Second, a theophany (3:3–7). Habakkuk is either describing how God came from Sinai to help his people during the exodus or he is describing what will happen when God comes again to rescue his people from the oppressor. Third, the battle between God and the forces of creation and history is described in "mythological" language (3:8–15). Finally we have the climactic response of faith on the part of the prophet. He says that he will trust God regardless of what happens (3:16–19).

Brevard Childs has called attention to the autobiographical framework of the book. The superscription designates Habakkuk as the one who received the vision. The complaint in 1:2–4 is the prophet's complaint and the response in 1:5–11 is Yahweh's response to Habakkuk's question and complaint. The same is true of Habakkuk's second complaint (1:12–17) and God's response to it (2:1–5). Even chap. 3 is introduced by Habakkuk's appeal to Yahweh to renew his works of holy history (3:1–2) and is concluded with Habakkuk's commitment in faith to Yahweh even if there are no outward evidences of God's care (3:16–19).

Many scholars see a cultic setting for the book of Habakkuk, but Childs suggests that this autobiographical framework does not lend itself to a cultic setting (Childs, *Introduction*, 452).

The Text

The Hebrew text of Habakkuk is in fair shape. There are some very obscure passages, e.g. 3:13–14. There are at least four hapax legomena (מעקל, 1:4; מגמת, 1:9; כפים, 2:11; and חביון, 3:4) which are of uncertain meaning. A pronoun or a noun has evidently dropped out of 1:5; and 2:4. An obvious case of transposition of consonants occurs in 2:16. יחית is inexplicable in 2:17. Albright proposed thirty-eight corrections, no deletions, but five insertions in the text of chap. 3 alone (*OT Prophecy*, 10). Procksch proposed thirty-seven emendations plus three omissions for chap. 3 in *BHK*. Brownlee lists at least nineteen major variants between the MT and DSH (cf. *the Text of Habakkuk*, 109–112). There are numerous differences between the MT and the LXX. Three of these differences show up in the NT where the NT always follows the LXX rather than the MT (cf. Hab 1:4; Isa 25:8; 1 Cor 15:54; Hab 1:5; Acts 13:41; and Hab 2:4; Rom 1:17; Gal 3:11; Heb 10:38).

The Message of Habakkuk

The message of Habakkuk was directed to the nation of Judah during the crisis which led to the fall of Jerusalem, the destruction of the temple, and the deportation of many people. The crisis was internal as well as external. Internally the nation was torn with strife expressed in the abuse of the righteous by the wicked. The law was ineffective.

An even more serious problem for Habakkuk was the seeming inactivity of God in the face of unrelenting evil. The problem of theodicy was great for the conscientious, thoughtful worshipers of Yahweh. Why would a righteous, sovereign God continually allow sin to go unpunished? The answer came from God and is capsulated in 2:4–5. The sinner is arrogant; he thinks too highly of himself. He will not survive. But the righteous shall live abundantly in his faithfulness. The ultimate fate of the righteous and the wicked may be slow in appearing, but the outcome is certain because of the nature of God. The righteous will live; the wicked will perish. In the meantime the righteous is to keep on trusting God and keeping his commandments even if there is no visible sign of God's presence or favor.

Habakkuk and Nahum Compared

Habakkuk and Nahum were contemporaries, Habakkuk slightly later than Nahum. There are similarities between their books and messages as well as contrasts. Each of their books consist of three chapters. Nahum begins with a psalm; Habakkuk ends with one. Each spoke to a crisis situation and was convinced that Yahweh was Lord of the universe and history. Nahum wrote to assure his people that Nineveh was going to fall. Her enemy and oppressor would be overthrown. Nahum's message was basically an oracle against a foreign nation. Although Habakkuk addressed five woes to Babylon, his primary message was one of commitment to Yahweh even when a cruel, godless tyrant was poised on the border ready to overrun one's land.

OUTLINE

Superscription 1:1
1. Habakkuk's first complaint 1:2–4
2. Yahweh's response to Habakkuk's first complaint 1:5–11
3. Habakkuk's second lament 1:12–17
4. Yahweh's answer to Habakkuk's second complaint 2:1–5
5. Five woes 2:6–20
6. A prayer 3:1–19
   a. Superscription 3:1
   b. Petition 3:2
   c. A theophany 3:3–7
   d. A battle 3:8–15
   e. A response of faith 3:16–19

Superscription (1:1)

Translation

The oracle (burden) which Habakkuk the prophet saw.

Comment

"The burden" (המשא) seems to be a technical term to introduce prophetic oracles on foreign nations (cf. Isa 13:1; 14:28; 15:1; 17:1; 19:1; Nah 1:1). The burden of Habakkuk is not directed primarily to a foreign nation but it does assert that the foreign tyrant will ultimately be overthrown (2:4, 16–17). Habakkuk's name may be an Akkadian word. If so, it would show a strong foreign influence in Israel at this time. Habakkuk is one of only three prophets who are called prophets in the superscription to their books. The other two are Haggai and Zechariah. The word "see" is חזה which in the noun form means "visions" (cf. 2:3).

Habakkuk's First Complaint (1:2–4)

Translation

² *How long, Yahweh, shall I cry*	3+2
and you will not hear?	
I cry to you, "Violence!"	3+2
and you do not save.	
³ *Why do you cause me to see iniquity*	3+2
and cause me to look upon trouble?	
Destruction ᵃ *and violence are before me,*	3+4
and there is strife, and contention arises.	
⁴ *Therefore, the law is numb*	3+3
and justice never ᵃ *goes forth,*	
because the wicked hems in ᵇ *the righteous*	4+4
therefore justice goes forth distorted. ᶜ	

Notes

3.a. Omit ו.

4.a. נצח usually means "forever"; however in late Hebrew and Aramic it meant "victory." See 1 Chr 29:11 and Paul's translation of Isa 25:8 as "victory" in 1 Cor 15:54. NEB reads "victorious" (Hab 1:4).

4.b. מכתיר "to hem in" might be an example of transposition of consonants. Nowack proposed reading מכרית "cut off."

4.c. מעקל is a pu. part. of a root that only occurs here in the OT.

Form/Structure/Setting

The form is a complaint or a lament. It begins with the words "how long" (cf. Ps 13:1–2), and addresses Yahweh. The opening lines are 3+2 meter. V 3 begins with "why" followed by a description of the unjust situation. The pericope closes with "therefore" which introduces the consequence of the miscarriage of justice. The complaint might have been spoken in the temple as Solomon suggested in his prayer at the dedication of the temple (1 Kgs 8:28–53).

Comment

Most of the debate about this pericope has concerned the identification of the wicked (v 4). Are they Israelites or are they a foreign nation? There is nothing in this passage that points to a foreign nation. Those who hold such a view do so on other grounds. They argue that since the wicked "who swallows the righteous" in 1:13 are the Chaldeans, the wicked in 1:4 should be the same. However, it is better to understand the wicked as Israelites in 1:4.

This pericope graphically portrays the sick and decadent society of Habakkuk's times. There was a growing crime rate. Physical violence (חמם) was rampant. Strife (ריב) and contention (מדון) grew like wild fire. The law was either misapplied ("distorted" v 4) or was not enforced at all. Even God seemed not to be concerned. Perhaps the key issue here is theodicy. The prophet was concerned about the unchecked power of evil, but that fact caused him to question the nature of his God who permitted such evil to go unpunished.

V 4 mentions the "righteous" and the "wicked." Eduard Nielsen has reviewed the biblical and extra-biblical uses of these terms both as cultic and as historical terms. Nielsen believes that the terms are used in Habakkuk to refer to the pro-Jehoahaz (Shallum), Josianic party as over against the pro-Jehoiakim Egyptian party. He sees Jehoiakim as the tyrant to be destroyed (2:4). Nielsen believes that the misery of the people mentioned in 1:1–4 "is due to their lack of a rightful ruler" (*ST* 6 [1953] 71). There is not enough evidence to support Nielsen's conclusions. It is better to take a historical view and see the wicked in v 4 as oppressors in Israel and the wicked in v 13 as the Babylonians.

Yahweh's Response to Habakkuk's Complaint (1:5–11)

Translation

⁵ *Look among the nations* ᵃ *and see.*
  Be stunned, be astonished,   3+2

because I [b] am working a work in your days	4+4
which you would not believe if	
it were told.	
[6] For behold I am raising up the Chaldeans,[a]	3+3
that bitter and impetuous nation,	
the one marching across the wide world	3+3
to possess dwellings that are not his.	
[7] He is terrifying and fearsome.	3+4
His justice [a] and his dignity go out	
from himself.	
[8] His horses are swifter than leopards.	3+3
They are quicker than evening wolves.	
His horses paw the ground;	2+3
they spring forward; [a]	
they come from afar;	
they fly like eagles;	2+2
he hastens to devour.	
[9] Everyone comes for violence,	3+3+3
all [a] of their faces are forward,[b]	
and he gathers captives as sand.	
[10] He makes fun of kings,	3+3
and laughs at rulers.	
He laughs at every fortress	3+3
and piles up dirt and captures it.	
[11] Then he passes by like wind [a]	4+4
and passes on. [b]	
He became guilty, [c] this one whose	
strength is his god.	

Notes

5.a. Many scholars prefer to read בּוֹגְדִים "treacherous ones," for בַּגּוֹים "among the nations" on the basis of the LXX and 1:13; 2:5. This line is missing in DSH. Acts 13:41 follows the emendations and LXX.

5.b. "I" is not in MT but in LXX.

6.a. The reading הכשדים is well established even though Duhm, Torrey, and DSH propose הכתיאים "the Kittim."

7.a. משפט can be "law."

8.a. Read וּפָרְשׁוּ for וּפָרָשָׁיו with DSH and NEB.

9.a. מגמת a hapax, "all of him" (cf. CHAL 182; BDB, 169).

9.b. קָדִימָה the "he directive" could make the reading "eastward." It can also mean "forward."

11.a. רוּחַ "wind," "spirit," or "mind." It cannot be the subject of the verb חלף because רוּחַ is fem.

11.b. ויעבר could read "and he transgressed."

11.c. ואשם is a 3rd mas. sing. qal pf. אשם "and he became guilty." However DSH has וישם G. R. Driver regards both אשם and ישם as probable dialectical forms of שמם "to be desolate, or appalled, horrified" (cf. Brownlee, Text, 22–24); NEB follows Driver's reading.

Form/Structure/Setting

Yahweh's response is in the form of an oracle. Childs calls this an unusual *Heilsorokal* offered as a word of divine comfort that has been turned on its head. "It does not offer the usual comfort but announces an attack by a cruel nation which will set Israel's wickedness right by a devastating judgment" (*Introduction,* 451). The prophet tells the people to look among the nations. They will see an incredible thing happening (v 5). God speaks through the prophet to describe the Chaldeans or Babylonians. They are proud and powerful. They respect nothing but their own strength (vv 6–11). The oracle does not have the messenger formula or an announcement of judgment. It has two simple parts: a call to look among the nations, and a description of the Chaldeans. One is left to assume that the coming of the Chaldeans is to punish Judah for the evil described in 1:2–4. There is no evidence that the setting of the oracle was the New Year festival as Nielsen suggests (*ST* 6 [1953] 74).

Comment

The prophet says that the coming of the Chaldeans would be surprising to some in Judah. If we read with the LXX, 1:13 and Acts 13:41 בּוֹגְדִים "the traitors," or "unscrupulous ones" in v 5 instead of בַגוֹים "among the nations," we might understand the surprise and consternation of the traitors. The traitors were probably the advisers and supporters of Jehoiakim who had put their trust in Egypt. They would have been shocked and dismayed when the Babylonians came. But this passage seems to be addressed to a broader group than "the traitors." This is a general oracle to the nation of Judah. The people are to look among the nations (גוֹים) to see that a new nation was on the march. Perhaps they expected Assyria to be the nemesis. Habakkuk says that it will be Babylon (the Chaldeans).

The word translated Chaldeans in v 6 is כשׂדים "Kasdim." The land of the "Kasdim" is called Kaldû in the Assyrian tablets. Kaldû was a country situated along the Euphrates and the Tigris rivers between the Persian Gulf and the southernmost cities of Babylonia. It was a region of swamps, canebrakes and lakes with few urban areas. The inhabitants seemed to have relied on fishing, hunting, small-scale agriculture and some cattle breeding for their livelihood.

The region was divided into tribal areas. The people lived in loosely organized tribal groups and were fiercely independent of each other and especially of the major cities to the north, such as Babylon and Nineveh. They were natural enemies of all urbanized societies. When Assyria placed garrisons in the cities in an attempt to police the tribal lands, the Chaldeans became the leaders and carriers of an Anti-Assyrian movement and champions of national independence.

Merodach-Baladan, who fought Tiglath-pileser III, Sargon II, and Sennacherib, but died in Elam, was one of the first strong Chaldean leaders. About a hundred years later another strong Chaldean leader, Nabopolassar, the founder of the Chaldean dynasty with its capital in Babylon, led the attack that captured Nineveh in 612 B.C. During the reigns of Nabopolassar and his son Nebuchadnezzar the Chaldeans were called Babylonians (cf. *IDB*, 1962 ed., S. V. "Chaldea").

B. Duhm changed the word כשׂדים "Chaldeans" to כתיאים "Kittim," meaning "Greeks." Duhm believed that the oppressor in 1:5–11 was Alexander the Great. He dated the book in the fourth century believing that it was directed against Alexander's attempt to conquer the world. Duhm supported his position by pointing out that the rise of the Chaldeans should not have surprised anyone in Judah in the seventh century; and by interpreting קדימה in 1:9 to mean "toward the east wind," instead of "forward" (cf. Wade, 158). The Qumran pesher on Hab 1:6 reads כתיאים rather than כשדים. The Covenanters of Qumran, however, interpreted כתיאים "Kittim" to refer to the Roman oppressors of their day.

Explanation

Babylon is described by Habakkuk as bitter (harsh) and rash (v 6), a nation marching through the whole earth following a scorched earth policy. The Babylonian makes his own laws (v 7). His military force is ominous and ready to strike (vv 8–9). He makes fun of kings and laughs at others' defenses (v 10). Then after one fell swoop he goes on, but he is guilty because he worships his own power and strength (v 11). God allows tyrants to spring up and flourish for a little while, but they become guilty by the abuse of their power and, like a plant before it is firmly rooted, God blows on them and they wither. A tempest carries them away like stubble (Isa 40:24).

Habakkuk's Second Complaint (1:12–17)

Translation

12 *Are you not from of old,*   4+4
  Yahweh my God, my Holy one?
  You shall not die. [a]

Yahweh, you appointed him for judgment,   3+3
  O Rock, you destined him for reproof.
13 *Your eyes are too pure to gaze on evil,*   4+4
  and you are not able to look on wrong.

Why do you look upon the faithless ones,   3+5
  and remain silent while the wicked
    swallows one more righteous than he?
14 *You made men like the fish of the sea,*   3+3
  like the creeper without a ruler.
15 *He brings them* [a] *all up with a hook;*   3+2
  he drags them [a] *out with his net*
    and gathers him in his fish net.   2+3
  Therefore he rejoices and sings for joy.
16 *Therefore he sacrifices to his net*   3+2
  and burns incense to his fish net,
    because by these his portion is luxurious, [a]   3+3
    and his food plentiful. [a]

¹⁷ *Is he,*^a *therefore, to empty his net* ^b *forever,*   4+4
  and slaughter nations without pity?

Notes

12.a. לֹא נָמוּת "we shall not die" is one of eighteen passages in the OT called *tiqqune soferim* "corrections of the Scribes" by the Masoretes. The scribes were supposed to have corrected the original reading. The original reading of this passage was probably לֹא תָמוּת "you shall not die," referring to God. Even though there is no manuscript or version support for תָמוּת it is probably the best reading.

15.a. The first two pro. suf. in v 15 are sing. but should be pl.

16.a. שָׁמֵן "luxurious" and בראה "plentiful" both basically mean "fat."

17.a. The ה interrog. is not in DSH.

17.b. Wellhausen, G. A. Smith and Marti suggested חרב "sword" for חרם "net." DSH has חרב and NEB reads "to unsheathe the sword" following the scroll. This expression is parallel with "slaying the nations" in the next line. But "emptying his net" is a suitable metaphor here.

Form/Structure/Setting

The form of this second lament is much like that of the first. The pericope begins with a question: "Are you not from everlasting?" God, who is holy, eternal, and pure, has appointed and destined a wicked instrument to punish one who is more righteous than the punisher. A second question asks why this is true (v 13). The prophet complains about the ruthless conduct of the oppressor (vv 14–16) and asks finally, how long such persecution will continue (v 17).

Traditionally this lament has been interpreted as a question of theodicy raised by Yahweh's use of the Babylonians to punish the wicked in Israel. However, scholars who have recently argued that Habakkuk was a cultic prophet believe that this second lament was part of a cultic liturgy used in the New Year festival in Jerusalem ca. 601/02 to protest Jehoiakim's usurpation of the role of Jehoahaz. This theory leaves too much to imagination to be accepted as a viable option for the setting of this material.

Explanation

With Habakkuk, prophecy moves into the interrogative mood. Whereas former prophets had declared the certainties of God to man, Habakkuk began asking questions of God on behalf of man. Given a theology that assumes God's goodness, holiness and universal sovereignty, how does one explain God's standing aside while the wicked swallow the righteous (cf. v 13)? God is said to be "from of old" (v 12). The word קֶדֶם means "former" or "ancient" times. The Hebrews did not think in abstract terms such as "eternal." If we reject the rabbis' emendation of תָמוּת to נָמוּת, this term simply expresses the same idea as the first line, that Yahweh never dies. He lives forever. Habakkuk addresses Yahweh as a rock, suggesting that he provides stability in an unstable age. The prophet believes that what was happening in his world was the work of God. God had appointed and ordained the Babylonians to reprove and bring judgment on his people (v 12). The word "appoint" (v 12) is the regular word "to set, place, or put." The word יסד (v 12) "ordain," literally means "to establish" in the sense of laying a foundation. Yahweh had established the Babylonians "to reprove" Judah for her sins. But the judgment and the reproof seemed to be too harsh, too long and from an undesirable agent. Instead of reproof it appears that the Babylonians aim at extinction of their victims.

After acknowledging Yahweh's antiquity, holiness, immortality, purity, and the fact that Yahweh was using Babylon to discipline his people (v 12), the prophet asks why Yahweh remains silent when the wicked swallows the righteous. Times when God is silent (when we think he should be vocal or active avenging the wrong and judging evil) are hard to understand. Job, Jeremiah and countless sufferers have asked this same question. Why does God not do something? Hosea said that like a lion God would rend and go away . . . "I will return again to my place until they acknowledge their guilt and seek my face" (Hos 5:14b–15a). Sometimes the silences of God can be explained by the people's sins and their failure to repent. But that is not always true.

Here Habakkuk compares Babylon's treatment of captives to a fisherman's treatment of fish. His military machinery is compared to the fisherman's hooks, nets, and seines. The English word seine comes from the Greek word σαγήνη used by the LXX to translate מכמרה "fish net" (v 15). Fish are helpless and disorganized against such devices. The Babylonian rejoices and shouts for joy because of his success. Then he worships those things that make him rich and successful. How prone are people today to worship whatever makes them rich and successful? Habakkuk asks if the wicked will continue to oppress the righteous endlessly or if Yahweh will break his silence and act on behalf of his people.

Yahweh's Second Response (2:1–5)

Bibliography

Brownlee, Wm. H. "The Placarded Revelation of Habakkuk." *JBL* 82 (1963) 319–25. **Clifford, R. J.** "The Use of HÔY in the Prophets." *CBQ* 28 (1966) 458–64. **Emerton, J. A.** "The Textual and Linguistic Problems of Habakkuk II. 4–5." *JTS* 28 (1977) 1–18. **Holt, J. M.** "So He May Run Who Reads It." *JBL* 83 (1964) 298–303. **van der Woude, A. S.** "Habakkuk 2.4." *ZAW* 82 (1970) 281–82.

Translation

[1] I will stand upon my guard,	2+2
and I will take my position on the tower,	
and I will watch to see what he will speak with me,	3+3
and what he [a] will reply concerning my complaint.	
[2] And Yahweh answered me and said,	3+2
"Write the vision and make it plain upon the tablets	4+4
so that the one reading it may run.	

³ *For the vision is yet for an appointed time.*   4+4
   It hurries ᵃ *to the end and it will not lie.*
If it tarries, ᵇ *wait for it,*   3+3+2
   because it will surely come.
   It will not be late."
⁴ *Behold,* (*the oppressor*) ᵃ *is puffed up,* ᵇ   2+3+3
   his soul is not upright in him,
   but the righteous shall live by his faithfulness.
⁵ *And furthermore,* ᵃ *wine* ᵇ *is treacherous.*   3+4
   The arrogant ᶜ *man will not survive,* ᵈ
who ᵉ *widens his throat like sheol,*   4+4
   and like death is not satisfied.
He has gathered unto himself all nations,   3+3
   and has collected for himself all peoples.

Notes

1.a. Read "he" with the Peshitta. MT has, "what I will reply."

3.a. ויפח 3rd mas. sing. hiph. impf. פוח "to blow hard" (see Brownlee, *Text*, 41). GKC (par. 72,dd) takes ויפח as a rhythmically shortened form of יפיח from פוח.

3.b. יתמהמה 3rd mas. sing. hithpael מהה "delays."

4.a. The subject has fallen out. Read העגל "the oppressor" with Wellhausen and others.

4.b. Read עפלה "is puffed up," 3rd fem. sing. pu. pf. of עפל with BDB root I. NEB prefers root meaning II of BDB "the reckless." Emerton (*JTS* 28 [1977] 1–18) divides the consonants עף לה and reads עף as a qal part. of עוף "to fly away," that is "to die."

5.a. ואף בי "and furthermore" is not in the LXX or the Peshitta but should be retained.

5.b. היין "the wine" is חון "wealth" in DSH.

5.c. יהיר is only found here and Prov 21:24 and probably means "arrogant."

5.d. ינוה is a hapax. Emerton (Ibid.) takes it as an Arabic root נוי "to purpose, aim, intent," so "he will not reach his goal or be successful." Brownlee suggests a root נוה "to abide" (*JBL* 82 [1963] 323). It should read "shall not survive."

5.e. Take אשר as a relative "who." Brownlee takes it to be a reference to Asshur or Assyria (cf. "The Composition of Habakkuk," in *Hommages*, 259).

Form/Structure/Setting

The form is that of an oracle of response. The prophet says that he will wait on his watchtower "to see" what God will "say" to him in response to his complaint (v 1). Yahweh answers and tells him to write the answer on tablets so plainly that anyone passing by can read it (v 2). The answer or vision is for an appointed time (מועד). The prophet is to wait patiently for the fulfillment of the oracle. It may seem slow but it will surely come (v 3). The answer is in vv 4–5, and says that the arrogant man (Babylon) will not survive, but the righteous will live by his faithfulness (vv 4–5).

Comment

There is no more important passage in Habakkuk than this one, and few in the OT more significant because of the later use of it by the apostle Paul and Martin Luther. There are several textual and critical problems with this passage. The first problem one encounters in dealing with this pericope is its limit. Does the passage end with v 4, v 5a, or v 5? S. R. Driver (77), Eissfeldt (*Intro.*, 420), and Fohrer (*Intro.*, 452) limit the passage to 2:1–4. Humbert and Brownlee (*JBL* 82 [1963] 319–25) end the pericope at 2:5a. Brownlee then reads אשׁר "Assyria" in 2:5b instead of "who" or "which" in the MT. Most English translations (RSV, NEB) end the pericope at 2:5 and begin the series of woes with 2:6. Actually v 5 should be seen as a transitional verse. It relates to both v 4 and v 6.

A second problem in 2:1–5 is: who is the arrogant one? Is he a foreign invader or a wicked Israelite oppressor? If he is a foreigner, is he Babylonian, Assyrian, or Greek? All of these viewpoints have been defended by various OT scholars. It is impossible to give a definite answer to these questions. It is probably best to understand the wicked or arrogant one in 2:4–5 as the Babylonian. A third problem in the pericope is the omission of the subject in line one of 2:4. The text has probably suffered some corruption in transmission across the years. Many emendations and alternative readings of the text have been suggested. The easiest solution (which is not necessarily the best) is to insert העוּל "the evildoer" as the subject.

Explanation

This second oracle must be considered as God's answer to Habakkuk's second complaint about how a holy God can allow a wicked oppressor to continue devouring the righteous. Assuming that the wicked refers to the Babylonian and the righteous refers to Judah, we understand that Habakkuk is looking for Yahweh to punish Babylon. The second complaint and oracle must be dated later than the first complaint and oracle because there Babylon was just appearing on the scene as a conqueror. Now he is seen as a ruthless oppressor.

Like a watchman Habakkuk ascends his tower to scan the horizon. Other prophets have been referred to as watchmen (Isa 21:6–12; Ezek 3:17–21; 33:1–9; Hos 9:8). He says that he will wait to see what he will speak. To see a word is an unusual experience unless one is a prophet. What Habakkuk saw was a vision in the form of a message that he was to write on tablets. Writing on huge wooden tablets for public display was a form of publication. Isaiah was commanded to write some of his oracles on large tablets (Isa 8:1; 30:8). This may have been an early stage of writing notices on public walls. Such practice is still carried on in China and the Orient. The writing was to be plain. The verb בּאר only occurs three times in the OT. In Deut 1:5 Moses begins to "explain" the law. He was to make it so clear that anyone could understand what the law said. In Deut 27:8 Moses commanded the people to write the words of "this law" on the stones which they were to set up at Mt. Ebal when they came into Canaan. They were to write the words "very plainly" (RSV). The meaning was that the writing was to be very legible. In Hab 2:2 the vision was to be written and made plain on tablets.

How shall we interpret the expression, "so he may run who reads it"? S. R. Driver (75) understood the expression to mean that the writing was to be so clear and distinct that a person on the run could read the message. In 1964, J. M. Holt argued that Habakkuk was not using the word "run" literally for running off in haste or in alarm, but as a poetic device to refer to the way one was to live (walk, or run) in obedience to God (*JBL*, 82 [1964] 301). According to Holt, Habbakuk was saying that the writing was to be published so that the reader would know how "to run," i.e. how to live according to the will of God. Brownlee notes that the verb "run" is used for the work of a prophet in Jer 23:21. Therefore he suggests that "runners" here were all those who passed by and read the message to the illiterate who came along (*Hommages*, 263).

Yahweh gave Habakkuk one more word of caution before he told him the answer to his question of theodicy. He said that Habakkuk needed to learn to wait. God's time is not necessarily man's time. Habakkuk wanted his answer immediately. He wanted God to punish the Babylonians and put an end to evil and oppression right then. God said that he had appointed a time for all that to happen but it might not happen immediately. Habakkuk, like all of us, was living "between the times," between the promise and the fulfillment. Habakkuk was to wait in faith for God to act. He was assured that judgment on evil would surely come. It will not be late (v 3). But Habakkuk was not to wait with folded hands and bated breath for all this to happen. He was to live a life of faithfulness (v 4). The evil one is puffed up with pride and he will fall (vv 4, 5), but the righteous will live by being faithful to his covenant with God. Raymond Calkins said, "The summons is from speculation to action, from questioning to conduct, from brooding to duty. God is attending to His business, and Habakkuk must attend to his. Running the universe is not his task. That burden belongs to God. But Habakkuk has his task, and let him faithfully perform it. Thus he will live in moral sincerity and in moral security that righteous living brings in the midst of external calamities. That is the way for a righteous man to live in an evil world" (*The Modern Message of the Minor Prophets* [New York: Harper and Row, 1947] 97).

If Habakkuk was to live by his faithfulness, steadfastness, or trustworthiness, how do the NT writers get a doctrine of salvation by faith in Christ out of these words? The answer is to be found in the way the LXX translated these verses. 2:3b–4 are quoted from the LXX in Heb 10:37–38 and by Paul in Rom 1:17 and Gal 3:11. The longer quotation in Heb 10:37–38 reads: ὁ ἐρχόμενος ἥξει καὶ οὐ χρονίσει·ὁ δὲ δίκαιός μου ἐκ πίστεως ζήσεται, καὶ ἐὰν ὑποστείληται, οὐκ εὐδοκεῖ ἡ ψυχή μου ἐν αὐτῷ "The coming one will come and he will not tarry. But my righteous one shall live by faith, and if he shrinks back my soul has no pleasure in him." The writer of Hebrews was interested in this passage because of the LXX's use of "shrinking back." He was trying to get his readers not to "shrink back." He put no emphasis on living by faith. But Paul quoted only a portion of this passage, ὁ δὲ δίκαιος ἐκ πίστεως ζήσεται, left out the pronoun μου and read "but the righteous shall live by faith" (Rom 1:17; Gal 3:11). NT writers adapted OT scriptures to fit their purposes.

Evidently only 2:4 was written on the tablets. V 5 is an additional explanation by the prophet. "Furthermore" is the translation of אַף כִּי which is omitted in the Peshitta and the LXX, but it fits the context. Many would either omit הַיַּיִן "the wine" with the Peshitta or emend it to הוֹן "wealth" with DSH, or הוֹי "woe" and consider it the first of six "woes." But 5a is still talking about the arrogant man. He will not survive. The transition to v 5b is rough, but it is best to take v 5b as still talking about the arrogant man. Just as wine is treacherous (v 5a) so the proud oppressor opens his mouth as wide as Sheol (the place of the dead) and is never satisfied. Death never takes a holiday. The Babylonian, like death, continues to sweep the nations into his net (cf. 1:15).

The Five Woes   (2:6–20)

Translation

First Woe 2:6–8

6 *Will not these,* a *all of them, take up against him*
a taunt, an allusion, a riddle for him,
   and say, b

  "Woe to the one increasing that which   3+3
    is not his—how long?—
and loading himself with goods taken in pledge."
7 *Will not your creditors suddenly arise,*   3+2+3
   and those who make you tremble awake?
   Then you will become plunder for them.
8 *Because you have spoiled many nations,*   3+3
  all the rest of the nations will spoil you,
   because of the blood of men and violence to the land,   3+3
    the city and all her inhabitants.

Second Woe 2:9–11

9 *Woe to the one seeking an illegal profit for his house,*   4+3+2
  to set his nest on the height,
  to deliver himself from the evil hand.
10 *Your counsel* a *has brought shame to your house,*   3+3+2
  by putting an end to many people
   and sinning against your life.
11 *For a stone will cry out from the wall*   3+3
  and the beam a *answers from the woodwork.*

Third Woe 2:12–14

12 *Woe to the one building a city with blood,*   3+3
  and establishing a town with injustice.
13 *Behold, is not this from Yahweh of hosts,*
  that the nations grow weary to satisfy the fire,   3+3+3
  and the people exhaust themselves for emptiness.

14 *Because the earth shall be full*   3+3+3
of the knowledge of the glory of Yahweh,
as waters cover the sea.

Fourth Woe 2:15–17

15 *Woe to the one causing his neighbor to drink*   4+4
from the bowl [a] *of thy wrath,*
and making them drunk in order
to look upon their nakedness.
16 *You are satiated with shame*   3+3
rather than glory.
Drink you also, and stagger. [a]
The cup of Yahweh's right hand   3+3
will come round to you,
and disgrace will cover your glory.
17 *For the violence done to Lebanon shall*   4+3
cover you,
and the destruction of the beasts
will terrify you. [a]
Because of the blood of man, and violence   3+3
to the land, city and all her
inhabitants.

Fifth Woe 2:18–20

18 *What profit is an idol*   3+3+3
when its maker has formed it—
a molten image and a teacher [a] *of lies?*
For one trusts what he fashions   4+3
when he makes worthless dumb idols.
19 *Woe to the one saying to wood, "Awake,"*   4+3+2
"Stir yourself," to the silent stone.
Shall that teach? [a]
Behold it is overlaid with gold and silver,   3+3
but there is no spirit within it.
20 *But Yahweh is in his holy temple.*   3+3
Hush before him, all the earth.

Notes

6.a. אלה "these" is not in DSH. כלם "all of them" probably should be כלה "everyone" as 1:9, 15.

6.b. ויאמר is sing. It does not agree with pls. אלה and כלם.

10.a. יעצת lit. "you counseled."

11.a. כפיס a hapax. The meaning is uncertain.

15.a. מספח should read מסף "from bowl of."

16.a. הערל "to leave uncircumcised" should read in context הרעל "and stagger." Cf. the LXX of Zech 12:2.

17.a. יחיתן is inexplicable. The LXX and Peshitta read יחתך "it shall terrify you." The final ן should be ך.

18.a. מורה is a hiph. pt. of ירה III (*CHAL*, 144).

19.a. יורה is often omitted as a gloss (cf. NEB).

Form/Structure/Setting

Here is a series of woe oracles. The form is common in the prophets (cf. Isa 5:8–23; 10:1, 5; 28:1; 29:15; 30:1; 31:1; 33:1; Amos 5:18; 6:1, 4). The interjection הוי or אוי probably originated as an expression of grief in the funeral dirge (1 Kgs 13:30; Jer 22:18; 34:5), but in the prophets it introduces an oracle of judgment. There are five woes in 2:6–20. Each oracle begins with הוי followed by a participle describing the sin. The second part of each oracle announces the judgment to come on the sinner, and the third part often introduced by כי (when it is included) states the reason for the judgment.

Comment

Several questions arise when one begins reading this section. Who is the speaker? Who is the guilty one against whom the woes are pronounced? What is the relationship of this section to that which goes before and that which follows? Is there unity within this section?

The speaker in this section seems to be the nations. 2:6 says, "Will not these, all of them, take up against him a taunt-song . . . and say, 'Woe,' "? However, there is no antecedent to "these, all of them" in v 6. The "nations" and "peoples" in v 5 seem to be the antecedent. But is it logical for the pagan nations to be pronouncing "woe" on the guilty one in the name of Yahweh of hosts (v 13)? Would the nations speak about the earth being filled with the knowledge of God as waters cover the sea (v 14), or would they condemn the making of idols? Probably not. If the words of the woes are inconsistent in the mouths of the nations how do we explain "these" and "all of them" in v 6?

Some scholars have used drastic surgery in answering this question. Stade, Cornill and Ward only accepted the first woe as genuine and rejected vv 9–20 as a later addition. Brownlee believes that only the first three woes are non-prophetic, i.e. from the nations, and the last two are from Habakkuk (*Hommages*, 269–271). F. C. Eiselen says, "These woes are placed in the mouth of the nations; in reality the prophet is the speaker" (*The Minor Prophets*, 488). David Garland says, "The phrase 'all these' is not a reference to Judah only. As does 'the righteous' in 2:4, this term includes all nations experiencing the full weight of oppression, whoever the oppressor may be" (Garland, *BBC* 7, 259).

The expressions "these" and "all of them" are ambiguous. "These" is not in DSH and כלם "all of them" may be a scribal error for כלה "everyone" (1:9, 15). The form ויאמר is sing. Just before the "woe" in v 6. Therefore it is possible that the speaker is not the nations, but the prophet or "everyone." The nations are spoken of in the passage and nowhere do they speak directly.

If we cannot be certain about the speaker in this section, who is spoken of? Again we are not told. The person or nation addressed is guilty of robbery, oppression, debauchery, and idolatry, but we are never told his name. Traditionally, the oppressor has been identified with the Babylonian. Brownlee thinks it is Assyria. Humbert and Nielsen think it is Jehoiakim. It is impossible to determine at this point the identity of the oppressor. Perhaps this is providential because the passage is applicable to any situation of oppression, greed, debauchery, and idolatry.

Is there a unity within this section, and between this section and that which precedes and follows? The answer is probably yes, but to marshall the evidence for such a conclusion would require much space and time. We will try to point out some evidence in the *Explanation*.

Explanation

This series of woes is designed to show that ultimately sin, evil, crime, greed, oppression, debauchery, and idolatry are doomed to destruction. Often people look at the power and structures of evil and become depressed. Is this really God's world? Has it gotten away from him? Does he still have control over the world and its inhabitants? Habakkuk says, "Yes."

The first woe is the doom of the robber, thief, the embezzler, the dishonest person, the one who appropriates for himself that which belongs to another. Such a person may continue in such actions but sooner or later, like creditors, the oppressed people will rise up against their oppressor and make him pay the last penny. A man will reap what he sows (v 8).

The second woe is the doom of the exploiters and extortioners. The term "to get evil gain" comes from a weaver's term "to cut off the threads" (בצע). It is used several times in the OT in the sense of evil gain (Gen 37:26; Jer 6:13; Mic 4:13; Hab 2:9), "to make one's cut." We still use the expression, "to get one's cut" in a bad sense. Those who get their wealth by illegal methods feel the need for security. They build their nest on some high, secluded spot guarded by every security device available. But the stone in the walls of the house and the wood in the beams will cry out against them.

The third woe is the doom of evil and violence. The tyrant builds his society the bulldozer way. He runs roughshod over anyone who gets in his way (v 12). But such a tyrant will not succeed, because Yahweh of hosts will see to it that social structures built on violence and bloodshed will amount to nothing. They will be consumed in the flames (v 14). But a kingdom built on the glory of God will cover the whole earth (v 14).

The fourth woe is the doom of debauchery. The guilty ones here are those who ruin their fellow men by strong drink in order to gaze on their shame. The story of Noah's drunkenness comes immediately to mind (cf. Gen 9:20–25). Strong drink, crime, immorality often go together. Unquestionably, drink and drugs have been the path of doom for many. Habakkuk says that the one who makes his neighbor drunk will himself drink the cup of the wrath of God. V 17 must be dated after the Babylonian came through Lebanon and ravaged the forests of cedar, and the herds of wild animals. Is there an ecological message in this verse for us?

The fifth woe is the doom of idolatry. The prophet asks: What use is an idol? It has no power. It is man-made. Idols are instruments of lies and deception. Many people think idols are something that they are not. An idol is as silent as the stone out of which it is made. It cannot teach or give directions. It may look expensive but it is not alive.

In contrast to the idol, Yahweh is in his holy temple, let all the earth bow in hushed silence before him. So all of the forces that oppose God will ultimately be silenced. Now the forces of evil still rage. The righteous is still faithful. The battle continues. Yet there is a power in the world "greater than armies, bombs, bribery, and torture, and it is he who thwarts the efforts of the wicked and gives to the righteous another kind of power to enable them to resist and endure" (Gowan, *Perspective* 9 [1968] 166).

A Prayer (*3:1–19*)

Bibliography

Albright, W. F. "The Psalm of Habakkuk." *Studies of Old Testament Prophecy,* ed. H. H. Rowley. Edinburgh: T. & T. Clark, 1950 1–18. **Eaton, J. H.** "The Origin and Meaning of Habakkuk 3." *ZAW* 76 (1964) 144–70. **Margulis, B.** "The Psalm of Habakkuk: A Reconstruction and Interpretation." *ZAW* 82 (1970) 409–41.

Translation

Title 3:1

1 *A prayer of Habakkuk the prophet*
  on the shigionoth.

Petition 3:2

2 *Yahweh, I have heard the report of thee,*	3+3
I fear a *thy work.*	
In the midst of the years revive it; b	
in the midst of the years make known. c	3+3
In wrath remember mercy.	

A Theophany 3:3–7

3 *Eloah comes from Teman*	3+3
and the holy one from Mount Paran, Selah. a	
His radiance covers the heavens,	3+3
and his praise b *fills the earth.*	
4 *His brightness is as the light.*	3+3+3
Twin rays are in his hand,	
and there is the covering a *of his power.*	

5 *Before him goes the pestilence*   3+3
  and behind him goes the plague. [a]
6 *He stands and he measures* [a] *the earth,*   3+3
  he looks and makes the nations jump.
  Then the eternal mountains crumble   3+3+2
  and the everlasting hills sink.
  Everlasting paths are his.
7 *I see the tents of Cushan* [a] *under evil.*   5+4
  The tent curtains of the land of Midian shake.

The Battle 3:8–15

8 *Is it against the rivers that it burns, O Yahweh?*   3+3+2
  Is your anger against the rivers?
  Is your wrath against the sea?
  That you ride upon your horses,   3+2
  your chariot of salvation?
9 *Your bow has bared itself.*   3+3+2
  The stave is charged by a word, Selah.
  You break open rivers in the earth.
10 *The mountains see you and writhe,*   3+3
   the torrent of water overflows.
   The deep gives its voice.   3+3
   It lifts its hands on high.
11 *Sun, moon, halt in their dwelling place.* [a]   4+3+3
   For light your arrows go out
   for shining the flash of your spear.
12 *In indignation you tread the earth,*   3+3
   in anger you trample the nations.
13 *You go out to save your people*   3+2
   for the salvation of your anointed.
   You smote the head of the house of the wicked   4+3
   to lay him bare from tail [a] *to neck, Selah.*
14 *With his lances you pierced the head*
   of his hordes,
   they stormed out to scatter me. [a]   4+3+4
   They rejoiced as they devoured
   the poor in secret.
15 *You trampled the sea with your horses*   3+3
   foaming the mighty waters.

The Response of Faith 3:16–19

16 *I have heard and my belly quakes,*   3+3
   my lips quiver at the sound,
   rottenness comes into my bones,   3+3
   my steps tremble under me.

> I will wait calmly [a] for the day of distress   3+3
> to come upon the people attacking us.
> 17 If the fig tree does not blossom,   3+3
> and no fruit is on the vines;
> the labor of the olive fails,   3+3
> and the fields make no food;
> and the flock is cut off from the pen,   3+3
> and no ox is in the stall;
> 18 yet I will exult in Yahweh,   3+3
> I will rejoice in the God of my salvation!
> 19a Yahweh is lord of my strength,   3+3+2
> and he makes my feet like does' feet
> and causes me to walk on high places.

A Subscription 3:19b:
To the choirmaster on the stringed instruments.

Notes

2.a. Many emend יראתי "I fear" to ראיתי "I see" to be parallel with שמעתי but that is not necessary. LXX supports MT "fear."

2.b. הייהו could mean "give him (the king) life." But it is better to take the pro. suf. to refer to "work."

2.c. תודיע means "make your work known" or one could read a nif. תודע with the LXX, "make yourself known."

3.a. Selah occurs three times in this chapter, vv 3, 9, 13 and nowhere else in the OT except Psalms. The meaning is uncertain.

3.b. תהלתו is often translated "splendor" rather than "praise" on the basis of הלל II in BDB (p. 240).

4.a. חביון is a hapax. The meaning "covering" is very uncertain. Albright divides this word and combines it with the words before and after to read ושמח ביום עזה "rejoicing in the day of his triumph."

5.a. רשף is the name of a Canaanite deity (cf. Albright, *Archeology and the Religion of Israel.* [Baltimore: Johns Hopkins, 1942] 79, 81, 87, 91).

6.a. מדד means "measure." Some take the root as מיד "to shake."

7.a. כושן only occurs here in the OT. It must have been near or identical with Midian.

11.a. זבל usually refers to the exalted dwelling place of God (1 Kgs 8:13; Isa 63:15; 2 Chr 6:2). Here it is the dwelling place for the sun and moon.

13.a. יסוד according to Albright (*OT Prophecy,* 17), can mean "foundation," "thigh," or "tail."

14.a. v 14 is very difficult. Albright does not attempt to translate part of it!

16.a. There seems to be a shift in the prophet's attitude at v 16c. אנוח carries the idea of resting and waiting until distress comes on the oppressor of his people. But יגודנו could mean "attack him," or "attack us."

Form/Structure/Setting

Chap. 3 is a psalm in the form of a prayer. It is an intercessory prayer designed to be sung by the congregation or by one representing the congregation. It is a prayer on behalf of the king and his people that God will renew or revive his saving acts in the present. It is difficult to classify the psalm by type. Is it a hymn, a lament, a song of thanksgiving, a liturgy, or a royal psalm? It has elements of all of these types in it. It is probably best classified as a liturgy and was probably used on many occasions in the temple worship during the Fall festival.

Comment

The psalm in chap. 3 is made up of a superscription (v 1), a petition (v 2), a theophany (vv 3–7), a description of the battle between Yahweh and nature and the enemies of God (vv 8–15), the response of faith of the prophet (vv 16–19), and a subscription (v 19b).

The fact that chap. 3 has a separate title implies that at times it circulated separately and was used apart from the rest of the book. The fact that Habakkuk's name is attached to it preserves the tradition that he composed the psalm. The terms "shigionoth" (v 1) and "niginoth" (v 19) indicate that the psalm was set to music. Watts suggests that shigionoth may indicate the tune or mood for the presentation of the prayer as music suitable for a lament (Watts 144).

The petition (v 3) is for God to renew his awesome work of salvation of his people which had become only a report in Habakkuk's time. There may be a prayer for the king in 3b.

The theophany is an appearance of God although God himself is never seen in the OT (except in the patriarchal "epiphanic visitations") either because there is either too much or too little light (cf. S. L. Terrien, *The Elusive Presence* [San Francisco: Harper & Row, 1978] 69). Terrien does not like the word "theophany" because there is too much of the idea of Greek and Canaanite mythology in it. Undoubtedly old mythological language is used in the description of the Sinai type theophanies in the OT. The theophanies in Judg 5:4–5; Hab 3:3–7; Ps 18:7–15; 50:2–3; 69:1–2; 77:16–19; 97:3–5 are all of the Sinai type.

Often in association with an appearance of God in the OT there is a description of a battle between Yahweh and his enemies represented sometimes as "the deep" (תְּהוֹם), the "waters," "rivers," "sea," or as "the nations." Some scholars have posited a New Year festival in Israel each fall at which time a mock battle between the king and the nations was fought. The king was victorious over his enemies and Yahweh was proclaimed King of the universe again. Evidence for such an elaborate New Year festival in Israel is minimal but language similar to that which might have been used in such a cultic setting does occur in Hab 3 and elsewhere in the OT.

The response of faith on the part of the prophet is an indication that this chapter is a liturgy. This last section of Habakkuk (3:16–19) is one of the greatest expressions of faith in the Bible.

Explanation

Chap. 3 is part of the answer to the questions the prophet asked in chap. 1. Why does God allow the wicked to go unpunished? He does not. God is still on the throne. He acted in the past to overcome his enemies (3:2a), he will do it again at the request of his prophet (3:2b). God is coming from Teman as he did before (3:3). His power is described as that of a warrior

God with lightnings and thunder accompanying him (3:4). Pestilence and plague flee from him because of his power (3:5). He is sovereign over the universe, including the nations of the world (3:6).

God's wrath is poured out upon the "waters" that oppose him (3:8). God's coming is for the salvation of his people and his king (3:13).

3:3-15 is a vision of Habakkuk much like the vision God promised him in 2:3. Habakkuk may have had an ecstatic experience in which he "saw" God coming to defeat his enemies. In response to Habakkuk's petition in v 2, an appearance of God is described in vv 3-7. The Hebrew word for God here (אֱלוֹהַּ) is sing. and is used again in 1:11; Deut 32:15, 17; Ps 18:32 [Eng. 31]; 50:22; and Prov 30:5. God, in these verses, is pictured as coming from the South (Teman and Mount Paran). Normally the reader would expect God to come from the temple in Jerusalem or from his dwelling place in heaven. Here the prophet probably is remembering an earlier time when God came from Sinai to rescue his people at the Reed Sea and in the Wilderness (cf. Deut 33:2; Judg 5:4-5). Teman was a district in northwest Edom. Mount Paran refers to the hilly region stretching along the western border of the Gulf of Akaba (cf. Gen 21:21; Num 12:16; Deut 33:2).

God's coming is compared to a thunderstorm. The whole sky is lit with his radiance (v 3). The lightning flashes from the cloud are symbols of his power, but his real essence or power is covered or hidden (v 4). In most theophanies in the OT God's presence and power is very real—almost too real. But no one ever sees what God in himself actually looks like (cf. Ezek 1:1-28). The figure shifts a little in vv 5-7. God is pictured as a king with "pestilence" going before him and the "plague" behind him (v 5). He stands like a great man on the earth and surveys (measures) the scene. He looks and makes the nations jump. The effect of God's power is seen in the crumbling mountains and the sinking hills (v 6). The tents (homes) of Chushan and Midian will tremble at Yahweh's coming (v 7).

Why is God coming? The answer is in 3:8-15. He is coming to defeat his enemy represented by rivers, water, and sea, and the enemy of his people. Yahweh the warrior bares his bow (v 9). The rivers like the ancient Tiamat are split asunder. The mountains watch the battle in fear (v 10). Even the sun and moon stay in their dwelling place and do not come out (cf. Josh 10:12-14; Ps 19:4). The last part of v 11 is ambiguous. The meaning seems to be that even though the sun and moon do not shine, the lightning flashes from God's presence furnish enough light for the battle. God is angry with the nations (Assyria and Babylon) and has come to save his people and his anointed (vv 12-13). "Your anointed" probably refers to the Davidic king in Jerusalem. "From tail to neck" (v 13) appears to be a reference to the enemy in the form of a dragon. The enemy was still devouring the poor victims in supposed secrecy when Yahweh struck his fatal blow (v 14).

When the vision was over we hear Habakkuk's response (3:16-19). He describes his shattering experience in 3:16ab. V 16c is difficult to interpret. Does it mean that Habakkuk is still waiting for the oppressor to attack him and his people again and again? This idea is consistent with the first part of this verse. This is the way Albright, ASV, and NASV understand 3:16c:

Painful to me is the day of distress,
When a people comes up to attack me (Albright).

Because I must wait quietly for the
    day of trouble,
for the coming up of the people that
    invadeth us (ASV).

Because I must wait quietly for the
    day of distress,
for the people to arise who will invade us (NASV).

It must be admitted that the Hebrew permits all of the above interpretations.

But somewhere in this last section Habakkuk's fear is changed to faith and the change probably comes in 3:16c. He says that he was frightened when he heard about the works of God. He knows that the time of God's victory over the enemy might be long in coming. But he says

I will wait calmly for the day of distress
    to come upon the people attacking us (cf. RSV).

And while he waits for the ultimate victory, he says that he will rejoice and exult in the Lord even though there may not be any visible or external signs of his presence or favor. The words "rejoice" and "exult" each have the cohorative attached. This is the strongest possible way to say that one is determined to rejoice in the Lord regardless of what does or does not happen. Faith means loving and serving God regardless of circumstances. For the just to live by faith means that he is to be faithful to God in his living.

Zephaniah

Introduction

Bibliography

Books

Gaster, T. H. *Myth, Legend, and Custom in the Old Testament.* New York: Harper and Row, 1969. Hyatt, J. P. "Zephaniah." *PCB.* London: Thomas Nelson and Sons, 1962. Kapelrud, A. S. *The Message of the Prophet Zephaniah.* Oslo: Universitetsforlaget, 1975. Rice, T. T. *The Scythians.* London: Thames and Hudson, 1957. Sabottka, L. *Zephanja.* Rome: Biblical Institute Press, 1972. Taylor, C. L. "Zephaniah." *IB* 6, 1956.

Articles

Clifford, R. J. "The Use of Hôy in the Prophets." *CBQ* 28 (1966) 458–64. Fensham, F. C. "The Book of Zephaniah." *IDBSup* (1970) 983–84. Gerstenberger, E. "The Woe-Oracles of the Prophets." *JBL* 81 (1962) 249–63. Hayes, J. "The Usage of Oracles Against Foreign Nations in Ancient Israel." *JBL* 87 (1968) 81–92. Hyatt, J. P. "The Date and Background of Zephaniah." *JBL* 7 (1949) 25–29. Smith, L. P. and Lacheman, E. R. "The Authorship of the Book of Zephaniah." *JNES* 9 (1950) 137–42. von Rad, G. "The Origin of the Concept 'Day of Yahweh.'" *JSS* (1959) 97–108. Williams, D. L. "The Date of Zephaniah." *JBL* 82 (1963) 77–88.

The Place in the Canon

The book of Zephaniah occupies the ninth place among "The Twelve" in all forms of the OT, following Habakkuk and preceding Haggai.

The Man

Zephaniah was a prophet in Judah during the reign of Josiah (640–609 B.C.). His name can mean "Yahweh hides" and may reflect the terror of the days of Manasseh at the time of Zephaniah's birth. Sabottka, J. M. P. Smith, and J. D. W. Watts point out that the name might also be derived from a combination of *Zaphon* and *Yah* (an abbreviation for Yahweh). Zaphon was an important Canaanite deity who gave his name to the mythical mountain in the north where the gods were supposed to have lived. The combination of Zaphon and Yah could be translated, "Zaphon is Yahweh." Such a confession would claim that the real God which some people call Zaphon is Yahweh. Zaphon is also a common semitic word for "north" (Gen 13:14; Exod 26:20; 40:22; Jer 1:14; Isa 14:13, 31; Ezek 8:14; Ps 48:3; 89:13; Job 26:7).

The name Zephaniah occurs ten times in the OT and is spelled two different ways: צְפַנְיָה (Jer 21:1; 29:25, 29; 52:24; Zeph 1:1; Zech 6:10, 14; 1 Chr 6:21) and צְפַנְיָהוּ (2 Kgs 25:18; Jer 37:3). Perhaps four different people are called Zephaniah in the OT: (1) The prophet whose book bears his name

(1:1); (2) a priest, the son of Maaseiah (Jer 21:1; 29:25, 29; 37:3; 52:24; 2 Kgs 25:18); (3) a Kohathite, son of Tahath (1 Chr 6:36); (4) a priest, father of Josiah or Hen (Zech 6:10, 14). Donald L. Williams believes that (2) Zephaniah the priest, the son of Maaseiah, and (4) Zephaniah the father of Josiah are the same as (1) the prophet (cf. *JBL* 82 [1963] 85–88).

The Times

There was a period of silence in the history of OT prophecy during the first three-quarters of the seventh century B.C. (698–626). No prophetic voice is recorded in the OT between the times of Isaiah and Micah at the close of the eighth century B.C. and the times of Zephaniah, Nahum and Jeremiah (ca. 626 B.C.). This silence was probably due to the fact that Judah and her kings, Manasseh and Amon, were controlled by the Assyrian empire and her pagan religions. Much of Manasseh's reign (687–642 B.C.) coincided with the period of Assyria's greatest power and glory. In Judah, persecution, idolatry and child sacrifice were rampant (2 Kgs 21:1–9, 16).

Sennacherib, one of Assyria's great kings, was murdered in 681 B.C. and was succeeded by his son Esarhaddon. Esarhaddon was a strong king. He extended the empire as far west as Egypt by capturing Memphis in 671 B.C. The next Assyrian king, Ashurbanipal, strengthened Assyria's hold on Egypt by conquering Thebes, 440 miles down the Nile from Memphis, in 663 B.C. But that was the last major act of aggression by the Assyrians. When Ashurbanipal died in 626 B.C., Assyria's power crumbled. That opened the door for Josiah's reform in Judah (621 B.C.) and also for the rise of the Babylonians under their strong men Nabopolassar (625–605 B.C.) and his son, Nebuchadrezzar (605–562 B.C.).

Zephaniah was probably born during the dark days of Manasseh, when Assyria's influence was at its height, but began his ministry about the time of the death of Ashurbanipal (626 B.C.).

The Date

In the light of the words of the superscription (1:1) that Zephaniah prophesied during the days of Josiah (640–609 B.C.) one might suppose that there would be no problem in dating the book. But that is not the case. There is a problem as to when, in Josiah's reign, Zephaniah prophesied. Was it before the reform in 621 B.C. or after it? J. P. Hyatt and D. L. Williams have argued that Zephaniah's ministry was not in Josiah's time at all, but during the days of Jehoiakim, Josiah's successor. Louise P. Smith and E. R. Lacheman assigned the book in its final form to 200 B.C. counting only 1:4–13 the authentic message of Zephaniah.

Most scholars prefer a date before Josiah's reform in 621 B.C. for Zephaniah's ministry because Zephaniah denounced the syncretistic practices, Baal worship, and child sacrifice which were prevalent during Manasseh's reign (1:4–9, 11–12; 3:1–4). By denouncing such practices Zephaniah could have been a contributing influence in bringing about reform. However, some scholars have noted that the text says, "the remnant of Baal" (1:4), suggesting that the reform came and failed, and a remnant of Baalism persisted. J. Phillip Hyatt (*PCB*, 642) and Donald L. Williams (*JBL* 82 [1963] 83–85) argue for a date in the time of Jehoiakim, But their arguments and those of Smith and Lacheman are not convincing.

Kapelrud supports the traditional early date. He points to the reference to Nineveh (2:13–15) which had not yet fallen. Nineveh fell in 612 B.C. The syncretistic worship reflected in 1:4–5 also points to a pre-reform date as does the references to Moab, Ammon and the Philistine cities. Kapelrud says, "All features considered, it seems reasonable to conclude that the Prophet Zephaniah preached in Jerusalem in the years between 635 and 625 B.C." (*The Message*, 42). J. D. W. Watts notes that many previous scholars have seen parts of Zephaniah as later additions, largely because they could not allow the same prophet to preach messages of judgment and hope. But Watts remarks that current studies of worship and prophetic forms in Judah during the seventh century find less difficulty in combining words of judgment and words of assurance than previous generations. Watts concludes, "It is possible that Zephaniah planned the entire prophecy for temple services within the decade before Josiah's reform . . ." (Watts 155).

The problem of the Scythian invasion is related to the question of the date of Zephaniah. It is generally recognized that Zephaniah expected the imminent destruction of Jerusalem by a foreign enemy (1:4, 10–11; 2:1; 3:1–4). When historians began exploring the Josianic era for a possible enemy capable of bringing such destruction, the strongest candidate was the Scythians. But the Scythians are not mentioned in the OT. The suggestion of a Scythian invasion of Palestine in the time of Josiah comes from Herodotus (Bk 1, 41). But even here the evidence that the Scythians were a threat to Judah is very meager. The only city he mentions is Ashkelon where the Scythians sacked only the temple of Venus. A recent work on the Scythians dates this invasion of Palestine in 611 B.C. (T. T. Rice, *The Scythians* 45). Such a date after Josiah's reform and the fall of Nineveh would virtually eliminate the possibility that the Scythians are the enemy in Zephaniah.

If the enemies were not the Scythians, who were they? The Assyrians were impotent after 626 B.C. The Babylonians did not flex their muscles as a world power until 605 B.C. Hyatt and Donald Williams consider the Babylonians to be the enemy and assign the book of Zephaniah to the time of Jehoiakim (609–597 B.C.). They consider the words in the superscription, "in the days of Josiah," as incorrect (*JBL* 82 [1963] 84). Some scholars such as Horst and T. H. Robinson claim that no specific enemy needs to be found. Zephaniah was a successor to a whole line of prophets who preached about imminent judgment on Israel. More recent scholars interpret the enemy as a part of the drama or cult that was acted out during the fall New Year festival when a mock battle was engaged between the king and his enemies. The enthronement psalms (47, 95, 97, 98, 99) probably have their setting in such a ceremony. Smith and Lacheman saw the enemy as part of the work of the apocalyptist who wrote the book about 200 B.C. (*JNES* 9 [1950] 141). In light of our present information it is probably best to see Assyria as the enemy and assign a date of ca. 627 B.C. to the book of Zephaniah.

The Book

The book of Zephaniah opens with a judgment oracle on the whole world (1:2–3). This is not as unusual as it may appear. Micah does the same thing. It was one way to get the attention of the hearers. The oracle against the whole world is followed by one against Judah because of her syncretistic worship, indifference, and skepticism (1:4–6). The day of Yahweh is the subject of the next section (1:7–2:3). Zephaniah emphasizes the imminence of the day as well as the severity of the judgment that it will bring. The origin of the day of Yahweh has been the subject of much debate. Amos seems to have been the first OT prophet to use the term. He emphasized the judgment aspect of the day. Isaiah probably was the first to stress its nearness (13:6). Zephaniah is familiar with both these aspects of the day. It will be a day of darkness, clouds, and deep darkness. After Zephaniah, Obadiah (v 15), Ezekiel (7:7, 30:3), and Joel (1:15) took up the message against Judah. Many theories have been advanced to explain the origin of the idea of the day of Yahweh. Gunkel and Mowinckel supposed that there were ancient mythological ideas behind the prophets' preaching about the day (cf. Kapelrud, 83). Mowinckel saw the day of Yahweh as a part of the cultic drama during the New Year festival. It was the day of the theophany when God would come and restore the fortunes of his people. Cerny rejects Mowinckel's theory and finds the origin of the day in Israel's early experience of the dreadful God in the desert (cf. *The Day of Yahweh and Some Relevant Problems*, [Prague: University of Karlova, 1948]). G. von Rad believes that the idea of the day grew out of the concept of Holy War (cf. "The Origin of the Day of Yahweh." *JSS* 4 [1959] 97–108; *OTT* II, 119–125).

Some have doubted that Zephaniah 2:1–3 is a part of the pericope on the day of Yahweh. However, the expression "the day of the wrath of Yahweh" is found twice in this section (2:2, 3), and the prophet is warning the people to brace themselves for the blow. There is no general call for repentance here. It seems the prophet has given up hope for the immediate deliverance of Judah as a whole. Only a remnant of the humble seekers after Yahweh might be hidden from the wrath of God on that day.

The pericope on the day of Yahweh is followed by words of doom over foreign nations (2:4–15). The nations mentioned were traditional enemies like Philistia, Moab and Ammon, Assyria, and Ethiopians or Egyptians. A part of these oracles of judgment upon the foreign nations is the promise of hope for the remnant of Judah. The remnant will eventually possess the lands of their enemies (2:7, 9). Following the oracles on foreign nations, Zephaniah addresses the immediate situation in Jerusalem involving the faithlessness of the leaders (3:1–5). In 3:6–8 Yahweh says that the purpose of the judgment on the nations was to cause Judah to accept correction, but she refused. However, in spite of Judah's corruption, Zephaniah believed

that Yahweh could and would change the fortunes of his people. In 3:9–13
the change includes all the peoples of the world who eventually will become
worshipers of Yahweh. The remnant of Judah and Israel (3:13) will be humbled
and cleansed. Yahweh will dwell with his people and will be their king and
defender (3:15). He will destroy their enemies and they will sing and exult
in his love (3:14–20).

The Text

The text of Zephaniah is difficult in many places. The grammar is often
irregular (1:2, 14). Several rare words are used (2:14). Some words have
been divided improperly in the MT (1:14). Some secondary meanings of
words found in Egyptian and Ugaritic materials are used in the text (1:14).
All of these problems have contributed to many differences in modern translations. These problems are discussed thoroughly in the textual notes at the
end of the translation of each pericope. Sabottka has a thorough work on
the text of Zephaniah.

OUTLINE

Superscription 1:1
1. An announcement of universal judgment 1:2–6
2. An announcement of the day of Yahweh 1:7–2:3
3. Oracles against the nations 2:4–15
   a. Oracle against Philistia 2:4–7
   b. Oracle against Moab and Ammon 2:8–11
   c. Oracle against Ethiopia 2:12
   d. Oracle against Assyria 2:13–15
4. Judgment on Jerusalem 3:1–5
5. Judgment on the nations 3:6–8
6. A great change coming 3:9–13
7. A new song 3:14–20

Superscription (1:1)

Translation

¹ *The word of Yahweh which came to Zephaniah, son of Cushi, son of Gedaliah,
son of Amariah, son of Hezekiah, in the days of Josiah son of Amon, king of Judah.*

Form/Structure/Setting

The form of the superscription of Zephaniah is similar to that of Hosea,
Joel, Micah, Haggai, and Zechariah. In all of these books the message is
identified as "the word of Yahweh." The name of each prophet's father is

given (except for Micah) and the time of the prophecy is indicated by the name of the reigning king (except in Joel).

Comment

The superscription of Zephaniah is unique in that the prophet's lineage is traced back through four generations. This may indicate that Zephaniah's great, great grandfather was the famous King Hezekiah. However, if the Hezekiah of the superscription had been the king, that probably would have been made clear. Kapelrud points out that Hezekiah was a common name in Judah (1 Chr 3:23; Ezra 2:16; Neh 7:21), so this Hezekiah could have been someone other than the king. There were only two generations between Hezekiah and Josiah according to 2 Kgs 21–22 (Manasseh and Amon) not three as Zephaniah's superscription would have it if Hezekiah were the king. Also, Amariah is not attested as one of Hezekiah's sons.

Zephaniah's name probably means "Yahweh hides" or "Yahweh treasures." Some scholars (Sabottka, J. M. P. Smith, and J. D. W. Watts) point to the fact that "Zaphon" was the name of a Canaanite god. Zephaniah could mean "Zaphon is Yahweh."

Cushi is Zephaniah's father. Cush is usually identified in the OT as Ethiopia. Does that mean that Zephaniah's father was an Ethiopian? Probably not. The fact that the three ancestors before Cushi have good Hebrew names indicates that Zephaniah's family was Judean even though there might have been some intermarriage in or foreign influence on the family.

The time of Zephaniah's ministry is given as the days of Josiah. The majority of scholars have understood that Zephaniah delivered his messages before Josiah's reform in 621 B.C. The enemy in that case could be the Scythians or the Assyrians. J. Phillip Hyatt and D. L. Williams argue that the time of Zephaniah's ministry was really during the reign of Jehoiakim (609–597 B.C.), because of the expression "the remnant of Baal" (1:4) and other factors. Eissfeldt and Kapelrud defend the earlier view.

An Announcement of Universal Judgment   (1:2–6)

Translation

² *I will again sweep away* ᵃ *everything*   3+3+2
   from the surface of the ground,
      oracle of Yahweh.
³ *I will sweep away men and cattle,*   3+3+2
   I will sweep away birds of the heavens and fish of the sea
      and the stumbling blocks ᵃ *with the wicked.*

And I will cut off man
from the surface of the ground,
oracle of Yahweh.   2+2+2
⁴ *And I will stretch out my hand upon Judah*   3+3
and upon all the inhabitants of Jerusalem.
And I will cut off from this place   3+2+3
the remnant of Baal,
the name of the heathen ᵃ *priests, with the priests.* ᵇ
⁵ *And the ones bowing down on the roofs*   2+2
to the host of heaven,
and the ones bowing down ᵃ *and swearing by Yahweh*
and the ones swearing by their king, ᵇ
⁶ *and the ones turning away from following Yahweh*   3+3
who do not seek Yahweh nor inquire of him.

Notes

2.a. The terms אֹסֵף אָסֵף are difficult. אֹסֵף appears to be a qal. inf. abs. of אָסַף "to gather." אָסֵף can only be a hiph. juss. impf. of סוף "to sweep away," "to put an end to." The inf. abs. of one root coming before a different root is rare in the OT. It occurs in Isa 28:28 אָדוֹשׁ יְדוּשֶׁנּוּ but the text may be corrupt. If the words are read as they stand they could mean "I will utterly sweep away." Sabottka reads אֹסֵף as אָסִיף (1st com. sing. hiph. impf. of יסף "to add," or, "to do it again,") and אָסֵף as אָסוֹף (1st com. sing. qal. impf. of סוף "to sweep away"), אָסִיף אָסוֹף "I will again sweep away." The "again" refers to the "again" in Gen 8:21 (see *Explanation* below).

3.a. וְהַמַּכְשֵׁלוֹת אֶת-הָרְשָׁעִים is not in LXX. Many emend the text to וְהִכְשַׁלְתִּי "and I will cause (the wicked) to stumble." (BDB 506).

4.a. הַכְּמָרִים denotes priests of pagan gods in 2 Kgs 23:5; Hos 10:5, and in Aramaic, Syriac and Ugaritic.

4.b. עִם-הַכֹּהֲנִים "with the priests" is not in the LXX and may be a gloss.

5.a. הַמִּשְׁתַּחֲוִים "the ones bowing down" and הַנִּשְׁבָּעִים "the ones swearing" both occur twice in v 5. The second הַמִּשְׁתַּחֲוִים is not in the LXX but may be in the MT for effect.

5.b. RSV, NEB and others read מַלְכָּם after Lucian's ver. of LXX, Syr. and Vg.

Form/Structure/Setting

This pericope is in the form of a judgment oracle. Yahweh speaks in the first person. The piece is tied together by repetition of key words. Some have questioned the unity of vv 2-6 on the ground that vv 2-3 are universal and 4-6 are directed toward Judah. But Micah and Amos both begin with a broader group before addressing Israel directly. The words "sweep away" occur three times, "cut off" twice, "ones bowing down" and "swearing" twice, and "oracle of Yahweh" twice. The setting is definitely cultic because of the references to the priests, bowing down, and failing to seek Yahweh.

T. H. Gaster believes that these opening words were spoken at the autumnal Feast of Ingathering ('*asif*), and that the words are a parody on the syncretistic ritual of the fall festival.

Explanation

In this opening oracle the prophet announces a judgment which is about to sweep over the whole earth. Sabottka may be right in seeing a veiled reference to the flood story. Twice in vv 2-3 Zephaniah refers to the face of the ground. This reminds one of the threat in Gen 6:7; 7:4; 8:8. In Gen 8:21 the Lord says that he will "never again" (אֹסִיף) "curse the ground" (הָאֲדָמָה) "because of man." Jeremiah spoke of judgment in terms of creation reverting to chaos (4:23–26). All of Zephaniah is poetry with the exception of 1:1 and 2:10–11. Poetry uses exalted and extravagant languages and should not be pressed literally. The prophet is saying in vv 2–6 that God is about to bring judgment against the whole world, and that judgment will affect Judah and Jerusalem directly. Certain groups in Judah are identified as those on whom the judgment will come: "the stumbling blocks and the wicked" (v 3), the remnant of Baal and the idolatrous priests (v 4), those who worship the hosts of heaven and swear by Baal their king (v 5), those who have turned away from following Yahweh and are seeking other gods (v 6).

The expression "remnant of Baal" (v 4) does not necessarily suggest that only a remnant of the former followers of Baal were left. The LXX omits the word "remnant." Kapelrud believes that Zephaniah borrowed an oracle from Isa 14:22 about "Babel and his remnant" and used it against "Baal and his remnant" (p. 57).

Three specific groups in Judah are named as the objects of judgment: (1) those worshiping the hosts of heaven on roofs, (2) those who swear by Yahweh and by Baal, and (3) those who have turned aside from following Yahweh. The first group were those who worshiped the stars and the moon. Astral worship was common in Babylon and Canaan. It became very prevalent in Judah in the closing days of the monarchy (Deut 4:19; 2 Kings 21:3, 5; Jer 8:2; 19:13; 44:8–10, 16–19).

The second group were those whose religion was syncretistic. They worshiped Yahweh and Baal, even though this violated the first commandment and broke the covenant. The third group were those who no longer sought Yahweh or inquired of him. These two Hebrew words, בקשׁ "to seek," and דרשׁ "to inquire," are often used in a cultic context (Deut 4:29; Pss 9:11; 24:6). However, in Deuteronomy and the prophets the emphasis is always on seeking God with one's heart and not just observing some ritual (Deut 4:29; Amos 5:4–6; Jer 20:13).

An Announcement of the Day of Yahweh (1:7–2:3)

Bibliography

Gray, J. "A Metaphor from Building in Zeph 2:1." *VT* 3 (1953) 404–7. **Rainey, A. F.** "The Soldier-Scribe in Papyrus Anastasis I." *JNES* 26 (1967) 58–60. **Raitt, T. M.** "The Prophetic Summons to Repentance." *ZAW* 83 (1971) 30–49.

Translation

⁷ *Be silent before the Lord God!*
   Because the day of Yahweh is near,

4+4

because Yahweh has prepared a sacrifice	3+2
he has sanctified his guests. [a]	
[8] And it shall be in the day of Yahweh's sacrifice,	4
I will punish the princes	2+2
and the king's sons,	
and all those who are putting on	2+2
the clothing of the foreigner.	
[9] And I will punish everyone jumping	4+4
over the threshold [a] in that day,	
and those filling their Master's house	3+2
with violence and deceit.	
[10] And in that day, oracle of Yahweh, there shall be	4
the sound of a cry from the fish gate,	2+2+3
and a howling from the second quarter	
and a great crashing from the hills.	
[11] Howl, O inhabitants of Quarry,	3+4+3
for all the people of Canaan are destroyed;	
all the weighers of silver have been cut off.	
[12] And in that day	3+4
I will search Jerusalem with lamps,	
and I will punish men who are settled on their dregs;	4
the ones saying in their hearts,	2+3
"Yahweh will not do good or evil."	
[13] Their wealth shall be plundered	3+2
and their houses a desolation.	
They shall build houses	2+2
but not dwell in them.	
They shall plant vineyards	2+2
but not drink their wine.	
[14] The great day of Yahweh is near.	3+3
It is near and hurrying fast. [a]	
Hark, [b] the day of Yahweh is bitter. [c]	3+3
There [d] the mighty man gives the war-cry.	
[15] That day is a day of wrath,	2+2
a day of anguish and affliction,	
a day of storm and desolation,	2+2+2
a day of darkness and gloom,	
a day of clouds and thick darkness,	
[16] A day of trumpet and battle cry	2+2+2
over the fortified cities	
and the high towers. [a]	
[17] I will cause distress for men	2+2
and they shall walk like the blind,	
because they have sinned against Yahweh	3+3+2
their blood will be poured out as dust	
and their sap [a] of life as dung.	
[18] Neither their silver nor gold	2+2+3
will be able to save them	

> *in the day of the wrath of Yahweh.*
> *By the fire of his jealousy*   2+2
> *all the earth will be consumed,*
> *for he will make an end, yea a hasty* [a] *end will he make*   3+3
> *of all the inhabitants of the earth.*
> ²:¹ *Gather together and assemble,*   2+2
> *O shameless* [a] *nation,*
> ² *before the decree* [a] *takes effect,* [b]   3+3
> *like chaff a day passes,*
> *before "nothing"* [c] *comes upon you—*   3+2
> *the burning anger of Yahweh.*
> *before "nothing" comes upon you—*   3+2
> *the day of Yahweh's anger.*
> ³ *Seek Yahweh,*   2+2+3
> *all you humble of the earth,*
> *who carry out his ordinances.*
> *Seek righteousness, seek humility.*   4+2+2
> *Perhaps you may be hidden*
> *in the day of Yahweh's wrath.*

Notes

1.7.a. קְרֻאָיו qal. pass. pt. "his called ones."

1.9.a. מִפְתָּן may refer to the temple podium or terrace (cf. NEB).

1.14.a. V 14 is very difficult. מַהֵר is usually considered a piel inf. used as adv. "hurrying." New evidence from the Egyptian Papyrus Anastasi I, Ugaritic, Phoenician, and El Amarna suggests מהר was a Semitic term for soldier (cf. Rainey, *JNES* 26 [1967] 58–60).

1.14.b. קוֹל "voice" can be an interj. "hark" (cf. NEB, ICC, Isa 40:3, 6; *CHAL*, 315).

1.14.c. NEB, Gaster (683), BHS emend the text by dropping one letter and dividing the others differently.

1.14.d. שָׁם usually adv. "there." Sabottka, Dahood, Watts, consider it from Akkadian *summa* "behold," "see" (Dahood, *Psalms* I, 81).

1.16.a. פִּנּוֹת lit. "corners."

1.17.a. לַחְמָם noun לַח "sap of life." The final ם is enclitic.

1.18.a. נִבְהָלָה niph. pt., usually means "terrifying," here "hasty." "End" is not in the text.

2.1.a. נִכְסָף "shameless" niph. pt., lit. "not longed for." Watts translates, "nations that cared for nothing" (p. 164).

2.2.a. חֹק "decree." Watts and others take it as חֵיק "womb" which fits with the preceding word לדת "to be born."

2.2.b. NEB changes לדת חק "to give birth to a decree" to תרחקו "be sent far away."

2.2.c. לא is translated "nothing" by Watts and refers back to the idea expressed in 1:12, "the Lord will do nothing."

Form/Structure/Setting

The form of 1:7–2:3 is that of a judgment oracle made up of several small segments. Kapelrud and Sabottka believe that it was given in one speech by Zephaniah. Kapelrud identifies some phrases such as "in that day," or "in that time" in 1:8, 9, 10, 12 as being added by a disciple. But for the most part the whole passage (1:7–2:3) was delivered by Zephaniah on one occasion. Some scholars such as Gunkel and Wolff want to isolate the smallest unit of speech and see some redactor weaving them together. Kapelrud says, "Our interest is not directed towards finding the least, indissoluble elements of his message. Instead we want to see this message in its life situation, see what it meant and how it worked" (*Message* 29).

Concerning the idea that the prophet spoke only isolated and disjointed sentences Kapelrud remarks, "It is about time now to get rid of the picture of the prophet as some kind of a maniac, appearing on the temple square or the market place more or less in ecstasy, crying out a few words and then disappearing again. If we were to believe most of the literary analyses of the prophet's books, this is what would have appeared to have happened" (*Message* 29).

Even though 1:7–2:3 was probably all one speech, there are divisions within it. It has one dominating and unifying theme: "the day of Yahweh." It opens with an appeal for silence before the Lord God אֲדֹנָי יְהוִה (the only place the combined name occurs in the book). The appeal for silence is followed by a warning that the day of Yahweh is near. Although it will come on everyone, certain groups in Jerusalem will make up Yahweh's sacrifice: the princes and the king's sons; those who have adopted foreign customs and religions; and the indifferent and stagnant men (1:12). A fuller description of the day of Yahweh is given in 1:14–18. It will be a day of darkness, distress, and gloom. It will be a day of war, blaring trumpets and battle cries, bloodshed, helplessness and death. In 2:1–3 Zephaniah calls on his people to gather together and seek the Lord, but he has no word of assurance for them. He says, "Perhaps, if you seek righteousness and humility you may be hidden in the day of wrath" (2:3).

What is the setting of this oracle? Gaster may be correct in assuming that it was delivered at the temple in Jerusalem during the feast of harvest (âsif), but we should not consider Zephaniah a cultic prophet even though he used cultic language such as sacrifice, priests, "cut off," and so on (cf. Kapelrud, 51).

Comment

The oracle on the day of Yahweh begins with the word הַס, an interj. "hush." The word is used sparingly in the OT (Judg 3:19; Neh 8:11; Amos 6:10; 8:3; Hab 2:20; Zech 2:17). It is a call for silence in the presence of God. Judgment is imminent. The people of Judah are going to become like sacrificial lambs for God's invited guests (cf. 1 Sam 9:22; 2 Sam 15:11) who probably are the enemy armies. The reasons for judgment on the day of the Lord are: (1) the princes (officials) and the king's sons had adopted foreign customs and attire; (2) some had adopted foreign religions as evidenced by jumping over the threshold for fear of demons (1 Sam 5:5); and (3) some were filling their master's house with violence and deceit. The reference is to the king's palace and not the temple. The charge is not that the palace is being used as a storage place for stolen goods, nor that the royal treasury is being enriched by fraud and oppression; but that the conduct and character of the king's sons are a symbol and synonym for all that is bad. Violence and deceit left unchecked will bring down any government.

Various sections and groups in the city will bear the brunt of the attack. The fish gate was probably the main gate on the north side of the city. Attacks on Jerusalem always came from the north. The second quarter of the city was the new city, an addition to the original city. The hills may refer to a suburb outside the city toward the north. The quarry or lower town was probably on the south edge of the city, representing the opposite side geographically. It too would experience destruction. The merchants (the people of Canaan) would be cut off. The term Canaanite often denoted a trader or merchant (Hos 12:8; Isa 23:8; Ezek 16:29; 17:4; Prov 31:24; Job 41:6 and perhaps Zech 14:21).

The day of Yahweh will reach every dark corner of the earth and the hidden recesses of men's minds and hearts. Yahweh will search (in piel) Jerusalem with lamps and will punish all who sit in a stupor over the dregs of their wine and say, "Yahweh will do nothing, good or bad" (v 12 NEB). The end result will be that the people's wealth will be plundered and their homes destroyed. Their dreams of a stable and prosperous life will be shattered (cf. Amos 5:11).

A new description of the day of Yahweh begins in 1:14. The first line is clear enough. It reiterates that the day is near (1:7). The next phrase וּמַהֵר מְאֹד is difficult. מַהֵר appears to be a piel inf. used as an adv. "hurrying." מְאֹד is an adv. "exceedingly." The phrase has traditionally been read "hastening fast." But that is a loose translation of the Hebrew and seemingly a needless repetition of the first line. In recent years the semitic word מֶהֶר has been found in the Egyptian Papyrus Anastasi I and in Akkadian, Ugaritic, Phoenician, Greek and Latin sources meaning, "soldier" (cf. Rainey, *JNES* 26 [1967] 60). Sabottka, following Dahood, argues that מְאֹד should be read מָאֹד "grand" (cf. Dahood, *Psalms III.* AB. Garden City, NY: Doubleday, 1970. xxvi). The conj. ו on מהר, according to Sabottka, is emphatic so he translates וּמַהֵר מְאֹד "the grand hero himself" (*Zephanja*, 50).

The last part of 1:14 is as difficult as the first. The first phrase קוֹל יוֹם יהוה, "the voice of the day of Yahweh," is unclear. Sabottka and Watts translate it, "the noise of the day of Yahweh," which is clearer but stretches the meaning of קוֹל. Line 2 of v 14 קוֹל יוֹם יהוה מַר צֹרֵחַ שָׁם גִּבּוֹר is usually translated "the sound of the day of Yahweh is bitter, the one crying there is the hero." The meaning of such a statement is very ambiguous. Many emendations have been suggested. By changing the ר in צרח to a ל and making a new word division, BHS reads קל יום יהוה מרץ וחש מגבור "swifter than a runner and speedier than a hero is the day of Yahweh." NEB adopts this reading but changes the last word from גבור "hero" to גדוד "raiding party." Sabottka and Watts translate קוֹל "noise" and מר "strong" or "overpowering" rather than "bitter" to get the reading, "the noise of the day of Yahweh is overpowering."

The day of Yahweh is a major motif in Zephaniah. He was not the first or last to use the term. Amos was probably the first prophet to use the term and Zephaniah shows signs of being familiar with Amos' prophecies. Amos and Zephaniah both used the term הַס "hush" in referring to the day. Amos uses the words חשׁך "darkness" (5:18, 20), אפל "gloom" (5:20), and מר "bitter" (8:10) to describe the day. Amos did not speak of the day as קרוֹב

"near." Isaiah was possibly the first to use the term קָרֹוב in connection
with the day of Yahweh (13:6, cf. Kapelrud, 61–62). But after Zephaniah
others use it (Ezek 7:7; 30:3; Joel 1:15; Obad 15).

The language in Zeph 1:15–18 is cultic language combined with that of
holy war. Yahweh is pictured as a warrior who is coming to destroy his people
and to judge the world. George Adam Smith said that in Zephaniah we have
the first tinge of apocalypticism. The expression "a day of clouds and deep
darkness" are words that were used to describe an appearance of God (theophany) (Exod 19:16; 20:21; Deut 4:11). Zephaniah combines these words
of revelation with the words for war ("trumpet," "battle cry," "fortified cities")
to describe the day of Yahweh.

A new sub-section begins with v 17. It is a speech of Yahweh in which
all of the earth is included in the day of Yahweh (v 18). This universal element
takes us back to the opening verses of the chapter where God is about to
sweep away all flesh. Some scholars such as Gerleman, Elliger and Fohrer
believe that the universal elements are not the work of Zephaniah, but Kapelrud defends this section for Zephaniah by pointing out that the next chapter
leaves no doubt that the prophet expected a destruction of peoples and cities
other than Judah and Jerusalem (*Message* 31).

Should 2:1–3 be included with 1:7–18 under the heading "the day of Yahweh" It certainly would seem so. Vv 2 and 3 use the phrase "the day of
the wrath of Yahweh." However, this pericope has special problems. V 1 is
very short and the language is very difficult. The imperatives הִתְקֹושְׁשׁוּ "gather
yourselves together," and וָקֹושּׁוּ "assemble" come from the root קֹשׁשׁ and
only occur here, once in the hithpolel and once in the qal. The meaning
must be derived from the other uses of the root in Exod 5:7, 12 about collect-
ing sticks.

Is this cultic language? It may be, but it is not the kind of cultic language
one finds in Joel 2:15–16.

The term וְנִכְסָף is a niph. pt. from כסף which means, "long for" in the
only other places it is used in the OT (Gen 31:30; Ps 84:3). Literally it means
here "not longed for," but it is usually translated "shameless" (RSV) or "un-
ruly" (NEB) from the meaning of the root in Aramaic. The LXX ἀπαίδευτον
"silly," "uninstructed," "unprofitable," reflects this interpretation. John Gray
proposes a change in the text from כסף to כפס and reads "without cohesion,"
but this is only a conjecture.

The first line in 2:2 is no easier than the previous one (see discussion in
the notes above). The prophet ironically says that that which you thought
was "nothing" will destroy you. The shameless nation is not identified in
the pericope. From v 3 we must assume that the reference is to Judah because
of the admonition to seek Yahweh and to seek righteousness.

V 3 is a call to repentance. There seems to be a promise or a hope that
the threat will be withdrawn. The call to seek Yahweh is addressed to the
humble and righteous—those who do his ordinances. The word אוּלַי "perhaps" speaks volumes. The prophet would not presume on the prerogative
of Yahweh to determine who would or would not be hidden. Zephaniah,
like Amos (cf. 5:15), knew that not even righteousness nor humility could
guarantee a person's safety. That was all in the hand of Yahweh.

Should v 4 be included in this pericope? RSV and NEB include v 4 in this section because of the conjunction כִּי. It is a transition verse connecting the idea of the day of Yahweh with the oracles against the foreign nations.

Oracles against the Nations   (2:4–15)

Bibliography

Kselman, J. S. "A Note on Jer 49:20 and Zeph 2:6–7." *CBQ* 32 (1970) 579–81. **Thomas, D. W.** "A Pun on the Name Ashdod in Zeph 2:4." *ExpTim* 74 (1962/63) 63.

Translation

Oracle against Philistia 2:4–7

[4] *Yes, indeed,*[a] *Gaza shall be forsaken*	3+2
and Ashkelon desolate.	
At noon Ashdod shall be driven out	3+2
and Ekron shall be uprooted.	
[5] *Woe, you dwellers on the border of the sea,*	3+2
nation of the Cherethites,	
The word of Yahweh is against you,	2+3+3
O Canaan,[a] *land of the Philistines,*	
I will cause you to perish without an inhabitant.	
[6] *And the border of the sea shall become*	3+3+2
pastures, meadows of shepherds	
and folds for sheep.	
[7] *And the border shall be*	2+3+2
for the remnant of the house of Judah,	
their young[a] *shall feed.*	
On the estates[b] *of Ashkelon,*	2+2
they will lie down in the evening,	
because Yahweh their God will visit them	4+2
and restore their fortunes.	

Oracle against Moab and Ammon 2:8–11

[8] *I heard the insult of Moab*	3+2
and the revilings of the sons of Ammon,	
how they reproached my people	3+2
and enlarged[a] *their borders.*	
[9] *Therefore, as I live, oracle of Yahweh*	
of hosts, God of Israel,	
Moab shall become like Sodom	3+3
and the sons of Ammon like Gomorrah,	
a pile of weed,	2+2+2
a pit of salt,	
and a desolation forever.	

A remnant of my people shall plunder them,   3+3
and the remainder of my nation shall disinherit them.

10 *Shame* [a] *to them instead of pride,*   4+3+3
    because they insulted and grew great
    against the people of Yahweh of hosts.

11 *Yahweh will come upon them with terror*   3+2+3
    because he weakened [a]
all the gods of the earth
and every man will worship him   3+3
    from his place among the islands [b] *of the nations.*

Oracle against Ethiopia 2:12

12 *You also, O Cushites,*   2+2
    they are [a] *pierced by my sword.*

Oracle against Assyria 2:13–15

13 *He will stretch out his hand over the north*   3+2
    and will cause Assyria to perish.
And he will make Nineveh   3+2
    a desolation as dry as a desert.

14 *Herds shall lie down in her,*   3+2
    all the beasts [a] *of the field.* [b]
Also the vulture, [c] *also the owl* [d]   2+2
    shall roost on her capitals.
The owl shall hoot in the window,   3+2+3
    desolation [e] *on the porch,*
    for he will lay bare her cedar [f] *paneling.*

15 *This is the exultant city,*   3+2
    the one dwelling securely,
the one saying in her heart,   2+2
    I am and there is no one else.
Again what a desolation she is,   3+2
    a haunt for beasts.
Everyone passing her   3+2
    shall whistle and shake his fist. [a]

Notes

4.a. Emphatic כִּי "yes, indeed."

5.a. כְּנַעַן "Canaan" is strange in reference to the Philistines. Many read אכנעך "I will subdue you" (cf. NEB).

7.a. עֲלֵיהֶם "upon them." Kselman (579–81) suggests pointing עֲלֵיהֶם or עָלִיהֶם from עוּל "give suck" (BDB 732; cf. 1 Sam 6:7, 10; also in Jer 49:20; 50:45).

7.b. Lit. "houses of."

8.a. וַיַּגְדִּילוּ hiph. of גדל means "to make great" or "to enlarge" their borders as in Amos 1:13; Jer 49:1.

10.a. וֹ את normally a demonstrative "this," but Dahood (*Psalms* I. AB. [Garden City, NY: Doubleday, 1966] 42) and Sabottka (89) argue for a substantive "shame" and cite other examples in Deut 32:6; Ps 7:4; 44:18; 74:18; Job 2:11; 17:8; Mal 2:13.

11.a. רָזָה is difficult. It is a hapax. The basic meaning seems to be "to shrink away."

11.b. אִיֵּי "Islands" can mean "jackals" which represent "ghosts" or "demons" (cf. Watts, 171).

12.a. הֵמָּה is a 3 mas. pl. pro. Sabottka takes it as הִגֵּה "behold" (p. 94).

14.a. חַיָתוֹ old cst. form of חַיָה; the וֹ is not a suf.

14.b. גּוֹי "nation" should be גִּיא "valley" or "field." James Barr (*Comparative Philology*, 144, 324) says "nation" and "field" are homonyms.

14.c&d. קָאַת and קִפּד are unusual words probably referring to different kinds of owls.

14.e. חֹרֶב "desolation." LXX (Vg) κόρακες "raven" = עֹרֵב.

14.f. The last three Hebrew words are often omitted as a dittography (cf. Kapelrud, 34).

15.a. יָדוֹ "his hand."

Form/Structure/Setting

This section 2:4–15 is made up of a series of oracles against foreign nations. All eighth and seventh century writing prophets except Hosea have sections on foreign nations. In form these oracles are similar to the judgment oracles on Israel because they announce judgment on the nations. However, Westermann (*Basic Forms of Prophetic Speech*, trans. J. C. White [Philadelphia: Westminster Press, 1967] 205) says that they belong in the line of salvation-speeches because they imply salvation for Israel in the light of the situation in which they were uttered.

These four oracles are not the same in form or length. They are mostly poetry but 2:10–11 is prose. Sometimes the prophet speaks, sometimes Yahweh, and once Assyria speaks (2:15). The oracle on Philistia is an announcement of judgment on the coastlands of Philistia, but the remnant of Judah will eventually occupy their territory (2:7). Moab and Ammon on the east side of Israel reviled Israel and encroached on her territory (2:8), but a remnant of Judah will disinherit them. The oracle against Ethiopia to the south is very brief. The oracle against Assyria is an oracle of judgment. God will stretch out his hand (as in Isa 5:25; 9:12, 17, 21; 10:4) and Assyria will perish. Nineveh will become a desert and a habitat for all kinds of wild beasts and vultures.

The prophets sometimes use puns or plays on words. Isaiah said, "Yahweh looked for 'justice' (מִשְׁפָּט) and behold 'bloodshed' (מִשְׂפָּח), for 'righteousness' (צְדָקָה) and behold 'a cry' " (צְעָקָה) (5:7). Amos' vision of the "summer fruit" (קָיִץ) suggested the "end" (קֵץ) for Israel (8:2). Zephaniah used similar sounding words to announce judgment on Gaza and Ekron (2:4). Gaza (עַזָּה) will be "forsaken" (עֲזוּבָה) and Ekron (עֶקְרוֹן) will be "uprooted" (תֵּעָקֵר). D. Winton Thomas believes there may be a play on the names of the other two city names (Ashkelon and Ashdod) in this verse. Ashkelon is similar in sound to the word for "waste." But Thomas sees a closer similarity between Ashdod and another word שׁדד which he takes to mean "expel," "eject," "drive out."

Comment

Judgment against Judah's neighbors is the major motif of this section. Philistia on the west, Moab and Ammon on the east, Ethiopia or Egypt on the south, and Assyria to the north will all experience the judgment of Yahweh. Even though Judah's near neighbors were infringing on her borders, she

(Judah) would eventually dispossess them. Nothing is said about Israel possessing the land of Assyria. Ethiopian Pharaohs ruled Egypt during the twenty-fifth dynasty (ca. 716–663 B.C.). This dynasty was already off the scene by Zephaniah's time. This raised a question about the date of the oracle against Ethiopia.

The time of the destruction of Nineveh is still in the future in 2:13–15. Therefore the oracle must be before 612 B.C. If that is the case those who hold a date for this material to be during the days of Jehoiakim (609–597 B.C.) have a problem. Hyatt suggests that this is "a prophecy after the event" (*Zephanja* 641).

The expression וְשָׁב שְׁבוּתָם "and he will restore their fortune" (2:7) is an eschatological term which has been widely debated. The expression occurs in Deuteronomy, Job, Psalms, and the Prophets in slightly different forms (Deut 30:3; Job 42:10; Pss 14:7; 53:7; 85:2; 126:1; Jer 29:14; 30:3, 18; 31:22, 23; 32:44; 33:7, 11, 26; 48:47; 49:6, 39; Ezek 16:53; 29:14; 34:16; 39:25; Hos 6:11; Joel 4:1; Amos 9:14; Zeph 2:7; 3:20). The MT takes שבותם from the root שבית "captivity." The traditional translation of שב שבותם was "turn the captivity." This view takes the phrase as a reference to the return from Babylonian exile. But it is obvious in passages like Job 42:10; Ps 85; 126; Ezek 16:53 that the reference is not to a return from captivity. Mowinckel believes that the term was used in the enthronement festival as Yahweh comes to restore the right order (cf. *The Psalms in Israel's Worship*, trans. D. R. Thomas [Oxford: Blackwell, 1962] I, 146–47; II, 249–50; E. Jacob. *Theology of the OT*, trans. A. Heathcote and J. Allcock [New York: Harper, 1958] 320). A. R. Johnson argues that the root of שבות is not שבה "to take captive" or שוב "to return" but שבת "to be firm," "at rest" and translates the phrase "to restore one's well-being or confidence." He points out that the Arabic root of this word is used of the Christian rite of "confirmation" (*The Cultic Prophet in Ancient Israel* [Cardiff: University of Wales Press, 1944] 67 n.4).

Explanation

Oracles against foreign nations seem to be an important element in OT prophecy. These oracles were not spoken or written for the benefit or response of the nations. The message was directed primarily to Israel or Judah. They emphasize Yahweh's sovereignty over the nations and the nation's responsibility and accountability to Yahweh. Often some reference to Israel or Judah is made in the oracle. Two of these oracles indicate that the foreign nations (Philistia, Moab, and Ammon) will be disposed of and Israel occupy their land.

Judgment on Jerusalem (3:1–5)

Translation

[1] *Woe, O obstinate,*[a] *impure*[b]   3+2
oppressive city.

² *She obeyed no voice;*   2+2
   she accepted no discipline;
she does not trust Yahweh   2+2
   nor come near her God.
³ *Her princes within her*   3+2
   are roaring lions.
Her judges are evening wolves,   3+3
   *They leave nothing to gnaw on in the morning.*ª
⁴ *Her prophets are insolent,*   2+2
   treacherous men.
Her priests profane the holy place;   3+2
   they do violence to the law.
⁵ *Yahweh is righteous in the midst of her,*   3+2
   he does no wrong.
Morning by morning   2+2
   he gives his judgment.
At the sunrise ª *he does not fail,*   2+3
   *but the evil-doer knows no shame.*ᵇ

Notes

1.a. מראה fem. qal act. pt. מרא or מרה "obstinate" (cf. *Chal*, 213).

1.b. וְנִגְאָלָה nif. pt. גאל "become impure" in niph. (cf. Barr, *Comparative Philology* 148).

3.a. יגמו appears to be 3rd com pl. qal pf. גרם, but the meaning is very uncertain. גרם only occurs two other times in the OT (Num 24:8; Ezek 23:34). It seems to mean "to crush," "crunch," or "gnaw." Judges, as evening wolves, devour their victims' bones before morning.

5.a. לָאוֹר lit. "to the light." Here the context suggests "light of the new day."

5.b. NEB omits the last three Hebrew words because the meaning is unclear (cf. *Comment* below).

Form/Structure/Setting

This pericope is a woe oracle of judgment on Jerusalem. V 1 addresses the city (presumably Jerusalem) as obstinate, impure, and violent. Vv 2–4 accuse the people and leaders of faithlessness and oppression. In contrast to the unfaithfulness of the people, God's faithfulness is like the sunrise. The limits of the passage are hard to determine. Vv 6–8 could be a part of the passage if an oracle of judgment on the nations can be included with one on Jerusalem. We did that in 1:2–6 but the connection was more obvious there. There seems to be a definite break between 3:5 and 3:6. In 3:1–5 the prophet speaks to Jerusalem; in 3:6–8 Yahweh speaks about his judgment on the nations.

Comment

The prophet turns from Nineveh to Jerusalem. In fact the epithets in 3:1 fit both cities. Even though Jerusalem is not named, references to prophets, priests, Torah and instructions of Yahweh in 3:2–4 make it clear that the oracle is addressed to Jerusalem. She does not hear or obey. She does not receive instruction or discipline. מוּסָר is a wisdom word. She is foolish in her conduct. She does not trust her God nor come near to worship him. Her officials (princes, judges, prophets, and priests) are greedy, profane, treacherous men. But Yahweh is righteous, that is, he is true to his covenant. He does no wrong. God's justice is compared to the light, suggesting that it is positive and pure in contrast to the activities of the judges who carry on their foul actions during the night. ולא־יודע עול בשת is a very difficult phrase. It may be read in various ways. NEB prefers not to translate it at all. Sabottka takes בשת as a paraphrase for Baal, changes the word order, and reads, "doch der Schandgott erkennt nicht den Frevler" (yet the shameful god does not recognize the offender). Kapelrud (107) cannot decide whether this line is a dittography or not, so he puts his translation in parenthesis ("but the unjust does not know shame").

Explanation

In 2:4–15 Zephaniah described God's judgment on the foreign nations. Now he turns to Judah. She is as guilty as the nations and will not escape God's judgment (3:5). Judah's sins are even more heinous than those of the nations because God had spoken to her in a special way. He had tried to teach her but she rebelled. She did not trust her God or worship him (v 2). Her leaders had violated the basic principles of their offices. Her political leaders, "princes" who were supposed to care for the people, had devoured them like a lion. Her judicial leaders, who were to administer justice, spent their nights gnawing the bones of the people. Her prophets, who were to declare faithfully the word of God, were insolent or reckless with the truth. They were false prophets who spoke the message the people wanted to hear (Mic 2:11). Her priests who were to teach the people how to distinguish between the clean and the unclean, between the holy and the common (Lev 10:10–11) have profaned, i.e., made common the holy things. Nothing was sacred anymore.

But Yahweh was still in her midst and he is righteous. He does no wrong. In contrast to the wicked judges who prowl all night, Yahweh, morning by morning, brings to light his judgment. "Morning by morning" suggests the dependability of Yahweh. His conduct is as regular as the sunrise. Hosea said, "His going forth is as sure as the dawn" (Hos 6:3). The writer of Lamentations said,

> *"The steadfast love of the Lord never ceases,*
> *his mercies never come to an end;*
> *they are new every morning;*
> *great is thy faithfulness"* (Lam 3:22–23 RSV).

Judgment on the Nations   (3:6–8)

Translation

6 *I cut off nations,* [a]	2+2
their corner towers were destroyed.	
I made their streets a desert	2+2
with no one passing by.	
Devastated [b] *are their cities;*	2+3
without a man, without inhabitant.	
7 *I said, "Only fear me,*	3+2
receive instruction,	
that her dwelling place [a] *not be cut off*	3+3
from all that I have planned [b] *for her.*	
Nevertheless, they rose up early	3+2
and corrupted all their deeds.	
8 *Therefore, wait* [a] *for me, oracle of Yahweh,*	3+3
for the day when I arise as a witness. [b]	
Because it is my decision [c] *to gather nations,*	3+2
to collect kingdoms,	
to pour out upon them my fierce anger,	3+3
all the heat of my anger,	
because with fire of my jealousy	3
all the earth shall be devoured.	

Notes

6.a. NEB and others read גֵּאִים "proud" (following LXX) instead of גֵּים "nations."

6.b. נִצְדּוּ is a hapax possibly, 3rd c pl. niph. pf. צדה II (*CHAL*, 303).

7.a. Some read מְעִינָהּ "her eyes," for מְעוֹנָהּ "her dwelling place" following LXX; cf. RSV "she will not lose sight."

7.b. This is an unusual use of פקד "planned."

8.a. חַכּוּ 2nd mas. pl. piel impv. חכה

8.b. לְעֵד "for a witness" rather than לְעַד "for a prey" following LXX.

8.c. משפט is usually translated "justice" or "judgment." Here it refers to Yahweh's judicial decision to act in judgment.

Form/Structure/Setting

An oracle of judgment. A progression of thought can be detected in 3:6–8. First there is a reminder of how God acted in history to bring judgment on the nations at the exodus and conquest (cf. Amos 2:9; Micah 6:5). Second, there is a call for Jerusalem to worship ("fear") Yahweh and accept his discipline (v 7a). Third, there is a warning or an expression of hope that Israel would fear Yahweh so that he would not have to punish her (v 7b). Fourth, there is the acknowledgment that Israel refused to "fear" Yahweh, but lost no time in corrupting themselves (v 7c). Finally there is Yahweh's decision to gather the nations perhaps including Israel or Judah and pour out his fierce anger on the whole world (3:8).

Comment

One could make a case for dividing chap. 3 in various ways. 3:6–8 seems to be a logical division (cf. Kapelrud and Watts). Yahweh speaks abruptly in the first person without introduction reminding his people of the judgment he had already brought against the nations, thinking that Israel might be persuaded to worship him and accept his discipline. But the reminder only accelerated their self corruption. Therefore Yahweh had no choice. He would initiate world judgment.

Explanation

The nations in v 6 are not identified. The reference may be to the Canaanites and the other inhabitants of the land that Yahweh cut off before Israel when she came into the land (Amos 2:9; Mic 6:5). NEB follows the LXX and reads "the proud," but "the nations" is the focus of the entire verse. Yahweh points out that the desolation is so complete that their defensive "corners" (cf. 1:16) are in ruins, their streets are empty, their cities are devastated, without an inhabitant (cf. Isa 5:9; 6:11; Jer 2:15; 4:7; 9:11; 26:9; 33:10; 34:22; 46:19; 51:29, 37). Nothing but "ghost towns" were left of the "nations." Such judgments on the nations should have caused Judah to fear the Lord, but it seems only to spur her on to sin more and more. The word for "deeds" may refer to good or bad actions but frequently the word has an evil connotation (cf. 3:11; Ezek 14:22, 23; 20:43–44; 21:29; 24:14; 36:17, 19). Unquestionably the deeds of the nations here were corrupt.

Therefore Yahweh says, "Wait for me." The command is a 2nd mas. pl. piel imperative seemingly addressed to the nations. But the transition between vv 7 and 8 may be so rough that those being addressed are not the nations but the pious remnant in Judah (cf. Taylor, 1030; S. R. Driver, 134). *JB* says, "Expect me." Yahweh is a witness against the sinners. He is also the judge. He has decided to gather the nations together to pour out his fierce wrath upon them (cf. Joel 3:2, 12, 14). This language comes very close to being apocalyptic.

A Great Change Coming (3:9–13)

Translation

A Change for the Peoples 3:9–10

[9] *Yes, then I will give* [a] *the peoples*	3+2
a pure lip, [b]	
to call, all of them, on the name of Yahweh,	3+3
to serve him with one shoulder.	

¹⁰ *From beyond the rivers of Ethiopia*   3+2+2
my suppliants,^a *my scattered* ^b *ones,*
shall bring my offering.

A Change for Jerusalem 3:11–13

¹¹ *On that day, you shall not be*   2+4+3
ashamed for all your deeds
by which you rebelled against me.
Because then I will clear away from your midst   3+2
your haughty exultant ones.
And you shall never again be haughty   3+2
in my holy mountain.
¹² *But I will leave in your midst*   2+3+3
a people afflicted and poor.
who will seek refuge in the name of Yahweh.
¹³ *The remnant of Israel*   2+2+2
shall do no wrong
and shall speak no lies.
No tongue of deceit shall be found   2+2
in their mouth;
but they shall feed and lie down,   3+2
and nothing shall startle them.

Notes

9.a. הפך means "to turn," "change," "overturn." It expressed a sudden change (cf. Amos 4:11; 5:7; 6:12; 8:10; Jer 13:23; 23:36; 31:13).
9.b. שפה lit. "lip," here means "language" (Gen 11:1).
10.a. עֶתְרִי supposedly is a noun from the root עתר "to pray," or "plead." The noun עתר means "fragrance" the only other time it is used in the OT.
10.b. בַּת פוּצַי lit. "daughter of my scattered ones." This phrase is very difficult to understand (cf. comment below).

Form/Structure/Setting

This is a promise of salvation both for the peoples vv 9–10 and the people of Israel (11–13). Israel seems to be addressed in both parts. In vv 9–10 Israel is told that the language of the peoples of the world will be purified (it was corrupted in Gen 11). They will call on the name of the Lord and worship him as one people. People from a distant land (Cush) shall offer sacrifice to Yahweh. Israel herself will be cleansed of the proud, arrogant, rebellious element. This remnant of the humble, trusting Israelites will do no wrong, speak no lies, and will dwell in peace and security (vv 11–13).

Comment

Various scholars have questioned the unity and date of this passage. C. Taylor (*IB* 6, 1031) says, "Another spirit, more kindly and less grim, breathes through these two (9–10) verses." But there is no evidence that requires an author other than Zephaniah or his disciples. The basic ideas of the passage fit well into Zephaniah's times. Zephaniah was probably familiar with the Yahwist's account of the tower of Babel (Gen 11). Gen 11:1 says that all the earth had "one lip," that is "one language" (שָׂפָה). The prophet Isaiah had said that his lips (שְׂפָתִים) were "unclean" (טמא), a cultic term. Zephaniah seems to have combined the ideas in Gen 11 and Isa 6 and looked for a time when all of the uncleanness and impurity on the lips of the peoples of the world would be removed and they would come to worship Yahweh with one accord. The "scattered ones" (בַּת פוּצַי) in v 4 may be an addition to the text. Its meaning is obscure. The word "daughter" (בַת) does not fit the context. "My scattered ones" (פוּצַי) could refer to the scattered Israelites or to the scattered nations (Gen 11). Probably the latter. Sabottka and Kapelrud follow Dahood who reads בַּת "woven garment" (cf. 2 Kgs 23:7) and בוּצִי instead of פוּצַי because ב and פ were interchangeable in some Hebrew, Ugaritic and Phoenician texts. בּוּץ is used in Ezek 27:16 for a costly fine white linen. So בת בוצי could refer to "linen garment" brought as a gift.

But the idea of the scattered ones seems to be in line with the first part of v 9 which speaks of the change in the nations. The change will include the conversion of the nations and the renewal and purification of the remnant of Jerusalem.

In 2:3 Zephaniah had called for the poor and humble to seek the Lord, suggesting that they might be hidden on the day of the Lord's wrath. Now in 3:11–12 he promises that in the new age there will be no haughty or proud people left in the kingdom of God, only the afflicted and poor. It is true that "the poor" or "the poor in spirit" took on eschatological significance during the last days of the OT period. Words for the "poor" and "the oppressed" occur often in the Qumran texts as designations for the pious (cf. H. Ringgren. *The Faith of Qumran.* Trans. E. T. Sanders [Philadelphia: Fortress Press, 1963] 141). Jesus made the poor the subject of his first beatitude (Matt 5:3; Luke 6:20). Although the idea of God saving only the humble is magnified in the post OT era, the concept is an old one. It is found in the psalms and prophets (Pss 22:27 [Eng. 26]; 25:9; 34:3 [Eng. 2]; 37:11; 69:34 [Eng. 33]; 147:6; 149:4; Amos 2:7; 8:4; Isa 11:4; 29:19; 32:7; 61:1), some of which are older than Zephaniah.

A New Song   (3:14–20)

Bibliography

Lowenstamm, S. E. "The Hebrew Root *hrš* in the Light of the Ugaritic Texts." *JJS* 10 (1959) 63–65.

Translation

14 *Sing, daughter of Zion:*   4+4+2
    Shout, Israel;
  Rejoice and exult with all your heart,
  daughter of Jerusalem.

¹⁵ Yahweh has removed your judgments.^a　　　　　　　　3+2
　　He turned aside your enemy.
　　The king of Israel, Yahweh, is in your midst.　　　　　　4+3
　　You shall not fear evil ever again.
¹⁶ In that day　　　　　　　　　　　　　　　　　　　2+2
　　it shall be said to Jerusalem,
　　Fear not, Zion,　　　　　　　　　　　　　　　　　2+2
　　let not your hands be slack.
¹⁷ Yahweh your God is in your midst.　　　　　　　　　3+2
　　A hero—he will deliver.
　　He will rejoice over you with joy.　　　　　　　　　3+2+3
　　He will rest ^a in his love.
　　He will rejoice over you with singing.
¹⁸ Those who went away ^a from the festival I have swept away ^b from you.　4+4
　　They were heaping disgrace upon her.
¹⁹ Behold, I am about to deal with all of your afflictors.　　3+2
　　In that time,
　　I will save the lame,　　　　　　　　　　　　　2+2
　　And the outcast I will gather.
　　And I will give them praise and fame　　　　　　　3+2
　　whose shame has been in all the earth.
²⁰ In that time I will bring you in,　　　　　　　　　4+3
　　and in the time that I gather you,
　　because I will give you a name and a praise　　　　　4+2
　　among all peoples of the earth,
　　When I change your fortune before your eyes,　　　3+2
　　says Yahweh.

Notes

15.a. NEB and others read משפטיך "your adversaries," as a piel or poel part. as Job 9:15 (55b).

17.a. יחריש is a very difficult form to understand here. חרש normally means "to plough," or "engrave." A second meaning seems to be "to be silent." Neither of these meanings seem to fit the context. Sabottka and Kapelrud point to another meaning of the root in Ugaritic, "to compose" (cf. Dahood, *Psalms* I, 270; Lowenstamm, *JJS* 10 [1959] 63–65). RSV changes חרש to חדש "to renew," which is a viable option. F. C. Eiselen suggests transposing two letters רחש "to overflow" which is also a good possibility. Perhaps the best interpretation is to take the second meaning of "silent" in the sense of "rest" in his love.

18.a. נוגי is a very difficult form. Traditionally it has been read as a mas. pl. niph. part. of יבה "afflicted ones" (cf. Lam 1:4). The root seems to mean "carry off" in the hif. in 2 Sam 20:13. If it had that meaning in the niph. it could mean, "those carried off." Watts, Sabottka, and Kapelrud, on the basis of Ugaritic, read "have gone away." RSV and *CHAL* (230) change נוגי ממועד to כיום מועד "as the day of the feast." NEB follows LXX and reads כימי מעד "as in days long ago" and assigns it to end of v 17.

18.b. אספתי usually means "I gathered." Kapelrud takes it to be from the root סוף "to sweep away." That seems to be appropriate in the light of 1:2–3.

Form/Structure/Setting

This pericope is not an enthronement song but it has the structure and vocabulary similar to the enthronement Psalms (47; 95; 97). It is an oracle

of salvation probably delivered during the New Year festival, on the enthronement day. The call to singing, the victory over the enemies, the presence
of Yahweh as king in their midst are all motifs common to the enthronement
festival. Many scholars have considered all or parts of vv 14–20 as postexilic
because of the references to the gathering of the exiles (vv 19–20). Some
consider the passage late because they consider the enthronement festival
to be a post-exilic festival. Westermann calls these psalms, "eschatological
Songs of Praise." He lists as examples of the type, Isa 12:4–6; 52:9–10; Jer
20:13; 31:7; Joel 2:21; Nah 2:1, 3a [Eng. 1:15; 2:2]; Zeph 3:14–15; Zech 2:4;
9:9–10. Then he says, "It cannot be asserted that any of these passages are
preexilic in origin. In the passages in Jeremiah, Nahum and Zephaniah we
are dealing with later additions, as in Isa 12" (*The Praise of God in the Psalms,*
144–45).

But Kapelrud says that there is a misinterpretation behind the rejection
of the passage as non-Zephanian. Kapelrud (*Message,* 89) believes that the
prophet has already advanced his setting into the future when only a remnant
of the humble purified ones will survive, and in spirit addresses the words
of praise and promise in vv 14–20 to them.

The structure of the passage includes: (1) imperatives to sing, shout, and
rejoice addressed to the daughter of Zion, Israel, and the daughter of Jerusalem. Israel is included because future hope for the nation always included
the undivided kingdom (v 14); (2) a statement that Yahweh reigns as king
and has cast out all of the enemies (v 14); (3) an assurance that Yahweh is in
their midst, therefore they should not fear (v 16); (4) an announcement that
Yahweh is victorious and loves his people (v 17); and (5) a promise that
the lame and the outcasts will be brought back home to live in peace and
security. That will be done in their lifetime "before your eyes" (vv 18–20).

Comment

One can imagine the prophet Zephaniah in Jerusalem during the fall enthronement festival preaching in the court of the temple. He had already
preached his message of doom about the imminent day of Yahweh. He had
probably used the term אֹסֵף as a play on words to emphasize God was
about to sweep away all sinners from the earth. Now at the end of his message
he counterbalances his message of doom with a message of hope (3:14–20).
Kapelrud (*Message,* 90) notes that it is a psychological error on the part of
modern scholars who do not understand the need for such a counterbalance.
The kind of message which the day of Yahweh represents was not easy to
accept. The people might have rejected it completely if it had not been accompanied by the promise of hope and restoration after the destruction. There
were enemies to fear. Their hands were hanging down (v 16; cf. 2 Sam 4:1;
Isa 13:7; Jer 6:24; 50:43; Ezek 7:17; 21:12; 2 Chr 15:7; Heb 12:12). Zephaniah
leaves no room to doubt that there would be a new day when fear would
be cast out and shame changed to praise and fame. This would happen according to Zephaniah in the near future, "before your eyes" (v 20). Because
Yahweh had changed the fortunes of his people before, he could and would
do it again.

Haggai

Introduction

Bibliography

Books

Ackroyd, P. R. "Haggai." *PCB*. London: Thomas Nelson and Sons, 1962. 643–45. **Benoit, P., Milik, J. T.,** and **de Vaux, R.** *Les Grottes De Murabba'at*. Oxford: The Clarendon Press, 1961. 50, 203–4. **Beuken, W. A. M.** *Haggai-Sacharja 1–8*. Assen: Van Gorcum an Co., 1967. **Beyse, K. M.** *Serrubbabel und die königserwartungender Propheten Haggai und Sacharja*. Stuttgart: Calver, 1972. **Coggins, R. J.** *Samaritans and Jews*. Atlanta: John Knox Press, 1975. 45–56. **Hanson, P. D.** *The Dawn of Apocalyptic*. Philadelphia: Fortress Press, 1975. 173–75, 245–50. **Johnson A. R.** *The Vitality of the Individual in the Thought of Ancient Israel*. Cardiff: Univ. of Wales Press, 1949. 25–6. **Matthews, I. G.** "Haggai." *An American Commentary*. Philadelphia: The American Baptist Publication Society, 1935. **Parker, R. A.** and **W. H. Dubberstein.** *Babylonian Chronology 626 B.C.–A.D. 45*. Chicago: University of Chicago Press, 1946. **Rad, G. von.** *The Problem of the Hexateuch*. Edinburgh: Oliver and Boyd, 1966. 232–42. **Thomas, D. W.** "The Book of Haggai." *IB*. 6. Nashville: Abingdon Press, 1956. 1037–49. **Wolff, R.** *Book of Haggai: A Study Manual*. Grand Rapids: Baker, 1967.

Articles

Ackroyd, P. R. "Studies in the Book of Haggai." *JSS* 2 (1951) 163–75. ———. "Studies in the Book of Haggai." *JSS* 3 (1952) 1–13. ———. "The Book of Haggai and Zechariah I–VIII." *JSS* 3 (1952) 151–56. ———. "Some Interpretative Glosses in the Book of Haggai." *JJS* 7 (1956) 163–168. ———. "Two Historical Problems of the Early Persian Period." *JNES* 17 (1958) 13–22, 23–27. **Bloomhardt, P. F.** "The Poems of Haggai." *HUCA* 5 (1928) 153–95. **Bruce, F. F.** "The Earliest Old Testament Interpretation." *Oudtestamentische Studien* 17 (1972) 38–89 No. 3. **Budde, K.** "Zum Text der drei letzten kleinen Propheten." *ZAW* 26 (1906) 1–28. **Cook, S. A.** "The Age of Zerubbabel." *Studies in Old Testament Prophecy Presented to T. H. Robinson*. Ed. by H. H. Rowley. Edinburgh: T. & T. Clark, 1950. **Hamerton-Kelley, R. G.** "The Temple and the Origins of Jewish-Apocalyptic." *VT* 20 (1970) 12. **James, F.** "Thoughts on Haggai and Zechariah." *JBL* 53 (1934) 229–35. **Koch, K.** "Haggai's unreines Volk." *ZAW* 79 (1967) 52–66. **Loewe, R.** "The Earliest Allusions to Coined Money." *PEQ* 87 (1955) 141–50. **Mason, R. A.** "The Purpose of the Editorial Framework of the Book of Haggai." *VT* 27 (1977) 415–21. **North, F. S.** "Critical Analysis of the Book of Haggai." *ZAW* 79 (1967) 52–66. **Petersen, D. L.** "Zerubbabel and Jerusalem Temple Restoration." *CBQ* 36 (1974) 366–72. **Siebeneck, R. T.** "Messianism of Aggaeus and Proto-Zacharias." *CBQ* 19 (1957) 312–28. **Waterman, L.** "The Camouflaged Purge of Three Messianic Conspirators." *JNES* 13 (1954) 73–78. **Wolff, H. W.** "Die Begrundungen der prophetischen Heils- und Unheilsspruche." *ZAW* 52 (1934) 1–22.

The Prophet

There are only two references to Haggai in the Bible outside of his own book (Ezra 5:1; 6:14). Nothing is known about his age or his ancestry. He preached in Jerusalem for about four months in 520 B.C., but how he got there and whether or not he had been an exile in Babylon are moot questions. He is called "the prophet" in his book and in Ezra, a fact that might indicate the scarcity of prophets in his day. He is called the "messenger" or "angel" of Yahweh one time (1:13).

Some scholars have argued that Haggai was a priest, on the grounds that he appealed to the priest to answer a question on one occasion (2:11); that he was vitally interested in rebuilding the temple; and that his name was connected to some of the psalms in the ancient versions (LXX, 87, 145–148; Vul. 111, 145; Pesh. 125, 126, 145–148). Others have considered Haggai a layman, almost a super patriot. Paul Bloomhardt wrote, "There is more reason to regard him as a layman who was deeply interested in the political conditions of his time, especially the restoration of the political independence of his people, than as a priest" (HUCA 5 [1928] 154). According to Bloomhardt the rebuilding of the temple was advocated by Haggai for political reasons. The phrase "throne of the kingdoms" in 2:22 is a clear reference to the dominion of the Persian empire. The whole oracle in 2:21–23 breathes a spirit of revolution. 2:6 refers not to a physical catastrophe but to a religious and political upheaval in which battles are to be fought on land and sea HUCA 5 [1928] 166–170). Ackroyd rejects Bloomhardt's interpretation saying that it is too reminiscent of a formerly popular style of exegesis of the psalms, in which exact historical backgrounds are discovered, for it to be acceptable today. "In particular the allusion found to sea and land warfare in 2:6 is obviously far from being the correct interpretation of the passage" (JJS 3 [1952] 10).

At the other extreme Bentzen called Haggai a religious quietist. He did not call for a rebellion against his Persian overlords but announced Yahweh's intervention in nature and history (2:6–7, 21–22). Bentzen's view has more to commend it than that of Bloomhardt.

Paul Hanson called Haggai a hierocrat. In his development of a new theory on the origins of apocalyptic in Israel, Hanson said that apocalyptic had its beginning in the last part of the sixth century B.C. in the tension between the visionary followers of Deutero-Isaiah and the priestly hierocratic party interested in proper cultic worship in the temple. Hanson admits that Haggai had some visionary concepts about the temple and eschatology, but then says that "The most energetic champion of the temple party's cause known to us through the surviving literature was Haggai" (The Dawn of Apocalyptic, 173). According to Hanson, Haggai's oracles "comprise a powerful propaganda piece for the official restoration program presided over by Zerubbabel and Joshua" (Dawn, 176).

Peter Ackroyd aptly criticizes Hanson's assignment of Haggai to the side of the hierocrats. He says, "one suspects that the two prophets [Haggai and Zechariah] are in an oversimple manner put on one side of a controversy, where it might be more just to see them as revealing two attitudes, and these not identical, towards the very complex political and religious issues of their time" ("Apocalyptic in its Social Setting." Int 30 [1976] 414).

The Date

Four dates for Haggai's preaching are given in this brief book: (1) the first day of the sixth month of the second year of Darius I marks the date for Haggai's first oracle (1:1); (2) the twenty-fourth day of the sixth month and the second year of Darius is the time of the resumption of work on the second temple (1:15a); (3) the twenty-first day of the ninth month of the second year of Darius is the date of Haggai's second oracle (1:15b–2:1); and (4) the twenty-fourth day of the ninth month of the second year of Darius is the date of Haggai's message of assurance to the people and to Zerubbabel (2:19, 20). Jack Finegan gives the dates for Haggai's first two oracles in the Julian calendar as: (1) Aug. 29, 520 B.C.; (2) Sept. 21, 520 B.C.; (*Handbook of Biblical Chronology* [Princeton, NJ: Princeton University Press, 1964] 212–13). R. A. Parker and W. H. Dubberstein give the last date in Haggai as Dec. 18, 520 B.C. (*Babylonian Chronology 626 B.C.–A.D. 45* [Chicago: University of Chicago Press, 1946]).

By 520 B.C. some of the Jews had been back in Jerusalem from Babylon several years. Cyrus, the first king of Persia, conquered Babylon in 538 B.C. He issued a decree that all of Babylon's captives could return to their homes. Ezra 1–6 tells of the first group of Jews to make that trip. They came at great sacrifice but also with high hopes which had been aroused by the preaching of Deutero-Isaiah. But when they arrived in Jerusalem ca. 536 B.C. there was nothing but ruins, poverty, and opposition from the Samaritans and the local population. Consequently nothing was done about rebuilding the temple from 536 until 520 B.C., when Haggai came on the scene. Haggai had adopted Ezekiel's idea that the Glory of Yahweh which abandoned the temple in 592 B.C. (Ezek 10:19; 11:22) would return and usher in the "messianic age" when the temple was restored (Ezek 43). Although W. A. M. Beuken suggests that Haggai was a peasant from Judah rather than Jerusalem and had never been in exile, it is easier to believe that Haggai had been in Babylon. There he could have become familiar with Ezekiel's thought and been inspired to make the trip to Jerusalem to accomplish this task. If he had been in Jerusalem all of the years of idleness it would be hard to explain his sudden zeal.

If his book contains all of his sermons, his ministry only lasted fifteen weeks. God calls some people for spot jobs. Haggai's job was to inspire the people to initiate the rebuilding of the temple and to continue the work in the midst of discouragement. This he did with great effectiveness.

The Book

The book of Haggai contains thirty-eight verses divided into two chapters. It consists of a framework (1:1, 3, 12, 15; 2:1, 10, 20) plus the oracles of Haggai. The oracles are reported in the third person. There is no superscription, but dates and explanations of various kinds are included in the editorial framework. Haggai could have written the framework and referred to himself in the third person but it is more likely that a disciple or an acquaintance put the book together during or near Haggai's lifetime (cf. Eissfeldt, *Introduction*, 428; Baldwin, 30).

The book of Haggai is primarily prose, although scholars such as Bloomhardt and Ackroyd have argued that the original form was poetic. There is
a definite rhythmic pattern in some verses (1:4, 6–11; 2:4, 8). Perhaps it is
best to describe the style of Haggai's oracles as "poetic prose" (Ackroyd,
JJS 2 [1952] 164–65).

The text is in a fairly good state of preservation. There are some obscure
words and strange constructions (see notes under each pericope). There is
some confusion in 1:15. The word בַּשֵּׁנִי is probably misplaced. Some scholars
transpose 2:15–19 to follow 1:15a on the grounds that the content of these
verses agrees with those in 1:9–11, and that they were spoken on the day
the foundation of the temple was laid (1:15a; 2:18). But there is no ms evidence
that the material was ever arranged differently than it is in the MT. The
Murabba'at Scroll supports the present text (cf. Benoit, Milik, and de Vaux,
Les Grottes De Murabba'at, 203).

The book of Haggai was probably compiled soon after Haggai spoke, either
by the prophet himself or by a disciple. However, W. A. M. Beuken, Rex
Mason, and P. Ackroyd argue that the book as it stands now shows signs of
having been edited by someone sympathetic with the Chronicler to prove
that the worship of the second temple is evidence of the renewed covenant
between Yahweh and his people (cf. Ackroyd, *JJS* 3 [1952] 2; Beuken, *Haggai-
Sacharja 1–8,* 11–15; Mason, 10).

The Message of Haggai

Haggai has been criticized by some for being concerned almost entirely
with the construction of a building. Amos and Isaiah had criticized the perfunc-
tory offering of sacrifices as unacceptable to Yahweh, and Micah and Jeremiah
had predicted the destruction of the temple. Now Haggai believes that the
temple must be restored before Yahweh's blessings can come in. Why? Because Ezekiel had drawn the blueprint for the future kingdom of God. It
would be a nationalistic, political kingdom of all the tribes of Israel with a
temple at its center in Jerusalem. Haggai's understanding was colored by
his times and circumstances. He could not imagine the kingdom of Yahweh
without a temple and the twelve tribes of Israel. He knew that Yahweh was
not pleased with the present circumstances (1:8–9; 2:17). He believed that
the temple must be rebuilt so the glory of the Lord might return and dwell
with his people. Any person who longs for the presence of the Lord is a
good man. It is granted that Haggai did not preach repentance, although
Haggai recognized that there had to be a change in the people's attitude
before they responded to Haggai's call. Haggai could be accused of provincial-
ism and materialism in his announcement that the treasures of the nations
would be brought into the temple. But Haggai was looking for the eschaton
in his day. He believed that Yahweh was sovereign over nature and history
and that he was going to do something on a grand scale. He was going to
shake the heavens and the earth and the rule of Yahweh would come in.
That rule would be centered in Jerusalem, and Zerubbabel would be Yahweh's
signet ring.

Haggai's perspective was limited but he was on the right track. He was dissatisfied with the status quo. He called for action. He could not see that the temple would eventually be replaced with a cross, and the ring with a crown of thorns.

OUTLINE

1. A message of rebuke and exhortation 1:1–11
2. The response of the people 1:12–15a
3. A message of encouragement 1:15b–2:9
4. Messages of instruction and assurance 2:10–19
5. A message of assurance for Zerubbabel 2:20–23

A Message of Rebuke and Exhortation
(1:1–11)

Bibliography

Ackroyd, P. R. *Exile and Restoration.* 153–70. **Coggins, R. J.** *Samaritans and Jews.* Atlanta: John Knox Press (1975) 42–54. **Loewe, R.** "The Earliest Allusions to Coined Money." *PEQ* 87 (1955) 141–50. **Steck, O. H.** "Zu Haggai 1:2–11." *ZAW* 83 (1971) 355–79. **Whedbee, J. W.** "A Question-Answer Schema in Haggai 1: The Form and Function of Haggai 1:9–11." *Biblical and Near Eastern Studies: Essays in Honor of Wm. S. LaSor.* Ed. G. A. Tuttle. Grand Rapids: Eerdmans, 1978.

Translation

¹ *In the second year of Darius the king, in the sixth month, on the first day of the month, the word of Yahweh came by the hand of Haggai the prophet unto Zerubbabel, son of Shealtiel, governor of Judah and to Joshua, son of Jehozadak, the high priest,* [a] *saying,*

² *Thus says Yahweh of hosts,*
　 "*This people says, the time* [a] *has not come to build the house of Yahweh.*"
³ *And the word of Yahweh came by the hand of Haggai the prophet, saying,*
⁴ "*Is it time for you yourselves to dwell in your panelled* [a] *houses when this house lies in ruins?*"
⁵ *And now thus says Yahweh of hosts,*
　 "*Consider* [a] *your ways.*
⁶ *You have sown much and bring in little.*
　 One eats, but to no satisfaction;
　 drinks, but to no exhilaration;
　 puts on clothes but cannot get warm;
　 and the one earning wages, earns wages for a bag [a] *with holes.*"

7 *Thus says Yahweh of hosts,*
  "Consider your ways.
8 *Go up the mountain and bring wood,*
  and build the house,
  that I might take pleasure in it,
  that I may get glory," says Yahweh.
9 *"You were expecting much, and behold, little.*
  You brought it in and I blew it away,"
  oracle of Yahweh of hosts.
  "Why? ᵃ *Because my house is in ruins*
  and each of you is busy ᵇ *with his own affairs."* ᶜ
10 *Therefore the heavens over you* ᵃ *withheld dew,* ᵇ
  and the earth withheld her produce.
11 *"And I called for a drought* ᵃ *upon the earth*
  and upon the mountains,
  and upon the grain,
  and upon the new wine,
  and upon the olive oil,
  and upon that which the ground brings forth,
  and upon man, ᵇ *and upon the cattle,*
  and upon all of the labor of your hands."

Notes

1.a. הכהן הגדול lit. "the great priest" is usually translated "high priest" (cf. Lev 21:10; Num 35:25, 28; 2 Kgs 12:11; 22:4, 8; 23:4). כֹּהֵן הָרֹאשׁ "head" or "chief priest" is used in 2 Kgs 25:18.

2.a. עֵת בֹּא is not in LXX. If retained the inf. בֹּא must be read as a perf. בָּא. D. W. Thomas proposes reading עֵת "time" as עתה "now."

4.a. סְפוּנִים a qal pass. part. ספן "cover," "roof," "ceiling" (only in 1 Kgs 6:9, 15; 7:3; Hag 1:4). D. W. Thomas argues for "roof," Ackroyd argues persuasively for "paneled" suggesting "luxury."

5.a. שִׂימוּ לבבכם "set to heart" (used five times in Haggai 1:5, 7; 2:15, 18). It is an exhortation to think. The heart was the seat of the intellect or volition for the Hebrews.

6.a. צְרוֹר "bundle." Silver and valuables were wrapped in bundles before coins were invented. With the minting of coins came purses. Here צְרוֹר must mean "purse" or a receptacle of some kind because of the adj. "pierced" (cf. Loewe, *PEQ* 87 [1955] 149).

9.a. Instead of a question as in *BHS* (יַעַן מֶה), LXX translates with διὰ τοῦτο . . . ("by this . . .").

9.b. רצים qal act. pt. mas. pl. of רוץ "ones running."

9.c. לביתו "to his house." בית can mean "household" or "affairs" (cf. Ackroyd, *Exile*, 158).

10.a. LXX does not translate עֲלֵיכֶם "on you"; *BHS* suggests deletion.

10.b. מִטָּל "from dew"? The מ seems to be misplaced, or a possible dittography after שמים. Some place the מ at the end of טָל to read טלם "their dew." The Tg reads מטר "rain" which fits the context very well.

11.a. LXX apparently misread חֶרֶב "sword" for חֹרֶב "drought," and so translated ἐπάξω ῥομφαίαν "I will cause a sword to come."

11.b. LXX reads ἀνθρώπους "men" for הָאָדָם "the man."

Form/Structure/Setting

The form of 1:1–11 is that of a dispute and an oracle of judgment. The dispute is between Yahweh and the people of Jerusalem. Haggai is Yahweh's spokesman. The people were saying that it was not time to rebuild the temple. Haggai, trying to prick their conscience, asked if it was time to build their own elaborate houses and not time to build the house of God. He calls on them to consider their situation. They were in the midst of a crop failure, drought, high inflation (1:5–6, 11). Why has all this evil come upon them? Haggai asserts that it is because they have neglected the temple (1:9). He exhorts them to go to the mountains and bring timber and rebuild the temple that Yahweh might take pleasure in it and be glorified.

The structure of this pericope is that of a series of oracles bracketed by an editorial framework. The oracles are the words of Haggai reported by a disciple or some third person, or by Haggai himself (cf. Eissfeldt, *Introduction*, 428). The framework of the pericope consists of vv 1 and 3.

The probable setting of this first pericope was the temple area or the palace on a holiday. The first day of every month was the new moon and a holiday for the Jews of the postexilic period. It was a time of rest (Amos 8:5) and rejoicing (Hos 2:11). The message is addressed to Zerubbabel the governor and Joshua the high priest (v 1), but obviously the people were included in the message either directly or indirectly (1:9).

Comment

The date is given as the second year of Darius the king. This king was Darius I Hystaspes who seized the throne of Persia after Cambyses' death (522–21 B.C.). Two accounts of how Darius became king of Persia have survived: (1) A romantic version by Herodotus, *History* III, 171–80; and (2) The Behistun Stone (cf. J. Finegan, *Light from the Ancient Past* [Princeton, NJ: Princeton University Press, 1946] 234–35). The source or authority of the word of Haggai is indicated by the expression, "the word of Yahweh came by the hand of Haggai the prophet." That is, Haggai was the instrument through whom the word of Yahweh came. This construction "by the hand of . . ." is rare in the prophets. It is found only in Hag 1:1, 3; 2:1; and Mal 1:1. It is used in this sense frequently in the Pentateuch (Lev 8:36; 10:11; Num 4:37, 45) and in the Deuteronomic history (Josh 14:2; Judg 3:4; 1 Kings 12:15; 16:7). The more common expression, "The word of Yahweh came *unto* (אֶל) Haggai," is found in 2:10, 20 and in 2:1 in the Murabba'at scroll. No distinction should be made between the two expressions.

Zerubbabel's name probably comes from a Babylonian expression meaning "seed of Babylon," or "shoot from Babylon" (S. Mowinckel, *He That Cometh*, Tr. G. W. Anderson [New York: Abingdon, 1954] 119). Zerubbabel is called the son of Shealtiel five times in this book (1:1, 12, 14; 2:2, 23). However, according to 1 Chr 3:19, he was the son of Pedaiah, the brother of Shealtiel and son of Jehoiachin. In any case Zerubbabel was the grandson of Jehoiachin, of the line of David. He is called governor of Judah in 1:1, 14; 2:2, 21. The word פַּחַת "governor" is a construct form of the noun פֶּחָה which probably comes from a Persian or an Akkadian word designating a high government official. It is used mainly in postexilic literature in the OT. However, one possible early use is found in 1 Kgs 10:15. Since Joshua the high priest is named almost every time Zerubbabel is, the local authority and leadership seems to have been shared by the Jewish governor and the high priest, but both of them were under the authority of the Persian king.

Haggai believed that there was an authority greater than that of the Persian king. That was "Yahweh of hosts." This term "Yahweh of hosts" is used fourteen times in this short book. It is also used fifty-three times in Zechariah and twenty-four times in Malachi. Whether the term "hosts" mean "angels," "stars," or "the armies of Israel," it is used by these prophets to emphasize God's greatness and might.

Explanation

Haggai's first oracle begins with the words "this people say." Haggai calls the people in Jerusalem "this people," not "my people," or "God's people." Earlier prophets had used the term as a reproach and as a sign of rejection by Yahweh (Isa 6:9, 10; cf. Hos 1:9). Haggai used it in the same way. Haggai knew that his people were saying that the time was not right to rebuild the temple. He asks with mild sarcasm, "Is it then time for you to build your own paneled houses?" The term סְפוּנִים can mean "covering," or "roofs." D. W. Thomas believes that Haggai is using the word here to contrast the roofed houses of the people to the unroofed ruined temple (*IB* 6, 104). However, the word סָפֻן is often used in the OT for ceiling or paneling as a sign of ornamentation and luxury (1 Kgs 7:3; Jer 22:14). Ackroyd says that the stress in this passage is on ornamentation of private homes.

We do not know how many private homes were elaborately decorated. Zerubbabel and Joshua may have been living in mansions. The people for the most part seem to be suffering dire poverty. They suffered from drought, crop failures, food shortages, and inflation. The people might have used their hardships as an excuse for not rebuilding the temple. But Haggai said that their sufferings were the judgment of God because they had not rebuilt the temple.

Haggai's theology was grounded in the curses and blessings of covenant theology (cf. Lev 26; Deut 28). Specifically poor harvests (Deut 28:38), insufficient food (Deut 8:10), inadequate clothes (Deut 10:18) were the result of failure to keep the covenant.

Haggai tells his listeners that they should go up to the mountain and bring wood and build the house, then Yahweh will be pleased with it and "allow himself to be glorified," or he will "glorify himself." The word אֶכָּבְדָ is a 1cs coh. niph. impf. of כבד. The niphal stem can be either reflexive or passive. The reflexive use would be translated, "I will allow myself to be glorified or honored." Those who prefer this reading interpret the passage as saying that acceptable worship will be offered in the rebuilt temple (cf. Ackroyd, *Exile*, 160). Those who take the passive meaning, "I will be glorified," usually understand the reference to be to the coming of the messianic age (cf. Mitchell, 48; D. W. Thomas, *IB* 6, 1042; Ezek 43:4).

The Response of the People (1:12–15a)

Bibliography

Mason, R. A. *The Books of Haggai, Zechariah and Malachi.*

Translation

¹² *And Zerubbabel son of Shealtiel, and Joshua son of Jehozadak the high priest and all the remnant of the people hearkened* ᵃ *to the voice of Yahweh their God* ᵇ *and to the words of Haggai the prophet as Yahweh their God sent him. And the people feared before Yahweh.* ¹³ *And Haggai Yahweh's messenger* ᵃ *spoke Yahweh's message* ᵇ *to the people saying,* ᶜ *"I am with you," oracle of Yahweh.* ¹⁴ *And Yahweh stirred up the spirit of Zerubbabel son of Shealtiel, governor of Judah, and the spirit of Joshua son of Jehozadak the high priest, and the spirit of all the remnant of the people, and they worked on the house of Yahweh of hosts their God,* ¹⁵ᵃ *in the twenty-fourth day of the sixth* ᵃ *month.*

Notes

12.a. שמע means "to hear and obey."
12.b. LXX (Gott.) reads אֱלֹהֵיהֶם "their God" as אֲלֵהֶם "unto them" (transl. πρὸς αὐτούς). LXX (Rah.) adds πρὸς αὐτούς *after* אֱלֹהֵיהֶם.
13.a. מַלְאַךְ "angel" is frequently used for the "angel of Yahweh" but only here of a prophet.
13.b. מַלְאֲכוּת "message" is a hapax; omitted by the LXX.
13.c. LXX does not translate לֵאמֹר "saying."
15.a. לַחֹדֶשׁ בַּשִּׁשִּׁי "to the month in the sixth" is a very awkward construct. See *Comment* for a discussion of the problem.

Form/Structure/Setting

This section is in the form of a report of the people's response to Haggai's first oracle. The response was enthusiastic and seemingly unanimous. The governor, high priest, and people obeyed the voice of Yahweh and Haggai. They manifested an attitude of fear, respect, and honor for Yahweh and they began to work on the house of Yahweh in the twenty-fourth day of the sixth month. Haggai delivers a brief oracle of assurance, "I am with you" (v 13). V 13 has sometimes been thought to be an interpolation because of the oracle. But the oracle fits the situation. Israel had been unresponsive so long, now that they have turned around in their attitude and action, Yahweh, as his name suggests, will be with them.

Comment

It is clear in the report of the response to Haggai's first message that the people were among those addressed. They along with their leaders responded positively to the message. The people had been called "this people" in v 2. Now they are called "the remnant" (1:12, 14). Isaiah, Micah and Zephaniah had spoken about a chastened, humble, obedient remnant that would return to be the people of Yahweh. Since these people have obeyed the voice of Yahweh and Haggai, they are now called "the remnant." Yahweh renewed his promise "to be with them" as he promised Moses (Exod 3:12).

Haggai is called the "messenger" or "angel" of Yahweh. (1:13). This is a strange and enigmatic expression. Jerome mentions that some people in his day thought that Haggai, John the Baptist, and Malachi were really angels and possessed bodies in appearance only (S. Hieronymus. *Commentarium in Aggaeum Prophetam.* Corpus Christianorum. Series Latina, vol. 76a. [Turnholti: Brepols, 1970.] 726).

Rex Mason sees a close resemblance between vv 14–15 and the account of Moses calling on the people to build the tabernacle (Exod 35:20–36:3). But there it is the people's hearts that stirs them to action. Here it is Yahweh. This turnaround on the part of the people is God's work. Perhaps a better parallel to what happened here is God stirring up Cyrus to conquer Babylon (Isa 41:25; 44:28).

"Who says of Cyrus, 'He is my shepherd,
   and he shall fulfill all my purpose';
saying of Jerusalem, 'She shall be built,'
   and of the temple, 'Your foundation
      shall be laid'" (Isa 44:28).

Scholars have debated the meaning of v 15 since Talmudic days. The Rabbis taught that the non-Jewish king's reigns were reckoned from the seventh month. R. Joseph pointed to Haggai 1:15 and 2:1 and said if that were true of Darius "the seventh month" of his reign (2:1) should have been his third year not his second (cf. M. L. Rodkinson, *Babylonian Talmud,* vol. 4, tract "Rosh Hashana" [Boston: Talmud Society, 1918] 4–5). The problem seems to be that two sentences dating two different events occur back to back (1:15 and 2:1). 1:15a gives the date for the response of the people in beginning work on the temple and comes at the end of the report. 1:15b and 2:1 introduce Haggai's second oracle by giving the date at the beginning of that oracle. When the two dates come together it is difficult to know how much of the language goes with one date and how much with the other. The crux of the problem is with the word בַּשִּׁשִׁי "in the sixth." This is odd after לַחֹדֶשׁ "to the month." Logically it should stand at the beginning of verse 15 or perhaps בַּשִּׁשִׁי "in the sixth" should be changed to הַשִּׁשִׁי "the sixth." 1:15 should be divided and the first part 1:15a assigned to the people's response and 1:15b to the second oracle which follows.

The Message of Encouragement
(1:15b–2:1–9)

Bibliography

Ackroyd, P. R. "Some Interpretative Glosses in the Book of Haggai." *JJS* 7 (1956) 163–64. **Krause, G.** " 'Aller Heiden Trost' Haggai 2:7." *Solange es heute heisst.* Festgabe für R. Hermann. Berlin, 1957. **von Rad, G.** "The City on the Hill." *The Problem of the Hexateuch.* Trans. E. W. T. Dicken. New York: McGraw-Hill, 1966, 232–42.

Translation

15b *In the second* [a] *year of Darius the king,* **1** *in the twenty-first day of the seventh month the word of Yahweh came by the hand of Haggai saying,* **2** *"Speak now to Zerubbabel son of Shealtiel, governor of Judah and unto Joshua son of Jehozadaek the high priest and unto the remnant of the people saying,* **3** *'Who among you is left who saw this house in its former glory? How are you seeing it now? Is it nothing in your eyes?'* **4** *And now be strong, O Zerubbabel, oracle of Yahweh. And be strong Joshua, son of Jehozadak the high priest, and be strong all the people of the land, oracle of Yahweh, and work, because I am with you, oracle of Yahweh of hosts,* **5** *—the word* [a] *which I cut with you when you came out of Egypt. My Spirit is standing in your midst. Do not fear.* **6** *Because, thus says Yahweh of hosts, yet, once more, in a little while,* [a] *I will shake the heavens and the earth, the sea and the dry land.* **7** *And I will shake all nations, and the desirable things* [a] *of all nations shall come, and I will fill this house with glory, says Yahweh of hosts.* **8** *Mine is the silver, mine is the gold, oracle of Yahweh of hosts.* **9** *The latter glory of this house shall be greater than the former, says Yahweh of hosts. In this place I will give peace, oracle of Yahweh.* [a]

Notes

15.a. 1:15b could be considered part of the previous date, but in that case chap. 1 would have two notices that the date was the sixth month of the second year of Darius and the second oracle in chap. 2 would have no year of the king's reign given. So it is best to divide 1:15 and take 1:15a with chap. 1, and 1:15b, "In the second year of Darius the king," with chap. 2.

5.a. "The word which I cut" is very strange. Usually the expression is "the covenant" בְּרִית "which I cut." דָּבָר can be translated "word," "thing," or "matter." But it is best to take "the word which I cut with you when you came out of Egypt" as a scribal gloss because of the awkward construct, "word which I cut," and because it interrupts the thought between the parallel expressions, "I am with you" (2:4) and "My spirit is in your midst" (2:5). The LXX, NEB and JB omit 2:5a. There is some MS support for the phrase in question (cf. critical apparatus, LXX [Gott.]). Origen and Cyrillus Alexandrinus also include it.

6.a. עוֹד אַחַת מְעַט הִיא is a cryptic phrase. Literally it reads, "yet one, and it is little (or small)." Baldwin translates it, "Wait, just one little while" (p. 47). Jones reads it, "once again and that soon" (p. 47). NEB translates it, "one thing more," and then adds in a footnote "and that a little thing." The LXX omits מְעַט הִיא; Tg includes it! The expression occurs frequently in eschatological passages (cf. Ps 37:10; Isa 10:25; Jer 51:33; Hos 1:4; John 14:19; 16:16, 19; Heb 12:26).

7.a. KJV and Martin Luther took this messianically as "the Desire of all nations." But that reading has been abandoned almost universally. חֶמְדַּת is sing., but should be plural because it is the subject of a plural verb. The reference to the silver and gold in the next verse dictates the understanding of "desire" in terms of "treasures." LXX reverses the problem of וּבָאוּ חֶמְדַּת "the desire will come (pl.)" by translating τὰ ἐκλεκτά "the choice" with the singular ἥξει "will come."

9.a. LXX adds extensive interpretive gloss: καὶ εἰρήνην ψυχῆς εἰς περιποίησιν παντὶ τῷ κτίζοντι τοῦ ἀναστῆσαι τὸν ναὸν τοῦτον "and peace of soul as a possession to everyone from the creator of the restoration of this Holy Place."

Form/Structure/Setting

The pericope is a message of encouragement addressed primarily to those who remembered the splendor of the first temple. They must have been terribly depressed and dejected when they saw the smallness of the reconstruction. The depression of the elders seems to have infected the attitude of the leaders and the other people. Haggai recognized the need to encourage the group to continue rebuilding.

The first part of the paragraph gives the date and the address (vv 1–2). The expression of dejection takes the form of three questions (v 3): "Who saw this house in its former glory? How do you see it now? And is it not as nothing?" The message of encouragement is presented first as an exhortation to be strong and not fear (vv 4–5). This language recalls God's words to Joshua when he became the leader after Moses' death (Josh 1:5–9). Just as God promised Moses and Joshua that he would be with them, Haggai assures his people that Yahweh is with them even though the temple had not been rebuilt. Then he says that the present condition of the temple might be unimpressive, but in the near future it will be transformed. Its future glory will be greater than the glory of Solomon's temple (vv 6–9).

Explanation

The date in 2:1 gives the month and day but not the year, so it is best to take the last part of 1:15 as a part of this section giving the date as the second year of Darius. If the date is the second year of Darius (520 B.C.), there would have been very few people left who had seen the temple before it was destroyed in 586 B.C. (v 3). Those who had seen the former temple would remember it through their eyes as children. Childhood memories of older adults are often fuzzy and sometimes exaggerated. These people might have remembered the former temple as greater and more splendid than it really was. This could have added to their dejection when they saw the smallness of the new temple.

One of the strengths of the book of Haggai is this message of encouragement for the rebuilders of the temple. It is easy to become discouraged in the work of God. Haggai three times used the imperative חֲזַק "Be strong" in addressing every segment of his people. He encouraged them to work. With the right kind of motivation and encouragement people will work. Haggai had the ability to motivate people. He assured them that Yahweh was already with them in a very real sense.

An awkward construction occurs in the beginning of v 5. Either Haggai or a copyist recalled the exodus from Egypt and remembered that Yahweh promised Moses that he would be with him. The vocabulary is strange ("the word which I cut") but the thought is correct. Yahweh was with his people during the exodus from Egypt. He will be with them now as they face the task of rebuilding the temple in the midst of opposition and poverty. They should not fear (v 5).

Then Haggai turns to the future. "In a little while," he says, "God is going to shake the heavens and the earth, the treasures of the nations will come into the temple because they all belong to Yahweh, and the temple will be filled with glory." What is this shaking of the nations to which Haggai refers? Is it the disturbance surrounding the death of Cambyses and the struggle for his throne? Was Haggai a political activist inciting rebellion against Persia as Bloomhardt and Waterman suggest? Or was he a religious quietist who used the old language of holy war to speak of Yahweh's work of overturning the worldly powers? This passage is eschatological. Haggai expects the culmination of history in his time. The phrase, "yet, in a little while," is the clue to the eschaton. The day of Yahweh is near. Haggai does not speak of popular rebellion but of Yahweh's intervention.

The political upheavals of 522/21 B.C. might have been a model for Haggai's thought of what God would do in an even greater and more magnificent way. Von Rad compares this passage with two other similar passages in which the temple plays a leading role in relationship to the nations in the eschaton (Isa 2:2-4 and Isa 60:1-22). In Isa 2:2-4 the interest is upon the nations and the significance the new Jerusalem and the temple will have for them. In Isa 60:1-22 the emphasis is upon the light of the new Jerusalem to which the nations in darkness come bringing their sacrifices and treasures which brings an end to violence and the beginning of universal peace. Now Haggai speaks of a cosmic disturbance, and the nations, shaken by such an event, will come into Jerusalem bringing their treasures. Von Rad calls v 8 a starkly challenging sentence which proclaims Yahweh's exclusive right to the silver and gold of the world. He says, "It is as if they have been hitherto on temporary loan, and are still held back from their true purpose as property of Yahweh. In the eschaton, however, they will return from this misappropriation with the exclusive control of Yahweh, their rightful owner" (*Hexateuch*, 240). There is no materialism or avarice on the part of Haggai here. It is a bold prediction of the complete recognition of Yahweh's sovereignty over the whole world. Then Yahweh will bring "peace" (שָׁלוֹם) in this "place" (מָקוֹם).

D. R. Jones sees in the Gentiles' contribution to the temple an implication that "the Jews are no longer sufficient of themselves to fulfill the purpose for which they exist. They do not simply receive tribute, as masters of the world. They accept contributions in order to create the full glory of God's house in Zion" (pp. 34-35). In another place Jones said of v 9, "In the most literal sense the prophet's vision was not and could not be fulfilled, and it is no part of the Christian scheme to build a universal Temple on the physical Zion. But in principle this was a glorious and permanent insight" (p. 47). The vision was fulfilled in the universal scope of the "One, Holy and Apostolic Church." But no single communion can establish the latter and greater glory without the contribution of other communions; "nor is it possible without the contribution of Africa, Asia and the East" (Jones 47).

Messages of Instruction and Assurance (2:10-19)

Bibliography

Ackroyd, P. R. "Some Interpretative Glosses in the Book of Haggai." *JJS* 7 (1956) 166–67. Coggins, R. J. "The Interpretation of Ezra 4:4" *JTS* 16 (1965) 124–47. Johnson, A. R. *Vitality of the Individual in Ancient Israel.* Cardiff: Univ. of Wales Press (1949)

25. **May, H. G.** "This people and this nation in Haggai." *VT* 18 (1968) 190–97.
Townsend, T. N. "Additional Comments on Haggai 2:10–19." *VT* 18 (1968) 559.

Translation

¹⁰ *In the twenty-fourth day of the ninth month in the second year of Darius, the word of Yahweh came to Haggai the prophet saying,* ¹¹ *"Thus says Yahweh of hosts, Please ask of the priests a directive.*ᵃ ¹² *If a man takes holy flesh in the skirt of his garment and touches with his skirt bread, pottage, wine, oil, or any food, will it become holy?" And the priests answered, "No."* ¹³ *And Haggai said, "If it touch an unclean corpse* ᵃ *with all of these will it become unclean?"* ¹⁴ *And Haggai answered, "So this people,*ᵃ *and so this nation, is unclean, and so is all the work* ᵇ *of their hands and that which they bring near, oracle of Yahweh."* ᶜ ¹⁵ ᵃ *And now, consider your ways, from this day forward,*ᵇ *before one stone was set upon another in the temple of Yahweh,* ¹⁶ *How did you fare?* ᵃ *One came to a heap of twenty measures, and there was ten. He came to the wine-press to draw fifty measures from* ᵇ *the trough and there was twenty.* ¹⁷ *I smote you and all the work of your hands with scorching, with rust, and with hail, and you were nothing to me,*ᵃ *oracle of Yahweh.* ¹⁸ *Consider it. From this day forward, from the twenty-fourth day of the ninth month, from the day on which the temple of Yahweh was founded,*ᵃ *consider it.* ¹⁹ *Is the seed* ᵃ *still in the granary? Has the vine, the fig tree, the pomegranate, and the olive tree not yet* ᵇ *borne (fruit)? From this day forward I will bless you.*

Notes

11.a. Lit. "a torah," "law," "teaching."

13.a. נפש "soul" or "life" is used of a dead body (Num 6:6; 19:11, 13; Lev 21:11 cf. Johnson, *Vitality* 25). LXX adds a preposition, ἐπὶ ψυχῇ "on the soul."

14.a. "This people" probably refers to the Jews in Jerusalem (cf. 1:2), although several scholars see it as a reference to the Samaritans.

14.b. The regular construction for "work of their hands" מעשה ידיהם. A different phrase יגיע כפים is used in 1:11.

14.c. The LXX adds an additional clause to the end of 2:14 and concludes with the words from Amos 5:10 καὶ εμισεῖτε ἐν πύλαις ἐλέγχοντας "and they hate in the gates one that reproveth."

15.a. 2:15–19 is often transposed to follow 1:15a without ms evidence.

15.b. מעלה is sometimes translated "backwards" but without grammatical evidence.

16.a. מהיותם "since their to be" must be emended with the LXX to מה הייתם "how did you fare?" See *BHS.*

16.b. Read מפורה "from the trough" instead of פורה taking the מ from the end of the previous word as a result of haplography.

17.a. This whole verse 2:17 is a paraphrase of Amos 4:9 plus a reconstruction of Amos' expression, "yet you did not return to me." The construction ואין-אתכם אלי is subject to various interpretations (see *Comment*). On the basis of the LXX καὶ οὐκ ἐπεστρέψατε "and you did not turn back" Ginsburg suggests emending to וְלֹא שַׁבְתֶּם "you did not return" (supported by Vg and Tg Jon.).

18.a. יֻסַּד a pual pf. of יסד, usually means "to found." Here it may mean "to restore."

19.a. LXX omits הזרה "the seed" and reads εἰ ἔτι ἐπιγνωσθήσεται ἐπὶ τῆς ἅλω "if it will still be perceived on the threshing floor."

19.b. Read עוֹד "yet" for עַד "until."

Form/Structure/Setting

2:10–19 is made up of two parts which seem to be unrelated: (1) 2:10–14 is didactic. The people are referred to in the third person. The Priests are asked to decide a question of the influence of holiness and uncleanness; but (2) 2:15–19 is a promise that the blessings of God are on the way. The people are addressed. There is a problem in that there is no immediate antecedent for "this day" in v 15.

These two passages are bound together in our present text by the date "the twenty-fourth day of the ninth month in the second year of Darius" in each section (2:10, 18). However, 2:15–19 seems to refer to the laying of the foundation stone of the restored temple (2:15, 18). 1:15a places the beginning of the work on the restored temple on the twenty-fourth day of the sixth month. Now if 2:15–19 deals with an oracle given at the laying of the foundation of the restored temple and that event occurred on the twenty-fourth day of the sixth month, then the date in v 18 should be the "sixth" month and move 2:15–19 to follow 1:15a on the grounds that it has a close affinity with chap. 1 in that they both speak about the bad harvests during the days when the temple was in ruins.

But 2:15–19 is different from chap. 1 also. It does speak about bad harvests but its main thrust is that all of the bad harvests are in the past. From this time forth, God's blessings are coming. So rather than being spoken on the twenty-fourth day of the "sixth" month, it was probably spoken on the twenty-fourth day of the ninth month as the text says. The people had been working three months (cf. 1:15a; 2:10, 18), and they saw no evidence of God's blessings. Haggai addressed a new oracle of encouragement to them. H. G. May observes that the arguments for the transposition of vv 15–19 lose some of their force if it can be shown that 2:14 refers to the same people as those addressed in vv 15–19, and if it is presumed that the community needed strong prodding several times. May points out that a month after the work began Haggai found it necessary to give encouragement (2:3–4). Two months later he prodded them again by declaring that the people were unclean due to their laxity in rebuilding the temple (2:15–19, 20–23). The content of Zech 8:9–13 closely parallels Hag 2:15–19. May notes that the Zechariah passage can hardly be as early as Hag 1:15a for Zechariah had not yet begun to prophesy. "In view of this, Hag 2:15–19 may not be out of place at a time later than the date in 1:15a" (*VT* 18 [1968] 191).

Comment

After the people had worked for three months, from October to December, they must have become discouraged again. In an attempt to encourage the people and to explain the absence of any promised blessings from God, Haggai appeals to a lesson from the priests. He asks them for a ruling. If a man carries holy flesh (a sacrifice) in his skirt, does anything the skirt touch become holy? The answer is, "No." Holiness is not transferable. The holy flesh makes the skirt "holy" but the "holy" skirt cannot make anything else "holy." But impurity is transferable. If a person touches a dead body he becomes unclean and everything he touches is unclean, and so on.

"So," Haggai says, "this nation and all of the work of their hands and their sacrifices are unclean." Haggai seems to be saying that just restoring the temple building is not enough. The temple was no fetish. Its presence did not guarantee God's blessings. Jeremiah in his temple sermon made it clear that the people's right actions and attitudes brought security and blessings (Jer 7). "This people" of Haggai was rebuilding the temple, but probably had not reformed their lives.

In 1908 J. W. Rothstein set out a new theory about the identity of "this people" and "this nation" which has been adopted by D. W. Thomas, (*IB* 6, 1047) and others. He argued that "this people" and "this nation" in 2:14 does not refer to the returned exiles but to the Samaritans who offered to help rebuild the temple in Jerusalem (Ezra 4:1–5). According to this theory, Haggai was saying that everything about the Samaritans was unclean. Those who accept Rothstein's theory that "this people" in 2:14 refers to the Samaritans take Ezra 4:1–5 as the background to this passage. There "the people of the land (Samaritans) discovered the people of Judah and made them afraid to build" (Ezra 4:4). Haggai never mentions the Samaritans. There is no basis for Rothstein's theory in the text of Haggai and there is no evidence that 2:15–19 ever followed 1:15a as Rothstein suggested. The Murabba'at Scroll follows the same order of the material as the Masoretic text does. May points to some significant analogies to Haggai's use of "nation" and "people" as referring to Judah or Israel as a "sinful nation and a blessed people" (cf. Isa 1:4; 10:6; Exod 33:13; Ps 33:12). "For Haggai the blessed nation—people had become, as it were, unclean, and its offerings unacceptable. But the way to holiness was ready at hand" (May, *VT* 18 [1968] 194). The way to holiness was not in simply rebuilding the temple, but in acknowledging Yahweh as their Lord and honoring him in worship and in consistent ethical conduct (p. 194–95).

In 2:15–19 Haggai asks the builders to take another look backward. He reminds them that while the temple was in ruins, the harvests were skimpy and disappointing (2:16). 2:17 depends heavily on Amos 4:9. In fact some scholars see this verse as a scribal gloss from Amos (cf. Ackroyd, *Exile*, 158). Whether it is a scribal gloss or not it is very similar to Amos 4:9. The last part of the verse is very difficult to translate. ואין־אתכם אלי literally means, "and nothing you to me." Is Yahweh saying that during those days Israel was "as nothing" to God? The standard English versions including KJV have read this part of the verse as Amos 4:9 has it, "Yet you did not return to me." One has to emend the text to get that reading. In any case 2:17 describes the state of the people before the rebuilding of the temple. They were "as nothing," or they had not "returned to Yahweh." Now, in 2:19 Haggai promises "from this day forward Yahweh will bless you." What day was "this day?" Supposedly it was the day of laying the foundation stone of the temple and that date here is the twenty-fourth day of the ninth month. However, work on the temple began on the twenty-fourth day of the sixth month. Does this mean that the foundation (corner) stone was not laid until three months after the work was resumed? Or, does the word יֻסַּד have to be translated "founded"? Baldwin argues that the verb can and should be translated here "build" (p. 53). So the date does not have to be that of the laying of the foundation stone.

2:19 gives Haggai's evidence for his belief in the coming of God's blessings. He says, "The seed is not still in the granary, is it?" It has been planted. It is not yet time for the harvest. They were between the times, but Haggai was confident from that day forward, perhaps the day of the sowing of the seed, God would bless them.

A Message of Assurance to Zerubbabel (2:20–23)

Bibliography

Ackroyd, P. *Exile and Restoration.* 163–66. ———. "Studies in the Book of Haggai." *JJS* 3 (1952) 10–11. **Bruce, F. F.** "The Earliest OT Interpretation." *OTS* 17 (1972), 38–39n. **Hanson, P. D.** *The Dawn of Apocalyptic.* 175–76.

Translation

[20] *The word of Yahweh came a second time to Haggai in the twenty-fourth day of the month saying,* [21] *"Speak to Zerubbabel, governor of Judah saying, 'I am about to shake the heavens and the earth,*[a] [22] *and I will overturn the throne of the kingdoms and I will destroy the strength of the kingdoms of the nations. And I will overthrow the chariots and the ones riding in them, and the horses and their riders shall go down each by the sword of his brother.'* [23] *"In that day," oracle of Yahweh of hosts, "I will take you, Zerubbabel my servant, oracle of Yahweh, and I will set you as a signet ring, because I have chosen you," oracle of Yahweh of hosts.*

Notes

21.a. LXX adds καὶ τὴν θάλασσαν καὶ τὴν ξηράν "and the sea and the dry land."

Form/Structure/Setting

This is an oracle of salvation addressed to Zerubbabel. Perhaps Zerubbabel wanted to know what role he was to play in the future. Would he always be a governor and never a king? This is an eschatological oracle of salvation. Haggai refers to that same earth-shaking event which he alluded to earlier in 2:6–9 in which all the treasures of the nations would be brought to the temple. Now he says that in the shaking of the earth the power and dominion of the world kingdoms will be broken and the prophecy of Jeremiah about Jehoiachin would be reversed. Jeremiah had said to Jehoiachin that though he wore the signet ring on Yahweh's right hand, he would tear it off and give it to Nebuchadrezzar (Jer 22:24–25). Two generations later Haggai takes up that language of Jeremiah, reverses it, and says to Zerubbabel, Jehoiachin's grandson, "On that day, says Yahweh of hosts, I will take you Zerubbabel son of Shealtiel my servant and will wear you as a signet-ring, for you it is I have chosen" (cf. Bruce, 39).

Explanation

How are we to interpret this passage? We must remember that Haggai was speaking eschatologically to a definite circumstance. There was a big difference between things as they were and things as they would be. Things then were small, difficult and discouraging. The temple was being restored but very slowly. The new structure in no way matched the splendor of the former temple. The harvests were small. Drought and mildew plagued the workers. Zerubbabel of the line of David was only a Persian governor of a tiny community. But it would not always be that way. Yahweh was going to shake the nations. Their power would be broken, their wealth would be brought to the restored temple. The future glory of that temple would be greater than the former, and Zerubbabel, God's servant, would become God's authorized representative on the earth.

None of these things happened in the lifetime of those who heard Haggai. The temple was finished in 516 B.C. (Ezra 6:15), but the treasures of the nations were never brought in an eschatological sense. The temple was destroyed in 70 A.D. Zerubbabel dropped out of sight in a very few years with no explanation of what happened to him. Was Haggai wrong? His words were not fulfilled in the way or within the time he expected. The fulfillment tarried many centuries, then with the coming of Christ, in a spiritual but no less real way, Haggai's hopes for the temple and for Zerubbabel were fulfilled. Of course the new age has not yet reached its culmination. The power of worldly kingdoms is still strong but the outcome of history is sure.

Zechariah

Introduction

Bibliography

Books

Bič, M. *Das Buch Sacharja.* Berlin: Evangelische Verlagsanstalt, 1962. ———. *Die Nacht-gesichte des Sacharja.* Biblische Studien 42. Neukirchen: Verlag des Erziehungsvereins, 1964. **Gaide, G.** *Jérusalem, voici ton Roi. Commentaire de Zacharie 9–14.* Paris: Leditions Cerf, 1968. **Jansma, T.** *Inquiry into the Hebrew Text and the Ancient Versions of Zechariah ix–xiv.* OTS (1950) 1–142. **Jeremias, C.** *Die Nachtgesichte des Sacharja.* Göttingen: Van-denhoeck und Ruprecht, 1977. **Lamarche, P.** *Zacharie i–xiv: Structure, Litteraire, et Mes-sianisme.* Paris: J. Gabalda et Cie, 1961. **Lutz, J.** *Jahwe, Jerusalem und die Völker.* Assen: van Gorcum, 1968. **Otzen, B.** *Studien über Deutero–Sacharja.* Copenhagen: Munksgaard, 1964. **Petitjean, A.** *Les Oracles du Proto-Zacharie.* Paris: Gabalda, 1969. **Plöger, O.** *The-ocracy and Eschatology.* Trans. S. Rudman. Richmond: John Knox, 1968. **Rignell, L. G.** *Die Nachgesichte des Sacharja.* Lund: Gleerup, 1950. **Rothstein, J. W.** *Die Nachgesichte des Sacharja.* BWANT 8, 1910. **Saebø, M.** *Sacharja 9–14.* WMANT 34, 1969. **Thomas, D. W.** and **Dentan, R. C.** "The Book of Zechariah." *IB* 6. Nashville: Abingdon, 1956. **Watts, J. D. W.** "Zechariah." *BBC* 7. Nashville: Broadman, 1972. **Willi-Plein, I.** *Prophetie am Ende. Untersuchungen zu Sacharja 9–14.* BBB 42, 1974.

Articles

Eichrodt, W. "Vom Symbol zum Typus. Ein Beitrag zur Sacharja-Exegese." *TZ* 13 (1957) 509–22. **Feinberg, C. L.** "Exegetical Studies in Zechariah." *BS* 97–103 (1940–1946). **Galling, K.** "Die Exilwende in der Sicht das Propheten Sacharja." *VT* 2 (1952) 18–36 = *Studien zur Geschichte Israel im persischen Zeitalter* (Tübingen 1964) 109–26. ———. "Serubbabel und der Wiederaufbau des Tempels in Jerusalem." *Verbannung und Heimkehr, FS W. Rudolph.* Tübingen (1961) 67–96. ———. "Serubbabel und der Hohepriester beim Wiederaufbau des Tempels in Jerusalem." *Studien zur Geschichte Israel in persischer Zeitalter* 127–148. **Gese, H.** "Anfang und Ende der Apokalyptik, dar-gestellt am Sacharjabuch." *ZTK* 70 (1973) 20–49 = *Vom Sinai zum Zion* (Munich 1974) 202–230. **Jones, D. R.** "A Fresh Interpretation of Zech. ix–xi." *VT* 12 (1962) 241–59. **Lipiński, É.** "Recherches sur le livre de Zacharie." *VT* 20 (1970) 25–55. **Mason, R. A.** "The Relation of Zech. 9–14 to Proto Zechariah." *ZAW* 88 (1976) 227–39. **Ridday, Y. T.** and **Wickmann, D.** "The Unity of Zechariah Examined in the light of Statistical Linguistics." *ZAW* 87 (1975) 30–55. **Saebø, M.** "Die deuterosacharjanische Frage. Eine forschungsgeschichtliche Studie." *StTh* 23 (1969) 115–40. **Sauer, G.** "Ser-ubbabel in der sicht Haggai und Sacharjas." *Das ferne und nahe Wort, FS L. Rost.* BZAW 105 (1967) 199–207. **Seybold, K.** "Spätprophetische Hoffnungen auf die Wiederkunft des davidischen Zeitalters in Sach. 9–14." *Jud* 29 (1973) 99–111.

Zechariah is the longest and the most obscure book among the Minor Prophets. It has fourteen chapters and 211 verses, while Hosea the second longest book of the Minor Prophets has fourteen chapters and 197 verses. At the beginning of the fifth century A.D. Jerome called Zechariah "the obscurest and longest of the twelve prophets" (J. Steinmann, *Saint Jerome*, trans. R. Matthews [London: Geoffrey Chapman, 1950] 298). In the Middle Ages two Jewish scholars called attention to the obscurity of this book. Arabanel (d. 1508) said, "The prophecies of Zechariah are so obscure that no expositors however skilled have found their hands in the explanation." And Solomon ben Isaac, better known as Rashi (1040–1105) said, "The prophecy is very abstruse, for it contains visions resembling dreams which want interpreting; and we shall never be able to discover the true interpretation until the teacher of righteousness arrives" (cf. T. W. Chambers, *Zechariah,* trans. P. Schaff [Lange's Commentary on Scriptures. New York: Ch. Scribner, 1874] 7). The evident obscurity of the book of Zechariah has spawned many theories concerning its date, authorship, unity, and interpretation.

The book of Zechariah is very closely related to the NT. In 1961, Paul Lamarche published his studies on the structure and messianism of Zech 9–14 and concluded that Zech 9–14 is the most quoted section of the prophets in the passion narratives of the Gospels, and other than Ezekiel, Zechariah has influenced the author of the Revelation more than any other OT book (*Zacharie i–xiv* 8, 9). If for no other reason the book of Zechariah deserves careful study because of its influence on NT writings.

The Prophet

The name Zechariah (זכריה) probably means, "Yahweh remembers." It is a common name in the OT, especially among the priests and Levites in the post-exilic period. T. M. Mauch lists thirty different people in the OT with the name of Zechariah (cf. "Zechariah," *IDB* IV 941–43). Some of the more familiar of these people are: (1) a son of the high priest Jehoiada who was slain in the court of the house of the Lord by the order of King Joash (837–800 B.C.). This Zechariah denounced the apostasy of Judah and preached God's judgment upon her (2 Chr 24:20–22). Jesus seems to refer to this incident but he calls the prophet the son of Berechiah the last of the martyrs among the prophets (Matt 23:35; cf. Luke 11:51); (2) a king of the Northern Kingdom of Israel, the son of Jeroboam II who reigned only six months before being murdered in 745 B.C. (2 Kgs 14:29; 15:8, 11); (3) a Zechariah the son of Jeberechiah, one of two men Isaiah chose to witness his writing the words *Maher-shalal-hash-baz* on a large tablet (Isa 8:2); and (4) the prophet Zechariah who began prophesying in Judah about 520 B.C. This prophet is called "the son of Berechiah, the son of Iddo" in two places (Zech 1:1, 7) and simply "the son of Iddo" in two places (Ezra 5:1 and 6:14).

The question of whether Zechariah's father's name was Berechiah or Iddo has received much attention. Using allegory, Jerome claimed that Berechiah was the prophet's father in the "flesh" and Iddo was his father in the "Spirit" (cf. S. Bullough, *CCHS* 689). Hengstenberg believed that Berechiah was Zechariah's father who probably died while Zechariah was young, and that the grandfather Iddo reared Zechariah. The word "son" in Hebrew can mean "grandson" or "descendant." However, there is no evidence that Berechiah died during Zechariah's youth. The JB takes "the son of Berechiah" as a gloss and puts it in parentheses. Many scholars believe that the name Berechiah in Zechariah 1:1 is the result of a confusion of the prophet, the son of Iddo, with the Zechariah son of Jeberechiah, Isaiah's reliable witness (Mitchell, *ICC* 82; Mauch, *IDB* IV 942; Jones, *TBC* 54). It is hard to understand how such a chronological mistake could be made since the two Zechariahs lived 300 years apart, but evidently this happened. One copy of Epiphanius (codex Augustanus) says that Zechariah the prophet was put to death by Joash, king of Israel, and the Targum to Lamentations 2:30 calls the martyred prophet "Zechariah, the son of Iddo" (cf. Mitchell, *ICC* 83). Chrysostom and Jerome both identified our prophet with the son of Jehoida but C. H. H. Wright calls this a gross anachronism (Wright, *Zechariah and His Prophecies.* [London: Hodder and Stoughton, 1889] xviii).

Some continental scholars beginning with A. Bertholdt (1814) explained the confusion of the two names of Zechariah's father by suggesting that Zech 9–14 was written by Zechariah ben Jeberechiah, Isaiah's companion, and Zech 1–8 was written by Zechariah ben Iddo. Later these two sections were put together and the two Zechariahs became father and son (cf. Eissfeldt, *Introduction* 435). After Stade's articles appeared in the *ZAW* 1881–82, assigning much of Zech 9–14 to the Greek period, the name Zechariah ben Berechiah, attached to those chapters was considered a pseudonym (cf. E. Sellin 478–79; F. Horst, HAT 217). There is still no adequate explanation for the listing of two different names for Zechariah's father. The relationship of 1–8 to 9–14 will be discussed more fully below.

Statements in Neh 12:4, 10, 16, suggest that Zechariah was a priest or a Levite and that he became the head of the house of Iddo in his later life. However it is not certain that the Zechariah in Neh 12 is the same as the prophet in the book of Zechariah. Yet it seems evident that Zechariah the prophet, like Ezekiel, was from a priestly family and was also called to be a prophet (cf. Mason, *CNEB* 27).

Nothing is known about Zechariah's age. An early Christian tradition represented by Pseudo-Epiphanius, Dorotheus, and Hesychius claimed that the prophet was already well advanced in years when he came to Jerusalem from Babylon and that he had already proved his prophetic ability by predicting the births of Joshua the high priest and Zerubbabel the governor, and by predicting Cyrus' victory over Croesus (C. H. H. Wright, *Zechariah and His Prophecies* xvii–xviiii). But many other scholars believe that Zechariah was a young man when he returned to Jerusalem. As evidence they claim that the prophet is the young man (נער) in 2:4, 2:8 (Heb.) (cf. J. Calvin, *Commentaries on the Twelve Minor Prophets*, trans. J. Owen, V 61 [Grand Rapids: Eerdmans, 1950]; M. Luther, *Minor Prophets III Zechariah*, ed. H. C. Oswald, 26; T. W. Chambers, *Minor Prophets* 6). If the Zechariah in Neh 12:16 is the post-exilic prophet, he lived at least until the high priest Joshua died. The last dateable reference to Zechariah in his book is in the fourth year of Darius (518 B.C.) when men came from Bethel to ask about fasting (7:1–2).

According to some ancient versions Zechariah was a poet as well as a prophet. His name is in the titles of Pss 137, 145–50 in the LXX; in the titles of Pss 111, 145 in the Vulgate; and in the titles to Pss 125, 145–48 in the Syriac.

The Book

Date

The first part of the book of Zechariah (chaps. 1–8) is well dated. The first date is "the eighth month of the second year of Darius" (1:1) which would be October, 520 B.C. This is the only place among the seven dates given in Haggai and Zechariah 1–8, where the day of the month is omitted. The Syriac version supplies the day by adding the phrase "in the first day of the month," which may or may not be correct. At any rate, "the eighth month of the second year of Darius" puts the beginning of Zechariah's ministry one month before Haggai delivered his last two oracles (cf. Hag 2:18, 20). The second date in Zechariah is "the twenty-fourth day of the eleventh month, which is the month Shebat, in the second year of Darius" (1:7). This date corresponds to February 15, 519 B.C. This second date seems to suggest that Zechariah saw his eight visions in one night. But Rex Mason, following W. A. M. Beuken and P. R. Ackroyd, notes that the verse (1:7) is editorial and in the third person, whereas most of the vision accounts that follow are in the first person. Mason says, "although they (all of the visions) have now been joined in a series and are all related to one theme and occasion, there are indications within them of a more varied origin" (Mason 35). J. D. W. Watts suggests that 1:7–6:15 is "a speech (or writing) put together and delivered by the prophet at this time" (Watts 314).

The third and last date in Zechariah is in 7:1, "in the fourth year of King Darius, in the fourth day of the ninth month which is Chislev." Our equivalent would be December 7, 518 B.C. This verse too is editorial and introduces Zechariah's ethical and eschatological oracles about the true meaning of fasting (chaps. 7–8). Chaps. 7 and 8 seem to be made up of a number of short sayings introduced by "thus says Yahweh" (7:9; 8:1, 4, 7, 9, 14, 18, 20). These sayings probably were delivered over a period of several months or even years.

When we turn from chap. 8 to chap. 9 of Zechariah we leave all dates behind. No dates are given in Zechariah 9–14. Zechariah's name is never mentioned in these last chapters. Times have changed. There are no more references to Darius the king or to any king. The temple is standing (9:8; 11:13–14, 14:21). A note of controversy is sounded in 10:1–3a with its denunciation of the shepherds; in 11:4–17 as the prophet acts as a rejected shepherd; and in another oracle against "my shepherd" in 13:7–9. A time of peace (chaps. 1–8) gives way to a time of war (9–14).

Many different dates have been suggested for Zech 9–14. Those scholars who hold that they are the work of Zechariah ben Jeberechiah date them in the eighth century B.C. Scholars who believe that Zech 9–14 are the work of Jeremiah (cf. Matt 27:9) date them in the seventh century. Those who hold the unity of the book and attribute the whole to Zechariah date this last part in the sixth century, and those who argue that the reference to an invasion in 9:1–8 is to Alexander the Great's invasion of Palestine in 333 B.C. date chaps. 9–14 in the last part of the fourth century B.C.

B. Otzen assigns different dates to the various chapters in 9–14. He believes that chaps. 9–10 come out of the crises in the time of King Josiah. Chap. 11 stems from the immediate time of the fall of the kingdom of Judah. Chaps. 12–13 come out of the crisis of the early post-exilic period, and "chap. 14 carries an apocalyptic character reminding one most of Trito-Isaiah and its late post-exilic time" (cf. B. Otzen 212). Paul Hanson also assigns different dates to the various chapters in the 9–14 section. In his book, *The Dawn of Apocalyptic,* he dates chap. 9 in the mid-sixth century (p. 324); chap. 10 in the third quarter of the sixth century (p. 334); chap. 11:1–17, and 13:7–9 in the end of the sixth or the beginning of the fifth century (p. 353); chap. 12:1–13:6 in the first half of the fifth century (p. 368); and chap. 14 from 475 to 425 B.C. (p. 400). Chaps. 9–14 probably were produced in Palestine by a disciple of Zechariah at the end of the sixth or the beginning of the fifth century B.C.

Unity

There was a time when a reference to the unity of a book or section of the Bible was understood as a reference to a single authorship of that book or section. Thus the unity of Isaiah meant that Isaiah of Jerusalem wrote all sixty-six chapters of the book. Now with the rise of redaction criticism, the unity of a book or section of the Bible is often viewed from the standpoint of the final editor or redactor.

The problem of the unity of Zechariah represents one of the earliest critical problems in OT studies. No serious question was raised against Zechariah's authorship of the entire book until the seventeenth century. In A.D. 1638 a learned and pious Cambridge theologian pointed out that Matt 27:9 quotes Zech 11:12 as having been written by Jeremiah rather than Zechariah. Mede departed from the tradition that Zechariah wrote the whole book and said, "there is reason to suspect that the Holy Spirit (through Matthew) desired to claim these three chapters 9, 10, 11 for their real author" (cf. Mitchell 252).

At first Mede denied that Zechariah wrote all of this book on a scriptural basis. He said, "There is no scripture sayeth they (chaps. 9–11) are Zachary's, but there is scripture saith they are Jeremy's as this of the evangelists" (cf. F. C. Eiselen, *The Prophetic Books of the Old Testament* [New York: Methodist Book Concern, 1923] 560). But Mede did not base his view of Jeremiah's authorship of Zech 9–11 on Matthew's reference alone. He also argued on the basis of internal evidence in these chapters that they were earlier than the exilic period. He said, "Certainly, if a man weighs the contents of some of them, they should in likelihood be of an elder date than the time of Zachary, namely, before the captivity, for the subjects of some of them were scarce in being after that time" (Eiselen 560).

Mede's modest suggestion did not attract attention until 1699 when Richard Kidder, Lord Bishop of Bath and Wells, wrote, "That *Jeremy* wrote chapters 9, 10, 11, 12, 13, and 14 of *Zechary* is a very probable Opinion. This is certain, that such things are contained in those Chapters, as agree with the time of *Jeremy,* but by no means with that of *Zechary,* e.g. that the *Pride of*

Assyria shall be brought down, and the *Septre of Egypt depart,* is foretold Zech 10:11. It is well known that this was past in *Zechary's* time. And tho' *Jeremy* might, *Zechary* could not predict this" (Richard Kidder, *A Demonstration of the Messiah* I–III [London: 1684, 1700] 199 cited by B. Otzen, 14).

A controversy ensued in England, Germany, and America concerning the last part of Zechariah. In 1784, Flugge in an anonymous work (*Die Weissagungen welche bey den Schriften des Propheten Sacharjas beygebogen sind,* 1784) divided Zech 9–14 into nine distinct prophecies: 9, 10:1, 2; 10:3–12; 11:1–3; 11:4–17, 12:1–9; 12:10–13:6; 13:7–9, 14; to which he assigned various dates. He explains their appearance in this book by supposing that Zechariah collected and preserved them here (cf. Mitchell 245).

The first scholar to assign chaps. 9–14 to a date later than Zechariah was Corrodi in 1792 (cf. Mitchell 250). Corrodi assigned chap. 9 to the time of Alexander the Great and chapter 14 to the time of Antiochus Epiphanes. A similar view was adopted by Eichhorn in 1824. In 1881, B. Stade published the results of his exhaustive studies in two articles, "Deuterozacharja. Eine kritische Studie" (*ZAW* 1 [1881] 1–96; 2 [1882] 151–72, 275–309). Stade concluded that chaps. 9–14 are the work of one author who wrote during the second half of the period of the wars of the Diadochi, between 306 and 278 B.C. Interest in the unity of Zechariah was brisk through the rest of the nineteenth century. George L. Robinson, writing in the *AJSL* 12 (1895), listed 103 authors who had treated the subject in one or more publications since the days of Mede.

The unity of the book of Zechariah has been studied in more recent years on literary, historical, and theological bases. In 1961 Paul Lamarche published his studies of Zech 9–14 in which he argued that a single author living about 500–480 B.C. arranged a group of seemingly diverse pericopes into a chiastic pattern. Lamarche believes that the author of Zech 9–14 used four themes arranged chiastically to portray the ultimate victory of the kingdom of God. The day of Yahweh would be brought in by the messianic king. The surrounding nations, as well as Judah and Jerusalem, would be judged and purged by war. Idolatry would cease and Yahweh would be universally worshiped in Jerusalem.

Joyce Baldwin (pp. 80–81) was so impressed with Lamarche's arguments that she not only believed that all of Zech 9–14 was written by one man, but she suggested that that one man was the prophet Zechariah because she found a chiastic arrangement in the first part of Zechariah (chaps. 1–8) as well. But other scholars have not been as impressed with Lamarche's view of the unity of Zech 9–14. Walter Harrelson said, "The larger thesis—that the entire six chapters come from one author—seems to me difficult if not impossible to maintain, and the author's analysis of the pattern of ideas purported to show the integral relation among the several parts remains unconvincing" (*JBL* 82 [1963] 116).

Recently, computers have been invoked to try to settle the issue. With the aid of a computer, Y. T. Radday and D. Wickmann from the Institute of Technology in Haifa, Israel, studied the book of Zechariah on the basis of statistical linguistics. These same men had used the same methods to study the unity of Isaiah. They found that the chances of Isaiah 40–66 being written by the author of 1–35 were 1:100,000. In analyzing the book of Zechariah they divided the book into four parts:

Section IA: Chap 1–4—843 words
Section IB: Chap 5–8—898 words
Section II: Chap 9–11—642 words
Section III: Chap 12–14—739 words

The question posed was: With what probability may one assume that Sections II and III were written by the author of Section I? They studied such evidence as sentence length, syllable criteria, word length, phonemes, particles, parts of speech, transitions between word categories, vocabulary richness, vocabulary concentration, vocabulary eccentricity, and comparisons with other OT writings such as Ezekiel. The conclusions reached on the basis of linguistic analyses alone were that there was insufficient evidence to postulate a break between chaps. 8 and 9. But the chances for the same author of 1–11 and 12–14 are 2:1,000 (*ZAW* 87 [1975] 30–54).

Rex Mason wrote a doctoral thesis for the University of London called, "The Use of Earlier Biblical Material in Zech 9–14: A Study in Inner Biblical Exegesis" (June, 1973). Growing out of that study was a commentary on Haggai, Zechariah, and Malachi in *CNEB* (1977) and an article, "The Relation of Zech 9–14 to Proto-Zechariah" (*ZAW* 88 [1976] 227–38). Mason studied the similarities between Zech 1–8 and 9–14 around five main emphases: the prominence of the Zion tradition; the divine cleansing of the community; universalism; the appeal to the earlier prophets; and the provision of leadership as a sign of the new age. Mason found evidence of all five emphases in chaps. 1–8 and 9–14 but concluded that the differences between the two parts suggest that chaps 9–14 "are from different and later hands than Zechariah" (Mason, 79).

Brevard Childs has dealt with the book of Zechariah recently from the standpoint of the canon. At first Childs emphasizes the differences between chaps. 1–8; 9–11; and 12–14. He says that it appears clear that chaps. 9–14 do not exhibit any features that would cause one to assign them to the same redactional level as that of chaps. 1–8. In fact, chaps. 9–14 are divided into two parts by superscriptions (cf. 9:1; 12:1) with each section (9–11 and 12–14) circulating independently of chaps. 1–8 and of each other. Childs concludes that there is no direct literary dependence of 9–14 and 1–8 such as a conscious patterning, a midrashic expansion, or a prophecy-fulfillment relationship. Childs believes that the canonical process which shaped the book of Zechariah "was of very different order from that which fashioned the Isaianic corpus" (Childs, 480).

Even though Childs sees a need to handle the two sections of the book of Zechariah separately, he acknowledges a surprising compatibility between the two sections. Childs believes that this compatibility is due to the fact that the same authoritative scriptures, Isaiah, Jeremiah, and Ezekiel, lie behind both sections. Some of the elements of congruity that Childs (*Introduction* 482–83) sees in both parts of Zechariah are: (1) a new Jerusalem without walls which experiences divine protection (2:5; 9:8; 14:11); (2) the return of paradisal fertility (8:6; 14:6, 8); (3) the ancient covenant promise (8:8; 13:9); (4) the curse in 5:3 is removed in 14:11; (5) divine judgment on the nations (2:1–2; 14:6) and the conversion of the nations (2:15; 8:22; 14:6); (6) the gathering of the exiles (8:7; 10:9–10); (7) new cultic rites for the new age (8:18–19; 14:20); (8) the outpouring of the Spirit which brings cleansing and transformation (4:6; 5:4; 12:10; 13:3); (9) an humble messianic figure (3:8; 4:6; 9:6–7).

Childs notes that the vocabulary in the two sections is different, and the highly structured chiasmus arrangement of chaps. 9–14 does not convince him of the unity of the two sections. Nevertheless, there is according to Childs a significant linkage between 1–8 and 9–14 brought about by redactors (Childs, *Introduction* 483). So most modern scholars agree that there is "unity" in the whole book of Zechariah but there is little agreement about what constitutes the "unity" and how that "unity" came about.

Literary Form

There are a number of literary forms in the book of Zechariah. It is written primarily in prose, yet it contains some poetry (chaps. 9–10). It has exhortations (1:1–6), visions (1:7–6:8), symbolic actions (6:9–15), and oracles (7:1–14:21). One of the most debated issues concerning the literary form of Zechariah is: Is it apocalyptic? One's answer to that question depends largely on one's definition of apocalyptic, and there seems to be no general agreement among scholars as to what apocalyptic is. J. M. Schmidt has recently published a revised edition of his comprehensive study of the history of the investigation of Jewish apocalyptic, (J. M. Schmidt, *Die jüdische Aopcalyptik, die Geschichthte ihrer Erforschung von den Anfängen bis zu den Textfunden von Qumran*, rev. ed. [Neukirchen-Vluyn: Neukirchener Verlag, 1976]), in which he sets out the great variety of opinions scholars have expressed about the nature of apocalyptic literature since the late eighteenth century. Schmidt noted that Eichhorn called attention to Ezekiel's uniqueness in his third edition (1783) to his *Introduction to the Old Testament*, 218. "No other prophet let his phantasy run so freely that he created so many kinds of poetry. Therein he clearly lifted himself from the old prophets and at the same time showed his nearness to Daniel and the apocalypse of John" (p. 32). Eichhorn seems to make the use of fantasy or artistic imagination the clue to apocalyptic. Schmidt said that the transition from prophecy to apocalyptic did not take place suddenly, but the visions of Zechariah were a part of that transition (p. 34). Schmidt refers to Hermann Schultz approvingly as one who considered Zechariah's visions as apocalyptic (p. 33). Schultz said, "Prophecy did not change into this new form (apocalyptic) all of a sudden. Already in the visions of Ezekiel and Zechariah the pictures are, without a doubt, mainly artistic, produced by a conscious effort of the imagination, and reference is, of set purpose, made to earlier prophecies. But this tendency is evidently worked out in an altogether different fashion in Daniel" (H. Schultz, *Old Testament Theology*, I [Edinburg: T and T Clark, 1898] 421). One can detect in Schultz's writings two prominent characteristics of apocalyptic: (1) it is highly imaginative, and (2) it makes much use of earlier prophecies.

What is apocalyptic? The word "apocalypse" is from a Greek word for "revelation" and does not appear in the OT. If one takes the NT book of

Revelation as the model for apocalyptic literature, he may recognize some characteristics of this literary genre. Robert North believes that it is the weird imagery and arcane puzzles in the book of Revelation that distinguishes this book from other NT books and links it to Daniel in the OT. The frequency and variety of *angels* as vehicle or interpreter of revelation may be a characteristic of apocalyptic (Robert North, "Prophecy to Apocalyptic via Zechariah" in VTSup 22 [1971] 53). But Revelation and Daniel have a framework or pattern of distinct "eons" into which history is divided and which give a unified "meaning" to its totality. R. North does not believe that this feature occurs in Ezekiel or in either part of Zechariah (North 53).

However Helmut Gese does believe that a system of "eons" can be found in the book of Zechariah and he agrees with E. Sellin that Zechariah was the first apocalyptist (H. Gese, "Anfang und Ende der apokalyptik, dargestellt am Sacharjabuch," *ZTK* 70 [1973] 24). After arguing that only seven of the night visions were original Gese arranged them in a pattern which moved from evening to midnight and then to the morning. Then he said, "We stand fast [in the belief that] here is not a collection of seven visions laid out before us, but a *system* of seven visions of the night, and I myself believe that here is a full apocalypse, a sevenfold revelation of the invasion of a new eon, the kingdom of God" (*ZTK* 70 [1973] 37).

Paul Hanson rejects Gese's conclusion that Zechariah was the first apocalyptist. Hanson is not willing to define "apocalyptic" strictly on the basis of literary types (*Dawn* 250). Hanson argues that "apocalyptic eschatology" has its origin in the struggle between the visionary succession of the prophets and the hierocratic rulers in the early post-exilic period. When the second temple was built the priests gained control of the religious and political life of the community. The priestly rulers had no need for future eschatology because for them eschatology was "realized" in their priest-state. So the successors of the classical prophets despaired of the restoration of God's people as the holy community in a glorified Zion under a hierocratic state. They began to look for a cosmic intervention of Yahweh on behalf of his people in terms of the old Divine Warrior motif (*Dawn* 11, 26–27).

Hanson's work has been critiqued by Robert P. Carroll (*JSOT* 14 [1979] 3–35). After listing some strengths of Hanson's work, such as his sociological analysis and form-critical approach, Carroll notes several weaknesses. He thinks that Hanson's unwillingness to base one's view of apocalyptic on definitions is "begging the question." He believes that Hanson uses excessive polarization in his approach and that his view of the two parties' (visionaries and hierocratic) use of myth and history is not clear.

Some scholars make visions, imagination, and use of angels indicators of apocalyptic. Others make the reinterpretation of earlier prophecies the clue. Zechariah 9–14 makes much use of earlier prophetic sayings. Some scholars see dualism, "eons," or the idea of "two ages" as being the sure sign of apocalyptic.

Gerhard von Rad tried to change the whole debate about the nature and origin of apocalyptic by arguing that it was a sapiential or wisdom genre. In view of its keen interest in eschatology and its use of visions and dreams one might understand apocalyptic literature as a child of prophecy. But von

Rad says, "To my mind, however, this is completely out of the question. . . . The decisive factor, as I see it, is the incompatibility between apocalyptic literature's view of history and that of the prophets" (G. von Rad, *Old Testament Theology* II, trans. D. M G. Stalker. [Edinburgh: Oliner and Boyd, 1965] 303). Von Rad makes no reference to Zechariah as apocalyptic literature.

Whether or not Zechariah is apocalyptic depends on one's definition of apocalyptic. It contains visions, interpreting angels, and reinterpretation of earlier prophecies. There are strong eschatological emphases in the book. But whether or not they are "dualistic" in their view of history is debatable. Perhaps Samuel Amsler is correct when he says that "in his visions Zechariah revealed himself as one of the precursors of the movement which raised the challenge to the history of the first and second centuries (S. Amsler, "Zacharie et l'origine de l'apocalyptic," VTSup 22 [1971] 231). If Zech 9–14 is not apocalyptic, it represents the forerunner of that type of literature.

The Text

The Masoretic text of the book of Zechariah is in relatively good condition. It contains a number of the normal textual problems such as the omission of a word (6:6) or the addition of a word (1:7 "saying"). There are problematical pronominal suffixes and words without antecedents. Some obscure passages occur. Unfortunately the DSS do not help with the text of Zechariah. Only one small fragment of Zechariah (1:1–4) was found in the Hebrew scroll from the cave at Murabba'at (cf. Benoit, Milik, de Vaux, *Les Grottes de Murabba'at* [Oxford: Clarendon Press, 1961] 50,205). Another scroll of the Minor Prophets in Greek was found probably in the wadi Khabra. This scroll was published by D. Barthélemy in *Les Devanciers d'Aguila* (VTSup 10, 1963). The scroll contains Zech 1:1, 3, 4, 13, 14; 2:2, 7, 16, 17; 3:1, 4–7; 8:19–21, 23; 9:1–4. Barthélemy dated the scroll in the second half of the first century A.D. and argued that it was a reworked form of the Palestinian LXX in accord with developing rabbinic hermeneutical principles in order to bring the Greek text more closely into line with the Hebrew Mss in use in the first century A.D. (cf. P. W. Skehan, "The Biblical Scrolls from Qumran and the Text of the Old Testament," in *Qumran and the History of the Biblical Texts*, eds. F. M. Cross and S. Talmon [Harvard Univ. Press, 1975] 269).

In 1950 T. Jansma published a substantial work on the text of Zechariah 9–14 (T. Jansma, "Inquiry into the Hebrew Text and the Ancient Versions," *OTS* 7 [1950] 1–142). Jansma devotes a separate chapter of this work to the study of the variants in different mss of the Targum, Peshitta, LXX and the MT. Then he goes through the text of Zech 9–14 verse by verse and discusses the variant readings in all of the different text types. This is a very valuable contribution to the textual criticism of this part of the OT. Unfortunately it was done before the Qumran materials became available to scholars.

The Messiah in Zechariah

From the beginning of the Christian movement some passages in Zechariah have been interpreted messianically. On the night he was betrayed Jesus led

his disciples out to Gethsemane and said to them, "You will fall away, for
it is written, I will smite the shepherd and the sheep will be scattered" (Zech
13:7 quoted in Mark 14:27). F. F. Bruce says that there is "no doubt about
the application of the passage in Mark's passion: the smitten shepherd is
Jesus. Moreover, according to Mark, it is Jesus Himself who makes the identification. I have no doubt at all that Mark is right in ascribing this interpretation
of the prophecy to Jesus" (F. F. Bruce, *New Testament Development of Old Testament
Themes* [Grand Rapids: Eerdmans, 1968] 104). Undoubtedly Jesus' understanding of his ministry was influenced by several passages in Zechariah along
with many other OT passages. In 1952 C. H. Dodd published a work, *According
to the Scriptures* (New York: Scribners, 1953) in which he argued that early
Christians circulated orally a list of OT scriptures which served as the basis
of the Gospel for many NT writers. Among this list are a number of passages
from Zech 9–14. For example, 9:9 is quoted in Mt 21:5 and Jn 12:15; 11:13
is quoted in Mt 27:9; 12:3 is quoted in Lu 21:24; 12:10 is quoted in Jn
19:37 and Rev 1:7; 13:7 is quoted in Mark 14:27. Compare also Zech 14:5
with 1 Thess 3:13; 14:8 with Jn 7:38; and 14:21 with Jn 2:16 (pp. 64–67).
There is ample evidence in the NT that many references in the book of
Zechariah were interpreted messianically.

Not only is there evidence that a list of OT scriptures pointing to the
person and work of Christ was circulated by early Christians before the NT
was written but there is evidence of such a list in the writings of the early
church fathers such as Cyprian, Tertullian, Irenaeus, and Justin. In the middle
of the third century Cyprian published such a list under the title *Testimonia*.
The passages were arranged and classified for the use of Christian apologists
(p. 24).

Jerome (331–419 B.C.) wrote a commentary on five minor prophets (Zechariah, Malachi, Hosea, Joel, and Amos) in A.D. 406. His Zechariah commentary
was the longest of the five and consisted of three books. He claims to have
used as sources Origen, Hippolytus, Didymus of Alexandria, and Apollinarius.
Almost all of these commentaries have disappeared, but Didymus' five-book
commentary on Zechariah was discovered at Toura in Egypt in 1941 and
shows the enormous extent of Jerome's indebtedness to him (cf. J. N. D.
Kelly, *Jerome: His Life, Writings, and Controversies* [London: Duckworth, 1975]
292; L. Doutreleaus, *Didyme l'Avengle sur Zacharie* [3 vols, Paris, 1962]).

Jerome's plan for his commentary was to give a double translation for
each verse or group of verses: one from the Hebrew which served as the
basis of a literal or "historical" exposition; and another from the LXX which
served as the basis of a "spiritual" exposition. Kelly says that Zechariah's
apocalyptic visions "invited exuberant allegorising" (p. 291). The man whom
Zechariah saw riding on a red horse (Zech 1:8) was "Christ made flesh"
(pp. 292–94), and the four horns in 1:18 were "the four passions: grief, joy,
hope and fear which according to Stoic doctrine throw men's souls into tur-
moil" (p. 294).

Even though most modern scholars use the historical-grammatical method
of interpreting scripture, one can still find examples of typological or "spiritual" interpretations of Zechariah. A. C. Gaebelein took the same approach
as Jerome toward "the man on the red horse." "The first question which

arises in the interpretation of this vision is concerning the person who leads the angelic hosts. He is called a man riding on a red horse. This does not mean that he was nothing but a man, but it means that he appeared in the vision to Zechariah as a man, he had a human body. Later he is called the Angel of the Lord, and as such, he acts as successful intercessor for Jerusalem, and receives a loving answer from Jehovah. The leader must have been a divine person incarnate. The name Angel of the Lord is one of the Old Testament names for the *Son of God*, and there can be only one satisfactory interpretation of who the rider on the red horse is, and that is, he must be the Son of God" (A. C. Gaebelein, *Studies in Zechariah* 4th ed. [New York: Francis E. Fitch, 1905] 10–11).

Such extreme examples of eisegesis led some scholars to the opposite view of denying any messianic references in Zechariah. Such scholars prefer to interpret any reference to a future king as a reference to some historical character in the time of the prophet. For example, Mitchell (p. 104) says, "Zechariah follows Haggai in recognizing Zerubbabel as the Messiah and the restorer of the Davidic dynasty." In contrast to Mitchell's view, Rex Mason (p. 75) says, "If Zechariah had attached messianic hopes to Zerubbabel, these have now disappeared. He is seen only as a temple builder with little political and no military significance. The messianic references are detached from him and cast into the future. . . ." Caution is advised in interpreting OT passages messianically. Mason (*ZAW* 88 [1976] 236) sounds such a note of caution about certain passages in Zech 9–14: "The celebrated passage concerning the coming king in 9:9f is so detached a unit as to make it difficult to be sure of its significance, but also it is ambiguous concerning the nature of the king." It is not at all clear, according to Mason, whether or not "the corner-stone, tent-peg and battle bow" in 10:4 refer to leaders emerging from the community or from Yahweh:

> It is illegitimate to detect a Messianic figure elsewhere in deutero-Zechariah. Whatever be made of the promise concerning David in 12:8, it cannot be overlooked that the house of David needs to share in the general act of penitence which follows, nor that the context specifically states that victory will be clearly Yahweh's so that the glory of the house of David and the inhabitants of Jerusalem shall not be unduly exalted above that of the rest of the community (v 7). Even if v 8 is secondary in its present position, this does not suggest that the circle responsible for the final form of these oracles saw the house of David in a traditionally Messianic way. Nor can the "pierced one" of v 10 be pressed into service here, however he be understood, for neither he nor his sufferings are the *means* of the people's penitence. They mourn for their treatment of him as a *result* of a direct, regenerative act of Yahweh's Spirit. Nor is the "shepherd" of 13:7 to be equated with the "good shepherd." Traditio-critical considerations make it clear that the burden here is one of judgment of Yahweh against faithless leadership and community in the spirit of 11:17. No reference to human leadership of any kind is found in ch. 14 (*ZAW* 88 [1976] 237).

It is easy to read too much of the experiences of Jesus into some of the passages in Zech 9–14. F. F. Bruce quotes with approval T. V. Moore's saying that anyone who tries to interpret the words "wounds between his hands" in Zech 13:6 as a prophecy of the nail-wounds in our Lord's hands is guilty of "the grossest misapprehension of its meaning." Bruce also says, "it is astonishing that so able a Hebraist as E. B. Pusey should have been capable of this misinterpretation" (F. F. Bruce, *New Testament Development* 114).

In recent years scholars have returned to a study of the "messianic" passages in the OT. Much of the renewed emphasis of this study has been on how the NT writers and the people of Qumran used these OT scriptures.

The revival of interest in the NT's use of the OT began in earnest with C. H. Dodd's *According to the Scriptures* (1952). Actually Dodd built on the earlier work of Rendel Harris, *Testimonies* (1916, 1920). Harris argued that there was a "testimony book" of OT quotations used widely in the early church. Dodd selects fifteen important OT texts which are used more than once in the OT and argues that these fifteen texts which were circulated orally were the basis of early Christian theology. Dodd also maintains that there was agreement on the methods of exegesis and other uses of those texts. Isolated quotations are not intended as proof-texts, but as pointers to whole OT contexts, knowledge of which is assumed. D. Moody Smith, Jr., says, "In opposition to much modern critical opinion concerning the use of the Old Testament by the New Testament writers, Dodd contends that it was not fundamentally arbitrary: 'In general . . . the writers of the New Testament, in making use of passages from the Old Testament, remain true to the main intention of their writers' " (D. M. Smith, Jr. "The Use of the Old Testament in the New and Other Essays," FS for W. F. Stinespring, ed. J. M. Efird [Durham, N.C.: Duke Univ. Press, 1972] 28–29). Dodd saw that the NT's method of interpreting the OT was already discernible in the OT itself. Martin Noth and Gerhard von Rad have since developed the theory of "representation" as a method of studying the NT's use of the Old. But Dodd did not make use of the Qumran materials in his writing. F. F. Bruce and others have noted the similarities and differences between the NT and Qumran's use of OT texts (F. F. Bruce, *Biblical Exegesis in the Qumran Texts* [London: The Tyndale Press, 1959]; D. M. Smith, Jr., "The Use of the Old Testament" 18–20).

In 1956 Helmer Ringgren published *The Messiah in the Old Testament* in which he espoused the cultic interpretation of certain Psalms and other OT passages including Zech 9:9–10. Ringgren accepts Mowinckel's hypothesis of a New Year (or covenant) festival being observed in Israel in which the king is the anointed Yahweh and is proclaimed as God's son. Ringgren believes that as time went on the hopes connected to contemporary kings were transferred to a future king who would come and bring in the universal reign of God. Ringgren says, "This idea of divine kingship is the background and the necessary condition of the belief in the coming Messiah, it is the soil from which the messianic hope has grown (H. Ringgren, *The Messiah in the Old Testament* [London: SCM Press, 1956] 21). Although Mowinckel and Ringgren might have gone too far in cultic interpretation of "messianic" passages, it is undeniable that many of these passages have cultic backgrounds. F. F. Bruce, dealing with Zech 13:7–9, says "The language of the oracle may well have a life-setting in the national cultus, in the liturgical role of the king. The presence of such liturgical language in prophetic oracles is well enough established" (*New Testament Development* 102).

In 1961 Paul Lamarche published *Zacharie IX–XIV*. He begins by noting the obscurity of this passage of scripture. He calls attention to the myriad of different theories for dates and authorship for the various parts of this material. Then he proposes a solution to the problems in these passages, a solution based on a literary form (chiasmus) which he says displays a remarkable unity of the material from 9:1–14:21. Along with the detailed structural analysis, Lamarche provides an interpretation of the author's thought in relation to post-exilic messianic ideas and to the servant poems of Second Isaiah.

Lamarche suggests that the figure of Zerubbabel may have influenced the author's messianic views. He finds a single messianic expectation in the portrayal of the coming king (9:9–10), the good shepherd rejected by his people (11:4–17), Yahweh's representative who was pierced (12:10–13:1) and the smitten shepherd (13:7–9). The historical personality upon whom the author fixed his hopes was at the same time, however, one in the line of descendants of David, from which line the messianic king would appear. Thus the messianic references are at once related to a historical figure and to one who will arise at the end of days. After reviewing Lamarche's book, Walter Harrelson found the author's thesis about the messianic passages attractive but was not convinced of the correctness of Lamarche's literary analysis (cf. W. Harrelson, "Review of Zacharie IX–XIV by Paul Lamarche," *JBL* 82 [1963] 116).

In 1968 F. F. Bruce published his Payton Lectures given at Fuller Theological Seminary in which he considers the NT "as a fresh presentation and interpretation of Old Testament theology—fresh, in the light of the 'new thing' that God did in the earth when His Son became man for man's salvation" (Bruce, *NT Development* 18). In the last chapter, "The Shepherd King," Bruce deals effectively with seven passages from Zech 9–14 in which Jesus saw his own role as the messiah. The passages are: 13:7–9, the smitten shepherd and the scattered sheep; 9:16, the thankless flock; 9:9–10, Behold, your king; 14:4, the Day of the Lord; 11:12 thirty pieces of silver; 12:10, the pierced one; 14:21 the expulsion of traders from the temple. One of Bruce's contributions to the field of the interpretation of scripture is his work with the Qumran materials. Bruce sees both similarity and dissimilarity between Qumran's and the NT's use of OT prophetic materials. They are similar in that they reinterpret OT texts in the light of their own situation. They each believe that the OT prophets were speaking of the last days and that they (Qumran people and NT Christians) were the ones to witness the fulfillment of the earlier prophecies. Both believed that there was something mysterious about the earlier prophecies that was revealed to their leaders (the teacher of righteousness and Jesus) in the last days. Both communities were atomistic and allegoristic in their use of OT prophecies. However, the Qumran community used such practices much more than did the NT writers. Both communities "chose that form of the biblical text which lent itself best to their interpretation" (F. F. Bruce, *Biblical Exegesis in the Qumran Texts* 80). Again, Bruce says, "in neither community are events created to fit the scriptures—on the contrary, the scriptures are interpreted in the light of events" (Bruce, *N.T. Development* 114). The primary difference between Qumran's interpretation of OT prophecies and that of the NT writers is that "although the Qumran community believed that the last days of the current age had set in, nowhere in the Qumran literature, so far as it has been published, is the coming messianic era viewed as having been inaugurated . . . , but whereas the latest Qumran texts are still waiting for the messianic age to dawn, for the early Christians it has dawned in Jesus" (F. F. Bruce, "The Theology and Interpretation of the Old Testament," in *Tradition and Interpretation,* ed. G. W. Anderson [Oxford: Clarendon Press, 1979] 411–412). Another great difference between the interpretation of Qumran and NT writers is that the NT writers understood that the Gentiles were included in the Abrahamic promise (cf. Rom 9:25; 1 Pet 2:10; Hos 2:23). "Such an application of Old Testament scripture, extending to Gentiles equal privileges within the Abrahamic covenant, would have been unacceptable to the Qumran sect" (Bruce, *NT Development* 79). Thus Qumran leaders and NT writers reinterpreted many OT prophecies in terms of their own situations and experiences.

H. Cunliffe-Jones in 1973 published a lecture in which he goes a step beyond Bruce. He says that three questions may be asked of an OT passage that has influenced the NT: (1) What is its historic meaning in its own setting? This is the foundation of everything else. (2) How does the NT actually use the OT passage? (3) How may the passage rightly be used to convey truth in the writer's (or reader's) own century? Cunliffe-Jones said that since Jesus found help in these chapters in clarifying his own conviction about the nature and outcome of his own vocation, and the primitive church turned to these chapters to interpret the life, death and resurrection of Jesus, we may find some elements in these chapters that have a universal meaning (H. Cunliffe-Jones, *A Word for Our Time?* [London: The Athlone Press, 1973] 6). One universal truth he finds in Zech 9:9 is that Jesus by entering Jerusalem as a victorious king riding on a donkey built onto his conception of the kingdom of God a transvaluation of authority. The word righteous "does not mean a careful balancing of merit and defect but a leaning over to rescue the wrongdoer from his sinning" (p. 7). Cunliffe-Jones said that in the teaching of Jesus authority is not repudiated: it is reinforced as in Matt 6:24; Mark 9:35; 10:45. Under the heading of the Day of the Lord based on passages from Zech 12 and 14, Cunliffe-Jones says that there are four elements for our positive reflection: Triumph, Transformation, Worship, and Holiness. The triumph of God comes in the conquest of evil (p. 19). The transformation of nature points to a transformed world in which there will be universal worship of the Lord and holiness will be universal.

In summary, Cunliffe-Jones stresses the value of Zech 9–14 and appeals for continued in-depth study of it:

> This little booklet Zechariah 9–14 sounds both the depths and the heights of human life. It bids us reckon with the exceeding sinfulness of sin, which goes far to wreck the very foundations of human life. It asks us also to take with equal seriousness the triumph of the eternal God. It is a great pity that the historical background of almost all of it is so uncertain, and we may hope that continued historical study will clarify this. It is a section of the Old Testament on which Jesus himself mediated to clarify his conception of his own mission, and to which his interpreters turned to explain it. There is in it a universal meaning, as well as a localized one, and we need concerted intellectual study, here as elsewhere in the Bible, of the kind of use which can be made of it today, alert to all that historical scholarship has to say about it, and compatible with intellectual integrity.

It is out of such concerted intellectual study that a satisfactory general use of the Bible will grow (p. 24).

A. OUTLINE OF ZECHARIAH 1–8

1. Superscription and first oracle   1:1–6
2. Eight night visions and oracles   1:7–6:8
   a. First vision—A man on a red horse and an accompanying oracle   1:7–17
   b. Second vision—Four horns and four smiths   2:1–4 (Eng. 1:18–21)
   c. Third vision—The man with a measuring line and an accompanying vision   2:5–17 (Eng. 2:1–13)
   d. Fourth vision—The accusation of the high priest and accompanying oracles   3:1–10
   e. Fifth vision—A golden lampstand, two olive trees and accompanying oracles   4:1–14
   f. Sixth vision—The flying scroll   5:1–4
   g. Seventh vision—A woman in an ephah   5:5–11
   h. Eighth vision—The chariots and the four winds—6:1–8
3. The symbolic crowning of Joshua   6:9–15
4. The question of fasting and morality   7:1–8:23
   a. The question about fasting   7:1–6
   b. Reiteration of the words of the Former Prophets   7:7–14
   c. A decalogue of promises   8:1–23
      (1) Five brief messages of hope   8:1–8
      (2) A sermon including two promises and exhortations   8:9–17
      (3) Three brief messages about the future   8:18–23

B. OUTLINE OF ZECHARIAH 9–14

1. The first burden   9:1–11:17
   a. Yahweh's kingdom in Syria, Phoenicia and Philistia   9:1–8
   b. The coming of a new king   9:9–10
   c. Freeing the captives   9:11–17
   d. A prophetic admonition (Mahnwort)   10:1–2
   e. Restoration of Judah and Joseph   10:3–12
   f. A fable-like taunt song against tyrants   11:1–3
   g. The shepherd rejected   11:4–17
2. The second burden   12:1–14:21
   a. The attack on Jerusalem by the nations   12:1–8
   b. Weeping in Jerusalem over one they had pierced   12:9–14
   c. Cleansing Jerusalem from sin, idols, and false prophets   13:1–6
   d. The smitten shepherd, a remnant spared   13:7–9
   e. The day of battle for Jerusalem   14:1–5
   f. The new Jerusalem   14:6–11
   g. The plague on those who war against Jerusalem   14:12–15
   h. The pilgrimage of the nations to Jerusalem   14:16–21

Superscription and First Oracle (1:1-6)

Translation

¹ *In the eighth month in the second year of Darius, the word of Yahweh came to Zechariah son of Berechiah son of Iddo the prophet saying,* ² *Yahweh was very angry* ^a *with your fathers.* ³ *And you shall say to them, Thus says Yahweh of hosts, Return to me, oracle of Yahweh of hosts, and I will return to you, says Yahweh of hosts.* ⁴ *Do not be like your fathers to whom the former prophets preached* ^a *saying, Thus says Yahweh of hosts, O turn from your evil ways and your evil deeds. But they did not hear and they did not listen to me, oracle of Yahweh.* ⁵ *Where are your fathers? Did the prophets live forever?* ⁶ *Surely, did not my words and my statutes which I commanded you by my servants the prophets overtake* ^a *your fathers? And they* ^b *repented and said, as Yahweh of hosts purposed to do to us, according to our ways and according to our deeds, so he has done with us.*

Notes

2.a. The translation "very angry" refers to the verb קצף and its cognate accusative.
4.a. קראו lit. "they called." In postexilic times it meant "preach" (cf. Jon 1:2; 3:2).
6.a. השיגו 3 c pl. hiph. pf. נשג "to overtake" (cf. Deut 28:15, 45).
6.b. The antecedent of "they" is unclear. See *Comment*.

Form/Structure/Setting

1:1–6 is an introductory pericope which serves as a part of the framework for the eight visions in Zech 1–6. The form is that of a sermon addressed to those who returned from Babylon in 536 B.C. and perhaps was reinterpreted and addressed to the generation of the Chronicler. The structure contains a superscription (1:1) which is an editor's note of the date, "the eighth month of the second year of Darius"; the source and nature of the message, "the word of Yahweh"; and the identity of the messenger, "Zechariah son of Berechiah, son of Iddo." The superscription is followed by a sermon in three parts: (1) Yahweh's anger with the fathers (1:2); (2) a call for the present generation to repent (1:3–4); and (3) a statement that man is mortal but God's word is eternal (1:5–6). The former prophets called for the fathers to repent of their evil ways and deeds, but they did not repent. The word of Yahweh spoken by the prophets overtook the fathers, and the implication is that the same fate awaits the present generation unless it repents. The setting might have been some festival or an anniversary of the renewal of the work on the temple.

Comment

The superscription in 1:1 differs from the superscriptions attached to most of the other OT prophetic books. In the first place it appears that an editor has changed the beginning of Zechariah's oracle from the first person, "the word of Yahweh came unto me" as in 6:9; 7:4; 8:1, 18, to the third person, "the word of Yahweh came to Zechariah" (cf. Mitchell 108; J. Baldwin 88). A second difference in the superscription is exactness of the date, "the eighth month of the second year of Darius." Most OT books of the prophets are dated generally by the names of kings who were reigning during the prophet's ministry (cf. Amos, Hosea, Isaiah, Micah, Jeremiah, Ezekiel, Zephaniah).

Exact dates (month, day, and year) are rare in the books of OT prophets. There are no exact dates in Amos, Hosea, Isaiah, Micah, or Jeremiah (cf. P. R. Ackroyd, *JJS* 2 [1950–51] 171). However, Ezekiel contains eleven passages which give the exact month, date, and year of certain events (cf. 1:2; 8:1; 20:1; 24:1, 17; 30:20; 31:1; 32:1; 33:21; 40:1). One date in Ezekiel (32:17) omits the month. There are seven exact dates in Haggai and Zechariah (Hag 1:1, 15; 2:1, 10, 20; Zech 1:1, 7; 7:1). The date in Zech 1:1 is the only one that does not give the day. It is a little surprising that the exact day of the beginning of Zechariah is not given. The Syriac version does give the exact day as "the first day of the eighth month" which seems plausible since the first day of the month would have been a holy day. But Baldwin points out that a comparison between the order of the Syriac version and that of the other dates in Haggai-Zechariah "shows that the Syriac is out of step in putting month, day, year." The other dates are in the order "day, month, year, or year, month, day" (Baldwin 87). She concludes that in view of the tendency of the Syriac version to clarify, amplify, and harmonize verses, "it seems likely that in this case the original did not include the day of the month" (Ibid).

Twice in the book of Zechariah the prophet is called "the son of Berechiah, son of Iddo" (1:1, 7), but in Ezra 5:1 and 6:14 he is referred to only as "the son of Iddo." No mention is made of Berechiah in Ezra, but a number of men named Berechiah appear in Chronicles, none of which can be related to our prophet (cf. 1 Chr 3:20; 6:39; 9:16; 15:17, 23; 2 Chr 28:12; Neh 3:4, 30; 6:18). Berechiah could have been Zechariah's father's name. Then Iddo would have been his grandfather. The term "son" is often used in the OT to mean, "descendant," "heir," "successor" and not necessarily an immediate son. Many other theories have been used to explain the absence of Berechiah's name in the Ezra passages. Jerome suggested that Berechiah was the father according to the flesh and Iddo was the father according to the Spirit (cf. S. Bullough, *CCHS* 689). H. G. Mitchell suggested that the phrase is from someone who identified our prophet with a certain Zechariah, the son of Jeberechiah in Isa 8:2. It is often noted that an Iddo and a Zechariah are mentioned in Neh 12:4, 16, but there is no certainty that the people there are the ones referred to in this book.

Zechariah is the only prophet to use the expression "former prophets" (1:4; 7:7, 12). The former prophets had become almost canonical for Zechariah. Many later prophets and apocalyptists are familiar with and are influenced by the former prophets. When Zechariah says that Yahweh had sent his servant the prophets to call the fathers to repent, he seems to refer to Jeremiah 35:17, and possibly 25:4, 5 and 18:11. Beuken (91) and Mason (32) see a strong similarity to 2 Chr 30:6–9.

Some ambiguity exists in 1:6b, "and they repented and said, as Yahweh purposed to do to us, according to our ways and our doings so has he done to us." Who are "they" and "us"? Are "they" the fathers who repented? If so, 1:4 says that they did not repent. Are "they" the present generation who repents? If so, we do not have any previous word in this book that they had been threatened with judgment. R. Kittel believed that 1:6b referred to the present generation and emended the text in BH from אבתיכם "your fathers" to אתכם "you." P. R. Ackroyd believes that Zechariah's contemporaries are addressed in 1:6 as an ideal generation (*Exile and Restoration*, 202–203). R. Mason (33) believes that is the more likely view. W. Beuken and A. Petijean take 1:6 as a part of a cultic confession used by the fathers but continued after the exile, so the words could be applicable to both generations (cf. Baldwin 92).

If we take 1:6 as a part of a cultic confession used by the fathers, we must assume that the fathers did not repent until tragedy struck (1:4). The confession also says that Yahweh did exactly what he said he would do (1:6; 8:14–15). S. R. Driver (183) said that the fathers turned "not at the warning, but at the judgment, which forced them when it was too late, to acknowledge the truth of what the prophet had said."

Explanation

Why did Zechariah or an editor begin his book with a call to repentance? Repentance was a prominent theme in Jeremiah and Ezekiel who were Zechariah's models. D. R. Jones says that "the opening section is placed here deliberately to set the visions that follow in the widest context of God's wrath upon his people, especially that final destruction of Judah in 586, which seemed to many like the Day of the Lord" (p. 54). Joyce Baldwin comments, "If the hortatory tone, the reminder of judgment and reference to the anger of the Lord appear to be an inappropriate way to encourage a downcast people and spur them to action, the purpose is to provide solid ground for the promises to come" (p. 87).

Zechariah was a prophet of unrealized hopes, and although work on the temple had already started when he began his ministry, he placed his work against the background of the exile and its causes. The exile had been due to the father's rejection of God's word to turn from their evil ways. Now Zechariah addresses another generation and asks them to learn from the past. One measure of a true prophet is the way he looks at the past. George Adam Smith says that the development of religion consists of a struggle between two tempers, both of which appeal to the past, but from opposite motives. "The one proves its devotion to the older prophets by adopting the exact formulas of their doctrine, counts these sacred to the letter and would enforce them in detail upon the minds and the circumstances of the new generation. It conceives that truth has been promulgated once and for all in forms as enduring as the principles they contain. It fences ancient rites, cherishes old customs and institutions, and when these are questioned it becomes alarmed and even savage. The other temper is no whit behind this one in its devotion to the past, but it seeks the ancient prophets not so

much for what they have said as for what they have been, not for what they
enforced but for what they encountered, suffered, and confessed. It asks not
for dogmas but for experience and testimony" (*EXB* 14, 624). This latter
view represents that of Zechariah.

Eight Night Visions and Oracles   (1:7–6:8)

Bibliography

Jeremias, C. *Die Nachtgesichte des Sacharja.* FRLANT 117 (1976). **May, H. G.** "A Key
to the Interpretation of Zechariah's Visions." *JBL* 57 (1938) 173–184. **Rignell,
L. G.** *Die Nachtgesichte des Sacharja.* Lund: Gleerup, 1950.

It is widely agreed that the eight night visions of Zechariah belong together,
but there is some debate about the nature of the visions, the date of each
vision, and the basic principle that holds them together. Older scholars tried
to arrange the visions by subject matter. Mitchell (102, 115) sees three groups
of visions: The first three depicting the return from captivity; the fourth and
fifth dealing with the anointed of Yahweh; and the last three with the removal
of sin. S. R. Driver (179) divided the eight visions into two groups: (1) Three
visions (1, 2, and 8) dealing with the relation of Israel to the heathen world
without, and (2) the remaining five visions (3, 4, 5, 6, 7) dealing with the
future of Israel as a nation. Joyce Baldwin (80, 93) believes that the arrangement of the visions follows a chiastic pattern a/b/b/c/c/b/b/a. The first and
last are alike in that they speak of horses and chariots used to patrol the
earth and the earth is at rest. The second and third speak about the threat
of the nations against Judah and God's defense of his people. The fourth
and fifth deal with the two anointed leaders of the post-exilic community,
and the sixth and seventh describe the cleansing of the land of sin and sinners.
    Some questions have been raised about the nature of the night visions
in 1:7–6:16. H. G. Mitchell (117) argued that the vision accounts were not
the record of what Zechariah saw in a dream while he was asleep or in an
ecstatic condition. He said they must be classed with those of Amos 7:1,
Jer 1:11, and Ezek 8 "as literary forms in which the prophet clothed his
ideas, whatever their origin, for the purpose of securing for them prompter
attention among those whom he sought to instruct and influence" (see also
H. G. May, *JBL* 57 [1938] 173). Robert North argued that the account of
the series of visions is artistically constructed. He suggests that the account
was composed in writing intended for silent, reflective reading rather than
preaching aloud. "The prophet is simply conveying in a form which he deemed
suitable certain convictions acquired from reasoning rather than from any
real dream either irrational or miraculous" (R. North, "Prophecy to Apocalyptic Via Zechariah," VTSup 22 [1971] 49). We may make allowance for stero-
type literary forms in reporting the "vision" experiences of OT prophets

and still believe that the experience was revelational. Rex Mason said that Zechariah might have been drawing on older motifs and traditions in his vision accounts, but "it would not do on account of this to dismiss the 'night visions' as a mere literary convention, if by that we mean that they do not reflect a genuine conviction of God's message. Just as great poets can use conventional forms, such as the sonnet, to express genuine feeling, so the true prophet can express what he felt intensely and deeply to be true through stereotyped forms" (Mason 31).

An examination of the structure of the visions reveals a general pattern with some variety. The general pattern includes (1) an introduction which reports in one form or another that Zechariah saw some person or a happening; (2) a description of what he saw; (3) the prophet's questions about the meaning of what he saw; and (4) an interpreting angel's interpretation. All of the visions fit this general pattern except the fourth (the cleansing of Joshua the high priest 3:1–5). In the fourth vision everything is different. The introductory phrase, "and he showed me," occurs only here in the book (3:1). There are no questions from the prophet or answers from an interpreting angel.

Christian Jeremias following a number of OT scholars (K. Elliger 118–22; A. Jepsen, "Kleine Beitrage zum Zwolfprophetenbuch III," *ZAW* 61 [1945/48] 95–96; T. Chary (73) doubts whether the fourth vision belongs to the original series at all. Jeremias believes that this fourth vision is so different that it should be considered as outside the cycle of seven night visions and discusses it at the end of his book. It is true that on the basis of form, vision four is very different from the others, but the content and theme fit the themes of the others (N. L. A. Tidwell, "wā ōmar [Zech. 3:5] and the Genre of Zechariah's Fourth Vision." *JBL* 94 [1975] 346). It is best to try to understand the eight visions in their present positions rather than rearranging them as the NEB has done. The NEB moves 4:1–3; 11–14 to a position between chaps. 2 and 3, and makes 4:4–10 follow chap. 3 on the assumption that the oracle in 4:4–10 does not relate to either vision four or five (cf. Mason 45–46).

Interspersed in four of the vision accounts are various oracles. In vision one the oracle is in 1:13–17; in vision three the oracle is in 2:10–17 (Eng. 2:6–13); in vision four the oracles are in 3:6–10; and in vision five the oracles are in 4:5–10. All of the oracles follow the vision to which they are attached except the last one. The oracles in 4:4–10 interrupt the vision of the two olive trees in 4:1–3, 11–14. The relationship of the original form of the oracles to the visions accounts is a matter of debate.

All eight visions seem to have occurred in a single night, "the twenty-fourth day of the eleventh month of the second year of Darius" (Feb 15, 520 B.C.). Gerhard von Rad remarked that "these pictures had appeared to his spirit during the course of a single night" (*The Message of the Prophets.* Tr. D. M. G. Stalker [London: SCM, 1965] 254).

H. G. May believed that the date "the twenty-fourth day of the eleventh month" was the key to the interpretation of Zechariah's visions because of its proximity to the spring New Year, a little more than a month later (H. G. May, *JBL* 57 [1938] 173). May believed that Zechariah was planning to hold a secret coronation of Zerubbabel on that New Year's day. Joshua too would be involved in the ceremony as demonstrated in the fourth vision 3:1-5. According to May, Zechariah drew his symbolism from his familiarity with the Babylonian New Year festival and its influences on Israel's pre-exilic rituals. May sees the influence of the worship of the sun-god in the references to the horses and chariots in visions one and eight.

First Vision—A Man on a Red Horse and an Accompanying Oracle (1:7-17)

Bibliography

Ackroyd, P. R. "Two Old Testament Historical Problems of the Early Persian Period." *JNES* 17 (1958) 23-27. **McHardy, W. D.** "The Horses in Zechariah." *In Memoriam Paul Kahle*, eds. M. Black and G. Fohrer. Berlin: Verlag Alfred Topelmann, (1968). 174-79. **Orr, A.** "The Seventy Years of Babylon." *VT* 6 (1956) 304-06. **Whitley, C. F.** "The Term Seventy Years Captivity." *VT* 4 (1954) 60-72.

Translation

⁷ In the twenty-fourth day of the eleventh month, it was the month Shebat,[a] *in the second year of Darius, the word of Yahweh came to Zechariah son of Berechiah son of Iddo the prophet*[b] *saying,* ⁸ *"I saw in the night and behold a man was riding upon a red horse. He was standing among the myrtles*[a] *which were in the hollow,*[b] *and behind him were horses, red, sorrel, and white.* ⁹ *And I said, 'What are these, my lord?' And the angel speaking with me said to me, 'I will show you what these are.'* ¹⁰ *And the man standing among the myrtles answered and said, 'These are the ones that Yahweh sent to patrol the earth.'* ¹¹ *And they answered the angel of Yahweh, the one standing among the myrtles, and said, 'We have walked through the earth and behold all the earth sits and rests.'* ¹² *And the angel of Yahweh answered and said, 'O Yahweh of hosts, how long will you not show compassion on Jerusalem and on the cities of Judah against which you have had indignation these seventy years?'*

¹³ *"And Yahweh answered the angel speaking with me good words, comforting words.* ¹⁴ *And the angel speaking with me said to me, 'Preach, thus says Yahweh of hosts, I have been jealous for Jerusalem and for Zion with a great jealousy,* ¹⁵ *and I am very angry with the nations who are at ease, against whom I was angry a little, but they furthered*[e] *the disaster.* ¹⁶ *Therefore,' thus says Yahweh, 'I have returned to Jerusalem with compassion. My house*[a] *will be built in her, oracle of Yahweh of hosts, and a measuring line will be stretched over Jerusalem.* ¹⁷ *Again, Cry, saying, thus says Yahweh of hosts, 'Again my cities shall overflow*[a] *with good things and Yahweh will again comfort Zion and again choose Jerusalem.'"*

Notes

7.a. שבט "Shebat" is the Babylonian name for the eleventh month and only occurs here in the OT. Since Haggai and earlier books use numbers for the months and the Chronicler consistently uses Babylonian names for them, many scholars see "Shebat" (1:7) and "Chislev" (7:1) as later insertions into the book of Zechariah (cf. J. Baldwin, 94, 141).

7.b. הנביא "the prophet" refers to Zechariah, not Iddo.

8.a. ההדסים "The myrtle" is an evergreen flowering shrub that is common throughout Palestine. In the later part of the OT it is mentioned among the trees that testify to the prosperity of the messianic age (Isa 41:19; 55:13). There is no need to change ההרסים for ההרים "mountains" with the LXX.

8.b. במצלה "in the hollow" or "deep" probably refers to the lowest part of the Kidron Valley where there was a garden in pre-exilic times (2 Kgs 25:4). But the word may have a symbolic meaning here also for "distress" of the people (cf. Ps 88:6; Jonah 2:4). JB translates the phrase "deep rooted myrtles."

15.a. עזרו basically means "they helped." Here it probably means that the nations carried the evil judgment on Judah too far (cf. Ackroyd 176 n. 20).

16.a. בית "house" is used for the temple five times in Zech (1:16; 4:9; 7:3; 8:9; 11:13) while היכל is used also five times (6:12, 13, 14, 15; 8:9). Cf. G. W. Ahlstrom, *Joel and the Temple Cult of Jerusalem* (Leiden: E. S. Brill, 1971) 19.

17.a. פוץ normally means "scatter" in defeat (Ezek 34:45; Zech 13:7), but here all Eng. vers. read "overflow." Rignell (53) translates it here "despoiled" (cf. Ackroyd, *Exile* 177, n. 20).

Form/Structure/Setting

The form of 1:7–17 is that of a vision report (vv. 7–15) plus an oracle (vv 16–17). V 7 is a superscription intended for the whole section 1:7–6:8. In 1:8, Zechariah reports that he saw a man on a red horse among the myrtles in the hollow (presumably on the south side of Jerusalem). Other horses of various colors were behind him. 1:9–13 contains a conversation between Zechariah and the interpreting angel (1:9–10); between the horsemen and the angel of Yahweh (1:11); and between Yahweh and the interpreting angel (1:12–13). Zechariah asks about the identity of the horsemen. The interpreting angel says that they have been on patrol through the earth. They report that the whole earth is quiet with no sign of an upheaval that might signal Yahweh's coming. Then the angel of Yahweh intercedes for Jerusalem and the cities of Judah (1:12), and Yahweh answers with comforting words. 1:14–15 contains Zechariah's commission. He is to preach that Yahweh is jealous for Jerusalem and is very angry with the nations that had punished her (1:15). The oracle said that Yahweh has returned to Jerusalem with compassion. The temple and Jerusalem will be rebuilt. The cities of Judah will overflow with good things because Yahweh has again chosen Jerusalem (1:16–17).

The setting of the first vision is impossible to determine. The date of the twenty-fourth day of the eleventh month might suggest that Zechariah was thinking of the anniversary of the resumption of the work on the temple five months before. The visions might have taken place in the temple area although the temple had not yet been rebuilt. D. R. Jones (57) suggests that the myrtle trees probably were in the forecourt of the temple area and were translated in the vision to the gate of heaven. There is much in the visions to indicate that Zechariah was standing in the heavenly council. The patrol of horsemen is similar to the rovings of Satan in Job 1–2 except the functions are different. Satan's accusation of Joshua the high priest in chap. 3, and the chariots coming out from the two mountains in chap. 6, suggest a setting of the visions in the temple area which has been transported to heaven. Of course what Zechariah saw taking place in heaven had its counterpart on earth. Yahweh would return to Jerusalem; the temple would be rebuilt; the nations would be defeated or converted, the priests, people, and the land would be cleansed; and the rule of Yahweh would be established in the whole earth.

Comment

Rex Mason believes that the expression "in the night" (v 8) suggests the idea of the prophet as a watchman for the dawn or for the enemy. He points to Hab 2:1–3 which portrays the prophet on a watchtower waiting for a word from God; to Ezek 3:17 where the prophet was assigned the role of a watchman, and to Isaiah 21:6–9 and 11–12 where a prophet stands on a watchtower day and night and finally sees men coming in "two-horse chariots" (NEB). The night often symbolizes a time of suffering and distress, while the dawn can refer to the time of God's deliverance (Pss 30:5; 46:5). In the first vision Zechariah appears as a watchman through the long night of distress and is informed of the first signs of God's return to his people and land.

One characteristic of Zechariah's materials is the presence of an interpreting angel. An interpreting angel is found elsewhere in the OT in Ezekiel 40–48 and in Daniel. Some have seen the use of the interpreting angel as an indication that the book of Zechariah is apocalyptic literature. Hartmut Gese sees seven of Zechariah's night visions as symbols of the various phases of the night. Visions 1–3 represent the evening; vision 5 represents midnight; and visions 6–8 represent the morning (the restoration of the world). (See chart in H. Gese, "Anfang und Ende der Apokalyptik, dargestellt am Sacharjabuch," *ZTK* 70 [1973] 36). He calls the night visions of Zechariah "the oldest and best known apocalypse" partly on the grounds of the presence of an interpreting angel in them (p. 24). Paul Hanson (*Dawn* 250) says that Zechariah utilized a genre—the vision with the *angelus interpres*—that later was adopted by apocalyptic writers to communicate their message. But one genre is not a sufficient basis on which to identify a piece of literature as apocalyptic.

There seems to be some confusion over the identification of the principal characters in the first vision. There is a "man" riding a red horse standing among the myrtles; behind him are other horses presumably with angelic riders (v 8). There is an angel speaking with the prophet (v 9); there is a man standing among the myrtles (nothing is said about a horse, v 10); there is an angel of Yahweh (vv 11, 12). Although some earlier critics resorted to drastic emendations and deletions to "correct" the text (see S. R. Driver, 186–87), it is probably best to consider the "man" in vv 8 and 10 as the leader of the patrol and as the angel of Yahweh in verses 11 and 12. "These" and "they" in vv 9, 10, and 11 are the other angelic riders in the patrol.

The angel of Yahweh is not to be identified as Yahweh in this case. Because of his intercession in v 12 he may represent a forerunner of Michael, the patron angel of Israel (Dan 10:21; 12:1). The horses and riders may be an influence of the Persian post-system but more likely the messengers are those who were members of the heavenly council (cf. Ackroyd, *Exile* 176). There is no way to determine how many horses were involved in the vision. No significance should be attached to the various colors of the horses (for a discussion of the colors see 6:1-8).

Is there evidence of a mythological background behind some of the visions of Zechariah? T. Chary sees a mythological background to the "hollow" or "deep" (v 8) (Chary 57). Others see a similarity between visions 1 and 8 at the point of the horses and chariots. In vision 8, four chariots come out from between the two bronze mountains. The two mountains represent the dwelling place of God. R. J. Clifford has pointed out that in Canaan and in the OT some mountains are given religious veneration. Such mountains "can be the meeting place of the gods, the sources of water and fertility, the battle-ground of conflicting natural forces, the meeting place of heaven and earth, the place where effective decrees are issued. In these senses, the mountains are cosmic, that is, involved in the government and stability of the cosmos" (R. J. Clifford, *The Cosmic Mountain in Canaan and the Old Testament* [Cambridge, Mass.: Harvard University Press, 1972] 3). Clifford notes that in the Hebrew Bible, the cosmic mountain motif can be seen in the beliefs surrounding Mt. Zion. This "mountain" on which the temple stood was God's earthly dwelling place, a place protected from his enemies who could only stand at its base and rage, the place where God's enemies will be defeated in battle and where streams of living water begin. These and other "mythological" motifs perhaps provide some of the background for Zechariah's visions and his book.

Paul Hanson distinguishes between prophetic and apocalyptic eschatology partially on the basis of the use of myth. Hanson argues that Israel's religion contrasted sharply with that of the major city-states of Mesopotamia and Canaan. The cults of the latter centered around a pantheon of cosmic deities charged with regulating the cycles of the natural order, and the ritual of these cults was tied to the royal house giving cosmic legitimacy to the current dynasty. Although much of Israel's early hymnic literature was influenced by this ancient ritual, it presents "a new view of reality which has cut the heart from the nature myth of the Canaanites. The God of Israel, Yahweh, is not in the first instance identified with the rainstorm in its yearly struggle to overcome the threat of drought. . . . Rather he is recognized in events leading up to Israel's emergence as a people" (Hanson 13). For Hanson the difference between prophetic eschatology and apocalyptic eschatology was that the prophets always translated their cosmic view of reality into real history, whereas the apocalyptists left their visions of God's future actions on behalf of his people in the cosmic realm. Robert P. Carroll criticizes Hanson's view of myth at the point of his polarization of the prophet's and apocalyptists' view of myth and history. Carroll says that Hanson's analysis "leads to false antitheses and to an overly simplified presentation of material that is even more complex and complicated than Hanson allows (R. P. Carroll, "Twilight of Prophecy or Dawn of Apocalyptic?" *JSOT* 14 [1979] 19). Carroll does not deny that there are mythological motifs in Zechariah and other OT materials. But he does say that the treatment of myth throughout Hanson's book is unsatisfactory (p. 20).

The major thrust of the first vision is in its message of comfort and assurance that Yahweh is about to act to restore the temple, the cities, and the prosperity of his people. Perhaps we can see in the use of the word "comfort" in vv 13 and 17 a deliberate reference to Isa 40:1. Even though no visible signs of the intervention of Yahweh on behalf of his people were evident at this time, the message of Yahweh was clear—the long night of waiting ("seventy years") was over. Yahweh still had compassion and was jealous for Israel. (For a discussion of the jealousy and wrath of Yahweh in the OT see earlier explanation in Nahum 1:2).

The long night of waiting is referred to as "seventy years" in length (v 12). The term "seventy years" occurs a number of times in the OT and in some extrabiblical materials. In Jer 25:11–12 and 29:10 it refers to the period of Babylonian rule over Israel. In Zech 1:12 and 7:5 it refers to the period of Jerusalem's destruction. In Isa 23:15–17 Tyre was to be laid waste for "seventy years," and in 2 Chr 36:21 and perhaps in Dan 9:2 the "seventy years" was a period where Israel was keeping the sabbaths she had missed. Whitley thinks that "the seventy years" in Zechariah is a reference to a specific date of 586–516 B.C. but was an insertion by a later editor (C. F. Whitley, "The Term Seventy Years Captivity," *VT* 4 [1954] 72). Avigdor Orr admits that the term "seventy years" in Zechariah may be a specific date and may be the work of a later editor, but the date according to Orr refers to 605–539 B.C. Orr believes that the date referred to the rule of Babylon and the *terminus post quem* could not be later than 539 B.C. (A. Orr, "The Seventy Years of Babylon," *VT* 6 [1956] 306). E. Lipinski has recently called attention to an inscription on the black stone of Esarhaddon (681–669 B.C.) that the god Marduk should have been angry with his land until "seventy years had been accomplished." But in fact Marduk had mercy on Babylon and restored her after eleven years. Lipinski's conclusion was that seventy years constituted a period of divine anger against a city or sanctuary (E. Lipinski, "Recherches sur le Livre de Zacharie," *VT* 20 [1970] 38).

The themes of judgment on the nations, the measuring line stretched over Jerusalem, and the overflowing population of the city will be taken up in the following visions. The use of the term עוֹד "again" four times in v 17 is significant. At the beginning of the verse it simply means that the prophet is to repeat what he had been told to say (vv 14–16). There is a problem about the use of the second עוֹד. It can mean "again" or "while," depending on one's interpretation of the whole clause. Does the clause say, "Again my cities shall overflow with good things," or does it say, "While my cities are scattered (or deprived from) the good"? (cf. Ackroyd 177 n. 20). Both translations are possible. This second use of עוֹד may be a reference to the current unfortunate situation in Jerusalem. However the third and fourth occurrences of עוֹד in this verse definitely mean "again." Yahweh will again comfort Jerusalem after a period of suffering and he will again "choose" Jerusalem. He had chosen Zion once as his dwelling place when he made a covenant with David (cf. 3:2; 1 Kgs 8:44, 48; Isa 44:26–28; 2 Chr 6:6, 34, 38).

Second Vision—Four Horns and Four Smiths (2:1-4 [Eng. 1:18-21])

Translation

1(18)a *And I lifted up my eyes and behold I saw four horns.* 2(19) *And I said to the angel who spoke with me, "What are these?" And he said to me, "These are the horns which scattered Judah, Israel, and Jerusalem."* 3(20) *Then Yahweh caused me to see four craftsmen,* a 4(21) *and I said, "What are these coming to do?" And he said, "These are the horns which scattered Judah so that* a *not a man lifted up his head. And these (craftsmen) came to rout* b *them, to throw down* c *the horns of the nations, who lift up a horn against the land of Judah to scatter her."*

Notes

1.a. At this point the chapter and verse numbers differ in the Hebrew and English texts. 1:18 in English is 2:1 in Hebrew. Verse divisions probably go back to ca. A.D. 200 (cf. R. Pfeiffer, *Introduction to the Old Testament* [New York: Harper Bros. 1941] 80) but no numbers were assigned to them until medieval times (cf. I. M. Price, *The Ancestry of Our English Bible*, eds. W. A. Irwin and A. P. Wikgren, 2nd rev. ed. [New York: Harper Bros., 1949] 24). The chapter divisions were not standardized in the Hebrew text until the first half of the tenth century A.D. (Pfeiffer 80).

3.a. חרשים "smiths" or "craftsmen" of any sort, stoneworker (Exod 28:11), carpenter (1 Kgs 12:12), metalworker (1 Sam 13:19).

4.a. כפי is an idiom, lit. "according to the mouths of" (cf. Lev 25:52).

4.b. להחריד appears to be a hiph. inf. cst. חרד "to frighten," or "terrify." The LXX τοῦ ὀξῦναι "to sharpen" translates חדד. The NEB "to reunite" seems to be from יחד.

4.c. לידות "to throw down," a pi. inf. cst. ידה (*CHAL* 128).

Form/Structure/Setting

The form of the second vision is essentially the same as that of vision 1 without the concluding oracle. First there is the report of a vision, "I lifted up my eyes and I saw and behold" (cf. 2:2; 5:1; 6:1). Secondly, there is the description of what Zechariah saw, "four horns" (2:1) and "four smiths" (2:3) followed by the prophet's questions, "What are these?" and "What are these coming to do?" Finally the interpreting angel answers both questions. The four horns are four nations, powers, or kingdoms that scattered Judah, Israel and Jerusalem, and the four smiths have come to terrify and to cast down the nations (horns) because they scattered Israel. There is nothing in this brief vision account to indicate any setting different from that of the first.

Comment

This second vision takes up the theme of the wrath of God on the nations which was set out in vision 1. In the introduction God's wrath was upon Israel (1:2). Yahweh had given them into the hands of the nations who abused and despoiled them and carried them into exile. Now God's wrath is turned against the nations who went beyond Yahweh's intentions for them in the punishment of Israel (1:15). The nations are represented by four horns, either ox horns or horns of iron. Deut 33:17 pictures the strength of Joseph with this metaphor.

> His firstling bull has majesty,
> and his horns are the horns of a wild ox;
> with them he shall push the peoples,
> all of them, to the end of the earth.

When a wild ox or bull was captured or defeated his horns would be cut off. Yahweh would do this to the nations.

> All the horns of the wicked he will cut off,
> but the horns of the righteous shall be exalted (Ps 75:10).

Sometimes horns representing nations were made of brass (cf. Mic 4:13) which might explain the reference to the smiths coming to cut down the horns. Smiths were metal workers. The prophet speaking for Yahweh in Isa 54:16–17a says,

> Behold, I have created the smith
> who blows the fire of coals,
> and produces a weapon for its purpose.
> I have created the ravager to destroy;
> no weapon that is fashioned
> against you shall prosper,
> and you shall confute every tongue
> that rises against you in judgment.

The nations to be cut off are not named. The number four probably corresponds to the four horsemen in the first vision and the four chariots of the last, and indicates the totality of enemy nations in every direction that had oppressed Israel.

The expression "Judah, Israel, and Jerusalem" is a little unusual. "Israel" is not in the LXX. The BHS and NEB and many scholars take it as a gloss. J. D. W. Watts suggests that Judah is being defined by Israel and Jerusalem so that she is presented as the heir of Abraham, Moses, and David (*BBC* 7, 316). Perhaps Israel is included here because the prophets always spoke of the restoration of all the tribes in the new age. Watts notes that there is no oracle attached to this vision, but suggests that the short message in 2:9 is more appropriate here than after 2:8 (p. 317).

The thrust of the second vision is the same as that of the first. It is a message of comfort and assurance that Yahweh is about to act on behalf of his people.

Third Vision—The Man with a Measuring Line and Accompanying Oracles (2:5-17 [Eng. 2:1-13])

Bibliography

Robertson, E. "The Apple of the Eye in the Masoretic Text." *JTS* 38 (1937) 57–59. **Scott, R. B. Y.** "Secondary Meaning of '*Ahar.*" *JTS* 50 (1949) 178–79. **Stinespring, W. F.** "No Daughter of Babylon." *Encounter* 26 (1965) 133–41. **Vriezen, T. C.** "Two Old Cruces." *OTS* (1948) 80–91.

Translation

5(Eng. 2:1) *And I lifted up my eyes and behold I saw a man, and in his hand was a measuring line.* 6(2) *Then I said, "Where are you going?" And he said to me, "To measure Jerusalem to see what its width and length should be."* 7(3) *And behold the angel speaking with me was going out and another was going out to meet him.* 8(4) *And he said to him, "Run, speak to this* a *youth, Jerusalem shall be inhabited like open country* b *because of the multitude of men and cattle in her midst.* 9(5) *And I will be to her, oracle of Yahweh, a wall of fire around her and glory in the midst of her."*

10(6) *Oh, oh, flee from the land of the North, Oracle of Yahweh, because I have scattered* a *you like four winds of heaven, oracle of Yahweh.* 11(7) *Oh, Zion,* a *inhabitant of the Maiden* b *Babylon, escape!* 12(8) *Because, thus says Yahweh of hosts, after glory* a *he sent me to the nations who were plundering you. The one who touches you touches the apple of his eye.* b

13(9) *"For behold I am about to shake* a *my hand against them, And they shall be plunder for their servants, And you shall know that Yahweh of hosts has sent me.* 14(10) *Sing and rejoice, maiden Zion, For behold I am coming and I will dwell in your midst, oracle of Yahweh.* 15(11) *And many nations shall join* a *themselves to Yahweh in that day, And they shall become my people, And I will dwell in your midst. Then you shall know that Yahweh of hosts has sent me to you.* 16(12) *And Yahweh will inherit Judah as his portion upon the holy land, and he will again choose Jerusalem.* 17(13) *Hush, all flesh before Yahweh, because he is rousing himself from his holy dwelling-place."*

Notes

8.a. הֵלָז an unusual form of the dem. pron. זֶה plus prep. and art. (cf. GKC 340).
8.b. פְּרָזוֹת open country as opposed to walled cities (Ezek 38:11; Esth 9:19).
10.a. LXX reads "from the four winds I will gather you." This meaning fits the context but it involves reading מֵאַרְבַּע "from four" for כְּאַרְבַּע "as four," and אֶסְפְּתִי "I will gather" for פֵּרַשְׂתִּי "I scattered." Ackroyd (179) translates פֵּרַשְׂתִּי "I caused you to take wings" in the sense of "spread out," which is parallel to return.

11.a. rsv follows LXX εἰς Σειών "to Zion" rather than MT which makes Zion a vocative.

11.b. בת בבל should not be translated "daughter of Babylon" but as an appositional genitive, "maiden Babylon" (cf. Stinespring 133–141).

12.a. אחר כבוד "after glory" is very difficult to interpret in this context. See comment for various theories.

12.b. בבת עינו "the apple(?) of his eye" only occurs here, but a similar expression עינו אישׁ "little man of his eye" occurs in Deut 32:10; Ps 17:8. בבת according to BDB (p. 92) is from בבה or בבא "gate." CHAL 33 takes the whole phrase to mean "eyeball." עינו "his eye" is one of the 18 *tiqqune sopherim*, "corrections of the scribes." The original reading was probably עיני "my eye" (cf. Mitchell 146).

13.a. מניף hiph. part. נוף. The part. probably expresses imminent judgment.

15.a. ונלוו 3 c pl niph. pf. לוה (CHAL 174) "and they will join themselves" not to Israel but to Yahweh.

Form/Structure/Setting

The form of this pericope is that of a vision report (2:5–9, Eng. 2:1–5), a group of oracles (2:10–16, Eng. 2:6–10), and a call for silence and reverence before Yahweh (2:17, Eng. 2:13). Zechariah sees a man with a measuring line in his hand. The prophet asks the man where he is going, and he replies that he is going to measure the size of Jerusalem. Then the interpreting angel goes forth and another angel goes out to meet him to tell him to run and tell the youth that Jerusalem would be rebuilt without walls, as open country because of its vast population and because God would be her external protection. "A wall of fire about her," and her inner glory.

The oracles seem to be made up of four sayings: (1) an exhortation to flee from Babylon (2:10–11, Eng. 2:6–7); (2) reasons for leaving Babylon: (a) Yahweh guards Israel as the pupil of his eye, and (b) Yahweh is shaking his hands against them (2:12–13, Eng. 2:8–9). J. D. W. Watts (318) and P. R. Ackroyd (*PCB* 647) suggest that 2:12–13 (Eng. 2:8–9) links closely with 1:18–21 explaining the reversal of Judah's fortunes; (3) a call for rejoicing because Yahweh is coming to dwell with his people, both Jews and Gentiles, 2:14–16, (Eng. 2:10–12); and (4) a call for silence and reverence before Yahweh as he rouses himself to accomplish his purpose (2:17, Eng. 2:13).

Comment

This third vision amplifies a remark made in 1:16 that a measuring line would be stretched over Jerusalem, which means that Jerusalem will be rebuilt. Ambiguity still prevails in this vision. The identity of the man with the measuring line is not clear. Some scholars think he is the prophet (D. R. Jones 63; Jerome; cf. *PCB*, 647). Others say he is an angel or that his identity is unimportant. If the young man were the prophet that would tell us something about his age. But no solid evidence for the prophet's age can be derived from this reference. It seems that the young man was going to rebuild Jerusalem along the lines of the former city, with definite boundaries or walls for protection from enemies. But, the angel said to the youth that the new Jerusalem would be built as villages without walls. The only wall she would need would be the wall of the fire of Yahweh around her. Yahweh would protect her and she would be free to enlarge her boundaries to take in the influx of people who had been scattered by the nations, and the nations who would come and join themselves to Yahweh (2:15, Eng. 2:11). The idea of a great population may be related to Yahweh's promise to Abraham of a great posterity (Gen. 12:1-3; cf. Isa 54:1-3).

It seems clear that the "land of the north" in 2:10 refers to Babylon (cf. 2:11; Jer 3:18; 16:15; 23:8; 31:8). Although Babylon was east of Judah, travelers from Babylon had to enter Judah from the north because of the desert between them.

The expression אחר כבוד שלחני "after glory he sent me" is the most puzzling clause in the book. Is it to be taken as a purpose clause to mean that Yahweh sent Zechariah to get glory; or as a temporal clause "after the glory i.e. the vision, Yahweh sent me. . ."? Does "glory" refer to Yahweh as the RSV indicates; or to the vision (KJV); or to heaviness or insistence, as Chary and Baldwin believe? כבוד basically means "to be heavy." Baldwin suggests "with insistence he sent me" (p. 109). Others emend or transpose the text in order to get a clear reading. NEB changes אחר to ארח and reads "a glorious mission (way)." D. W. Thomas changes אחר to אשר and reads "whose glory sent me" (IB 1066). R. B. Y. Scott reads אחר "with" instead of "after." Vriezen believes that אחר כבוד is an editor's note, which means that v 12 should come after כבוד at the end of v 9 (Eng. v 5). Watts and Ackroyd move 2:12-13 (Eng. 2:8-9) to follow 1:21. George A. Smith omits them. F. C. Eiselen translates כבוד as "honor" and thinks it refers to the honor that comes to the prophet when his words are fulfilled (Minor Prophets, 617).

Paul Hanson notes that the terms כבוד "glory" and שכן "to tent" are two key concepts shared by Ezekiel and Zechariah. שכן is used in Ezekiel to express the covenant conditions under which Yahweh will be present with his people (37:24-27; 43:7-9). It is used in the same sense twice in this passage of Zechariah (2:14-15, Eng. 2:10-11).

The word כבוד "glory" is used in Ezekiel to refer to the tabernacling presence of Yahweh with his people. The "glory" of the God of Israel abandoned Jerusalem just before its destruction (Ezek 10:18-19; 11:22-24), and would return to inaugurate the new age (Ezek 43:4; 44:4). Hanson thinks that the term is used in the same technical sense in Zech 2:9 and 12 (Eng. 2:5 and 8). If "glory" here refers to the returning presence of God to the rebuilt temple, then Zechariah is tying his call and commission to the fulfillments of his prophecies (cf. Ezek 2:5). Twice in this passage the prophet says the people will know that Yahweh has sent him. Once when the enemy nations will be plundered (2:13, Eng. 2:9) and once when many nations will be converted and God comes to dwell with his people (2:15, Eng. 2:11). Two other times Zechariah points to the verification of his commission at the time the temple is built (4:9; 6:5).

The last part of the pericope (2:14-17, Eng. 2:10-13) probably was used in some cultic setting. Yahweh will appear in a theophany to be greeted with shouts of joy (cf. Ps 47:1-9). But when he comes all flesh is to be silenced (cf. Hab 2:20; Zeph 1:7) because Yahweh is "awakening" or "rousing himself" (2:17, Eng. 2:12).

Explanation

Vv 4 and 5 present one of the most amazing texts in the OT. At a time when others such as Nehemiah were interested in rebuilding the walls of Jerusalem and excluding from the community those who had divorced their wives and married young foreign girls (Ezra 10:2–3), Zechariah sees a vision of the future Jerusalem as a broad, spreading metropolis with the wall of God's presence around her and the glory of his presence within her. The church's greatest defense is still God's presence around her and his glory within her. The word נֵעוֹר 3rd mas. sing. niph. perf. of עוּר "awake" is frequently used in the Psalms in a cultic setting (Ps 7:6; 35:23; 44:23; 57:8; 59:4). It means that Yahweh is about to act on behalf of his people and his name. The only occurrence of the expression "holy land" in the OT is in 2:16 (Eng 2:12).

Fourth Vision—The Accusation of the High Priest and Accompanying Oracles   (3:1–10)

Bibliography

Baldwin, J. G. "*Ṣemaḥ* as a Technical Term in the Prophets," *VT* 14 (1964) 93–97. **Davis, J. D.** "The Reclothing and Coronation of Joshua, Zech III and VI." *Princeton Theological Review* 18 (1920) 256–68. **Jeremias, C.** *Die Nachtgesichte des Sacharja*, 201–225. **Lipinski, E.** "Recherches sur le livre de Zacharie." *VT* 20 (1970) 25–29. **Thomas, D. W.** "A Note on מחלצות in Zech 3:4." *JTS* 34 (1932) 279–80. **Tidwell, L. A.** "*Wā'ōmar* (Zech 3:5) and the Genre of Zechariah's Fourth Vision." *JBL* 94 (1975) 343–55.

Translation

[1] *And he showed me Joshua the high priest standing before the angel of Yahweh, and Satan* [a] *was standing upon his right to accuse him.* [2] *And Yahweh said to the Satan, "Yahweh rebukes you, Satan, Yahweh who chose Jerusalem rebukes you. Is not this a brand snatched from fire?"* [3] *Now Joshua was clothed in filthy* [a] *garments and standing before the angel.* [4] *And he answered and said to the ones standing before him saying, Remove the filthy garments from him. And he said to him, "See I have put away* [a] *from you your iniquity and I will clothe you* [b] *with white garments."* [5] *And I* [a] *said, "Let them put a clean turban on his head." So they put a clean turban on his head and they clothed him with garments. And the angel of Yahweh was standing by.* [b]

[6] *And the angel of Yahweh charged* [a] *Joshua saying,* [7] *"Thus says Yahweh of hosts, If in my ways you walk and my service you guard, then* [a] *you shall rule my house and shall guard my courts, and I will give you access* [b] *among these (angels) standing here.* [8] *Hear, please, Joshua the high priest, you and your friends who are sitting before you, because they are men of a sign, for behold I am about to bring my servant the Branch,* [9] *for behold the stone which I set before Joshua. Upon one*

stone are seven fountains. [a] *Behold I am opening* [b] *its opening,* [c] *oracle of Yahweh of hosts. And I will remove the iniquity of that land in one day.* [10] *In that day, oracle of Yahweh of hosts, a man will invite his neighbor under the vine and the fig tree."*

Notes

1.a. השׂטן "the Satan" or "adversary" always has the article in the OT except in 1 Chron 21:1. The verb שׂטן means "to oppose or accuse" (3:1). The LXX translates השׂטן, διάβολος "the false accuser."

3.a. צוֹאִים "filthy" only occurs in this form in vv 3 and 4. It means to be fouled with human excrement (BDB, 844; CHAL 302).

4.a. העברתי "I will put away," lit. "I will cause to pass over."

4.b. הלבשׁ inf. used as impf. "I will clothe (you)."

5.a. ואמר "and I said" is unexpected. We would expect "and he said" referring to the angel. If the 1st per. is retained it must refer to the prophet interrupting the vision to call for the turban to be put on the head of the high priest.

5.b. The last clause is awkward and is omitted in the LXX.

6.a. ויעד 3ms hiph. impf. עוד "to witness," "warn," "charge."

7.a. V 7 is a conditional sentence without a sharp demarcation line between the protasis and apodosis. Are there four parts to the protasis: "If you walk in my ways, keep my charge, rule my house, and keep my courts," or are there only two (the first 2)? The *waw* conjunction can be translated "and" or "then." Most scholars opt for two parts to the protasis leaving three parts for the apodosis.

7.b. מהלכים "access" may be an Aramaic *aphael* (ph.) part. meaning "passageways."

9.a. עינים "eyes" can mean "facets." Here it probably means "fountains" since it is related to the removal of iniquity.

9.b. מפתח "opening" a pi. part. usually translated with the secondary meaning of "engraving." Here it probably has the primary meaning of "opening."

9.c. פִּתָחָהּ is pointed to mean "its engraving" or "inscription," but with different vowels it can mean "its opening" (cf. Lipinski 25–29).

Form/Structure/Setting

The form is that of a vision report (3:1–7) plus an accompanying oracle (3:8–10). The structure of this vision report is very different from the other seven in that there is no interpreting angel, and no questions from the prophet. The prophet seems to interrupt the proceedings in v 5. Zechariah sees Joshua the high priest standing clothed in filthy garments before the angel of Yahweh and the Satan is standing at his right side accusing him. Yahweh rebukes the Satan. The angel commands that Joshua's filthy garments be removed and clean, white garments be put on him because his iniquity has been taken away. Then the prophet says, "let them put a clean turban on his head," and it was done. Vv 6–7 seem to be a part of the vision. The angel of Yahweh promises Joshua that he will have complete charge over the temple and have access to the heavenly council if he walks in his ways and guards his service.

The oracle in 3:8–10 is addressed to Joshua and the priests. They are to be signs of the coming of Yahweh's servant, the Branch, and of the stone with seven (eyes) fountains through which the iniquity of the land will be removed on one day.

When the Branch comes and the seven fountains of atonement are opened then every man will dwell in peace, security and plenty. The setting for the vision and oracle is in the heavenly council.

Comment

Many European scholars (T. Chary 73; H. Gese 26; K. Elliger 103; F. Horst 210; Jeremias 201–25) do not consider this fourth vision a part of the original cycle of visions because of its differences in form from that of the other visions. There is no ms evidence to show that this fourth vision ever stood in any place in the text other than its present location. However, the NEB reverses the order of visions 4 and 5 and rearranges the text to restore its "original" order. The order of the material in the NEB after chap. 2 is: 4:1–3 the vision of the lampstand and the two olive trees; 4:11–14 the explanation of the vision in 4:1–3; 3:1–8, 9c–10 the vision of the cleansing of Joshua the high priest and the following oracle; 3:9ab; 4:4–10 an address to Zerubbabel that does not relate directly to either vision 4 or 5. This is rather drastic surgery in order to rearrange the text without any supportive external evidence.

The first three visions were designed to comfort Zion and to assure the people that God was about to act to fulfill the promises he had made through Ezekiel (40–48) and the prophet in Isa 40–55. Visions 4 and 5 concentrate on the spiritual and political leaders of the community for the new age. Joshua is referred to as the הַגָּדוֹל הַכֹּהֵן "the high or great priest" (cf. Hag 1:1, 12, 14; 2:2, 4; Zech 3:1, 8; 6:11) a term that is used mainly in the post-exilic period. It probably reflects the increased power and authority of the office of chief priest in Israel after the fall of the monarchy.

The thrust of the fourth vision is the cleansing of the priests (v 4) and the land (v 9) of עָוֹן "iniquity or guilt." Even though the people had returned from Babylon and had started to rebuild the temple, there was still the contamination of iniquity that had not been purged. Was the iniquity only that of Joshua personally (cf. J. Smart, *History and Theology in Second Isaiah* [Philadelphia: Westminster Press, 1965] 285)? Or did Joshua's filthy garments (3:3, 4) represent the contamination of all the people? The latter seems to be the proper meaning. Just as Aaron and his sons were cleansed and clothed properly at the institution of the priesthood (Lev 8:5–7) so Joshua was to be cleansed in order to be acceptable before God in his role as priest.

The role of Satan becomes clear if we understand the setting of the vision to be that of the meeting of the heavenly council. Satan was a member of the heavenly council in Job 1 and 2. There are a number of similarities between this passage and the heavenly council scenes in Job 1 and 2: (1) Satan appears before the Lord as an accuser in both passages (v 1); (2) Yahweh speaks to Satan (v 2); (3) the presence of other "angels" in the group (vv 4, 6). N. L. A. Tidwell (347) sees the seven eyes of Yahweh ranging through the whole earth (4:10b) as corresponding to the function of Satan in Job 1 and 2. There can be no doubt that the scene is that of the heavenly council. The expression "and I said" in verse 5 is also an indication that Zechariah was standing in the council and interrupted the proceedings by saying, "Put a clean turban on his head." For other references to prophets and the heavenly council see 1 Kgs 22:19–22; Isa 6:1–13; Jer 23:18, 22; Amos 3:8.

The term "the Satan" is used here as a title of an accuser before Yahweh rather than as a personal name. "The fuller development of the doctrine of

a personal and devilish opponent of God is a feature of the New Testament"
(Baldwin 113).

The cleansing, reinstatement, and recommissioning of Joshua is represented by a change in clothing. The filthy robes were removed and a fine
white festival garment מחלצות was put on him (cf. Thomas, *JTS* [1932] 279–
80). The reason given for the cleansing of the high priest and Israel is that
God has chosen Israel (3:2; cf. 1:17; 2:16, Eng. 2:12). Yahweh had snatched
the high priest and Israel from destruction as a piece of wood is snatched
from the fire (3:2; cf. Amos 4:11).

After Joshua's clothes were changed, apparently Zechariah noticed that
the high priest had nothing on his head. Then the prophet (or the angel)
said, "Let them put a clean turban on his head." The word "turban" צניף
comes from the root צנף "to wind around." It is used of the turbans of
rich women (Isa. 3:23) and of royal or eminent persons (Isa 62:3; Job 29:14).
It is used here as the mark of the new dignity conferred on the high priest
rather than the regular word מצנפת for the priest's mitre (cf. Exod 28:4).
With his head covered the priest was properly clothed to approach Yahweh.
Then the angel promises Joshua that he would "rule" or "judge" דין the
house of God and have access to the heavenly council if he walks in the
ways of Yahweh (moral injunctions) and attends his service (ceremonial functions).

The oracle that follows (3:8–10) is an eschatological passage. Many questions arise in interpreting this passage. Should מופת be translated "signs"
or "witnesses" to? Who is the branch? What is the meaning of the stone?
Is it an engraved, precious gem worn on the turban of the high priest? Is it
a reference to the top or corner stone of the temple? Could it be a reference
to the rock in the wilderness from which flowed living water (Exod 17:6;
Num 20:7–11)? Should עינים be translated "eyes" or "fountains"? Is there
any relationship between the seven "eyes" of the stone (3:9) and the seven
eyes of Yahweh (4:10c)? These are the more important questions that have
been raised about this passage. We cannot discuss all of the proposals that
have been made in answering these questions.

מופת should be translated "signs" instead of witnesses. Perhaps the priests
would witness the coming of the messianic age but until it came they were
to be signs of its coming. Ackroyd (189) says, "The existence of the priestly
order is a divine sign of the favor which God is about to show to his people."
The priests then were the signs of the coming messianic age, not of the
building of the temple or the verification of the words of the prophet. S. R.
Driver (197) says, "The restored priesthood is a pledge of the approach of
the Messianic kingdom." The sign apparently is related to the branch and
the stone (3:8–9). The branch or shoot צֶמַח was used by Jeremiah (23:5;
33:15) to refer to the coming of a new king from the line of David. Isaiah
spoke of this new king as a shoot and branch from the line of David using
different words:

"And a shoot חֹטֶר shall go out
      from the stump of Jesse,
and a branch נֵצֶר shall grow
      out of his roots" (Isa 11:1).

Ezekiel had used the expression "my servant David" to refer to the king of the new age in 34:24 and 37:24. Now Zechariah combines the ideas of branch and servant and says, "for behold I am about to bring my servant the Branch" (Zech 3:9). Since Zerubbabel is called "my servant" in Hag 2:23 many scholars have assumed that Haggai and Zechariah identified Zerubbabel as the branch of David. But the expression "my servant" is used in many different ways in the OT. It can refer to individuals such as Abraham, Isaac, and Jacob (Deut 9:27); Moses (Num 12:7–8); David (2 Sam 3:18); Nebuchadnezzar (Jer 27:6); the nation Israel (Isa 41:8; 44:21); and a future suffering servant (Isa 53). It is possible that Zechariah or an editor combined Isaiah's, Jeremiah's, and Ezekiel's concept of the Branch of the line of David with Deutero-Isaiah's idea of the suffering servant to refer to the coming Messiah. Although H. G. Mitchell (156) argues that Zechariah identified Zerubbabel with the branch there is no evidence in the text as it stands now that Zerubbabel was to be the expected Messiah. He was supposed to finish the temple (4:7–10a). But there is nothing to indicate that Zerubbabel would be a suffering servant or have anything to do with cleansing the land of sin. That was to be the work of the suffering servant (Isa 53:5–6).

Whatever the symbolism, the purpose of the stone is related to the removal of "guilt" or "iniquity" עָוֹן in one day (3:9). The stone will have seven "eyes," "facets," or "fountains." The Hebrew word עֵינַיִם can mean "eyes" (Gen 3:7) or "springs" or "fountains" (Gen 16:7; Num 33:9).

It is not at all clear how the meaning "eyes" could relate to the role of the stone as a cleansing agent. If the stone represents some precious jewel with seven facets on the turban of the high priest, the reflection of light by seven facets of the stone could conceivably refer to the seven (complete number of perfection) eyes of God which would express God's care for the completion of the temple. But if the "eyes" of the stone were seven "fountains" through which the water of life could flow as it did when Moses struck the rock in the wilderness (Exod 17:6; Num 20:7), then the rock would be closely related to the Messiah's role of cleansing the land.

Some scholars solve the problem of the relation of the seven "eyes" on the stone to the cleansing of the land by rearranging the text. For example NEB removes the statement in 3:9bc, "Here is the stone that I set before Joshua, a stone in which there are seven eyes. I will reveal its meaning to you," from its context in chap. 3 and places it just before 4:4a.

It seems by using the two metaphors of "branch" and "stone" to refer to the coming Messiah, Zechariah or the editor saw him as both king and priest. The idea of a priest-king may go back to the ancient concept of the priesthood of Melchizedek, king of Salem (cf. Gen 14; Ps 110). Later in the Dead Sea Scrolls and in the Testament of the Twelve the people looked forward to two messiahs, one from the family of Aaron who would function as a priest and one from the tribe of Judah who would be a king (cf. H. Ringgren, *The Faith of Qumran*, trans. E. T. Sander [Philadelphia: Fortress, 1963] 167–82).

E. Lipinski (26) has made a good case for translating עֵינַיִם "springs" or "fountains." He says that the masculine plural form is an influence of Aramaic on the language at this point. Lipinski argues that normally in Hebrew when

עין refers to springs or fountains the feminine plural is used (cf. Deut 8:7; 2 Chr 32:3) but in the Aramaic Targums the masculine plural is used. He also points out that the LXX supports the reading "springs" or "fountains" because it translates פתחה here and פתח in Josh 8:29 with βόθρον "gate" or "opening" (p. 28). Therefore, Lipinski connects the seven fountains in Zech 3:9 and 4:10 with the idea of the rock which Moses struck in the wilderness and the fountain that flows from the temple in Ezek 47 and Zech 14. We need to remember that the apostle Paul interpreted the rock in the wilderness as referring to Christ (1 Cor 10:4).

When the Messiah comes the seven fountains will be opened and Yahweh will remove the iniquity of that land "in one day" (3:9; cf. 13:1). S. R. Driver (198) said that "Freedom from sin is one of the standing traits of the ideal future, as depicted by the prophets: cf. Isa 1:26, 4:3–4, 32:1–8, 33:24; Jer 31:33f; Dan 9:24." It is clear that by NT times this passage was understood as messianic. For example Luke 1:78, probably depending on the LXX translation of צמח "shoot" as ἀνατολή "a rising" (Zech 3:8; 6:12), refers to the birth of Christ as an ἀνατολή, a "dayspring."

Lipinski and D. R. Jones have opposite opinions about the relationship of the last verse (v 10) to the rest of chap. 3. Jones says that v 10 is an independent word of prophecy added by a catch-word "in one day" used as a convenient suture. But Lipinski argues that "in one day" should be translated "on the same day." So on the day the land is cleansed of iniquity it will be watered by seven copious springs, bringing in an era of peace and prosperity. The idea of every man sitting under his own vine and fig tree hearkens back to the reign of Solomon (1 Kgs 4:25) and forward to the coming of the Messiah (Mic 4:4; John 1:48–50).

Each man will have his own property but he will live in close fellowship with his neighbor. They will "invite" תקראו 3rd com. pl. qal imperf. of קרא, each other from time to time (imperfect action) to sit under their own vines and fig trees. The rabbis extended the meaning of this verse "to indicate that the study of the law should be under the vine and under the fig tree" (see Ackroyd 191, n. 69).

Fifth Vision—A Golden Lampstand, Two Olive Trees and Accompanying Oracles (4:1-14)

Bibliography

Lipinski, E. "Recherches sur le Livre de Zacharie." *VT* 20 (1970) 30–33. **North, R.** "Zechariah's Seven-Spout Lampstand." *Bib* 51 (1970) 183–206. **Rost, L.** "Bemerkungen zu Sacharja 4" *ZAW* 63 (1951) 216–21.

Translation

¹ *And the angel speaking with me returned and waked me as a man that is wakened from his sleep.* ² *And he said to me, "What do you see?" And I* ᵃ *said, "Behold I see a lampstand* ᵇ *all of gold, and a basin upon the top of it and seven lamps upon it and seven spouts to the lamps which are on top of it.* ³ *And two olive trees were beside it, one on the right of the basin and one on the left."* ⁴ *And I answered and said to the one speaking with me, "What are these, my lord?"* ⁵ *And the angel speaking with me said to me, "Do you not know what these are?" And I said, "No, my lord!"* ⁶ *And he answered and said to me saying, "This is the word of Yahweh to Zerubbabel saying, Not by might and not by power, but by my Spirit says Yahweh of hosts.* ⁷ *Who are you, O great mountain? Before Zerubbabel you shall become a plain, and he shall cause the top stone to go up amid shouts of 'Grace, grace to it!'"* ⁸ *And the word of Yahweh came to me saying,* ⁹ *"The hands of Zerubbabel founded this house and his hands shall complete it, and you shall know that Yahweh of hosts sent me to you.* ¹⁰ᵃ *For who has despised the day of small things? They shall rejoice and see the plummet* ᵃ *in the hand of Zerubbabel.*

¹⁰ᵇ *"These seven fountains* ᵇ *of Yahweh, they flood* ᶜ *the whole earth."* ¹¹ *And I answered and said to him, "What are these two olive trees on the right of the lampstand and on its left?"* ¹² *And I answered a second time and said to him, "What are the two twigs* ᵃ *of the olive trees which are in the hand of the two golden pipes which pour out gold(en) oil?"* ᵇ ¹³ *And he said to me, "Do you not know what these are?" And I said, "No, my lord!"* ¹⁴ *And he said, "These are two sons of oil who stand by the Lord of all the earth."*

Notes

2.a. MT ויאמר "and he said," but next line has 1st. per. ראיתי.

2.b. מְנוֹרַת menurat comes from נֵר "lamp."

10.a. הָאֶבֶן הַבְּדִיל lit. "the lead (or tin) stone," see *Comment.*

10.b. עֵינֵי can mean "fountains" as in 3:9.

10.c. משטטים a pôlel pt. of שׁוּט. שׁוּט regularly means "to rove about" (Num 11:8; 2 Sam 24:2; Amos 8:12). But in late Hebrew it referred to flood waters (cf. Isa 28:15, 18; Job 9:23).

12.a. שבלי "twigs," "branches" (a hapax)?

12.b. The text simply says "gold" (cf. R. North 187; Mitchell 167).

Form/Structure/Setting

The form of this chapter is that of a vision account (4:1–5, 11–14) interrupted by two oracles addressed to Zerubbabel (4:6–10). The vision account begins with the report that the interpreting angel had to awaken the prophet from his sleep (v 1). The usual questions of the angel and the prophet follow. The prophet describes what he sees. He sees a golden lampstand with a basin on the top. Seven lamps are also said to be on top of the lampstand. Each lamp has seven spouts, which are probably places for the wicks. Then he sees two olive trees: one on the right and one on the left of the lampstand (v 3). The prophet asks for the meaning of what he saw (v 4) but his question is followed by another question of the angel (v 5).

It is generally agreed that two oracles (4:6–10) interrupt the vision report

which concludes in 4:11–14. In 4:10b the angel explains the meaning of the
עיני "eyes" or "fountains," but refers to the seven lamps or the "openings"
on the stone in 3:9. The angel simply says that the seven "eyes" of Yahweh
rove throughout the whole earth or the seven "fountains" of Yahweh flood
the whole earth. If the lampstand represents the presence of Yahweh in the
midst of his people, and the seven lamps represent the eyes of the Lord, v
12 presents a problem because it seems to say that the two olive trees furnish
the oil for the lamps. This would make Yahweh dependent on the leaders
of the people. See *Comment* for a discussion of this problem. Finally in v
14, the two olive trees are identified as two sons of oil who stand by (to
serve) the Lord of the whole earth.

The two oracles addressed to Zerubbabel (4:6–10) may or may not be
related to this vision of the lampstand and the two olive trees. They do
have essentially the same message, that is, Yahweh is with Zerubbabel and
he will be able to finish the temple. The first oracle (4:6–8) stresses the
divine power by which all opposition to the rebuilding of the temple will
be removed and the rejoicing which will come at its completion. The second
oracle (4:9–10) promises success to Zerubbabel and authentication for Zechariah.

The setting of the vision probably is the temple in a time of depression.
Opposition to rebuilding the temple is described as a great mountain (4:7).
There were some who despised the day of small things (4:10).

Comment

The thrust of this fifth vision with its accompanying oracles is clear. Its
purpose is to assure Zerubbabel that he will complete the temple through
the Spirit of Yahweh. The details of the vision and oracles are unclear at
times. Three primary problems meet the interpreter of this passage: (1) Why
do the oracles in 4:6–10 interrupt the account of the vision of the lampstand
and the two olive trees? (2) Does the lampstand represent the temple, the
nation of Israel or Yahweh, and do the seven "eyes" or "fountains" in 4:10b
refer to the seven lamps (4:2) or the stone in 3:9? And (3) How does one
deal with v 12? Is it an interpolation or an original part of the vision account?

Many modern translations of the OT try to solve some of these problems
by rearranging the text of chaps. 3 and 4. The NEB probably has the most
drastic rearrangement of these materials. The order of the material in the
NEB after chap. 2 is: 4:1–3, 11–14; 3:1–8, 9b–10; 3:9a; 4:10b; 4:4–10a. In JB
the order is 3:1–4a, 5, 4b, 6–9a, 8, 9b–10; 4:1–6a, 10b, 11–14, 6b–10a. The
TEV moves 4:6–10a to the end of chap. 4 "to retain the natural sequence of
the narrative."

Long before modern versions rearranged the text many commentaries suggested such changes. S. R. Driver (203) following Wellhausen suggested that
chap 4 should be read: 4:1–4, 6a, 10b–14, 6b–10a. The American Translation
(1941) edited by J. M. P. Smith of the University of Chicago made the same
changes as Driver. H. G. Mitchell (190–194) removed 4:6–10a and placed it
after 6:14. Surely there is some confusion in the MT as it stands.

If "these seven eyes" of Yahweh in 4:10b refer to the seven lamps on the lampstand in 4:2, the lampstand must represent the presence of Yahweh. But eight verses stand between "these" (eyes) in 4:10b and its supposed antecedent (lamps) in 4:2. Of course, if the oracle to Zerubbabel in 4:4–10a is removed as many scholars suggest, then the distance between "these" and its antecedent would not be so great. However, it would be possible to arrange the material so that the antecedent is the "seven fountains" in the rock in 3:9 (cf. NEB and Lipinski 29). If "these seven eyes" or fountains (4:10) refer to the opening in the rock (3:9) the emphasis would be on world-wide cleansing but that would still not solve the problem of the symbolism of the lampstand with seven lamps.

If one turns to the account of the building of the candlestick (lampstand) for the tabernacle (Exod 25:31–40; 37:17–24) for its symbolism he will be disappointed because none is suggested in the text. Josephus believed that the seven lamps represented the seven planets including the sun (*Ant* iii, 6,7; 7,7; *Wars* v 5,5). J. J. Owens seems to accept this theory *BBC* 2, "Numbers" 105; see also H. G. May, "A Key . . . ," 182. But S. R. Driver said that any symbolism proposed for the candlestick is "in danger of being far-fetched, or of being read into the description as an afterthought: but—whether this was its *original* intention, or not—the candlestick may perhaps be most easily regarded as symbolizing the people of Israel, shining with the light of divine truth (cf. the figure of 'light' in Is li. 4, Mt v 16 f., Phil ii.15; and Rev i. 12, 20, where the seven golden candlesticks seen in the vision are said to denote the seven churches). The interpretation of Zech. iv.1–4, 11–13 is too uncertain to be used in explaining the symbolism of the candlestick in the Tabernacle: moreover, the candlestick there is differently constructed, and the lamps are differently supplied with oil" (*Exodus,* CB 261).

Robert North made a thorough study of the shapes and sizes of many lamps and lampstands found by archeologists in Egypt and Palestine. Lampstands with round bases with a bowl and seven spouts at the top have been found at Ugarit as early as 1450–1365 B.C. Similar lampstands have been found at Dan, Gezer, and Lachish dating from 1400–700 B.C. None of these lampstands were similar in appearance to the famous Menorah on the Titus Arch in Rome (R. North *Bib* 51 [1970] 183–206).

V 12 is very difficult to interpret. In the first place two new terms are introduced in this verse which are not used anywhere else in the Bible in the way they appear here. (1) שבלי "branches" or "twigs" elsewhere means "grain." Here it must refer to the fruit-laden ends of olive branches. (2) עֹנתרות "pipes" only occurs in this verse. The expression at the end of the verse "the ones (pipes) emptying themselves gold" is very strange. The meaning probably is that the olive branches furnish golden olive oil through the golden pipes, presumably to the seven lamps. If this is the meaning, then the lamps represent Israel and not Yahweh. The two olive trees in vv 2 and 11 probably represent Zerubbabel and Joshua, the political and religious leaders. They are described in v 14 as "sons of oil," that is, they were the anointed leaders who "stand by," or "wait upon," or "serve" the Lord אדון of all the earth. Although it is doubtful that Zerubbabel was ever officially anointed,

Zechariah might have expected him to be (cf. May, 173–84). At least this passage supports a dyarchy in Israel.

However, the oracles in the middle of chap. 4 say nothing about the role of Joshua, the high priest. It may be that his role had been explained in connection with the fourth vision so that vision 5 could relate to the role of Zerubbabel.

The section 4:6–10a can stand where it is if the reader is aware of the break in the discussion about the lampstand and the two olive trees. What follows in 4:6–10 is not an answer to the question, What are these? (4:4–5), but a word of Yahweh concerning the temple and Zerubbabel's role in rebuilding it. There are really two words from Yahweh here (4:6–7 and 8–10a) but they both say essentially the same thing. One, the temple will be built. Zerubbabel started the rebuilding and he will finish it. Two, strength to finish the temple will not be man's physical ability חיל or military might כֹּחַ, but will be by the power of the Spirit of Yahweh of hosts (4:6).

There seems to have been opposition to the rebuilding of the temple. The opposition is referred to as a great mountain (4:7). The opposition might have come from the "adversaries of Judah and Benjamin" referred to in Ezra 4:1–16. The mountain of opposition might have been the discouraged group who despised the day of small things (Hag 2:3; Zech 4:10). Or the mountain of opposition might have been a deep schism within the community concerning the rebuilding of the temple. Paul Hanson believes that in the early post-exilic community there was a bitter struggle between two groups for control of the restoration cult. Before the beginning of the restoration of the temple the conditions were described as a time when "there was no wage for man or any wage for beast, neither was there safety from the foe for him who went out or came in; for I set every man against his fellow" (Zech 8:10). Whatever the opposition and regardless of its size or power Zechariah assured Zerubbabel that he would finish the temple. At the midnight hour when the opposition appeared to be a mountain the word of God to Zerubbabel was that the mountain would become a plain מִישֹׁר. The similarity of the language of Zech 4:7 and that of Isa 40:4 and 42:16 is unmistakable. The language is eschatological. Zechariah was speaking about more than just rebuilding the temple. He was thinking of the coming of the kingdom of God. The idea of moving mountains of opposition to the kingdom of God is prominent in the NT (Matt 17:20; 21:21–22; Mark 11:22–23; Luke 17:6; 1 Cor 13:2).

Sixth Vision—The Flying Scroll (5:1-4)

Bibliography

Beuken, W. A. M. *Haggai-Sacharja 1–8*, 255–58. Brichto, H. C. "The Problem of the 'Curse' in the Hebrew Bible." *JBL* Monograph Series 13 (1963) 22–71. Jeremias, C. *Die Nachtgesichte des Sacharja*, 188–95. Scharbert, J. "אלה." *TDOT*, vol I, 261–66.

Translation

¹ *And I turned and lifted up my eyes and behold, I saw a flying* ᵃ *scroll.* ² *And he said to me, "What do you see?" And I said, "I see a flying* ᵃ *scroll. Its length is twenty cubits* ᵇ *and its width is ten cubits."* ³ *And he said to me, "This is the curse* ᵃ *that is going out over the face of all the land* ᵇ *for every thief according to it* ᶜ *shall be purged* ᵈ *and the one swearing (falsely* ᵉ*) according to it* ᶜ *shall be cut off.* ᵈ ⁴ *And I will send it out, oracle of Yahweh of hosts, and it will enter into the house of the thief and into the house of the one swearing to a lie by my name, and it shall lodge in the midst of his house and put an end to it and its wood and its stone."*

Notes

1.a.2.a. עפה is a fem. sing. qal act. part. of עוף used adjectivally. The "flying" suggests the quickness of the coming judgment.

2.b. באמה lit. "by the cubit."

3.a. אלה is not the usual ארר Heb. word for "curse." אלה is usually translated "oath" in a covenant context. See comments below for details.

3.b. ארץ means "land of Israel" here rather than "earth."

3.c. מזה כמוה lit. "from this" (point in time, or curse), "according to it." Ackroyd (203 n. 9) says "the phrase is very odd." The phrase could refer to a time frame. H. G. Mitchell (171) following Wellhausen emends the text to זה כמה "already how long?" as in 7:3 (cf. Brichto 68; Beuchen 257). The assumption is that already too long the thief and the false swearer has been declared innocent. The phrase מזה כמוה could refer to האלה "the curse" and read "from it" (this curse). The TEV and Delcor (SB) think the phrase means "from this (side)" and "from that side," that is, one curse was written on one side of the scroll and the other on the opposite side. The meaning of the phrase מזה כמוה depends on the meaning of the verb נקה. See note 3.d.

3.d. The word נקה is used twice in this verse in the niph. perf. Traditionally these forms and the one in Isa 3:26 have been taken as prophetic perfects used in the "original" meaning of the root "to be emptied out." So here and in Isa 3:26 the word could mean "will be punished," "cut off," "purged." But Mitchell (171) and most modern scholars say that there is no evidence for such a rendering. H. Brichto (16) says that the noun never occurs as an antonym of אלה. "The verb which expresses the idea of being free of, or freed from, the effects of an *'ālā* is the *niph ʿal* of the stem *nqh* (**nqy*)."

3.e. "falsely" is supplied in this verse from the reading in v 4.

Form/Structure/Setting

The form of this sixth vision account is similar to that of the second and third visions. The prophet lifts up his eyes and sees a flying scroll (v 1). The interpreting angel (the words "who was speaking to me" [2:19; 3:13; 4:1] are not present here) asks, "What do you see?" The prophet repeats the words from v 1 that he saw a flying scroll and says that it had huge dimensions. Then the angel interprets the meaning and significance of the scroll (vv 3–4). The scroll is a written curse, the result of an "oath" which the people gave when they made the covenant with Yahweh (cf. Deut 29:11, 13, 18). The people of Israel broke the covenant and seemingly even the exile was not enough of a curse for breaking their covenant. The sins of theft and false swearing still remain. These two sins are usually associated with the idea of taking a conditional oath אלה. See Prov 29:24; Judg 17:2;

1 Kgs 8:31–32; Job 31:29–30; Lev 5:21–24; Ps 24:4–5. The setting of the vision is the same as the others.

Comment

The flying scroll suggests not only its speed but its source. The scroll was in the air, suggesting that it was from God. Perhaps Ezekiel's influence on Zechariah can be seen here (cf. Ezek 2:1–3). The scroll must have been unrolled because the dimensions are given. It was huge (10×20 cubits or 20×30 feet). The scroll was the same size as the porch of Solomon's temple and the holy place in the tabernacle. However, no special significance should be given to that fact. The dimensions serve to show the vastness and the power of the curse. The scroll was gigantic, overwhelming, and fearful.

The people of the ancient world were afraid of curses. They felt that if a curse were written on papyrus or parchment, washed off into the water of bitterness and drunk by an accused adulteress, dire consequences would come upon her if she was guilty (Num 5:11–24). Although such ideas may have their root in magic, for the most part in the OT the "realm of magic is left behind and everything is subordinated to the power of God" (Brichto 7). Brichto acknowledges that Mowinckel may be right in seeing traces of magical practices in the Psalms; the outstanding battle in the OT is to suppress sorcery and witchcraft. Yahweh is in control. If the curses of the covenant become effective, if the people repent and turn to Yahweh in obedience he will forgive (Deut 30:1–4).

There might have been many curses written on the scroll Zechariah saw, but the two groups of sinners singled out for judgment were thieves and swearers to lies in the name of Yahweh. Do these two groups represent offenses against the two parts of the Decalogue? The clue to understanding this vision probably can be found in the oath of innocence. When someone's property was stolen or missing in ancient Israel a curse was often pronounced against the person who took it (cf. Judg 17:2; Lev 5:1; Prov 29:24). In many cases the guilty party confessed (Judg 17:2) or judgment came upon him. If a person was accused of stealing and/or of unfaithfulness in the matter of a pledge, that person was brought before God in the temple and made to swear under the threat of a curse that he was innocent. The idea was that if the accused was guilty the curse of Yahweh would be upon him (Num 5:11–28; 1 Kgs 8:31; Job 31:29–30; Lev 5:21–24; Ps 24:4–5; Jer 7:9).

Haggai and Zechariah, following Ezekiel (7:1–27; 36:23–36) taught that the land and the people of Judah had been defiled a long time and the curse of breaking the covenant had been overlooked. Now Yahweh was going to act to rebuild his temple, to cleanse the people and the land. This was the oracle (נְאֻם) of Yahweh of hosts. The curse in the form of the scroll was about to fly through the land. God was causing it to go forth (הוֹצֵאת a com. sing. hiph. perf. of יצא "to go out"). It would enter the house of every thief (anyone who had wronged his neighbor) and the house of the one who swore falsely in Yahweh's name that he was innocent, when he was guilty. The curse would lodge in every sinner's house and destroy it completely (wood and stone, 5:4).

Seventh Vision—A Woman in an Ephah (5:5-11)

Bibliography

Jeremias, C. *Die Nachtgesichte* . . . , 195–200. **Marenof, S.** "Note Concerning the Meaning of the Word Ephah, Zechariah 5:5–11." *AJSL* 48 (1931/32) 264–67. **Rost, A. L.** "Erwagugen zu Sacharjas 7. Nachtgesicht." *ZAW* 58 (1940–41) 223–28.

Translation

⁵ *And the angel talking with me went out and said to me, "Lift up your eyes please and see what this thing is that is going forth."* ⁶ *And I said, "What is it?" And he said, "This is an ephah* ᵃ *going forth." And he said, "This is their eye* ᵇ *in all the earth."* ⁷ *And behold the cover of lead was lifted up and this woman was* ᵃ *sitting in the midst of the ephah.* ⁸ *And he said, "This is wickedness." And he thrust her into the midst of ephah and he thrust the stone—the lead cover over its* ᵃ *mouth.* ⁹ *And I lifted up my eyes and behold, I saw two women going forth and the wind was in their wings and their wings were as the wings of the stork. And they lifted up the ephah between the earth and between the heavens.* ¹⁰ *And I said to the angel speaking with me, "Where are they taking the ephah?"* ¹¹ *And he said to me, "To build for it a house in the land of Shinar, and when it is ready* ᵃ *they will place* ᵇ *it there on its pedestal."* ᶜ

Notes

6.a. האיפה "the ephah" was a dry measuring basket with a capacity of about nine gallons (cf. D. R. Jones, *Haggai, Zechariah, Malachi* 83). Many English versions translate it "barrel." Marenof and Mitchell have suggested that the e in ephah might be suggested by the Babylonian word for temple, such as "E-kur," the house of the mountain, or "E-temen-anki" the house of the foundation of heaven and earth. So E-phah would be the house of Phah.

6.b. עינם "their eye" is strange here. Most modern translators emend the text with the LXX and the Syr to עוֹנם "their iniquity" to make the idea parallel with רשעה "wickedness" in v 7. However, D. R. Jones defends the KJV reading "their resemblance" meaning "what they see." Eye can mean "what one sees" (cf. Exod 10:5; Lev 13:55). This is probably an idiom meaning, "This is what one sees through the whole land." Just as the flying scroll was to be seen by everyone, so the removal of wickedness in an ephah was to be witnessed by everyone. L. G. Rignell translates עינם "what they see," taking the final ם not as a suffix but a form expressing totality (cf. Ackroyd 204 n. 112).

7.a. Lit. "and this woman, one sitting in the midst of the ephah."

8.a. פיה lit. "her mouth." The meaning is the ephah's mouth, not the woman's mouth.

11.a. והוכן a 3rd mas. sing. hoph. pf. of כון "and being ready." The LXX καὶ ἑτοιμάσαι "to make ready," "prepare" suggests an active form. Ackroyd notes that the subject of הוכן is not clear in the MT. We assume that בית "house" or "temple" is the subject.

11.b. וְהֻנִּיחָה should be read וְהִנִּיחָה (*CHAL* 331).

11.c. מְכֻנָתָהּ "her base" is the word used for the ten-wheeled bases or stands for the ten lavers in the temple (1 Kgs 7:27–37; cf. Jer 52:17; Ezra 2:68; 3:3).

Form/Structure/Setting

The seventh vision varies slightly in form from the other visions. The angel initiates the conversation by calling the prophet's attention to an approaching object. The prophet asks about its identity and is told that an ephah is coming. The heavy lid of the ephah is raised slightly and a woman can be seen sitting in the ephah. The woman represents wickedness. She appears to try to escape. She is thrust back into the ephah and the heavy cover is put back in place. Like the second vision of the horns and the smiths this vision has two parts. In the second part of the vision the prophet lifts his eyes again and sees two other women coming with wind in their wings to carry the ephah to the land of Shinar far away from Israel where "wickedness" is enshrined in a temple and made an object of worship. The setting appears to be the same as that of the previous visions, the temple courtyard which has cosmological overtones.

Comment

Some early commentaries treated this vision account as a part of the previous one in order to reduce the number of visions to seven the perfect number (cf. Mitchell 171–72). We have already seen that many modern scholars regard the fourth vision (Joshua before Yahweh) as outside the original seven visions on the basis of form rather than any regard for a perfect number. But there are no grounds for eliminating the fourth or the seventh visions from their place in the original series of visions.

The seventh vision is a companion of the sixth. They both deal with cleansing the land of sin and sinners. In the sixth vision the sinners and their houses were destroyed within the land of Judah. In the seventh vision "wickedness" personified is removed from Judah to Babylon where a temple is built for it as an object of worship.

If the ephah is understood literally to be a basket holding no more than five to nine gallons of grain, it would not be large enough to contain a normal size woman. Therefore some have suggested that the woman in the basket was a fertility goddess that had to be kept "bottled" up.

Why is "wickedness" represented here as a woman? The text does not say but many writers have speculated about the subject. Joyce Baldwin (129) says simply, "Because the Hebrew word is feminine, wickedness is personified as a woman." Mitchell (173) says that Zechariah was simply following earlier prophets who identified "wickedness" with idolatry and presented it under the figure of prostitution (cf. Hos 2:2; Jer 23:1, Ezek 16:1). Rex Mason sees the clue to the use of a woman to represent evil in Ezekiel's words, "Son of Man, when the house of Israel dwelt in their own land, they defiled it by their ways and their doings; their conduct before me was like the uncleanness of a woman in her impurity" (Ezek 36:17). Jeremias (197) finds the clue in a passage in Jer 44:17–19 where the "Queen of Heaven" was being worshiped by the women in Judah after Jerusalem was destroyed. The "Queen of Heaven" evidently was considered a Babylonian deity. Zechariah says that the Babylonian goddess will be taken to the land of Shinar.

In the first part of the seventh vision "wickedness" is personified as a woman. In the second part she is removed by two women. It is easier to explain on the basis of other scriptures how wickedness could be represented as a woman than to understand how those who removed wickedness from the land could be represented as women. The removal of sin and/or iniquity was usually the work of a priest. Once, in Leviticus, birds are used in a symbolic way to carry away the uncleanness of the leper (Lev 14:1-7, 48-53).

The two women in Zechariah's vision who carried away the Ephah containing "wickedness" had wings like a stork (5:9). Storks were very common in Palestine especially in the spring (March and April) when they migrated to Europe (Jer 8:7). Although the word חסידה is usually translated "stork," it could include other large, long-legged wading birds (cf. McCullough, "Stork," IDB, vol 4, 447). The word "stork" might have been suggested to Zechariah because of the similarity of חסידה to חסיד "the devoted" or "faithful" one. These two women flew with the wind in their wings, suggesting a rapid and easy flight. But the word for wind רוח also means "spirit." Some have seen here a suggestion that the removal of wickedness from the land was the work of the Spirit of God. Before one accepts this viewpoint too readily, he needs to know that other interpreters have viewed storks as evil and unclean birds on the basis of Lev 11:19, and Deut 14:18.

Jeremias explains the two women carrying away the ephah to Babylon as an influence of Ezekiel's first vision of the cherubim carrying the throne of Yahweh to Babylon. Jeremias notes the following parallels between the two women in Zechariah 5:9 and the cherubim in Ezek 1. (1) They were both partly human in nature, with wings; (2) their function was to transport a deity; (3) they moved through the air from Judah to Babylon.

Shinar was the old name for Babylon (Gen 10:10; 11:1). The people who had recently returned from Babylon to Jerusalem probably had been greatly offended by the idolatry of that land. Now Zechariah says that which ranks as idolatrous in the holy land will become an object of worship in Babylon. So by divine action (3:9) the community will be purged of social evils and religious apostasy.

Eighth Vision—The Chariots and the Four Winds (6:1-8)

Bibliography

Clifford, R. J. *The Cosmic Mountain in Canaan and the Old Testament.* Cambridge, Mass.: Harvard University Press, 1972. **Gese, Harmut.** "Anfang und Ende der Apokalyptik, dargestellt am Sacharjabuch." *ZTK* 70 (1973) 20–49. **Jeremias, C.** *Die Nachtgesichte des Sacharja,* 110–155. **McHardy, W. D.** "The Horses in Zechariah." *BZAW* 103 (1968) 174–79.

Translation

¹ *And I turned and lifted my eyes and behold, I saw four chariots going out from two mountains and the mountains were mountains of bronze.* ² *With the first chariot were red horses and with the second chariot were black horses,* ³ *and with the third chariot white horses, and with the fourth chariot dappled strong* ᵃ *horses.* ⁴ *And I answered and said to the angel speaking with me, "What are these, my Lord?"* ⁵ *And he answered and said to me, "These are the four winds* ᵃ *of heaven going out from appearing* ᵇ *before the Lord of the whole earth.* ⁶ *Whereupon* ᵃ *(the chariot) with the black horses are going to the land of the north, and the white (horses) go after* ᵇ *them and the dappled horses go to the land of the south."* ⁷ *And the strong* ᵃ *(horses) went out anxious to go to patrol the earth. And he said, "Go, patrol the earth." And they patrolled* ᵇ *the earth.* ⁸ *And he cried to me and said, "See, the ones going out to the land of the north have caused my spirit to rest in the land of the north."*

Notes

3.a. אמצים usually means "strong," but because it occurs in a list of colors of horses in 6:3, 7, and because the LXX and the Tg read a color here, many modern translations read "gray" (RSV; "piebald" JB). Holladay gives "flesh-colored," "piebald" (*CHAL* 21). It is omitted by the Syr and NEB in v 3 and changed by the Syr to אדם "red" in v 7. Gese reads "strong ones" in both places (52; cf. Jeremias 127 n.94).

5.a. רוחות "winds" or "spirits." Mitchell (179) says that the prophet was not thinking about the winds themselves, much less the spirits, but of the cardinal points from which the winds blow. He cites 1 Chr 9:24 for support. But these winds are coming out from the mountain of God going toward the four points of the compass. Winds are spoken of as the messengers or ministers of God (Ps 103:20).

5.b. מהתיצב is a hithpael inf. meaning, "to present oneself before another."

6.a. V 6 begins with אשר, a relative particle without an expressed antecedent. Literally the first phrase אשרבה הסוסים השחרים reads, "which with it the black horses." Obviously something has fallen out of the text. The RSV supplies "the chariot"—with the black horses—"goes." The NEB and JB, noting that there is no reference to red horses or to the east country, assume that a statement like "the red horses going to the east country" has fallen out and include it in their translations. But such an insertion is not necessary because all four points of the compass need not be included. The word chariot does not appear in this verse or in the remainder of the pericope because the distinguishing factor was the different color of the horses not the chariots.

6.b. אחריהם "after them" is the normal reading. But the white horses are said "to go after them" (the black horses). Does "after them" mean "in the same direction" to the north country, or does it mean "after them" in the point of time even though they might have gone in another direction? Some scholars think that all four directions should be in v 6, and since north and south are expressed in the text, and east presumably has fallen out with the red horses, then the west is missing. Consequently (they) the NEB, RSV, JB, and TEV emend the text from אחריהם "after them" to אחרי ים "toward the sea." Again there is no real reason to emend the text here (cf Ackroyd 182; Mason 60).

7.a. See 3.a.

7.b. ותתהלכנה "and they patrolled." The fem. form may be due to the influence of the vision in Ezek 1:13.

Form/Structure/Setting

The form of this eighth vision account is similar to the previous ones (except the fourth). The prophet lifts his eyes and sees four chariots going out between two brass mountains. The four chariots are distinguished by the different colors of horses hitched to each chariot. Nothing is said at this point about directions. The prophet asks what these four chariots with their horses mean. The interpreting angel replies that they represent the four winds or spirits of heaven who are going out from a meeting of the heavenly council. The black horses are to go toward the land of the north (Babylon) with the white horses following them, and the dappled horses are to go to the land of the south. The strong (all the horses) were ready and anxious to begin their missions of patrolling the earth (v 7). Then they were given the signal to start their journeys. Again one cried to the prophet, "See the horses going to the north country have established the rule of God in the power center of the world." The setting of this vision obviously is the heavenly council on the cosmic mountain. It seems to occur at sunrise. The bronze mountains gleamed in the morning light as a symbol of hope and a new day.

Comment

There are several similarities between the first and the eighth visions. Each speaks of horses of various colors patrolling the earth. However, the horses in the first vision are accompanied by riders returning from their patrol. In the eighth vision the colors of the horses are not the same. Nothing is said about riders. Instead the horses are joined to chariots in vision 8 and they are just beginning their patrol. Both visions refer to a "rest." In the first vision the angel laments that the world was still at rest. There were no signs of a world revolution that some (Hag 2:6–8) expected to happen and usher in the messianic age. In the last vision the "spirits" that went to the north country had established God's "rest" (sovereignty) over the north country which probably referred to world and cosmic powers. Other similarities might be seen if the word for "myrtle" in 1:8 is emended to read "mountain" as in 6:1.

The two bronze mountains between which the chariots came forth are mentioned only here in the OT. However, they probably represent the dwelling place of God. Many people in the ancient world believed their gods lived on mountain tops. The Hebrews spoke of Yahweh dwelling on Mt. Zion (Ps 48:1–3; 132:13–14) and coming from Mt. Sinai (Judg 5:4–5; Hab 3:3). The Canaanites believed that their deities lived on Mt. Zaphon in the north of Palestine. "Zaphon" is used in the Hebrew Bible to mean "north" (Gen 13:14; Isa 14:13; Ps 48:2; 89:13; Job 26:7; Ezek 32:30). Zechariah's language about the two bronze mountains must be understood against this background. He was saying that Yahweh is the king of all the earth. The winds are his chariots not only to take his message but to establish his sovereignty over the whole world. Therefore the two bronze mountains represent Zion and especially the temple.

There was always a danger that the adoption of language and concepts from other cultures could lead to perverted concepts of deity and worship. Consider the presence of chariots and horses in the Jerusalem temple dedicated to the sun (1 Kgs 23:11). W. F. Albright argued that the bronze altar in the court of the temple represented the cosmic mountain as the dwelling place of God because it is called har 'el "the mountain of God" in Ezek 43:15 (Albright, *Archaeology and the Religion of Israel* [Baltimore: Johns Hopkins

Press, 1942] 151–52; cf. H. Ringgren, *Israelite Religion*, trans. D. E. Green
[Philadelphia: Fortress, 1966] 161). Others have seen the two huge, bronze
pillars, Jachin and Boaz, which stood at the front of Solomon's temple (1
Kgs 7:13–22), as representative of the two bronze mountains (Mason, 59;
Baldwin, 131).

How shall we understand the various colors of the horses? Too much
importance should not be given to them. They may have no other significance
than simply distinguishing the various groups of God's ministers. However,
the "meaning" of the various colors has been the object of much speculation
through the centuries. Evidently the writer of Revelation in the NT was familiar
with this passage (cf. Rev 6:1–8). Before trying to determine any theological
significance these various colors might have, we should look at some of the
problems, namely: (1) What actual colors are indicated by the various Hebrew
words? (2) Why are there six different terms? (3) Why are the colors not
the same in each of the three lists? (4) Why are not all four points of the
compass mentioned in 6:6? (5) Is there any special significance in the various
colors? Below is a list of the six words, their translation, and location:

אדם	red	1:8, 8	6:2	
שרק	sorrel	1:8		
לבן	white	1:8	6:3	6:6
שחר	black		6:2	6:6
ברד	dappled		6:3	6:6
אמץ	strong		6:3	6:7

W. H. McHardy argues that originally only four words were in the list (אדם,
שרק, לבן, שחר). He believes that these words were not written fully at first
but were indicated by their initials or by the first letter. Through much copying
the initials were misunderstood and two extra words (ברד from Gen 31:10,
12, and אמץ confused with אדם) crept into the text. If this theory is true
then the four original colors were אדם "red," שרק "sorrel" (or ירק "green"),
לבן "white" and שחר "black." Two other Scripture passages seem to support
this hypothesis. The prophet Joel compares a plague of locusts to horses
(2:4) and the book of Revelation remarks that their flight is similar to the
noise of the sound of chariots and of many horses rushing to war. Again
the book of Revelation speaks about four horses—white, red, black, and pale
(gray or greenish yellow). S. R. Driver quotes an Arab saying in a note on
the locusts in the book of Joel, "The Arabs say that there are different kinds
of locusts, yellow, white, red, and black" (Driver, *Joel and Amos*, 88 n.1).

Is there any special significance in the various colors? The book of Revelation evidently used white to represent victory (6:2), red to represent war
and bloodshed (6:4), black to represent famine (6:5–6) and pale (gray or
yellowish green) to represent death (6:8). Some commentaries have speculated
that the four colors represent four world kingdoms with various characteristics.
The north country probably refers to Babylon or Persia and the south country
could refer to Egypt, Edom, or Ethiopia (cf. F. W. Farrar, *The Minor Prophets*
[London: Nisbet, 1890] 204).

H. Gese (34–35) thinks that there may be a geographical and meteorological
connection with Zechariah's use of colors. He points to an old tradition found
in Herodotus (iv, 42) and other ancient writings about the teaching of the
existence of three continents. The continents were Asia, Europe, and Africa

represented by three colors: brown, bright red and white. Asia is the most fruitful, Europe represents the cold north but blessed a little, and Africa is the type of unfruitful lands. The various winds in the OT are seen in terms of hot or cold, dry or wet (cf. Prov 25:23; Jer 47:2; Job 37:17; Zech 9:14; Luke 12:55).

The word הֵנִיחוּ is a 3rd com. pl. hiph. pf. of נוּח and can mean (1) "to settle down on" (Ezek 44:30), or (2) "to satisfy or appease" (one's anger, Ezek 5:13). Ackroyd (183) says it is possible that both judgment and promise are intended. T. Chary suggests a link with 6:15 and understands that the spirit of God will come upon the people and stimulate them to rebuild the temple (Chary, *Les Prophe'tes et le culte a partir de l'exil* [Tournai: Desclée, 1955] 143; see Ackroyd 183 n.40).

The last vision ends on a note of victory. Rex Mason (60–61) says, "It is as though we have been brought to the last act of a play in which all the tensions and conflicts have been resolved . . . Babylon has been judged and the exiles liberated." The sun of righteousness (victory) has risen with healing in its wings (Mal 4:2). It is time to think about crowning the new king. D. R. Jones (89) says, 'The four spirits' are the spirits of Yahweh, and the spirit that went to the north is the spirit of Yahweh. *Have quieted* means 'have caused to rest' in the sense of 'settle.' This is an affirmation of faith that the power of Yahweh is active and present in the very centre of the world-power in the north. In the very origin of world disturbance and destruction is the controlling power of the whole earth. There is nothing to unlearn here, once the strange biblical imagery is decoded. According to Christian faith the spirit of God will, if he chooses, rest in the midst of the Kremlin and the Pentagon, for he is the Lord of the whole earth."

One note of caution perhaps needs to be sounded here. It would be easy to get the impression from Zechariah's language about horses and chariots in 6:1–8 that he is advocating rebellion against the Persian empire. He is not speaking here about earthly armies or rebellion. He is referring to Yahweh's intervention. Warfare is not the way to the messianic kingdom (4:6; See Ackroyd, *JSS* 3 [1952] 11).

The Symbolic Crowning of Joshua (6:9–15)

Bibliography

Ackroyd, P. R. *Exile and Revelation,* 174–75, 194–200. **Beuken, W. A. M.** *Haggai-Sacharja 1–8,* 275–82. **Lipinski, E.** "Recherches . . ." *VT* 20 (1970) 33–35. **May, H. G.** "A Key to the Interpretation of Zechariah's Visions." *JBL* 57 (1938) 173–84. **Wallis, G.** "Erwagungen zu Sacharja VI 9–15." *SVT* 22 (1972) 232–37.

Translation

⁹ *And the word of Yahweh came unto me saying,* ¹⁰ *"Take* ᵃ *a gift* ᵇ *from the captivity, from Heldai, and from Tobiah and from Jedaiah and you shall go in,*

you, in that day you shall go into ᶜ *the house of Josiah son of Zephaniah, who came* ᵈ *from Babylon.* ¹¹ *And take silver and gold and make a crown* ᵃ *and set it on the head of Joshua son of Jehozadak the high priest.* ¹² *And you shall say to him saying, 'Thus says Yahweh of hosts saying,*

"Behold a man, Branch is his name,
Out of his place ᵃ *he shall sprout,*
And he shall build the temple of Yahweh.

¹³ *And he* ᵃ *shall build the temple of Yahweh, and he* ᵃ *shall bear honor. And he shall sit and rule on his throne, and he shall be a priest upon his throne. And a counsel of peace shall be between the two of them."'* ¹⁴ *And the crown* ᵃ *shall be for Helem,* ᵇ *and for Tobiah, and for Jedaiah, and for Hen* ᶜ *son of Zephaniah for a memorial in the temple of Yahweh.*

¹⁵ *"And the far off ones shall come and build the temple of Yahweh, and you shall know that Yahweh of hosts has sent me unto you. And it shall happen if you obey the voice of Yahweh your God."*

Notes

10.a. לקוֹח is an inf. abs. of לקח and can be used as an imperative "take." Lipinski (33–34) shows that on the basis of Qumran materials and medieval Hebrew grammar the *matres lectionis* (ו) is not a sign of the inf. abs. but of the imperative.

10.b. There is no object of the verb "take" expressed in the text. Most translations supply the word "gift" (TEV, Wallis, 235), "offering" (JB), or "silver and gold" (NEB).

10.c. בָאת "you shall go in" is repeated in the verse.

10.d. בָאוּ the pl. indicates that all four men came from Babylon.

11.a. עטרות here and in v 14 probably should be read as a sing. "crown." The LXX has the sing. and in v 14 the Syr has sing. both times. The Tg has sing. here and another meaning in v 14 (cf. Wallis, 232). The verb with "crowns" is sing. in v 14.

12.a. וּמתחתיו "and from under him" is difficult to interpret. Beuken calls צמח יצמח an explanatory clause that hints that the sprout is Zerubbabel, because his name means "shoot of Babylon." S. R. Driver (213) says that תחתיו "underneath oneself" is a Hebrew idiom for "where one stands" (cf. Hab 3:16). Ackroyd reads, "where he is, there is sprouting up" (*PCB* 649), *or "where he is, there is flourishing" (Exile and Restoration,* 174). Joyce Baldwin (135) thinks that the expression is a pun on the word "branch." But she probably reads too much into the text when she says that "he will come where there is little promise of new life, unexpectedly, like the root out of a dry ground."

13.a. The pronoun הוא is emphatic, perhaps suggesting the proper names Zerubbabel and Joshua are intended (cf. D. R. Jones 92; Ackroyd, *PCB* 649):
"And he (Zerubbabel) shall build the temple . . . ,
and he (Joshua) shall bear sacral glory."
Baldwin (*136*) rejects this view.

14.a. See 11.a. above.

14.b. חֶלֶם "Helem" stands here in the place of חֶלְדָּי "Heldai" (cf. 1 Chr 7:35)

14.c. חֵן "grace." One expects the name "Josiah" here as in v 10. The Syr has "Josiah." D. W. Thomas suggests that חן belongs after זכרון "a memorial" as a "sign of favor." חן does occur twice in 4:7 (*IDB* 6, 1081). Baldwin (137) suggests that the change to "grace" from "Josiah" is due to a scribal error.

Form/Structure/Setting

The form of this pericope is that of a sign-oracle. OT prophets often acted out their sermons. Isaiah walked around Jerusalem "naked and barefoot" for three years as a sign against trusting in Egypt's help (Isa 20:2–4). Jeremiah wore a yoke around his neck to portray the submission Judah should give to Nebuchadnezzar (Jer 27:2–7). Ezekiel carried his baggage through a hole in the wall of Jerusalem to symbolize the capture of the city and the exile of her citizens (Ezek 12:1–12). Oracles were usually attached to such signs like the one in vv 12–13.

The introductory formula, "Now the word of Yahweh came unto me," identifies the pericope as an oracle, but it is a special kind of oracle—a sign-oracle. There are two parts to the sign: (1) Zechariah is to take gold and silver from some men who had just returned from Babylon, make a crown out of it, and set it on the head of Joshua the high priest, probably as a sign of the coming branch (cf. 3:8); (2) the crown was to be placed in the temple as a memorial from the men who returned from Babylon to remind Yahweh of his promised blessings (Ackroyd 200).

Included in these sign accounts is an oracle that "the branch will build the temple" and he will rule on his throne. Although the text is not absolutely clear it appears that v 13 anticipates that time when both Zerubbabel and Joshua will sit on a throne, and the "two of them shall have a counsel of peace between them."

Three things are reported in v 15: (1) those that are far off (the diaspora) will come and build the temple; (2) when that happens Zechariah's role as a prophet will be authenticated; and (3) this will all happen when and if the people truly obey the voice of their God.

Although there is no direct structural tie to the eighth vision (6:1–8) in which God's Spirit was made to rest in the north country so that the temple could be rebuilt and the exiles in Babylon could return to Jerusalem, this pericope (6:9–15) addresses both those issues. The temple will be built by the branch and some men have already returned with silver and gold.

The tradition-history behind the pericope is uncertain. Gerhard Wallis (233–4) thinks that the words of Zechariah originally were in two sections: (1) the symbolic act of crowning Joshua (6:9–10ab, 11, 14) and (2) the messianic prophecy (6:10c, 12–13, 15). Wallis (233–34), Beuken (281), and Ackroyd (*PCB* 649) believe that Zechariah's original prophecy has been adapted to a later age, perhaps the age of the Chronicler, to comfort and encourage the people of God who knew that Zerubbabel was not the true branch. Insofar as they stood under the authority of the high priest as the true people of God to worship in the second temple, the promises of God were fulfilled. But as Beuken points out (281) there were other prophecies that had not been fulfilled. "The throne of David was empty. Zerubbabel, the Davidic heir, had disappeared. That part of Yahweh's word which dealt with 'the Branch' awaited a new fulfillment."

Comment

Many questions face the interpreter of this pericope. In the first place, who were the men who came from Babylon? Were there four or more of them? Was Josiah a goldsmith or silversmith? A problem arises in trying to identify the men who came from Babylon. Were their names Heldai, Tobiah, and Jedaiah and Josiah (v 10)? Or were they Helem, Tobiah, Jedaiah, and

Hen (v 14)? D. W. Thomas (*IB* 6, 1080) notes that only the name Josiah the son of Zephaniah is considered a proper name by the LXX. The other "names" are treated as appellatives and are translated as such. For example Heldai is translated by τῶν ἀρχόντον "the chiefs, rulers." If the first three "names" are titles, there might have been many more than three or four returnees in the group. It is not explained why they went in to the house of Josiah, the son of Zephaniah. Nothing is said about his being a worker of metals. It does appear from the MT that he was a part of the group because the relative clause with a plural verb "who came from Babylon" follows his name. The important thing about vv 10 and 11 is that exiles were free to return with money to crown the new king and rebuild the temple. The second exodus had begun like the first with the "despoiling" of their captors (cf. Ackroyd 195).

Were there two crowns or one? The word appears to be plural each time it occurs in the text (vv 11, 14) but the verb is singular in v 14. The plural form could refer to the various rings around one crown. Lipinski (34) points out that the fem. pl. ending ות is used of wisdom in the book of Proverbs in the sing. (Prov 1:20; 9:1). However v 13 may suggest that both Zerubbabel and Joshua were crowned.

Beuken, Ackroyd and D. R. Jones believe that Zechariah was speaking to Zerubbabel and Joshua alternatively in v 13:

And he (Zerubbabel) shall build the temple,
And he (Joshua) shall put on splendor,
And he (Zerubbabel) shall sit and rule upon his throne;
And he (Joshua) shall be priest upon his throne;
And a counsel of peace shall be between them.

If both Zerubbabel and Joshua sit on a throne, that would suggest a dyarchy in Judah in post-exilic times. The idea would be similar to that of the fifth vision of the golden lampstand and two olive trees.

The real issue is: Did Zechariah identify Zerubbabel as the messianic king and expect the new age to begin in his lifetime? Or did he say that the time is coming when the branch or shoot of David (the Messiah) will come and be both king and priest? Joyce Baldwin holds the latter view. She says (136–37), "The symbolic coronation and the enigmatic term 'Branch' referred to a future leader, who would fulfil to perfection the offices of priest and king, and build the future Temple with all appropriate splendour (Hag 2:6–9). In this way the priestly and royal offices will be unified. The old interpretation that Messiah is meant has not been displaced. Nowhere else in the OT is it made so plain that the coming Davidic king will also be a priest. It is for this reason that the passage has occasioned so much questioning." Perhaps Baldwin is overzealous in defending the old messianic interpretation. At one stage of the tradition the prophet probably thought of both Zerubbabel and Joshua being co-rulers. The "counsel of peace" between the two of them means that they would not only work together harmoniously, but they would execute the counsel of God which would be peace (שלום) indeed. However the text says that the crown was to be put on the head of Joshua as a sign of the branch. It was then to be put in the temple as a reminder of God's promises. When and if and to what extent the passage was edited is impossible to tell. Zerubbabel was not the king of the new age. He rebuilt the temple, but it appears that another temple is to be built by those who were "afar off" (v 15).

Rex Mason (63) suggests that the temple to be built by those who were afar off was a temple in the sense of the community of God's faithful people. The "afar off" ones is generally understood to refer to Jews scattered throughout the world (cf. Isa 60:4, 9; see Mason 63; Thomas 1081; D. R. Jones 93). But Mitchell (193), Ackroyd (213), and Baldwin see it as referring to the nations as well as Jews. Again, Baldwin says (137–8), "The building of Zerubbabel's Temple can hardly have been meant because it was already well on the way to completion, and those 'far off' are not necessarily confined to Jews of the dispersion (cf. 2:11; 8:22). The 'Book of Visions' looked farther afield than the rebuilding in Jerusalem, and embraced all nations. Like many other prophetic passages it was concerned with the focal point of all history, the coming of the Davidic king, who would transform the concepts of Temple and of leadership."

The last part of v 15, "And it shall be if you truly hearken to the voice of Yahweh your God," appears to be an incomplete quotation of Deut 28:1. Deut 28 is the chapter that sets out the blessings and curses of the covenant. Zechariah or the redactor wanted to remind the reader that the promises of God's blessings are covenant promises. Faithfulness to the covenant was essential. The expression "obey" or "truly hearken" is שָׁמוֹעַ תִּשְׁמְעוּן lit. "hearing you shall hear." It is the strongest grammatical way to express certainty in the Hebrew language (an inf. abs. preceding a finite verb). So the book of Zechariah opened with a call for the people to turn back to Yahweh (1:1–6). This part of the book closes with a reminder that the blessings (rebuilding the temple and the messianic age) are coming (וְהָיָה "and it will be"), but they are dependent on a proper response to the voice of Yahweh expressed in the covenant (cf. 8:8).

The Question of Fasting and Morality (7:1–8:23)

Chaps. 7 and 8 of Zechariah contain a collection of oracles and/or sermons from Zechariah probably arranged and adapted by an editor in the time of the Chronicler. The date at the beginning of chapter 7, "the fourth day of the ninth month (Chislev) of the fourth year of Darius the king," is probably the date of the coming of the delegation to Jerusalem and not the date of the various oracles and sermons in these chapters. The date in 7:1 is almost two years after the date given in 1:7 for the eight visions. This date indicates that Zechariah continued to preach after his visions.

There may be a loose connection between the materials in chaps. 7 and 8 and the last section of chap. 6 (6:9–15). Both sections begin with a reference to a delegation from Babylon and Bethel. In 6:10 some Jewish exiles had returned to Jerusalem from Babylon with some silver and gold for a crown. In 7:1 a delegation from Bethel or Babylon came to Jerusalem with a question about fasting. The names of the people in both groups are problematical.

In both sections there is the assurance that the temple will be rebuilt (6:12; 8:3, 9). Great stress is placed on hearing the voice of God and obeying (6:15c; 7:8–14; 8:16). Both sections refer to the nations coming to Zion to participate in the blessings of the new age.

The arrangement of the materials in chaps. 7 and 8 is rough. For example, in 7:1–3 a delegation from somewhere comes to Jerusalem "to entreat the favor of Yahweh" and to ask the priests and the prophets at the temple whether they should continue to fast in the fifth month as they had done so long. Logically, the priests and the prophets should reply to the delegation's question in 7:4–6. But what we find is a word from Yahweh through Zechariah to "all the people of the land" about the true meaning of all fasting (not just the fast of the fifth month).

Then we have a sermonette much like the one in 1:1–6 about the preaching of the former prophets, the (fathers') response and Yahweh's wrath (7:7–14). Actually it is difficult to tell who is preaching in 7:7–14. We read of words proclaimed by the former prophets in 7:7, but in 7:8 we are told that the words that follow in 7:9–10 are the word of Yahweh through Zechariah. It is possible that Zechariah or an editor is simply reiterating the words of the former prophets.

It appears that the fathers were the ones who refused to obey in 7:11 but the word "fathers" is not in the text. "They" at the beginning of v 11 has no antecedent. The reference to the role of the Spirit of Yahweh inspiring the former prophets seems to be a postexilic emphasis (cf. Neh 9:30).

The mood shifts in chap. 8 from judgment to hope and from the past to the present. S. R. Driver (220) calls chap. 8 "a decalogue of promises each introduced by 'Thus sayeth Yahweh of hosts,'" and each containing some word of brightness and hope for the Jerusalem of the future.

The materials in chaps. 7 and 8 can best be divided into three broad sections: (1) The question about fasting 7:1–6; (2) reiteration of the words of the former prophets 7:7–14; (3) a Decalogue of promises 8:1–23.

The Question about Fasting (7:1–6)

Bibliography

Hyatt, J. P. "A Neo-Babylonian Parallel to Bethel-Sar-ezer, Zech 7:2." *JBL* 56 (1937) 387–94. Nickolson, E. W. "The Meaning of the Expression *'am ha'ares* in the Old Testament." *JSS* 10 (1965) 59–66.

Translation

¹ *Now it happened in the fourth year of Darius the king, the word of Yahweh came to Zechariah in the fourth day of the ninth month in Chislev.* ² *Now Bethel* ᵃ *sent Sharezer* ᵇ *and Regem-melek* ᶜ *and his men to entreat* ᵈ *the face of Yahweh,* ³ *to say to the priests who were of* ᵃ *the house of Yahweh, and to the prophets saying, "Shall I weep in the fifth month, separating* ᵇ *myself already* ᶜ *how many years?"* ⁴ *And the word of Yahweh of hosts came to me saying,* ⁵ *"Say to all the people of the land and to the priests, when you fasted and mourned in the fifth and in the seventh months these seventy years, did you really* ᵃ *fast for me?* ⁶ *And when you ate and when you drank were not you the ones eating and you the ones drinking?"*

Notes

2.a. Bethel could be a part of a man's name, Bethel-sharezer, or the name of the town about twelve miles north of Jerusalem used as the subject of the verb "sent." Bethel could be the object of "sent" in which case the king Darius might be the subject (cf. Lipinski 37). The supposed motive for Darius' sending a delegation to Jerusalem would be to determine how his contributions to the Jerusalem temple were being used. The KJV follows the LXX and Vg, and makes Bethel the object of the verb "sent" but translated Bethel as the "house of God." This reading is almost certainly wrong here. It is best to follow the ASV, RSV, and JB and read "the people of Bethel sent."

2.b. Sharezer could be part of the combined subject (Bethel-sharezer) or the object of the verb "sent." The usual sign of the accusative is not present.

2.c. Regem-melek appears to be a Babylonian name, presumably of a Jewish proselyte in Babylon. The Syr at this point has Rab-Mag, a chief spokesman of the king (cf. Jer 39:3, 13).

2.d. חלות is a piel inf. of חלה meaning "to stroke" the face, i.e. "to entreat the favor of."

3.a. The prep. ל means that the official priests were attached to the temple at Jerusalem.

3.b. הנזר a niphal inf. of נזר "to separate oneself." It is the root of the Hebrew word Nazirite (cf. Num 6:1, 2, 3, 4, 5, 6, 7, 8).

3.c. זו "already." Mitchell (198) calls זו an enclitic here (cf. *CHAL* 184).

5.a. הצום צמתני אני a qal inf. abs. followed by a finite verb, "fasting did you fast for me?" This is the strongest way of asking, "Did you really do it for me or for yourself?"

Form/Structure/Setting

The opening verse (7:1) is a superscription much like 1:1 and 1:6. It gives the date of the coming of a delegation to Jerusalem to ask about fasting, and it states that the word of Yahweh came to Zechariah at that time. There is no mention of Zechariah's father or grandfather here. A delegation comes to Jerusalem to entreat the favor of Yahweh (7:2) and to ask if they (the delegation and/or the people of Bethel) should continue the fast of the fifth month (7:3). Zechariah's initial response to the question is in 7:4–6. He asks all the people of the land a question about their motives in fasting. Did they fast for Yahweh or for themselves? He also broadened the question to include not just one fast (in the fifth month) but all fasts (the one in the seventh month as well).

Beuken notes that Würthwein (120) calls this section a *Kultbescheid* "cult answer" but does not give any reasons for doing so. It is obvious that the delegation came to Jerusalem to ask the priests and the prophets a question.

This suggests that the people were not free to make changes in religious practices without some authenticating word from Yahweh.

The setting obviously was in the temple in Jerusalem. Although the building was not complete at this point, evidently sacrifices were being offered and worship was conducted. Whether or not Zechariah was a cultic prophet cannot be determined on the basis of this passage alone.

Comment

The point of departure and the make-up of the delegation that came to Jerusalem to ask about the fast of the fifth month is sticky. We cannot tell from the text whether they came from Bethel or Babylon, or what their names were. D. R. Jones (96) put the problem in proper perspective, though, when he said, "For the readers of the prophet, intent upon his message, it does not greatly matter who asked the question." The names seem to be Babylonian, and Bethel seems so close. Why would anyone remember a delegation from Bethel coming to Jerusalem? That probably happened every day. J. Baldwin argues that the time span from the fifth month, which was the date of the fast remembering the destruction of the temple, and the ninth month, which probably was the date of the arrival of the delegation in Jerusalem, suggests that the group came from Babylon because a trip between those two points usually took about that long. But that is reading too much into the text. For this reason Baldwin (142) opts for Babylon as the departure point for the delegation. But Bethel was an old and significant worship center in Israel. It was the place where Jacob had his vision (Gen 28:19). It was the site of a temple of the northern kingdom during the divided monarchy period (Amos 4:4; 7:13). D. Winton Thomas (1083) suggests that Zechariah rebuffed the delegation from Bethel by telling them that their fasts had no value, and they should live the good life which Yahweh had demanded through the earlier prophets. Thomas thinks that Zechariah's answer exhibits an unfriendly attitude toward the people from the north because they were Samaritans. Such an assumption is without evidence in this text.

The delegation actually does not use the term "fast." They use the terms בכה "to weep" and נזר "to separate oneself." In his reply to their question Zechariah uses the formal term צום for "fast." Fasting was often associated with weeping, mourning, entreating, and repenting. The origin of fasting has been lost in antiquity. The purpose of fasting is not always clear. Fasting can be personal and individualistic as in the case of David mourning because of the death of his first son by Bathsheba (2 Sam 12:16), or it can be public and institutional as in the case of the observance of the Day of Atonement (Lev 16). The word "fast" does not occur in Lev 16. The expression "to afflict one's soul" is found twice (Lev 16:29, 31). Fasting became very common in postexilic times. Perhaps the only reference to fasting in preexilic prophecy is in Jer 14:12. But there are many references to fasting in what is generally regarded as postexilic prophecy (Jon 3:5; Joel 2:12–13; Isa 58:3–4; Zech 7:5). By NT times fasting by individuals had become a work of merit (cf. H. H. Guthrie, "Fast, Fasting," *IDB* e-j 241–44).

Four different fasts are mentioned by Zechariah: one in the fourth month

(8:18), the fifth month (7:3; 8:18), the seventh month (7:5, 8:18), and the tenth month (8:18). Zechariah does not identify the specific day of each of these four months on which the fasts were held or the occasion(s) commemorated by the fasts. Ackroyd (207) suggests that the fast of the tenth month was in memory of the siege of Jerusalem in 588 B.C. (cf. 2 Kgs 25:1). The fast of the fourth month probably commemorated the capture of Jerusalem in 587 B.C. (cf. 2 Kgs 25:2–3; Jer 39:2). The fast of the fifth month was for the burning of the temple in 587 B.C. (2 Kgs 25:8), and the fast of the seventh month was probably for remembering the assassination of Gedaliah, the governor of Judah after the fall of Jerusalem (2 Kgs 25:25; Jer 41:1–2). However, the fast of the seventh month could refer to the Day of Atonement.

The expression עם הארץ "people of the land" seems to refer to all of the Jews living in Judah and Jerusalem (cf. Baldwin 144). But the expression can be a technical term to refer to a very specific group of people (Ackroyd 150 n.50). The term is used between sixty and seventy times in the OT and its meanings are varied (E. W. Nickolson, *JSS* 10 [1965] 59). Sometimes it refers to the indigenous people of a land (cf. Gen 23:7; 42:6; Num 14:9). At times it refers to the entire population of a country (Lev 20:1, 4). The term can refer to a group of free, property-owning male, full citizens of Israel who played a prominent role in the political, economic, and military affairs of the nations (2 Kgs 11:18; 21:24; 23:30). In Ezra 4:4 "the people of the land" refers to the group of Jews who were left in Judah at the time of the exile.

It is very possible that behind Zechariah's use of the term "all the people of the land" there lurked the controversy over ownership of the land between those who returned from captivity and those who remained in Judah. Paul Hanson (240) believes that "those having a part in the rebuilding of Yahweh's temple, and thereby establishing their membership in his temple community, would be entitled to a share in Yahweh's land; those excluded from the rebuilding and from the temple community would forfeit that claim." He cites Ezekiel 11:14–17 as an indication of the struggle between the two groups for title to the land:

> And the word of the Lord came to me: "Son of man, your brethren, even your brethren, your fellow exiles, the whole house of Israel, all of them, are those of whom the inhabitants of Jerusalem have said, 'They have gone far from the Lord; to us this land is given for a possession.' Therefore say, 'Thus says the Lord God: Though I removed them far off among the nations, and though I scattered them among the countries, yet I have been a sanctuary to them for a while in the countries where they have gone.' Therefore say, 'Thus says the Lord God: I will gather you from the peoples, and assemble you out of the countries where you have been scattered, and I will give you the land of Israel' " (Ezek 11:14–17, RSV).

In Zechariah's response to the inquiry about fasting he asked why the people were fasting. What was their motive? Was it for themselves or for Yahweh? And he broadened the question of fasting to include other fasts. We do not know how long these fasts lasted. They might have lasted one day or a month. Did the fast mean total abstinence from food, drink, work, and sex? For Muslims fasting is obligatory during the twenty-eight days of the ninth month, Ramadan. "During Ramadan all adult male and female Muslims must fast during the day-time from the first light of dawn until complete darkness at night" (E. G. Parrinder, *Worship in the World's Religions* [London: Faber and Faber, 1961] 195). Evidently the fasts in Zechariah's time permitted some consumption of food and drink (7:6).

The heart of the matter concerning fasting is motive and attitude. A fast should be an outward sign of an inner disposition of humility and of a heart turned toward God.

Reiteration of the Words of the Former Prophets (7:7–14)

Bibliography

Hoftijzer, J. "The Particle יד in Classical Hebrew." *OTS* 14 (1965) 76–77.

Translation

7 *Are not these* [a] *the words that Yahweh proclaimed by the hand of the former prophets while Jerusalem was inhabited and undisturbed and her cities surrounding her, the Negeb and the Shephelah were inhabited?*

8 *And the word of Yahweh came to Zechariah* [a] *saying,* 9 *"Thus says Yahweh of hosts,*

'You judge with justice and truth,
and act with loyalty and compassion
each man with his brother.

10 *And do not oppress the widow and orphan,*
the stranger and the poor.
And let not a one of you devise
evil in your heart against [a] *his brother.'"*

11 *But they* [a] *refused to listen, and they* [a] *gave a stubborn shoulder and their ears were heavy of hearing.* 12 *And they made their heart like a diamond from hearing the torah* [a] *and the words that Yahweh of hosts sent by his spirit, by the hand of the former prophets. And there was great anger from Yahweh of hosts.* 13 *And as he called and they did not hear, so they will call and he will not hear, says Yahweh of hosts.* 14 *And I will* [a] *blow them away among* [b] *all the nations that they did not know. And the land was made desolate behind them, so that there was no going or coming,* [c] *and they made the land of desire a desolation.*

Notes

7.a. The particle את creates a problem here. It is normally used as a sign of the def. direct object and it may be used that way here. We expect the word אלה "these" and the LXX οὗτοι supports that reading even though there is no evidence from Heb. Mss to support it. J. Hoftijzer sees את as a key word in the connection of v 7 to the previous passage. He reads, "Are you then not these who did eat and drink the words which God has spoken . . . ?" (*OTS* 14 [1965] 76–77). But Beuken (121) is probably right in regarding this verse as the beginning of an independent tradition about the teaching of the former prophets.

8.a. The use of Zechariah's name in 7:1, 7 is a part of the editorial framework. When Zechariah speaks he says, "the word of Yahweh came to me" (7:4).

10.a. The expression ורעת איש אחיו "and evil a man his brother" is difficult. Mitchell (204–5) devotes more than a page of fine print to his discussion of it. He says that the peculiar construction found here only occurs one other time (Gen 9:5) where ביד איש אחיו is, "at the hand of every man his brother." The Syr has the prep. על "against." This makes the meaning clear.

11.a. The subject "they" has no expressed antecedent. The assumption is that "they" refers to the hearers of the words of the former prophets.

12.a. Most scholars take התורה "the Torah" in the sense of the "teaching" or "instruction" along with the words of the prophets, but the Heb. text would allow the reading "the law and the words . . . of the prophets."

14.a. The tense of ואסערם "and I will blow them away" is unclear. The Hebrew pointing suggests a future tense but the other verbs in the verse are pointed to be read in the past tense.

14.b. על "upon" should be read as אל "unto" or "among" according to LXX εἰς.

14.c. The מ on מעבר can mean "without" (cf. GKC. 119, 3, d).

Form/Structure/Setting

The form is that of a sermon, much like 1:1–6. The structure falls naturally into four parts: (1) a summary of the teaching of the former prophets (7:7–10; v 8 is an editorial gloss); (2) the negative response of the people (7:11–12a); (3) the wrath of God (7:12b–14a); and (4) conclusion (7:14b). The setting depends on the relationship of this pericope to the previous one about fasting. If it is closely connected with that one, the setting would be in the temple.

Comment

(1) A Summary of the Teachings of the Former Prophets 7:7–10

7:7–10 provides one of the finest summaries of the teaching of the former prophets. It has a strong emphasis on social justice. But it is not social justice for social justice's sake. Social justice is God's requirement. "Thus says Yahweh of hosts" (7:9). They refused to hearken to the words of Yahweh that he gave by his spirit through the former prophets (7:12). God requires social justice between brothers (7:10) and toward the disadvantaged (widows, orphans, aliens, and poor 7:10). The verbs are imperatives שפטו "judge" and עשו "do, or act." They are commands from Yahweh.

These great terms אמת "truth," משפט "justice," חסד "covenant-love," רחם "compassion" remind one of the words of Hosea, Amos, and Micah. Hosea said,

There is not truth (אמת) or covenant love (חסד) in the land (4:1b).

Amos said,

And let justice (משפט) roll down like water,

and righteousness (צדקה) like a perennial stream (5:24).

Micah said,

He has declared to you, O man, what is good,
And what Yahweh seeks from you,
but to do justice (משפט) and love covenant-love (חסד),
and to walk humbly with your God (6:8).

Right relationship between God and man, and between man and man, go together. It is not individual piety expressed in fasting that keeps the fabric of society secure, but honesty, integrity, compassion, faithfulness expressed in one's conduct, and attitude toward other people.

There is a group of people in every society that requires special care. They are the unfortunate, the helpless, the disenfranchised ones. They are identified by Zechariah as the widow, orphan, alien, and poor (7:10). Isaiah admonished his hearers "to seek justice, correct oppression, defend the father-less, plead for the widow" (1:17). Amos spoke of those who "trample on the needy and bring the poor of the land to an end" (2:6–7; 8:4). D. R. Jones observes that the widow had no husband to speak for her, orphans had no parents to love and care for them, the alien had no country to protect and sustain them, and no shopkeeper had a legal responsibility to provide food and clothes to those without money to pay for them. Then Jones (100) says, "It is exactly in this area of life, beyond the limits of legal duty, that men and women sort themselves out, as to what they are in their innermost being, and in the sight of God."

Zechariah put his finger on the root of man's problem when he said, "And let not one of you devise evil in your heart against his brother" (7:10c). Human actions and expressed attitudes are the outward manifestations of the state of the heart. The wise said,

"Keep your heart with all vigilance for from it flow the springs of life"
(Prov 4:23).

Jeremiah said,

"The heart is deceitful above all things, and desperately corrupt;
who can understand it?" (17:9).

Jesus said,

"What comes out of the mouth proceeds from the heart" (Matt 15:18). Micah warned his listeners not to devise evil against a neighbor at night and put it into effect the next morning, because Yahweh would devise evil against such a people from which they could not remove their neck (Mic 2:1–3).

So in the sense that outward conduct is the expression of one's inner disposition, social justice is related to true piety.

What does fasting have to do with social justice? Is there any relationship between 7:1–6 and 7:7–14? A glance at the Heb. text suggests that there is some connection between the two passages. The last part of v 6 and the first part of v 7 each begins with the word הלוא "is not," which is the beginning of a rhetorical question. But v 7 definitely is a part of the sermon in 7:7–14 about the words of the former prophets. The former prophets had almost nothing to say about fasting. Their main concern was social justice, but as we have seen social justice is a corollary of piety and in turn fasting. Although the former prophets did not relate the two, Zechariah and Deutero-Isaiah

certainly did (cf. Isa 58:1–9). There is a striking similarity between the passage
in Deutero-Isaiah and this one in Zechariah.

(2) *The Negative Response of the People* (*7:11–12a*)

Zechariah follows his profound analysis of the ethical teachings of the
former prophets with an analysis of the people's response. Using three different metaphors, he charges them with refusing to hear, listen to, and obey
the voice of God given to them by the former prophets as they were speaking
by the spirit of Yahweh. The three metaphors are: (a) "they turned a stubborn
shoulder" (cf. Neh 9:29). The figure is that of a stubborn ox that will not
allow a yoke on its neck (cf. Hos 4:16). (b) "They made their ears heavy so
they could not hear." Isaiah was told that his preaching would make the
people's ears heavy or hard so they could not hear (Isa 6:10). The prophet
in Isa 59:1 asks if Yahweh's ears are heavy that he cannot hear. The word
כבד "heavy or hard" is used of hardening the heart of Pharaoh (Exod 7:14;
8:11, 28; 9:7, 34; 10:1). (c) "They made their heart like a diamond." The
word שמיר "diamond" is only used three times in the OT: once in Jer 17:1,
"The sin of Judah is written with a pen of iron; with a point diamond it
is engraved on the tablet of their heart and on the horns of their altars";
again in Ezek 3:9, "Like a diamond harder than flint have I made your fore-
head."

The story of Israel was one of rebellion against Yahweh. Whole chapters
in the OT are recitals of Israel's rebellion and obduracy. They rebelled at
Horeb. They rebelled at Kadesh. They rebelled in their own land (cf. Deut
9; Pss 78; 106; Ezek 16; 20). The wrath of God always came upon them as
a consequence of their rebellion.

(3) *The Wrath of God* (*7:12b–14a*)

"And there was a great anger from Yahweh of hosts." The word for wrath
קצף means "outburst" (E. Jacob, *Theology of the Old Testament*, trans. A. W.
Heathcote and P. J. Allcock [New York: Harper, 1958] 114) or "splintering"
(cf. Joel 1:7 of a fig tree; and Hos 10:7 of Samaria's helpless king). This
word is used in Zech 1:2, 15; 7:12; 8:14.

The wrath of God expresses itself in Zechariah in three ways: (a) in God's
withdrawal, "They will call and I will not answer"; (b) in exile for the people,
"and I will blow them away among all nations"; (c) and in the beautiful
land becoming a waste and desolation without inhabitant.

God's withdrawal reminds us of Hos 5:15,

"I will return again to my place,
  until they acknowledge their guilt and
  seek my face."

The use of the word קרא "call" here and in 1:4 is evidence that we are
dealing with a sermon genre. The same expression is used in the wisdom
sermon in Prov 1:24–28. The tenses change in the middle of v 13. "He called
and they did not hear" is in the past tense, suggesting the reference is to

Israel's experience before the exile. But "so they will call and I will not hear" is in the imperfect tense. Does this refer to Zechariah's time, to the time of the redactor, or to the eschaton? There is no satisfactory answer to this question. However, there must have been a warning here for Zechariah's people. Fasting and temple-building are not enough. The heart and actions of God's people must be right or God will withdraw.

Another prophet of the same era said,

Seek the Lord while he may be
    found,
call upon him while he is near;
let the wicked forsake his way,
    and the unrighteous man his
        thoughts;
let him return to the Lord, that he
    may have mercy on him,
and to our God, for he will
    abundantly pardon (Isa 55:6–7).

Another expression of the wrath of God will be exile for the people. God will blow them away as with a whirlwind (סער) among people they have not known. The reference "have not known" does not mean intellectual knowledge, but has to do with Israel not acknowledging the gods of these other people (cf. Deut 11:28; 13:3, 7, 14; 28:64; 29:25; 32:17; Jer 15:14; 16:13; 17:4; 22:28).

But the worst expression of the wrath of God is the desolation of pleasant land. The ideal picture of the land of Canaan is given in Deut 8:7–10:

For the Lord your God is bringing you into a good land, a land of brooks of water, of fountains and springs, flowing forth in valleys and hills, a land of wheat and barley, of vines and fig trees and pomegranates, a land of olive trees and honey, a land in which you will eat bread without scarcity, in which you will lack nothing, a land whose stones are iron, and out of whose hills you can dig copper. And you shall eat and be full, and you shall bless the Lord your God for the good land he has given you (RSV).

But now the land will be desolate again without inhabitant. Again the tense is a problem in v 14. The first verb ואסערם is imperfect "and I will blow them away." But the verbs in the last part of the verse are perfects, as if the desolation of the land had become a reality. It is probably best to understand these passages as referring both to the Babylonian captivity and to possible future occurrences of the judgment of God.

The conclusion 7:14b, "and they made the pleasant land a desolation," is a terse report of the fact. The only question is, Who is "they"? Who made the land desolate, invaders or the people who refused to hear the former prophets? The RSV and NEB put the blame on the people of God, "Thus the land they left was desolate . . . and the pleasant land was made desolate" (RSV). But this is a very free translation. The expression "the land they left was desolate" is והארץ נשמה אחריהם in Hebrew. The verb is a niphal, therefore passive, and the preposition means "after them" or "behind them," probably referring to the "nations." Therefore it is best to understand that "they" in the last clause refers to the nations (cf. D. W. Thomas 1084).

A Decalogue of Promises *(8:1–23)*

The last word of God is not judgment, but promise, salvation, hope, forgiveness. God's wrath is real and certain, but it is limited by his love and compassion. God's wrath is a sure word of prophecy but it is not the last word. The pattern of salvation history in the OT is: judgment—hope; sin—salvation; rebellion—return. Those chapters that recite Israel's rebellion against God also emphasize his compassion and forgiveness.

37 Their heart was not steadfast
    toward him;
  they were not true to his covenant.
38 Yet he, being compassionate,
    forgave their iniquity,
    and did not destroy them;
  he restrained his anger often,
    and did not stir up all his wrath.
39 He remembered that they were but
  flesh,
  a wind that passes and comes not again (Ps 78:37–39 RSV).

43 Many times he delivered them,
    but they were rebellious in their purposes,
  and were brought low through their iniquity.
44 Nevertheless he regarded their distress,
    when he heard their cry.
45 He remembered for their sake his covenant,
    and relented according to the
      abundance of his steadfast love.
46 He caused them to be pitied
    by all those who held them captive (Ps 106:43–46 RSV).

Yea, thus says the Lord God: I will deal with you as you have done, who have despised the oath in breaking the covenant, 60 yet I will remember my covenant with you in the days of your youth, and I will establish with you an everlasting covenant (Ezek 16:59–60 RSV).

Practically all of the books of the prophets end on a note of hope. If chap. 8 is the last of Zechariah's words in this book, as many believe, it is appropriate that this chapter contain a message of hope.

Five Brief Messages of Hope (8:1–8)

Bibliography

Porteous, N. W. "Jerusalem—Zion: The Growth of a Symbol." *Living the Mysteries.* Oxford: Blackwell (1967) 93–111.

Translation

¹ *And the word of Yahweh came* [a] *saying,*
² *"Thus says Yahweh of hosts,*
I am jealous for Zion, greatly jealous,   2+2
and with great wrath I am jealous for her.   2+2
³ *Thus says Yahweh,* [a]
I have returned to Zion,
I will dwell in the midst of Jerusalem   2+2
and Jerusalem shall be called the faithful city
and the mountain of Yahweh of hosts, the holy mountain,   3+3
⁴ *Thus says Yahweh of hosts,*
Again old men and old women shall sit
in the streets of Jerusalem,   3+2
And each one will have his staff in his hand
because of the multitude of ways,   3+2
⁵ *And the streets of the city will be full of boys*
and girls playing [a] *in her streets.*   3+2+2
⁶ *Thus says Yahweh of hosts,*
If it is a marvel [a] *in the eyes of the*
remnant of this people,   2+3
(In those days) [b] *will it also be a marvel in my eye,*
oracle of Yahweh of hosts?   2+2
⁷ *Thus says Yahweh of hosts,*
Behold I am about to save my people
from the land of the sunrise
and from the setting of the sun.   3+2+3
⁸ *And I will cause them to come in*
and they shall dwell in the midst of Jerusalem   2+2
and they shall be for me a people
and I will be God for them in truth
and in righteousness."   3+4+2

Notes

1.a. V 1 is an editorial comment. It asserts that what follows is the word of Yahweh, but Zechariah is not mentioned by name, and the words "unto me" which might be expected are not present.

3.a. This is the only one of the ten messenger formulas in this chapter that omits ". . . of hosts."

5.a. מְשַׂחֲקִים a pi. part. The word can mean "laugh, play, entertain, joke, be happy, hold a tournament" (cf. *CHAL* 350).

6.a. The basic idea of the word פלא is "wonder," "astonishment," "miracle," sometimes unusual and almost impossible.

6.b. בַּיָּמִים הָהֵם "in those days" is often omitted as a gloss (cf. NEB, JB, Ackroyd 213 n. 137).

Form/Structure/Setting

The form of this passage evidently is a collection of sayings of Zechariah from different times in his ministry and arranged in a series. After a superscription which identifies the sayings as the word of Yahweh of hosts, each of the next five sayings (except the second) is introduced with the messenger formula, "Thus says Yahweh of hosts." The "of hosts" is omitted in 8:3. Each saying is one or two verses in length and contains a message of encouragement for the remnant that returned from Babylon (8:6). It is possible to detect a kind of poetry in this passage. It contains a type of parallelism, but not of the regular synonymous or antithetic type that one sees in Psalms, Proverbs, Job, or some other prophetic oracles. BHK, RSV and NEB do not set out this passage as poetry, but JB and Ackroyd do. Since this passage is probably a collection of sayings spoken on various occasions, it is impossible to detect one setting for all of them.

Comment

(a) The First Saying: Yahweh Is Jealous for Zion (8:2)

This verse is similar to 1:14. There the interpreting angel spoke the assuring words that Yahweh was jealous for Jerusalem and Zion. Here the prophet proclaims the message once again that Yahweh cares deeply about his chosen city. Jealousy is an ambivalent term. It is a strong emotion expressed in an intolerance of rivals. It can be good or evil, depending on the legitimacy of the rival. God had chosen Israel and made a covenant with her. He bound her to himself in an exclusive relationship of God and people. "You shall have no other gods before me" (Exod 20:3). Zion and/or Jerusalem was the chosen earthly dwelling place of Yahweh (Ps 132), and Zion became in the biblical materials a symbol for the kingdom of God (Isa 65:17–18). After reviewing the place of Zion in many OT passages, Norman Porteous says, "We have been watching the process in the Old Testament by which Jerusalem, the chosen city of God, not just the chosen city of David, gradually gave its name as a symbol of the transcendent action of God in creating a people for himself in the world, that is, in bringing in his kingdom" (*Living the Mystery*, 109). Yahweh is often presented as a jealous God in the OT. Yahweh's jealousy caused him to bring great hardships on Israel when she broke her covenant with him (Deut 29:20–28; Ezek 5:13; 16:38, 42; 23:25). But here and in 1:14, God's jealousy is for Jerusalem and against the nations that had grossly abused her.

(b) *The Second Saying: Yahweh Has Returned to Zion* (8:3)

Ezekiel said that Yahweh abandoned the temple and his city, allowing Jerusalem to be destroyed by the Babylonians (Ezek 10:18–19; 11:22–23). Yahweh was a sanctuary to his people in Babylon for a little while (Ezek 16:16). Now Yahweh is returning to Jerusalem just as Ezekiel (43:1–5) and Haggai (1:8) said he would. He will tabernacle שׁכן in the midst of Jerusalem as he had done in the wilderness (Zech 8:3). Perhaps there is a reference here also to the promise in 2:9 that Yahweh would be a glory in the midst of the new Jerusalem.

The renaming of Jerusalem is in line with a number of other passages in the OT about renaming. The term קרא "to call" can be a technical term for naming or renaming (cf. O. Eissfeldt, "Renaming in the Old Testament," *Words and Meaning,* eds. P. R. Ackroyd and B. Lindars [London: Cambridge University Press, 1968] 69–79). Eissfeldt suggests that people, places, and institutions (such as a prophet, 1 Sam 9:9) are renamed when there is a change of status. The right to name or rename someone or something expresses authority. Such authority may express itself in exploitation or in protection. Obviously in this case it is protection that Zechariah has in mind.

The new names for Jerusalem in 8:3 are: "a faithful city" and "a holy mountain." The suggestion is that whereas previously Jerusalem has been unfaithful, now she is to be faithful as Isaiah had promised (Isa 1:26). The word אמת actually means "to be firm," "dependable," "truthful." Jerusalem is also to become the holy mountain. The root of the word קדשׁ "holy" means to be separate. Thus Jerusalem is to become the exclusive realm of Yahweh.

Two other passages in the OT speak of a new name for Jerusalem. In 48:35 Ezekiel uses a pun on the name of the city for her new name יהוה שׁמה "Yahweh is there." The new name emphasizes the presence of Yahweh in the city. The other passage that speaks of a new name for Zion and her land is Isa 62:2b–4:

> and you shall be called by a new
>   name
>   which the mouth of the Lord will
>   give.
> You shall be a crown of beauty in
>   the hand of the Lord,
>   and a royal diadem in the hand
>   of your God.
> You shall no more be termed
>   Forsaken,
>   and your land shall no more be
>   termed Desolate;
> but you shall be called My delight
>   is in her,
>   and your land Married;
> for the Lord delights in you,
>   and your land shall be married (Isa 62:2b–4; RSV).

(c) The Third Saying: The Streets of Jerusalem Will Be Full of Boys and Girls (8:4–5)

This passage begins with the word עוֹד "again." Beuken says that we probably have here a stereotyped form of a salvation prophecy. We saw it earlier in Hag 1:6 and in Zech 1:17. Beuken points to several passages in Jeremiah as the earliest references to the term "again" (Jer 31:23; 32:15; 33:10, 12, 13). Other references are found in Isa 14:1; 49:20; 56:8 and Zech 8:20.

The idea here is that once the streets of Jerusalem were filled with old men and women and children laughing and playing. But war, devastation, and destruction changed all that. The Babylonians had swept the city of its citizens, and the first to return were of necessity the age group that could withstand hardship and endure hard labor.

In one of the most amazing and challenging statements about measurement of the health of society, Zechariah suggests that we look at the place the old and the young have in that society. T. C. Speers says, "Too often men are apt to measure a city's significance by its business, professions, and industry, its buildings, its wealth, its art and culture. Zechariah suggests that we measure the significance of our cities by their effect upon two groups easily overlooked—the old and the young" (*IB* 6, 1085). Long life and children were thought of in the OT as blessings from God (Prov 3:2; 9:10–11; Pss 127:3; 128:3–4).

(d) The Fourth Saying: Is Anything Impossible for Yahweh? (8:6)

Beuken (176) classifies this fourth saying not as a salvation word but as a *streitfrage*, "a disputation question." He notes two other places where a question about Yahweh's ability or power to act is raised. One is in Sarah's dispute with Yahweh over the announcement of Isaac's birth. She did not believe that it was possible for her to have a child. The Lord said, "Why did Sarah laugh? . . . Is anything too hard (פלא "wonderful") for Yahweh?" (Gen 18:13–14). The other passage similar to this is in Jer 32. Jeremiah had bought a farm that was in territory occupied by the enemy (Babylon) to demonstrate his faith that Yahweh would restore the land to Israel again. Jeremiah said, "Nothing is too hard for thee" (32:17). But Jeremiah might have had some doubts himself of Yahweh's power to carry out his promise. So the word of Yahweh came to Jeremiah: "Behold, I am Yahweh, the God of all flesh, is there for me anything too hard (פלא)?" (32:26).

There is an element of dispute between the remnant and Yahweh here in Zech 8:6. It seems impossible to restore Jerusalem and to bring in peace. But Yahweh asks if it is impossible for him to do it. There is some difficulty in knowing whether the last part of the verse should be translated as a question, since there is no he interrogative present, or whether it should be understood as irony. If it is irony the Lord would be saying, "If it seems like a marvel to you, it even seems like a marvel to me also" (8:6).

The appearance of the term "oracle of Yahweh" probably indicates that at one point in the formation of this material this saying stood at the close of a unit (cf. 8:17; see Beuken 178; D. R. Jones 105). Calvin said, "Nothing is more preposterous than to seek to measure God's power by our own understanding" (cf. Jones 106).

(e) The Fifth Saying: Universal Ingathering and Renewal of the Covenant (8:7-8)

A universal ingathering of all of God's people is a frequent theme of post-exilic prophecy. The passage is clearly a salvation oracle. It begins with the words, "Behold I," followed by a hiphil participle "am saving." The construction suggests imminence. No nation is named from which the people will come. Rather from two extremities of the earth, the land of the rising and the land of the setting of the sun, they will come. We would say "from the east and the west." They will come and dwell in the midst of Jerusalem. It is easy to see here that Jerusalem has become a symbol of something much larger than an earthly city. The old covenant formula is used to describe the relationship between God and people. Two words are added to describe the nature of the relationship: אמת "faithful" and צדקה "righteous." They are the same two words which characterize the eschatological city in Isa 1:26b.

A Sermon: Strong Hands and Stout Hearts (8:9-17)

Bibliography

Brongers, H. "Bemerkungen zum Gegrauch des the Adverbialen Wᵉˑ attah im A.T." *VT* 15 (1965) 291-92. **Baltzer, K.** *The Covenant Formulary.* Trans. D. E. Green. Oxford: Basil Blackwell, 1971.

Translation

⁹ *Thus says Yahweh of Hosts, "Let your hands be strong, you that hear in these days these words from the mouth of the prophets who spoke* ᵃ *in the day the foundation of the house of Yahweh of hosts was laid to build the temple.* ¹⁰ *Because before those days there was no hire for man or beast, and for* ᵃ *the one going out or coming in there was no security from the enemy, and I sent every man each against his neighbor.* ¹¹ *But now not like the former days I will be to the remnant of this people, oracle of Yahweh of hosts,* ¹² *for they shall sow in peace.* ᵃ *The vine shall give her produce, and the heavens shall give their dew. And I will cause the remnant of this people to inherit all these things.* ¹³ *And it shall be as you, O house of Judah and the house of Israel, were a curse among the nations, so I will save you and you will be a blessing. Do not fear. Your hands be strong.*

¹³ᶜ *"Let your hands be strong,* ¹⁴ *for thus says Yahweh of hosts, as I purposed to do evil to you when your fathers provoked me to anger and I did not repent, says Yahweh of hosts,* ¹⁵ *so I turned, I have purposed in these days to do good to Jerusalem and to the house of Judah. Do not fear.* ¹⁶ *These are the things you shall do: Speak truth each to the other. Administer justice in your gates that is true and satisfying.* ¹⁷ *No person shall devise evil in his heart against a neighbor; and you shall not love a lying oath, because all those I hate, oracle of Yahweh."*

Notes

9.a. The word "spoke" is not in the text. No verb is in the text at this point. The prophets who were active at the time of the laying of the foundation for the temple are not identified. Haggai must have been one of them.

10.a. The prep. ל "for" is attached to the participles יוֹצֵא "one going out" and בָּא "one coming in" only here and in 2 Chr 15:1–7 which is parallel to this passage.

12.a. זֶרַע שָׁלוֹם "seed of peace." The idea seems to be a contrast with the former situation in which it was unsafe for a farmer to be outside to plant his seed.

Form/Structure/Setting

The form is that of a sermon similar to 7:4–14 and 2 Chr 15:1–7. The sermon is divided into three parts (vv 9–13c, 13d–15, 16–17). The first two parts begin with the messenger formula and end with an admonition, "Fear not." The two parts comprise sayings six and seven in the decalogue of sayings in this chapter. The various parts of the saying can be seen in the outline below.

First Saying	*Second Saying*
The messenger formula, v 9 Thus says Yahweh of hosts	v 14 Thus says Yahweh of hosts
Call to courage v 9 "Let your hands be strong"	v 13d Let your hands be strong.
Addresses v 9 You who heard the words of Yahweh from the prophets when the foundations of the temple was laid	
Unhappy conditions v 10 No secure employment no security from foreign enemies. No security from each other.	v 14 Fathers provoked me to anger
Turning point v 11 But now	v 15 So I turned
Covenant promises vv 12–13 agricultural and spiritual blessings	v 15 I will do good
Admonition not to fear v 13c fear not	v 15 fear not

The third part of the sermon (vv 16–17) is a summary of the moral and ethical duties of the people of God. And although the prophet was sure that the new age was coming, it remained contingent on the proper response of the people to the law of God and proper relations with each other.

Comment

The overall purpose of this sermon is encouragement. The form is one of admonition. Each section begins with "strengthen your hands" and ends with "fear not" (vv 14d, 15). Beuken shows that the expression "strengthen your hands" is an old term often used in the context of holy war (158). When Gideon was reluctant to go out against the Midianites the Lord told him to go down to their camp at night and listen to their conversation about him. That would strengthen his hands to go fight against them (Judg 7:9–11). Jonathan strengthened David's hands in God when Saul tried to kill him (1 Sam 23:15–17). Ezekiel says that Israel's hands will not be strengthened against Yahweh when he scatters them among the nations (Ezek 22:13–15).

There is some uncertainty concerning the recipients of this sermon. According to v 9 the sermon is addressed to "the ones hearing in these days these words from the mouth of the prophets who (preached) in the day the house of Yahweh of hosts was founded (in order to) build the temple." The sentence is long and involved. It is not clear whether Zechariah is speaking in 518 B.C. about the preaching of Haggai two years before, when the foundation of the temple was laid (Hag 2:18), or whether someone is speaking in the time of the Chronicler (ca. 400 B.C.) applying these words "in these days" to his own day. There is a strong similarity between this sermon and the one in 2 Chr 15:1–7. Rex Mason (70) says, "This suggests that here, as elsewhere, we have characteristic sermon material from the temple of about the same time of the Chronicler." Beuken (156–84) and Ackroyd (214) believe that the material was edited in the time of the Chronicler. But D. R. Jones takes an opposite view. Jones (107) says, "There is no reason why this short oracle should not be the summary of an appeal of Zechariah at the very end of his ministry." This matter cannot be settled on the basis of present evidence. However, it is true that the words of the prophets were applied to later situations many times in the Scriptures and extrabiblical materials.

Paul Hanson, in his book *The Dawn of Apocalyptic,* says that there was a bitter struggle in the early post-exilic community between two groups for the control of the restoration cult. One was a prophetic group, the heirs of Deutero-Isaiah, which was finally defeated and excluded, at least for a time, from the mainstream of post-exilic Judaism. The other group was a priestly group to be identified with the Zadokites and the hierocratic party. Hanson believes that Haggai and Zechariah supported the hierocratic party in rebuilding the temple. The temple was rebuilt but not without a struggle. Hanson (210, 243) sees graphic evidence of that struggle between the two parties in Zech 8:10: "For before those days (i.e. before the temple foundation had been laid) there was no wage for man or any wage for beast, neither was there any safety from the foe for him who went out or came in; for I set every man against his fellow." Hanson probably overstates his case but v 10 is a very good description of Jerusalem in the early post-exilic period. D. R. Jones (107–8) summarizes this verse in three points: (a) no secure employment; (b) no security from external enemies, and (c) no internal security. Beuken makes several observations by way of comparing 8:10 with 2 Chr 15:1–7. (a) He notes that the sub-expression, "cause to inherit all these things," is a consistent element in old covenant formulas (cf. Josh 24:13; Deut 6:10–11; Neh 9:24–25). The promise for keeping the covenant or treaty was not only the fruit of the land but the land itself. Ugarit tablet number 16138 lists as gifts from the gods, "land, castle, olive yards, vineyards, orchards, and all these other things" (Baltzer, *The Covenant Formulary* 20).

The turning point is seen again in v 13. Whereas before Israel was the object of the cursing among the nations, so (כֵּן) or now "I (Yahweh) will save you and you will be a blessing." Obviously we are still in covenant language. Blessings and curses were a part of the old covenant formula. The curse does not mean that Israel will be a curse on the nations. Rather it means that as Israel was scattered among the nations they were looked on as a curse and a by-word (cf. Deut 28:37; Jer 24:9; 25:18; 42:18; 44:8, 12; 49:13). The blessing will be the work of Yahweh, "I will save you." Some scholars see the name "Israel" in this verse as a gloss (cf. Beuken, 168). Ackroyd (215 n. 144) says that "the house of Israel is perhaps intrusive here; but it reveals the application of the message not only to the Judean community but to the ideal of a reunited people." But D. R. Jones (109) says, "This is no interpolation. The restoration of the scattered northern people is an integral part of Zechariah's hope of salvation."

The first part of the sermon ends with the exhortation, "Fear not," just as the second part does (v 15). The underlying purpose of the sermon shines through if we take the last clause of v 13 "Let your hands be strong" as the beginning of the second part. Then the first two parts begin and end with an exhortation to faith and courage.

The second part of the sermon then should begin with the words, "Let your hands be strong." Then follows the messenger formula introduced by the word "because" (כִּי). The (כִּי) "because" or "for" introduces the reason for strengthening the hands. The reason Zechariah gives in the second part of his sermon for strengthening the hands is the purpose (זָמַם) of Yahweh. God is true to his purpose, just as before he purposed to bring judgment on his people and he did. He did not repent (נָחַם) 8:14), but (כֵּן) now Yahweh has repented again (שַׁבְתִּי from שׁוּב 8:15). This time he has purposed (זָמַם, cf. 1:6) "to do good" (לְהֵיטִיב, a hiphil inf. const. יָטַב). "To do good" is often used in a covenant context (cf. Josh 24:20; Isa 1:17; Amos 5:6, 14; Zeph 1:12; Ezek 36:11). This time the promised blessing is for the house of Judah and Jerusalem. Nothing is said about Israel (v 15). The point of this saying is that God's purpose is sure. Ackroyd (215) says, "The certainty of divine judgement which has been experienced vouches for the certainty of divine deliverance which has been *promised.*"

The promise of blessing is assured because Yahweh has purposed it. However, the time and place of its fulfillment is conditioned by the people's response. Therefore Zechariah adds a statement about the moral and ethical responsibilities of the people very similar to the statement in the previous sermon (7:4–14, especially vv 9–10). There as here, external acts of social justice, integrity of mind and heart, and a proper regard for the word of Yahweh are included. A strong warning stands at the end of the sermon. "All these things (devising evil in one's heart against a neighbor and loving false oaths) I hate, oracle of Yahweh" (v 17).

Three Brief Messages about the Future (8:18–23)

Bibliography

Lipinski, E. "Recherches sur le Livre de Zacharie." *VT* 20 (1970) 42–46. **Rad, G. von,** *Old Testament Theology* II, 155–68; 292–96. **Wolff, H. W.** "The Kerygma of the Yahwist." *Int.* 20 (1966) 131–58.

Translation

[18] *Now the word of Yahweh of hosts came to me saying,* [19] *Thus says Yahweh of hosts; the fast of the fourth (month) and the fast of the fifth (month) and the fast of the seventh (month) and the fast of the tenth (month) shall be for the house of Judah for joy and gladness and for happy* [a] *festivals. But love truth and peace.* [20] *Thus says Yahweh of hosts again,*
Peoples will come in,
and the inhabitants of many cities.
[21] *The inhabitants of one shall go*
to another saying,
Let us go now [a] *to entreat the face of Yahweh*
and to seek Yahweh of hosts.
I am surely going, even I.
[22] *And many peoples and strong nations*
shall come
to seek Yahweh of hosts in Jerusalem
and to entreat the face of Yahweh.
[23] *Thus says Yahweh of hosts,*
In those days ten men from all
the tongues of the nations
shall seize the robe of a Judean man,
saying, Let us go with you
because we have heard that God is with you.

Notes

19.a. טובים lit. "good" but good has a wide range of meanings other than ethical. It can be used in the sense of that which is pleasing to the eye or feelings. Here it means "happy."
21.a. הלוֹךְ "going" the inf. abs. is used to intensify the meaning of the main verb נלכה "let us go" which is a very strong cohortative for itself.

Form/Structure/Setting

The last three sayings are set off from the previous saying by still another superscription (8:18). All of these superscriptions indicate separate collections that have been put together. The form of all three sayings includes a messenger formula at the beginning of each one (vv 19, 20, 23). The eighth saying is an answer to the previous question about fasting (7:1–3). The ninth saying is an announcement of coming of the nations to worship Yahweh of hosts (8:20–22). The form of the last (tenth) saying builds to a climax which gives the key to Zechariah's message, "We have heard that God is with you" (8:23).

Comment

This last section of chap. 8 is all about a happy future. The future will be happy for the Jews because there will be no need to continue to fast on certain days. God's blessings will be so abundant that sorrow and sadness will pass away. Every religious festival (מֹעֵד) will be happy (טוֹב "good"). But the people are reminded once again of the absolute necessity for faithfulness (אֱמֶת) and wholeness (שָׁלוֹם) in their lives.

The last two sayings (8:20–22; 8:23) are set off from the others by the adverb (עוֹד "again") as if these last two sayings are something special. They do speak about an unusual and very significant subject—the coming in of the Gentiles. It is almost universally agreed that these last verses of chap. 8 refer to Gentiles or pagan nations. However, E. Lipinski (43) argues (not successfully) that the passage has been added later and the reference to many nations and tongues here refer to Jews or proselytes of the diaspora. There is probably a reference here to an earlier passage in Zechariah (2:14–15, Eng. 2:10–11).

> Sing and rejoice O maiden Zion,
> because, behold I come
>   and I will dwell in your midst,
>   Oracle of Yahweh.
> And many nations shall join themselves
>   unto Yahweh in that day.
> And they shall become to be a people
>   and I will dwell in your midst.

Rex Mason (72) says that if 2:15(11) comes from Zechariah there is no reason to doubt that 8:20–23 do also. He notes that in both places Jerusalem and its people have the role of primacy as the medium of revelation to the nations. Zechariah does speak of Yahweh's judgment on the nations (1:15, 18–21; 2:9), but this judgment is due to those nations oppressing the people of God. But that was not Zechariah's last word about the nations. They too could come to Jerusalem and seek the face of Yahweh.

This picture of the pilgrimage of the nations is a part of the continuing strand of the Zion traditions. Gerhard von Rad sees two lines of traditions in the OT about the nations coming up to Jerusalem. One is a warlike tradition. It speaks of the nations coming to attack Jerusalem. Von Rad thinks that such a tradition may go back to the traditions in Jerusalem in pre-Davidic times (*Old Testament Theology* II, 157). However, Isaiah applied the tradition to the Assyrian attacks on Jerusalem (10:27b–34; 14:24–27; 17:12–13). Jere-

miah spoke about the enemy from the north (1:13; 4:6; 5:15–17; 6:1–5). Ezek
38–39 and Joel 4:9–17 (3:9–17) carry on the thought of the nations fighting
against Jerusalem. The culmination of this line of thinking is found in Zech
12 and 14 (von Rad 294).

But there is another cycle of concepts about the nations coming to Jerusalem. This cycle is peaceful. The nations come for salvation and not judgment
(von Rad 294). Perhaps the oldest expression of this thought is found in
Isa 2:1–4 and Mic 4:1–5. There the mountain in Jerusalem on which the
temple stands will rise and become the tallest mountain. All nations shall
flow into it to learn the law of Yahweh. He will decide difficult issues between
nations and they will be changed from warriors to peacemakers. Deutero-
Isaiah spoke about the nations coming to Jerusalem to comfort and sustain
her people (Isa 49:22–23). In Isa 45:14 we find a verse very similar to Zech
8:23, "God is with you only, and there is no other, no god besides him."

Von Rad sees the fullest development of this tradition in Trito-Isaiah. In
the beginning of Isa 60 the city of God is transfigured:

> Arise, shine; for your light has come,
>   and the glory of the Lord has risen
>   upon you.
> For behold, darkness shall cover the earth,
>   and thick darkness the peoples;
> but the Lord will arise upon you
>   and his glory will be seen upon you.
> And nations shall come to your light,
>   and kings to the brightness of your rising (Isa 60:1–3 RSV).

H. W. Wolff in a penetrating study of the "Kerygma of the Yahwist," shows
how God's promise that all the families of the earth would be blessed in
Abraham (Gen 12:3b) is the aim of the message of the Yahwist (*Int* 20 [1966]
138–39). Wolff (145) points out that the primeval history (Gen 1–11) explains
why the families of the earth need the blessing. He notes that the root אָרַר
"curse" occurs five times in these early chapters (3:14, 17; 4:11; 9:25; and
5:29). But the word "blessing" (on humanity) does not occur at all. It is
shown that curse destroys freedom and expels man from a fruitful life (4:11).
It thrusts him into aimless wandering and the tormenting fear of death (4:13).
It robs the ground of productivity and requires of man vain and agonizing
labor (3:17). But after Gen 12:3b we begin to see what it means for the
nations to gain a blessing. In a series of stories about the patriarchs the
Yahwist illustrates how the promised blessing to the peoples is realized. The
Moabites, Ammonites, Philistines, and Arameans all were blessed through
the patriarchs (Wolff 148–51). One verse in the story of Isaac and Abimelech
is very similar to Zech 8:23. Abimelech says, "We see plainly that Yahweh
is with you" (Gen 26:28).

Wolff traces this promise of blessing to the nations beyond the work of
the Yahwist. He sees evidences of it in Ps 47 and in Isa 19:23–25. A significant
change occurs in the concept in Jer 4:1–2. "If you return, O Israel, says
Yahweh, to me you may return. If you remove your abominations . . . and
if you swear, 'As Yahweh lives,' in justice and uprightness, then nations

shall gain blessing in her, and in her shall they glory." The important point
here is that Israel can only fulfill her commission of redemption in the world,
which has gone before her ever since Gen 12:3b, when she herself confesses
her God with undivided loyalty and uprightness of life (cf. Wolff 156–57).

Zech 8:23 leads one step further by offering a concrete example for the
eschatological fulfillment of the old message. Wolff comments, "The mission
to humanity is now illustrated in a single scene: one Israelite will draw ten
foreigners. In this the universal extent is not abandoned but rather clarified
in a new way. The ten foreigners come from the nations of every tongue,
as if the confusion of tongues at the end of the Babel narrative were standing
in the background (as in Gen 12:3). In a similar way the motive for the
foreigners coming—'we have heard that God is with you'—is reminiscent of
the Yahwist's pattern in the Abilmelech-Isaac narrative" (Wolff 157). So the
old promise is constantly being applied to new situations. The process did
not cease at the end of the OT. Paul saw the fulfillment of the promise in
the bringing in of the Gentiles to the kingdom of God (Gal 3:6–8).

Zechariah 9-14

Even the casual reader of the book of Zechariah can experience the differences between chaps. 1–8 and 9–14. At the beginning of chap. 9 is a new heading, "The burden of the word of the Lord." That term was not used in the first eight chapters. An observant reader will notice also that this same expression occurs in 12:1 and at the beginning of Malachi, the next book in the Hebrew Scriptures. This heading should be a clue that Zech 9 introduces something different from 1–8. The reader then will note that there is nothing in chaps. 9–14 about rebuilding the temple. The names Zechariah, Joshua, Zerubbabel, and Darius are not mentioned. There are no vision accounts or references to interpreting angels as we saw in 1–8.

The somewhat peaceful setting of 1–8 changes abruptly to one of war in chap. 9. Immediately the questions are raised: Did Zechariah write chaps. 9–14 of his book? What is the historical situation(s) reflected in these chapters? Is it possible that Zechariah could have written them near the end of his life? Or did some of his disciples or successors write them? There are some similarities between the two parts such as: (1) the significant role of Jerusalem and Zion (1:12–16; 2:1–13; 9:8–10; 12:1–13; 14:1–21). (2) The cleansing of the community as part of God's final act (3:1–9; 5:1–11; 10:9; 12:10; 13:1–2; 14:20–21). (3) The place of all the nations in the kingdom of God (2:11; 8:20–23; 9:7, 10; 14:16–19). (4) The use of the work of the former prophets (Amos 1:9–10, 5:27–62 in 9:1–8; Jer 25:34–38 in 11:1–3; Ezek 38–48 in 14:1–4). Practically all of Zech 9–14 is an interpretation of and application of earlier prophecies. Rex Mason said, "To some extent the prophet of the living word is giving way to the exegete of the written word" (Mason 80).

It was an English scholar at Cambridge who first raised the question of the date, unity, and authorship of the book of Zechariah. In 1653 Joseph Mede noted that Matt 27:9–10 attributed to Jeremiah the words found in Zech 11:13. It was Mede's opinion that the Holy Spirit was trying to correct a mistake of the Hebrew Masoretic scholars who attributed these words to Zechariah. "There is reason to suspect that the Holy Spirit (through Matthew) desired to claim these three chapters 9, 10, 11 for their real author. For there are a great many things in them which, if one carefully considers them, seem not to suit the time of Zechariah as well as that of Jeremiah" (Mede, *Dissetationum ecclesiast. triga,* 1653, quoted by Mitchell, 232). Mede's earliest followers differed from him only in extending his theory to include chaps. 12–14 as well as 9–11 to be the work of Jeremiah. In 1700 Richard Kidder, Lord Bishop of Bath and Wells, wrote "That *Jeremy* wrote 9, 10, 11, 12, 13, 14 chapters in *Zechary,* is a very probable opinion. This is certain, that such things are contained in those chapters, as agree well with the time of *Jeremy,* but by no means with that of *Zechary,* e.g. that the *Pride of Assyria shall be brought down,* and the *Septre of Egypt depart* is foretold in Zech 10:11. It is well known that this was past in *Zechary's* time; and tho' *Jeremy* might, *Zechary* could not predict this" (*A Demonstration of the Messiah 1–111* [London 1684–1700], cited by B. Otzen, *Studien* 14).

In 1785 William Newcome shifted the emphasis of the discussion of Zech 9–14 from that of the unity of this section and written by Jeremiah to the theory that chaps. 9–11 were written before the fall of the Northern Kingdom in 722 B.C., and chaps. 12–14 were written after Josiah's death but before the fall of Jerusalem in 586 B.C. (cf. Mitchell 244; Otzen, *Studien* 16; Hanson, *The Dawn of Apocalyptic* 288).

While Newcome was breaking new ground an anonymous work was published in Germany by an author later identified as Archdeacon Benedict Flugge of Hamburg. Flugge divided Zech 9–14 into nine different prophecies and assigned them to various dates on the basis of internal evidence. Flugge's pericopes and dates are:

1. Chap. 9 The time of Amos and Isaiah.
2. 10:1–2 Pre-exile. There was no idolatry after the exile.
3. 10:3–12 After 722 B.C.
4. 11:1–3 Before 722 B.C.
5. 11:4–17 Pre-exile. Reference to a king. Probably by Jeremiah.
6. 12:1–9 Undeterminable
7. 12:10–13:6 Same as number 2 above
8. and 9. 13:7–9; 14 Difficult, but probably 520 B.C. (cf. Mitchell 245; Otzen, *Studien* 18). In 1814 L. Berthold modified Flugge's theory by attributing 9–12 to Zechariah, the son of Jeberechiah, a contemporary of Isaiah (Isa 8:2), and 12–14 to an author of the period just before the fall of Jerusalem (Mitchell 245; Hanson, *Apocalyptic* 288; Baldwin, 64).

J. G. Eichhorn was the first to argue for a post-exilic date for all of 9–14. In the fourth edition of his *Introduction to the Old Testament* published in 1824 he argued that chaps. 9–10 should be placed in the period after Alexander the Great's conquest, with 13:7–14:21 coming from the Maccabean period (cf. Hanson, *Apocalyptic* 288; Otzen, *Studien* 19; Baldwin 64).

Eichhorn's thesis found little support until more than a half-century later (1881). Bernhard Stade built on Eichhorn's theory. He spent much time establishing his principles of interpretation and dating. He concluded that 9–14 are the work of one author who worked between the time of Alexander the Great and the struggle between the Diadochi about 300 B.C. (cf. Otzen 28; Mitchell 250). Stade's theory became the most popular solution for decades. Stade was the first editor of the prestigious *Zeitschrift fur die alttestamentliche Wissenschaft.* His influential articles appeared in the first two issues of that journal.

Until recently, most OT scholars have followed Stade's views rather closely. There have been some who have defended Zechariah's authorship of all fourteen chapters. George L. Robinson argued extensively for the unity of Zechariah in *The Prophecies of Zechariah* (Chicago, 1896). C. H. H. Wright (*Zechariah and His Prophecies* [London: Hodder & Stoughton, 1879]; E. B. Pusey (*The Minor Prophets* [New York: Funk and Wagnells, 1885] 4–37); A. Van Hoonacker ("Les chapitres IX–XIV du Livre Zecharie," *RB* 2 [1902] 61–62); E. J. Young (*An Introduction to the Old Testament* [Grand Rapids: Eerdmans, 1950] 273);

and R. K. Harrison (*Introduction to the Old Testament* [Grand Rapids: Eerdmans, 1970] 956), all have supported the concept that Zechariah son of Iddo was the author of the whole book of Zechariah.

Most modern scholars who have written on the book of Zechariah have taken a historical-critical approach to the book. They have tried to identify people, places, events, and customs in the book and to establish their historical and geographical location. For example references to the "sons of Greece" (9:13), "Judah and Joseph" (10:6), Ephraim (10:7), Tyre and Sidon (9:2), four Philistine cities (9:5–6), Egypt and Assyria (10:10), and Israel (9:1) have been isolated and identified in numerous ways. But this approach has not been entirely satisfactory because the data are subject to many different interpretations. For example, the historical situation in Zech 9:1–10 has been identified with almost every era from the time of Hezekiah to that of the Maccabees (cf. Hanson, *Apocalyptic* 289).

Because of the unsatisfactory results of using strictly the historical-critical method of interpreting Zech 9–14 some modern scholars have turned to other methods. Some, such as A. R. Johnson, have used the idea of the New Year festival and the theory of sacral kingship to unlock the secrets of Zech 9–14. Building on the work of Sigmund Mowinckel and S. H. Hooke, Johnson reconstructed a New Year festival in Israel similar in some ways to the New Year festival in ancient Babylon. On the basis of his study of several Psalms (72, 132, 89, 29, 93, 95, 99, 24, 68, 48, 149, 46, 97, 82, 98, 84, 101, 110) Johnson argued that a New Year festival was celebrated (in the seventh month) in Solomon's temple between the tenth and sixth centuries (1 Kings 8:2; *Sacral Kingship* [Cardiff: U. of Wales, 1955] 54, 124). The king of the house of David in Jerusalem represents Yahweh in a ritual drama in which the king, representing the forces of light, is attacked by "the nations," representing the powers of darkness or the waters of chaos. After the Davidic king is humiliated (Pss 2:1–3; 89:38–45), Yahweh saves his king, people, and Jerusalem. He demonstrates his power over chaos by giving rain on the earth.

Johnson acknowledges that there is little direct evidence of the ritual and mythology of this great autumnal festival "and even the little that is available is post-exilic in date" (*Sacral Kingship* 58). "Happily, however, there is a brief but important passage in the postexilic book of Zechariah which touches on the Feast of Tabernacles, and in so doing, yields a valuable clue to the indirect evidence which is available for the reconstruction of the ritual pattern as it existed in Jerusalem" (ibid.; cf. Zech 14:9, 12, 16–17). Johnson believes that the eschatological picture found in Zech 14 (he emphasizes the eschatological aspect of the covenant rather than the magical aspect seen by Mowinckel) is based on the already established complex of ideas associated with this festival in Jerusalem (*Sacral Kingship* 59).

Almost all contemporary OT scholars accept some kind of cultic influence on chaps. 9–14 of Zechariah. Otzen acknowledges that some of the language in Zech 9–14 had its origin in the cultic celebration of the New Year festival (cf. *Studien* 135–42).

F. F. Bruce does not doubt that Zech 9–14 had some historical life-setting but he does not believe that it can be identified. He says that "there are no more vexed problems in Old Testament criticism than the life-setting of Zech

9–14. . . . The historical contexts . . . can only be guessed at" (*New Testament Development of Old Testament Themes* 101). Bruce recognizes the cultic language behind much of this material. He sees the language about "smiting the shepherd and scattering the sheep" in 13:7–9 as cultic. Bruce says that whatever the historical life-setting was, however, the language of the oracle may well have a life-setting in the national cultus, "in the liturgical role of the king" (102). Again Bruce says about "the pierced one" (Zech 12:10) that the oracle could be drawn from the national liturgy, "and more particularly from the part played in that liturgy by the king" (p. 112).

Paul Hanson sees Zech 9–14 as the polemical literature of a dissident group of visionary followers of Deutero-Isaiah and a group of disenfranchised Levites who were struggling against the ruling hierocratic party for control of governmental and spiritual affairs of the early post-exilic community in Jerusalem. Hanson dates all of Zech 9–14 from about 550 to 475 B.C. (cf. *Apocalyptic* 27, 400). According to Hanson, the prophet-Levite coalition saw in the Persian sponsorship of the rebuilding of the temple a threat to the "autonomy and Lordship of Yahweh" (*Apocalyptic* 284). The coalition also viewed the hierocratic leaders as corrupt (cf. 10:2–3; 11:5, 16–17); and they believed that the hierocratic party was virtually indifferent toward eschatology (ibid).

But the prophetic party (the visionaries) continued to insist that the fulfillment of Israel's history would be a future event in which Yahweh himself would destroy the present structures, which the hierocrats had absolutized and supplanted, and replace them with a new and more glorious order. To explain how all this would happen, Hanson believes that the visionaries borrowed the old mythic Divine Warrior motifs, fusing the ritual conquest traditions of the old tribal league with the ritual procession of the royal cult (285).

Hanson's work has met with mixed reactions. It was reviewed by Ackroyd (*Int* 30 [1976] 412–15), who compliments Hanson's work because it "takes the texts seriously, examining their structure, analyzing their metrical form, and tracing the origin of the imagery and ideas to be found in them. . . . What Hanson does for the study of the use of imagery, particularly its relationship to much older patterns is particularly valuable" (413). But Ackroyd believes that Hanson's over-confident assignment of particular sections to the "visionaries" or the "hierocrats" can be dangerous (414).

The most thorough critique of Hanson's work was done by Robert P. Carroll in *JSOT* 14 (1979) 3–35. Again there is a positive evaluation of Hanson's work. Carroll says, "This is a formidable volume of textual exegesis, form-critical analysis and hermeneutic argumentation, and I doubt if there has been anything quite as substantial in biblical studies published in recent years" (16–17). But Carroll criticizes Hanson's work on a number of points. (1) He thinks Hanson begs the question in his definitions of prophetic and apocalyptic eschatology (18). (2) He finds Hanson's obsessive use of polarization disconcerting (19). (3) Hanson's false antithesis between myth and history is a major weakness of the work according to Carroll (20). (4) The visionaries' relationship to the cult is unclear in Hanson's work (22). (5) The issue about the hierocratic party lacking an eschatology is also more complex.

B. S. Childs seems to make a quick, negative critique of Hanson's work when he says, "To attempt to interpret the book as the result of a conflict between 'visionaries' and 'realists' can result in the worst kind of reductionism" (Childs, *IOTS* 486). Hanson's work has strong points and weak points. It has provided a method of interpretation that makes much of the language of Zech 9–14 understandable without identifying every specific "historical" reference. However the reader of Hanson's book gets the impression that he makes the biblical materials conform to his hypothesis, rather than deriving his hypothesis from a strict exegesis of those materials.

It is widely acknowledged that it is virtually impossible to explain the historical background of Zech 9–14. "The most satisfactory conclusion is that the writer is not taking any particular standpoint, but rather, in the manner characteristic of apocalyptic, is using past events to typify a supremely important future event" (Baldwin 158).

In July 1962 Douglas R. Jones of Durham advanced a fresh interpretation of Zech 9–11 (*VT* 12 [1962] 241–59). Jones argued that these chapters are the work of a prophet living in or near Damascus in the first half of the fifth century B.C. Jones believes that much of the material is autobiographical. This prophet had taken the pastoral oversight of a group of captives from the Northern Kingdom. Amos had spoken about Israel going into captivity near Harmon (perhaps Mt. Hermon 4:3). He had mentioned Hamath, in connection with Gath and the Philistines in 6:2. Ps 42:6 suggests that some sons of Korah were being held captive near Mt. Hermon. So this prophet looked for the time when Amos' prophecies about Tyre and the Philistines would be fulfilled. The flock in these chapters represents the people exiled around Mt. Hermon. The prophet is the good shepherd who is rejected (Zech 11:4–17).

Jones points out one other key to the understanding of these chapters. He believes that the reunion of the tribes under one Davidic king is a major motif of these chapters. This idea came to the prophet according to Jones while the prophet was meditating on the permanent meaning of 2 Sam 15–19 (the story of Absalom's rebellion against David). In that story Absalom rode on horses and in chariots (2 Sam 15:1) and David rode on an ass (2 Sam 16:1). Absalom's rebellion is seen also as a threat to the unity of all the tribes under David (2 Sam 16:3). But here in Zech 9–11 all of that will be reversed. A new king of the line of David will come with humility but power to return and to reunite his people. Jones elaborated on his theories in his commentary on Haggai, Zechariah, and Malachi in the *Torch Bible Commentary* Series (1962). His theories have not been widely adopted. He even warns the reader of his commentary that his theories are fresh and untried. At least they add to the already long list of possible backgrounds for this material.

As we have seen Paul Lamarche published a well organized study of the literary structure of Zech 9–14 in which he argues for a unity for all the materials in these chapters, probably as the work of a redactor. Lamarche found the clue to the organization of the material in the principle of chiasmus. Chiasmus is a classical term from the Greek letter *chi* which is in the form of a cross. When applied to a literary structure it refers to the reversal of the word order of two parts of a sentence or paragraph. A good example is found in Gen 9:6, "whoso sheddeth man's blood, by man shall his blood be shed." The pattern is described as abc c'b'a'. Lamarche isolated twelve pericopes in Zech 9–14 and detected in them a chiastic pattern which demonstrated to him their unity. He preferred a date for the work as 500–480 B.C., but he acknowledged that a date of 320 B.C. was possible (*Zacharie IX–XIV* 148).

Lamarche's chiastic arrangement is:

A. Judgment and salvation of neighboring peoples 9:1–8
  B. Arrival and description of the king 9:9–10
    C. War and victory of Israel 9:11–10:1
      D. Presence of idols; judgment 10:2–3a
    C ^{1} War and victory of Israel 10:3b–11:3
  B ^{1} The shepherd rejected by the people 11:4–17
    C ^{2} War and victory of Israel 12:1–9
  B ^{2} Yahweh's representative pierced; mourning and purification
    12:10–13:1
      D ^{1} Suppression of idols and false prophets 13:2–6
  B ^{3} Shepherd struck; people tested, purification and return
    to God 13:7–9
    C ^{3} War and victory of Israel 14:1–15
A ^{1} Judgment and salvation of all nations 14:16–21

Not many scholars have followed Lamarche's ideas completely. However, one who has done so is Joyce Baldwin. In fact, she has gone beyond Lamarche in seeing not only a chiastic arrangement for chaps. 9–14 but for chaps. 1–8 as well (cf. Baldwin 85–86). J. A. Soggin said that the work of Lamarche helps in an examination of the text. But even here, "Lamarche is perhaps too optimistic about the real condition of the traditional text, transferring the responsibility for the variants which appear to the ancient translations" (Soggin, *IOT* 350). Mason was probably referring to Lamarche's and Baldwin's works when he said, "It has been claimed that these chapters (Zech 9–14) reveal a clear and carefully formed structure and that this shows the essential unity of their final presentation. Such schemes, however, ignoring as they do the wide differences, argue more for the ingenuity of the commentator than for anything else" (Mason 78). So, even though there is something to be said about Lamarche's attempt to demonstrate the unity of Zech 9–14 he probably overstates his case and bends the materials to fit his mould.

A different kind of study of the book of Zechariah to determine its unity or the lack of it was made by Yehuda T. Radday and Dieter Wickmann (*ZAW* 87 [1975] 30–55). They had already made a study of the book of Isaiah (1973) and found that the chances of chaps. 40–66 of that book being written by the author of 1–35 were 1:100,000 (31). Radday and Wickmann used the same method of statistical analysis on the book of Zechariah and found that the difference in language behavior between chaps. 1–8 and 9–11 is not sufficient to postulate a change of authors between chaps. 8 and 9 (54).

But the chances that chaps. 1–11 were written by the same author(s) as 12–14 are 2:1,000. Of course, these figures do not prove that chaps. 1–11 are a unity, nor that 12–14 were not written by the author(s) of the first part.

One other method for understanding the book of Zechariah should be considered. That is the canonical method used by Brevard S. Childs who believes that the clue to the understanding of any part of the Bible is to be found in its final or canonical form (Childs *IOTS* 73). He argues that most of the literature has a history. In some cases it has undergone many changes so that the final form and message may be quite different from its original shape and meaning (74–79). In applying this canonical method to the book of Zechariah, Childs acknowledges that a definite historical reference was originally intended for much of the book. But now the language about Syria, Palestine, Egypt, and Assyria, and the shepherd allegory in chap. 11, can refer to the future as well as the past (480–81). "The inability of critical research to establish a convincing case for one period is further evidence that the present canonical text has been dislocated from its original moorings" (481). He traces the changes in the materials of the whole book to its final canonical form and argues that although chaps. 1–8 had different authors and redactors from those of chaps. 9–14 there is presently a unity among all the chapters. For Childs the stages of production of the book were: (1) a number of visions occurring at different times, some occurring before the deliverance of the exiles by Cyrus (477). (2) The eight visions were arranged in a series at the absolute time of the second year of Darius in order to allow the visions to perform a different role within the book of Zechariah. The deliverance from Babylon now lies in the past. Although the traditional language of the "second exodus" has been retained, it has been given a new reference. "The language of hope now points to a still (eschatological) future event in which Israel's deliverance lies" (477). Childs sees another sign of canonical shaping within chaps. 1–8 in the expansion of the various visions by the addition of oracles and in the sign-act of chap. 6 (478). Finally, in chaps. 7 and 8 a series of divine oracles occur between a question about fasting and its answer. These oracles also have an eschatological orientation but the ethical imperatives of the covenant remain intact.

According to Childs, chaps. 9–14 are from a different and later hand than that of chaps. 1–8 (482). "There is no direct literary dependence of 9–14 on 1–8 such as a conscious patterning, a midrashic expansion, or a promise-fulfillment relationship" (480). However, Childs sees "a surprising compatibility" between the two parts of the book (482). He does caution against Lamarche's overstating the compatibility of the material in chaps. 9–14 (483). Childs lists a number of elements of congruity between the two parts, including (1) Yahweh's protection of the New Jerusalem (2:5; 9:8; 14:11). (2) The return of a paradisal fertility (8:12; 14:8). (3) Renewal of the covenant (8:8; 13:9). (4) Divine judgment on the nations (2:1–4 [Eng. 1:18–24] 14:9) and their ultimate conversion (2:15 [Eng. 2:11]; 8:22; 14:9). (5) The gathering of the exiles (8:7; 10:9–10). (6) The outpouring of the spirit (4:6; 12:10) and cleansing (5:4; 13:3). (6) The messianic figure (3:8; 4:6; 9:9–10).

So Childs sees the original visions before the return from Babylon modified in 519 B.C. to mean that the new age would begin with the reconstructed temple. In turn that understanding was modified by the addition of chaps. 9–14 to give a prophetic word about the period before the end (483–84):

It is important to recognize that the editorial joining of the two parts of Zechariah not only serves to alter the reading of the first chapters in terms of the last, but the reverse dynamic is also set in motion. The presence of Proto-Zechariah significantly affected how the community heard the message of the last chapters. To suggest that the late apocalyptic writers had lost interest in the everyday ethical responsibilities of the covenant because of a fixation on the coming age fails to reckon with the canonical shape of the book as a whole. The strong imperatives of ch. 8 which the editors link inextricably with the coming age serve as a constant warning against misunderstanding the nature of the coming kingdom. Judah's repentance is described in 13.9 by a repetition of the same ancient covenant formula found explicit in 8.8. Thus ch. 8 provides the content to the imperatives which ch. 13 signals and links the two parts of the book closely together (484–85).

One may not agree with Childs about the dating of the visions before the return from Babylonian exile, but his emphasis on the necessity for a holistic reading of the book is welcome. We agree that any attempt to find a specific historical setting for the materials in Zech 9–14 will end in failure. That these materials originally had a specific historical setting should not be denied. But it is no longer possible to identify such a situation. As the material now stands it refers to the end time when God will judge the nations and his own people. After a fearful purging, Jerusalem will repent. God will save Jerusalem and the peoples of the earth will come to worship Yahweh in holiness.

The First Burden (9:1–11:17)

The last part of the book of Zechariah is divided almost equally between chaps. 9–11 and 12–14. There are forty-six verses in chaps. 9–11 and forty-four verses in chaps. 12–14. There are some similarities and differences between these two parts. In chaps. 9–11 the nations close to Israel are attacked. In chaps. 12–14 Jerusalem is attacked by all the nations of the world. In chaps. 9–11 the captives or exiles are freed and return to their homes, but nothing is said about the return of the exiles in chaps. 12–14. The shepherd motif is strong in chaps. 9–11 but may not appear at all in chaps. 12–14 if 13:7–9 belongs with chap. 11. Nothing is said about cleansing in chaps. 9–11 but a strong emphasis is made on weeping, cleansing, and holiness in chaps. 12–14. A new king is mentioned in 9:9–10, but the pierced one (12:10) and the slain shepherd (13:7) are not strictly identified as the new king. The nations are defeated in chaps. 9–11 but some of them are converted in 12–14.

Yahweh's Kingdom in Syria, Phoenicia, and Philistia (9:1–8)

Bibliography

Dahood, M. "Zecharia 9:1, 'En 'Adam." *CBQ* 25 (1963) 123–24. **Hanson, P.** "Zechariah 9 and the Recapitulation of an Ancient Ritual Pattern." *JBL* 92 (1973) 37–59. **Zolli, E.** "Eyn 'Adam (Zach IX.I)." *VT* 5 (1955) 90–92.

Translation

[1] A Burden [a]

The word of Yahweh 　is [b] against the land of Hadrach, and Damascus is [b] its resting place [c].	2+2+2
Because the eye of man [d] belongs to Yahweh, 　and the eye of all the tribes of Israel.	4+3
[2] And also Hamath which borders 　on her, Tyre, and Sidon, 　although she [a] is very wise.	2+2+3
[3] And Tyre built a rampart for herself. 　She heaped up silver like the dust, 　and gold like dirt of the streets.	4+3+3
[4] Behold the Lord will possess her 　and he will knock her wealth into the sea 　and she will be consumed with fire.	3+3+3
[5] Askelon shall see and be terrified; 　and Gaza shall writhe exceedingly; 　and Ekron, because her hope will 　　be ruined.	3+3+3
And the king from Gaza will perish. And Askelon will not be inhabited.	3+3
[6] And a half-breed [a] will dwell in Ashdod. 　And I will cut off the pride of the Philistines.	3+3
[7] And I will remove his blood from his mouth, 　and his detestable things from between his teeth.	3+3
And even he shall be a remnant for our God. 　And he shall be like a clan [a] in Judah. 　And Ekron shall be like the Jebusite.	3+3+2
[8] And I will encamp before my house 　as a guard [a] against the one who would 　　go in or out,	2+3
And no oppressor will come upon them again because now I see with my eyes. [b]	4+4

Notes

1.a. מַשָּׂא is often translated "oracle" or "burden." The term is often used in the OT in a technical sense to introduce an oracle of a prophet (cf. Isa 13:1; 14:28; 15:1; 17:1; 19:1; Ezek 12:10; Nah 1:1; Hab 1:1; Zech 9:1; 12:1; Mal 1:1). It lays stress on the feeling of the prophet. His message is something placed on him which he must accept and deliver to others (cf. Jer 20:9; Paul de Boer, "An enquiry into the meaning of the term Massā'." *OTS* 5 [1948] 197–214; R. B. Y. Scott, "The Meaning of Massā' as an Oracle Title." *JBL* 67 [1948] 5–6).

1.b. There is no verb in the Hebrew text. Consequently this first verse is read in different ways. The RSV considers מַשָּׂא as the title of chaps. 9–11 and separates it from "the word of Yahweh" that follows. However, Hanson reads מַשָּׂא דבר יהוה as a construct chain with the LXX, Vg and Tg "The oracle of Yahweh's word" (*Apocalyptic*, 296). The NEB has "An oracle: the word of the Lord." Hanson follows Otzen and others and assumes that a second יהוה has dropped out and reads "Yahweh is against Hadrach." The NEB reads בָּא אֶרֶץ "he has come to the land of . . ." for בָּאָרֶץ "in" or "against the land of . . . ."

1.c. מְנֻחָתוֹ "its resting place," if the subject is "the word of Yahweh," but if the subject is Yahweh, which is supplied by adding a second יְהוָה, the translation is "his resting place." Hanson translates מְנֻחַת "his throne dais" on the basis of 1 Chr 28:2; Isa 66:1; Ps 132:8, 14; Isa 11:10 (Hanson, *Apocalyptic* 297).

1.d. עֵין אָדָם "eye of man" is a crux (Otzen 235). If the text is correct as it stands "the eye of man (*adam*)," it is difficult to understand its meaning. Should we take it as an objective genitive as Otzen does (236) and read, "Yahweh has his eye on man and especially on all the tribes of Israel"? Or should we read it as a subjective genitive, "Man has his eye on Yahweh and so does all the tribes of Israel"? The form suggests the latter meaning. However, the RSV along with many scholars emend the text from עֵין אָדָם to עָרֵי אֲרָם "cities of Aram" (Syria). M. Dahood thinks אָדָם is a mas. form of אֲדָמָה "ground" in Gen 16:12; Job 11:12; 36:28; Prov 30:14b; Jer 32:20; Zech 13:5, and translates "surface of the earth." E. Zolli thinks the "Eyn Adam" is a village place name near Mt. Hermon (cf. Josh 3:16; Ps 68:19; Eng. 68:18). It is probably best to retain the difficult reading "eye of man" and understand it as a subjective genitive, "belong to Yahweh," i.e. "the eyes of Gentiles and all the tribes of Israel should be on Yahweh."

2.a. כִּי חָכְמָה מְאֹד "although she is very wise." The problem is that the subject "Tyre and Sidon" is pl. but the verb is sing. Otzen (237) explains three possible ways of understanding the construction. (1) Consider the verb in agreement with the last subject. (2) Tyre and Sidon may, as a word-pair, be considered sing. (3) חָכְמָה could be an old fem. pl. form. The NEB omits Tyre to solve the problem. The RSV would read the pl. חָכְמוּ with LXX and Vg.

6.a. מַמְזֵר JB and RV translated "bastard." The term only occurs here and Deut 23:3 (Eng. 23:2). The term is of uncertain origin. The rabbis understood it to refer to one born out of an incestuous marriage (S. R. Driver 238). It probably refers to a mixed race situation similar to that described in Neh 13:23–25.

7.a. בְּאַלֻּף "as a clan-chief" (Gen 36:15–19; Exod 15:15) is usually repointed כְּאֶלֶף "as a clan."

8.a. מִצָּבָה seems to be the noun צָבָא "host" or "army" plus the prep. מִן. But most scholars prefer to read מַצָּבָה "outpost" as 1 Sam 14:12.

8.b. בְּעֵינַי "with my eyes." Are these Yahweh's eyes (Otzen 240; Baldwin 158,161), or are they the prophet's eyes (Jones 129; NEB)? It is probably best to understand that they are Yahweh's eyes in the sense of enforcing his judgments (cf. Jer 7:11).

Form/Structure/Setting

The form of 9:1–8 seems to be a prophetic judgment oracle against Syria, Phoenicia, and Philistia. Hanson calls the whole chap. 9 a Divine Warrior hymn. The pericope begins by announcing that the word of Yahweh is against the land of Hadrach and Damascus (v 1). It is also against Tyre and Sidon. In spite of their wisdom (v 2), defenses (v 3), and wealth (v 3), Yahweh will destroy them (v 4). The Philistine cities will fear and be overcome (vv 5–6) but then Philistia will be cleansed and will become like a clan in Judah (v 7). Finally, Yahweh will camp at his house to protect his people from potential enemies (v 8).

The setting of this passage is almost impossible to determine. D. R. Jones argues that these are the words of a prophet in exile near Mt. Hermon. The prophet is simply asserting that Yahweh has spoken to him in Syria. Yahweh's word is not directed toward Damascus, but toward Tyre and Philistia (*VT* 12 [1962] 124).

Paul Hanson sees 9:1–8 as a part of one unit which encompasses all of chap. 9. He thinks that it is the work of the visionary group in Jerusalem using the language of holy war and the cosmic myth to assert Yahweh's victory over the nations, the coming of a new king of the line of David, the return of the exile, and a restoration of fertility to the earth. The influence of the cosmic myth can be seen in Yahweh's throne dais being located in the north as the old Baal cultic myths had their gods enthroned on Mt. Zaphon. Hanson recognizes that very few other scholars have viewed 9:1–17 as a unit. He notes that Sellin maintained that the oracle extends through v 17 but only after deleting vv 9–10 (Hanson, *Apocalyptic* 293).

The setting probably was in Jerusalem about the middle of the sixth century B.C. Evidently the temple had not yet been restored. A change in the language of prophecy toward a strong emphasis on eschatology was beginning.

Comment

B. Otzen's statement that "already the first word gives us several problems" (233) is an indication of the difficulty one encounters in trying to interpret the last six chapters of Zechariah. One of the first questions one should decide in interpreting 9:1–8 is: Does this material refer to an invasion of Palestine by an earthly king such as Alexander the Great, Nebuchadnezzar or one of Assyria's kings? Our answer is no. Hanson is surely correct in saying, "No specific historical conquest by a specific historical conqueror is being described, nor is there anywhere in these verses so much as a hint that a foreign king is being used by Yahweh as his instrument" (*Apocalyptic,* 316). It is Yahweh who is about to come and do these things.

A second question the interpreter of this passage should answer is: Is the word of Yahweh against Damascus and the land of Hadrach, or is Hadrach thought of as the sacred mountain, the dwelling place of Yahweh from which his word comes? It may seem strange to speak about Damascus being the dwelling place of Yahweh. But such an idea probably was not strange to the Damascus-covenanters who chose Damascus as their home in the second century B.C. while others of the same persuasion chose Qumran.

Although Israel seldom occupied the territories of Syria, Tyre, and Philistia, the ideal borders of her territory included these regions (cf. Num 13:21–24; 34:1–12; Deut 1:7; Josh 1:3–4; 1 Kgs 4:21, 24; 2 Kgs 14:25, 28). The Targum and some rabbis understood v 2 to say that Yahweh would dwell in Damascus. H. G. Mitchell quotes one rabbi, "I take heaven and earth to witness that I am from Damascus, and that there is there a place called Hadrach. But how do I justify the words, *and Damascus shall be his resting-place?*

Jerusalem will one day extend to Damascus; for it says, *and Damascus shall be his resting-place,* and his *resting-place,* according to the Scripture, *this is my rest forever,* is none other than Jerusalem" (*ICC* 263). It is impossible to decide whether the word of Yahweh is favorable or negative for Syria. In either case Yahweh's rule over Syria is certain (cf. Isa 17:1–3).

The last part of 9:1 is also an enigma. Is the eye of man on Yahweh or is Yahweh's eye on man (אדם), or should אדם be changed to אדם? Again, it is impossible to answer this question decisively. Theologically it would be better to take this expression and that at the end of 9:8 to say that Yahweh has his eye on the whole world. But one cannot say dogmatically that this is what the texts say.

The meaning of vv 2, 3, 4 is clearer. Tyre and Sidon, though they are wise, strong defensively (rampart, v 3), and rich, will not be able to withstand the judgment of Yahweh. Some word-play typical of this passage is seen in this verse: "stronghold" מצור echoes "Tyre" צור; "dust" עפר echoes צבר "heaped up"; and "streets" חוצות echoes חרוץ "fine gold." The judgment on Tyre (v 4) almost certainly is influenced by Amos 1:10.

> I will send a fire on the wall of Tyre,
> and it shall devour her strongholds.

Tyre's downfall will cause the cities of Philistia to tremble. Four of the five Philistine cities are named in this passage as they are in Amos 1:6–8; Zeph 2:4 (cf. Jer 47:1–7). Gath is the one Philistine city missing from the list. It seems to have been destroyed in the time of Uzziah (2 Chr 26:6; cf. Amos 6:2). The four remaining cities are to be severely judged. Here it is Gaza that will lose its king, not Askelon as in Amos 1:8; and Askelon will be without inhabitants, not Ashdod as in Amos.

A change occurs in the middle of the brief v 6 from third person to first person and from judgment to hope (Mason 86). Yahweh is the speaker. He will cut off the pride of the Philistines (v 6). He will cleanse them from pagan customs of drinking blood and eating forbidden meat like dogs, pigs, and mice (Isa 65:4; 66:3, 17). Then in the middle of v 7 another remarkable change occurs. The Philistine is to become a remnant for Yahweh (v 7). It seems to have surprised the prophet himself. He says, "and even he (the Philistine) shall be a remnant to our God." D. R. Jones says that this idea is an amplification of the teaching of Zech 2:11 and 8:23, but "It challenges the nationalistic instincts of the Jews to the core" (Jones 128). The Philistines, who in the days of Samuel were the archenemy now will become a remnant of God and like a clan in Judah!

The reference to the Jebusite here is significant. It supports the theory that David did not put all the indigenous Jebusites to death when he captured Jerusalem (cf. 2 Sam 5:6–9; 1 Chr 11:4–9). The prophet here says that just as the Jebusites became part of the people of God in David's time so will the Philistines become like a clan in Judah (cf. Isa 17:3). It is important to notice, however, that there is no compromise on the issue of pagan practices. The remnant will be purified by fire.

V 8 is difficult. To what does "my house" refer? Does the word מצבה

mean "army" or should it be emended to "outpost"? Should the two participles with a prefixed prep. מן be deleted? Does the last line refer to the
prophet's eyes or Yahweh's? Again it is impossible to give a definitive answer
to any of these questions. However, Hanson says that "it is totally unjustifiable
to remove v 8 as a later addition" (*Apocalyptic* 320). He sees this verse as
an integral part of the ritual-conquest pattern. The conquest is described
in vv 1–7 and in v 8 the conqueror Yahweh reaches his goal—the temple
from which he will protect his people. But does לביתי mean "temple"? The
word is not היכל, the technical term for temple, but בית "house." Otzen
(239) says it can mean "temple," "Jerusalem," or "Judah" (Hos 8:1; 9:15;
Jer 12:7). Jones says it refers to God's people (129). The last line of v 8
probably should be understood as referring to Yahweh's eyes looking in judgment on offenders.

Explanation

In spite of its difficulties, this passage (9:1–8) is an appropriate beginning
for the eschatological oracles in chaps. 9–14. It asserts that the territory of
the nations will become God's territory. Many of the peoples will be brought
into his covenant. It links this final section with the first eight chapters of
Zechariah and shows that earlier prophecies (like those of Amos) will be
fulfilled. There is in these verses not only a note of Yahweh's victory but
an emphasis on cleansing (v 7). Mason says about this passage, "If there is
hope for the Philistines, there is hope for all" (87).

The Coming of a New King   (9:9–10)

Bibliography

Lipinski, E. "Recherches sur le livre de Zacharie." *VT* 20 (1970) 50–53.

Translation

[9] *Rejoice greatly, daughter Zion!*	3+3
Shout, daughter Jerusalem!	
Behold your king comes to you,	3+3
righteous and delivered. [a]	
He is poor and riding upon a donkey,	3+2
and upon a colt [b] *of an ass, son of a she-ass.*	
[10] *And I* [a] *will cut off the chariot from Ephraim,*	3+2
and the horse from Jerusalem.	
And the war-bow will be cut off.	3+3
And he will speak peace to the nations,	
and he will rule [b] *from sea to sea*	3+3
and from the river to the ends of the earth.	

Notes

9.a. ונושׁע is a niph. pt. and should be translated "saved" or "victorious." Traditionally the word has been translated as an active form, "having salvation." But the point here is not what the king can do for others (save them) but what Yahweh has done for him. He has saved him from some ordeal. Therefore he (the king) is victorious (cf. Isa 49:4; 50:8; 53:12; Ps 18:4, 50; 33:16; 89:39–45; 118:15–18).

9.b. עיר "colt." Holladay reads "stallion." This passage has probably been influenced by Gen 49:10b–11. There the reference is to one "whose right it is" (probably a messianic reference) and he will bind his foal (עיר) to a vine. The fertility of the land will be so great that a vine can serve as a hitching post, and his ass's colt (בני אתנו) tied to a choice vine. The poetic parallelism is very obvious in Gen 49:11, as it is in Zech 9:9. The language of the two passages is essentially the same. Matthew and John both refer to this passage and treat it with unusual freedom (cf. Mitchell 276). Matthew seems to understand that the prophet spoke of two animals (Matt 21:7), but John understands the reference to be only to one animal (John 12:15). John's interpretation is correct.

10.a. There is a change from 3rd to 1st person. NEB follows the LXX and reads, "he (the king) will cut off the chariot from Ephraim."

10.b. Lit. "his rule shall be."

Form/Structure/Setting

The form is that of an entrance liturgy. The pericope begins with a call to Jerusalem to sing, rejoice, and shout greatly because her king is coming (cf. Zeph 3:14; Zech 2:10). The character of the king is then described as righteous, victorious (saved), and humble (v 9b). Then Yahweh (or the king, JB, NEB) will cut off the instruments of war (v 10a), and the king will bring in his universal reign of peace (v 10b). Although the form as well as the language is cultic, the setting does not have to be in the cult. D. R. Jones imagines the setting as that of a prophet speaking to Jewish exiles in Syria in the fifth century. This is the prophet's vision of peace under the rule of a new David in Jerusalem. The passage is probably post-exilic and is the work of a prophet speaking eschatologically. What is the relationship of 9:9–10 to the rest of chap. 9? E. G. Kraeling considers 9:1–10 a separate oracle because "the resumption of war after the coming of the king of Peace is unbearable" ("The Historical Situation in Zech 9:1–10," *AJSL* 41 [1924–25] 24–33). E. Sellin maintains that the oracle extends through 17, but only after deleting vv 9–10 (496, n. 5). (Vv 9 and 10 do have a different meter from the rest of the chapter.) Hanson defends the unity of chap. 9 in spite of a different meter in vv 9–10. He says, "the stepped-up tempo in verses 9–10 is completely consonant with the crescendo of excitement at this point in the unit" (*Apocalyptic*, 293).

Comment

This is one of the most familiar passages in Zech 9–14. Undoubtedly it is an eschatological passage. The prophet picks up the language of the new king from the eighth century prophets (Isa 9:6–7; 11:1–5 and Mic 5:2–4), the New Year festival (Ps 72:1–11; 89:38–45) and the promise to Judah in Gen 49:10–11.

The shouting of the people greeting the coming of the king is characteristic

of cultic situations. But this situation is different. The king comes riding on
a donkey which may suggest humility, rather than on a horse which probably
would have been indicative of militarism. D. R. Jones has made a good case
for seeing part of the background of this passage, Absalom's rebellion against
David and David's return to Jerusalem after Absalom's death (cf. 2 Sam 15–
19; Jones, *VT* 12 [1962] 256–59).

The king comes to Jerusalem after Yahweh's reign is established in Syria,
Phoenicia, and Philistia, although nothing is said about any part the king
might have had in that conquest. The king is described with three Hebrew
terms צדיק נושע עני "righteous," "saved," and "humble" or "poor." The
word "righteous" refers to the conduct of the king in accordance with his
proper relationship with Yahweh and with his people. He is to keep his covenant with Yahweh (2 Sam 23:1–7). He is to rule his people in righteousness,
which includes justice משפט for the poor. Such action on the part of the
king will result in rain (fertility) and peace (שלום) (Ps 72:1–7).

The word "saved" does not mean primarily "having salvation" (KJV), but
it refers to the act of being saved by Yahweh's action from some ordeal. It
is the same word found in Ps 33:16–17.

> A king is not saved by his great army;
>   a warrior is not delivered by his great strength.
> The war horse is a vain hope for victory,
>   and by its great might it cannot save.

The idea is the same here in Zech 9:9 except that here the prophet is speaking
of an eschatological king. He will be saved by Yahweh. The thought is that
the king will receive divine help and favor so that whatever he does will
prosper. He will keep his covenant and rule righteously. He will be "humble,"
or "poor," not proud and haughty as Absalom was when he got himself "a
chariot and horses and fifty men to run before him" (2 Sam 15:1; cf. Esth
6:6–9).

A. R. Johnson suggests that Ps 118:22–27a is a short hymn of welcome
to the Messiah. The cry "Hosanna" (הושיעה נא "grant salvation") in v 25
is addressed to the Messiah (*Sacral Kingship*, 127).

The third term used here to characterize the new king is "humble" or
"poor." The word seems to be interchangeable in the Qere-kethib with ענו
(cf. S. R. Driver, "Poor" *HDB;* cf. Mitchell 276). The significance of this
characteristic is that it presents the Messiah as meek and lowly, not proud
and boastful. There could be some connection here with the idea of Moses'
meekness (ענו Num 12:3) and with the suffering of the servant (מענה Isa
53:4).

V 10 has three major motifs. (1) The new king will destroy every implement
and semblance of war. Here as elsewhere in the OT the eschaton will be a
time when wars will cease.

> I will cut off the chariot from Ephraim
>   and the horse from Jerusalem.
> And the war-bow will be cut off (v 10a,b).

Both northern Israel and southern Judah are included in this total disarmament program. The language sounds very much like Mic 5:10; Hos 2:20 (Eng. 2:18); Isa 2:4; Mic 4:3; Isa 9:5; Ps 46:9. (2) A second motif in v 10 is that the new king will speak "peace" (שלום) to the nations (לגוים). This idea is in line with the prophecy of Isa 2:4 and Mic 4:3. "Peace" means "blessing," "wholeness." The prophet sees the new king extending the blessings of Yahweh, which the psalmist reserved for Israel (72:7–11), to all the world. (3) The third motif is similar to the second. The new king will rule from sea to sea and from the river to the ends of the earth (cf. Ps 72:8). Again, the assertion is made of the universal reign of Yahweh's king. But there is quite a difference between this prophet's concept of the place of the Gentiles in the new kingdom and the concept of the writer of Ps 72. After the psalmist asserted Yahweh's universal rule he prayed for his foes and enemies to lick the dust before him (cf. Ps 72:9–11). Here the prophet stops after quoting Ps 72:8. He believes that the universal reign of the Messiah will include all nations and will be one of peace.

The word for "rule" in Ps 72:8 is וירד, a qal impf. from רדה which means "to tread" as in a winepress (Joel 4:13). In Zech 9:10 the word for rule is משל which is a general word for "rule."

The relationship of Zech 9:10 to Ps 72:8 is interesting from the vantage of earlier and later commentaries. C. A. Briggs believes that the psalmist in Ps 72 is copying Zechariah (*Psalms* 2. ICC [Edinburgh: T & T Clark, 1907] 134, 138). But Artur Weiser thinks the order is reversed. It is the prophet who borrows from the psalmist (Weiser, *Psalms* [Philadelphia: Westminster Press, 1962] 502–504).

Almost all commentaries understand the reference to "the river" in Zech 9:10 and Ps 72:8 to be a reference to the Euphrates (Driver 242). But A. R. Johnson says "the reference, far from being an allusion to the Euphrates, is really an allusion to the current of the great cosmic sea which nourishes the holy city" (cf. Ps 46:4; Ezek 47:1; Zech 14:8; Johnson, *Sacral Kingship* 9).

Vv 9 and 10 were probably part of the "testimonies" of the early Christian. No doubt this passage had a great influence on Jesus. He seems to have deliberately modeled his "triumphal entry" into Jerusalem according to its outline. The peaceful and universal reign of God was his goal.

Freeing the Captives   (9:11–17)

Translation

11 *As for you (daughter of Zion)* ᵃ*, because of the blood of*   3+3+3
    your covenant,
      I will ᵇ *send your captives from the waterless* ᶜ *pit.*
12 *Return to your stronghold,* ᵃ   2+2
      O prisoners of hope.

Even today, I am declaring a second time	3+2
I will return to you,	
13 *Because I will draw Judah to me as a bow,*	3+3
filled with (the arrow a *) of Ephraim.*	
And I will brandish b *your sons, O Zion,*	3+2+3
over your sons, O Javan, c	
and I will wield you like the sword of a mighty man.	
14 *And Yahweh shall be seen above them;*	3+3
and his arrow will go out as the lightning.	
And the Lord God shall blow the trumpet, a	4+3
and he shall go out with the storms of Teman.	
15 *Yahweh of hosts will protect them,*	4+4+4
they will eat a *and tread down the sling stones.*	
And they will drink and make noise like wine-bibbers. b	
They shall be full like a bowl,	2+2
like the corner of the altar.	
16 *And Yahweh their God will save them*	3+2+2
on that day,	
as the flock of his people,	
because like the stones of a diadem a	2+2
they shine b *upon his land.*	
17 *Yea, how good and how fair it* a *will be.*	3+2+3
Grain will strengthen the young men,	
and new wine the maidens.	

Notes

11.a. "Daughter of Zion" is not in the text but the fem. pronoun shows that she is still being addressed (v 9).

11.b. שלחתי should be regarded as a prophetic perfect, "I will send."

11.c. אין מים בו "with no water in it" is often considered a gloss because it lengthens the line too much metrically and it is a mixed metaphor with "pit." A pit is expected to be dry (Jones 135). But the writer or editor was probably thinking of Joseph's experience of being put into a waterless pit (cf. Gen 37:24; Jer 38:6).

12.a. בצרון "stronghold" only occurs here, although another form of the word (בצר) is used in Isa 22:10 to refer to the walls of Jerusalem. KB (143) and *CHAL* (45) transpose the consonants צברון and read "in multitudes."

13.a. "The arrow of" is not expressed but implied in the idioms (Ps 7:12–13; Jer 9:10; Lam 2:4; Isa 49:2).

13.b ועוררתי "and I will brandish," a polel pf. of עור "to stir up." But when used of a weapon it means "brandish" (2 Sam 23:18. *CHAL* 268).

13.c. יון "Javan," "Greeks," or "Ionians," the name by which the Greeks were known to the Hebrews (Gen 10:2, 4; Ezek 27:13; Isa 66:19; Joel 3:6 [4:6, Eng.]; Dan 8:21; 11:2).

14.a. Lit. שופר "shophar."

15.a. NEB reads ויכלו "and they shall prevail," for MT ואכלו "and they will eat." There is no evidence or necessity for doing this. The picture is that of a banquet, "not the ruthless devouring of the enemy."

15.b. ושתו המו כמו־יין is very difficult. Literally it reads "and they shall drink and make noise like wine." Some scholars follow LXX and read דמם "their blood" for המו "they make noise." It is better to maintain the MT text and consider המו a 3rd com. pl. qal pf. המה "to make noise." The idea of a boisterous banquet is being presented.

16.a. אבני־נזר "stones of a crown" cf. Isa 62:3.

16.b. מתנוססות is a hithpalel part. of נסס and means "to lift up" as a banner. But the reference here is to a crown of jewels. So the meaning should be "to sparkle or shine." A very similiar word נָצַץ means "to shine" in Ezek 1:7. However KB (620) gives sparkle as a possible meaning of נָסַס.

17.a. The pronoun is mas. Some take it to refer to Yahweh and read "How good and fair is Yahweh." But Yahweh is not called "fair" anywhere else in the OT. Wellhausen and many others have emended the text to make the pronouns fem., understanding them as a reference to the land.

Form/Structure/Setting

The form is a salvation oracle. Yahweh speaks to Jerusalem and the prisoners of hope in vv 11–13. In vv 14–17 the prophet continues the message of hope, referring to Yahweh in the third person. The language is poetic and metaphorical. The place of exile is called "a waterless pit" (v 11). Jerusalem is called a stronghold (v 12). The language of vv 13–15 is largely the language of holy war. Vv 16–17 use pastoral language primarily. The beginning of the pericope is clear. The fem. pronoun in v 11 clearly refers back to the daughter of Zion in v 9. But the conclusion of the pericope is indefinite. V 16 could go with vv 11–15 as a peaceful conclusion to a war-like pericope. Or it could be a new beginning which might extend through 10:2. We will consider v 17 as the conclusion to the pericope about the return of the captives (vv 11–17). The setting is probably the New Year festival.

Comment

A part of the post-exilic eschatological hope included the return of the remaining exiles from Judah and Ephraim to Jerusalem (vv 11–13). Yahweh tells Jerusalem that her captives (אֲסִירֵךְ "prisoners") will be set free (lit. "sent") from the waterless pit, i.e. the place of death (cf. Gen 37:24; Jer 38:6). The basis for the return of the captives is not the coming of the new king (v 9), but Yahweh's covenant of blood with Jerusalem (v 11). The renewal of Yahweh's covenant with David and Jerusalem evidently was part of the New Year festival. Unlike the Sinai covenant, which was more closely related to obeying the statutes and ordinances, Yahweh's covenant with David and Jerusalem is often called an "everlasting covenant" (2 Sam 23:5; Pss 89:4, 29; 132:11). Paul Hanson suggests that the "unconditional" covenant might have come into use in the OT through the Mesopotamian "covenant of grant" which made a covenant available forever, but not guaranteed forever (Hanson, *Apocalyptic* 304 n. 16).

The expression "the blood of my covenant" only occurs here and in Exod 24:8 in the OT. Jesus used similar language at the institution of the last supper (Mk 14:24).

In v 12 Yahweh addresses the prisoners of hope (exiles) and commands them to return to Jerusalem which would be their stronghold (cf. Zech 2:10–11, Eng. 2:6–7). Another element in Yahweh's promise to the returned captives was that they would have twice as much as before (cf Isa 40:2; 61:7).

Beginning with v 13 the language of holy war or the Divine Warrior becomes prominent. Judah becomes Yahweh's bow and Ephraim his arrow. The sons of Javan (Greece) are the target. V 14 is a theophany account. Yahweh appears above the army of Israel. The lightning is his arrow (cf. Hab 3:4, 9, 11).

He comes from Teman as he did in the theophany in Habakkuk (3:3). The
Lord of hosts will protect them (|ג׳ from |גג), and they will celebrate with
a banquet (not with a violent destruction of their enemies, v 15). Yahweh
their God will save them on that day as a shepherd saves his flock. Like a
jeweled crown they will sparkle on his land again (v 16). The fertility of the
land will be restored and it will cause the young men and women to flourish
(v 17).

Although the language of holy war is used here, there is no description
of a battle between the forces of Israel and her enemies. Even the sons of
Greece were referred to in passing in the original text, if at all. The NEB
considers the reference a gloss. Obviously too much has been made of this
reference to the "sons of Javan." No system of dating chaps. 9–14 should
hinge on this reference. Yahweh is the hero here. He is the protector (v
15). His presence is seen in the theophany. The theophany was a vital part
of the New Year festival. His appearance and the blowing of the trumpet
were a part of the theophany.

> "God has gone up with a shout,
>   the Lord with the sound of the trumpet" (Ps 47:5).

V 15 is the most difficult verse in this pericope. The verse has often been
considered corrupt and an expression of unparalleled ferocity on the part
of Israel. Many interpreters and translators have Israel eating the slingers
of stones (RSV) and drinking their enemies' blood. But this is a misunderstanding of the text based on an emendation "their blood" from the LXX. The
picture here is not one of a ruthless destruction of other people, but a description of a banquet celebrating a great victory with wine. Thus, "They will
eat and tread down the stones which were slung against them. They will
drink (wine, not blood) and they will be full as the basins and altar are full
of blood during times of sacrifice." Hanson surely goes too far in saying
that "we are dealing with a *rite de passage,* where the victory alone does not
restore the fertility of the earth, necessary in addition is a bloody sacrifice
of the enemy's warriors, whereby the shedding of their blood has the effect
of releasing the earth's fertility which had been suppressed during the enemy's
reign" (Hanson, *Apocalyptic* 322).

A Prophetic Admonition (Mahnwort)
(10:1-2)

Translation

¹ *Ask from Yahweh rain*   3+2
    in the time of the spring ^a *rain!*

> Yahweh is the one making the thunder ^b clouds   3+3+3
>   and gives to them ^c heavy rain,
>   and to each plant in the field.
> ² Because the Teraphim speak emptily,   3+3
>   and the diviners see a lie,
> and the dreamers speak falsely,   3+2
>   they comfort vainly.
> Therefore they ^a wander as sheep;   3+3
>   they are afflicted because there is no shepherd.

Notes

1.a. מלקוש "latter rain." This is the rain that usually comes in Mar–Apr in Israel as opposed to the former rains (יורה) which come in autumn. The two rainy seasons are usually mentioned together in the OT (Deut 11:14; Hos 6:3; Joel 2:23). The NEB includes "autumn rains" here on the basis of the LXX. The New Year Festival was a fall festival and was concerned with the former rains (Zech 14:17).

1.b. חזיזים can mean "lightning" or "thunder" (cf Job 28:26; 38:25). Here it must refer to the rain-bearing clouds.

1.c. להם "to them" NEB follows the Syriac and reads "to you." RSV follows Mitchell (286) and understands the reference to be to "men." JB reads לחם "bread" for להם "to them."

2.a. The 3rd com. pl. form of the verb נסע must be a reference to the people.

Form/Structure/Setting

The form of this short pericope is that of a *Mahnwort* (admonition). The writer returns from his look at the eschatological future salvation, to the present evil age. At the end of chap. 9 he had spoken of a time when the people of Israel would be in their land again, sparkling like jewels in a crown. The land would be fruitful and produce grain and wine. One thing was necessary before the land could produce abundantly. That one thing was rain. But rain comes from Yahweh. From the time Israel entered Canaan there had been a struggle between the forces of Yahweh and Baal about who gives the rain. Now in the post-exilic period there is no more reference to Baal. The false gods here are the Teraphim. Perhaps the teraphim here and in Ezek 21:21 have been downgraded from household gods to an instrument for divination (cf. JB, n. 10a). It is obvious, however, that the rains were related to the proper observance of the fall festival (Zech 14:17; Joel 2:23).

The prophet here admonishes his hearers to ask rain of Yahweh, who controls the clouds, and not from the teraphim. A further warning is given in v 2 against diviners and dreamers who speak falsely. They deceive their hearers and their alleged "comfort" is vanity (חבל). The pericope ends with an observation that the people wander aimlessly because they have no shepherd to guide them in the right path. The pericope is short and must be regarded as separate from chap. 9 and 10:3–12, even though there are catch words and phrases that tie it to that which precedes and follows. The setting may be a prophetic admonition during the New Year festival about 500 B.C.

Comment

The admonition to the people in this pericope was to remember that it was only Yahweh who gave the rain. Jeremiah (27:9) and Ezekiel (21:21; 22:28) both referred to false prophets, diviners, and soothsayers. No doubt such false leaders continued into the postexilic period. Such false leadership had a devastating effect on the people. They strayed as shepherdless sheep and were afflicted because they had no one to care for them.

Restoration of Judah and Joseph (10:3–12)

Translation

3 My anger burns against the shepherds;	3+2
and I will bring a judgment ᵃ against the he-goats	
because Yahweh of hosts cares for his flock,	4+2
the house of Judah,	
he will set them like his royal horse	4+1
in battle.	
4 From them a cornerstone,	2+2
from them a tent-peg,	
from them a battle-bow,	3+4
from them every overseer ᵃ shall come out together. ᵇ	
5 And they shall be like heroes	2+4
trampling in the mud of the streets in the battle;	
And they shall fight because Yahweh is with them;	4+3
and they shall put to shame riders of horses.	
6 And I will strengthen the house of Judah;	3+3
and I will save the house of Joseph.	
And I will restore ᵃ them because I have	3+3
compassion on them.	
And they shall be as though I had not	
rejected them,	
because I am Yahweh their God,	4+1
and I will answer them.	
7 And Ephraim shall be ᵃ as a hero,	3+3
and their heart shall be glad as with wine,	
and their sons shall see and rejoice.	3+3
So shall their hearts rejoice in Yahweh.	
8 I will whistle to them and I will gather them,	3+2+3
for I have ransomed them	
and they shall multiply like they multiplied.	
9 I will sow ᵃ them among the peoples,	2+2
Yet they will remember me in distant places.	
They will cause their sons to live (survive), ᵇ	2+1
and they will return.	

¹⁰ *And I will restore* ^a *them from the land*   3+2
   of Egypt
   And I will gather them from Ashur.
   And to the land of Gilead and to Lebanon   2+2+3
     I will bring them in,
     and (room) shall not be found for them.
¹¹ *And he* ^a *will pass through the sea of distress,*^b   3+3+4
   and one will smite ^c *the waves of the sea,*
   and all the depths of the Nile will be
     dried up.
   And the pride of Ashur shall be brought down,   3+3
     and the scepter of Egypt shall depart.
¹² *And I will make them strong in Yahweh,*   2+2+2
   and they will walk in his name,
     oracle of Yahweh.

Notes

3.a. אֶפְקוֹד the word פקד means "to visit." It often carries the connotation of visiting judgment on someone as here and Amos 3:2. However, it can mean visit in the sense of caring for someone as it is used in the next line.

4.a. נוֹגֵשׂ a qal act. part. נגשׂ. The same form was translated "oppressor" in 9:8. It is used of a tax collector (Dan 11:20); of a taskmaster (Exod 5:6, 10); of a despot (Isa 14:2, 4). However, here it must denote a ruler or overseer as in Isa 3:12 and 60:17.

4.b. יַחְדָּו "together" refers to the corner stone, tent-peg and battle-bow "together," i.e. all shall come out of the house of Judah. RSV and others put "together" at the beginning of v 5.

6.a. וְהוֹשְׁבוֹתִים and וְהֲשִׁיבוֹתִים in 10:10 seems to be a conflation of two variants: the hiphil of שׁוּב "to return" and ישׁב "to dwell." "To restore" is a good translation.

7.a. הָיוּ a plural verb with a collective subject "Ephraim."

9.a. וְאֶזְרָעֵם "and I will sow/scatter them." The verb זרע can mean either "sow" or "scatter." The question is: Is the prophet speaking of the past (RSV) or the future (RV)? The imperfect form supports the future understanding. Even after the exile a further scattering of Israel was anticipated.

9.b. וְחָיוּ is a qal perf. of חיה "to live." The following syntax is awkward. אֶת בְּנֵיהֶם supposes a hiphil or piel verb preceding it. So we should read וְחָיוּ as a piel, "and they shall cause their sons to live or survive" the Diaspora.

10.a. See 6.a. above.

11.a. Many translations read with the LXX וְעָבְרוּ for עבר.

11.b. The word צָרָה "distress" is often emended (RSV, Hanson, *Apocalyptic* 327) to מִצְרִים "Egypt." But the emendation is unnecessary.

11.c. וְהִכָּה is a hiphil pf. of נכה "one will smite." Hanson and RSV read וְהֻכּוּ as a hophal, "they will be smitten."

Form/Structure/Setting

The beginning of the pericope is difficult to determine. V 2 ends with the statement that the people of God are scattered and afflicted because they have no shepherd. V 3 opens with the words "my anger is kindled against the shepherds." That is quite a transition unless the "no shepherd" (v 2) refers to a native ruler and the shepherds and he-goats in v 3 refer to foreign rulers. D. R. Jones says that there is no need to think of foreign rulers. He believes that the Hebrew tenses need to be taken seriously. "Was kindled" refers to Yahweh's judgment against his rulers and people in the exile. "I *will* punish the he-goats" is an allusion to the present unsatisfactory leadership which will be the subject of chap. 11 (Jones 142). He may be right, but the perfect tense at the beginning can be read as a present tense (RSV, NEB).

Saebo divides the material in this pericope between the words of God (vv 3a, 6, and 8–10) and the words of the prophet (vv 3b–5, 7, 11–12). The pericope opens with the words of Yahweh announcing his judgment against the shepherds (whoever they are). This seems to be eschatological language. Yahweh will judge the unjust rulers because he cares for his flock, the house of Judah. From Judah will come reliable leaders: a cornerstone, a tent-peg, a battle-bow, and a beneficent overseer (v 4). V 5 tells of the future victory of Judah over the riders of horses. Vv 6–10 refer to the restoration of both Judah and Israel. Victory over the sea and the nations is the theme of v 11. V 12 repeats the theme of v 6. The people will be strengthened in the Lord. Rex Mason sees a possible influence of Isa 40:31 on this passage.

Comment

This pericope picks up the shepherd motif first mentioned in 10:2. The idea of a king serving in the role of a shepherd is old in the Ancient Near East. An Egyptian writer Ipu-wer before 2000 B.C. described an ideal king who would be called "the herdsman of all men. Evil is not in his heart. Though his herds may be small, still he has spent the day caring for them" (*ANET*, 443). Hammurabi identified himself in the prologue to his laws as "the Shepherd, called by Enlil" (*ANET* 164). Yahweh is referred to as a shepherd in Jacob's blessing (Gen 49:24). Moses prayed for a successor so that the congregation be not as sheep without a shepherd (Num 27:17). Several psalms present Yahweh as a shepherd (Pss 23:1; 74:1; 78:52; 79:13; 80:1; 95:7; 100:3). The theme of a ruler as a shepherd is common in the prophets (Isa 40:11; 44:28; Jer 6:3; 23:2–4; Ezek 34; and 37:24). So the prophet in Zech 10:2–3a was using a long-standing metaphor.

Rulers as shepherds were often commended for their care of their people but more often they were condemned for devouring their flock (Jer 2:8; Ezek 34:2–6). The word "leaders" or "he-goats" (עתודים) is used in Ezek 34:17 and Isa 14:9.

Yahweh is presented here as a good shepherd who "cares for" (פקד "visits" in the good sense) his flock." He will turn the frightened, passive, shepherdless sheep into an active, proud, brave war-horse.

"The house of Judah" is considered a gloss by Mitchell (288) and Hanson (*Apocalyptic*, 324–46) because it overloads the line and is inconsistent with v 6 where Ephraim is the object of Yahweh's favor. But Judah and Ephraim constitute the two divisions of Israel in the prophet's mind. The house of Judah becomes prominent in chaps. 12–14, and the ruler will come as a cornerstone out of Judah, not Ephraim. All these things argue for the authenticity of the "house of Judah" in the text.

Three rather unusual metaphors for rulers are found in v 4: a cornerstone, a tent-peg, and a battle-bow. Cornerstone (פנה) was used in Isa (19:13) and by the psalmist (118:22) of present or future rulers. The idea of comparing a ruler to a cornerstone emphasized the stability and the adhesive power that a good ruler gives to his people (cf. Eph 2:20). The NT picks up the idea of the cornerstone from the OT and uses it messianically. 1 Pet 2:5–8 refers to Isa 28:16; Ps 118:22–23; and Isa 8:14–15. Peter interprets all three references in the light of Christ and makes the point that to those who believe, he is precious. But those who do not believe have rejected the head of the corner and will stumble and fall. In Acts 4:11 Peter says that the Sanhedrin has rejected the cornerstone. Jesus used Ps 118:22 in connection with this parable of the vineyard to emphasize and interpret his rejection by the people (Mark 12:10). Paul conflates Isa 8:14–15 with 28:16 in Rom 9:32–33 to indicate Israel's refusal of the gospel. And in Luke's account of the parable of the vineyard Jesus conflates Ps 118:22 with the stone cut out of the mountain without hands in Dan 2:34–35 (cf. F. F. Bruce, *New Testament Development* 65–66). A tent-peg (יתד) suggests security, reliability and in this case leadership (cf. Isa 22:23–24). The battle-bow is not used elsewhere in the OT to refer to the king, but it was a common royal designation in the Near East (cf. Mason 100). These metaphorical references are all to a new leader who is to come out of Judah.

Obviously 5 uses the language of holy war, but the MT is not as brutal as RSV makes it. Notice that the language is poetic and Judah is *like* an army. The RSV inserts the words "the foe" probably because of Mic 7:10; Ps 18:42. But the MT says they shall be trampling "in the mud of the streets" not "on the foes." V 5 ends on a note of victory. The foot soldiers of Judah will be able to overcome the enemies' cavalry.

Vv 6–10 are primarily about the restoration of Ephraim. Judah has already returned from exile. She will be strengthened (v 6a). But what about those Israelites who were carried away by the Assyrians when they captured Samaria in 722 B.C.? Two possible answers are given by OT prophets. Some prophets taught that these northern tribes would ultimately be brought back to Jerusalem and be reunited with Judah (Isa 11:12–13; Jer 3:12, 18; 31:4–9, 15–20; Ezek 37:15–22; Zech 8:13; 9:10, 13; 10:6–10). However, Zech 11:14 speaks of a time when the brotherhood between Judah and Israel will be annulled.

In v 6 Yahweh tells what he will do for the northern tribes (the house of Joseph). He will save (ישׁע) them. He will restore (הושׁב). The element of repentance may be implied in the root שׁוב. He has compassion (רחם) on them. The new relationship between Yahweh and the northern tribes will be as though nothing had ever happened to cause Yahweh to reject them. Yahweh will be their God (in a covenant sense) and will answer them. Yahweh's answer implies a call to him which is a complete reversal of a threat in Zech 7:13.

V 7 describes the joy of such restoration, although it might be a long way off because of the reference to "the son" experiencing such joy (cf. D. R. Jones, 145). Yahweh will whistle (cf. Isa 5:26; 7:18) for the exiles and he will gather them for he has ransomed (פדה) them. And they will multiply according to the command at creation (Gen 1:28) and Yahweh's promise to Abraham (Gen 12:2; 15:5).

V 9 presents a slight problem. The MT has ואזרעם "and I will sow them" (as seed) among the peoples. But the context (vv 8 and 10) speaks about a return, not a sowing or scattering. Many scholars and translations (RSV) emend the text slightly to וארדם (a waw consecutive from the root זרה) "and though I have scattered them . . . ." The problem is in knowing whether the scatter-

ing has already happened or is yet to happen. The results are the same.
The emphasis is on the return.

In v 10 Egypt and Ashur are to be taken as symbols of nations and places
from which the captives will return. Lebanon and Gilead represent places
in or near the promised land where the returnees will settle. There will be
plenty of room.

Brevard Childs sees in v 11 an example of the *Urzeit-Endzeit* pattern of
thought in the OT. He says "the entire redemptive history of Israel repeats
itself in the eschatological age. There is to be a redemption again from Egypt
and a passing through the sea" (Isa 10:26; Zech 10:10–11; Isa 43:16–17; cf.
B. S. Childs, *Myth and Reality in the OT* [Naperville: Allenson, 1960] 76).
There is no need to emend the text or add "the sea of Egypt" with JB and
RSV. This prophet is using old mythological language to describe an eschatological event.

V 12 returns to the theme of v 6. Yahweh will strengthen his people, or
they will be strengthened in Yahweh, and they will walk in his name. The
RSV and others follow the LXX and Syriac and change תהלכו "they will walk"
to יתהללו "they will glory" in his name (cf. Pss 34:2; 105:3).

A Fable-like Taunt Song against Tyrants
(11:1-3)

Translation

¹ *Open your doors, Lebanon,*	3+3
and fire will devour your cedars. [a]	
² *Howl, O juniper, because the cedar has fallen,*	4+3
because [a] *the mighty are devastated.*	
Howl, oaks of Bashan	3+4
because the thick [b] *forest has come down.*	
³ *Hark,* [a] *the howl of the shepherds,*	3+3
because their splendor [b] *is devastated.*	
Hark, the roar of the lions	3+4
because the pride [c] *of the Jordan is devastated.*	

Notes

1.a. בארזיך "your cedars." The ב is a substitute for את the sign of the object in late Heb.
(*CHAL* 32).

2.a. אשר is causal (cf. GKC § 158).

2.b. הבצור. This form is irregular. As an adj. it has an article when the preceding noun
has none. The Qere and Kethib have different vowels. It is probably best to translate it "thick"
or "impenetrable." The KJV, which follows the margin of MT and reads "forest of vintage," is
obscure.

3.a. קול when it stands at the beginning of a sentence followed by a genitive should be
considered an exclamation (GKC § 146).

3.b. אדרתם "their splendor," is often translated "rich pasture" (*CHAL* 5). But we should not miss the notion of "pride."

3.c. גאון again, the specific reference is to the jungle of the Jordan, but the basic meaning of pride shines through.

Form/Structure/Setting

11:1–3 is a short transitional pericope. It may be considered the close of 10:3–12 or the introduction to 11:4–17 (see S. R. Driver 251). It picks up the word Lebanon from 10:10 and uses the term shepherd which is the theme of 11:4–17. Rex Mason says, "Whatever its origin this taunt-song has been placed at the end of the oracles of chaps. 9–10 to express the conviction that all their hopes will be realized since all that opposes the will of God will be destroyed" (103). But Hanson says, "it forms a suitable introduction to the commissioning narrative in 11:4ff." (Hanson, *Apocalyptic* 334).

The form is that of a taunt-song against the proud leaders (probably of Israel) who are represented by trees, shepherds, and lions. So the passage is a parable or a fable since trees and animals represent people. Yet the form is not narrative but a threat of approaching judgment. The form is poetical and the structure is symmetrical. The opening sentence is a command for Lebanon to open her doors so that fire can destroy her cedars. Fire here should be considered symbolical of destruction. 11:2–3 are introduced by "Howl" and "Hark" followed by reasons for the laments and consternation. The pride of the leaders will be devastated.

Comment

There is some similarity of this pericope to Zech 9:1–6. There seems to be an implied invasion of Lebanon, Bashan, and the Jordan valley here. In 9:1–6 the invasion was of Hadrach, Tyre and Philistia. In both instances the invader seems to be Yahweh as judge and not as a foreign power. There is a strong similarity between the language here and that of Jer 25:34–38; Isa 10:34; and Ezek 27:5–6. Three strong and valuable types of trees (cedar, juniper or cypress, and oak) representing proud rulers are to be devastated. The devastation will cause the shepherds and the lions in the jungle of the Jordan to bow. Hanson is probably right in seeing these proud rulers as the priestly leaders about 500 B.C. (*Apocalyptic,* 347). There may be a connection between this announcement of judgment on Lebanon, Bashan, and the Jordan Valley and the promise in 10:10 that there would be plenty of room for the restored captives of Northern Israel.

The Shepherd Rejected (11:4–17)

Bibliography

Delcor, M. "Deux Passages Difficiles: Zecharie 12:11 et 11:13." *VT* 3 (1953) 67–77. **Torrey, C. C.** "The Foundry of the Second Temple at Jerusalem." *JBL* 55 (1936) 247–60.

Translation

⁴ *Thus says Yahweh my God, "Shepherd* ª *the flock doomed for slaughter.* ⁵ *The ones who buy them slaughter them and they are not guilty,* ª *and the ones selling them say, 'Blessed be Yahweh, I have become rich.' And their shepherds have no compassion upon them.* ⁶ *For I will not have compassion again on the inhabitants of this land,* ª *Oracle of Yahweh. And behold I am about to cause each man to go into the hand of his neighbor (or shepherd) and into the hand of his king. And they shall crush the earth and I will not snatch (anyone) from their hand (power)."*

⁷ *So I shepherded the flock doomed for slaughter for the sheep dealer* ª *and I took two staffs; one I called Pleasant and one I called Union. So I shepherded the flock.* ⁸ *And I removed three shepherds in one month. I was impatient* ª *and their soul became tired* ᵇ *of me.* ⁹ *And I said, "I will not be your shepherd. The dying* ª *shall die. The ones about to be destroyed shall be destroyed and the ones that remain let each one devour the flesh of her neighbor."* ¹⁰ *So I took my staff, Pleasant, and I broke it, in order to break Yahweh's covenant which he cut with all the peoples.* ¹¹ *So it was broken in that day, and the sheep dealers* ª *watching me knew that this was the word of Yahweh.* ¹² *And I said to them, "If it is good in your eyes give me my hire, but if not leave it off." And they weighed my hire, thirty (shekels) of silver.* ¹³ *Then Yahweh said to me, "Throw the noble price which I was paid by them to the moulder,"* ª *and I took the thirty (shekels) of silver and threw them into the moulder* ª *of the house of Yahweh.* ¹⁴ *So I broke my second staff, Union, in order to annul the brotherhood between Judah and Israel.*

¹⁵ *Then Yahweh said to me, "Again take the instruments of the foolish shepherd.* ¹⁶ *For behold I am about to raise up a shepherd in the land who will not care for the perishing, seek the young,* ª *heal the broken, nourish the weak,* ᵇ *but one who will eat the flesh of the fat and tear off their hoofs.* ¹⁷ *Woe to my foolish shepherd who deserts* ª *the flock.*

A sword (shall fall) upon his arm	3+2
and upon his right eye.	3+2
His arm shall surely wither	
and his right eye be utterly expressionless."	3+4

Notes

4.a. רעה is an imper. and means "to feed" or "shepherd" sheep. In 11:6 it is parallel to "king."

5.a. ולא אשמו "and they are not guilty" is irony, as is "Blessed be Yahweh, I am rich."

6.a. הארץ could mean "earth."

7.a. לכן עניי here and in v 11 in MT seems to refer to "the poor of the flock." Most modern scholars follow the LXX (εἰς τὴν χαναανῖτιν) and combine the two words to read לכנעניי "to the Canaanites" or "traders." Canaan does mean merchant or trader in some OT references (cf Hos 12:7; Prov 31:24; Job 40:30 [Eng 41:6]; Zeph 1:11; Ezek 17:4).

8.a. Lit. "my soul was short."

8.b. בחלה is a hapax legomenon. Its meaning is uncertain.

9.a. המתה is a fem. sing. qal act. pt. of מות "the dying."

11.a. Cf. 7.a. above.

13.a. יוֹצֵר is often emended to אוֹצָר "treasury" following the Syr. C. C. Torrey argued convincingly that there was a foundry in the second temple which melted the gold and silver that was given to the temple. The minor temple official responsible for the "money" was יוֹצֵר "moulder."

16.a. הַנַּעַר "the young" doesn't seem to fit. S. R. Driver (260) says that נַעַר is never used of young animals in the OT. Some emend the text and read נִדַּחַת for נַעַר "that which is driven away," or נֶעְדָּרָה "that which is lacking."

16.b. הַנִּצָּבָה "the wretched, exhausted" (cf. *CHAL* 243). Hanson reads "the sound (healthy)" from נָצַב "to stand."

17.a. עֹזְבִי is a qal pt. of עֹזֵב with a *yod compagnis* (connective) cf. GKC § 90; Hos 10:11.

Form/Structure/Setting

Paul Hanson may be right in calling the form of this pericope a commissioning narrative. Yahweh commands the prophet to assume the role of the shepherd of the flock (political leader of the people) in v 4, because the present shepherds (leaders) buy and sell the people with impunity (v 5). However, Yahweh has already determined that the flock is doomed to be slaughtered (vv 4, 6). In vv 7–14 the prophet reports that he became the shepherd of the people on behalf of the "sheep dealers" (v 7). He took two staffs: one, Pleasant, and one, Union. He removed three shepherds in one month (presumably these three shepherds opposed him). But soon he and his employers became dissatisfied with each other. The prophet quit being a shepherd and asked for his wages. His employers (the sheep dealers) gave him the glorious sum of thirty (shekels) of silver. He in turn tossed it to the moulder (smelter) in the temple. In the process he broke both staffs. The first staff, Pleasant, represented Yahweh's covenant with the peoples and the second, Union, represented the brotherhood between Northern Israel and Judah. This report of the commissioning narrative appears to have the form of a prophetic symbolic action such as Isaiah's going naked for three years (Isa 20:2); Jeremiah's wearing a yoke on his neck (Jer 27:2); and Ezekiel's being commanded not to weep when his wife died (Ezek 24:16).

In vv 15–16 the prophet is recommissioned as a worthless shepherd to represent one who would come who would be everything a shepherd should not be. The pericope ends with a "woe" pronounced against the worthless shepherd.

Many scholars since Ewald have considered 13:7–9 as a misplaced conclusion to 11:4–17 (cf. Saebo 276; Driver 271). The NEB transfers the text of 13:7–9 to follow 11:17. Hanson does the same thing (*Apocalyptic,* 339). Those who see 13:7–9 as a conclusion of 11:4–17 understand the shepherd in 13:7 to be the "foolish shepherd" of 11:15. But that is not necessarily true. Eissfeldt (*IOT* 435) says, "Ewald proposed placing the section xiii, 7–9, which appears to be meaningless in its present position, after xi, 17, where it would continue the threat against the shepherd of xi, 17 in a satisfactory manner, and is itself intelligible in this position." Eissfeldt later stated that "Ewald's suggestion treating xiii, 7–9, as its conclusion cannot be proved to be correct" (438). R. C. Dentan says, "My shepherd in this oracle (13:7–9) has no connection with the shepherd of 11:15–17" (*IB* 6, 1109). See *Comment* on 13:7–9.

Comment

S. R. Driver says that this prophecy is the most enigmatic in the OT (253). It is obviously an allegory. Leaders are referred to as shepherds who buy, sell, and consume the sheep (people). But the allegory is not interpreted or apparent. Many attempts have been made to identify those buying and selling the sheep, "and the three shepherds that were cut off in one month" (v 8). Mitchell in 1912 said that there were at least forty conjectures about the identity of the three shepherds who were cut off, covering the whole field of Hebrew history from the exodus to the conquest of Palestine by the Romans (306). Among the suggestions for the three shepherds are: Moses, Aaron, and Miriam; three kings of Israel—Zechariah, Shallum, and Menahem; three world empires—Assyrians, Babylonians, and Persians; Persians, Greeks, and Romans; kings, prophets, and priests; three high priests—Jason, Menclaus, and Lysimachus; the Pharisees, Sadducees and Essenes. A. F. Kirkpatrick was probably correct in suggesting that no precise meaning should be given to the expression. The three shepherds are "a part of the furniture of the allegory, and their removal by the prophet within a month is intended to signify God's intention to deal promptly and effectually with the oppressors of His people, whoever they may be" (*The Doctrine of the Prophets* [New York: Macmillan, 1892] 467). The "three shepherds" in 11:8 are like the "three" transgressions of nations in Amos 1–2. Three is a complete number. All of the evil shepherds were removed. The word כחד means "removed" or "expelled" in this context, not "destroyed" as the RSV has it (cf. D. R. Jones 153; Baldwin 183). It is possible that 11:8a is an interpretative gloss by someone in the Maccabean period relating the events of chap. 11 to the happenings of his own times. The reference to three shepherds and their removal is very terse and unexplained (cf. Baldwin 183; R. C. Dentan, 1102; Mason 107; Mitchell 306–307).

After the prophet assumed the role of the shepherd of the people he soon learned that any attempt to govern them favorably and graciously would be met with rejection. So his soul (נפש) became short with them—a Hebrew metaphor for impatience (cf. Num 21:4; Mic 2:7; Job 21:4). Vv 9 and 15 set out in negative terms the role of a shepherd, no doubt the role the prophet intended to follow, but because of the people's rejection he decided not to serve as their shepherd. He would not rescue the perishing, seek the wandering, heal the broken, nourish the weak, and treat them with integrity.

When the prophet assumed the role of shepherd he took two staffs, instruments that good shepherds should have. One was a short rod or club to ward off wild beasts (cf. S. R. Driver 256). This one he called "Pleasant." It referred to Yahweh's covenant with the nations that they would allow his people to go free. The other staff was called "Union," referring to the reunion of the northern and southern tribes of Israel. These were to be the objectives of the new David according to Ezek 37:16–28. But whereas Ezekiel saw the staffs as indicators of saving events, the prophet in Zech 11 sees them as symbols of doom and judgment.

Paul Hanson believes that Zech 11:7–17 is a conscious polemic against those who were building their leadership claims on Ezekiel's vision. Instead of the broken staff being united, the united staff would be broken; instead of perfect peace and harmony, there would be total destruction; instead of an ingathering from the nations, the annulment of the covenant with the nations; instead of an ideal shepherd caring for his flock, a worthless shepherd who would lead his sheep to their destruction. Even as the promise of brilliant restoration in Ezekiel comes as the word of Yahweh, so too does the message of doom come as Yahweh's word to the visionary of Zech 11 (Hanson, *Apocalyptic* 344).

Also there seems to be a different interpretation of the future in Zech 11 and Ezek 34. Whereas in Ezek 34 Yahweh himself will save the sheep (34:9–16), in Zechariah, Yahweh will deliver them into the hands of the shepherds to be scattered (11:6). In Ezek 34:23 Yahweh promises to raise up a shepherd who will feed them; in Zech 11:16 he says he will raise up a shepherd diametrically opposed to the well-being of the sheep. In Ezek 34:25 Yahweh promises to establish a covenant of peace with them; in Zech 11:10, 14 he breaks his covenants of peace and union. In Ezek 34:26–31 spectacular blessings are promised—in Zech 11:16 incredible doom and desolation. For the followers of Ezekiel the glorious new age was at the point of fulfillment, but for the prophet of Zech 11 the eschatological time table does not anticipate the direct movement from the present situation to the glories of the eschaton. Instead he seems to anticipate a very grim period indeed (11:16–17).

After the prophet is rejected by the people he asks for the wages he earned as their shepherd, leaving the amount up to his employers. They weighed (verb שָׁקַל, "shekeled") out "thirty" (shekels = a unit of weight) of silver. Then Yahweh commanded him to cast it (his wages) to the potter (יוֹצֵר MT). The Syriac has treasury אֹצָר. So the prophet took the noble price (irony) and cast it to the potter (יוֹצֵר) in the house of Yahweh.

The term יוֹצֵר "potter" in v 13 in the MT has caused some consternation for many interpreters. Why would the prophet cast his wages to the potter? Was there a potter working in the temple? Can the word יוֹצֵר refer to a shaper of metals as well as to a shaper of clay? Was the word in the original text אוֹצָר "treasury" (cf. Neh 10:39; Jer 38:11), as the Syriac has it, rather than יוֹצֵר "potter"? The overwhelming weight of the evidence favors יוֹצֵר "potter" as the original reading. But according to Torrey it can mean "one who melts and moulds metal." Torrey cites the example of Aaron taking gold from the people, casting it in the fire and with an engraving tool fashioning (יצר) it into an idol (Exod 32:2–4, 24). Torrey also refers to Herodotus' account (111, 96) of Darius Hystaspis' melting metal and storing it in earthen jars. When it was needed the jars were broken and the metal was cut in pieces and used. Torrey says, "The same process was required for the Hebrew temple, and the official in charge bore the title יוֹצֵר" ("The Foundry of the Second Temple at Jerusalem," *JBL* 55 [1936] 256). If Torrey is correct one can see how the potter and the treasury were connected.

But M. Delcor does not think that Torrey's theory explains the irony of "the noble price." He links the verse to Judg 17:4 where two hundred shekels of silver were made into a molten image. By comparison thirty shekels would only make a figurine and therein lies the irony (Delcor, "Deux Passages Difficiles . . ." *VT* 3 [1953] 74). M. Saebo concludes that יוֹצֵר in our present

MT text is a compromise form from אוֹצָר reflected in the Syriac, Vulgate, and Targum, and צוֹרְרִי/יוֹצֵק reflected in the LXX Χωνφυτήριον "furnace" (1 Kgs 8:51; Mal 3:2; Saebo 78–82).

V 13 is quoted with variations from both the MT and the LXX in Matt 27:9–10 and applied to the purchase of a potter's field with the money Judas received from betraying Jesus. Acts 1:16–20 also refers to Judas buying a "potter's" field with the reward of his wickedness. But the Acts account looks to Psalms (presumably 69:25; 109:8) as the scriptures that were fulfilled by Judas' act. According to Torrey (253) and Bruce (110), Matthew probably knew both traditions (potter and treasury) behind Zech 11:13. According to Matthew the chief priests took the pieces of silver and said, "It is not lawful to put them into the treasury (אוֹצָר) . . . so they bought with them the potter's (יוֹצֵר) field" (Matt 27:6–7). The idea of buying a field may be in some way related to Jeremiah's buying his cousin's field (Jer 32:6–9).

Although NT writers connect this passage about the thirty pieces of silver paid to the prophet for his unappreciated service as a shepherd to his people to the money Judas received for betraying Jesus, the original passage makes no reference to a future Messiah. S. R. Driver says that the evangelist (Matthew) makes the connection because he "follows the exegetical methods current among the Jews of his time" (cf. Matt 2:15, 18; Driver 259).

Although no strict messianic view should be seen in the original passage, the quality of leadership is its central theme. Here is a people who had Yahweh's own choice to be their shepherd. He wanted to rescue the perishing, care for the injured, and feed the hungry. But the people rejected him. So Yahweh told the shepherd to take again the gear of a foolish shepherd who would consume the sheep. The lesson of the parable is that if a people will not follow good leaders they are doomed to suffer under evil ones. But "the arm of the foolish shepherd will wither and his right eye will be expressionless." The arm of the leader represented "strength for defense" and the right eye was the one used to see over the shield in aiming his arrow. Thus the people under a foolish shepherd will be defenseless (v 17).

The Second Burden (12:1–14:21) The Attack on Jerusalem by the Nations 12:1–8

Bibliography

Driver, G. R. "Linguistic and Textual Problems: Minor Prophets." *JTS* 39 (1938) 393–405. **Honeyman, A. M.** "Hebrew סַף 'basin, goblet.'" *JTS* 37 (1936) 56–59. **Lutz, H.** *Jahwe, Jerusalem und die Volker* 10–19.

Translation

1 *A Burden. The word of Yahweh concerning Israel* [a], *oracle of Yahweh:*
    The One stretching out the heavens,   2+2+3
    and establishing the earth,
    and forming the spirit of man within him.

2 *Behold I am about to make Jerusalem a cup of staggering* [a] *to all the surrounding peoples, and it will also be upon* [b] *Judah in the siege upon Jerusalem.*

3 *And in that day I will make Jerusalem a heavy stone to all the peoples. Everyone lifting her will surely be torn, and all nations of the earth will be gathered against her.*

4 *In that day, oracle of Yahweh, I will smite every horse with confusion and his rider with madness. But upon the house of Judah I will open my eyes and I will smite every horse of the peoples with blindness.* 5 *And the clans of Judah will say in their heart, The ones dwelling in Jerusalem are a strength* [a] *to me, in Yahweh of hosts their God.*

6 *In that day I will make the clans of Judah like a brazier of fire in the trees and like a fire among the sheaves, and they shall devour all the surrounding people on the right and on the left. And Jerusalem shall be inhabited again in its place, in Jerusalem.* 7 *And Yahweh will save the tents of Judah first so that the glory of the house of David and the glory of the inhabitants of Jerusalem may not be exalted over Judah.*

8 *In that day Yahweh will put a shield around the inhabitant* [a] *of Jerusalem, and the one stumbling among them shall be like David and the house of David like God, like the angel of Yahweh before all the nations coming against Israel.*

Notes

1.a. Israel refers to all the tribes of Israel, not just those of the Northern Kingdom (cf. 9:1).

2.a. סף רעל usually translated "cup of staggering." This figure of speech means that Jerusalem would become a strong drink for the nations which would make them reel. However סף means "bowl" or "basin." The regular word for "cup" is כוס (cf. Isa 51:17). Another meaning of סף is "threshold." Honeyman suggests that the following figure "stone of burden" favors reading סף רעל as a "threshold stone of reeling" as the LXX πρόθυρα σαλευόμενα. The threshold stone of reeling refers to a threshold that an inebriated person would have difficulty crossing, or to the door-lintel which deals a stunning blow to the person who will not stoop on entering (cf. Honeyman *JTS* 37 [1936] 58). The NEB has "steep approaches."

2.b. The words וגם על יהודה are difficult to interpret. They read "and also upon Judah." But does that mean that the cup of reeling or the threshold of reeling will come upon Judah as it will come upon the surrounding peoples? If so, then Judah must be opposed to Jerusalem, and participates in the siege against her. Paul Hanson, following Otzen's suggestion, believes that the MT has a conflated reading combining features of one tradition preserved in Tg and Vg and another represented by syr and LXX. The first tradition omits על before Judah and would read "and also Judah will be in the siege against Jerusalem." The other tradition omits the ב before מצור "siege." It would read "and upon Judah there will be a siege upon Jerusalem." The text is problematical as it stands. The question is, did Judah join the peoples in their siege of Jerusalem or did the peoples attack both Judah and Jerusalem? The kjv is very specific. It reads, "when they (peoples) shall be in the siege both against Judah and against Jerusalem." The asv has, ". . . and upon Judah also it shall be in the siege against Jerusalem." The rsv says, ". . . it will be against Judah also in the siege . . ." The neb reads, ". . . and Judah will be caught up in the siege of Jerusalem."

5.a. The words אמצה לי ישבי ירושלם "strength to me inhabitants of Jerusalem" are ambiguous. As the text stands it probably means that Judah says that the inhabitants of Jerusalem are her strength through Yahweh of Hosts. That can be the meaning although the construction is awkward. G. R. Driver follows Tg and Wellhausen and reads אמצה לישבי ירושלם "strength *is* to the inhabitants of Jerusalem . . ." (*JTS* 39 [1938] 403). Paul Hanson has an interesting reconstruction. He changes one י (yodh) to a ו (waw) and divides two words differently and gets a different reading. He reads אם צהל(ו) ישבי ירושלם "If only the inhabitants of Jerusalem would raise a shout (צהל) for Yahweh," i.e., the threatened inhabitants of Jerusalem should shout to Yahweh for help (cf. Isa 24:14; Jer 31:7. Hanson, *Apocalyptic* 357).

8.a. Pl. in the LXX.

Form/Structure/Setting

V 1 is a superscription probably for the entire section of chaps. 12–14. Vv 2–8 are an oracle of judgment on the nations that attack Jerusalem. Yahweh speaks of the imminence of the approaching battle and judgment as seen in the use of the participle (v 2). It is not clear whether Judah is for or against Jerusalem at the beginning of the battle (v 2). Two figures of speech are used to indicate Jerusalem's adverse effect on those who oppose her: (1) a cup of reeling or a threshold of reeling, and (2) a heavy stone (v 3). Yahweh will blind the horses of the enemy but will open his eyes over the house of Judah. Judah will recognize that Jerusalem's strength is in Yahweh her God and he is Judah's strength also (v 5). Then the clans of Judah will destroy the nations approaching Jerusalem like fire in a field of grain and Jerusalem will be saved (v 6). Judah will get the credit for the victory so that neither the house of David nor Jerusalem would glory over Judah (v 7). Then Yahweh will put a mighty shield around the inhabitants of Jerusalem and the weakest ones will be like David and the house of David will be like the angel of the Lord (v 8). V 9 is difficult. Mitchell (329) attaches it to the next pericope.

The structure is simple: a superscription for the whole section, chaps. 12–14 (v 1); an announcement of the judgment coming on the peoples surrounding Jerusalem (vv 2–4); the victory will come through Judah ((vv 5–7); divine protection for Jerusalem (v 8); and an announcement of judgment on all nations who attack Jerusalem (v 9).

The setting of these verses is debatable. The language of the nation's attacking Jerusalem probably goes back to the Royal-Zion festival in Jerusalem to celebrate the inviolability of Zion. The motif is strong in Pss 2, 46, 48 and 76. Isaiah, a prophet intimately acquainted with the royal court, draws heavily upon this tradition (cf. Isa 7:4–9; 8:9–10; 14:29, 32; 17:12–14; 28:14–18). The language here in Zech 12 is eschatological and possibly apocalyptic. In this early postexilic period (Hanson [368] dates it about the middle of the fifth century) there is a tension between the rural tribes of Judah and the house of David along with the priesthood in the temple in Jerusalem. The priests thought that the future was bright. But the prophet says that Yahweh is about to bring the peoples against Jerusalem for battle. Jerusalem will be spared through the efforts of the clans of Judah as they are strengthened by Yahweh.

The picture of Yahweh leading foreign armies against Jerusalem only to destroy them is fairly common in the OT (cf. Isa 10:5–19; Jer 25:8–14; Isa 29:1–8; Mic 4:11–13; Ezek 38:1–23; Joel 3:9–14). This theme becomes more eschatological toward the end of the OT. This is Armageddon, the last great battle of earth (cf. Rev 16:16).

Comment

Chap. 12 begins with the title משא "a burden" (cf. also 9:1 and Mal 1:1). This title was probably put in these places by the redactor of the book of the twelve minor prophets. The following statement identifies this burden with the "word of Yahweh" concerning Israel. The use of the term Israel here is surprising since it does not occur again in chaps. 12–14 and since it is generally understood as a reference to the Northern Kingdom. In order to stand here Israel must refer to all the tribes in a religious sense.

V 1b is a hymn fragment or a doxology identifying Yahweh as the Creator of the world and man. The words are similar to Isa 42:5; 44:24; 45:12; 51:13; Amos 4:13. Yahweh is the One who stretches out (participle) the heavens; the One who establishes (participle) the earth; the One who forms (participle) the spirit within man. Because Yahweh is the Creator he is the sovereign over creation and the Lord of history. Therefore when he gives his word about the future he has the power to bring it to fruition.

Rex Mason sees this doxology as an expression of the view that "the final act of salvation is to be an act of re-creation of a cosmic renewal" (Mason 115). Yahweh through the prophet tells what is about to happen. The people surrounding Jerusalem are going to bring a siege against Jerusalem. Judah's role in the siege is not clear. She may fight with the other peoples or against them (see note b above). But it is clear that the peoples will not succeed in their attempt to capture Jerusalem. She will be a "cup of reeling" and a "heavy stone" to them. Yahweh will bring confusion on Jerusalem's attackers (v 4). He will strike their horses with blindness but he will open his eyes over Judah.

A distinction is made between the tribe of Judah and Jerusalem and the house of David. The clans of Judah will win the victory over the peoples and save Jerusalem (vv 6–7). But Judah will recognize that her strength comes from Yahweh (v 5). The victory really is Yahweh's.

The rivalry between Judah and the inhabitants of Jerusalem is evident in vv 4–8. Judah will be the instrument through which Yahweh will save Jerusalem (v 6). Yahweh will save Judah first so that Jerusalem and the house of David cannot boast (v 7). Yet the weakest (the stumbling) one in Jerusalem will become as strong as David, and the house of David (the succession of David's heirs) will become like God. This last expression is very bold, but it is not new here. Notice that the text does not say that the house of David will become God, but "will be *like* God." Then there are the words "like the angel of Yahweh before them." Obviously the reference here is to Yahweh or the angel of Yahweh going before the tribes as they marched through the wilderness on their way to the promised land (Exod 32:34; 23:20; Judg 6:11; 2 Sam 14:17). The house of David, probably represented by a prince or a governor, would regain his leadership role.

Has there been some editing of this passage? It appears that the original form of the passage made Judah primary, then a later redactor said that eventually Jerusalem and the house of David would regain their lost preeminence. No personal Messiah is singled out in this passage. V 9 changes the language of the enemy from "peoples" to "nations." For this reason Mitchell (329), Plöger (*Theocracy* 83, 92), and Saebo (266–67) make v 9 the beginning of the next pericope. It probably is a transitional sentence. The purpose of v 9 is to assure Israel that Yahweh will protect her in the day of the Lord against all enemies.

Weeping in Jerusalem Over One They Had Pierced (12:9–14)

Bibliography

Ap-Thomas, D. R. "Some Aspects of the Root HNN in the Old Testament." *JSS* 2 (1957) 128–48. **Mason, Rex.** "The Relation of Zech 9–14 to Proto-Zechariah." *ZAW* 88 (1976) 227–38.

Translation

⁹ *And it shall be in that day I will purpose* ᵃ *to destroy all nations coming against Jerusalem.* ¹⁰ *And I will pour out on the house of David and upon the inhabitants of Jerusalem a spirit of grace and supplication. And they will look to me* ᵃ *whom they pierced, and they shall mourn over him like the mourning for an only child, and weep bitterly over him as one weeps bitterly over an only son.* ¹¹ *And the weeping in Jerusalem shall be great in that day as the weeping of Hadad-rimmon in the plain of Megiddo.* ¹² *And the land shall mourn family by family, by itself; the family of David alone, and their wives alone; the family of the house of Nathan alone and their wives alone;* ¹³ *the family of Levi alone and their wives alone; the family of Shemeites alone and their wives alone;* ¹⁴ *and all of the remaining families family by family alone, and their wives alone.*

Notes

9.a. אבקש "I will seek" means here "I purpose" (cf. Ackroyd, *PCB* 654).

10.a. אלי "unto me" is often emended to אליו "unto him." S. R. Driver said that about fifty MSS support אליו "unto him" (Driver 266). The context supports אליו. The fifth word in MT beyond this one is עליו "upon him." John 19:37 and Rev 1:7 read "upon him whom they pierced." However, Yahweh may be the speaker and may be saying that the people had pierced him metaphorically by their rebellion and ingratitude, or they pierced him when they attacked his representative (perhaps some unidentified martyr). The NEB keeps both pronouns and reads ". . . on me, on him whom they have pierced." D. R. Jones understands the passage to mean that the people of Jerusalem will look upon Yahweh (in prayer) touching those whom they (the nations) have slain (Jones 161). J. D. W. Watts follows Jones and translates v 10, "when they look to me (in prayer) regarding (those) whom they (the nations) have pierced (i.e. soldiers of Judah), they shall mourn for him (a collective)" (Watts 357).

Form/Structure/Setting

The form of this brief pericope is that of a mourning rite. In *that* day Yahweh will pour out on the house of David and the inhabitants of Jerusalem a spirit of eagerness to obtain "grace" (forgiveness). Then they will look on me (Yahweh) or on him (an unknown martyr) whom they have pierced and will weep bitterly. The weeping will involve all the families in Jerusalem—two royal families, David and his son, Nathan (1 Chr 14:4); two priestly families, Levi and his grandson Shimei (Num 3:16; 1 Chr 6:17); and all other families. Or the reference may be to royal (David), prophetic (Nathan), priestly (Levi) and wise-counselor (Shimei) families. The mourners are to be separated by families and by sexes within the families. The setting of this pericope is uncertain but the language seems to come from the national liturgy and from the part played in that liturgy by the king. F. F. Bruce says that "it has even been suggested that the first person singular of the Massoretic text ('. . . on *me* whom they have pierced') is taken verbatim from a royal utterance in the liturgy" (Bruce, *NT Development* 112).

Comment

The pericope probably begins with the words in v 9 וְהָיָה בַיּוֹם הַהוּא "and it shall be in that day." These words occur in vv 3, 9, and 13:2. V 9 seems to be a transition sentence. V 10 begins with a waw conjunction וֹ which suggests that what follows is directly related to that which immediately precedes it. The normal meaning of אֲבַקֵּשׁ "I will seek" is awkward here and may suggest uncertainty about the outcome. P. R. Ackroyd says, "V 9 should read 'I purpose to destroy' rather than 'seek' " (*PCB* 654). 12:1–8 looks at the external events that will take place in Jerusalem "in that day." 12:9–14 looks at the internal condition of the people in Jerusalem. Yahweh will pour out on them a spirit of "grace and supplication." The idea is that they will humble themselves and recognize that they were saved by another whom they pierced.

Scholars are divided on their interpretation of the possibility of vicarious suffering being involved in the people's repentance. D. R. Jones sees a possible connection of the passage with the suffering servant passage in Isa 53. He says, "The correspondence of thought is so close, that these words may be allowed to suggest the sort of supplications with which Zion 'looked unto God.' This unknown prophet of Zech 12 thus touches on the mystery of vicarious suffering and, to that extent, anticipates the central mystery of Christ's atoning death" (Jones 163). However, Rex Mason advises caution in assigning a vicarious role to the death of this figure. He observes that (a) what is described is a work of Yahweh, a work of regeneration and renewal; (b) it is effected by the Spirit of Yahweh and results in, it is not occasioned by, their repentance; (c) the weeping is the result, not the cause of Yahweh's regenerative work, and (d) since the emphasis is on return to Yahweh, the "they shall look to *me*" (אֵלַי) of the MT seems right and no emendation is necessary. All this is very close to Ezekiel's emphasis in chap. 36, which also regards repentance as a consequence of Yahweh's regenerating work (v 31). The fact that the spirit of "grace and supplication" (repentance) is poured out on women as well as men reminds one of Joel 2:28–29; 3:1–2 (cf. Mason, *ZAW* 88 [1976] 232–233).

If Mason is correct in his understanding that the weeping (repenting) is the work of God, the result of the outpouring of a spirit of "grace and supplication," then the role of the "one whom they had pierced" is unclear. The passage does not say specifically that the tears of repentance resulted from the death of the one the people had pierced. It does say that the tears of repentance were the result of the outpouring of Yahweh's spirit of "grace and supplication." What does all this have to do with identifying "the one they have pierced"? It certainly does not solve the problem. Numerous theories have been advanced about the identity of "the one pierced." Some say it was Josiah, the good king slain by Pharaoh Necho. Others say it was Onias III, a high priest who might have been murdered about 170 B.C. Paul Hanson thinks that the "pierced one refers to the visionary successors of Deutero-Isaiah who were persecuted by the hierocrats" (*Apocalyptic,* 365). The text seems to indicate it was Yahweh who was pierced. Some think the pierced one is the same as the suffering servant of Isa 53. Both the Babylonian and Palestinian Talmuds take the reference to be to the Messiah (cf. F. F. Bruce, *NT Development* 112). The fourth Gospel (John 19:33–37) and Rev 1:7 identify the pierced one with Jesus.

Undoubtedly this passage in Zech 12 is eschatological. It speaks of the "end-time" as far as the prophet was concerned. He was familiar with Ezekiel's prophecy in chap. 36 that in the "end-time" Yahweh would cleanse his people, give them a new heart and put a new spirit within them (Ezek 36:25–26). The idea of a pierced one may have come from the ritual in the Royal-Zion festival when the king was beaten by the enemy nations. However, Bruce is correct in saying that the prophet in Zech 12:10 suggests something that is more than what appears on the surface.

> The prophet compares the mourning over the pierced one to "the mourning for Hadad-rimmon in the plain of Megiddo"; but now the annually repeated lamentation for a fertility deity, never finished and always fruitless, has been swallowed up by the compassionate tears of penitent suppliants for a victim pierced once for all, never to be struck again. Moreover, whatever be the original reference of the piercing and the mourning, in the passion narrative it has by implication been brought into close association with the oracle of Zechariah 13:7; the pierced one and the smitten shepherd are both recognized as pointing to Jesus, scourged and crucified as "the king of the Jews" (Bruce, *NT Development* 113).

V 11 says that the weeping of Jerusalem in the "end-time" will be as great as the weeping of (for) Hadad-rimmon in the plain of Megiddon. The reference is to some great public lamentation which might have been repeated annually in the plain of Megiddon, but we are not told the precise nature of the event. The name Hadad-rimmon does not occur elsewhere in the OT. In the past many scholars following Jerome took Hadad-rimmon as a place name (cf S. R. Driver 267; J. Baldwin 192). But it is better to understand Hadad-rimmon as the name of a god. Hadad in Ben-hadad (1 Kgs 20:1, 2, 5, 9 etc.) and in Hadadezer (2 Sam 8:3, 5, 7, 8, 9, 10, 12; 1 Kgs 11:23) probably refers to the god Hadad. Some think the weeping in the plain of Megiddon was for Josiah who was killed there in 609 B.C. by Pharaoh Necho. The Chronicler mentions the fact that Jeremiah uttered a lament for Josiah and the custom was continued "to this day" (i.e. to the day Chronicles was edited 2 Chr 35:25). But Zech 12:11 speaks of the "mourning of" Hadad-rimmon as if this were a pagan ritual. Various attempts have been made to avoid acknowledging the presence of a pagan rite in Megiddo. T. Jansma notes that the Targum states that Hadadrimmon the son of Thabrimmon killed Ahab the son of Omri (cf 1 Kgs 22:34, T. Jansma, "Inquiry into the Heb. Text . . . of Zech 9–14." *OTS* 7 [1950] 118). M. Delcor finds the idea of mourning for a pagan deity on the same level as mourning before the Lord repugnant. He believes that the consonants א and ר of the Aramaic word רמון "Rimmon" and אמון were confused, and proposes the translation, "the mourning of that day will be like the mourning for the son of Amon (i.e. Josiah) in the plain of Megiddon" (M. Delcor, "Deux passages difficiles: Zacharie 12:1 et 11:13." *VT* 3 [1953] 67–73). Delcor's proposal has not gained wide acceptance. It is probably best to understand the prophet here as saying, the eschatological weeping will be as loud and deep as the pagan's wailing for their fertility gods.

Cleansing Jerusalem from Sin, Idols, and False Prophets   (13:1–6)

Translation

¹ *In that day a fountain* ᵃ *shall be open continuously* ᵇ *for the house of David and for the inhabitants of Jerusalem for sin and for uncleanness* ᶜ. ² *And it shall happen in that day, the oracle of Yahweh of hosts, I will cut off the names of the idols from the land that they be remembered no more. And I will cause the prophets* ᵃ *and the unclean* ᵇ *spirits to pass from the land.*

³ *"And it shall be if anyone again* ᵃ *prophesies, then his father and mother, the ones who bore him, shall say to him, 'You shall not live, because you have spoken a lie in the name of Yahweh.' And his father and mother who bore him shall pierce him when he prophesies.* ⁴ *And it will be in that day that every prophet will be ashamed of his vision when he prophesies and he will not put on a hairy mantle in order to deceive.* ⁵ *And he will say, 'I am no prophet. I am a tiller of the ground, because man has possessed me* ᵃ *from my youth.'* ⁶ *And one* ᵃ *shall say to him, 'What are these wounds between your hands* ᵇ *?' And he shall say, 'Those with which I was wounded in the house of my lovers* ᶜ*.'"*

Notes

1.a. מקור "fountain." In the original paradise there was a river. Yahweh has the fountain of life (מקור חיים Ps 36:10 [Eng. 36:9]). Yahweh is the fountain of living waters (Jer 2:13).

The river of life flows from under the altar of the temple in the city of God (Ezek 47:1-12; Joel 3:18; Ps 46:4; Zech 14:8). Here (13:1), as in 3:9 where another word עין which can mean fountain is used, the purpose is to cleanse the land and its people of sin.

1.b. נפתח "shall be open." A niphal part. which along with the verb היה implies that the fountain is to be open continuously (cf. S. R. Driver 268).

1.c. נדה a technical term covering ritual and sexual impurity (Lev 12:2 15:19; Ezek 18:6; 22:10; 36:17).

2.a. הנביאים "prophets" in general not just false prophets, although the LXX has τὰς ψευδιπροφήτης. Prophets were in disrepute at this time, suggesting a late date for this material. Of course some prophets were in disrepute in earlier times but here they are associated with "the unclean spirit."

2.b. רוח הטמאה "the unclean spirit" only occurs here in the OT, but many times in the Gospels. The implication here is that the prophets were speaking for unclean spirits (cf 1 Kgs 22:22).

3.a. עוד "again" or "still." The idea probably is that if anyone continues to prophesy in this late period, drastic actions based on Deut 13:1-5, should be taken. The man's father and mother should thrust him through.

5.a. אדם הקנני "man has possessed me." The verb is 3rd mas. sing. hiph. perf. of קנה with a 1st com. sing. suff. The meaning would be that the prophet impersonator would say, "I am a servant of the ground (עבד אדמה) man (not God) has possessed (owned) me." Many scholars have followed Wellhausen's suggestion and emended the text to read אדמה קניני "the ground has been my possession" (CHAL 320; RSV). The NEB evidently takes הקנני from קנא "to be jealous," and reads "who has been schooled in lust from boyhood." The Peshitta reads "a man has inflamed me from my youth" (cf. Otzen 265). The LXX εγέννησέν usually translates הוליד "to begat." Otzen believes that the reference here may be to the prophet's connection with the Baal fertility cult (Studien 266).

6.a. Lit. "he."

6.b. בין ידיך "between your hands" is generally understood to mean "between your arms," i.e. "on the chest or back."

6.c. Cf. note 5.a.

Form/Structure/Setting

There is some question about whether 13:1 is the end of the previous pericope about weeping or the beginning of this pericope about cleansing the land of idols, false prophets, and unclean spirits. It is related to the previous pericope by the reference to the house of David and the inhabitants of Jerusalem. But its emphasis on a fountain being opened for the cleansing of sin and uncleanness ties it on to 13:2-6. The form of this pericope is that of a salvation oracle or an oracle of eschatological cleansing. The promise of a cleansing fountain is in 13:1. Idols, (false) prophets, and the unclean spirit are the targets for cleansing in 13:2. The identification and removal of the (false) prophet is in 13:3-6. The language of the pericope is cultic. The "fountain" probably builds on the "water of expiation" (Num 8:7) or "water of impurity" (Num 19:1-9, 13, 20, 21, 31:23; Ezek 36:25). The word נדה is a technical term for ceremonial uncleanness due to menstruation (Lev 12:2; 15:19; Ezek 18:6; 22:10; 36:17) or due to contact with a dead body (Num 19:11-13).

Comments

The problem of sin is the central problem in the OT. It began in the garden of Eden and will not be eradicated until the final day of Yahweh. In the previous pericope great wailing and penitent weeping is described (12:10–14). But no amount of weeping alone can cleanse. Cleansing from sin can only come from God. Here (13:1) "a supernatural means is provided for purifying community life from its corruptions . . . and most remarkable of all—from the institution of prophecy" (R. C. Dentan, 1108). The supernatural means of cleansing is a continuously flowing fountain.

The cleansing of idolatry will be radical. The "names" or reality of the images will be "cut off" (eradicated) and the memory of them will be forgotten (v 2). The prophets and the unclean spirit will be "removed" from the land. The expression "unclean spirit," another sign of a cultic background, is only found here in the OT. The idea seems to have developed in the inter-testamental period. Unclean spirits abound in the Gospels.

The inclusion of prophets with idolatry and the unclean spirit as corrupting influences shows how far prophecy had fallen (cf. Neh 6:12–14). Anyone prophesying was to be accused of lying in the name of Yahweh and put to death (v 3). Consequently any prophet would be ashamed of his vision and not put on the hairy mantle in order to deceive (v 4). He will deny that he is a prophet and claim to be a farmer instead. It is tempting to read the emended text with the RSV "the land has been my possession from my youth" (cf. Baldwin 196; S. R. Driver 270; Dentan 1109).

The wounds between the prophet's hands were probably wounds made in an ecstatic orgy (1 Kgs 18:28). The wounds or scars would have been visible in the summer. Such a prophet would deny that they were the marks of a prophet. Dentan observes that "Ecstatic prophecy had always been easily subject to perversion by the fanatic or charlatan, and while capable of being used for higher ends, had in these times become an object of universal contempt" (Dentan 1109).

C. H. Dodd observes that Zech 13:1–6 shows no contact with the NT even though v 6 was later associated with the passion of Christ (Dodd, *According to the Scriptures* 65). F. F. Bruce also thinks that it is significant that no NT writer tries to interpret v 6 as a prophecy of the nail-wounds in our Lord's hands, "in the grossest misapprehension of its meaning" (Bruce, *NT Development* 114). Bruce says that it is astonishing that so able a Hebraist as E. B. Pusey should have been capable of this misinterpretation (ibid).

The Shepherd Smitten, a Remnant Spared (13:7–9)

Translation

7 "O sword, awake against my shepherd,
    against the man, my fellow,[a]"
    oracle of Yahweh of hosts.
"Smite the shepherd, and the sheep will be scattered,
    and I will turn my hand against the little ones.[b]

3+3+3

4+3

[8] *And it shall be in all the land,* *oracle of Yahweh,*	3+2

two thirds [a] *shall be cut off.*
    They shall expire,
    and a third will be left in it.
	2+2+3

[9] *And I will bring this third into the fire,*
    and I will refine them as one refines silver,
    and I will test them as one tests gold.
	3+3

They [a] *shall call on my name,* *and I will answer,*	3+3
'I will [b] *say, they* [a] *are my people,* *and he will say, Yahweh is our God.'* "	3+4

Notes

7.a. עֲמִית is found only here and in the priestly document in the Pentateuch (Lev 5:21 [Eng. 6:2]; 18:20; 19:11, 15, 17; 24:19; 25:14, 15, 17). There it is often translated "neighbor" or "another." It implies companionship and association.

7.b. צְעִרִים comes from a root meaning small. It is used two other times in the OT (Jer 30:19; Job 14:21) "be insignificant," and here meaning "small ones," referring either to shepherd boys or to small sheep.

8.a. פִּישְׁנִים lit. "mouth of two," an idiom for "two parts" or "two thirds" (Deut 21:17; 2 Kgs 2:9; cf. CHAL 289).

9.a. הוּא "he" is used collectively and should be translated "they."

9.b. אָמַרְתִּי "I said" should be read with the LXX with a waw consecutive וְאָמַרְתִּי "I will say."

Form/Structure/Setting

This is a brief pericope (three verses), somewhat independent of the previous oracle of cleansing the land of sin, uncleanness, unclean spirits, and false prophets. It takes up the earlier motif of the shepherd (9:16; 10:2–3; 11:3–17).

Because of the reference to a sword in 11:17 and because the shepherd motif is prominent in Zech 9–11 but is not mentioned in chaps. 12–14 other than this passage (13:7–9), Ewald suggested moving 13:7–9 to a position following 11:17 where it "supplied the natural close to 11:4–17" (cf. S. R. Driver 271). Many scholars have followed Ewald's suggestion. NEB transposes 13:7–9 to follow 11:17. Rex Mason (110) and Paul Hanson (*Apocalyptic* 338–39; 344; 348) concur with this position. Those who transpose 13:7–9 and attach it to 11:4–17 understand the smitten shepherd in 13:7 to be the worthless shepherd of 11:15. But 13:7–9 does not identify the shepherd except as the "fellow" or "associate" of Yahweh. C. A. Briggs said that "This shepherd is a ruler of the people, rather than a prophet. . . . He is engaged in war at the head of his flock, and is defeated by the enemy. . . . His fall results in the flight of his army, and great suffering" (C. A. Briggs, *Messianic Prophecy* [New York: Scribner's, 1891] 463).

Many scholars have resisted moving 13:7–9 to follow 11:17. Friedrich Bleek in 1875 said that Ewald and Ortenberg were quite wrong in separating 13:7–9 from 13:7—14:21, and looking upon it as the close of the prophecy in chap. 11 (F. Bleek, *Introduction to the OT,* trans. G. H. Venables [London: G. Bell, 1875] II, 171). D. R. Jones believes that 13:7–9 is linked with 13:1–6 in that Yahweh was going to do to his shepherd and people (smite and scatter them) what the people had done to the false prophets (Jones 168–69). Otto Plöger thinks that 13:7–9 might have belonged to another context originally, but now it serves as an expansion and a "deliberate sharpening of perspective" (Plöger, *Theocracy* 88). According to Plöger this sharpening of perspective is revealed in the fact that Yahweh calls for his sword to smite his shepherd and scatter the sheep. In 1 Kgs 22:17 Israel is spoken of as sheep without a shepherd. There the shepherd undoubtedly refers to the king. Here (13:7) in the framework of the Jewish theocracy, Plöger believes that the shepherd is the high priest who represented the Jewish community before the Persian king and before Yahweh—"*geber*ʿᵃ*miti* in xiii need not signify anything more" (Plöger 88).

This idea of a sword as a symbol of judgment may have originated with Jeremiah. The expression "sword, famine, and pestilence" was a favorite of his (14:12, 13, 15, 18; 21:7, 9; 24:10). Ezekiel uses Jeremiah's term "sword, famine, and pestilence" and adds "wild beasts" to it (14:1–23). In Ezek 21:1–22 there is a "song of the sword" predicting judgment on Judah. Here (Zech 13:7) the sword strikes Yahweh's king, governor, or high priest, which results in a period of tribulation for the people. Two thirds of them will be slain but a remnant will be spared (v 8). Then the remaining one third will be tested by fire and refined after which they will call on the name of Yahweh and he will make a new covenant with them (v 9).

Although this brief pericope has some similarity to 11:17, which could lead some to see 13:7–9 as a sequel, it also has a relationship to 13:1–6 and to 14:1–21. It is an eschatological oracle of hope and salvation which will be fulfilled after a period of tribulation.

The setting of this eschatological oracle of salvation was probably in the national cultus, "in the liturgical role of the king" (Bruce, *NT Development* 102). The striking of the king in the cultus occurs in a number of OT oracles (Mic 5:1; Isa 50:6).

Comment

Even though the relationship of 13:7–9 to its context may not be clear, its meaning is that the day is coming when God's appointed leader in Israel will be cut off and the people will be scattered. Paul Hanson (*Apocalyptic* 338–53) believes that the writer identified the shepherd of 13:7 with the worthless shepherd of 11:17 who was the leader of the hierocratic party in post-exilic Jerusalem. Plöger identifies the purified remnant of this passage with "those who think and hope eschatologically, men of insight; in contrast to their co-religionists, who also take divine judgments into full consideration but expect the purification in a formal, ritualistic manner without painful intervention and have thus occupied a supposedly secure position in the van of eschatological decisions" (*Theocracy* 89).

Whatever the historical setting of the oracle was, Jesus interpreted it eschatologically. He saw himself as the "smitten shepherd" and interpreted his ministry along the lines of this passage. In Mark 14:27 Jesus told his disciples as they were on their way to the garden of Gethsemane, "You will all fall away; for it is written, I will strike the shepherd, and the sheep will be scattered" (cf. Matt 26:31). In other places Jesus spoke of the people as "sheep without a shepherd" (Mark 6:34; Matt 9:36). Perhaps Jesus also interpreted the "falling away" of his followers in the light of the expression "the little ones" (Zech 13:7). In Luke 12:32 Jesus said to his disciples, "Fear not, little flock, for it is your father's good pleasure to give you the kingdom" (cf. Luke 22:28). It is interesting to note that one of the Zadokite Documents found in the Cairo Genizah and published in 1910 quotes Zech 13:7 followed by the phrase "and those who were watching him are the poor of the flock" (cf. notes on 11:11 above; cf. Bruce, *NT Development* 103; C. Rabin, *The Zadokite Documents* [Oxford: Clarendon Press, 1954] 31). Rabin suggests that the Zadokite Document may refer here to the Teacher of Righteousness. Ibn Ezra refers the events of Zech 13:7 to the time after the death of "Messiah ben Joseph," the precursor-Messiah. For the Karaite Moses Dar'i (twelfth–thirteenth cent) the passage refers to the Messiah (ibid. 31).

The Day of the Battle for Jerusalem
(14:1-5)

Bibliography

Abel, F. M., "Asal dans Zacharie XIV 5." *RB* 45 (1936) 385–400. **de Vaux, R.** "The Remnant of Israel According to the Prophets." *The Bible and the Ancient Near East,* Ed. G. E. Wright. Garden City, N.Y.: Doubleday, 1961. 15–30. **Noth, M.** "The Holy Ones of the Most High," *The Laws in the Pentateuch.* Trans. D. R. Ap-Thomas. London: Oliver & Boyd, 1966. 215–28.

Translation

¹ *Behold a day (is) coming* [a] *for Yahweh when your spoil will be divided in your midst.* ² *And I will gather all the nations to Jerusalem for war and the city will be captured. The houses will be plundered and the women raped. Half of the city will go into exile but the rest* [a] *of the people shall not be cut off from the city.* ³ *And Yahweh will go out and fight against those nations like the day of his fighting* [a] *in the day of battle.* ⁴ *And his feet shall stand in that day on the Mount of Olives which is in front of Jerusalem from the east, and the Mount of Olives will be split in half* [a] *by a very great valley from east to west. And half of the valley shall withdraw northward and half southward.* ⁵ *And you shall flee* [a] *by the valley of my mountains, because it shall touch the valley of my mountains* [b] *unto Asal.* [c] *And you will flee as you fled before the earthquake in the days of Uzziah, king of Judah. And Yahweh my God will come and all his* [d] *holy ones with you.* [e]

Notes

1.a. בָּא is a qal act. pl. of בּוֹא "coming."

2.a. יתר "rest" is not the regular word for remnant (שאֵרת), which means "to be leftover." יתר is a noun and means, "that which is over and above," "in excess" (De Vaux 17 n.16).

3.a. הלחמו lit. "his to fight" a niph. inf. cst. of לחם.

4.a. מחצין lit. "from its half."

5.a. וְנַסְתֶּם "and you shall flee," a 2nd mas. pl. qal pf. of נוס with a waw consecutive. But many scholars read וְנִסְתַּם "and shall be stopped up," a 3rd mes. sing. niph. pf. with waw consecutive from סתם.

5.b. גֵּי הרים "valley of the mountains" is often read גֵּי הנם "valley of Hinoam."

5.c. אָצַל is taken by KJV, NEB and others as a place name "Asal" (cf. Abel, *RB* 45 [1936] 385) but many emend it אצלו "its side" with Sym meaning the side of the mountain or the side of the "spring."

5.d. conj ו (waw) is supplied from LXX and Syr.

5.e. עמָן "with you" is often emended with the LXX עמּוֹ "with him."

Form/Structure/Setting

With Zech 14 we reach "full-blown" apocalyptic literature (cf. Hanson, *Apocalyptic* 369). Hanson sees in vv 6–8 a view of time that distinguishes between the present evil order and a future order of salvation. The present order was so permeated by evil that nothing seemed untainted (376). The days of restoration and the return to paradisical purity had to wait for a cosmic battle with the forces of evil. "The dualism and the related doctrine of the two eras . . . are here revitalized in the visionary tradition" (ibid. 379). D. R. Jones also sees this time (in vv 6–9) as "the time of the end" (Jones 174).

The form of this brief pericope is that of an announcement of a future battle over Jerusalem between Yahweh and the nations. Yahweh will gather all the nations to fight against Jerusalem (v 2; cf. Ezek 38:4, 17; Joel 4:2, 12 [Eng. 3:2, 12]); the city will be captured by the enemy amid great suffering and loss (v 2). Then Yahweh will appear as a huge man on the Mount of Olives. The mountain will split under his feet and a valley will appear east and west through the mountain. The newly formed valley will serve as a means of escape for the remnant in Jerusalem and as a way of Yahweh's victorious processional to Zion (v 5).

This passage may well reflect views in the post-exilic period of the leader or leaders of a band of visionaries (successors to the classical prophets) who despaired of hope in this present evil age apart from a personal intervention of Yahweh to put down all the forces of evil and bring in a paradisical purification and the kingdom of Yahweh. The language is mainly cultic from the Royal-Zion festival reflecting the battle of Yahweh with his enemies, the theophany, victory and the celebration by a processional.

Comment

The words, "Behold a day is coming (or "about to come") for Yahweh *to act*," indicate that what follows is eschatological. The language is weighted heavily with terms related to holy war. שלל "spoil," חלק "divided," מלחמה

"war," לכד "capture," שסס "plunder," גּוֹלָה "exile," כּרת "cut off" are holy war terms. 14:1-2 is a dramatic reversal of the promise made to Jerusalem in 2:8-9 (Eng. 2:4-5). There Jerusalem was to have a large population which would not need a wall for protection. It is a pastoral scene of peaceful security. Here the city is actually attacked, pillaged, and ravaged. Half the people will be taken captive.

The theme of Jerusalem being attacked by the other nations may go back to Sennacherib's attack on the city in 701 B.C. Yahweh spared the city at that time (Isa 36-39). Micah saw the time when Jerusalem would be plowed as a field (3:12). Jeremiah spoke often of the enemy from the north as a threat to Jerusalem's security. But in his famous temple sermon Jeremiah said that Israel's real security was in Yahweh and their keeping covenant with him. Ezekiel (38-39) spoke of the battle between Gog of Magog and Yahweh over Jerusalem. Much of this language of holy war and the nation's attack of Jerusalem can be seen in the royal psalms, the enthronement psalms and the songs of Zion (2, 46, 47, 48, 93, 96, 97, 99).

In 14:1 the time is "a day for Yahweh." It will be Yahweh's day. He will reveal his power (cf. Zech 4:6). Here Yahweh's power is described in a theophany. He will fight like he did when he fought the Egyptians at the Red Sea (Exod 15) and other enemies on numerous occasions (cf. Hab 3:3-15). Here his feet will stand on the Mount of Olives (v 4). The location of the Mount of Olives is given probably for the benefit of readers who were not familiar with the environs of Jerusalem. The name Mount of Olives is mentioned here for the first time in the OT. In 2 Sam 15:30 David flees Jerusalem because of Absalom's rebellion and ascends the "slope of Olives." Ezekiel also speaks of the cherubim abandoning the temple and "standing on the mountain which is on the east side of the city" (Ezek 11:23). Both these passages—David's ascent of the slope of Olives and the departure of the cherubim from the mountain east of Jerusalem—may have been in the background of the writer's thinking at this point.

In Mic 1:3-4 Yahweh comes down and treads on the high places of the earth, the mountains melt like wax and the valleys are cleft. In Amos 4:13 and 9:5 Yahweh treads on the high places and the earth melts. All this imagery expresses Yahweh's power over the natural world. But Zech 14:1-5 stresses Yahweh's power over history and the peoples of the world. He will fight against the nations. The nations are undifferentiated here. The Mount of Olives will split and a valley will be formed across it from east to west so that the rest of the people in Jerusalem can find refuge and a way of escape.

There is some confusion in v 5. Some of the confusion involves the word נַסְתֶּם which is used three times in this verse. When it is pointed as the MT points it, it is a 2nd mas. pl. qal perf. from נוּס "and you shall flee." But the same consonants with different vowels נִסְתַּם is a 3rd mas. sing. niphal perf. of סתם "and it shall be stopped up." This reading is supported by the LXX, Tg, and Sym, so the verse may be saying to the remnant in Jerusalem, "you shall flee (into or through) the valley of my mountains like you fled before the earthquake in the days of Uzziah king of Judah." Or, the verse may be saying, "The valley of my mountains shall be stopped up (blocked) and it shall touch the valley of my mountains unto Azel as it was blocked in the face of the earthquake in the time of Uzziah." The first reading is clearer and has fewer problems.

The last sentence in v 5 refers to a triumphal entrance procession into Jerusalem by Yahweh, his holy ones, and the remnant who were saved in the battle with the nations. Martin Noth is probably correct in understanding "the holy ones" to refer to the "angels" or "heavenly beings" (*The Laws in the Pent.* 215–28). עמך "with you" is often emended with the LXX and Syriac to עמו "with him," but the "you" can refer to the inhabitants of Jerusalem who were spared.

The New Jerusalem (14:6–11)

Bibliography

Clifford, R. J. *The Cosmic Mountain.* Cambridge, Mass: Harvard University Press, 1972. **McBride, S. D., Jr.** "The Yoke of the Kingdom." *Int* 27 (1973) 272–306. **Montefiore, C. G.** and **Loewe, H.** *A Rabbinic Anthology.* New York: Meridian, 1960. 104, 640–42. **Porteous, N. W.** "Jerusalem-Zion: The Growth of a Symbol." *Living the Mystery. Collected Essays.* Oxford: University Press, 1967. 93–112.

Translation

⁶ *And in that day there shall be neither heat* ᵃ *nor cold.* ᵇ ⁷ *And the day shall be one (it is known to Yahweh). It shall be neither day nor night but it shall be light even at the time of the evening.* ⁸ *And it shall be in that day the water of life shall go out from Jerusalem, half unto the eastern sea and half unto the western sea in the summer and in winter.* ⁹ *And Yahweh will be king over all the earth, in that day Yahweh shall be one and his name one.* ¹⁰ *And all the land shall be transformed* ᵃ *as the Arabah from Geba to Rimmon south of Jerusalem and she (Jerusalem) shall tower high,* ᵇ *and shall dwell in her place.* ¹¹ *People* ᵃ *shall dwell in her and there shall not be a ban* ᵇ *again. And Jerusalem shall dwell in trust (securely).*

Notes

6.a. אור means "light," but the context is incongruent with the idea of "no light." 14:1–5 spoke of Yahweh's theophany, an event usually associated with brilliant light rather than no light. However there are passages in the OT which speak of the day of Yahweh as a day of darkness and not light (Amos 5:18; Zeph 1:15). This could be the idea here. But the rest of the pericope (vv 7–11) speaks of blessings rather than evil or judgment. V 7 refers to the water of life. V 9 refers to the day when Yahweh will be proclaimed king over all the earth. So it is better to read אור "flame," "fire," or "heat" for אור and read קרות "cold" for יְקָרוֹת "precious things." So the verse would say, "There shall be neither heat nor cold."

6.b. יְקָרוֹת usually means "precious things" from יקר (*CHAL* 142). But change the י (yodh) to a ו (waw) and make the root קרר or קרה mean "cold" (cf. קר Gen 8:22). יקפאון most translations read the קרי (וקפאון "frost") cf. *CHAL* 321. The LXX, Syr, and Sym read "cold and frost."

10.a. יסוב 3rd mas. sing. qal impf. of סבב "turn," or "be transformed" (*CHAL* 252). The idea is that all the mountains surrounding Jerusalem will be leveled or smoothed out so that the city will tower over them as she would the floor of the Arabah.

10.b. וראמה a 3rd fem. sing. qal pf. of ראם with waw consecutive. A hapax (*CHAL* 329).

11.a. "people" is from the 3rd com. pl. form of the verb ישבו. Not men only.

11.b. חרם "ban," or "destruction." Holy war will be ended. There will be a ban on the ban.

Form/Structure/Setting

Vv 6–11 are made up of a series of apocalyptic sayings beginning in vv 6, 8, 9, and 10. The first saying talks about the change in seasons and in day and night. The implication is that conditions in the universe will revert back to prediluvian times before "the fall." The second saying describes a perennial source of living water for the land. The third saying looks toward the day when the universal kingdom of God will become a reality. And the fourth saying speaks of the physical exaltation of Jerusalem and the leveling of the countryside around her.

The boundaries of the new capital are first given as those of Judah—from Geba to Rimmon (1 Kgs 15:22; 2 Kgs 23:8). Then the four corners of the immediate city are given as: the Gate of Benjamin (NE corner, Jer 37:12, 13); the corner gate (on the west side); the Tower of Hananel (on the north, Neh 3:1; 12:39); and the king's winepress (on the south, Neh 2:14; 3:15). The pericope closes with the promise that there will be no more חרם, "ban." The חרם was the act of slaying the captives in holy war. When the חרם is discontinued there will be no more war.

The connection of this pericope with the one before it and the one following is uncertain. However it fits the overall picture of the New Jerusalem presented in the entire chapter.

Comment

V 6 is very difficult. Certainty about its precise meaning is impossible at this point. It seems to be a transition verse between the theophany in vv 3–5 and the description of the transformation of the times, seasons and geological situation of the New Jerusalem and the surrounding environs. Although the MT says there shall be "no light" (אור) it is best to read אור "flame" or "heat." There seems to be cosmic change perhaps related to the Noachian covenant (Gen 8:22). In Gen 8:22 God promised Noah and all mankind that there would always be "seedtime and harvest, cold and heat, summer and winter, day and night." This promise was to assure mankind of the regularity of nature. Man needed that assurance because of the great destruction and death caused by the flood which in turn was caused by man's sins. Now in this last day of Yahweh there will be no need of such a promise because the curse of sin will be removed. There will be no extremes in temperature (cold or hot), no darkness and light, or day and night, no extremes of brightness. It will always be light. There will be one continuous day (Isa 60:19–20). John picks up this theme in Rev 21:22–25—

And I saw no temple in the city, for its temple is the Lord God the Almighty and the Lamb. And the city has no need of sun or moon to shine upon it, for the glory of God is its light, and its lamp is the Lamb. By its light shall the nations walk; and the kings of the earth shall bring their glory into it, and its gates shall never be shut by day—and there shall be no night there (RSV).

With continuous day there will be no clouds and no rain. The land will be watered by a stream of living water flowing out of Jerusalem (cf. Ezek 47:1–12; Joel 3:18; Rev 22:1–2). Here in Zech 14 the living water will flow to the Dead Sea and to the Mediterranean Sea. The stream will never run dry. It will flow in summer and in winter. And Yahweh will be proclaimed king over all the earth. In the New Year festival celebrated every fall in Jerusalem there probably was a ceremony in which the king (high priest or some official) was crowned to symbolize Yahweh's kingship of the whole world (cf. Ps 47:5–9; 93:1–2; 95:2–5; 96:10; 97:1–5; 99:1–5). Now that which had been anticipated will become a reality. "Yahweh will become king over all the earth" (Zech 14:9; Mason 128). "And he shall be one and his name one." Obviously this is Deuteronomic language and theology. It is strange that the *shema* (Deut 6:4) which came to be "the watchword of Judaism" by the beginning of the Christian era, is only mentioned once in the OT. However, here in Zech 14:9 the prophet sees the time coming when the unity and the uniqueness of Yahweh will be acknowledged and accepted by all of the nations of the world. Yahweh's kingdom will be complete, total, and real on earth as it is in heaven. Yahweh's name stands for God's revealed presence on earth. By NT times the recital of the *shema* twice a day included not only Deut 6:4 but also 11:13–21. To orthodox Jews this meant taking on oneself the yoke of the kingdom of heaven (Montefiore and Lowe, *Rabbinic Anthology* 3). Dean McBride believes that Zechariah 14:9 may be a comment on Deut 6:4.

Zech 14:9 which may indeed be an early comment on Deut 6:4, reads: "And Yahweh will become king over the whole earth in that day; Yahweh will be ' eḥād (sole, unique, alone) and his name ' eḥād." Hence the rabbis derived that the words *yahweh* *ᵉlōhênû* in Deut 6:4 express the primary, intimate relationship between Yahweh and Israel ("our God"), and that *yahweh* *ᵉḥād* affirms the universal eschatological rule of God over the nations. It seems quite likely this interpretation is reflected by Paul in Romans 3:29f., though modified in the light of his own mission and eschatology (*Int* 27 [1973] 278 n.10).

The exaltation of Zion is the theme of v 10. Isa 2:2, Mic 4:1, Ezek 40:2, and Pss 46:2–3 and 48:1–2 speak of Zion as a city on a very high mountain. This imagery probably goes back to the cultic celebration of the New Year festival in Jerusalem. The language is reminiscent of the "cosmic mountain" motif in the Ugaritic materials where Zaphon, the high mountain in the far north, was the dwelling place of the gods (cf. R. J. Clifford, *The Cosmic Mountain* 153–160). Here in Zech 14:10 the geographical boundaries of the new kingdom are surprisingly small, so much so that Rex Mason says that v 10 must be a separate oracle from v 9. The northern and southern boundaries seem to be those of the former tribe of Judah (2 Kgs 23:8). Perhaps these boundaries refer only to the New Jerusalem. V 11 speaks about Jerusalem as being a place inhabited, that is a place not under the ban, but a place full of people fully trusting (בטח) in Yahweh.

The Plague on Those Who War Against Jerusalem   (14:12–15)

Translation

¹² *And this shall be the plague with which Yahweh shall smite all the peoples who warred against Jerusalem: their* ^a *flesh shall rot* ^b *while they* ^a *stand on their* ^a *feet, and their* ^a *eyes shall rot in their sockets and their* ^a *tongue shall rot in their mouth.* ¹³ *And there shall be on that day a great panic from Yahweh among them. And each man shall seize the hand of his neighbor and shall raise his hand against his neighbor.* ¹⁴ *And also Judah will fight in* ^a *Jerusalem, and the wealth of the surrounding nations, gold and silver and garments in great abundance will be gathered.* ¹⁵ *And so the plague shall be on the horse, the mule, the camel, the ass, and all the cattle that are in that camp like this* ^a *plague.*

Notes

12.a. The pronominal suf. on "flesh," "stand," "feet," "eyes," and "tongue," in sing.

12.b. הָמֵק a hiph. inf. abs. of מקק "to rot." The niphal is used in Lev 26:39; Ps 38:6 (Eng. 38:5); Isa 34:4; Ezek 4:17; 24:23 and means "to pine away" in Lev, Pss, and Ezek.

14.a. The prep ב can mean "in," "on," or "against." Most modern translations including RSV read "against." The KJV reads "at." The NEB reads "Judah too shall join the fray."

15.a. "This plague" refers to the plague on the "peoples" in v 12.

Form/Structure/Setting

Paul Hanson considers vv 12–15 to be covenant curses falling on people warring against Jerusalem. Another word for plague (מַגֵּבָה) is used in the covenant curses in Lev 26:21. The word מהומה "panic" in v 13 is used in the covenant curses in Deut 28:20. The source of the idea of the plagues may go back to the plagues of Egypt (Exod 7–11) or to the sudden rout of Sennacherib (2 Kgs 19:35). There is no evidence that either of these events was celebrated in any annual festival. However, the covenant curses were probably recited each year in the New Year festival (cf. Lev 26:16–39; Deut 28:16–45). The language is horrifying. R. C. Dentan says that this language is typical of the savagery which is part of the literary stock of apocalyptic (cf. Rev 19:17–18; Ezek 39:17–20). Panic shall seize the invaders of Jerusalem and they will kill each other in their attempts to escape (cf. Hag 2:22; Zech 11:9).

Did Judah fight *against* Jerusalem or *in* Jerusalem? The RSV reads "against Jerusalem" in v 14, but that does not seem to fit the context. Nothing else in this passage suggests that Judah and Jerusalem are at odds with one another. KJV reads "Judah will fight at Jerusalem," which is possible but not the usual meaning. The NEB may capture the meaning of the phrase, "Judah too will join in the fray in Jerusalem." Paul Hanson explains that since vv 12–19 are concerned with Jerusalem "vis-à-vis the foreign nations," 14a may be an intrusive element stemming from further reflection on the relationship between Judah and Jerusalem in chaps. 12 and 14 (Hanson, *Apocalyptic* 371).

The bringing of the wealth of the nations to Jerusalem in the eschaton is a part of the larger theme of the pilgrimage of the nations to Jerusalem. Isa 2:2–4 and Mic 4:1–4 envision the nations coming to Jerusalem after it has become the highest mountain. There the nations come to be taught the law of Yahweh, which in turn will bring in a period of universal peace. In Isa 49:22–23 and Mic 7:17 the prophets speak of a change in fortune between Zion and the nation. Whereas Judah had been in exile and the nations their masters, now the nations will be the servants and Zion shall be the victor. In Isa 60:1–22 Zion is the light to which all nations come. They will bring their treasure by land and sea (vv 6–9). In Hag 2:6–8 the treasures of the nations will be brought to Jerusalem and the latter splendor of the temple will be greater than that of Solomon's temple. One should note that in almost all of these passages, the place of the temple is stressed. But in Zech 2:11; 8:22–23; 14:14, 16 the nations come to Jerusalem to worship Yahweh but nothing is said about the temple. In Rev 21:22 the new Jerusalem has no temple, for the Lord God the Almighty and the Lamb are the temple. Notice that garments make up some of the wealth of the nations (cf. Matt 6:19).

The Pilgrimage of the Nations to Jerusalem (14:16–21)

Translation

16 *And it shall be that every survivor from all the nations coming against Jerusalem shall go up year after year to worship the king, Yahweh of hosts, and to celebrate* [a] *the feast of Tabernacles.* 17 *And it shall be that it will not rain upon the families of the earth which will not go up to Jerusalem to worship the King Yahweh of Hosts.* 18 *And if the family of Egypt will not go up and will not come in, then upon them* [a] *will be the plague with which Yahweh will smite the nations who do not go up to celebrate the feast of Tabernacles.* 19 *This shall be the punishment* [a] *of Egypt and the punishment of all the nations who will not go up to celebrate the feast of Tabernacles.*

20 *In that day there shall be on the bells of the horses, "Holy to Yahweh." And the pots in the house of Yahweh shall be like the bowls before the altar.* 21 *And every pot in Jerusalem and in Judah shall be "Holy to Yahweh of hosts." And all those sacrificing shall take from them and shall cook in them. And there shall not be a trader* [a] *in the house of Yahweh of hosts in that day.*

Notes

16.a. ולחג "and to celebrate a festival," qal inf. of חגג.

18.a. The לא "not" before עליהם in the MT probably should be omitted with the LXX,

Syr, RSV, JB and NEB. The meaning surely is not that Yahweh will not bring the plague upon Egypt. Ackroyd suggests the לֹא could be left in the text if it were understood as part of a question, "shall there not be a plague upon them (the Egyptians)?" (P. R. Ackroyd, *PCB* 655). Mitchell follows Marti in omitting the third negative in v 18 along with the relative clause, "who will not go up to celebrate the Feast of Tabernacles." Mitchell argues that this clause is out of place here but is used correctly in v 19.

19.a. חטאת lit. "sin" but here it also refers to the punishment of sin (cf. Num 32:23; Gen 4:7).

21.a. כְּנַעֲנִי lit. "a Canaanite." The term "canaanite" was used often by the prophets to refer to "traders" in Israel (cf. Hos 12:8 [Eng. 12:7]; Zeph 1:11; Zech 11:7, 11). The reference here (Zech 14:21) is to the unworthy merchants who were using unscrupulous business methods in the temple area. In the eschaton all such practices will be eliminated (cf. Mark 11:15–18; Matt 21:12–13).

Form/Structure/Setting

The final pericope in Zechariah is made up of two parts: (1) the pilgrimage of the nations to Jerusalem to observe the feast of Tabernacles (vv 16–19) and (2) the sanctification of all things in the eschaton (vv 20–21). V 16 is a connecting link to 14:1–15. It tells what will happen to the remnant of the nations that fought against Jerusalem in the final battle. Some of them will be converted to a worship of Yahweh and will come to Jerusalem annually to observe the feast of Tabernacles (v 16), but those who will not worship Yahweh will suffer from the plague and drought (vv 17–19). In the last two verses (20–21) everything will become holy. The bells on the war horses and ordinary cooking pots will be as holy as the turban of the high priest (cf. Exod 28:36; 39:30) and the sacred vessels in the temple (cf. Ezek 46:21–24). And the unscrupulous "canaanite" will never again be in the temple of Yahweh of hosts. Paul Hanson is probably correct when he says that "Zechariah 14 is cast in the form of the new hybrid salvation-judgment oracle, which levels salvation and judgment words simultaneously against two different segments within a divided nation" (*Apocalyptic* 391).

Comment

The last scene in the book of Zechariah is a picture of the world after Armageddon. It will be a new world not entirely unrelated to the previous world. A remnant of the nations that participated in the last battle against Jerusalem shall survive. And that remnant of the Gentiles will be divided between those who become worshipers of Yahweh of hosts and make the pilgrimage to Zion to celebrate the Feast of Tabernacles, and those who will not go up to Jerusalem for the feast. Those who go up and worship Yahweh will become a part of Yahweh's kingdom. Those who do not will suffer the same kind of plague that the original invaders of Jerusalem suffered (14:12) and will experience a death-wielding drought (14:17–18). Egypt seems to be singled out for special attention in vv 18 and 19, perhaps because the threat of a plague reminded the author of the earlier plagues of Egypt at the time of the exodus, but also because Egypt would not naturally be affected by the lack of rain because she depended almost entirely upon the Nile for her water supply.

There could not be more shocking words for an OT priest than those in vv 19–20. The writer says that there will come a time when every distinction between the holy and the profane will be eliminated. Those warlike horses that had been instruments of the invaders of Zion will become as holy as the turban of the high priest (cf. Exod 28:36–38), and ordinary cooking utensils will be like the sacred vessels in the temple. There will be no difference between the Jew and the Gentile, the clean and the unclean. That which will matter will not be race or nationality but whether one worships Yahweh as king, the lord of hosts (cf. Hanson, *Apocalyptic* 386–87). R. C. Dentan takes an opposite view of this passage from Hanson and sees these verses as the work of a priest in the post-exilic period (cf. Dentan 1114).

With Zech 14 we have reached apocalyptic eschatology "without stricture or qualification." Hanson, who dates this chapter about 425 B.C., says, "Internal development would continue to occur, but the essentials of apocalyptic eschatology are all present" (*Apocalyptic*, 396). There is the battle against Zion and Yahweh's judgment on his enemies. There is the apocalyptic woes (vv 12–15), the new age (vv 6–7) and the mystery of the time known only to God (v 7). There is no vision of restoration of the entire nation of Israel in chap. 14. "The last ties with a conception of salvation along the lines defined by nationalism seem to be severed, yielding to a new dualism distinguishing not between nations but between evil and good on a broader scale" (Hanson, *Apocalyptic* 391). Mason suggests that Zech 14 represents a disillusion with, and hostility toward, the official Judaism of the day. Reform is no longer an option. Temple and cult must be renewed through drastic judgment and divine deliverance. The temple no longer occupies the place it once did since all of life will be sacralized. The writer was a member of a "sect" type community within Judaism who kept alight the torch of the pure prophetic faith through a time of persecution, apostasy, and crisis. Such a group was a forerunner of the Qumran community, and in some way, the early Christian church. The emphasis on the new age and the universal kingdom of God probably accounts for the many uses of and references to Zech 9–14 in the NT.

Malachi

Malachi

Bibliography

Books and Commentaries

(See also *General Bibliography* for commentaries on more than one book. Also see commentaries on all or more than one of the twelve prophets.) **Bennett, T. M.** "Malachi." *BBC* 7. Nashville: Broadman Press, 1972. **Delaughter, T. J.** *Malachi: Messenger of Divine Love.* New Orleans: Insight Press, 1976. **Dentan, R. C.** "Malachi." *IB* 6. New York: Abingdon Press, 1956. **Hvidberg, F. F.** *Weeping and Laughter in the Old Testament.* Leiden: Brill, 1962. **Isbell, C. D.** *Malachi.* Grand Rapids: Zondervan, 1980. **Matthews, I. G.** "Malachi." *An American Commentary.* Philadelphia: Judson Press, 1935. **Myers, J. M.** *The World of the Restoration.* Englewood Cliffs, NJ: Prentice-Hall, 1968. **Petersen, D. L.** *Late Israelite Prophecy.* Missoula, MT: Scholars Press, 1977.

Articles

Boeker, H. J. "Bemerkungen zu formgeschichtlichen Terminologie des Buches Maleachi." *ZAW* 78 (1966) 78–80. **Budde, K.** "Zum Text der drier letzen Propheten." *ZAW* 26 (1906) 1–28. **Dumbrell, W. J.** "Malachi and the Ezra-Nehemiah Reforms." *RTR* 35 (1976) 42–52. **Elliger, K.** "Maleachi und die kirchliche Tradition." *Tradition und Situation.* Artur Weiser's Festschrift. Eds. Wurthwein und Kaiser. Göttingen: Vandenhoek und Ruprecht, 1963. **Kruse-Blinkenberg, L.** "The Book of Malachi according to Codex Syro-Hexaplaris Ambrosianus." *ST* 21 (1967) 62–82. ———. "The Peshitta of the Book of Malachi." *ST* 20 (1966) 95–119. **Margalioth, E.** "Eschatology in the Book of Malachi." In *Sepher M. H. Segal.* Jerusalem (1964) 139–143. (Hebrew). **Radday, V. T.** and **Pollatschek, Moshe A.** "Vocabulary Richness in Post-Exilic Prophetic Books." *ZAW* 92 (1980) 333–46. **Rudolph, W.** "Zu Mal 2:10–16." *ZAW* (1981) 85–90. **Torrey, C. C.** "The Prophecy of Malachi." *JBL* 17 (1898) 1–15. **Wallis, G.** "Wesen und Struktur der Botschaft Maleachis." In *Das Ferne und Nahe Wort.* Leonard Rost's Festschrift. Ed. Fritz Maass. Berlin: Töpelmann (1967) 229–237.

Introduction

Malachi is the twelfth and last book of the Minor Prophets. How the material in this book became the twelfth book in that collection is a matter of debate. Since the expression משא דבר יהוה "Oracle. The word of Yahweh" only occurs three times in the OT, and those three references appear together at the end of the book of the twelve (Zech 9:1; 12:1; Mal 1:1), it is often assumed that an editor took three anonymous oracles and placed them at the end of the prophetic canon of the OT. In the course of transmission the first two oracles became attached to Zechariah and the third one achieved an independent status and became the book of Malachi (cf. Bennett, "Malachi," BBC 7, 366; Childs, *Introduction* 489; Eissfeldt, *OT Introduction* 440; Dentan, "Malachi," *IB* 6, 1117).

Radday and Pollatschek examined the books of the post-exilic prophets with the aid of a computer. On the basis of frequency lists of vocabulary words they discovered that chaps. 1 and 2 displayed a completely uniform behavior, but chap. 3 was "wholly out of step with them." They concluded that the editor of the Book of the Twelve had a post-exilic collection of materials left after he had finished the books from Hosea to Zech 8. "This small library consisted of several short but distinct manuscripts, three of which bore the title 'An Oracle. The Word of the Lord.' Following the size principle, he attached them after Zech 1–8. The two longer ones (3 chaps. each) coalesced with Zech 1–8 to become 9–11 and 12–14. He then attached two chapters, Mal 1–2. Finally the editor was left with what perhaps amounted to a page or two. These, originally nameless and later to become Mal 3, he added at the very end. Then he or another editor keen on presenting a collection of prophetic books whose number corresponded to that of the twelve tribes may have inserted the words, 'by the hand of Malachi' in 1:1 thus turning a word he found three times in his last chapters into a name of a hitherto unknown prophet" (Y. T. Radday and M. A. Pollatschek. "Vocabulary Richness in Post-Exilic Prophetic Books." *ZAW* 92 [1980] 333–46).

Brevard Childs does not agree that because the same expression occurs in Zech 9:1; 12:1; Mal 1:1 we can conclude that three anonymous oracles were arbitrarily assigned to their present place in the canon. He notes that the first word מַשָּׂא "oracle" is probably used in its absolute form as a separate superscription in Mal 1:1. Moreover, Mal 1:1 has features that Zech 9:1 and 12:1 do not have, such as אֶל "to," rather than עַל "upon" and בְּיַד "by the hand of." These expressions alone would be enough to argue for an independent tradition behind Mal 1:1. Childs concludes that the three passages had a history independent of one another and says, "the present independent status of Malachi did not arise from an arbitrary decision which separated it from the book of Zechariah. Rather its separate status is deeply rooted in the book's own tradition" (Childs, *Introduction* 492).

The Prophet

Little is known about Malachi apart from what may be gleaned from this book. He is not mentioned anywhere else in the Old or New Testaments. Malachi is included in the *Lives of the Prophets*, a collection of Jewish traditions dating from about the fourth century A.D. There it is said that he was born in Sopha (a place otherwise unknown) after the exile. "Even in boyhood he lived a blameless life, and since all the people paid him honor for his piety and mildness they called him 'Malachi' (angel); he was also fair to look upon. Moreover, whatever things he uttered in prophecy were repeated on that same day by an angel of God who appeared; as had happened in the days when there was no king in Israel, as it is written in the book of Judges (2:1–4; 5:23; 6:11–22; 13:3–21)" (*The Lives of the Prophets*. JBL Monograph 1 [1946] 45). Although these traditions are interesting and may reflect the thinking of some Jews in the fourth century A.D., they are according to F. C. Eiselen, "late and without value" (Eiselen, *Minor Prophets* 688).

Name

Malachi might have been the personal name of this prophet or it might have been a title, Malachi = "my messenger." The LXX took it as a title and read "his messenger" rather than "my messenger." The Targum adds, ". . . by the hand of my angel whose name is called Ezra the scribe." But many recent scholars have supported the view that Malachi is a proper name (cf. Childs, *Introduction* 493–94; Rudolph, 247–48).

Whether or not Malachi was the name or the title of this prophet is not important. What is important is whether or not the prophet or the editor thought that he was the messenger Yahweh was going to send to prepare the way for his coming (3:1). If that is true as T. C. Vriezen and Karl Elliger believe, then the coming of Yahweh was considered to be imminent. However, the prophet makes no statements that indicate he considered himself to be that forerunner (cf. T. C. Vriezen, [Bibliography to 1:2–5]).

Date

We can only estimate the date of Malachi's ministry. No kings are named in the superscription or in the book which might give us a clue to the date. No historical incident such as a battle or earthquake is mentioned to give us a historical context. However we know that the time was post-exilic because of the use of the Persian word פחת "governor" (1:8). The temple had been rebuilt (1:10; 3:1, 10). The Edomites had suffered a crushing blow evidently from some invader. Many scholars believe that the crushing blow refers to the invasion of Edom by the Nabatean (Joyce Baldwin 223; R. C. Dentan 1124; J. M. P. Smith 6). Unfortunately we cannot date this invasion precisely. Baldwin dates the Nabatean invasion possibly as early as the sixth century, while Dentan and Smith date it in the middle of the fifth century. According to Diodorus Siculus, Southern Judah was called Idumaea (from Edom) in 312 B.C. indicating that the Nabateans had driven Edom from her stronghold in Petra into Southern Judah (*Biblotheca Historica* 19, 94–100). (For a recent study of the Nabataeans see Gary Baldwin's unpublished Ph.D. Dissertation, Southwestern Baptist Seminary, Ft. Worth, 1982.)

There is a kinship between the book of Malachi and that of Nehemiah. The same social and religious conditions prevail in both, and Nehemiah instigates a reform to correct some of the social and religious abuses perhaps under the impetus of Malachi (Mal 3:5; Neh 5:1–13). Tithing is stressed in both (Mal 3:7–10; Neh 10:37–39). Divorce and mixed marriages were a problem in both (Mal 2:10–16; Neh 10:30; 13:23–29). J. M. P. Smith says, "the Book of Malachi fits the situation amid which Nehemiah worked as snugly as a bone fits its socket" (Smith 7). Nehemiah's first return to Jerusalem from Babylon can be definitely dated in 444 B.C. Therefore Malachi should be dated in the first half of the fifth century B.C.

Not everyone would agree with this date for Malachi. A. C. Welch has an unusual view of the date of this prophet. He argues in his *Post-Exilic Judaism* that Malachi was a contemporary of Haggai and Zechariah about 520 B.C. He believes that the proof that the temple had been rebuilt is not convincing

(118–19), and that 2:10–16 does not refer to divorce and mixed marriages but to the worship of a foreign deity (119–21). He says that "it is much more natural to connect this picture with the time which preceded than with the time which followed the restoration of the temple" (A. C. Welch, *Post-Exilic Judaism* [Edinburgh: Blackwood, 1935] 113–25). Perhaps it should be noted that Welch in an earlier article in *Hastings Dictionary of the Bible* supported the traditional date for Malachi.

While Welch argued for an early date for Malachi (520 B.C.), some scholars proposed a much later date for the prophet and the book. C. C. Torrey says that the apocalyptic passages (3:1–2; 19–24; Eng. 4:1–6) with their conception of the day of judgment as a day of separation of the righteous from the wicked reminds one of the late psalms and wisdom literature. He says that we may "assign the book with some confidence to the first half of the fourth century" (C. C. Torrey, *JBL* 17 [1898] 14–15). I. G. Matthews supports a date for the book at the beginning of the fourth century B.C. Again, the strong apocalyptic tone and the existence of a schism have heavily influenced his decision. Matthews says that the facts do not suggest that the book "was a creation of the Greek era and certainly there is little basis for the assertion that the governor mentioned in 1:8 was Jason, who in 174 was high priest (2 Macc 4:8), and that the crux of the book, 2:10–16, was an attack on the false worship introduced into Jerusalem by Antiochus Epiphanes" (Matthews ix–x). The book could not possibly be later than 180 B.C. because Ben Sira refers to it in Sir 48:10; and 49:10.

The Book

The book of Malachi is made up of a superscription (1:1); six disputations between Malachi/Yahweh and the addressees (1:2–3:21, Eng. 4:3); and two appendices (3:22, Eng. 4:4; 3:23–24, Eng. 4:5–6). The six disputations are:
1. A dispute about God's love   (1:2–5)
2. A dispute about God's honor and fear   (1:6–2:9)
3. A dispute about faithlessness   (2:10–16)
4. A dispute about God's justice   (2:17–3:5)
5. A dispute about repentance   (3:6–12)
6. A dispute about speaking against God   (3:13–21, Eng. 3:13–4:3)
The two appendices are (1) an admonition to remember the law of Moses (3:22, Eng. 4:4) and (2) the announcement that Yahweh is sending Elijah to turn the hearts of children to parents and vice-versa before the great and terrible day of the Lord comes (3:23–24, Eng. 4:5–6).

One can readily see from a glance at the outline that the prophet's concern was to reassure his people that God still loved them. The post-exilic period was a discouraging time for the people who returned to Jerusalem from Babylon with such high hopes. The prophet in Isa 40–55 painted the future of those repatriated people in such glowing terms, that they expected the messianic age to dawn immediately. Haggai and Zechariah added to these hopes by assuring the people that if they would rebuild the temple the "glory of the Lord" would come with unprecedented blessings. They built the temple and waited and waited but there was no glory. Instead, there was famine, poverty, oppression, unfaithfulness to marriage vows, and to covenant vows. Moral and spiritual laxity, pride, indifference, permissiveness, and skepticism were rife. Malachi tried to rekindle the fires of faith in the hearts of his discouraged people. He assured his people that Yahweh still loved them (1:2–5)—that the covenant was still in force. But God expected them to honor and fear him as a suzerain party to a covenant is feared and honored (1:6–2:9). God expected faithfulness on the part of the people in covenant with him and with one another (2:10–16). God defended his justice by saying that he was coming to purge and purify the Levitical priests and to judge the guilty sinners among his people (2:17–3:5). The people should repent of their evil deeds and of their wrong attitudes before he returns. If they repent he will pour out on them an unprecedented blessing (3:6–12). But there is no sign of repentance. Murmurings against Yahweh are heard (3:13–15). However some God-fearers encourage one another in faithfulness. They are God's special possession and will be spared in the day of judgment (3:16–21, Eng. 4:3).

The language and ideas of Malachi are deeply influenced by the Deuteronomic materials. "Love," "fear," "faithfulness" are motifs occurring frequently in Deuteronomy and in Deuteronomic history. The idea that the Levites could serve as priests is Deuteronomic (Deut 17:9; 18:1). The storehouse tithe is the Deuteronomic tithe (14:28–29; 26:12–14). The "law of Moses," "Horeb," "all Israel" in Mal 3:22 (Eng. 4:4) is Deuteronomic.

The style of the book of Malachi is that of disputations. Some have called it "discussions." Others call it "Socratic," or "catechetical," or question and answer style. But dispute is probably the best word to use to characterize the style. The disputation style is not new or unique to Malachi. Mic 2:6–11 is a classical example of Micah's dispute with the false prophets. Jeremiah had his disputes with his contemporaries (2:23–25, 29–32) and the false prophet (28:1–11; 29:24–32). Admittedly the form of the disputation passages is more standardized than that in previous passages. The prophet or Yahweh makes a statement containing a general premise: "I have loved you, says Yahweh"; "a son honors his father and a servant his Lord." Each premise seems to be an indictment of Israel's failure at that point. Israel has failed to understand that God still loves her; that God expects honor, fear, and faithfulness. In each dispute the people ask, "Wherein have we done, or not done what is charged?" (1:2, 6; 2:10, 14, 17; 3:7, 13). Then the prophet or Yahweh marshalls overwhelming evidence of Israel's guilt. But Malachi has a pastoral concern for the people. The major thrust of the book is love, comfort, assurance, and hope.

There are some serious textual problems in the book of Malachi. Does לתנות in 1:3 mean "jackals," or "pastures"? Two supposedly hophal participles appear together in 1:11. The word נִיבוֹ "fruit" in 1:12 is a problem. The meaning of the inf. להיות in 2:4 is uncertain. The words ער וענה in 2:12 are very difficult. 2:15 is probably the most difficult verse in the book. "One" could be either the subject or object of the verb "make." The expression "remnant of the spirit" is ambiguous. The verse is subject to a number of different translations. There have been a number of studies published on the text of Malachi. Karl Buddes', "Zum Text der drier letzen Prophetens" (ZAW 26 [1906] 1–28) is still helpful. Lars Kruse Blinkenberg's two recent articles, "The Peshitta of the Book of Malachi," *ST* 20 (1966) 95–119, and "The Syro-Hexapla of the Book of Malachi," *ST* 21 (1967) 62–82, are very helpful. To indicate something of the vastness of the problem of the text of Malachi, Kruse-Blinkenberg lists 111 divergencies between Syr and MT (*ST* 20 [1966] 109), and 96 divergencies between the LXX and MT (*ST* 21 [1967] 73). However, few of these divergencies are of a serious nature. Unfortunately to this point very little light has been shed on the text of Malachi by the materials from Qumran.

Is the book of Malachi poetry or prose? For many years most English speaking scholars have considered it to be prose. The RSV, NEB, and JB translate it as prose. But German scholars often consider it to be a type of poetry. Marti, Sievers, and Nowack emended the text to produce poetic forms (cf. Smith 25). W. Rudolph considers the book a kind of poetry and translates it in verse form without resorting to much emendation. S. R. Driver said, "The style of Malachi is more prosaic than that of the prophets generally, though his sentences often fall into the rythmical parallelism which is such a constant feature in the more elevated oratory of the prophets. He does not possess the eloquence or the imaginative power of some of the older prophets: but his words are always forcible and direct: and the similes and imagery which he uses are effective and to the point" (Driver 297–98). The *Translation* will reflect the "free verse" nature of this book.

The Message of Malachi

Again the prophet's purpose was to assure his people that Yahweh still loved them and was keeping his covenant with them (1:2–5). But he demanded honor, respect, and faithfulness (1:6). The people and priests were not honoring Yahweh. They were dishonoring him with their worship, by their unfaithfulness to marriage vows (2:10–16), by their social injustices (3:5), and by their harsh words bordering on blasphemy (3:13–14). Malachi assures his people that Yahweh knows those who fear him and those who do not. Yahweh calls for his people to repent and return to him (3:7). If they do not return he will come and smite the land with a curse (ban). Since the last word of this book is one of judgment, it should claim the attention of everyone who reads it.

Superscription (1:1)

Translation

[1] *A burden (oracle),*[a] *the word of Yahweh unto Israel, by the hand of Malachi.*[b]

Notes

1.a. משא is often translated "oracle" or "burden." See discussion on Zech 9:1. It is best to read it here as "burden" referring to something the prophet must accept, carry, and deliver to others.

1.b. מלאכי The LXX reads (מלאכו), ἐν χειρὶ ἀγγέλου αὐτοῦ "by (in) the hand of his angel." Tg reads, "by the hand of my angel whose name is called Ezra the scribe."

Form/Structure/Setting

The form of this superscription is similar to that in Hab 1:1; Zech 9:1; 12:1; Nah 1:1; Isa 13:1; 17:1; 19:1. It has three parts: (1) a description of that which follows, "oracle," "burden," "the word of Yahweh"; (2) the recipient of the burden—Israel; and (3) the agent carrying the message—"by the hand of" Malachi. The setting of the superscription is simply that of identifying the source of this literary material. The superscriptions of prophetic books probably are the work of a later editor, in this case one who put the materials of the twelve minor prophets together (cf. Isbell 28; also see my comment on Mic 1:1).

Comment

Scholars have debated whether משא means "burden," or "an utterance." BDB (672) and *CHAL* (217) give both meanings. The ideas are related. The utterance of the prophet was often considered a burden. Jeremiah spoke of God's word as "fire in my bones" (Jer 20:9). Most scholars consider the word משא at the beginning of Zech 9, 12 and Mal 1 as an indication that three floating anonymous oracles were arbitrarily assigned to their present position in the canon. The third and last of these was isolated and given the name of Malachi from a word in 3:1 in order to make twelve minor prophets. All three passages begin with the same three words משא דבר יהוה, but beyond that they are different. Zech 9:1 reads: דבר יהוה בארץ חדרך משא "a burden of the word of Yahweh against the land of Hadrack"; Zech 12:1 reads משא דבר יהוה על-ישראל נאם יהוה "a burden the word of Yahweh upon Israel, oracle of Yahweh"; Mal 1:1 reads משא דבר יהוה אל-ישראל ביד מלאכדי "a burden the word of Yahweh unto Israel by the hand of Malachi." Brevard Childs says that there are "striking differences in both form and function" between the three passages, and there is an indication that they are independent of each other. "The present independent status of Malachi did not arise from an arbitrary decision . . . rather its separate status is deeply rooted in the book's own tradition" (*IOTS* 492).

The second part of the superscription says that it was addressed to Israel. "Israel" was the name for the Northern Kingdom during the time of the divided monarchy. But when Israel fell, the people of Judah took over the name because it was a "dignified religious name" (Rudolph 253). J. M. Myers says that Malachi employs the cultic term Israel which occurs three times (1:1; 2:11; 3:22, Eng. 4:4) whereas Judah and Jerusalem only occur in 2:11 and 3:4 (Myers 102). Brevard Childs notes that the superscription designates the addressee of the book as Israel. "The editors of the final form are consistent in maintaining this perspective throughout the whole composition" (Childs, *IOTS* 494). Childs says that there is no evidence to support the theory of Wellhausen and Sellin that the harsh words of rejection (3:19, Eng. 4:1) were directed to the Samaritans who were outside of Israel. "The prophetic message of Malachi is addressed solely to Israel" (ibid).

Dumbrell sees a very close similarity between Malachi's and Deuteronomy's use of "Israel." These two books are the only books in the OT to begin with an address to "all Israel." (Deut 1:1 uses "all Israel." Mal 1:1 simply reads "Israel.") Malachi ends on a similar note (3:22, Eng 4:4). A similar use of "Israel" can be seen in the books of Ezekiel and Ezra. The name "Israel" occurs 186 times in Ezekiel as opposed to 15 for Judah. "Israel" occurs 24 times in the Ezra narratives while Judah occurs only four times (Dumbrell, *RTR* 35 [1976] 44–45). The emphasis in Malachi on the New Israel, made up of all the tribes, centers around a cleansed temple and a renewed covenant.

"By the hand of" (ביד) is a Hebrew idiom used many times in the OT to indicate the agent through whom Yahweh spoke (1 Sam 28:15; 1 Kgs 12:15; 16:12; 2 Kgs 17:13; 21:10; Hag 1:1; 2:1; Mal 1:1; 1 Chr 11:3; 2 Chr 10:15; 29:25; 36:15; Neh 9:30). Budde argued that this expression was late (*ZAW* 26 [1906] 1–28). Childs (*IOTS* 492) and Beuken (27) seem to agree that this expression is typical of late Hebrew. However, J. Lindblom recalls that the early prophets Elijah and Elisha were "inspired" by "the hand of Yahweh" in an ecstatic experience (1 Kgs 18:46; 2 Kgs 3:15. See Lindblom, *Prophecy in Ancient Israel* 48, 58).

The word מלאכי "my messenger" has been an enigma for centuries. Does it refer to a man's name, or is it a title? The LXX does not read it as "Malachi (my messenger)," but "Malacho, (his messenger)." The Targum reads it "my angel whose name is Ezra the scribe" (cf. Note[b]). Some have considered מלאכי "Malachi" as an abbreviation of a fuller name מלאכיה "Malachiyah," which could mean "Yah is my messenger." That is not very likely. However "Malachiyah" could also mean "messenger of Yah" which would be much more likely. We cannot solve the problem of the name of the author without additional information.

The superscription does not give a definite date or name for the author but it does stake a claim to be an authoritative word of God. Charles Isbell suggests that the term משא in Mal 1:1 means almost precisely what the English word *revelation* means in twentieth-century speech. He asserts that the superscription could be read, "what you are about to read (in this book known as Malachi) is divine revelation משא!" (Isbell 25). Isbell also points out that the superscription says that the divine revelation did not come in a mysterious, unearthly fashion. It came through a person, "by the hand of Malachi." The personality of the prophet was not squelched. "He was allowed to express things his own way" (Isbell 30).

A Dispute about God's Love   (1:2-5)

Bibliography

Baldwin, J. G. "Malachi 1:11 and the Worship of the Nations in the OT." *TB* 23 (1972) 117–24. **Cresson, B. C.** "The Condemnation of Edom." *The Use of the Old*

Testament in the New. W. F. Stinespring's Festschrift. Ed. J. M. Efird. Durham, N.C.: Duke University Press, 1972. 125–48. **Kooy, V. H.** "The Fear and Love of God in Deuteronomy." *Grace Upon Grace.* L. J. Kuyper's Festschrift. Ed. J. Cook. Grand Rapids: Eerdmans, 1975. 106–16. **Thompson, J. A.** "Israel's Haters." *VT* 29 (1979) 200–205. **Toombs, L. E.** "Love and Justice in Deuteronomy." *Int* 19 (1965) 399–411. **Vriezen, T. C.** "How to Understand Malachi 1:11." *Grace Upon Grace,* L. J. Kuyper's Festschrift. Ed. J. Cook. Grand Rapids: Eerdmans, 1975. 128–31.

Translation

2 "*I have loved you,*" *says Yahweh.*   4+3
    But you say, "In what way have you loved us?
  Is not Esau a brother to Jacob,   3+2+2
    oracle of Yahweh?
    And I have loved Jacob.
3 *But Esau I hated,*   2+3+3
  and I have made his mountain a desolation, and his inheritance a dwelling place [a]
    in a desert."
4 *When* [a] *Edom says, "We are beaten down*   3+3
  but we will return and rebuild."
  Thus says Yahweh of hosts.   4+4
  "*They may build but I will demolish.*   2+2
  And they shall call them the wicked country,   4+4
    and the people with whom Yahweh is angry forever." [b]
5 *And your eyes will see, and you will say,*   2+2
  "*Great is Yahweh beyond the border of Israel.*"   2+2

Notes

3.a. לתנות appears to be a fem. pl. form of תנים "jackals" with the prep ל. The word תנות "jackals" occurs in Isa 13:22; Mic 1:8; Lam 4:3 as mas. However the LXX here reads εἰς δόματα which is the equivalent of נות(ל) for "pastures" or "dwelling places of."

4.a. כי is used here with the conditional force "if," or "when."

4.b. עולם is sometimes translated "eternity." It is usually derived from עלם "to hide." But G. R. Driver and H. W. Robinson take it from a root "to be remote," or "farthest time." It usually does not refer to endless duration (cf. James Muilenburg. "The Biblical View of Time," in *Grace Upon Grace* 45).

Form/Structure/Setting

The form is a "prophetic dispute." There are many prophetic disputes in the OT. Some of them are disputes with other prophets (cf. Mic 2:6–11; Jer 28:1–17), and some are disputes with lay persons (Isa 40:27–28; Ezek 12:21–28). The style is often called the question-and-answer or "catechetical" style. Some have called it "Socratic" after the style of the Greek philosopher. The structure of this pericope is simple. The prophet first states a truth, then his disputants (lay persons in this pericope) state their objections by asking a question. Finally the prophet restates his premise and supports it with hard evidence. Some writers think that this device is purely literary. Joyce Baldwin says that it is "extremely unlikely that the words he [Malachi]

puts into the mouth of his opponents were in fact voiced. . . . Malachi reads
the attitudes of his people and intuitively puts their thoughts into words,
so gaining attention before driving home his word from the Lord" (Baldwin
214; cf. Isbell 9). There is no way to determine the precise setting of this
pericope. Lay persons in the sense of "all Israel" are being addressed. A
covenant renewal or New Year festival would be an appropriate setting.

Comment

Malachi begins his book with a message that God still loves Israel. "I
have loved you, says Yahweh." The word love (אהב) is a covenant word. It
is also an election word. God chose Israel because he loved her (Deut 7:8).
Love is peculiarly a Deuteronomic word in the OT (cf. Deut 4:37; 5:10; 6:5;
7:8, 9, 13; 10:12, 15, 18, 19; 11:1, 13, 22; 13:4, Eng. 13:3; 19:9; 21:15, 16;
23:6, Eng. 23:5; 30:16; cf. Toombs, *Int* 19 [1965] 402). Love is a domestic
word. Lawrence Toombs says that love (אהב) "describes the lover's attitude
to his beloved, the father's relationship to his child, and the friend's affection
for his closest companion" (ibid.). Toombs believes that the Deuteronomist
used אהב rather than Hosea's term חסד because of its idea of intensity,
totality, interiority, and its suggestion of a family bond (ibid. 403).

Love (אהב) is often used opposite the word שנא "hate" in the OT as it
is in this pericope (cf. Gen 29:31; Deut 7:10; 21:15; 2 Sam 19:7, Eng. 19:6;
Mic 3:2; Prov 8:36). Love and hate sometimes carry political and religious
overtones (1 Kgs 5:15, Eng. 5:1). In Hosea "lovers" refers to other gods
(Hos 2:7, 9, 12, 14, 15, Eng. 2:5, 7, 10, 12, 13). Enemies are "haters" in
Deut 33:11; 2 Chr 19:2; Lev 26:17 (cf. Thompson, *VT* 29 [1979] 200–05).

It is best to take Malachi's use of the terms "love" and "hate" in vv 2
and 3 as covenant language. When Yahweh says, "I have loved Jacob," he
means, "I chose Jacob," and when he says, "I hated Esau," he means, "I
did not choose Esau." J. M. Myers said, "Jacob was the chosen one; Esau
the rejected one. The usual rendering of the word, *san'e* (=hate), is too strong
here. As the antithetical parallelism appears to indicate, it is the equivalent
of 'not loved' (='not chosen,' 'rejected')" (Myers, *World of the Restoration* 97).
This certainly is election language. "Loved" means chosen and "hated" means
not chosen. But also there is probably an overtone of bitterness here directed
at Edom. Edom's origin is traced to Esau who was the older twin brother
of Jacob. There was a special antipathy between Israel and Edom. Bruce
Cresson, writing in W. F. Stinespring's *Festschrift* (125) says that Professor
Stinespring has explained to several decades of students that one of the characteristics of post-exilic prophecy is a "Damn-Edom" theology. Evidently the
Edomites participated with a furious and vindictive spirit against "Israel" in
the destruction of the temple by Nebuchadrezzar in 587 B.C. It is probably
to this event that the "Damn-Edom" theology is to be attributed. Edom is
condemned in many OT prophetic passages (Obad 1–14; Jer 49:7–22; Amos
1:12; Ezek 25:12–14; 35:1–15; Lam 4:21–22; Joel 3:21; Mal 1:2–5; Isa 21:11–
12; 34:5–17; 63:1–6; Ps 137:7; 60:8–9). In some of these passages (Isa 34
and 63) Edom has become a symbol for all the enemies of Judah (Cresson,
in *Use of the OT* 139). Rex Mason notes that no nation other than Edom is

spoken of in this way in the OT and it is possible that Edom is being used in a "typical" sense symbolizing a "realm of wickedness" on whom God's wrath would fall forever (Mason 141).

V 3 probably refers to some invasion and devastation of Edom by an enemy, but we cannot be certain about the incident. George L. Robinson argues that Edom was weakened by the army of Nebuchadrezzar in 587 (cf. Cresson, in *Use of the OT* 129, 132), but W. F. Lofthouse thinks that some Edomites fought with Nebuchadrezzar against Judah. Whatever their involvement the Edomites incurred the undying hatred of Judah. Edom became too weak to resist the incursion of the Nabatean Arabs into their territory. Evidence from Aramaic-inscribed vessels found at Tell Maskhuta in Lower Egypt suggests that a late sixth or early fifth century B.C. date may be assigned to the Nabatean invasion of Edom (see Rabinowitz, "Aramaic Inscriptions of the Fifth Century B.C.E. from a North Arab Shrine in Egypt," *JNES* 15 [1956] 2, 3). The only conclusive evidence is that Edom had migrated into the Negeb by 312 B.C. because in that year the Nabateans were in control of Petra, a former stronghold of Edom (See Diodorus Siculus, *Bibliotheca Historica* 19, 94; Cresson, in *Use of the OT* 132).

V 4 may reflect the determination of some Edomites to return to Petra to drive out the Nabateans but that never happened. Actually the Nabateans built a remarkable civilization of their own in Edom's former territory which lasted until they were conquered by the Romans in A.D. 106. The Edomites remained in the Negeb and became known as the Idumeans.

"Israel's" attitude toward Edom has been looked upon by some as a narrow nationalistic viewpoint. But v 5 gives us a broader perspective. Commenting on v 5 Baldwin says, "The Lord's domain is not restricted to Israel, says Malachi with irony" (*TB* 23 [1972] 124). "You will see and say, 'Great is Yahweh beyond the border of Israel.'" T. C. Vriezen points to a number of factors in the book of Malachi which indicate a broad aspect to his view of God. For example Malachi's use of the general names El, Elohim, Adonai for God, and such general designations as Father and King (1:6, 9, 14; 2:10; 3:8, 14), and his reference to creation (2:10) point to a God greater than a local deity (*Grace upon Grace* 130). Vriezen also thinks it is remarkable that Malachi speaks of "one God" a term that recalls the *Shema* (Deut 6:4). It reminds one of the thought in Isa 45:14 that Yahweh is God, he alone, and the nations will acknowledge him as the only God. Vriezen says that it is a misunderstanding to contrast the seemingly universalistic view of such passages as Mal 1:11 and 2:10 with the alleged particularism of 1:2–4. Vriezen concludes that "Malachi is anything but a purely particularistic preacher, the comforting words at the beginning of the book do not contrast with the latter message" (Vriezen, in *Grace upon Grace* 131).

Rex Mason thinks the first oracle may not be as comfortable as it has often been understood to be. H. J. Boecher says the introduction (1:1–5) forms not a positive affirmation but "a statement of the opening of a dialogue" ("Bermerkungen zur formsgeschichtlichen Terminologie des Buches Malachi," *ZAW* 78 [1966] 77–80). The reminder of their election may be to emphasize God's freedom to choose or reject. He does not reject arbitrarily, but he does reject those who create a domain for wickedness. Paul quotes 1:2,

3 in a context which stresses the freedom of God to choose or reject whom
he will (Rom 9:13, 18). This seems to be the meaning in 3:24 (Eng. 4:6),
"lest I come and smite the land with a curse."

A Dispute about God's Honor and Fear   (1:6–2:9)

Bibliography

Baldwin, J. "Malachi 1:11 and the Worship of the Nations in the OT." *TB* 23 (1972)
117–24. **Bamberger, B. J.** "Fear and Love of God in the Old Testament." *HUCA* 6
(1929) 39–53. **Devescovi, U.** "L'alleanza di Jahvé con Levi (Mal 2:1–9)." *BibO* 4 (1962)
205–18. **Kooy, V. H.** "The Fear and Love of God in Deuteronomy." *Grace Upon
Grace.* L. J. Kuyper's Festschrift. Ed. J. I. Cook. Grand Rapids: Eerdman's, 1975.
106–16. **Kruse-Blinkenberg, L.** "The Peshitta of the Book of Malachi." *ST* 20 (1966)
87–90. **Rehm, M.** "Das Opfer der Völker nach Mal 1:11." *Lex tua Veritas.* Festschrift
für Herbert Junker: Trier, 1961. 193–96. **Sutcliffe, E. F.** "Malachy's Prophecy of the
Eucharistic Sacrifice." *IER* 5 (1922) 502–13. **Swetnam, J.** "Malachi 1:11: An Interpretation." *CBQ* 31 (1969) 200–209. **Toombs, L. E.** "Love and Justice in Deuteronomy."
Int 19 (1965) 399–411. **Verhoeff, P. A.** "Some Notes on Mal 1:11." *OTWSA* (1966)
163–72. **Vriezen, T. C.** "How to Understand Malachi 1:11." (See Bibliography to
1:2–5).

Translation

6 *"A son honors his* [a] *father and a*	3+2
servant fears [b] *his lord.*	
Then if I am a father where is my honor?	2+2
And if I am a lord, [c] *where is my fear?*	2+2
Yahweh of hosts says	3+4+4
to your priests, despisers of my name.	
But you say, 'In what way have we despised your name?'	
7 *You are offering upon my altar polluted bread.*	4+3
And you say, 'In what way have we polluted you? [a] *'*	
By saying, Yahweh's table?	3+2
We may despise it.	
8 *And when you offer the blind as sacrifice,*	3+2
is it not evil?	
And when you offer the lame and sick,	3+3
is it not evil?	
Offer it please to your governor.	3
Will he be pleased with you,	1+3+3
or will he lift up your face,	
says Yahweh of hosts?	

⁹ *And now, entreat* ᵃ *please the face of God* ᵇ   3+1
   that he might be gracious to us.

Is this from your hand?   3+3+3
   Will he lift up your faces,
     says Yahweh of hosts?

¹⁰ *O,* ᵃ *that one among you would shut the doors*   4+3
   that you might not kindle the fire
     of my altar in vain.

I have no delight in you,   3+3+3
   says Yahweh of hosts,
   and I will not accept an offering
     from your hand.

¹¹ *But* ᵃ *from the rising of the sun even*   3+2+3
   until its going down,

   great is ᵇ *my name among the nations,*   3+4+3
and in every place   2+3+2
   an oblation ᶜ *is offered*

to my name—a pure offering,
because my name is great among the nations,   3+3
says Yahweh of hosts.

¹² *But you are profaning me* ᵃ *by saying,*   3+1
   the table of the Lord is polluted,   4+3
     it and its fruit ᵇ *are despised.*

¹³ *And you say, 'Behold what a nuisance.* ᵃ '   3+2
   And you ᵇ *puff at it,*
     says Yahweh of hosts.

And you bring in the torn   2+2+2
   and the lame; and the sick
     you bring as an offering.

Shall I accept it from your hand, says Yahweh?   3+2
¹⁴ *Cursed be the cheater*   2+2
   when there is in his flock a male,
   and he sacrifices the blemished to   2+2
     the Lord.

I am a great king,   4+3+3
   says Yahweh of hosts
and my name is feared among the nations.

2:1 *"And now, O priests, this commandment is for you.*

² *If you will not hear,*   2+3
   and if you will not set it to heart
to give glory to my name,   3+3
   says Yahweh of hosts,
then I will send on you the curse.   3+2
   And I will curse your blessings.
Indeed I have cursed them,   2+4
   because you do not set it to heart.

³ *Behold I am rebuking* ᵃ *your seed,*ᵇ   4+3
    and I will smear offal ᶜ *on your face,*
the offal of your festivals,   2+3
    and he ᵈ *will carry you to it.*
⁴ *And you shall know that I sent*   4+2
    this commandment,
*that my covenant with Levi should be maintained,*ᵃ   3+3
    says Yahweh of hosts.
⁵ *My covenant was with him.*   3+2+3
    Life and peace,
    I gave them to him in fear and he feared me.
And before my name   2+2
    he was in awe.
⁶ *True teaching was in his mouth,*   4+3
    and wrong was not found on his lips.
    With peace and uprightness he walked   4+3
    with me,
    and he turned many from iniquity.
⁷ *Because the lips of a priest should guard knowledge,*   3+3+4
    and they should seek instruction from his mouth,
    because he is a messenger of Yahweh of hosts.
⁸ *But you have turned from the way.*   3+3
    You have caused many to stumble by ᵃ *your teaching.*
You have corrupted the covenant of Levi,   3+3
    says Yahweh of hosts.
⁹ *So I have made you despised and abased*   3+3
    before all the people   5+3
in as much as you have not kept my ways
and have shown partiality in your teaching.''

Notes

6.a. Read אביו "his father" for אב "father" with Syr and Tg.

6.b. Some LXX MSS add φοβηθήσεται "fears."

6.c. The pl. אדונים is probably a pl. of majesty (GKC § 124 i; Gen 39:2; 42:30; Deut 10:17; Isa 19:4; Hos 12:15; Ps 136:3).

7.a. גאלנוך "we have polluted you," is often read גאלנוה "we have polluted it" with LXX and Tg. The first meaning of גאל is "redeem" but a second meaning is "pollute" or "soil." It is similar to געל.

9.a. חלה in the piel often means "appease" or "stroke the face" of God as here (Zech 7:2; 8:21; 1 Kgs 13:6) and man (Ps 45:13).

9.b. אל "God."

10.a. מי גם־בכם "who among you" is used idiomatically in the optative mood to express a wish, "O that one among you . . . ."

11.a. כי is used as an adversative (cf. Swetnam, *CBQ* 31 [1969] 200).

11.b. No verb is expressed, hence the debate about pres. or fut. tense.

11.c. מקטר is a hophal pl. probably used here as a substantive.

12.a. אותו "it" is one of the eighteen *tiqqune sopherim* changed from אותי "me."

12.b. וניבו נבזה אכלו is difficult. ניב is used one time in Isa 57:19 metaphorically of the fruit of one's lips. It is not in the Tg or Syriac here and some Heb. MSS (Chary 246). Many take נִיב here to be a dittography of the next word נבזה "despised." אכלו "Its fruit" is unnecessary if נִיב is retained.

13.a. מתלאה a hapax. מה-תלאה "what a nuisance." *CHAL* 222.

13.b. והפחתם "you (pl.) blow" from נפח. Some LXX MSS have ἐξεφύσησα αὐτά "I blew on it." Syr supports this reading (cf. Kruse-Blinkenberg, *ST* 20 [1966] 95).

2:3.a גער qal pt. "rebuking" (cf. Nah 1:4; Zech 3:2). LXX reads ἀφορίζω = גדע "to cut off," "separate."

3.b. הזרע "the seed," or with different vowels, "the arm."

3.c. פרש "contents of the stomach" of animals (*CHAL* 299).

3.d. וכשא אתכם אליו is difficult. It does not fit the context well. Is Yahweh the subject of נשא or an indefinite "he"? "Yahweh will take you up" or "someone will take you up." Most translations read אליו "to it," but what is the "it"—a dung heap? Rudolph changes אליו to אלה "curse" with Num 5:21; Jer 29:18, and reads "one will take up a curse against you" (Rudolph 260). The LXX reads, "I will take you to the same."

4.a. להיות a qal inf. const. of היה "to be." Budde, Horst and others proposed a reading מהיות "from to be." The NEB and JB have adopted this reading, "My covenant with Levi falls to the ground." היה in the niphal can mean "come to an end" (Dan 2:1; 8:27) but the niphal is not used here. G. R. Driver says that היה is used as = to נפל "fall" (*JTS* 39 [1938] 399). cf. Prov 14:35.

8.a. בתורה "by the teaching." Peshitta has "against the law" (cf. Kruse-Blinkenberg, *ST* 20 [1966] 98).

Form/Structure/Setting

This is the longest section in the book of Malachi. It contains twenty-three out of a total of fifty-five verses in the book. It is a dispute with the priests. One verse is directed toward the laity (1:14). The passage begins with a statement of a premise that would have been considered universally true in the Ancient Near East. "A son honors (imperfect suggests repeated action) his father and a servant his lord." Since "his" is not in the text before father, the statement may mean that any son honors any father. But the implication is made that Yahweh is father and Lord to Israel and the people neither honor nor fear him (1:6b). This charge is addressed directly to the priests who are described as the ones who all the time (participle) are despising Yahweh's name. But the priests ask for specific evidence of their despising the name of God (1:6c). Such specific evidence is forthcoming in vv 7–8. They are accused of polluting the altar of God by offering polluted food on it. The nature of the pollution is spelled out as offering blind, lame, and sick animals as sacrifice, a practice directly prohibited in Deut 15:21; Lev 22:20–25. Then the prophet suggests that the Persian governor would not accept such animals as gifts or as payment of taxes (1:8c). V 9 is probably irony. The prophet advises the priests "to stroke the face of God and it may be he will be gracious to us." But that is not likely to happen. He will not accept such gifts or persons who offer such gifts. V 10 calls for closing the doors of the temple so that such a farce or travesty of worship will cease. V 11 suggests that much pagan worship is more acceptable than the worship of these priests in Jerusalem. Vv 12 and 13 repeat the charges against the priests and add that the priests consider their job a weariness or a nuisance.

The punishment phase of the pericope may begin with v 14 in which the layman who is a cheat is cursed. This verse may be a late addition to the book since it is the only reference to the laity in this pericope (cf. Chary

247–48). The authority for the judgment comes from Yahweh who is the great king. "Great king" is a phrase found in the old Hittite treaties referring to the Hittite emperor. The second part of the pericope is the announcement of judgment on the priests (2:1–9). If they do not hear and obey the words of warning (1:6–14), they will be cursed (2:2). Their person will be desecrated (2:3) and they will be removed from office (2:3).

How do the actions and character of the present priesthood compare to the earlier priests of the house of Levi? God made a covenant with Levi and those early priests served Yahweh and the people well (2:4–7). But the present priesthood has apostasized (2:9) and has become abased in the eyes of God and the people (2:9).

The form is a prophetic dispute, but the disputants have very little to say. They ask questions in 1:6, 7 and they say "What a nuisance" in 1:13. But in the other material either Yahweh or the prophet is issuing warnings, reviewing past blessings or failures, and announcing imminent judgment on the priests. The setting might have been a feast day in the rebuilt temple.

Comment

The second section of Malachi takes up another significant concept from Deuteronomy. The first pericope (1:2–5) was addressed to "all Israel" and dealt with the theme of "love" which is very prominent in Deuteronomy. Now the second section takes up the theme of "fear," another prominent theme in Deuteronomy. Some form of the word "fear" (ירא) occurs seven times in Malachi (1:6, 14; 2:5[twice]; 3:5, 16, 20). Another word for "fear" (נחת) "awe" (RSV) occurs in 2:5. B. J. Bamberger studied the words for "fear" in the OT and classified them according to their usage. He said, "Fear and love of God refer not so much to an inward emotional state as to some type of overt action" (Bamberger, *HUCA* 6 [1929] 39). Bamberger says that the fear and love of God as motives for righteous conduct are absent in the biblical literature. He cites Ps 130:4 and Exod 20:20 as examples of the term "fear" not meaning terror. In Malachi 1:6 "fear" is parallel to "honor," or "respect" which should be demonstrated by keeping the law of sacrifice. In 1:14 "fear" is used in connection with pagan worship. Two words, "fear" and "awe," are used in 2:5 describing the fear and awe Levi had toward God. In 3:5 "fear" of the Lord includes ethical conduct. Samuel Terrien said that the fear of God in the language of Hebrew religion meant supreme devotion (Terrien, *The Elusive Presence* 83).

The word "honor" (כבד) is parallel to "fear" in 1:6. The root כבד means "to be heavy, weighty, burdensome, honored." It is the word used in the fifth commandment, "Honor your father and mother" (Exod 20:12; Deut 5:16). That commandment might have been the basis of the premise stated in 1:6. The word כָּבֵד not only means "honor" but it also means "glory." It is characteristic of priestly theology (Exod 14:4, 17–18; 24:16–17; 33:18; 40:34–35). Glory stands for the awe-inspiring presence of God.

If "glory" is a priestly word, "name" is a Deuteronomic word. In Deuteronomy the name of God stands for his presence (Deut 12:5, 11, 21). The word "name" (שם) occurs eight times in this passage (1:6, 6, 11 [three times],

14; 2:2, 5) and is implied in v 12. Malachi accuses the priests of despising (בזה) and polluting (חלל) Yahweh's name (1:6, 7, 12). The word "despise" (בזה) means "to treat wickedly, unrighteously" (Görg, *TDOT* II, 60). It means "disdain" in Prov 1:7; 11:12; 15:20; 23:9, 22, and "contempt" in 2 Sam 12:9, 10. The opposite of "despise" frequently is "fear" (ירא), Prov 13:13; "to be kind" (חנן), Prov 14:21; "to be glad" (שמח), Prov 15:20; "to hear" (שמע); "to honor" (כבד), 1 Sam 2:30; and "to keep" (שמר). In Ezek 22:8 Jerusalem has despised (בזה) the holy things and profaned (חלל) the sabbath. When Malachi spells out how the priests have despised Yahweh's name, he points to the polluted bread and unclean animals being offered on the table or altar of God (1:8, 13), and to the priest's indifference and disrespect for the things of God (1:7, 13). The result of the priests' despising (בזה) Yahweh's name will be that he will make them despised (בזה) and abased (שפלים) before all people (2:9). The root (שפל) means "to be low," "sink down," "to be humble or abased" physically or socially. It is the root of the word Shephelah, "the lowland" (1 Kgs 10:27).

The attitude of the present priesthood toward the name of Yahweh stands in stark contrast to the previous attitude of Levi (early priests) and the Gentiles. Levi "feared Yahweh" and stood in awe (נחת) of his name (2:5), and the Gentiles regard God's name as great and fear him (1:11, 14). The present priests should give glory (כבד) to Yahweh's name and examine their conscience, "lay to heart" their attitude toward God and his worship.

The word "governor" (פחת) probably is a loan word from Akkadian. It is used mainly to refer to governors in the time of Jeremiah (51:28, 57) and Ezekiel (23:23), and the Persian governors in the time of Haggai (1:1; 2:21); Nehemiah (2:7, 9; 5:14); Esther (3:12; 8:9; 9:3). The use of the word here in Malachi makes it clear that the province of Samaria and/or Judea was being ruled by a governor appointed by the Great King of Persia. The governor might have been a Jew or a Samaritan but his authority came from Persia. This entire pericope deals with the proper attitude or response to authority: son-father, servant-lord, vassal-governor. Malachi accuses the priests with having more fear, respect, honor for the governor than they have for Yahweh.

In 1:10, Malachi expresses a personal wish on behalf of Yahweh that someone among the priests would have the courage and fortitude to shut the doors of the temple and not light the fire on Yahweh's altar, because the ritual that was being carried on there was not pleasing to God. "Doors" probably do not refer to the doors of the temple proper, but to the doors between the court of the priests and the great court (2 Chr 4:9). If these doors were closed no offerings could be made. Rex Mason comments that "excommunication should be their judgment" (Mason 144). The Qumran community picked up Mal 1:10 in its polemic against the temple. The Jerusalem priesthood is derisively called "closers of the doors" (cf. Dumbrell, 45 n. 12; Baldwin 227).

1:11 is one of the most difficult verses in the OT to interpret. The text is not clear. Two hophal participles (מקטר "is kindled," and מגש "is offered") occur together without a connecting word between them. The expression "my name (is) great among the nations" occurs twice in the verse without a verb. The conjunction 1 "and" before "pure sacrifice" is almost certainly out of place.

Another problem with 1:11 is its relation to its context. Is 1:6–14 a unity? In vv 6–10 the prophet criticizes the priests for accepting and offering inferior sacrifices. He says in v 10 that it would be better to close the doors of the temple and offer no sacrifices at all than to do what they were doing. In vv 12–14 there is a denunciation of those who bring such inferior animals when in some cases they have acceptable sacrificial animals in the stalls. Some regard 1:11 as a swing verse between 6–10 and 12–14. Vriezen suggests that it could have been an independent liturgical text, a kind of doxology put into Yahweh's mouth as self-glorification (Vriezen, *Grace upon Grace* 129; cf. Amos 4:13; 5:8–9; 9:6).

Some scholars have seen 1:11 as contradictory to the narrow particularistic view of 1:2–5 and have considered it along with vv 12–14 a later addition (F. Horst 265–67; K. Elliger 194–95; C. Kuhl, *The Prophets of Israel* 167–68). But it is not necessary to consider 1:11–14 as a late addition to this book or as a contradiction to the earlier passages (1:2–5). Vriezen wrote, "It is a misunderstanding to contrast the universalistic view of the former with the alleged purely particularistic character of the latter. To interpret Mal 1:2–5 in this way is to neglect the most important element in the text, namely, that the prophet is involved in a dispute with his compatriots and addresses persons among his people who were denying the love of God for Israel and the reality of any manifestation of his grace" (Vriezen, *Grace upon Grace* 131). Rex Mason says,

> The verse should not therefore be rejected as secondary because its "universalism" contradicts 1:3. It is not picturing a universal conversion to Yahwism any more than 1:3 is suggesting an outright rejection of all other nations. Neither should it be excluded because it interrupts the connection between verses 6–10 and 12–14. The whole oracle falls into two parts, verses 6–11 and verses 12–14, in each of which similar statements of the charges against the priests lead to a similar climax. The repetition is probably for emphasis (p. 145).

One might classify the various interpretations of 1:11 as follows: (a) the early Roman Catholic view that it refers to a prediction of the mass; (b) the view that it refers to the Jews of the Diaspora; (c) the syncretistic view that it refers to worship of the high God in all religions; (d) the metaphorical view that understands the prophet to be saying that some pagan worship is better than the present adulterated worship in the temple in Jerusalem; (e) the view of imminent eschatology.

Joseph Packard wrote in *Lange's Commentary on the Minor Prophets: Malachi* (p. 4). "The Church of Rome, it is well known, has found in the 'pure offering' of Malachi 1:11, its principal proof-text of the doctrine of the Mass." Carroll Stuhlmueller wrote in *JBC* (400), "In view of the words of the Council of Trent (DB 1742), A. Gelin (BJ65) regards as 'official' the interpretation that Malachi refers here to the perfect sacrifice of the Messianic era. We hold that the text looks forward to a ritual sacrifice of the Messianic age, a fulfillment and perfection of the Mosaic rite which will be offered by all men and accepted by God." E. F. Sutcliffe (*CCHS* 702) wrote: "The word 'for' shows the universal and pure oblation is to replace the existing Jewish sacrifices, a fact which of itself shows that Malachias is not thinking of any existing sacrifices but of a future Messianic age" (also see E. F. Sutcliffe, S. J., "Malachy's Prophecy of the Eucharistic Sacrifice" *Irish Ecclesiastical Record* 5 [1922] 502–13). A more recent Roman Catholic author has taken a different approach to 1:11. James Swetnam says, "Catholic commentators have frequently understood the text as a reference to the sacrifice of the Mass. Whatever may be said about this interpretation from the standpoint of Christian exegesis of the Old Testament (and the present writer suspects that quite a bit can be said), this interpretation could hardly have been the original one at the time the text was written. . . . Since the acceptance of the offerings made outside Jerusalem is contrasted with Yahweh's refusal . . . to accept the offerings made at Jerusalem, the natural inference is that the offerings made outside of Jerusalem are also contemporaneous" (Swetnam, *CBQ* 31 [1969] 203). He then argues for a metaphorical interpretation of the "pure oblation" as referring to prayer and the study of the law in Jewish synagogues in the time of Malachi (205–07).

So Swetnam introduces a second general interpretation of 1:11. It refers to the worship of the Jews of the Diaspora. The *Midrash Rabbah* of Num 13:4 interprets Mal 1:11 as referring to the prayer of the Diaspora (ibid 205). A comment in the Babylonian Talmud based on Mal 1:11 refers to the study of the law. "R. Samuel b. Nahmani said in the name of R. Jonathan, 'This refers to the scholars who devote themselves to the study of the Torah in whatever place they are. God says, I account it unto them as though they burnt and presented offerings to my name" (Swetnam, *CBQ* 31 [1967] 207; "Sacrifice (Jewish)," *ERE* 24–29). It is true that Jews were probably scattered from Persia to southern Egypt in Malachi's day. Remember the Jewish community at Elephantine in Egypt. But their worship was far from orthodox. Nothing is said in 1:11 about Jewish worship outside Israel. The expression "My name is great among the nations" must refer to Gentile worship (cf. Vriezen, in *Grace upon Grace* 133).

A third general interpretation of 1:11 is that it refers to a syncretistic view of the worship of the high God in all religions. Joyce Baldwin critiques this view very well. She says that on the face of it this verse appears to express divine approval of heathen worship "and indeed this is the way it has been taken by the majority of interpreters during the last hundred years" (Baldwin, *TB* 23 [1972] 117). She lists among those holding this view J. M. P. Smith, Hitzig, Wellhausen, C. C. Torrey, Nowack, Marti, Chief Rabbi J. H. Hertz, Rabbi Eli Cashdan, R. H. Pfeiffer, and R. C. Dentan. But Baldwin marshalls considerable evidence from the OT to show that pagan worship is never considered acceptable to Yahweh. She deals with Elijah's contest with the prophets of Baal on Mt. Carmel (1 Kgs 18:19–46) and concludes by saying that if the last three verses (Mal 3:22–24, Eng. 4:4–6) are an integral part of Malachi's book, "the prophet continues his uncompromising stand for exclusive witness to the one true God" (ibid. 119). One wonders what Baldwin would do with such passages as Deut 4:19b; 29:26; 32:8–9 RSV.

A fourth interpretation is a real possibility. This view suggests that the prophet is speaking metaphorically or using a hyperbole. R. H. Pfeiffer says, "the sacrifices that the heathen tender their gods are purer in his sight than these polluted offerings in Jerusalem (1:11)—an instance of religious liberalism unparalleled in the Old Testament; the author would have undoubtedly repudiated the implications of this utterance in a calmer and more reflective mood" (Pfeiffer, *IOT* 613). Johannes Blau says that the verse is meant "to accentuate the faithlessness of Israel; compared with Israel, the heathen are upright worshippers of Yahweh" (J. Blau, *The Missionary Nature of the Church* [London: Lutterworth, 1962] 142). I. G. Matthews says, "that he (Malachi) was ready to acknowledge that heathen who were sincere in their worship were more acceptable to Yahweh than the Jew who with greater light was indifferent to his heritage seems to be the point of this verse" (19). T. M. Bennett takes essentially the same position: "The prophet's purpose of course was not to praise the heathen in his worship but to shame the leaders of his own people" (Bennett 378). Rex Mason expresses the same view. He says, "It is interesting that no sacrifice involving blood is mentioned, but incense and cereal offerings. . . . The reference may therefore be to the fact that when men anywhere acknowledge the mystery of creation and give thanks for it they are in fact acknowledging the greatness of the Creator's name (cf. v 14b). Such worship, even if offered in ignorance of Yahweh's name, is more acceptable to him as offerings and gifts in their genuineness than the blood sacrifices offered by the priests in the temple in a spirit of indifference" (Mason 145).

One other interpretation of 1:11 which seems to be growing in popularity is the view of an imminent coming of the kingdom of God. Joyce Baldwin and T. C. Vriezen may be considered advocates of this view. Baldwin points out that the expression "from the rising of the sun to its setting" in Pss 50:1; 113:3 and in Isa 45:6; 59:19 is in contexts which look toward an eschatological demonstration of the Lord's person to the whole inhabited earth. "The prophet has in mind, not exceptions or limited groups, but large numbers, scattered over the earth" (Baldwin, *TB* 23 [1972] 122). Baldwin believes that the two hophal participles are participles of the immediate future. She says, "My contention is that the prophet was thinking of an imminent future event which was sure to happen" (ibid. 124).

T. C. Vriezen (in *Grace upon Grace* 132) also believes that 1:11 is best understood as a reference to the nearness of the revelation of God's kingdom which is already in the process of realization among the nations. He cites Morton Smith's article in which he points to Naaman, Jonah, Solomon's prayer (1 Kgs 8:41–43) and Isa 56:6–7 as evidence of foreigners converting to the worship of Yahweh (cf. M. Smith, *Palestinian Parties and the Politics that Shaped the Old Testament* [New York: Columbia University Press, 1971] 93–94). However, Vriezen does not share Smith's syncretistic view.

Vriezen agrees with Elliger that the messenger in 3:1 and in 1:10 is Malachi. "The prophet realizes that he is being called upon to prepare his people for the imminent coming of Yahweh, as is evident from 3:1a. . . . He is the messenger sent by Yahweh to prepare the way" (Vriezen, *Grace upon Grace* 132). The preparatory mission reminds one of the role of the messenger in Isa 40:3; 57:14; 62:10, except that there the preparation was for salvation. Here the preparation is for judgment and salvation.

Vriezen concludes his discussion of 1:11 by comparing Malachi with the Qumran community. He says that both lived in expectation of the nearness of God's kingdom, both emphasized the ideas of election and community, and both came into conflict with the priests of Jerusalem. But there are some important differences between them also. The Qumran community was a completely introverted community, whereas Malachi evidently remained open to the world outside Israel. Thus he said of Yahweh, "My name (is) great among the nations." Vriezen says that Dr. Verhoef is justified in referring in this connection to John 4:20–24. The same point can be seen in Matt 8:5–13; Acts 10 and following and Rom 1–3. "Thus, from a *Christian theological* point of view, there is some reason to place the collection of prophetic books at the end of the Old Testament canon (even though this order is no older than the reformation), so that the prophets and especially the last prophet, Malachi—are linked with the Gospels of the New Testament" (Vriezen *Grace upon Grace* 135).

Vv 12–14 are largely a repetition of the charges against the priests in 6–10. Again they are accused of polluting and despising Yahweh's table (v 12). But a new charge is leveled against the priests in v 13. They are accused of being bored with their work. They say, "What a nuisance (or weariness)!" They "sniff," "blow" at "it" (or "me"). They turn up their nose at Yahweh. The MT has אוֹתוֹ "at it," but the rabbis said that the original reading was אוֹתִי "at me" (God). Baldwin says that this is the notion of "cheap grace," summed up before that phrase was coined by Heine, "God will forgive me, it's his job" (cf. Baldwin 231).

In v 8 the sacrifices were unacceptable because the animals were blind, lame, or sick. Here (v 13b) the animals are torn, lame, or sick. "Torn" (גָּזוּל) is a qal pass. part. and refers to animals killed by wild beasts. Such animals were unfit for human consumption and sacrifice (Exod 22:30, Eng. 22:31; Lev 17:15).

1:14 speaks about a lay person or anyone who makes a vow to God while bringing some petition to him that if God grants his request he will offer a sacrifice of thanksgiving. Many psalms contain petitions and vows (Pss 7:6, 17; 35:17, 18; 54:1, 6; 56:1, 12; 57:1, 9). In Lev 22:18–20 the animal required for such a votive offering was a male without blemish of bulls, sheeps, or goats. However when the petition was granted the worshiper was often tempted to offer a cheap substitute for a sacrifice (Ps 76:11). The person who resorted to such a scheme was a "cheat" and was placed under the curse of Yahweh (Deut 27:26).

Yahweh was "the great king," the enforcer of the curse on anyone who cheated in paying his vows. In the ancient Hittite treaties their kings were often identified as "I . . . the great king." Israel did not often use the term מֶלֶךְ "king" in her early history to refer to Yahweh, possibly because other nations (Moab and Amon) used it to refer to their gods. However, Eichrodt points to some OT references, which may be dated early, that refer to Yahweh as King (cf. Num 23:21; 24:7; Exod 15:18; Deut 33:5; Eichrodt, *OTT* 1, 195). Other possibly early passages point to an idea of God as King (1 Sam 12:12; Ps 24:7–10; Judg 8:23; 1 Sam 8:7; 1 Kgs 22:19; Isa 6:5). The ark of the covenant is called Yahweh's throne (1 Sam 4:4; 2 Sam 6:2; 2 Kgs 19:15; Pss 80:1; 99:1; Jer 14:21; 17:12). There are a number of references to Yahweh as king in the Psalms (5:3, Eng. 5:2; 29:10, 48:3, Eng. 48:2; 68:25, Eng. 68:24; 74:12; 84:4, Eng. 84:3). The enthronement Psalms refer to Yahweh as king (47:3, 7, 8, 9, Eng. 2, 6, 7, 8; 93:1–2; 95:3; 96:10; 97:1; 98:6; 99:1). The classical prophets make little use of the title "king" for Yahweh (cf. Mic 2:13; 4:7; Obad 21; Jer 8:19; 10:10). Eichrodt says that the understanding of God's kingship underwent a creative development in such passages as Mal 1:14; Pss 103:19; 145:11–13. They refer to a universal reign of God, but the new note in them is that the universal kingdom is not so much a hope but a present reality. "It is this present reality which effectively orders the world here and now; it is to this that man has to bring himself into obedience" (Eichrodt, *OTT* 1, 199).

2:1–9 specify the terms of the judgment on the priests. Their persons, blessings and perhaps their offspring will be cursed (RSV v 3). Again the reason for the curse is the priests' attitude toward Yahweh and his service. They have not "set it to heart" (v 2). This expression reminds one of the words of Haggai (1:5, 7; 2:15, 18). The priests had not "glorified Yahweh's name." The words הנני גער לכם את-הזרע have been translated and interpreted in various ways. KJV and the RV take the words literally, "Behold I am rebuking for your seed," understanding seed to refer to grain or harvest. NAS and RSV understand זרע to mean "seed" in the sense of descendant. NEB and others change גער with the LXX to גדע "to cut off," and make זרע with different vowels read, "arm"—"I am cutting off your arm." The last clause in v 3 is difficult. It may mean "he will bear you (pl.) up to it (the dung heap)." See note 3.d. for a discussion of this clause.

The meaning of 2:4 is also debatable. Did Yahweh warn the priests to call them to repentance so that his covenant with Levi "might continue" (להיות)? Or was his warning to announce that his covenant with Levi had fallen to the ground (מהיות cf. note 3.d.)? S. R. Driver said, " 'Be,' it seems, must have the force of *continue* or *'be maintained'* " (Driver 309). G. R. Driver said that היה means "to fall" here and in 1 Sam 1:8; Prov 14:35 (G. R. Driver, *JTS* 39 [1938] 399). "Be maintained" is the best reading.

Another question in 2:4 is: what is meant by the covenant with Levi? Nothing is said in the Pentateuch about a covenant with Levi. There is a reference to a "covenant of peace" with Phineas in Num 25:12, but that covenant was not made with the Levites as a whole. Most writers believe the reference here is to Moses' blessing of Levi (Deut 33:8–11). The Deuteronomic materials allow all Levites to function as priests (cf. Deut 17:9; 18:1; Jer 33:21; Neh 13:29), while the priestly materials recognize only the sons of Zadok as priests (Num 16:40; Ezek 44:15).

Yahweh promised Levi "life and peace," and Levi and/or the priests were to fear and reverence Yahweh (2:5). Both Yahweh and the early priests kept their covenant. Levi must be a personification of the early Israelite priesthood. "True teaching was in his mouth." He walked with God in peace and uprightness and he turned many away from iniquity (2:6). Is it possible that the "many" here refer to a proto-eschatological group found in Isa 53:11; Dan

12:2–4, 10; the Qumran materials 1QS 6:8; Mk 10:45? (For a discussion of the "many" in the DSS, see F. F. Bruce, *Second Thoughts on the Dead Sea Scrolls* [London: Paternoster Press, 1956] 105.)

Malachi thought that the primary role of the priest was to "guard," "treasure," "conserve," or "keep" the knowledge of God. The knowledge of God should be kept true and pure from one generation to another not just for the priests but for the people as well. The priests were the guardians and instructors of the knowledge of God. A priest was a "messenger of God" (2:7), but not in the same sense a prophet was. God revealed his message to the prophet and the prophet was to proclaim it. The priest was the messenger of God in the sense that he was the guardian and teacher of a body of religious knowledge.

But the priests of Malachi's day no longer walked with God. They had turned aside from the way (2:8). They no longer turned many from iniquity. Instead they had caused many to stumble by their instruction or the lack of it. They had corrupted their covenant with Yahweh. The word "corrupted" here is different from "pollute" (1:12) and "profane" (1:12). This word means "corrupt" (Gen 6:12), "destroy" (Mal 3:11). Since the priests had despised Yahweh he will make them despised and abased before all the people. The priests had not kept or guarded the "way" of Yahweh and they had not treated all people the same way.

A Dispute about Faithlessness (2:10–16)

Bibliography

Adinolfi, A. "Il ripudio secondo Mal 2:14–16." *BeO* 12 (1970) 246–56. **Ahlstrom, G. W.** *Joel and the Temple Cult of Jerusalem.* Leiden: E. J. Brill, 1971. 49–50. **Althann, R.** "Malachi 2:13–14." *Biblica* 58 (1977) 418–21. **Hvidberg, F. F.** *Weeping and Laughter in the Old Testament.* Leiden: E. J. Brill, 1962. 120–23. **Myers, J. M.** *The World of the Restoration.* Englewood Cliffs, N.J.: Prentice-Hall, Inc., 1968. 96–102. **Rudolph, W.** "Zu Malachi 2:10–16." *ZAW* (1981) 85–90. **Schreiner, S.** "Mischehen-Ehebruch-Ehescheidung: Betrachtunges zu Malachi 2:10–16." *ZAW* 91 (1979) 207–28. **Torrey, C. C.** "The Prophecy of Malachi." *JBL* 17 (1898) 1–15. **Tosato, A.** "Il Ripudio: Delitto e Pena (Mal 2:10–16)." *Biblica* 59 (1978) 548–53. **Vaccari, A.** "Matrimonio e divorzio (Mal 2:15, 16)." *CC* 114 (1963) 357–58. **Wolmarans, H. P.** "What does Malachi say about Divorce?" (Africaans) *HTS* 22 (1967) 46–47.

Translation

[10] *Is there not one father for all of us?*   4+4
   Did not one God create us?
Why are we each faithless to his brother,   4+3
   profaning the covenant of our fathers?

¹¹ *Judah has been faithless*   2+2+2

   and an abominable thing has been done in Israel and in Jerusalem,

      because Judah has profaned   3+4+3

       the holy ^a *place of Yahweh which he loves,*

     and has married the daughter ^b *of a foreign god.*

¹² *May Yahweh cut off the man who does this,*   5+2

    the one who is awake and answers, ^a

   from the tents of Jacob,   2+2+2

    and who offers a gift ^b *to Yahweh of hosts.*

¹³ *And this you also* ^a *do,*   3+4+2

    you cover ^b *the altar of Yahweh with tears,*

      weeping and groaning,

^c *because he [Yahweh] will not turn toward the offering any more*   4+3

   or receive it with favor from your hand.

¹⁴ *But you say, "Why?"*   2

    Because Yahweh has witnessed between you   4+3+4

     and the wife of your youth

    with whom you have been faithless.

    Yet she is your companion   2+2

    and the wife of your covenant.

¹⁵ *Did* ^a *he not make one?*   2+3

    The (last) remnant of (the) Spirit (belongs) to him.

    And why does the One   2+3

     seek a godly seed?

    So guard yourselves in your spirit,   2+3

    and stop ^b *being faithless with the wife of your youth.*

¹⁶ *"Because I* ^a *hate divorce,* ^b   2+4

    says Yahweh God of Israel,

   And he (who) covers his garment with violence,   3+3

    says Yahweh of hosts.

    So guard yourselves in your spirit   2+2

    and do not be faithless."

Notes

11.a. The word קדש can mean "holy place," "holy thing," "holy one," or "holiness." Here it probably refers to the holy place or temple.

11.b. בת־אל נכר "daughter of a foreign god." This is the only time this expression occurs in the OT. Ahlstrom says that בת־אל נכר is parallel to the phrase בני אלים "and we could assume a goddess behind this phrase, a goddess that Judah is said to have married." If the prophet had meant to designate foreign women, "he would have used the phrase נשים נכריות" (Ahlstrom, *Joel and the Temple Cult* 49). However the Moabites are referred to as the "sons and daughters of Chemosh" (Num 21:29). Israelites are called "sons and daughters of Yahweh" (Deut 32:19).

12.a. The words עֵר וְעֹנֶה are very difficult to interpret. They are both qal act. part. (עֵר from עוּר), and literally mean "awake and answering." But what can such an expression mean when speaking about a person whom Yahweh cuts off? The KJV followed the Vg and read "the master and the scholar," assuming that the reference is to the rote learning of a pupil from his teacher. The RV translates the words literally "him that waketh and him that answers," referring to the sentries or watchmen making their rounds around the tents of Jacob (S. R.

Driver 314). The NEB translates them "nomads or settlers." James Barr discusses עֹנֶה in terms of "stay in place." The two words together could mean "gad about, stay at home" meaning "everyone" (Barr, *Comparative Philology and the Text of the Old Testament* [Oxford: Clarendon Press, 1968] 165, 243, 250, 333). The RSV emends the text and reads עֵד "witness" for עֵר. D. R. Jones says that a better reading which would also call for a slight emendation would be "Er and Onan," the sons of Judah and the Canaanite woman (Gen 38:2–4) both of whom were killed by the Lord (38:7, 10). "These would then be types of children born of the union of Judah with the daughter of a strange god" (Jones 195).

12.b. The word מנחה may mean "cereal offering or gift."

13.a. Robert Althann suggests on the basis of similar Ugaritic forms that זאת שנית be read as two nouns "indignity, gnashing of teeth." S. R. Driver (315) suggests שנית means lit. "a second thing," "again."

13.b. כסות is an inf. const. translated here as imperf. "to cover."

13.c. מאין עוד פנות The prep. מן can mean "because" (cf. *CHAL* 267). אין "there is not." עוד means "again." פנות is a qal inf. cst. of פנה "to face, or turn toward."

15.a. The expression ולא אחד עשה is very difficult. It is best to take it as a question, "Did he not make one?" D. R. Jones (196) reads these three words "not one has done." Schreiner and Tosato read לא אחד "no one."

15.b. אל-יבגד The אל can be the present negative, "stop being faithless."

16.a. שנא "he hates" should be read שנאתי "I hate." Rudolph takes it as a part. שנא.

16.b. שלח lit. means "sending (out)." This word is used of divorcing a wife in Deut 21:14. A harsher word (גרש) is used in Lev 21:7. The word generally translated "divorce" (כריתות), lit. "a cutting off," is found in Deut 24:1; Isa 50:1; Jer 3:8.

Form/Structure/Setting

The form is still that of a prophetic dispute. The disputants in this case seem to be the people of Israel including the priests. The passage is very difficult to outline. Rex Mason has argued that vv 11–12 are a later addition because they change the first person (v 10) to the third person (vv 11–12), and they interrupt the argument about faithlessness to the wives of their youth (cf. vv 13–16). As the text stands the pericope begins with a double question (v 10), which in fact states a premise. We all (Israel) have one father; one God created us; we should be one happy family. But, the truth is every man was dealing treacherously with the other, and profaning the covenant of the fathers (v 10). The expected retort of the people, "but you say," does not occur in v 11, but it occurs in v 14. Instead vv 11–12 level more charges against the people. Vv 11–12 identify the faithlessness with the marriage of foreign women, "the daughter of a foreign god" (2:11). (For the view that this expression may refer to the worship of a pagan goddess, see *Comment* below.) There were long-standing traditions as well as laws in Israel, for religious or cultic reasons, against marrying foreign women (Gen 24:3–4; Exod 34:12–16; Deut 7:3–4; Num 25:1; 1 Kgs 11:1–8).

2:13–16 return to the charge of "faithlessness." The people are described as weeping and moaning at the altar because Yahweh refuses to accept their sacrifices (v 13). When the people ask why Yahweh will not accept their sacrifices, the prophet replies that it is because Yahweh is a witness to the covenant which husbands made with their wives in their youth (v 14)—wives whom these husbands have now sent away (divorced, v 16). The prophet concludes by saying that Yahweh hates such sending away, and admonishes husbands to consider their actions and not be faithless to the wives of their youth (v

16). The setting of this dispute "remains in the dark" (cf. Schreiner, *ZAW* 91 [1979] 218).

Comment

This disputation passage has itself been the subject of much recent debate (cf. the two recent articles by Schreiner and Rudolph). Part of the debate concerns the state of the MT. It is generally admitted that this passage contains many textual problems. R. C. Dentan (1136) wrote about v 15, "In Hebrew this is one of the most obscure verses in the entire Old Testament. Almost every word raises a question." Joyce Baldwin says of this verse, "Here the text becomes difficult, having suffered perhaps at the hand of scribes who took exception to its teaching. . . . It is impossible to make sense of the Hebrew as it stands, and therefore, each translation, including the early versions, contains an element of interpretation" (Baldwin 240). Although there are many serious textual problems in this pericope, the situation is not as bad as A. C. Welch believed it to be. Welch said, "The text is so corrupt and the sense is so uncertain that the verses cannot form the basis of any sure conclusion" (A. C. Welch, *Post-Exilic Judaism* [London: Blackwood, 1935] 120).

The word אחד "one" occurs four times in this pericope (2:10, 10, 15, 16), and the word בגד "faithless," "deceitful," "treacherous" occurs five times (2:10, 11, 14, 15, 16). Perhaps these two words, "one" and "faithless," are the key to this passage. The word "one" probably refers to Yahweh in v 10 although some argue that it is a reference to Abraham (cf. D. R. Jones 193–94; J. Baldwin 237). Abraham is referred to as the father of Israel (Isa 51:2), and one of the patriarchs (Abraham or Jacob) was called the "wandering Aramean father" in Israel's early creed (Deut 26:5). But only God is "father" in the sense of "creator" (ברא, cf Deut 32:6; Isa 63:16; 64:8). So the "one" father and Creator in v 10 is Yahweh. The implication is that if people (in this case Israel) have one Creator, they should be one, "Did he not make one?" (v 15a). But they are not one! They treat each other treacherously. The fourth use of "one" in v 15 definitely refers to Yahweh, "And what does the one seek?" The answer is, "a godly seed." Some say the "one" here refers to Abraham's relations with Hagar (cf. Keil and Delitsch 453; S. R. Driver 316). But it is Yahweh who seeks a godly offspring; therefore faithfulness to one's marriage covenant is essential.

The other key word in this pericope is בגד "faithless," "deceitful," "treacherous." The word is used five times as a verb (2:10, 11, 14, 15, 16). Charles Isbell believes that the verb came from the noun form בֶּגֶד "garment." Isbell says, "As a verb, it originally meant the taking of a *beged* 'garment' but it soon came to describe other acts that were improper within the setting of a community composed of equal partners in covenant with God. Cheating, swindling the gullible, defrauding poor or helpless members of society, etc.—all were called *begeding* or 'garmenting' " (Isbell 50).

There are two examples of faithlessness in this passage. One has to do with "marrying the daughter of a foreign god" (v 11). The other involves divorcing the wife of one's youth—"the wife of the covenant" (v 14). But the meaning of these two acts is not clear. Does marrying "the daughter of a foreign god" mean marrying a foreign woman, or does it mean worshiping a female diety (idol)? Does divorcing the wife of one's youth refer to husbands divorcing their wives or does it refer to Israel's unfaithfulness to the covenant religion (cf. C. C. Torrey, *JBL* 17 [1898] 4–5)? In the past most scholars have accepted the literal meaning of the text. J. M. Myers takes the literal view and suggests that the husbands were marrying Samaritan women in order to reclaim the land which they had before the exile (Myers, *The World of the Restoration* 98; also see G. A. Smith).

In recent years another interpretation of "marrying the daughter of a foreign god" has gained some following. It may be called the cultic or typological interpretation. According to this interpretation, "the daughter of a foreign god" represents a pagan idol or goddess (Asherah). In support of this view it is often pointed out that the word "abomination" (תּוֹעֵבָה v 11) almost always refers to idolatry in Deuteronomy (7:25, 26; 12:31; 13:14; 17:1, 4; 18:12; 20:18; 22:5; 23:18; 24:4; 25:16; 27:15; 32:16). Could it be that some form of idolatry persisted into the post-exilic period? The reference to profaning Yahweh's holiness or his holy (temple) could easily be explained according to this view (v 11). Also the reference to covering the altar with tears (v 13) would fit into a cultic interpretation of the passage. F. F. Hvidberg says that this passage is "an attack on foreign cultic weeping in Jerusalem by which the temple was being profaned" (Hvidberg, *Weeping and Laughter in the Old Testament*, trans. N. Haislund [Leiden: Brill, 1962] 120). Ezek 8:14 speaks about women sitting in the temple "weeping for Tammuz."

In 1898 C. C. Torrey said that almost all interpreters since Jerome have seen in these verses (2:10–16) the prophet's rebuke of two evils: marriage with heathen women (see also Tg), and divorce. But according to Torrey this interpretation fails to meet the requirements of the text. "The rebuke is rather directed against the encroachment of some foreign cult in Israel. The unfaithfulness of a part of the people threatens to forfeit for all the covenant of the fathers (v 10). Judah has dealt falsely with the wife of his youth, the covenant religion, and is wedding a strange cult" (Torrey, *JBL* 17 [1898] 4–5).

In another place Torrey said that it is ridiculous to interpret literally such terms as בָּגַד "faithless," לְחַלֵּל "profane," בַּת-אֵל נֵכָר "daughter of a foreign god," בְּרִית אֲבוֹתֵנוּ "covenant of our fathers." To do so would involve insuperable difficulties. "There is one, and only one, admissible interpretation of the passage; namely that which recognizes the fact that the prophet is using figurative language. Judah, the faithless husband, has betrayed the wife of his youth, the covenant religion, by espousing the daughter of a strange god" (ibid. 9–10).

Hugo Winckler agreed with Torrey in interpreting the passage figuratively but he differed with him in dating it. Winckler argued that the passage was directed against innovations in the temple and the altar introduced by Antiochus Epiphanes during the early part of the second century B.C. (Winckler, *Altorientalische Forschungen*, II Reihe, Band III [1899] 531–39).

A. C. Welch supported the figurative interpretation of this passage. He claimed that the clause which has often appeared to give the general sense,

"Judah has married the daughter of a strange god, is unexampled as the description of a woman who worshipped a foreign deity" (Welch, *Post-Exilic Judaism* 120).

Recently, Abel Isaaksson has strongly supported the cultic interpretation of Mal 2:10–16. After reviewing the traditional or literal view that the passage refers to mixed marriages and divorce, Isaaksson lists five arguments for the cultic interpretation: (1) This portion of the text must not be interpreted from the words שׁלח שׂנא at the beginning of v 16 because its meaning is unclear. The subject of שׂנא is not stated, nor is the object of שׁלח. (2) The OT concept of בּרית "covenant" is incompatible with what marriage meant at this period. (3) The expression "covered the altar of Yahweh with tears" must be interpreted as alluding to ritual mourning. (4) No instance can be quoted of these verses being understood in earlier times as an attack on divorce. The LXX and the Tg take v 16 not as a prohibition against divorce but as a permission to divorce one's wife. And (5) interpreting this passage as an attack on apostasy to an alien cult is in agreement with the rest of the book of Malachi (Abel Isaaksson, *Marriage and Ministry in the New Temple* [Lund, 1965] 31–32).

It may be said in reply to Isaaksson's five arguments that: (1) even though the words שׁלח שׂנא are unclear, it is possible to read them "I hate divorce." Lars Kruse-Blinkenberg says, "In my opinion, the meaning of ii 16 is that Yahweh hates divorce. This is undoubtedly the most characteristic feature of M: First the author of M seems to protest against the dissolving of mixed marriages in his time; secondly, his proclamation contrasts with Deuteronomy that allows divorce" (Kruse-Blinkenberg, *ST* 20 [1966] 103–4). (2) Against Isaaksson, marriage is compatible with the concept of covenant in the OT. Hos 1–2, Ezek 16, and Prov 2:17 all use marriage as a type of covenant. W. Eichrodt, R. H. Pfeiffer, Martin Woudstra, T. C. Vriezen, and J. Ridderbos all have emphasized the use of the image of man and wife to describe the covenant relationship between God and his people (cf. Woudstra, "The Everlasting Covenant in Ezekiel 16:59–63." *CTJ* 6 [1971] 25; and H. W. Wolff, *Anthropology of the Old Testament,* trans. M. Kohl [Philadelphia: Fortress, 1974] 167). One other problem with the symbolic or cultic view is at this point. According to that view Yahweh would be "the wife of one's youth" (v 15b). Everywhere else Yahweh is father or husband but never the wife (cf. Dumbrell, *RTR* 35 [1976] 47). (3) Tears in the Scriptures are not often cultic tears. The only sure reference to cultic tears in the OT is Ezek 8:14, ". . . there sat women weeping for Tammuz." Ps 126:5–6 may use cultic language about weeping. The tears in Mal 2:13 that cover the altar are not cultic tears or the tears of the divorced wives, but the tears of the people whose offerings Yahweh refuses to accept. (4) Isaaksson is correct in saying that the LXX and Tg take 2:16 not as a prohibition against divorce but as a permission to divorce one's wife. But that is not what the MT text says. Lars Blinkenberg believes that the Targum, LXX and the Peshitta of 2:16 have all been corrected to bring them into line with Deuteronomy (See Blinkenberg, "The Peshitta of Malachi," *ST* 20 [1966] 103–04). (5) To consider this passage an attack on a pagan cult may make it agree with the rest of the book of Malachi, but everything in the book need not agree. The literal view is the one found

in most of the commentaries and the majority of articles on this passage
(Isaaksson, *Marriage and Ministry* 30).

The debate about the interpretation of this pericope continues. G. W.
Ahlstrom defended the cultic/symbolic view in his recent book, *Joel and the
Temple Cult.* Stephan Schreiner takes the literal view that the passage refers
to mixed marriages and divorce but he argues that the author accepted the
Deuteronomic law of divorce (Deut 24:1–2). But he believed that it sets a
high price on monogamy and considers a second marriage less ethically worthy
(Schreiner, *ZAW* 91 [1979] 228).

W. Rudolph refutes Schreiner's argument that this passage in Malachi is
based on Deuteronomic law. Rudolph says that Schreiner's "astonishing results" need checking. Rudolph notes that he had discussed these questions
in his commentary on Malachi (1976), but Schreiner is unfamiliar with it
(Rudolph, "Zu Mal 2:10–16." *ZAW* 93 [1981] 85). Rather than being based
on the Deuteronomic teaching on divorce (Deut 24:1–2), the ideas in Mal
2:15–16 go back to Yahweh's creation of the "one," man in Gen 2:18–24.
Rudolph also disagrees with Schreiner's translation of the first three words
in v 16. Schreiner reads שׁלח שׂנא "wenn einer nicht mehr liebt, Ehe scheiden,"
"when (if) one does not love anymore, divorce." But Rudolph says that those
two words may be translated "Denn ich hasse Scheidung"—"For I hate divorce" without any textual changes. Rudolph argues that שָׂנֵא is a verbal
adj. with the meaning of a participle, "I am hating." שלח is an infinitive
used as a substantive "divorce" (Rudolph 270). Rudolph notes that A. Tosato
agrees with his interpretation of v 16, but agrees with Schreiner's translation
"No one has so acted" (Rudolph, *ZAW* 93 [1981], 90).

2:15 is a difficult verse. R. C. Dentan says that this is one of the most
difficult verses in the OT (Dentan 1136). "One" could be the subject or
the object of the verb "make." We believe it is the object and translate
ולא אחד עשה "Did not he (God) make one (man = אדם, Gen 1:27, but he
created "Adam" male and female, Gen 1:27), therefore a man leaves his
father and mother and cleaves to his wife, and the two become one flesh"
(לבשׂר אחד, Gen 2:24).

The expression ושׁאר רוּח לו is vocalized in Hebrew to read, "and a remnant of the spirit (belonged) to him," but the meaning of that expression is
ambiguous. D. R. Jones (196) reads the first part of v 15, "Not one who
has any spirit left in him has done these things." Schreiner reads, "No one
does such things so far as he possesses a remnant of understanding." He
translates רוח as "understanding" (Schreiner, *ZAW* 91 [1979] 216–17). Tosato adopts the same reading (*Biblica* 59 [1978] 548–53). The problem with
these readings is that לא אחד should not be read "no one." The subject
of אחד is Yahweh. Thomas J. Delaughter says that a more natural interpretation is that "God has the spirit of life and could have given Adam several
wives if he had desired to do so. Monogamy was his intent, however, and it
was in order to raise up a godly seed for a covenant people" (Thomas J.
Delaughter, *Malachi, Messenger of Diving Love* [New Orleans: Insight Press,
1976] 101).

Rudolph calls v 15a the great crux of the book of Malachi. He changes
שְׁאָר "remnant" to שְׁאָר "flesh" and reads v 15, "He has not created one

individual being, but flesh out of his flesh as a supplement for it. And what does the One seek, a seed (after the will of) God" (Rudolph 270). "Flesh out of his flesh" refers to the creation of Eve. Chary (260–61), Baldwin (240), JB and NEB all change שְׁאָר "remnant" שְׁאֵר to "flesh."

Explanation

2:10–16 is one of the most important yet most difficult pericopes in the book of Malachi. The debate between the cultic/figurative and the literal interpretations will probably continue for some time. The literal view has a preponderance of evidence on its side. Malachi is speaking about the disastrous effects of mixed marriages and divorce. Malachi's ministry probably occurred just prior to that of Ezra and Nehemiah in the first part of the fifth century when mixed marriages and divorce were serious problems.

Malachi calls for faithfulness between husbands and wives because as Jews they all had one father—Yahweh; because marriage is grounded in a covenant between the husband and wife and Yahweh; and because God intended for a man and his wife to be one flesh for the benefit of a godly offspring. This passage does not seem to be based on Deut 24 but goes back to Gen 1–2 and is the forerunner of Jesus' teaching in Matt 5:31–32; 19:4–9.

A Dispute about God's Justice   (2:17–3:5)

Bibliography

Elliger, K. "Maleachi und die kirchliche Tradition," in *Tradition und Situation*. Eds. E. Wurthwein and O. Kaiser. Gottingen: Vandenhoeck & Ruprecht, 1963. 43–48. **Holladay, J. S.** "Assyrian Statecraft and the Prophets of Israel." *HTR* 63 (1970) 29–52. **Petersen, D. L.** *Late Israelite Prophecy.* Scholars Press 23, 1977. 38–45. **Robinson, A.** "God the Refiner of Silver." *CBQ* 11 (1949) 188–90.

Translation

2:17 *You have wearied Yahweh with your words,*	3+3
And you have said, "How have we wearied him?" [a]	
In your saying, "Everyone evil	3+3
is good in the eyes of Yahweh,	
And in them he delights."	3+4
Or, "Where is the God of justice?"	
3:1 *"Behold I am sending my messenger*	3+3
and he will clear the way before me.	
And suddenly he will come to his temple,	3+3
the Lord whom you are seeking.	
And the messenger [a] *of the covenant*	2+2+2
in whom you delight,	

Behold he is coming!	3
says Yahweh of hosts.	
² *But who can endure the day of his coming?*	4+3
And who can stand when he appears?	
Because he is like a refiner's fire	3+2
and like alkali ᵃ *of a fuller.*	
³ *And he will sit refining and purifying silver.*	4+3
And he will purify the sons of Levi.	
And he will strain ᵃ *them*	2+2
like gold and silver.	
And they shall become the offerers	2+3
of a righteous offering to Yahweh.	
⁴ *And the offering of Judah and Jerusalem*	2+3
will be pleasing ᵃ *to Yahweh*	
like days of old and like former years.	2+2
⁵ *Then I will draw near to you for judgment,*	3+3
and I will be a swift witness,	
against the ones practicing ᵃ *sorcery, and commiting* ᵃ *adultery,*	2+2
and against the ones swearing ᵃ *to a lie,*ᵇ	
and against the oppressors ᵃ *of the wages* ᶜ *of a hireling,*	4+2
widow and the fatherless,	
and those who turn aside ᵃ *the sojourner,*	2+2+3
and those who do not fear me,	
says Yahweh of hosts.	

Notes

17.a. "him" is not in the MT but the LXX reads αὐτοῦ.

3:1.a. Rudolph follows the LXX and reads "angel" of the covenant.

2.a. בֹּרִית only occurs twice in OT, here and Jer 2:22. It refers to the alkali that comes from the *mesembrianthemum cristallinum* (iceplant). Cf. *CHAL* 49.

3.a. זקק means "to strain, or wash" with water (Job 36:27); to "strain or wash" gold (Job 28:1), "to strain" wine (Isa 25:6).

4.a. ערבה comes from a root whose primary meaning may be "to stand surety." It is not the regular word חפץ "to delight in," or "be pleased with." It is translated "sweet" in Prov 3:24; Jer 6:20; 31:26; Ezek 16:37.

5.a. All of the words denoting sinners here are participles which suggests continuous or habitual conduct.

5.b. The LXX and many Heb mss add בשמי "by my name" (cf. David B. Freedman, "An Unpointed Support for a Variant to the MT of Mal 3:5" [*JBL* 98, 1979] 405–06).

5.c. שכר "wages of" is often omitted as dittography. For the legal basis of this warning see Lev 19:13; Deut 24:14–15.

Form/Structure/Setting

A new theme begins at 2:17 as indicated by the ס in the MT. Rudolph notes that the pericope ends with 3:5 because 3:6–12 is not eschatological. 2:17–3:5 is a prophetic dispute probably with the Levitical priests. However, the disputants were skeptical of Yahweh's justice whoever they were. At times

Yahweh is the speaker against the doubters rather than the prophet (3:1a, 5).

The structure is similar to previous pericopes. The prophet states his thesis that the people and/or the priests had wearied Yahweh with their words (2:17a). The disputants ask for proof that they had wearied Yahweh (2:17b) and the prophet cites the specific charge that they were saying that every evildoer was good in God's sight, or they were asking where is the God of justice (2:17c)?

Then the Lord answers the second question about the God of justice. He said that he was sending his messenger to clear the way for him. Then he would come suddenly to his temple along with the messenger of his covenant (3:1). But his coming would be one of judgment for the Levitical priests (3:3). The judgment on the priests would result in their cleansing and restoration to their position of offerers of righteous sacrifices (3:4), but it would be a day of reckoning for the wicked oppressors (3:5). Perhaps the covenant law-suit form shows through here. The terms "draw near," "judgment," and "witness," along with the presentation of evidence, suggests a court scene.

Comment

Earlier Malachi had castigated the prophets for their attitude and actions toward sacrifices and the altar. Now he says that the priests are expressing their skepticism and Yahweh is weary of them. The word יָגַע "weary" echoes the phrase in Isa 43:24b.

> "You have burdened me with your sins,
> You have wearied me with your iniquities."

The expression "all evildoers are good in the eyes of the Lord" is echoed again in 3:14–15. The Lord's answer to such skepticism appears in 3:16–18. There he assured his hearers that there is a difference between the righteous and the wicked, between those who fear God and those who do not fear him.

This question of the prosperity of the wicked is a question of theodicy. Habakkuk had raised it earlier. How can Yahweh, whose eyes are too pure to behold evil, allow the wicked to swallow someone more righteous than he (Hab 1:13)? That is the question of the psalmist (Ps 73) and Job (21:7–25).

The idea of Yahweh's failure to act in judgment and the confusion of moral values is reflected as early as Isaiah (5:18–20).

Yahweh does not let the challenge to his justice go unanswered. He says that he is about to send (the participle שֹׁלֵחַ expresses imminent action) "my messenger" (מַלְאָכִי), who will prepare or clear the way (cf. Isa 40:3) "before me" (3:1). The messenger is not identified by name or origin. We do not know if he was a man or an angel. Numerous theories have been suggested to identify this messenger-forerunner. Some have argued that he was Malachi the prophet (cf. Elliger). Vriezen said, "The prophet realized that he is being called upon to prepare his people for the imminent coming of Yahweh"

(Vriezen, *Grace upon Grace* 132). Others have seen the messenger in verse 1 as a figurative embodiment of the whole line of prophets (Hengstenberg) or an ideal figure (S. R. Driver 318).

There is a shift from the first person to the third person in the middle of 3:1. Yahweh begins by saying he is sending his messenger to prepare the way for his coming. Then the prophet says "and the Lord (הָאָדוֹן) whom you seek will suddenly come to his temple, and the messenger (מלאָך "angel") of the covenant which you desire."

What is the relationship between the messenger who prepares the way for Yahweh's coming, the Lord who comes, and the messenger of the covenant who comes? Isbell believes that all three could be "a single being" referred to "by three different titles." In this case the Lord (הָאָדוֹן) would not refer to Yahweh, but "to a person of noble station socially" (Isbell 59). But (אָדוֹן "lord") can refer to Yahweh (cf. Zech 4:14; 6:5). Here the Lord is coming or returning to his temple according to the word of Ezekiel (43:2–4); and Haggai (1:8). This passage in Malachi is eschatological. The idea of Yahweh's coming is based on Isa 40:3–5. There "the glory of the Lord shall be revealed and all flesh shall see it together." There his coming is for the salvation of Israel. Here his coming is for judgment. He will come to his temple as Ezekiel and Haggai expected, but it will not be for salvation but for cleansing and judgment.

If "lord" (אָדוֹן) is Yahweh, who is the messenger of the covenant? Again a definitive answer is not possible. However the best suggestion is that he is the "angel of Yahweh," who represents Yahweh many times in earlier references and who is interchangeable with him on some occasions (Gen 18:1, 2, 17, 22; 19:1). Wallis thinks that we should look to references such as the interpreting angel in Zech 1:13; 2:2; 4:4; 5:10; or to references to angels in Dan 7:16; 8:16; 9:21 for our clue. S. R. Driver may be right when he says, "The messenger of the covenant is a synonym of 'the Lord' (אָדוֹן),— notice 'whom ye desire,' parallel to 'whom ye seek'—i.e. Yahweh, not in Himself, however, but in a representative form" (Driver 318).

The "whom you seek" (אֲשֶׁר אַתֶּם מבקשׁים) and "in whom you delight" (אֲשֶׁר אַתֶּם חפצים) in 3:1 seem to refer to the "God of justice" in 2:17. The expression "messenger or angel of the covenant" only occurs here in the OT so there is no other context to aid our interpretation. Some have assumed that the covenant is the Sinai covenant. Others have argued that the reference is to the covenant with Levi mentioned in 2:10. The sons of Levi are to be purified and restored in 3:3. Others believe that the covenant here refers to the new covenant spoken of in Jer 31:31. This certainly would fit into the messianic or eschatological interpretation of 3:1–3.

The whole passage hangs on the charges attributed to the disputants in 2:17. They were wearying Yahweh by saying that everyone doing evil is good in the eyes of Yahweh and they were asking, "Where is the God of justice?" The word "weary" normally refers to the state of fatigue which results from overwork. But here and in Isa 43:22 and Micah 6:3 Yahweh says that they have not wearied themselves by serving him. Instead it is Yahweh who is weary because of their sins (Isa 43:22–24) and their words (Mal 2:17). They were saying, "Where is the God of justice?" But the prophet believed that it was not the justice of God that needed investigating but the impurity of the people needed to be purged.

Yahweh then answers for himself, "Behold I am sending my messenger and he will clear the way before me" (cf. Exod 23:20; Isa 40:3; 63:9). Then the Lord will come to cleanse his temple, and when that happens the disputants will not be anxious to see him for his coming will be sudden (an eschatological idea) and sure (3:1). Then the question will be not, "Will God never come?" but, "Are we prepared for his coming?" The implication of 3:2 is that no one will be able to stand (endure) his appearing for he is like a refiner's fire and fuller's soap. God's presence is often compared to fire (cf. Exod 3:2; 19:16; Mic 1:4; Nah 1:6; Pss 18:7–15; 68:2; 97:3). Fire purifies as well as destroys. Here the fire is that of a refiner. Yahweh is portrayed as a refiner who sits over a vessel containing silver ore until it is purged of every foreign substance and only silver remains.

Alan Robinson asks why silver is mentioned before gold? Was there ever a time when silver was more valuable than gold? He notes that in Egypt before the establishment of the New Kingdom in the sixteenth cent. B.C. silver was more highly prized than gold (A. Robinson, *CBQ* 11 [1949] 188). But by the time of Malachi, gold was surely more valuable than silver. Robinson then suggests that silver was still mentioned first because the process of refining silver is more delicate and anxious than the process of refining gold. He says, "When the silver becomes molten it gives off some twenty times its own volume of oxygen with a noticeable hissing and bubbling. This phenomenon is known as 'spitting.' But the task is not yet finished. Unless the molten silver is treated with carbon (charcoal was used by the ancients), the silver re-absorbs oxygen from the air and loses its sheen and purity" (ibid. 189). Robinson adds a second (eisegetical) comment on this passage. He says that a refiner knows that his metal is pure when he can see his own image reflected in the mirror-like surface of the metal. Then he observes that in view of the import of the book of Malachi and the celebrated Eucharistic text in 1:11, we must interpret 3:3 "as referring to the process of sanctification in the New Law. . . . God will know that His work has been completed when he sees reflected in the Christian soul His own image" (ibid 190; for a good description of the refining process see S. R. Driver 319–20).

The "right sacrifices" (מנחה בצדקה) remind one of the sacrifices in Ps 51:21 (Eng. 51:19) that conform to the norm of what sacrifices should be. Edmond Jacob says that objects which conform to a certain type are called צדק: just balances, just weights, just measures are objects in conformity with what they ought to be (Lev 19:36; Ezek 45:10); זבחי צדק "sacrifices of righteousness" (Deut 33:19; Pss 4:6; 51:21) or sacrifices offered according to the accustomed rites (Jacob, *Old Testament Theology*. Trans. A. W. Heathcote and P. J. Allcock [New York: Harper, 1958] 95).

The word "pleasing" or "sweet" (ערבה) is the third meaning of the root ערב in BDB (787). The first meaning is "mixed." The second meaning is "to give or take a pledge." The third meaning is used in Jer 31:26; Prov 3:24, "my sleep was sweet"; of lovers (Ezek 16:37); of sacrifice (Jer 6:20).

In 3:5 we return to Yahweh speaking in the first person. He says, "I will draw near to you." The priests and people had accused Yahweh of hiding, or refusing to act, or not returning to Jerusalem and the temple as Ezekiel and Haggai said he would. Justice for these people was the fulfillment of previous promises. Justice (משפט 2:17; 3:5) for Yahweh meant proper relationships with God and one's fellowman.

Yahweh said that his justice would be swift (ממהר), not slow as his critics had implied. They had accused God of injustice, now he lists their injustices: (1) practicing sorcery, (2) committing adultery, (3) swearing to a lie, (4) oppressing the hireling, widow and the fatherless, (5) turning aside the sojourner or alien, and (6) not fearing (respecting) Yahweh. The words are all participles, suggesting habitual conduct and attitudes. Most of the sins are sins against the covenant or the decalogue. The New Testament links 3:1–5 and 23 (Eng. 4:5) by identifying John the Baptist with the expected return of Elijah (cf. Matt 11:10, 14; Mark 1:2–3 combines Isa 40:3 and Mal 3:1). Dumbrell notes these references and says, "We are thus justified in seeing the total fulfillment of Mal 3:1–5 in a future Elijah figure who will come with a last message of covenant recall before the coming of God himself" (Dumbrell, *RTR* [1976] 48).

A Dispute about Repentance (3:6–12)

Bibliography

Driver, G. R. "Problems in Proverbs." *ZAW* 50 (1932) 145. **Waldmann, N. M.** "Some Notes on Malachi 3:6; 3:13; Psalm 42:11." *JBL* 93 (1974) 543–49.

Translation

⁶ "Because I (am) Yahweh, I do not change. ª	3+2
But you, sons of Jacob, have not come to an end. ᵇ	3+2
⁷ From the days of your fathers you have turned aside.	3+3
My statutes you have not kept.	
Return to me and I will return to you, says Yahweh of hosts.	2+2+3
But you say, How shall we return?	3
⁸ Will man rob ª God?	3+4
Yet you are robbing ᵇ me.	
But you say, How have we robbed you?	3+2
Tithes and offerings are (still with you). ᶜ	
⁹ With a curse you are being cursed. ª	3+3+2
Because it is me, you are robbing— this nation, all of it.	

¹⁰ *Bring all the tithe into the storehouse*   4+3
  in order that there be provisions ᵃ *in my house,*
and please test me in these (*things*),   3+3
  says Yahweh of hosts,
if I will not open for you   3+3+4
  the windows of heaven
  and pour out for you a blessing until nothing is lacking.
¹¹ *And I will rebuke the devourer*   3+4+4
  that it may not destroy for you the fruit of the ground,
  and the vine in the field may not miscarry,
says Yahweh of hosts.   3
¹² *And all the nations will bless you,*   3+4+3
  because you will be a land of delight,
  says Yahweh of hosts."

Notes

6.a. שניתי לא "I do not change," a *qal* pf. of שנה. God is not stating an abstract theological principle concerning the immutability of his nature. He is simply denying the charge of his disputants that he is unreliable, undependable, capricious. The question is about Yahweh's fidelity, not his nature. The unchangeableness of God's nature may be addressed in Ps 90:1; 102:26. Nahum Waldmann says that an Akkadian equivalent of שנה means, "to go back on one's word, change, renege." He translates this expression, "For I the Lord have not gone back on my word" (*JBL* 93 [1974] 544; cf. Prov 24:21).

6.b. The versions differ substantially from the MT in v 6b. The LXX combines v 6 with v 7 and reads καὶ ὑμεῖς υἱοὶ Ἰακωβ, οὐκ ἀπέχεσθε ἀπὸ τῶν ἀδικιῶν τῶν πατέρων ὑμῶν, "and you, sons of Jacob, have not abstained from the sins of your fathers." The Peshitta reads, "and you, sons of Jacob, have not departed from your injury."

8.a. The root is קבע "rob," but the LXX reads πτερνιεῖ "heel," or "cheat," = עקב. This latter word may be a play on the name "Jacob." Perhaps the idea of robbing God is stronger than cheating him so it should be maintained.

8.b. קבעים the participle suggests continuous action.

8.c. MT has only, "the tithes and offerings." Read with the LXX μεθ᾽ ὑμῶν εἰσιν "with you is." The meaning is, the people still had their tithes and offerings. They had not given them to the Lord as the law required.

9.a. נארים niphal pt. of ארר.

10.a. טרף literally means "prey" but here it means "provisions."

Form/Structure/Setting

This pericope is related to the previous one and to the one that follows in that all three are dispute dialogues between the people and Yahweh. However, this pericope (3:6–12) is not eschatological like the one before and the one after it. The premise is that Yahweh has not changed. Evidently some skeptics became weary of waiting for the promised return of Yahweh as Ezekiel and Haggai had promised. They were implying that God had changed his mind and was unfaithful to his word. But Yahweh says that he has not changed and they (the sons of Jacob) have not changed. The reason he has not returned (שׁוב) in glory to them is they have not returned, "repented" (שׁוב) toward Yahweh (v 7). Yahweh accuses them of not keeping his ordinances, of not repenting, and of robbing him. The people respond, How shall we return? How have we robbed you? Yahweh replies, In tithes

and offerings which you have withheld. Then Yahweh says that the whole
nation is guilty and is under a curse. But he invites his people at this point
to test him. If they bring the tithes to the temple, he will pour out on them
an immeasurable blessing and the nations will call them blessed (v 12).

Comment

כִּי "because" at the beginning of 3:6 suggests that in some way this verse
is connected to the previous pericope. The previous pericope (2:17–3:5) was
an announcement of imminent judgment. This paragraph 3:6–12 explains
the delay in the coming blessing. The opening verse (3:6) contrasts Yahweh
with the sons of Jacob. Two personal pronouns אני "I" and אתה "You"
are expressed. Yahweh does not change. The sons of Jacob have not changed
either. They persist in their sins but they continue to exist. Malachi says
that their continuance of rebellion goes back to the time of the fathers (3:7).
They have not kept Yahweh's statutes (חקות). The prophet issues a call for
Israel to repent, implying that Israel's failure to repent was responsible for
the delay in Yahweh's return in glory to his temple. The expression, "Return
to me and I will return to you," is a repetition of a part of Zech 1:3. The
situation is similar to that reflected in Isa 59:1–2

> Behold the Lord's hand is not shortened,
>   that it cannot save,
> Or his ear dull, that he cannot hear;
> but your iniquities have made a separation
>   between you and your God,
> and your sins have hid his face from you
>   so that he does not hear (rsv).

Repentance is an absolute necessity before sins can be forgiven, and sins
must be forgiven before God's kingdom can come in (Jer 4:1–4). But Israel
had no sense of guilt or shame. Their conscience was dulled by their long
history of disobedience. They asked, "Wherein shall we return or repent"
(שוב)?

Then the prophet asked a startling question, "Will a man rob God?" Robbing another man is serious enough. One of the ten commandments prohibited stealing another man or stealing from another man, but now the prophet
says these people were robbing God. It is altogether probable that these
people had never thought of withholding their tithes and offerings as "robbing
God." Raymond Calkins, writing on *The Modern Message of the Minor Prophets*
(140), spoke about the people of Malachi's day in words that are still true,
"The loose way in which many members wear their plain obligations to the
church . . . is a scandal which enormously weakens its influence. Desultory
church attendance, neglect of public worship, failure to identify oneself with
the church's work and mission in the world, niggardly gifts, lack of all personal
interest and loyalty: these are ways in which the laity of today rob God of
the honor to which He is entitled" (140).

The specific way these people were robbing God in Malachi's day was in

as justice, mercy, and faith (compare Mic 6:8). The central truth of
18:9–14 is that humility is more pleasing to God than a haughty and
actory performance of religious duties. In Malachi's day the people had
ed tithing and giving their offerings because of their attitude of neglect
things of God. Malachi said to them, "You are cursed with a curse."
e to love God and serve him results in a curse.

l invited the people of that day to test him (3:10). If they would bring
· tithe into the storehouse, God would open the windows of heaven
ess them immeasurably. The idea of God testing man is rather common
OT (Gen 22:1; Pss 11:5; 26:2; 66:10; 81:8, Eng. 81:7; 139:23; Prov
but the idea of man testing God is rare. Isaiah invited Ahaz to ask
ign (Isa 7:11–12). Gideon put out the fleece and God honored his
t (Judg 6:36–40). God gave Moses signs to increase his faith and the
f his people (Exod 4:1–9). God sent fire from heaven in answer to
prayer on Mt. Carmel (1 Kgs 18:22–39). Those were all unusual and
circumstances. It may be that this passage in Malachi should be under-
is a one-time, special act on God's part to renew the fires of faith in
of skepticism and indifference. If so, then this is not an open-ended
e to bless in a material way anyone and everyone who tithes his posses-
But Malachi's people like Ahaz did not accept Yahweh's challenge.
lid not bring all the tithes into the storehouse and the windows of
remained closed.

cannot presume upon God's goodness. We can test him only when
tes us. There is a great danger in testing God when our hearts are
it (Mal 3:15). The psalmist said,

> Harden not your hearts, as at Meribah,
>   as on the day at Massah in the wilderness,
> When your fathers tested me (נסה),
>   And put me to proof (בחן), though they
>   had seen my work.
> For forty years I loathed that generation
>   and said, "They are a people who err in heart,
>   and they do not regard my ways."
> Therefore I swore in my anger
>   that they should not enter my rest (Ps 95:8–11 RSV).

'windows of heaven" is a probable reference to rain coming from
Haggai had complained of poor harvests and drought (1:6; 2:16,
v, Malachi said, if the people will repent and bring their tithes and
in a spirit of faith and love, God will send rain and rebuke the
hat devour the crop. The fruit of the ground and the vine will be
l from the effects of the curse (perhaps, the reference is to the curse
round in Gen 3:17–19).
he blessing Yahweh promised Abraham (Gen 12:1–3) will come on
All the nations will call you blessed (אשר) because you will be a
lelight" (Mal 3:12). Material prosperity is a mark of the messianic
Israel (Cf. Amos 9:13–15).

tithes and offerings. Tithing is not one of the covenant sti[
mandments). Tithing was a very old custom in the ancien
Babylonians, Assyrians and Canaanites all practiced tithin
came a nation. References to tithing in the Bible are relati
and diverse. It is mentioned in only seventeen chapters
14, 28; Lev 27; Num 18; Deut 12, 14, 26; Amos 4:4; 2 C
13; Mal 3; Matt 23; Luke 11, 18; Heb 7). The first ref(
the OT is in connection with Abraham's giving a tenth
Melchizedek (Gen 14:20). The custom of paying a tith(
widespread in the ancient world (cf. Ralph L. Smith, "
Illustrator [Summer, 1981] 21). There is no reference to
earliest law code, "The Book of the Covenant" (Exod 2(
is enjoined in Deuteronomy (14:23) and in the priestly co(
warned those who asked for a king that he would take a
and of their vineyards and give it to his officers and to
8:15).

Did all of the people in the OT always tithe? It s(
periods in Israel's history, primarily periods of reform ar
gave their tithes faithfully and abundantly. Amos says tl
Northern Kingdom of Israel in his day "loved" to tit
not happy with them because of their social injustices
24). During Hezekiah's reform the people brought tit
the temple in abundance (2 Chr 31:5–10).

In the post-exilic period the people were not as fa
tithes. Nehemiah (around 444 B.C.) led his people to
with God and to vow to keep the law of Moses. Among
the people agreed to give the temple tax (Neh 10:32;
17:24), a wood offering, the firstfruits, and the tithe
people kept their promises to tithe and to make the v
little while (Neh 12:44–45). But when Nehemiah retur
in Babylon (Neh 13:6), he discovered among other t
had not been giving their tithes to the Levites, and tl
their own fields (Neh 13:10).

During the period between the testaments, several de
concerning the tithe. In the tract Zer'aim "Seeds" o[
details of the law of the tithe are spelled out. Grain
everything used for food which was cultivated and gr(
subject to the tithe. Three passages in the NT mentio
and its parallel, Luke 11:42, are the most important
of the publican and the Pharisee praying in the templ(
boast of giving more than the tithe (Luke 18:12). 1
mentions that Abraham paid tithes to Melchizedek (
order to prove that Jesus' priesthood is better than
Jesus' priesthood is like that of Melchizedek to whom
ham, paid tithes. In the three passages in the New Test;
to tithing, tithing is not the primary subject. In Matthe
a whole series of woes on the Pharisees, one of whi(
so legalistic in tithing and leaving aside the weight(

such
Luke
perfu
stopp
of th(
Failu

Gc
all th
and b
in the
17:3),
for a
reque
faith (
Elijah
specia
stood
an age
promi
sions.
They
heaver

We
he inv
not rig

The
heaven
19). No
offering
locusts
alleviate
on the ;
And
them, "
land of
hope in

A Dispute about Speaking against God   (3:13-22 [Eng. 3:13-4:3])

Bibliography

Gray, J. "The Day of Yahweh in Cultic Experience and Eschatological Prospect." *SEA* 39 (1974) 5. **Thomas, D. W.** "The Root עצב in Hebrew and the Meaning of in Mal 3:14." *JJS* 1 (1949) 182–88. **Waldman, N. M.** "Some Notes on Malachi 3:6; 3:13; and Psalm 42:11." *JBL* 93 (1974) 543–49. **Weinfeld, M.** "The Covenant of Grant in the Old Testament and Ancient Near East." *JAOS* 90 (1970) 95 n.103.

Translation

13 *Your words are strong* [a] *against me, says Yahweh.*	3+2+3
But you say, What have we spoken against you?	
14 *You said, It is vain* [a] *to serve God,*	1+3
and what profit is there that we have kept his charge,	4+3+3
and that we walked in mourning [b]	
before Yahweh of hosts?	
15 *And now we are calling the arrogant blessed;*	4+4+4
also evil doers are built up. [a]	
They even test God and escape.	
16 *Then the Yahweh fearers spoke with one another,* [a]	4+2
each with his friend.	
And Yahweh hearkened and heard	3+4
and a book of remembrance was written before him,	
for the Yahweh fearers	2+2
and for those who value his name.	
17 *Now they shall be mine,* [a] *says Yahweh of hosts*	2+3
for the day when I make a special treasure,	5
And I will spare them	2+3+3
as a man spares	
his son who serves him.	
18 *And you shall return and you shall discern* [a]	2+3
between the righteous and the wicked,	
between the one serving God	3+3
and the one who has not served him.	
19(4:1) *Because, behold the day is coming,*	3+2
burning like an oven,	
when all the arrogant	2+3
and every evil doer will become stubble.	
And the coming day shall burn them,	4+3
says Yahweh of hosts.	
And it will not leave them root or branch.	4+2

20(4:2) *And the sun of righteousness* [a]   2+2+2
        shall rise for you,
            fearers of my name.
        Healing (will be) in her wings.   2+2+2
            And you will go out and you will paw the ground [b]
            like a fattened calf.
21(4:3) *And you shall tread down the wicked,*   2+2+3
        for they will be ashes under your feet
        in the day I act, [a]   4+3
        says Yahweh of hosts.

Notes

13.a. חֲזְקוּ "they are strong." Waldman suggests that in the light of Akkadian and Mishnaic Heb parallels this term be read "your words *have been too much for me*" (*JBL* 93 [1974] 346).

14.a. שָׁוְא means, "vain," "empty." It is the word used in the Decalogue, "You shall not take the name of Yahweh in vain" (Exod 20:7).

14.b. The word קְדֹרַנִּית occurs only here in the OT. Traditionally it has been explained as coming from the root קָדַר "black." But D. W. Thomas suggests another eytmology. See *Comment.*

15.a. נִבְנוּ 3rd mas. pl. niph. pf. of בנה "to build." To build someone up is to encourage them, boast about them.

16.a. נִדְבְּרוּ 3rd mas. pl. niph. pf. of דבר used as a reflexive "they spoke with one another."

17.a. לִי lit. "for me."

18.a. וּרְאִיתֶם "and you shall see" in the sense of "discern."

20.a. שֶׁמֶשׁ צְדָקָה "sun of righteousness" only occurs here in the OT. John Gray sees this as the influence of Persian religion.

20.b. וּפִשְׁתֶּם 2nd mas. pl. qal pf. פּוּשׁ, "to paw the ground," "prance" (cf. Hab 1:8).

21.a. עֹשֶׂה a qal act. pt. of עשה "to do, make, act." Cf. also 3:17.

Form/Structure/Setting

The form is essentially the same as that of the previous pericopes. The premise is stated in v 13, "Your words are strong against me," says Yahweh. The people ask for proof of the charge. The evidence is their statements that it is vain (שָׁוְא) to serve God and there is no profit (בֶּצַע) in keeping his statutes (v 14). The doubters continue to speak in v 15, giving three strange beatitudes: (1) blessed are the arrogant; (2) blessed are the evildoers because they prosper; and (3) blessed are those who test God for they escape.

The focus shifts to a group of faithful Yahweh-fearers in v 16. They speak encouragement to one another, and Yahweh hears them. Their words are recorded in the book of remembrance before him. Yahweh assures them that they belong to him in a special way and they will be spared in the day of judgment (v 17). They and all others will see that there is a difference between the righteous and the wicked—between those who serve him and those who do not serve him (v 18). For a day of fire is coming when the wicked will be burned—root and branch (v 19), but another kind of heat, the Sun of Righteousness will rise with healing in its wings for those who fear Yahweh (v 20). They (the God-fearers) will triumph over the wicked (v 21).

Comment

In v 13 Yahweh accuses his people of "murmuring" against him. The murmuring motif was a significant one during the wilderness wanderings. The specific word "murmur" (לון) occurs only in Exod 15, 16, 17; Num 14, 16, 17; and Josh 9:18, but three other words יעד (Num 14:35; 16:11; 27:3), קהל (Exod 32:1; Num 16:3, 19; 17:7, Eng. 16:42; 20:2; Jer 26:9), and דבר (Num 21:5, 7; Ps 78:19) are also part of the murmuring motif. Malachi uses the fourth word (דבר) "to speak against." (For a thorough discussion of the murmuring motif in the OT see George Coats, *Rebellion in the Wilderness* [Nashville: Abingdon, 1968], esp. 24–25; 249.) Coats says that the murmuring motif is not designed to express a disgruntled complaint. Quite the contrary, it describes an open rebellion. The act of murmuring poses a challenge to the object of the murmuring, which, if unresolved, "demands loss of office, due punishment, and perhaps death" (ibid. 249). Coats also notes that the object of the murmuring is sometimes Moses and Aaron or the leaders of the people, and sometimes it is Yahweh (Exod 16:7, 8; Num 14:27, 29, 35; 16:11; 17:20, Eng. 17:5; 27:3). The object of the verb דבר "to speak against" is אֱלֹהִים "God" (Num 21:5; Ps 78:19) or Yahweh (Num 21:7). Malachi and his disputants could have had the murmuring of their ancestors in mind in this passage. If so, Malachi was charging his hearers with rebellion, the consequences of which were destruction.

The word "vain" (שָׁוְא) in v 14 supports the conclusion that the accusation was one of rebellion. This is the word used in Exod 20:7 and Deut 5:11 in the covenant stipulation about the use of Yahweh's name. "Keeping his charge" (שָׁמַרְנוּ מִשְׁמַרְתּוֹ) is also a covenant expression. It is used of Abraham (Gen 26:5); of Aaron and the priests (Lev 8:35), of the Levites in their service in the tabernacle (Num 1:53; 3:28); of the people (Num 9:19, 23; Lev 18:30; 22:9); of Reuben and Gad (Josh 22:3), and of Solomon (1 Kgs 2:3). The term is also used in 1 and 2 Chr, Ezek (40:45, 46; 44:8, 14, 15, 16; 48:11), and Zech (3:7). Malachi's disputants were asking, what profit is there in keeping Yahweh's charge (covenant)?

"Walking in mourning" is not exactly clear. The term קְדֹרַנִּית only occurs here in the OT. GKC takes it as an adverb from the root קדר "black" with the syllable ן added, plus the fem. ending ית, which elsewhere is used to form adverbs (cf. אֲחֹרַנִּית "backward" GKC § 100g). D. W. Thomas thinks that the idea of going about mournfully does not fit the context. What is required is a term parallel to "keeping his charge." He suggests that the root here is an Arabic root, "to measure," "estimate," "honor." The idea of "walking with God" in obedience is part of keeping the covenant (Gen 6:9; 17:1; 24:40; 48:15; 1 Kgs 2:3; 3:6; 14:8; 15:3).

In 3:15 the people were doing what they accused Yahweh of doing in 2:17. There they said that Yahweh was calling the evildoer good. Now they call the arrogant (זֵדִים) blessed. The arrogant are the enemies of the pious (cf. Pss 86:14; 119:21, 51, 69, 85, 122). They are haughty scorners who act with arrogant pride. BDB takes זֵד as a noun from the root זוד or זיד "to boil up, to seethe, act proudly, presumptuously, rebelliously" (BDB 267). The people here were speaking like the psalmist in 73:3; but they did not go into the sanctuary for an answer as the psalmist did. The prosperity of the wicked and the arrogant was a problem for the psalmist and for the people in Malachi's day. They were asking the same question Habakkuk asked, Why does Yahweh allow evil persons to prosper? They were saying, It does not pay to serve Yahweh.

"Then" אָז at the opening of v 16 may be a problem. The LXX translates this term ταῦτα ≡ זֶה "this." The Syr and Tg agree with the LXX. Smith (84) notes that the same confusion of אָז for זֶה occurs in Gen 4:26. Rudolph says that אָז must not be taken as an adverb here, but as a conjunction. He translates the sentence, "But since the God-fearers (so) spoke to one another Yahweh listened attentively." This interpretation implies that the God-fearers had been speaking in doubt and skepticism. Joyce Baldwin says that "those who feared Yahweh are not necessarily a different group from those who had been complaining, but they are those who have taken the rebuke, and they begin to encourage each other to renewed faith" (Baldwin 249). But it is better to take אָז as an adverb "then," and make the God-fearers a separate group from the skeptics who spoke in vv 14–15. F. C. Eiselen wrote, "It is not possible to identify the God-fearing persons of verse 16 with the persons who gave expression to their doubts in the language of verses 14 and 15; two distinct classes are meant" (Eiselen 733).

The "book of remembrance" only occurs here in the OT. There are other references to a book in which Yahweh records the names of his people (cf. Exod 32:32–33; Pss 69:28; 87:6; Dan 12:1). The practice of Persian kings recording incidents in their scrolls may be behind this reference to a book of remembrance. In the book of Esther, Mordecai discovered a plot on the king's life. The guilty men were put to death but Mordecai was not rewarded. Yet the incident was recorded in the king's book (Esth 2:23). Later the Persian king read about the incident and rewarded Mordecai (Esth 6:1–3). Here, Yahweh hears the words of those who fear him and who value his name rather than taking it in vain (v 16). God renewed his promise to them. In the coming day (בַּיּוֹם) they will belong to Yahweh in a special way. They will be his "special treasure" (סְגֻלָּה). The word סְגֻלָּה is also a covenant word. It occurs at the inauguration of the covenant in Exod 19:5. It occurs later in Deut 7:6; 14:2; 26:18; Ps 135:4. The idea is that all the earth belongs to Yahweh, but those who fear him and value his name will be his in a special sense. Moshe Weinfeld calls attention to the Akkadian equivalent of the Heb סְגֻלָּה. *Sikiltum* belongs to the treaty and covenant terminology, and is used to distinguish a special relationship of the suzerain to one of his vassals (M. Weinfeld, *JAOS* 90 [1970] 195 n. 103). For the NT use of this idea of a special possession see Titus 2:12–14.

One of the problems of Malachi's day was the blurring of moral and theological values. No one seemed to be able to distinguish right from wrong, or the righteous from the wicked. In 3:18 Yahweh makes it clear that there is a difference between the righteous and the wicked and the time will come when everyone will be able to discern that difference. "And you shall return" is a little ambiguous. The "you" is mas. pl. and may point to the doubters, to the faithful, or to anyone or everyone. The precise meaning of "return" (שׁוּב) here is not clear. Does it mean "repent" as it often does? Smith (79) suggests "you will return from your present state of mind and see." However most modern translations read it in an adverbial sense "again," (cf. NEB RSV, JB).

The expression "righteous and wicked" only occurs here in Malachi, but the contrast of those two groups is a major motif in Psalms (1, 37), Proverbs (10:6, 7, 11, 16, 20, 24, 28, 30; etc); and the Prophets (Hab 1:4, 13; 2:4; 3:13). A righteous man in the OT was a person who was faithful to his covenant relationships. The wicked were the enemies of the righteous who break their covenant and seek unlawful gain at the righteous man's expense. The wicked also break their covenant with God and are therefore "ungodly" (cf. Ed Nielsen, "The Righteous and the Wicked in Habaqquq," [*ST* 6, 1953] 64–65).

The righteous and the wicked in v 18 are parallel to those who serve (worship) God and those who do not serve (worship) him. BHK, following Sievers and Nowack, suggests omitting "between the righteous and the wicked" on the basis of meter. But there is no textual or manuscript evidence for doing so.

3:19 in Heb is 4:1 in the LXX, Vg and in English. The next three verses (3:19–21, Eng. 4:1–3) are about the coming day (הַיּוֹם בָּא) when the wicked and evildoers will be burned like stubble and left in ashes without root or branch. But the ones who fear Yahweh's name will be warmed and healed by the rays of the sun of God's presence. Like calves confined to the stall, when they are released they will run and jump. They will be victorious over the wicked who are their enemies (cf. Hab 2:17).

Malachi in the main portion of his book never uses the term "Day of Yahweh." Instead he speaks of "the coming day" (3:19, Eng. 4:1). Another unique expression of Malachi is "the sun of righteousness." Israel seems to avoid references to the sun in her religious literature, perhaps because the sun was worshiped by the majority of her neighbors. In Egypt and Mesopotamia the sun god was represented by a winged solar disc. In Persia Ahuramazda was represented as the god of justice or righteousness. John Gray sees here an influence of Zoroastrianism on Malachi: "In virtue of the date of Malachi in the Persian period and the association with the fiery consummation, a distinctive feature of Zoroastrian eschatology, we think it is the Persian conception that is reflected in Mal 3:19–22, Eng. 4:1–3" (John Gray, *SEA* 39 [1974] 5).

Whether the imagery of comparing Yahweh to the sun comes from Zoroastrianism or not it is rarely used in the OT. Ps 84:12, Eng. 84:11, speaks of God as "a sun and shield." However some scholars have suggested that (שֶׁמֶשׁ) "sun" be read as "buckler" or "battlement" (so Gunkel, G. R. Driver, NEB, JB; cf. A. A. Anderson, *Psalms 73–150*, NCB 606). Although the word "sun" does not appear in Ps 139:9 and Isa 60:1, the thought of Yahweh being like the sun is there. Surely the rays of the sun must be behind the expression, "the Lord make his face to shine upon you" in the priestly blessing (Num 6:24–26).

It is significant that the reference in Malachi is not just to the sun but to the Sun of Righteousness. I. G. Matthews says that the idea of righteousness passed over into the concept of triumph before the period of Malachi. He translates 4:2, "But to you, true worshipers of mine, the triumphant sun

with healing in his rays will break out, and freed, you will go out and like
stall-fed calves sport riotously" (Matthews 34). For evidence that צדק can
mean victory see Isa 41:2, 10; 45:21, 23; 46:13; 51:5, 6.

Two Appendices   (3:22–24, [Eng. 4:4–6])

Bibliography

Childs, B. S. "The Canonical Shape of the Prophetic Literature." *Int* 32 (1978) 51–
52. ———. *Memory and Tradition in Israel.* SBT 37. London: SCM Press, 1962. **Elliger,
K.** "Malachi und die kirchliche Tradition." In *Tradition und Situation.* Eds. Wurthwein
und Kaiser. Gottingen: Vandenhoeck & Ruprecht, 1963. 43–48. **Weiner, A.** *The Prophet
Elijah in the Development of Judaism.* London: Kegan Paul, 1978.

Translation

22a(4:4)	*Remember the Torah of Moses my servant*	4+3
	which I commanded him	
	on Horeb, concerning all Israel,	2+2
	statutes and ordinances.	
23 (4:5)	*Behold I am sending to you,*	4+3
	Elijah the prophet, [a]	
	before the coming of the great and terrible [b]	4+2
	day of Yahweh.	
24 (4:6)	*And he will turn the heart of the fathers unto the sons,*	3+3
	and the heart of the sons [a] *unto the fathers,*	
	lest I come and smite the land [b] *with a ban.* [c]	1+3

Notes

22.a. Some LXX manuscripts place v 22 (Eng. 4:4) after v 24 (Eng. 4:6) so that the book
will not end with a threat. The Massorah at the end of Malachi says that in the case of Isa,
Lam, Qoh, and Mal the next to the last verse would be read last in the synagogue.

23.a. LXX has Θεσβίτην "the Tishbite" following 1 Kgs. 17:1.

23.b. LXX has ἐπιφανῆ "glorious" from ראה rather than ירא.

24.a. LXX has καὶ καρδίαν ἀνθρώπου πρὸς τὸν πλησίον αὐτοῦ "and heart of a man to his neighbor."

24.b. ארץ should be understood as "land" or Judah, not the earth.

24.c. חרם "ban" means "an order to set aside for destruction."

Form/Structure/Setting

It is generally recognized that the form of 3:22–24 (Eng. 4:4–6) is quite
different from the form of the six disputes in the book. No longer are there
charges and countercharges, questions and answers. The dialogue is over.
V 22 (Eng. v 4) is an admonition to remember the Torah of Moses. It is
unrelated to anything that has gone before. Its language is Deuteronomic
and is probably an editorial addition by the redactor of the Book of the
Twelve. Vv 23–24 (Eng. vv 5–6) pick up the theme of a coming messenger
from 3:1 but differ from that passage in that these verses name the messenger

(Elijah) and assign him a different role. The messenger's role in 3:1 was to prepare the way for the coming of the Lord. Here the role is that of turning the hearts of fathers to children and vice versa, or perhaps turning the hearts of the people to the Lord.

Again the language is different. Here the expression is, "the day of Yahweh." In the body of the book it is "the coming day." The expression "great and terrible day of the Lord" is an echo of Joel 2:11b. The passage in Joel may be later than Malachi's time, but not necessarily later than this appendix. V 22 (Eng. v 4) looks back to the time of the exodus and Sinai and enjoins remembrance of the Torah of Moses by all Israel. Vv 23–24 (Eng. vv 5–6) look forward to the return of the first great prophet before that great and terrible day. So the law and the prophets appear together at the end of the OT (according to the LXX and English versions). The Hebrew Bible puts "the writings" after the prophets so it ends with 2 Chronicles. One would expect the joining of the law and the prophets at the end of the OT. Brevard Childs sees the last three verses as significant for his canonical view of the OT. It is generally recognized by critical scholarship that two appendices have been fixed to the conclusion of the book of Malachi. To dismiss these verses as a legalistic corrective of a disgruntled priestly editor is to misunderstand the canonical process. The first appendix reminds the nation that it still stands under the tradition of Moses. "The canonical effect of the first appendix to Malachi testifies that the law and the prophets are not to be heard as rivals but as an essential unity within the one diverse purpose. The effect of the second appendix (4:5–6) is to balance the memory of the past with the anticipation of the future" (Childs, *INT* 52 [1978] 51–52).

Comment

Rudolph sees Mal 3:22–24 (Eng. 4:4–6) as the conclusion to the entire prophetic canon which begins for the Hebrew Bible with Josh 1:1. He says that it is no accident that the last chapter in the Pentateuch (Deut 34), the first chapter of the prophetic canon (Josh 1:2) and Mal 3:22 (Eng. 4:4) all refer to Moses as the servant of Yahweh. This would bring the law and the prophets together. However, Childs finds Rudolph's argument here "unconvincing" (Childs, *IOTS* 495).

There are two conclusions to the book of Malachi. One is an imperative to remember the Torah of Moses. The exhortation to remember is Deuteronomic. It is used thirteen times in the book of Deuteronomy. To "remember" in the OT means far more than to recall or think about a past event. It always involves action. Childs says that God remembers and forgets (Pss 88:5, [Eng. 88:4]; 106:4; Jer 31:20; 44:21). Whoever Yahweh does not remember has no existence (Ps 88:6, Eng. 88:8). When God forgives sin, he forgets (Jer 31:34). Childs says, "there are no examples where this reflection does not issue in the objective intervention toward that which was remembered. Memory is not identical with action, but it is never divorced from it" (Childs, *Memory and Tradition* 33).

Later, when Israel was commanded to remember the law, statutes and ordinances of Moses, she was not merely to relive the past because much of that was painful. Memory served to link the commandments of Moses as events in the covenant history to the present and future obedience of Israel.

It should be noted that the words, "remember," "the law of Moses," "Horeb" and "all Israel" are all typically Deuteronomic in style.

The second appendix in 3:23–24 (Eng. 4:5–6) looks to the future and identifies the coming messenger of 3:1 as Elijah, who will reconcile or unify the people as he did in the time of Ahab and Jezebel. Elijah became a hero figure in later Judaism. There was some mystery about him in the original stories in 1 Kgs 17–2 Kgs 2:12. He appears unannounced as an adult and a prophet without ancestry or posterity. Instead of dying and being buried, Elijah was caught up in a chariot of fire by a whirlwind into heaven (2 Kgs 2:12). Aharon Wiener says that what is unexpected in Malachi's prophecy of Elijah is the prophecy of his return about 400 years after the end of his existence on earth. "It can be explained by the obvious assumption that his contemporaries did not consider Elijah to have died in the conventional sense" (Wiener, *The Prophet Elijah* 35).

Elijah became a very popular figure in Judaism after OT times. He is mentioned a number of times in the Apocrypha (Sir 48:10; 1 Enoch 89:51–52). 4 Ezra 7:109 mentions Elijah's prayers for rain and for the resuscitation of the child. The same book prophesies that the men who have been taken up and not tasted death from birth shall appear before the Messiah (6:26). The NT identifies Elijah with John the Baptist (Luke 1:16–17, 76–77; Mark 1:2–4; Matt 3:1–6), although on one occasion John the Baptist denied that he was Elijah, confessing that he was only a voice crying in the wilderness, "prepare ye the way of the Lord" (John 1:19–23).

Elijah still plays a significant role in Jewish liturgy and ritual. He is mentioned when grace is said after meals: "May God in his mercy send us the prophet Elijah." And in the benedictions after the weekly Sabbath reading of a chapter from the books of the prophets, the prayerbook says, "Let us rejoice, O Lord, through your servant, the prophet Elijah, and through the kingdom of David, your Messiah. May he come soon and rejoice our hearts." Elijah is mentioned in the circumcision ceremony and in the Passover seder. At the beginning of the celebration of the Passover a special cup of wine, called "Elijah's cup" is placed on the table. When grace is said after the meal, a child opens the door in expectation of Elijah's appearance and biblical passages are recited which express the hope of Jewish people for deliverance from oppression (Wiener, *The Prophet Elijah* 132–35).

The last word in the book of Malachi and in the Greek and English Bibles is "ban"—a word which could be translated "curse" or "anathema." This is a stark contrast with the book of Zechariah where one section of the last chapter ends by saying, "and there shall be no more ban" (Zech 14:11). The ominous ending of Malachi was not lost on the Masoretic scholars or the translators of the LXX. The MT directs the repetition of 3:23 (Eng. 4:5) after 3:24 (Eng. 4:6) to avoid the harsh conclusion. The LXX changes the order of the verses and makes our v 22 (Eng. 4:4) the last verse. But the word "ban" suggesting the annihilation of the land of Judah with its people says that, unless the Lord sends his messenger to change the hearts of his people, he will come to destroy them. However, his purpose is not destruction but repentance (Ezek 18:23, 30–32).

Index of Authors Cited

Subject Index

Index of Biblical References

A. Old Testament

B. The New Testament

C. The Apocrypha